Michigan Copper
The Untold Story

A History of Discovery

by C. Fred Rydholm

Winter Cabin

Books & Services

Michigan Copper
The Untold Story

A History of Discovery
by C. Fred Rydholm

Copyright: 2006
All rights reserved

Published by Winter Cabin Books & Services,
393 West Crescent St, Marquette, MI 49855,
by arrangement with the author.

Cover design by
Jeff Koval, Marquette, Michigan

Interior layout and design by
Stacey Wiley, Globe Printing, Ishpeming, Michigan

Printed by Edwards Brothers Inc.,
2500 South State Street, Ann Arbor, MI 48106

Other books and CDs by Fred Rydholm
are available from Top Water Productions
393 West Crescent Street, Marquette, MI 49855
(906-226-9849); www.superiorheartland.com.

Library of Congress Control Number: 2006925378

ISBN 0-9744679-2-8

All truth passes through three stages. First, it is ridiculed. Second, it is violently opposed. Third, it is accepted as being self evident.
-Schopenhauer

Dedication

Joseph Cuthbert Gannon
(1876-1965)

Dr. Roy Ward Drier
(1897-1974)

This book is dedicated to Joseph Gannon and Roy Drier, two local pioneers in the study of Michigan copper, both of whom were inspiration for and had great influence on this work.

Acknowledgments

Since the gathering of material for this book covered many years and the actual writing of it at least six or seven years, it is just impossible to list everyone who helped in one way or another along the way. It is hoped that those missed here will at least be mentioned in the text.

First and foremost, I must thank the editors who went over the work numerous times with a fine tooth comb, Jay Scriba and my son, Dan Rydholm. There were others who read the manuscript and caught many errors. John Henderson pointed out both technical and typographical errors Zena Halpern and Phylis Berg-Pegorsh who gave valuable overall additions and suggestions.

Then special thanks must go to Stacey Willey of Globe Printing for the layout work and to Beverly Pascoe for hours of getting my handwritten script onto a computer.

Artists Liz Yelland, Kathy Savu and Judy Johnson all had a part in the artwork.

Joe and Alma Cook, my thanks for the use of their library.

My good friend Warren Dexter overwhelmed me with his photograph collection. There were others such as Malcolm Pearson, Jack Deo, Jason Mikki, Robby Robinson, Tom Edgar, Judy Jones, Erick Mitchell, Hank Voori, Liz Yelland, Mim Newman, Walter Loope, Bill O'Boyle, Gloria Farley, Russell Burrows and my wife, June, and son, Kim, who supplied special photographs when needed.

I have always had a good feeling toward those amateurs and professionals who say "feel free to use anything I have as long as I am quoted correctly" or words to that effect. These would include Dr. Cyclone Covey, Dr. Joe Mahan, Dr. Jim Scherz, Dr. Gunnar Thompson, Dave Deal, Gloria Farley, Robby Robinson, Dr. Barry Fell, Marian Dahm, Bill Connor, Evan Hanson, Jim Grimes, Barry Hanson, Dr. Henriette Mertz, and Wayne May. They all radiate a feeling of honesty and generous cooperation not prevalent by some people and institutions I have contacted.

I also must thank readers of all or parts of the manuscript who have offered their suggestions and encouragements among whom would be Ginny Foreman, Ben Mukkala, Frank and Mary Smith and their son Warren, David Hoffman, Wilson Turner, Dr. Jim Scherz, Dr. Gunnar Thompson, Wayne May, Leslie

Bek, Phylis Berg-Pegorsh, Bill Weber, Kim Rydholm and a special thanks to journalist Meredith Timpson who has written book reviews and offered helpful suggestions. A Special thanks to Dr. John & Tory Parlin for their interest and generous support.

Others not mentioned above who have helped lending books and support are Dr. Allyn Roberts, Rudy Kastelic, Victor Kachur, Dr. John White, Beverly Moseley, Charlie Alvord, Bernie Arbit, Bill and Anne Manierre, Chuck Bailey, Howard Burtness, Robert Burcher, Jim Billings, Zelma Cahoon, Ila Conklin, Deb Chory, Bliss Calkins, Glen Devlaminck, Chuck DuCharme, Tom Edgar, Don Eckler, Clyde Elmblad, Julian Fell, James Guthrie, Marshal Payne, Zena Halpern, Lloyd Hornbostal, Stan Hess, George Hobson John and Judy Jones, Frank Joseph, Roger Jewell, Brian Jentoft, Peter Kittenville, George Kodan, Claude Le'gore', Bruce Marsh, Ray Meininger, Mary Jo Nadeau, Bill O'Boyle, Anne Parker, Vernon Peterson, Ron Priest, Judy Rudebusch, Ken Raisanen, Paula Sten, Joan Skelton, Duane Soine, Paul Shefranke, Rob Tuckerman, Scott Wolter, Marjorie Hornblower Johnson and Tom Wittman. And to those I have missed, I offer my apologies.

– C Fred Rydholm

Preface

Michigan Copper--The Untold Story, is an account of the Archaeology of North America and its ancient visitors. Emphasis is placed upon the waterways of the Great Lakes and the people who have labored tirelessly to preserve every piece of evidence supporting contact with the Eastern Hemisphere. There have been successes but, unfortunately, many artifacts and pristine sites have been lost to the settlement of the American frontier in all regions of the country. The Upper Peninsula of Michigan has been heavily trodden by the development of our European ancestors, yet there is much that has been passed over. Fred Rydholm is one of these people who have labored with great passion to discover, preserve and verify the ancient history of North America's Pre-Columbian visitors.

When this country was first heavily explored and then subjugated by the Old World powers, Central and South America were the first to be exploited. North American exploitation lingered in the background. Largely because there were no visible stone ruins and gold to fire-up the imagination of soldiers of fortune. Stone cities and temples of the south attracted the hemisphere's first "carpetbaggers" if you will.

The culture of Central and South America was ravaged and literally destroyed, especially the written records of the Aztec, Inca and Maya nations in the name of Christianity. The loss is immeasurable to the knowledge of these ancient cultures.

But, beneath the canopy of North America's forests, hidden from the eyes of the Old World conquerors, lies a magnificent history, every bit as exciting as our neighbors to the south: hundreds of earthen pyramids and platform mounds lying east to west from Georgia to Oklahoma; and thousands of mounds with fortifications revealing ditched walls of earth and stone covering Illinois to western New York. This mighty Mound Building culture, a name which is loosely used to cover all the mound activity of North America, was just as dynamic and culturally rich as any ancient civilization. They left behind in their mounds of earth and stone evidence of a vast trade network that existed from "sea to shining sea." Copper from the mines of the Keweenaw Peninsula can be traced to Central America, mica from the Carolina's is found in the burials of the very elite, obsidian from the rockies covers the land east of the Mississippi River, shells from the Gulf are in the mounds of the Great Lakes natives, etc... But what has become of this vast empire of Mound-Builders? We have degraded and treated them without respect for the obvious commercial and engineering capabilities they have left behind. Archaeoastronomy has shown they had tremendous knowledge of the stars and seasons as recorded in the tumuli of their sacred enclosures. Instead, we have largely ignored and positioned them as just a group of "hunter-gatherers" who settled together on occasion for convenience. Only small populations covered North America, we are told by those in authority. Nothing more could be so far from the truth!

The indigenous people of North America had a history so rich and full that we haven't grasped even a tenth of it. Oral history of the Native Americans is looked upon with much suspicion as mere tales for the campfire. Yet, how do we account for the numerous artifactual finds that support a more sophisticated past? Our professionals mostly disregard these unusual finds as mere hoaxes to fool the American public. Yet, what do the Native Americans tell us of their past? That the tribes, living from the Mississippi to the Atlantic seaboard, came from the land of the rising sun. That's across the Atlantic, not the land bridge of the northwest. Long ago they had books, but due to constant warfare, learning had to continue "mouth to ear." They tell us of many visits by strangers, coming into their countries, sometimes staying and assimilating with their people.

America has been a melting pot for centuries before Columbus landed. Fred Rydholm's collected works, in this book, of his years of dedicated search, is a crowning achievement. It does not cover every piece of evidence or every site but offers a tremendous resource to bring the American public up to speed and encourage them to "pick up the gauntlet" and pursue the discovery of the great history of this land, America. Rydholm's work is not to compete with numerous scholars other works but to encourage the reader and introduce him/her to the wealth of other books and sources to discover the great American story of the ancient people who lived here.

I am honored to have been able to associate with Fred Rydholm on his journey of discovery and fulfillment in bringing to light the antiquity of pre-historic North America. Remember, Columbus was last.

Wayne N. May
Publisher, *Ancient American Magazine*

Introduction

Some might wonder why I have gone out on a limb and taken the time and effort to write this book as an amateur in the field. I have several reasons.

The first is curiosity–being confronted with things for which there has been no logical explanation. In some cases I have been given an explanation that does not seem logical to me.

Second, because of my background of several generations on both sides of my family in the Upper Peninsula of Michigan, I became interested in writing a history of the area where I grew up. To me this seems like a natural, compelling force.

As I tried to connect the history in chronological order, further and further back into the unknown, I arrived at probably the most startling evidence: a tremendous amount of work done by ancient man right under our noses, which centers in the colossal era of the copper diggers, also with inadequate explanation.

Then there was the discovery that others, before me, some of whom I knew personally, had studied the same subject for years, but unfortunately had died without ever finding any solid proof for their theories.

With the benefit of their observations, I wanted to take over where they left off, at first by just keeping my eyes and ears open. In time I was able to make a few discoveries of my own and come to a few conclusions that seemingly no one else had noticed or thought of. I felt that my observations were valid when added to the picture as a whole.

Then, in the course of my part-time investigations, I met other amateur devotees, some of whom had made their own discoveries. A few had written them down, only to have their ideas, both good and bad, ridiculed and scoffed at by some of the professionals. Many of these professionals contributed little of their own but had spent a lifetime convincing the public that their predecessors were infallible and there was little left to learn. In some cases these professionals ignored or covered up the obvious. It reminds me of the account of the director of the U.S. Patent Office over a century ago who thought they should close the office down as surely everything had been invented.

In recent years, however, some of the ideas held by these amateurs are slowly gaining ground, not because of their work, but because gradually some of the professionals are arriving at the same ideas.

There are still many clues that have been missed and I am sure many new discoveries will come to light in the future. To further that possibility, I would like to add my two cents worth, without expecting any fame or fortune. We may never know the whole story, but there are a lot of people in the world with something important to add.

What we see depends on what we seek with an open mind.

– C Fred Rydholm

Contents

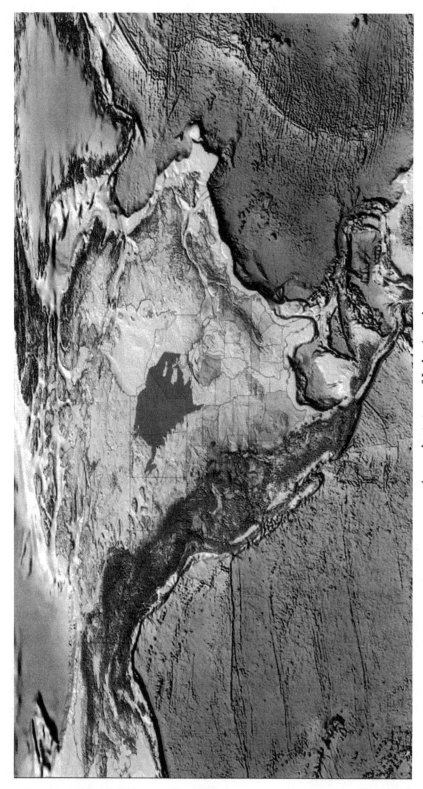

An ancient stage of Lake Agassiz

XIV

Chapter I

A Geological Sequence

Introduction

There are two basic methods of learning almost anything. One is to get the general (overall) picture and then go to the specifics. The other is to get very specific and then piece the specifics together.

In nearly everything I can think of, the first method is most logical. You learn to dog paddle before you learn the crawl or backstroke; you learn carpentry before you start cabinet making. You learn arithmetic before physics or you learn to sew before you learn petit-point.

It appears to me when looking over all the clues, ancient skeletons, gene studies, Clovis point arguments, ancient cities, etc., etc., that we are going at things backwards.

Where Did All the Copper Go?

As soon as the ancient diggings, pits and mines on Michigan's Keweenaw Peninsula and Isle Royale were discovered in the 1840's, the question arose: **where did all the copper go?**

That question still is on the lips of many today. It has been asked over and over for the last century and a half.

We're not talking about the millions of tons of Michigan copper mined with giant machinery from shafts that penetrate the earth two miles deep. That credit goes to modern industry, notably to supply the world's insatiable electric grids.

Neither do we mean the twenty or thirty tons (40,000 to 60,000 pounds) of Indian trade copper in those dusty North American museum cases with their copper knives, axes, spearheads, needles, awls and bits of jewelry, or the other twenty or thirty tons that may still lie buried and undiscovered. Much of that came from prehistorically recent North American mounds and burial sites.

These amounts could be equaled by a few large pieces of "float" copper that are still being found today. We're talking about somewhere between ten-million to fifty-million pounds, depending on whose estimate you go by (some go as high as a billion pounds that are unaccounted for). All of the figures used seem to get watered down as the years go by, especially by people who are unaware of the amounts of copper that are still being discovered and picked up today in Michigan's Copper Country.

Yet even the most skeptical archaeologists admit that, especially on Lake Superior's Isle Royale and Michigan's Keweenaw Peninsula, there remain to this day *thousands* of prehistoric copper pits, dug thousands of years ago by ancient peoples still unknown. Copper pits so large—many ten to thirty feet deep with connecting tunnels between—that one archaeologist estimated that their digging would take the equivalent of 10,000 men working for 1,000 years, working with little more than fire, stone hammers and calloused bare hands—a human feat of mind-boggling proportions.

And yet after nearly two centuries of speculation, no one has ever satisfactorily explained where the world's purist copper might have gone, as there has never been enough North American copper found to account for even 1% of it.

Meanwhile, of course, there was the global "Bronze Age," bronze being most (about 90%) copper with an admixture of tin. Yet worldwide, especially in Europe, copper has always been too scarce, at least in prehistoric times, to account for the unquestioned bronze riches of the ancient cultures of Egypt, Greece, Crete and Rome.

So, reader, once again, where did all the Northwoods copper go? If you love mystery and intrigue, keep reading.

Two Conflicting Ideas

There are two schools of thought concerning the mining, distribution and use of the vast deposits of pure copper in Michigan's Upper Peninsula during prehistoric times.

The scientific establishment (universities, museums, news media, textbooks, etc.) suggests that the ancient inhabitants of North America came to the Lake Superior region over thousands of years to mine and gather this copper, from which they fashioned tools and trinkets and traded with neighboring people. This hypothesis presupposes that the copper never left North America. This mainstream theory of prehistoric copper is called the "isolationist" view.[1a] *"But truth is not determined by majority vote"* (Doug Gwyn).

Then there is the conflicting argument that the Michigan copper went to Europe, Asia and Africa in ancient times. This concept, held by a few scholars and investigators over many years, has gradually gained the support of some scientists and historians as well as a sizable segment of the public. This group has been called "the diffusionists."

The isolationists hold that since no one apparently preceded Columbus, except possibly the Norse, all similar seeming artifacts or practices on either side of the oceans were either in place out of necessity or invented independently by different peoples. The diffusionists hold that unknown ancient peoples transported ideas and copper across the seas.

Among a small group of scholars, the argument on occasion has become heated and even reduced to name-calling. This book argues instead for a sober look at each side of the question.

While the mainstream or textbook[1a] view is well known and needs little explanation, the opposite or alternative story is relatively complicated and unknown and, therefore, needs much clarification.

[1a] For the professional view of the ancient mining see *"Wonderful Power - The Story of Ancient Copper Working in the Lake Superior Basin"* by Susan R. Martin. Wayne State University Press 1999.

As a contemporary researcher who is well versed in establishment views but at the same time having been exposed to the less popular views of pioneer researchers, I propose to take the reader on a journey. I would like you to accompany me on my lifelong inquiry into the mystery of North America's ancient copper diggings.

So that the reader won't throw up his or her hands in disgust in the early pages, I want to lead you gently into an ever-deepening abyss of knowledge in hopes of presenting a fresh new interest. I wish to warn you against the pitfalls of fact-versus-opinion, of so-called "experts" and others, entranced by their own thinking. I urge you, the reader, to make up your own mind, to form your own opinions.

In our free and open society, we should not degrade anyone for their opinions. Ridicule only reflects on the person who formulates it. Our mutual destination should be truth, and we should be ready and willing to hear all arguments.

In a speech given on the occasion of receiving the Nobel Peace Prize for 2001, United Nations Secretary General Kofi Annan stated, "The idea that there is one people in possession of the truth, one answer to the world's ills or one solution to humanities needs has done untold harm throughout history."

This seems to hold true in law, medicine, religion, politics and many divisions of science. In fact, when a belief holds unchangeably firm in an individual's mind, regardless of what or how much proof is presented against it, then it has become idolatrous. It is something one believes, no matter what the circumstances.

Science, however, should be in another category. A scientist, by his or her very nature, is one who is willing to explore a new idea and then be willing to concede when he thinks the new concept surpasses the old one. Then he is thinking objectively and scientifically. This is known as the "Scientific Method."

So this is the story of copper. First, we will inquire how and where this copper came from. Then we will look briefly, at what our recorded history tells us. I will relate my experiences, my quest for answers, even in the light of textbook learning, along with the people I met during that quest, the ideas that show promise and the questions that still remain.

As a science teacher years ago, I remember saying often, "Keep in mind that what we learn today might be wrong, or at least inadequate, tomorrow," so to begin we must realize why Upper Michigan's copper is so special and unique. Strangely, these facts are not generally known and have been "watered down" over the years. I have met many young people, native to the area, who didn't even know that copper was mined here.

Outer circle: where the copper deposits are.
Inner circle: area known as the "Copper Country".

Copper Country

A Sequence of Geologic Events

Many features about our local copper make it fascinating and unique. One of the most important of these is sheer quantity in the region. There is no other known place on earth that compares with it. The copper here is found in huge masses, millions of tons. It is believed to be in massive formations and pockets far out under Lake Superior, from Canada and Minnesota on its northwestern end and extending southeast under Michigan's Upper Peninsula. There is, in fact, such an immense concentration of copper that even after thousands of years of mining, some estimates claim that *over 90%* of it is still here.

Another unique feature of Michigan copper is its purity. Although copper ores of three percent to even one-half of one percent are profitable to mine, this

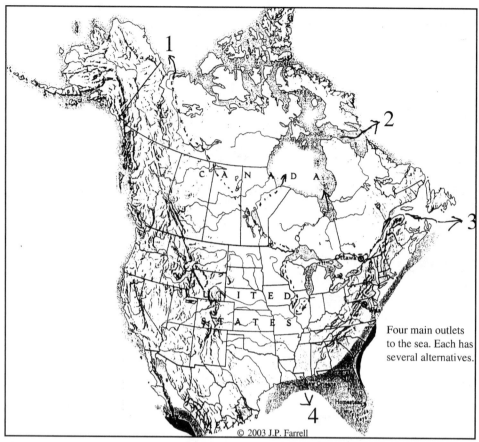

Four main outlets to the sea. Each has several alternatives.

© 2003 J.P. Farrell

is the only place where huge amounts of copper are found in a pure state, that is 99% or more pure, in pieces sometimes weighing many tons.

Still another phenomenon unique to the area is that huge amounts of this copper have already been freed from the surrounding matrix by Mother Nature. Glacial action broke it free from the native rock and spread it out on or just beneath the surface. Then the post glacial floods and accompanying rains washed sand and other glacial debris from it, leaving many pieces of the metal exposed high and dry, ready to be picked up.

Then we must add to these improbable circumstances the fact that the areas on which this copper is found are surrounded by water routes in every direction, especially east to the Atlantic. Certainly, in the past, routes were also open south to the Gulf of Mexico and northwest to the Pacific, as well as north to Hudson's Bay. It is my goal to relate a simple, complete tale, using laymen's language and few scientific terms. I hope it can be understood by average, intelligent people of school age and beyond. I believe this is the first step to understanding so that all may comprehend the dramatic history that follows.

While I am an advocate of the glacial theory that I learned as a student and taught for years, I have always had some doubts and concerns about it. It was one of those situations that you live with until something more logical comes along. Among the most baffling of these questions are:

1. *How do we explain old maps that show no ice around Antarctica, a condition that has never existed in historic times or an open polar sea in ancient times?*
2. *How do we explain the woolly mammoths found frozen in Siberia with grass and flowers in their mouths, and frozen so quickly and solidly that the meat is still fresh enough to be edible ten or twelve thousand years since they became extinct?*
3. *How do we explain evidence of glaciers where glaciers have never existed?*
4. *How do we explain the massive tangle of dead animals that have been found packed tight in caves around the world, and some tropical types in the Arctic?*
5. *There is evidence of much surface violence that does not seem explicable by a slow progressing and receding glacier. Also some of the disturbances seem too modern.*
6. *There are coal deposits in both the Arctic and Antarctic.*

A new alternative theory has been proposed by British scientists during recent years. The new theory needs much study, but is worth our consideration, as we shall see.

A Recent Challenge to the Glacial Theory

During the decade between 1830-1840, a Scottish geologist, Sir Charles Lyell, verified and popularized the geological views of J. Hutton, establishing "uniformitarianism" as the basis of modern geology. This theory is generally accepted and has gone unchallenged for over 150 years. It is the familiar story of global glaciation where, during a prolonged ice age, there was a building up of layers of snow and ice that formed glaciers which gradually crept south over the northern hemisphere, drastically altering the face of the earth, taking the tops off mountains, causing glacial scratches, and gouging out lakes and depositing glacial debris. Then, in an unexplained warming period, the rapid melting of these glaciers caused a great deluge. It is only recently that it has been determined that the melting of the last glaciers happened in a relatively short period of time, maybe a matter of only 15 or 20 years as compared with millions of years of build-up.

[1b] This could have been by a super-volcano

Now, near the end of the last millennium, two scholars from England, D. S. Allan and J. B. Delair proposed an alternate theory to the accepted glacial theory of Charles Lyell.

In a book published in 1997 (Bear & Company of Santa Fe, N.M.)[1] entitled "Cataclysm" and subtitled "Compelling Evidence of a Cosmic Catastrophe in 9500 B.C.," they outline their hypotheses. The foundations for this new theory have been around for years, but Allen and Delair have put these older ideas together in a very believable form.

Their theory suggests that a very large cosmic body sailed through our solar system from outer space about 11,500 years ago. It affected all the planets that were passing close to it, but it passed near enough to the earth to cause a shift in its axis of about 30°. This sudden shift, plus the effects of the gravitational pull of the intruder caused the up thrusting of mountain ranges, the rising and shrinking of land masses, gigantic volcanic eruptions, prolonged darkness and massive extinction of life. The cosmic visitor and its accompanying entourage of rock, ice and other debris, also caused great collisions and under slippage of the earth's tectonic plates. Of course, this caused massive flooding and churning of the oceans along with rains and violent winds. All of these powerful forces could have the same effects we now attribute to glaciers, but it would have happened swiftly and catastrophically, thus we have the two opposing theories, the slow "Uniformitarianism Principle" and the alternative "Catastrophism" theory.

Both of these theories concede that there were great floods and the people who survived these floods certainly were familiar with watercraft. Some may have gone to mountaintops and most would have become nomadic sea rovers or "people of the sea."

This author was brought up with the established glacial theory and it is not my purpose to argue the two here, but since the theme of these writings is to keep an open mind to new ideas and give them fair evaluation without dismissing them out of hand, I just want to call attention to the possibility that some day in the future, after years of careful scientific study with modern methods and new discoveries, our ideas of the distant past may change dramatically. Today we know so little, looking into the past is like walking into a dark room. It seems like the more we learn, the more there is to learn. The key to intelligence is curiosity and an open mind.

---

[1]This book was first published in 1995 under the title, "When the Earth Died" by Gateway Books, Bath, England. A book with further explanation should be out soon.

The Geology of Michigan Copper

Several theories suggest how and why great deposits of native, pure copper occur in the Lake Superior region.

One idea is that very early in the earth's formation, when the surface was still semi-molten and huge plates pushed against each other, great cracks appeared with volcanic action and frequent earthquakes. Thereupon a huge mass of molten copper rose up to fill every cavity, saturate spongy rock formations and, in some instances, formed great underground pools.

For a more scientific description of the formation of copper deposits, we quote from the *Journal of Metals,* Vol. 32, No. 1, January 1980, written by some world-renowned pioneers in the "fingerprinting" of copper deposits, Dr. George Rapp, Jr.[2], Dr. Eiler Hendrickson,[3] Michael Miller and Stanley Aschenbrenner:

> Native copper formed under reducing conditions is observed in several environments. It has been observed in modern swamps where it is believed to be forming as dilute copper bearing solutions encounter organic matter. Minor quantities of native copper found in some black shale and slates, such as at the White Pine Mine in Michigan and elsewhere, may be due to a similar mechanism. At other locations, native copper is associated with organic matter in sandstone. A fascinating decomposition of native copper as a replacement of parts of ancient mine timbers by migrating copper solutions can be seen on Cyprus.

# # #

Native copper found in Alaska will be mentioned later in these writings, from *Journal of Metals:* By far the most important of the native copper occurrences and the <u>only</u> major deposit of this type mined in the world, is the Lake Superior Copper District located in the northern peninsula of Michigan, on the southern shore of Lake Superior. The region is geologically unique, and the abundance of native copper is greater than anywhere else in the world. There is evidence to show that prehistoric mining was conducted as early as 6,000 B.C. from the large area of lava flows. Many of the lava flows are amygdaloidal in their upper portions,

---

[2] George Rapp, Jr., Professor of Geology and Archaeology, Directory of the Archaeometry Laboratory, University of Minnesota, Duluth.

[3] Eiler Hendrickson, Professor and Chairman, Department of Geology, Carleton College, Northfield, Minnesota.

and the majority of the copper occurs as vesicle fillings. Half the total copper mined in the area has come from such amygdaloids.

A second type of ore occupies at five to twenty foot thick pebble conglomerate with sandy matrix. The native copper interstices and replaces matrix and pebbles. Copper in the district ranges from abundant, small, irregular grains to extremely large masses, one of which weighs 480 tons. A third but minor type of native copper occurs in the district as fissure veins cutting the volcanics and intercalated sediments.

…Large masses weighing several tons are recorded. Such erratics might well have been utilized by ancient man in North America.

Other sporadic occurrences of native copper of primary origin similar to the Lake Superior District have been found in sandstone areas of eastern U.S., notably in New Jersey and in glacial drift overlying a similar area in Connecticut. Native copper deposited in red sandstone of Corocora District (Bolivia), southwest of La Paz, and an occurrence in Anarak, Iran, are also believed to be primary in origin.

A theory with a simple explanation is that the copper was held in solution by super-heated water and deposited among the rocks over millions of years. Other descriptions of this process will be forthcoming, I am sure.

In any event, when all this metal cooled and hardened, we were left with the only known spot in the world where copper, in all its forms, spread out in tremendous deposits in the earth's crust.

One anomaly remains a puzzle, namely, that an appreciable amount of pure silver was deposited with the copper.[3a] The quantity is insignificant compared to that of the copper, but strangely, the silver is not always mixed with the copper as an amalgam, instead being attached to it with a definite dividing line between the two metals. Small pieces of this copper-silver combination are locally called "half breeds." They are quite common.

This massive eruption of molten copper on the earth's surface was the first phase of a geologic sequence of events.

The second phase was its hardening in great masses relatively close to the surface, both in the pure state and in various ores.

The third phase probably would have taken place very slowly and less dramatically. Tremendous global forces on the earth's crust must have caused it to buckle, pressing a large area containing the bulk of the copper downward

---

[3a] West of Isle Royale on an island along the north shore of Lake Superior, two surveyors, Thomas McFarland and John Morgan in 1868 uncovered the richest silver mine in the world. A vein 20 ft. wide of rich silver ore produced millions of dollars worth of silver. Shares went from $50 to $125,000. The 1300 ft. shaft flooded after 13 years of mining.

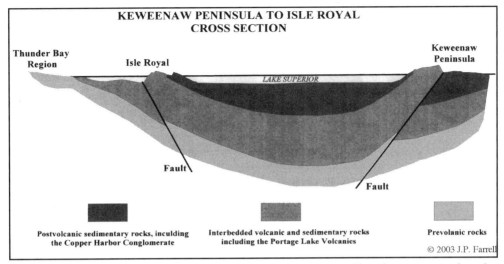

into a massive fold or syncline, some sixty or seventy miles from one end to the other.

As the extremities of this fold bent upward, they separated from the copper formations far down. Their upper edges, perhaps sixty miles wide on the northwest and even wider on the southeast end, rose to form what we know today as Isle Royale, an island just 15 miles from the Canadian shore, to the northwest and the Keweenaw Peninsula to the southeast, the latter barely connected to the Upper Peninsula of Michigan. The buckling of rock and the copper formation continue down the mainland for another seventy-five miles or so. These "ranges" come in the form of high mountain ridges, which expose millions of broken pieces of rock and copper of literally every size.

This step completed phase three of the geologic events, but this still is not enough to account for the copper phenomenon in the Lake Superior region. For during the mind-boggling passage of time since these events began, the earth's climate cooled and we passed into millions of years of ice ages. During this period, it is believed that one massive glacier after another covered large portions of the northern hemisphere.

In places far to the north, it is claimed that these glaciers could have been five or six miles thick and that the tremendous weight of the plastic ice slowly forced its edges outward. Over ages of time, these glacial tentacles slowly crept down over the sharp mountain ridges, scraping the tops off the high points as they advanced. The mountain rock was crushed to powder under the relentless pressure, but the copper, being malleable, simply bent and flattened or broke into smaller pieces. Nevertheless it was freed from its rock matrix and much of it carried along with the rest of the debris. As the glaciers slowly forced their way over the land, they gouged great channels and ravines and filled others with dirt, rock and pieces of copper.

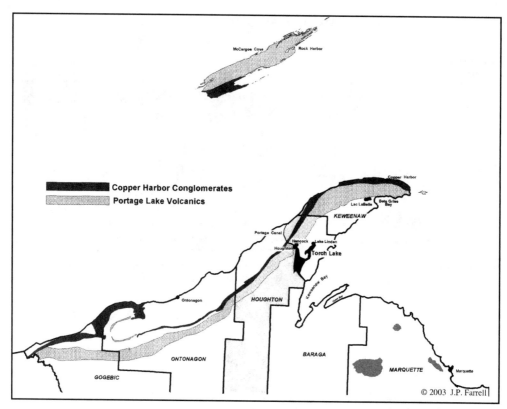

Copper Harbor Conglomerates
Portage Lake Volcanics

© 2003 J.P. Farrell

As the various advances of the glaciers pushed southward, the larger and deeper pieces of copper did not get carried as far, while the smaller pieces rolled on with the gravel for hundreds of miles. Most of the large chunks were left in Lake Superior and on the Keweenaw Peninsula.

This copper that floated with the glacier (float copper) is found in glacial moraines as far south as the farthest advances they made, into Ohio, Indiana and Illinois. Float copper is also found in southern Michigan and Wisconsin, but the vast majority of it is in Upper Michigan and especially the Keweenaw.

The Great Flood

But the enormous forces of nature were not done yet. There is still a fifth natural phenomenon, one most important in my thinking, but largely ignored. It was probably more dangerous to life than the previous two events combined. This event took place so recently in geologic time that it still lives in the legends of early man.

Consider that the earth's climate was going into a warming stage that we know as the Pleistocene. Huge amounts of the earth's water was locked in the frozen ice sheets; it has been estimated that at one time global sea levels were

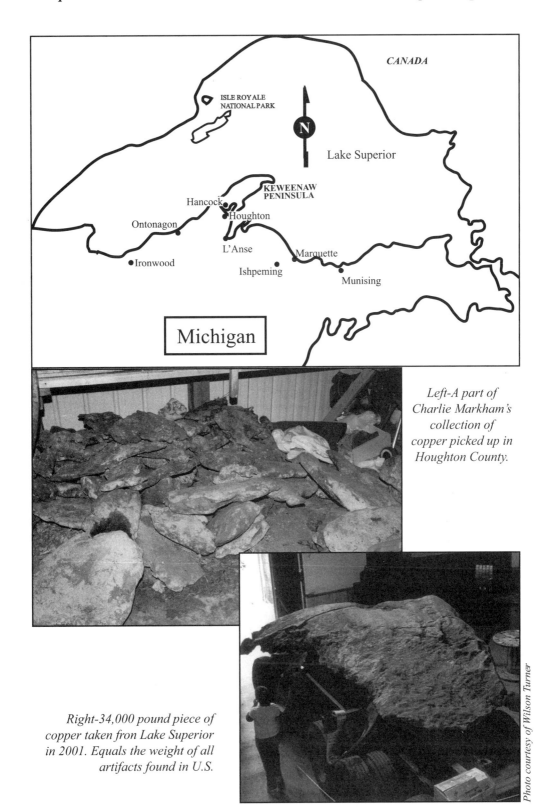

Left-A part of Charlie Markham's collection of copper picked up in Houghton County.

Right-34,000 pound piece of copper taken fron Lake Superior in 2001. Equals the weight of all artifacts found in U.S.

Photo courtesy of Wilson Turner

300 feet below present sea levels.

From the standpoint of the cataclysmic theory, the cosmic body (Phaeton) that passed through our solar system was accompanied by huge chunks of ice, some of these crashed into our earth causing a great swelling of our ocean systems thus raising the sea levels several hundred feet. This would also cause the other related catastrophic phenomena.

At just one hundred feet below today's sea levels, many more islands and land masses would have been exposed and the size of continental shelves would be increased. The weather was much warmer than today's arctic climate, so the ice melted rapidly. Thus the fifth great phenomenon was *water,* whole ocean volumes of it pouring off the glaciers in an unimaginable rush. Practically every ethnic history begins with tales of survivors of "the Great Flood", or people coming "out of the water" There actually must have been many floods. Each race has its own legendary stories and traditions concerning them.

One study by a geographer, John Shaw, from Queen's University in Kingston, Ontario, gives us a good example. He was studying drumlins (elongated or oval-shaped hills of glacial drift caused by currents of melting glaciers) near Livingston Lake in northern Saskatchewan. These were tall and narrow at the upstream end and low and broad-tailed at the downstream end.

Shaw proposed the theory that a drumlin field is the heritage of a vast, turbulent flood of melt water that surged beneath the glacial ice late in the ice age. These surges formed the pits that filled with sand and rock debris carried by the flood. Thus these deposits were molded into hills that remain for all to see and "read" some 10,000 years later.

John Shaw says the flood must have been of catastrophic proportions. In the area of his study, he feels the drumlins resulted from a single flood.

From the December issue (1989) of **Scientific American Magazine**, author Tim Appenseller writes:

> *From the total area of Livingston Lake, the drumlin field spans about 150 kilometers. Shaw estimated first the amount of ice that must have been removed to the cavities and then the amount of water it would have taken to erode them.*
>
> *He arrived at a figure of 84,000 cubic kilometers—about seven times the capacity of Lake Superior. When this sub-glacial flood burst from the edge of the ice sheet and drained to the Atlantic and Gulf of Mexico, it would have raised global sea levels by 23 centimeters. (Less than 10 inches.)*

Map Showing Ancient Drainage
Systems to Mississippi River
from Lake Superior and
Lake Michigan

SUPERIOR

HURON

MICHIGAN

MISSISSIPPI

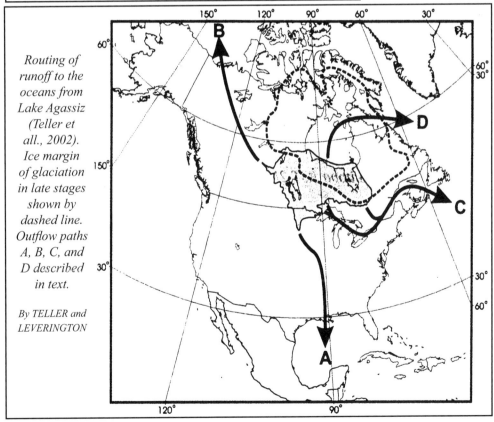

Routing of
runoff to the
oceans from
Lake Agassiz
(Teller et
all., 2002).
Ice margin
of glaciation
in late stages
shown by
dashed line.
Outflow paths
A, B, C, and
D described
in text.

By TELLER and
LEVERINGTON

But the sea levels have risen 300 feet. Jacques Cousteau found, in ocean surveys, caves 180 feet under water with stalactites and stalagmites. These could have taken thousands of years to form. Also, one doesn't have to be a geologist or geographer to notice the effects of floods that covered the entire Upper Peninsula of Michigan. Where hillsides have been eroded or where gravel has been taken from borrow pits, the water-washed gravel layers are fifty, sixty or more feet thick, marking literally hundreds of ancient river beds.

We must magnify Shaw's findings hundreds of times to get the true picture. There was water of great depths everywhere. The massive glacial floods and the rains that accompanied them over a period of many years scoured the earth's surface clean in some places and left massive deposits of debris in others. There were huge lakes and rivers and the land water levels were high.

On Isle Royale and the Keweenaw, these floods acted like a giant sluice, which separated the light gravel from the heavy copper. They also washed the light sand and rock away from the copper, which in large chunks is far heavier than iron.

Assorted pieces of copper, from one hundred tons to bits the size of a fingernail, were often left exposed on the surface, while most smaller pieces would have been washed along with the gravel to be deposited elsewhere. Pieces under one hundred pounds or so could have been moved great distances.

In those years of the great meltdown, there were huge glacial lakes in western Canada, which emptied to the north. These lakes extended into what are now Minnesota and the Dakotas, where there was an east to west continental divide. North of the divide, rivers and lakes drained northwest toward the great Mackenzie River, emptying into the Beaufort Sea and the Nelson River, which empties into the Hudson Bay. South of the divide, the water flowed to the Great Lakes and the Mississippi River system.

This is actually an oversimplified explanation for this ancient drainage. At one time, these huge volumes of water formed a gigantic lake, many times larger than Lake Superior, called Lake Agassiz. In fact, over a ten thousand year period, there was a whole series of glacial lakes. At different levels they had different names. A list of their names would include Duluth, Chicago, Lundy, Algonquin, Kirkfield, Minong, Chippewa, Stanley, Nippissing and Algoma. Larger than any of these glacial lakes was Lake Agassiz. It was named after Louis J. R. Agassiz and his son, Alexander, both of whom had done geological work in many parts of the world. [4]

This massive Lake Agassiz at one time (11,500 B.P.) covered great portions

---

[4]From Glacial Lake Agassiz, edited by J.T. Teller and Lee Clayton, Geological Association of Canada, Special Paper 26, 1983.

of Manitoba and Ontario in what is now Canada and a large area of eastern North Dakota and northern Minnesota. From about 10,900 and 9,500 B.P. (Before Present) it drained into Lake Superior through several channels. As the different lobes of the lake wasted away, the last drainage to Lake Superior was through the Lake Nipigon and Lake Winnipeg basins. The huge volumes of water took ages to drain (a process that still goes on today) as the land slowly rose in its glacial rebound. As the lakes disappeared, hundreds of islands began to appear, then finally the Great Plains. In the course of several thousand years, the route of the Mississippi swung back and forth from east to west over a 200 mile area. For many years one tributary came directly from the western end of Lake Superior and another from the southern end of Lake Michigan near today's Chicago. That same Continental Divide ranges from Minnesota, through Wisconsin and forms the south end of Lake Michigan. South Chicago is built on a debris-filled marsh. The rising of the land and the drying of the great rivers and lakes formed the topography of the land surface we know today. It has been fairly stable for about the last 750 years.

The one great change occurred when the ice left the St. Lawrence River valley and the drainage of the Great Lakes turned east to the North Atlantic instead of south to the Gulf of Mexico.

With this series of events in mind, it should be easier for the reader to follow the events, as I see them, which occurred later.

The one thing we should keep in mind is the fact that with all this water action, it stands to reason that there should have been many very large pieces of copper lying on the surface of the ground. They would have been hung up, so to speak, like rocks in a field after a rain. They should have been scattered all over the land on the Keweenaw Peninsula and the bottom of Lake Superior. Yet as far back as our recorded history, or even the legends beyond it go, there were none on the surface. There were many small pieces exposed, but the only large one came to light when the Ontonagon River became shallow enough for it to appear. That one piece became a sensation, even among the Indians who reported it to the early Europeans in the 1600's. For almost the next 150 years, the "Ontonagon Boulder" was the talk of the Lake Superior country. Many smaller pieces have been located just under the surface and in Lake Superior, but the large specimens that should have been there were gone!

During the early years of modern exploration (1848-1860), several large pieces of copper, much larger than the Ontonagon Boulder, were discovered (one weighing 30 tons). These were found resting on wooden cribbing, deep in holes that had been excavated around them. These were obviously in the process of being raised out of the ground to be taken away.

Our next step will be to examine what we do know. As we review the overall picture, some new concepts and insights may come to mind. At least you'll know more about the history of copper than you ever thought there was to know.

> *There must have been many other copper slabs that were raised and removed in this manner. These few that were found "part way in the process" must have been left to be worked on in another season. These hard working miners never returned. This has always been one of the mysteries.*

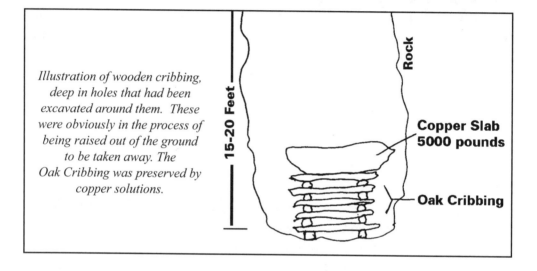

Illustration of wooden cribbing, deep in holes that had been excavated around them. These were obviously in the process of being raised out of the ground to be taken away. The Oak Cribbing was preserved by copper solutions.

15-20 Feet

Rock

Copper Slab 5000 pounds

Oak Cribbing

Ken Raisanen of Ontonagon, Michigan, standing beside a replica of the Ontonagon Boulder in the Ontonagon County Museum. The exact replica is made of paper mache.

Picture courtesy of Ken Raisanen

Chapter II

A Look at the Written History of Keweenaw Copper

Early History

Since the very earliest European penetration into North America during historic times, it has always been common knowledge that there was an abundance of pure copper on Isle Royale and the Keweenaw Peninsula.

Back in 1636, when the Lake Superior country was first being explored by the French, a man named Legarde reported mines from which a friend "showed him a copper ingot."

In 1640, a small volume published in Paris by Pierre Boucher told of finding mines in the Lake Superior region, where copper was found "all refined, and it is found in various places in large pieces."

The Jesuit Relations, a collection of letters and reports of Jesuit missionaries written between 1650 and 1660, frequently reported Lake Superior copper.

Father Claude Allouez, the first Jesuit stationed on Lake Superior, established the Mission of LaPointe in 1666 (now on an island off Bayfield, Wisconsin). He was told of Indians finding pieces of copper weighing 15 to 20 pounds, treasures which they held in great reverence.

In an article in the **Michigan History** magazine (Vol. 27, #5, Sept/Oct 1983), author John Halsey gives us an idea of the Indians' mystical feelings about copper.

> When a long-time friend, a trader, asked his old Indian acquaintance if he could buy a piece of copper, he replied, "Thou askest much of me, far more than if you had demanded one of my daughters. The lump of copper in the forest is a great treasure for me. It was so to my father and grandfather. It is our hope and our protection. Through its magic I have caught many beavers and killed many bears. It has made me victorious in all my battles and with it I have killed our foes. Through it, too, I have always remained healthy and reached that great age in which thou now findest me. I cannot give thee greater proof of my friendship than by showing thee the path to that treasure, and allowing thee to carry it away."[5]

---

[5] Johann G. Kohl, Kitchi Gami: Wanderings Round Lake Superior (Minneapolis: Ross & Haines, 1956, pp. 61 & 62, first published in 1860.)

These early investigators all noted that the local Indians knew nothing of the earlier people who left so much evidence of their collecting of copper, nor what it could have been used for, or where it all went. To them it was a curiosity, a gift from the Gods. Some Indian families of that era carried pieces of five and ten pounds and up to 20 pounds for years.

1671—New France and New England—1763

The upper lake region, the northern Great Lakes, including all the land around Lake Superior, was first mentioned to the Europeans as the "region of the Saguenay." The Saguenay River flows from the west into the St. Lawrence. The mouth of the Saguenay is about 150km northeast of Quebec City, just south of the present city of Tadoussac. The river is wide and impressive, flowing between high cliffs. Although it originates in Lake Saint Jean, a long distance east of Lake Superior, the Indians living along the St. Lawrence told Europeans that it came from a far western wonderland of precious stones. Following such reports, Cartier in 1635-36 sailed up the Saguenay in search of this wealth, but found nothing of value. In retrospect, stories suggest that the Indians were speaking of the pure, heavy, free copper far to the west.

Later on the Saguenay Region became better defined as the area around Lake Huron (Lake of the Hurons), known as Heronia.

It was during the period of the 1660's to 1760 that the main activity in the Lake Superior region was the very lucrative fur trade.

When the British took over the land, they also took over the fur trade. One of the first British fur traders to arrive at the Straits of Mackinac[5a] (St. Ignace) was 24-year-old Alexander Henry, disguised as a Frenchman for his safety. Within a few weeks he found himself embroiled in Pontiac's Indian uprising, which resulted in the capture of Fort Michilimackinac[5a]. This was the uprising that later became known as "Pontiac's Conspiracy." In it, Henry nearly lost his life.

During the English regime (1763-1783), both Alexander Henry and Jonathan Carver wrote descriptions of Lake Superior. They both mentioned the fabled land of native copper.

Alexander Henry, with a partner, Cadotte, spent the winter of 1765 at the head of Lake Superior. From his travels along the peninsula's waterways, Henry reported silver on the Iron River (western Lake Superior) and considerable virgin copper on Michipicoton Island. In 1770, he and Alexander Baxter returned to England to form the first mining company to exploit the region's silver and copper.

[5a] Always pronounced Macki*naw* with either ending "*ac*" or "*aw*".

Henry built a barge and a 40-ton sloop, the first ever to sail on Lake Superior. The purpose of this combination was to haul copper from a mining venture on the Ontonagon River in 1771 and 1772.

After establishing a camp and laying out the work, Henry returned to the Sault Ste. Marie for the winter. The next spring his schooner was loaded with supplies and dispatched to the mouth of the Ontonagon where, much to the surprise of those in charge, they found the entire party awaiting their arrival. The miners had dug a shaft (addit) horizontally into a clay bluff during the winter, and when the frost left the ground in the spring, it all caved in. That was the end of the venture. The mine location is said to have been just ten rods east of the NW quarter of Section 6, T-50, R, 40 on the site which later held the dam of the Victoria Mining Company.

The Ontonagon Boulder

Alexander Henry was the first white man to publicly describe large chunks of copper in the sand on the banks of the Ontonagon River. He also mentions the "Ontonagon Boulder." This huge piece of copper found on a sandbar, weighing upwards of 3,000 pounds, was shown to him by the local Indians. Henry had been very interested in the stories of unbelievable amounts of copper in the pure state, apparently unknown elsewhere in the world. While his Ontonagon venture failed, he later did mine some copper on Michipicoton Island in eastern Lake Superior, some of which was said to have reached England.

While there was much talk among the locals about the huge mass of copper in the Ontonagon River, news of it began to reach the outside world during the New England period (1763-1783). At first these stories took on an air of myth. Most believed they were just another backwoods exaggeration. However, after the Revolutionary War there was sufficient knowledge of Lake Superior copper in Washington for Ben Franklin to reconfigure the U.S. and Canadian borderline so that Isle Royale was included in the U.S., even though it was only 15 miles from the Canadian shore and nearly 50 miles from the tip of the American Keweenaw Peninsula.

It is legendary that Ben Franklin, when drawing the border in Lake Superior between the U.S. and Canada, hesitated about Lake Superior. But knowing about the copper on Isle Royale, he was said to have dipped his quill and drawn his line north of that island, so as to include it in U.S. territory. In going through the papers of the late Mr. Joseph Gannon, I found the following letter dated February 9, 1939. The writer was Edward A. Rumely of 205 East 42nd St., New York City. It was written to Mr. H. C. Dudley at 704 Linsdale Bldg., Duluth, Minn.

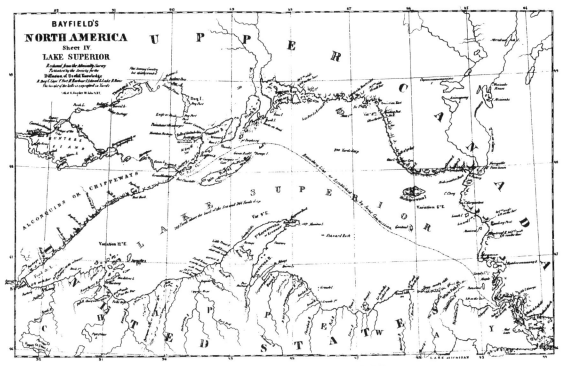

INTERNATIONAL BOARDER

Three paragraphs of that letter are footnoted here,[6] which outline the background of Franklin's decision.

In 1785, an ordinance was passed proclaiming the vast lands east of the Mississippi and north of the Ohio Rivers as the Northwest Territory and the subject of copper again came into the limelight.

------

[6] These facts I recall from conversation with E.H. Scott who was very methodical and painstakingly accurate in his reports. Unless he was misled by his investigation, this is the story.

The Jesuits saw the Indians in the Mississippi Valley using copper tools and at first were baffled in their efforts to find out the origin of the copper. After a considerable period, a Jesuit won the confidence of the Indians, was taken to Isle Royale and wrote home to France of the mining operations that he observed there. This correspondence was the occasion of the French claiming the Island in the way in which they did, and of its being called 'Isle Royale.'

When the French saw, as peace approached, that this small holding would be shut in between English territory and American territory, they preferred to have the Americans get it and tipped off Franklin of trading this in. Franklin is said to have enlisted the cooperation of Jefferson so that in drawing the boundary line, he would have started, if he made a concession of an island elsewhere in order to push the Lake Superior boundary north to the center of the Lake, which he did. Mrs. Rumely and her brother's family jointly still own about 1800 acres of the most beautiful islands and inlets and the site of one or two of the old mines on Isle Royale.

In 1818, Illinois became a state. By act of Congress, the Michigan Territory was extended to include part of Minnesota, all of present Wisconsin and the rest of the Upper Peninsula. Lewis Cass was appointed governor of this vast new Michigan Territory and at once he proposed a government expedition to look over the huge region for which he was responsible.

This expedition was undertaken in 1820. Its purposes were to gain the confidence of and become better acquainted with the Northern Indian tribes, to arrange for treaties and to investigate the reported mineral deposits along Lake Superior's south shore. Cass also wished to make an accurate map of the shorelines with some place names for references.

Accompanying Cass on the expedition as mineralogist was Henry R. Schoolcraft, who later married the daughter of John Johnston, an Irish fur trader from the Soo.[7]

The expedition left Detroit on May 24, 1820, and took two weeks to reach the fort on Mackinac Island. There the explorers picked up two more canoes and 22 soldiers provided by the commandant of the garrison for the Governor's protection. This brought the expedition to the full complement of 40.

Cass wanted to see the great copper boulder that had been described by Alexander Henry and others. He and his men reached the Ontonagon River on June 27 and started upstream by canoe and then on foot to find the curiosity. Cass eventually became exhausted as the journey was too strenuous for him and he sent the others on ahead. The copper was some 20 miles upstream, with Indian guides leading the way through the roughest terrain Cass had ever encountered, with tangled forest, steep hills and rocky footing.

Among the reports of people visiting the Ontonagon Boulder in early days, apparently some could not even find it. Some reported it protruding out of foot deep water while others found it high and dry on a sand bar in the middle of the river. Many noticed how many sand banks with huge trees had slid into the river during high water.

Most probably the boulder was at times under water, as there would have been many high water years over the centuries, with the amount of water slowly diminishing until the heaving earth subsided. Before the buckling land became stable, the copper boulder probably was never visible. Some have suggested that it may have fallen from a raft while ancient miners tried to move it to Lake

---

[7] John Johnston's wife was the daughter of the famous Chippewa Chief Wa-bo-geeg. She, as Schoolcraft's mother-in-law, told him many stories of the customs and culture of the Algonquin people, which Schoolcraft put down in six volumes. It was from this work that Henry Wadsworth Longfellow got his material to write the poem, "Song of Hiawatha" in 1855.

Governor Cass

Henry Rowe Schoolcraft

Colonel McKenney

Photos From a booklet "The Great Copper Boulder of Ontonagon by Gerin Faklstrom

Superior. Judging from various tools found nearby, many attempts had been made to get pieces off of it. Another suggestion is that it was just washed from the riverbank by high, fast water and left on the sandbar as the flood receded.

With the fame of the Ontonagon Boulder becoming more widespread, it seemed imperative that some attempt should be made to bring it to public attention. Its remote location, 20 miles up the Ontonagon River, kept this great natural phenomenon from the public eye.

By 1826, Governor Lewis Cass and Thomas L. McKenny were authorized by the United States government to negotiate a treaty with the Chippewa Indians at Fond du Lac (end of the lake—present location of Duluth, Minnesota). At the same time, they ordered George F. Porter, with a detachment of soldiers, to be sent to the Ontonagon to retrieve the famous mass of copper.

It was August of 1826 that this party of twenty arrived at the mouth of the river. The twenty miles "as the crow flies" constituted about twenty-eight miles of difficult river travel. The boulder trekkers had to abandon their boats and take to the hills, which stood from 100 to 300 feet high, with steep sides and deep bogs in the valleys. Unfortunately, when they finally reached the object of their search, they could see that it would take special equipment to move it, and so they were obliged to abandon the attempt and return to the Soo.

At the end of a long controversy over the "Toledo Strip", Michigan was an illegal state for a period of a few years. They had declared statehood but had not yet been admitted to the union by the United States Congress until 1837.

Claiming the Boulder

While Michigan was technically an illegal state in 1836, the Treaty of Washington was signed. In it, the Indians ceded to the federal government all

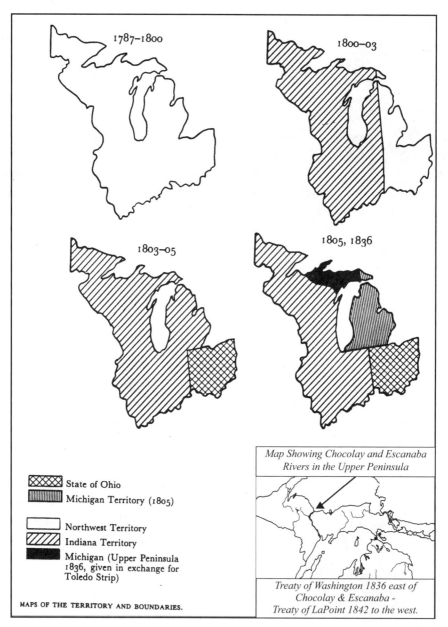

State of Ohio
Michigan Territory (1805)

Northwest Territory
Indiana Territory
Michigan (Upper Peninsula 1836, given in exchange for Toledo Strip)

MAPS OF THE TERRITORY AND BOUNDARIES.

Map Showing Chocolay and Escanaba Rivers in the Upper Peninsula

Treaty of Washington 1836 east of Chocolay & Escanaba - Treaty of LaPoint 1842 to the west.

the rest of the land not under treaty in the lower Peninsula of Michigan, plus all the land east of the Chocolay and Escanaba Rivers in the Upper Peninsula. Governor Cass had laid the groundwork for the treaty ahead of time, as he had been eager to clear title to the land to make room for settlers.

  Thus by the time Michigan became a state, all its lands were open to mineral exploration and settlement except those west of the Chocolay and Escanaba Rivers. Ironically, all the great deposits of copper and iron were in the portion yet unceded.

After Michigan became a state in 1837, steps were taken to open the Upper Peninsula. Dr. Douglas Houghton, who had been on the Schoolcraft Expedition in 1832, was appointed State Geologist in the first act of the legislature. He had accompanied Schoolcraft to Ontonagon to see the Ontonagon Boulder. He had managed to chip a piece off it and collect a loose piece or two. Pure native copper was always a curiosity, but more important, he had been excited to find traces of copper in many places on the Keweenaw.

In 1840, Houghton, now state geologist, brought Chief State Surveyor, Bela Hubbard, to see the famous "copper rock," as it had come to be known. At this time, Houghton seemed to foresee fully the potential great mining boom that awaited the Copper Country.

Although his report of 1841 warned that no quick riches lined the shore of Lake Superior, he did report the Keweenaw's vast copper deposits. This news spread quickly to the financial districts of the eastern seaboard and the rest of the nation. It also created much new curiosity concerning the Ontonagon Boulder.

There are several stories about the removal of the boulder, mainly concerning who actually did the work, James Paul, a former Wisconsin lead miner or Julius Eldred, a hardware merchant from Detroit. There seems to be some truth in all the accounts, and in all probability the boulder could not have been moved without the combined efforts of both men, thus the following version credits both.

Eldred had first heard about the boulder from a member of the Cass expedition and had given it much thought during the years preceding Houghton's report. So in 1841 he proceeded straight to the Ontonagon River. He believed that the huge piece of copper was so unique that it would indeed be a valuable attraction in the city. It was already famous, having been described by Alexander Henry, Louis Cass, Henry Schoolcraft and Douglas Houghton. The boulder was actually 50 inches long, 40 inches wide, about 18 inches thick and weighed a little over 3700 pounds, or just over a ton and a half.

Believing that the boulder belonged to the Indians, Eldred sought out a Chippewa chief in the area, Konteka, and paid him $150. After studying the boulder and its location that summer of 1841, he returned to Detroit to devise a method of removing it the next year. Upon his return in the summer of 1842, all his attempts to move the huge piece of copper proved futile, and he was forced to return to Detroit without it.

In those years, miners and prospectors were working illegally until the Treaty of LaPointe was signed in 1842, ceding the rest of the Upper Peninsula to the U.S. Government. This was the land west of the Chocolay and Escanaba Rivers all the way to the Mississippi, and it included all the great mineral

Courtesy of Bruce Johanson

James Paul

deposits of Michigan, Wisconsin and much of Minnesota.

In 1842, the land had not yet been surveyed, but temporary mineral claims were being issued pending the completion of the survey. Shortly after the treaty was signed, Colonel Hammond had taken out one of these temporary permits to mine the land where the Ontonagon Boulder lay. He sent James K. Paul and a party of miners from Wisconsin to the site.

Back in Detroit, during the winter of 1842-43, Eldred built a sturdy, flat cart just large enough for the boulder to rest on and

Photo courtesy-Smithsonian Institution Museum of Natural History

The famous Ontonagon Boulder, 3700 plus pound piece of float copper.

In an eight-page brochure that was handed out by the Smithsonian Institution in Washington, DC, the last sentence reads, "Such large masses of native copper are no longer found, and its likes is not to be seen elsewhere. The Ontonagon Copper Boulder is a unique specimen of its kind."

The Smithsonian brochure claiming these large pieces of copper are no longer found was printed in the early 1970s.

6000 plus pounds

400-600 plus pounds

over 5000 pounds

In the last 25 years, there have been at least 50 pieces of a ton or more found-some are many times larger than the Ontonagon Boulder.

Pictured here the giant Manitou copper boulder of Lake Superior weighing 8000 pounds. courtesy of Brian Schultz

30

All but a few of these pieces pictured are larger than the famous boulder. They range from 1/2 to 25 tons apiece.

over 9000 pounds

25 tons

Piece of Copper hanging form ceiling in mine shaft.

constructed some sections of strap railroad track. These were mounted on ties so that they could be leap-frogged in two sections, one ahead of the other.

In the summer of 1843, Eldred again returned to the Ontonagon with a crew of 20 men, his cart, rope, pulleys and other paraphernalia to accomplish his task. He had to get a permit to take copper from that land from General Walter Cunningham.

When he arrived at the site, he found Jim Paul and his miners guarding the boulder. Hammond's claim had been issued directly from the Secretary of War, so Eldred had no recourse but to purchase the boulder again, this time for $1,365.

At this point the early reports differ. It seems probable, since the two men had come to an agreement, that Eldred hired Paul with his leadership ability and experienced crew to help carry out the tremendous task of moving the huge chunk of copper down to Lake Superior.

Using greased skids and block and tackle, the crew slowly skidded the boulder up a 50-foot cliff and placed it on the waiting cart. This operation took a full week.

For over four miles, over hills and through valleys, hindered by thick underbrush and swarms of mosquitoes, they inched the cart along the sections of track, moving the sections of rail from back to front every 16 feet. It was a slow and laborious process, but at last the huge copper prize was placed on a river raft and floated down to Lake Superior.

By the time the boulder was ready to be loaded aboard a ship, the government agent had received orders from the Secretary of War to seize it. He did seize it, but after listening to Eldred's story of great expense and trouble, and realizing Eldred had taken every legal precaution and had the papers to prove it, he decided that Eldred was the rightful owner. Thereupon the agent let him load the boulder aboard ship and take it to Detroit.

An extract from the Buffalo Gazette for the year 1843 says:

> "The copper was shipped from Ontonagon on the schooner *Algonquin* to the head of the falls of the St. Mary's where it was transferred to a mackinaw boat and, after passing around the rapids, was shipped on the schooner *Brewster* to Detroit, where it arrived on October 11" (1843).

While in Detroit, the great natural phenomenon was put on public display in a tent set up on Jefferson Avenue for a fee of 25 cents per person.

Meanwhile in Washington there was a growing feeling that the boulder should be in the national capitol. An Englishman named Smithson had donated money for a national museum. He had actually left his fortune to a nephew with the stipulation that after his death the residue of the estate would go to the United States government for this purpose.

By this time the nephew had already died and plans were being completed to build the museum. The Ontonagon Boulder seemed to be just the kind of exhibit that should be in such a museum, a one-of-a-kind national treasure that should belong to all of the people, placed in the nation's capitol where all might view it.

Again the order came, this time from the U.S. District Attorney in Washington, D.C., that the boulder be confiscated. Over Eldred's protests, it was taken by soldiers and placed on the revenue cutter *Erie,* which took it to Buffalo.

The copper was then taken by rail to Washington with Eldred following every step of the way.

After much debate, which lasted some three years or more and with a great deal of publicity, the first session of the 28th Congress passed an act on January 26, 1847 authorizing the Secretary of War to make a settlement. Eldred and his sons were granted $5,664.98.

Photo Courtesy of Harold Banks, Jr., Museum Specialist, Division of Petroleum Smithsonian Institution

Ontonagon Boulder in the Smithsonian Institution

The boulder, now nationally famous, was temporarily placed in the yard of the Quartermaster's Bureau of the War Department, where it remained for eight years. In 1855, for some reason it was moved to the Patent Office and, finally, in 1858 found its home in the United States National Museum (now the Smithsonian).

A century later, in the 1960's, there was an uproar in Michigan to the effect that the Ontonagon Boulder had lost its identity. The staff at the museum didn't know what visitors were talking about when they asked to see it. Accusations were made that the exhibit was gathering dust somewhere in the vast labyrinth of halls in the Smithsonian, lost to history. There was talk of returning it to Michigan, possibly to the State Capitol Building in Lansing.

In 1971, the boulder was moved to the National Museum's "Our Restless Earth" display in the Physical Geology Hall. This seemed to satisfy everyone. The staff was brought up to date on its fascinating history at that time and the huge specimen was given a prominent viewing place.

In 1987, the people of Michigan were celebrating three historical events, the bicentennial of the Constitution of the United States (in Philadelphia), the bicentennial of the Northwest Ordinance, written in New York and the Sesquicentennial (150 years) of Michigan's becoming a state. As a part of these celebrations, after 144 years absence, the Ontonagon Boulder was returned to Ontonagon, Michigan, where it was featured in the annual Labor Day Parade. In beautiful

The Famous copper boulder in the 1987 Labor Day Parade in Ontonagon.

weather, huge crowds watched the famous 3,708 pound chunk of float copper carried down the street mounted on a raised platform on the back of a truck. From there it went on display at the A. E. Seaman Mineralogical Museum at Michigan Tech University in Houghton, where it remained for a month before being returned to the Smithsonian in Washington, D.C.

As a postscript to this 350 year history of the most famous piece of copper in the world, in the year 2000 there was a request by the Keweenaw Bay Indian community to have the Ontonagon Boulder returned to the Copper Country permanently. This, no doubt, was the result of action in 1997 proclaiming the Keweenaw Peninsula as a National Park. At this writing (2004), no action has been taken on this request.

On August 22, 1916, George F. Porter read a paper at the Keweenaw Historical Society meeting. It was later published in the Houghton Mining Gazette. The last portion of this paper is worth quoting, as it sums up the significance of this celebrated piece of copper.

> *I have seen this rock many times at the Smithsonian Institution in Washington, as I presume many thousands have done, but I do not remember if it bore on its surface anything to indicate its strange history and the various vicissitudes it has passed through before reaching its final resting place. If it does not, it seems to me that it should, considering the vast wealth it has heralded and the prospect of millions yet to come, the contemplation of which almost makes the senses reel.*
>
> *This silent rock, in its bed on the rugged shores of the Ontonagon, bore on its metallic face its story and its significance. The untutored savage read it partly, but it was left for the tale it had to tell and its great import. It seems that no mineral specimen in the world at this day possessed the interest and significance that this rock of copper does now, reposing so quietly in the halls of the Smithsonian and there should be some fitting recognition of the great part it played in making known to the nation the vast wealth that lay hidden in the copper region of Lake Superior, only waiting to be sought after.*

Today, a younger generation, not knowing its fascinating history, may be disappointed after traveling long distances to view this lifeless object. If only it could talk!

In a book entitled *Early Days in Detroit*, the author Friend Palmer wrote:

> The Ontonagon River copper rock arrived in Buffalo when I was residing there. I think it came in the fall of 1843. While in transit from the revenue cutter *Erie* to the railroad depot on Exchange Street, it was under the immediate charge of Capt. S. P. Heintzelman, United States quarter-

master (later major general in the U.S. Army during the Civil War), who was stationed in Buffalo at the time. The captain, to gratify the curiosity of the citizens, had it paraded up and down the principal part of the Main Street and down Exchange Street on a four-wheeled truck behind two span of horses and driver. The horses were gaily decorated.

Many of our citizens, eager to possess a clipping from the rock as a souvenir, provided themselves with hammers and chisels for that purpose, hoping to get a clip at it as it passed through the streets. But they were foiled in their attempts at this as Capt. Heintzelman was close to the rock on foot and it kept him busy keeping the people back.

Dr. Douglas Houghton

When Michigan became a state on January 26, 1837 (the 26th state of the Union), the first act of the legislature was to appoint Dr. Douglas Houghton to the position of State Geologist. It was his idea to do a geological survey of the state. He proposed four departments, geology, zoology, botany and topography. This was later revised to a combination of linear and geologic survey.[8]

From the time he was a young boy, Houghton was always interested in the natural sciences. It has been said that he had made several significant discoveries before he was 10 years old. His passion for the sciences was infectious

Photo Courtesy of Michigan Technological University Archives and Copper Country Historical Collections

Dr. Douglas Houghton

---

[8] It was during this linear and geological survey that Surveyor William Austin Burt discovered iron ore on September 19, 1844 near Teal Lake in Negaunee, Michigan.

and he was always surrounded by a group of young people eager to learn from him. While he had a remarkable life, it was a short one; he drowned in Lake Superior when he was only 36-years-old.

Douglas Houghton was born in Troy, New York on September 21, 1809. In 1828, he was graduated from the Van Rensselaer school in that city and was soon appointed assistant professor of chemistry and natural history under Professor Eaton of that same institution.

In 1830 General Lewis Cass and Major Wheting, both of Detroit, arrived at the school and asked Prof. Eaton to recommend someone who was qualified to deliver a course of public lectures on chemistry and geology. The professor highly recommended Douglas Houghton. Houghton was so young and slight that Cass and Wheting could hardly believe the professor could be serious.

Houghton accepted the challenge and his lectures were so popular that he was persuaded to make Michigan his home. He soon won the confidence of the high officials of the state.

Just as he was getting settled in a new office in Detroit, he was appointed by the Secretary of War as surgeon and botanist on the Schoolcraft Expedition to the source of the Mississippi. Over the next 15 years, he was elected Mayor of Detroit for two terms and was the president of the University of Michigan before he was 30 years old.

It was on the night of October 13, 1845 that Dr. Houghton lost his life on Lake Superior. In an open Mackinac sailboat, he was making his way to Eagle River over the rough waters of that lake. They were not far from land. A snow storm prevailed and the wind was blowing a gale. Houghton was anxious to get round a point of rock, a low broken promontory that shelved to a considerable distance seaward. He encouraged his men to brave the storm. The wind was increasing in fury and his companions proposed that they should go ashore, but Houghton, who had great confidence in his own skill, urged them to proceed. Amid the increasing violence of the gale, the boat was capsized. They all went under for a moment. Houghton was raised from the water by his trusted friend and companion, Peter, a half-breed who had been with him for several years, and was advised by him to cling to the keel, then uppermost.

"Never mind me," cried Houghton, "go ashore if you can. Be sure that I will get ashore well enough."

The boat was soon righted and all were at their oars again, but the interval was of brief duration. A moment later a wave struck them with such violence that the boat, receiving the blow at the stern, was dashed over end-wise and all were thrown again into the water. Two of the men were thrown on the beach in a helpless condition, but Houghton was drowned and his body was not found until the following spring.

A first-hand account from a historical pamphlet is quoted here.

> Houghton, his diminutive stature, his keen blue eyes, his quick and nervous motions, the strong sense of energy of words when dealing with matters of science, and his undaunted perseverance when carrying out his designs, made him a notable figure. He was no carpet knight of science and on his geological excursions never flinched from hard work and exposure. On these occasions he usually wore a suit of gray, the coat having large side pockets and hanging loosely from his small figure. His hands and feet were very small, but the latter were encased in boots that came almost to his thighs. His shockingly bad hat was broad-brimmed and slouched and his whole appearance was that of a tattered, weather-worn backwoods-man. I remember meeting him a few years later when his scientific mind and energetic body had unraveled the mysteries of the mineral region of Lake Superior—and when the great fame of that region had called hosts of scientists to those wild shores. He had just landed in Eagle River, fresh from one of his rough expeditions, and was at once hailed and surrounded by men known over the whole world for their scientific learning, to whose figures and bearing his own presented a most striking contrast. Yet these men bowed to his superior knowledge—sagacity I might term it—and one of them frankly said in my hearing that the rough-looking doctor carried more true knowledge in his cranium than all the big heads put together.

America's First Mineral Rush

Through 1843 and 1844, the Ontonagon Boulder received nationwide publicity and the eyes of the whole country were on that remote wasteland in the far north, Michigan's Upper Peninsula. While Houghton's last report was lost in the incident on Lake Superior, his first report published in 1841 was enough to spur interest in the region. With the great surge of publicity concerning the Ontonagon Boulder, prospectors, capitalists and adventurers turned their thoughts westward and northward and a small migration started toward the Copper Country. The land had not been surveyed, so no claims could be bought outright, but they could be leased for three years. The mineral leases were tracts of nine square miles, and six pounds of every hundred pounds of copper had to be paid to the government. Later, in 1847, when the survey had been completed, the sale of mineral lands in quarter sections (160 acres) was allowed.

Between 1843 and 1846, the first great mineral rush in the United States took place in the Copper Country of Michigan's Upper Peninsula. Hundreds of permits were issued and many companies were formed. Most of the speculators were from the east, especially New York and Boston.

The inevitable happened. Many of the new settlers were disillusioned, as everything (tools, food and equipment) was very expensive or unavailable. Supplies were slow to arrive or never arrived at all. The copper, even when found, was difficult to get out of the rock. The winters were longer and more severe than the fortune seekers had anticipated. Even in summer, life was complicated by poor maps, no roads, endless swamps and mosquitoes. But even under these conditions, ever-enthusiastic reports from some operations encouraged still more eastern investors.

In 1844, Dr. Charles T. Jackson, a geologist, was hired by a group of Boston financiers to operate the Lake Superior Copper Company. It and its successors operated at a loss before going bankrupt in 1849, but Jackson became well known on the Peninsula and did much to further the copper industry and later the iron industry.

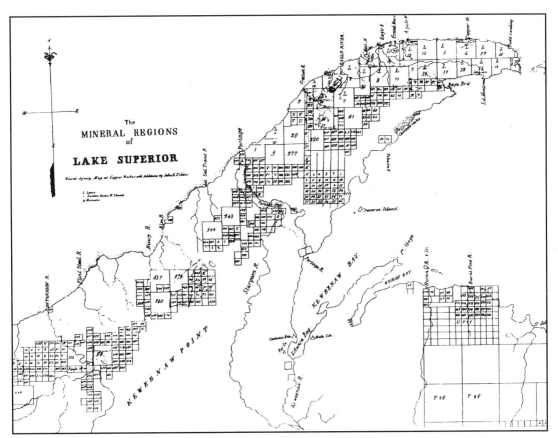

Mineral Claims in Upper Michigan by 1850

Fort Wilkins

Another company formed by men from Pittsburgh and Boston in 1844 was more fortunate. Near Eagle River, high on the Keweenaw Peninsula, they opened a vein which led to a mass of native copper. Later, along with other copper masses, they found silver. The Pittsburgh and Boston Company paid the district's first dividend in 1848.

Except for a few minor isolated incidents, there were no problems with the Indians when the first whites came to settle in the Upper Peninsula. Most of the Indians felt that they had been treated fairly and did not blame individuals if they weren't, and they were often helpful in the endeavors of the outsiders. However, with such an influx of miners to the Keweenaw Peninsula, many made it known in Washington that they felt a little uneasy about the Indians, no matter how peaceful they seemed. They felt the government should provide some protection.

In answer to these demands, in 1844 the U.S. built Fort Wilkins on the shores of Lake Fanny Hooe at the tip of the Keweenaw Peninsula, near Copper Harbor. The fort was named after the Secretary of War. The lake was named for the sister-in-law of Dan Ruggles who was stationed at the fort when she visited him in the early years.

Except possibly for the psychological well-being of some miners, Fort Wilkins proved to be a worthless expenditure, as the Indians continued to be friendly. The fort was in a bad location as well. It would have taken days to get help to stem an uprising that could have taken place in hours, and there was

Phoyo courtesy of Travel Michigan

Fort Wilkins at Copper Harbor as seen from Lake Fanny Hooe.

little or no means of communication. Besides, it was an extremely lonely and desolate post for the men to spend the winter. When the Mexican War broke out in 1846, the garrison, except for a skeleton caretaking force, was ordered away. The fort was finally evacuated in 1870 and the land purchased by Houghton and Keweenaw Counties. Later it was deeded to the State of Michigan.

The First Successful Copper Venture

John Hays - from the Book of Peter White.

From "The Honorable Peter White" by Ralph Williams, Panton Publishing Company, Cleveland, Ohio, 1907:

"Among those who were attracted by Houghton's report of the presence of copper in the Lake Superior country was John Hays of Cleveland, at the time residing in Pittsburgh. It is to John Hays that the credit belongs for making the first profit from a commercial venture in the new area. He had been engaged in the drug business for a number of years in Pittsburgh. He was determined to visit the Lake Superior region, primarily to regain his health and incidentally to inquire into the mineral deposits."

Early visitors and prospectors to the region discovered that one slept well and even when cold and wet, did not come down with a cold or other ailment. In fact, for the next century the delightful summer climate and pure air attracted people from the whole country and abroad for health and rest purposes.

Before leaving, Hays explained his purpose to Dr. C. G. Hussey of Pittsburgh. Hussey became much interested in the trip and agreed to pay half of Hays' expenses and to furnish half the funds required to take up leases of mineral lands. Hays accepted the proposition and on the 17th of August 1843 left Pittsburgh for Cleveland where he engaged passage on the steamer *Chesapeake* for Mackinac. The journey from Mackinac to Sault Ste. Marie was made by canoe. At the Soo, Hays boarded the schooner *Algonquin* and reached Copper Harbor in three days. There he made the acquaintance of a Mr. Raymond, a speculator from Boston, and General Cunningham, the government agent. Raymond had taken three leases, one at Copper Harbor, one at Eagle River and the third at Portage Lake. He was anxious to dispose of them, and Hays, being convinced upon examination that they were valuable, offered one thousand dollars for a one-sixth interest in the three leases on condition that his partner, Dr. Hussey, would ratify the deal. To this, Raymond agreed.

Hays then returned to Pittsburgh and reported the venture to Hussey, who was pleased with it, and so the bargain was closed. They concluded, however, that it would be well to control a larger interest in the leases, and Hays accordingly found three more investors, all men of means. They purchased an additional three-sixths interest in the Raymond leases. With a two-thirds interest in the leases, Hays was authorized by his partners to explore the lands and develop the properties.

In the spring of 1844, Hays left Pittsburgh for Lake Superior with nine men, eight laborers and one geologist, Mr. Alfred Rudolf. They chartered the *Algonquin* at the Soo to take them to Copper Harbor.

After examining the land, the party sank a shaft near Lake Fanny Hooe, where they uncovered a vein which proved to be the celebrated black oxide, yielding 86 percent pure copper. Hays and his men mined some twenty-six tons of this black oxide that first season.

On November 18, 1844, Hays discovered the Cliff mine near Eagle River. This mine was to become famous as the first mine ever developed in the Lake Superior country and the first in the world to yield pure native copper. This was considered a great discovery throughout the whole metallurgical world. In England the discovery could not be credited because the British Museum contained no specimens of metallic copper, as it was not known to exist.

THE CLIFF MINE IN THE SPRING OF 1845. FROM AN OLD ENGRAVING.

During the summer of 1845, Hays explored the Eagle River District and found a mass of copper weighing 3,100 pounds at the base of a cliff. Later, a mass of native copper weighing 81 tons was unearthed.

As the Cliff mine produced large amounts of copper in masses from one ton up to 81 tons, it became necessary to erect a smelting works in order to put it into marketable ingots weighing about ten pounds apiece. For this purpose, Hays went to England to examine English furnaces, carrying with him samples of copper, one piece weighing 3,852 pounds and others weighing from one to ten pounds. The large piece was sold to Kings College on the Strand and the smaller pieces were given to the British Museum.

There were, however, no furnaces in England for smelting mass copper. The English obtained their copper from ore combined with sulphur, known as sulphate of copper. The specimens that Hays left in England created great excitement among geologists and did much to enlist the interests of capitalists in the wonderful mineral region of Michigan.

Hays returned to the United States determined to construct a furnace with his own plan, provided that his associates were satisfied with it. The company at once decided to construct the furnace and it was completed at Pittsburgh in 1848. The top of the furnace was removed by a crane and masses of copper hoisted in by the same means. It proved to be a great success. Hays himself supervised the work for the first eighteen months.

The first batch of ingots was sold to Robert Fulton of Pittsburgh (son of the inventor). The first sheet copper to be rolled west of the Alleghenies was from one of Hays' ingots at Shoenberger's mill by Mr. William Lutton and his son, William H. Lutton.

The Cliff Mine proved to be a profitable venture for the Pittsburgh and Boston Mining Company. During a ten-year period (1846-1856), it earned $3,858,000 from the original $108,000 invested by its owners.

The Great Discovery

About the time that Hays' furnace first started producing copper ingots, prospectors were swarming all over the Keweenaw Peninsula and, indeed, along the whole north shore of Upper Michigan. They looked at rocks, dug test pits, staked out claims and looked for investors. Many had noticed strange ancient diggings here and there, but no one seemed curious about them or had any idea as to how they came about. Then an event took place that changed the method of prospecting for copper considerably.

During the winter of 1847-48, Mr. Samual O. Knapp, an agent for the Minnesota Mine near Rockland, Michigan, was doing some exploring and prospecting in the area.

One report says he was looking for a place to spend the night in the woods out of the weather. He was clearing out a cave in the side of a rock hill when he noticed that the material he was throwing out did not seem like natural fill. Curious, he continued digging the next day in good light. Among the debris he noticed some round stones with a definite man-made groove around their middle. As he continued to dig, more and more of the strange grooved stones turned up. Many were broken and from the scars and chips off the working ends of all the rocks. It was obvious to Knapp that these were the tools of ancient miners. Indeed, he deduced that prehistoric people must have been digging for copper there.

At a depth of 18 feet, he discovered the top of a huge mass of copper. Later it was discovered that the mass was resting on wooden cribbing. It had been cut free and raised at least five or six feet from the bottom of the hole. With further excavation, the piece of copper proved to be roughly 10 feet by 6 feet by 3 feet thick and weighed well over six tons.[9]

Knapp discovered many similar pits in the surrounding woods. All of them had copper and all of them had round, grooved rocks which turned out to be hammerstones. It was clear to him that intelligent people had done a tremendous amount of exploring and mining in the area. His discovery made prospecting much easier than the chance methods that had been used previously. All a prospector had to do was look for old pits: where there were hammerstones, there was copper.

Once ordinary people were told what to look for, it didn't take an expert to conclude that experienced miners had dug these holes. They knew exactly what they were doing. In fact, a 26-year-old Indian agent, J. Logon Chipman, viewing the Copper Country for the first time in 1853, wrote:

> *The changes which have marked the influx of the white population have been so like the witchery of a fairy tale that, instead of abating, they have increased the wonder of the world. Nothing has contributed so much to this result as the discovery of the vast works of the ancient miners. Scattered over the extent of hundreds of miles, evincing a degree of skill that seems to require utensils of a more effective nature than have yet been discovered, and a magnitude which, upon the hypothesis that their authors had no means of excavation, must have required the labor of a population as redundant as these states of antiquity, they will ever remain an impenetrable secret to science.*

---

[9] A piece of copper of this size would weigh 10 to 15 tons. *(Authors Opinion)*

The Calumet and Hecla and Quincy Mines

By 1864, the great Calumet and Hecla Mining Company was formed, consolidating with several other companies by 1871. While today there are some huge deposits of very low grade ore found in Finland, Russia and elsewhere as well as the United States, mainly Montana, Utah and Arizona, all are developed as open-pit mines. No other company in the world compared with the Calumet and Hecla in either the richness of its ores or profits. The amount of production has been exceeded recently by the Kennecott mines of Utah, but they mine extremely low grade ores of .5 to .8 percent. However, the volume and the methods of handling these low grade ores are so advanced that one modern 350-ton truck filled with .6 percent ore will produce over three tons of pure copper. The Kennicott Copper Mine in the mountains of Utah has out-produced any single mine in existence—but not the Calumet & Hecla, which closed in the 1920's.

In 1864, Edwin Hulbert and Amos H. Scott uncovered a vein of rich conglomerate bearing copper beneath a belt of amygdaloidal copper, a soft deposit containing an abundance of lump pure copper.

In a letter, John Hulbert, Jr. tells us of the famous discovery:

> In the fall of 1864, Mr. Hulbert directed Amos H. Scott and myself to go out into the woods to uncover a vein of copper that he believed and said existed, but never had been opened by anyone. He directed us to go to the Southwest corner of Section 13, Town 56 North, Range 33 West in Houghton County; to follow up the section line North about 1,500 feet; then run South 50°; and East about 250 feet, to a precise point indicated in a written order to us: there to sink an exploring pit for the vein.

Scott and Hulbert followed his directions and dug through some eight feet of drift before they came to rock. Working another ten feet northwesterly, they uncovered a vein of rich conglomerate bearing copper that was overlaid by a belt of amygdaloidal copper, a softer deposit containing an abundance of lump copper. In November of 1864, further excavations revealed an ancient pit 1200 feet southwest of the first opening. Over the next several months, Hulbert and his crew took twenty tons of loose green carbonate-of-copper from this cache as well as numerous birch bark baskets, buck skin and spruce-root strings, skeins for repairing the baskets, parts of wooden shovels and rock hammers.

This great storage pit, with its cache of thousands of pieces of copper, had obviously been collected and carried to this pit by many people long ago. The copper had carburized, one of the clues that triggered later scholars to think that these ancient miners had been collecting the copper so that it could be taken away in bulk quantities at a convenient time. Several more of these large storage pits were found later along the Keweenaw water way.

Edwin Hulbert's discoveries were the foundation for the great Calumet and Hecla Mine, which became world famous.

After a series of poor management decisions, Hulbert lost the confidence of his original Boston financial backers. In 1867, he was replaced as manager of the mine by Alexander Agassiz, the son of the famous geologist, Louis Agassiz (1807-1873), whose defense of the doctrine of a glacial period destroyed the last remnants of scientific opposition to Lyell's teachings.[10]

Alexander Agassiz was determined to make Calumet a model mining community. The company built homes, schools, streets, churches and hospitals. In addition, there was a public library, bathhouses, and an indoor swimming pool provided for the families. Calumet was by far the largest and most modern city in Michigan's Upper Peninsula and was even considered for being the state capitol. With its paved streets, electric lights, telephones and indoor plumbing, it attracted many high class merchants and shops. Its beautiful theater provided many worldly forms of entertainment. The famous old Calumet Theater has been restored and is still open for many events.

The main offices of the company were moved to Boston and controlled by Agassiz's brother-in-law, Quincy A. Shaw, Henry Lee Higginson and H. S. Russell.

Hulbert was compensated by being given land in the area and he pursued his profession as a surveyor, mining engineer and explorer in the region until 1876. He was elected to represent Houghton County in the State Legislature in 1874. He died at the age of 81.

The Calumet and Hecla main office was at 12 Ashburton Place in Boston with the main office in Calumet, Houghton County, Michigan. The mill office was at Lake Linden, with smelter's offices in Hubbell, all in Houghton County.

Another man connected with the C & H who became famous in the Copper Country was James McNaughton. Alexander Agassiz was president and he was general manager.

Dividends in C & H to December 31, 1907 were $105,850,000, the largest mining profits ever distributed by any incorporated mining company. Dividends were $5,000,000 in 1905, $7,000,000 in 1906 and $6,000,000 in 1907. Net earnings for the fiscal year ending April 3, 1907, were $11,297,390.

The land holdings of the Calumet and Hecla in Houghton, Keweenaw and Ontonagon Counties in 1907 amounted to 74,841 acres or 117 square miles.

Despite every precaution, the Calumet and Hecla had many underground fires. The amygdaloidal trap rock carrying native copper in chunks cannot burn

---

[10] (1) That the age of the earth is very great and (2) that in the processes in operation at the present may be found illustrations of most of the changes of the past.

like sulphide ore, but the old timbering eventually becomes nearly as flammable as tinder. The really serious mine fires, five in number, occurred once in 1884, in July and November of 1887, on November 30, 1888 and May 27, 1900.

Precautions against these mine fires involved fireproofing the mining timbers with zinc chloride solution, regular sprinkling of the shafts, strict maintenance of the water pipes and hydrants, fire hoses, chemical engines, electric alarm systems and 18 telephones at proper stations. The first fires that the mine experienced took a number of lives and caused losses of several million dollars.

There were 21 C & H shafts, some of them nearly two miles deep. The No. 4 shaft up until World War I contained some of the most powerful machinery ever built. The brick engine house, 62 feet by 146 feet, boasted a 4,700 horsepower Corliss engine "Superior," with 40-inch cylinders and 72-inch stroke, the engine "Mackinac," a 7,000 horsepower quadruple-cylinder triple expansion steel giant, and a 35-drill operating auxiliary compressor.

The machine shop, 225 feet by 250 feet, largely rebuilt in 1907, had equipment excelled only by a few of the largest mining shops in the country. It included a 25-ton electric traveling crane and mammoth planers.

Production in 1906 was 100,023,420 pounds of fine copper, leading all other mines in the world and the mighty C & H produced nearly the same rate of tonnage for the next four years.

Today a traveler driving north up the long Quincy Hill beyond the city of Hancock passes a famous Copper Country landmark. There, on the top of Quincy Hill, stands the unique Quincy shaft house No. 2, second of eight shafts sunk by the Quincy Mining Company between 1857 and 1900. This mine closed in 1931 at the beginning of the Great Depression. Back in 1909, however, it held extensive properties on the Pewabic lode, from the Hancock Mine on the north shore of Portage Lake to the Franklin Jr., halfway between Calumet and Hancock. The Quincy included lands formerly held by Quincy, Pewabic, Franklin, Mesnard, Pontiac and St. Mary's companies, south to north.

In the upper levels, immense masses of native copper were found, some of them up to 300 tons (600,000 lbs.) in weight. In 1906, the company employed 650 miners and had compressor capacity for 260 power drills. It produced 5,000 tons of stamp rock daily. This rock was then crushed to extract the copper.

The equipment from No. 7 shaft included an 8000 Allis-Chalmers Corliss hoist with 52-inch and 84-inch cylinders and winding drums 28-feet in diameter by 11 feet, 9 inches face carrying 8,000 feet of 1-1/2 inch steel cable. The main shaft cable weighed 120,000 pounds. The hoist could raise six ton skips from depths of 1-1/2 miles at a speed of 3,000 feet per minute. In later years, the great Quincy Hoist became known as "Old Reliable."

Calumet Hecla's "Old Reliable"

There were over 80 other mines working on the copper range during the last part of the 19th and early 20th centuries that provided 80 percent of the world's supply of copper.

Much of the copper was freed by huge stamp mills that produced millions of tons of stamp sand. Even today many beaches of the Keweenaw Peninsula are gray with finely ground stamp sand. Later many tons of this stamp sand were reworked and yielded as much as three pounds, or more copper per ton of sand. Most copper mines that are operating today produce ores of copper that are one percent or less.

On a trip through the Copper Country today, one can view many remains of these famous mineral workings.

Even with the phenomenal amount of copper available, the "strikes" of the modern prospectors that were able to pay more than the cost of developing

One of the old "mudsucker" barges, long abandoned on Torch Lake. It was used to reclaim stamp sand

a mine were not easy to find. Of more than 1,000 mines started in the Copper Country, only about 100 actually produced copper and many of these lost money. Only about 30 or so mines paid their way and only about half of these became really profitable. The real bonanzas were the Calumet and Hecla and the Quincy (Old Reliable). They paid far more than all the moneys spent on mine ventures in all of Michigan. The Calumet and Hecla eclipsed any mine in the world, irrespective of the metal or any other product mined in dollar value of the ores extracted. Between 1845 and 1969 the Copper Country mines produced over 12 billion pounds of copper worth 2.26 billion dollars.

One of the present attractions in the Copper Country is a ride on the Quincy Hoist which has been rebuilt for tourists. Another is a trip into the depths of the Arcadia Mine at Ripley near Hancock. Here visitors will be taken down into the depths of the mine over 300 feet on a trip that, when operating, extended for 3,000 feet below the richest copper bearing land in the country. The original Arcadia Mine opened in 1864.

The Italian Hall Disaster

What was undoubtedly the worst calamity ever to hit the Upper Peninsula took place on Christmas Eve of 1913. At that time the Copper Country was in the grip of a long and bitter strike.

While in the early years of Agassiz's benevolent paternalism, there were virtually no labor problems, but low pay, long hours and ethnic friction was causing some unrest. The Western Federation of Miners was making much of the fact that a handful of wealthy shareholders from Boston was reaping millions of dollars in dividends and this added fuel to the fire. They started a local union in 1908. On July 23, 1913, over 15,000 miners went idle when a general strike was called. That winter a Christmas party was being held in Calumet's Italian Hall, put on by the striking miners for their wives and children. The room was on the second floor with a long stairway leading down to the street where double doors opened in from the outside.

The party was called "A Christmas Tree Celebration," given by the Women's Auxiliary of the Western Federation of Miners for the strikers' children. There were about 700 people in the hall when at about 5:30 in the evening, someone, unknown to this day, yelled "fire" just as the presents were being distributed to the children.

An eyewitness account of the tragedy was given by Matt Saari to the newspapers.

He said the hall was crowded with women and children plus a few men. At the rear end of the hall were Christmas trees where children were crowding to get their presents.

Italian Hall in Calumet - stairwell at left.

Interior of Italian Hall - after the tragedy Christmas Day 1913.

Strikers Parade.

Funeral procession of dead.

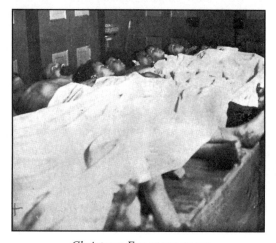

Christmas Eve at mortuary.

Line of hearses waiting at the church.

Saari said the cry of "fire" came from a group of men and women sitting at one side of the hall. Whether he realized the impending danger, he does not explain, but he said he left the building directly.

An article in the *Marquette Mining Journal* for Friday, December 26, 1913 says, in part:

> The Italian Hall is a long room of the familiar type of assembly room for lodges and societies of various sorts. It is reached by a long narrow stairway from the street, and this stairway ends at a small landing, with double doors opening into the auditorium.
>
> With the cry of fire, a stampede from the room began. Efforts were made by cooler heads to stem the tide flowing to certain death. Frightened women, fear-crazed children, boys and girls eager only for self preservation, men reduced to unthinking animals, all attempted to crowd through the narrow doorway to the stairs.
>
> One brave man, whose name will never be known, attempted to hold back the crowd. He was near the door and only a few women and children got past him before he made his effort. But the weight of the fear-maddened humanity was too much for him. With his voice and all his strength, he tried to calm the crowd to assure the panic-stricken that there was no danger. But the mass terror was uncontrollable and the brave man went to his death under an avalanche of little bodies. He literally was smothered to death by those he tried to save.
>
> The surge of humanity lost all individual identity as 700 people tried to surge through a pitiably inadequate passage. So great was the weight of humanity in back of those already on the stairs that even fugitives close to the street failed to emerge alive. The weight packed the crowd of children down onto the steps, pressed them outward against the walls of the stairway, bound them tight, until the mass jammed solid around the street door at the bottom.
>
> The awful tide crushed down until there was a causeway of quivering bodies over which many managed to escape by crawling and trampling and falling down into the street, heedless of everything except safety.
>
> All this took but a few minutes. The men in the saloon beneath the hall heard the death cries and ran out. A fire alarm was turned in. Citizens poured toward the sudden charnel house from every direction and a combined effort restored order so quickly that it seemed incredible so much destruction could have been wrought.
>
> The tangle of little bodies, with those of a few grown folk who also had perished, were so packed in the stairway that they formed almost a solid mass. It was impossible to release the jam of dead from the bottom of the stairway and the work had to be done from above.
>
> Hundreds of men and women seeking their children, and hundreds of children seeking their parents, mobbed the town hall in an effort to satisfy themselves, until they nearly caused another panic. The crowd was restrained with difficulty and hour after hour heart-rending scenes played out as family after family learned of their share of the disaster.
>
> Some few were found exhausted in the piles of dead and were revived. After the stampede, only the dead or the unconscious seemed to have been left in the hall as far as it has been able to be determined today.

The saddest Christmas Eve that Calumet ever knew was an echo of the great strike by the Western Federation of Miners. Though the Calumet community had tried in every way to give the children of the needy strikers just as merry a Christmas as any children of the district, the strikers' wives wanted to feel that they were contributing in some way to the Christmas cheer of their little ones. Thus, mothers died with their children.

This crowning act of calamity took the lives of thirty-four girls, twenty boys, twelve women and five men, a total of seventy-one lives in all, yet there was no sign of any fire.

General Manager McNaughton, of course, placed all the resources of the Calumet and Hecla Mining Company at the disposal of the injured, but there was such bitter resentment among the strikers that they announced they would accept no public aid.

The sadness and grief turned to anger. The WFM accused the pro-company Citizens Alliance of hollering "fire." Two days after the fire, Charles Moyer, the WFM president, was shot at the Scott Hotel in Hancock and put on a train to Chicago by a mob of union men. United States President Woodrow Wilson and Samual Gompers, President of the American Federation of Labor (AFL), and thousands of others sent condolences and money. (The union refused money from nonunion sources.)

Several mass funerals were held that were attended by over 32,000 people. There were dozens of investigations, but no one was ever prosecuted. Five Congressmen and Governor Ferris all visited the area during the investigations. The heart of the union had been broken. On January 12, 1914, the last of the National Guard went home. The companies refused to hire any union members and thousands of strikers left the area. There were thousands of nonunion workers who moved in to take over the vacant jobs. The strike ended on January 12, 1914. The stories of the violent union tactics that appeared in the press went a long way to defeat the union; it was the deathnell for the Western Federation of miners. Later, the American Federation of Labor moved in, but it was a long time before the C & H workers would have union representation.

The defeat of the union and the Italian Hall disaster were both a terrible blow to the whole Michigan copper industry and it never really fully recovered. Within the next few decades, the country was thrown into World War I and then the Great Depression, followed by World War II. By then, cheaper copper was being produced from the open-pit mines in Arizona and the mountains and hills of Utah and Montana, as well as other places in the world.

The Decline of the Copper Range

Production on the Michigan Copper Range slowly dwindled until there was but one mine operating. It was the White Pine Mine in Ontonagon. It was yielding 1% copper, but it was an underground mine with miles of underground roadways. The profit margin was just too narrow to compete and White Pine shut down in 1997.

Long-time Marquette resident Chuck Foreman tells a story that took place in 1964.

Chuck was touring the mine with Larry Garfield, Vice President of the White Pine Copper Mine. Mr. Garfield pointed to a neatly piled mass of cast ingots of copper and stated, "All of this is just break even. Our profit is from the silver by-product."

There were a few other metals, one of which was gold, that were taken from the copper and processed elsewhere.

Huge masses of pure copper still remain untouched in a massive syncline beneath Lake Superior from Isle Royale to the Keweenaw Peninsula, too deep

The most prolific writer of Copper Country history is Clarence J. Monette of Lake Linden, Michigan. He has written scores of well illustrated histories of nearly every village mine or location in the Copper Country. Books of his local history can be ordered by writing to: Clarence J. Monette 942 Ninth St. , Lake Linden MI 49945

and too expensive to mine today. But, as stated, there is much copper left in the area..

The future of the copper industry in the Copper Country does not look bright. In 1999 a new method of retrieving copper was rejected by the local inhabitants as too polluting. The idea was to pump acid into the ground in order to dissolve the copper. The solution would then be pumped out and the copper reclaimed.

Now, with new discoveries, it looks as if the next source of copper may be the sea floor. Massive deposits of mineral-rich sulphides have been located in many areas of sea bottom. These sediments are in layers up to 300 feet thick and contain iron, zinc, copper, lead, silver and gold.

Another development that will drastically reduce the need for copper in the future was described in "Technology," 1998, by Jeffrey Winters, as carbon nanotubes. These are cylindrical molecules of graphite which may be the material of the future as they conduct electricity with almost no resistance at room temperature and are about 100 times stronger than steel. Since much of copper production goes to the electrical industry, this would certainly curtail drastically the need for copper unless other uses are found. It will still have industrial uses such as roofing (flashing), etc., and it seems there will always be a demand in the form of art objects, statuary and bronze.

At present there is much experimentation going on in the underground tunnels of the White Pine Mine. Light can be perfectly controlled and temperature and humidity are fairly constant, thus food and medicinal plants are now being grown there.

Above: Copper Ingots on dock ready for shipment

Right: A single Ingot of Copper weighing 62 1/2 lbs, 20 inches long.

With this background in Copper Country history, I will now relate my lifelong interest in Upper Michigan copper. It is this knowledge from people and events that has compelled me to believe that there is much more to the history of copper than is told in our history books.

In my opinion, the history of Michigan copper involves the great civilizations that existed in Europe, Africa, Asia and China thousands of years ago. I am not the pioneer of this idea, but am one of many for whom I have tried to put the many pieces together. You will be introduced to those people and events that I have been closest to. For me it all started when I was a young boy.

Photo courtesy Liz Yelland

Ancient diggings along Lake Superior shores.

Chapter III
Early Indoctrination

Childhood Memories

In 1936, at a Boy Scout Camp known as Camp Miniyata in the central part of Michigan's Upper Peninsula, I listened to exciting tales of Isle Royale related by a group of Boy Scouts who had been camping there that summer. They told of a great forest fire that swept over half the island, of an airplane that crashed in Rock Harbor, and of paddling alongside swimming moose in order to jump astride. The boys would slide off the moose when they neared shore.

They told other intriguing stories of finding pure copper in the rocks, hunting for greenstones[11] on the gravel beaches, visiting lighthouses, hidden harbors, old mines and graves on Cemetery Island. The stories went on and on; I couldn't wait to go to Isle Royale. I am quite sure that I had never heard of the Lake Superior gem place before that summer of 1936, but the thought of a far-off wilderness island was more than enough to capture the imagination of any adventurous young boy.

My first experience as a camper at Camp Miniyata was in the summer of 1933 when it was a YMCA camp. I spent six days there with a group of 8 to 12-year-olds.

My dad drove us to the camp in our 1928 Buick and I remember I didn't want him to leave without me that first trip, but after finding a few school friends and seeing the tents we would be living in, my curiosity got the better of me. We were shown how to make our own straw ticks to sleep on and told we would be awakened by a bugle call. We also heard that we would be taking part in an Indian campfire ceremony, all exciting stuff for the 1930's. That first week was such a great experience and such fun that the next year my brother and I stayed for two ten-day sessions.

In 1935 Camp Miniyata was sold to the Boys Scouts of America. As a Scout Camp there was different leadership, of course, but the routine seemed pretty much the same as before. Because I had taken up the cornet in the school band, I became the assistant bugler that summer. My mentor, Hugo Pearson from Ishpeming, taught me all the standard Army bugle calls and often let me struggle through the appropriate call, or let me echo his evening taps from a distance.

---

[11] Greenstones—semi-precious stone, scientific name Cholersterlyte, state gemstone of Michigan.

By 1936 I was the head bugler and at 12 years old I was among the youngest of the boys; the age limits were 11 to 16. My brother and I were now old-timers who knew our way around.

My fondest memories at Camp Miniyata were the evening campfires and the Indian ceremonies that continued during both camps.

These events were held in a ceremonial ring built in a clearing out in a jackpine forest. We campers were all dressed in loin cloths and a blanket and at dusk we walked to the ring in a solemn column. In the distance we heard the beating of a tom-tom. Then a chief in a war bonnet and full Indian regalia began singing a long chant. At a certain signal, a carefully balanced pile of wood in the center of our circle seemed magically to burst into flame. It was all very impressive.

Another instructive campfire featured a South Sea Island explorer named Captain Salsbury who spoke of head-hunters and cannibals. He passed around spears, shields and other relics of primitive people. But of all the campfires over the years, nothing said or seen fired my imagination like the stories told of Isle Royale. Those scouts had been on a relatively nearby mysterious island. Maybe, I thought, I could go to this fabled place and share their thrilling experiences.

Getting to Isle Royale

The following year (1937), there was some doubt if there would be a trip to Isle Royale because of fire danger. During the summer of 1936, terrible fires had burned more than 35,000 acres of the island and the moose herd had dropped in number from about 3,000 head in 1929 to less than 500 animals. Because of the fire, there was concern that many more moose would starve to death that winter.

In an effort to further reduce the herd, 71 moose were live-trapped on the island and released east of Munising. At the time the numbers of moose on the mainland were negligible.

Late that summer of 1937 I received word through the scout office that a group of scouts from Wyandotte, Michigan, a city near Detroit, would be coming through Marquette headed for Isle Royale, and that they would be willing to take as many as 20 local boys with them.

Unfortunately, the flare of enthusiasm that I had noted among my friends the year before seemed to have passed. It seemed that I was the only one who still wanted to go. I was told that if I could round up three friends who could leave the next day, "Pop" Spurr, the local scout executive, would take us in his 1929 Model A Ford. The cost would be ten dollars for ten days, including everything. I rounded up the three friends and we left the next morning.

After picking up 200 loaves of bread at Corneliuson's Bakery in Ishpeming and dealing with six flat tires en route, we arrived at Copper Harbor late at night. It took a lot of asking around, but we finally located the downstate scouts camped in the woods just beyond Fort Wilkins. There was also a small group from Ishpeming and another from Hancock.

The next day we were very disappointed when we saw "our" boat leaving for the island with a small party of adults. But two days later the *Copper Queen* boarded our group and finally headed out for the forty-five mile trip.

Isle Royale is a narrow island, about 50 miles long and eight or nine miles wide at the widest part. It belongs to the State of Michigan, but is only 15 miles from the Canadian shore. There are several long, narrow harbors, especially on its southeast end, the longest being Rock Harbor, which was to be our campsite.

We set up our tents about a third of the way down Rock Harbor, at a clearing known as the Siskiwit Mine. Vance Hiney, a teacher in the Negaunee schools and a long-time friend of my family, was our cook. Since he knew me, he volunteered me to be his special helper, the official cookee.

When we first arrived at our campsite, Vance took me back into the woods and showed me a large hole in the ground. He told me we would be putting all the food that needed to be kept cold down in the bottom of that hole. Later, everyone pitched in to carry supplies up to the edge of the hole, while one or two boys would take the boxes and bags down inside.

It was afternoon when I took my first trip down. You didn't need a ladder; a steep path on rocks wound its way to the bottom. It was August, so I was amazed to find the bottom covered with ice, perfect for the fresh provisions. It became my job to bring things up as they were needed.

I became very curious about that hole and had a lot of questions every time I returned from it.

"That's a mine," I was told. It didn't seem like much of a mine to me as it was only 20 or 30 feet deep. I was used to stories of the iron mines near home where men went down hundreds of feet in shafts.

No one in the group seemed to know much about the mine or even seemed interested, but I was positively fascinated. When I was sent to get something down there I was always given a flashlight and several times I saw mice scampering around our food.

I asked what kind of a mine it was. "It's a copper mine," the leaders told me.

So I started looking for copper in the hole and sure enough there were small bits of copper glinting here and there. The more I looked, the more I found, but I couldn't chip any loose to take home. It was pure copper but imbedded in the rock.

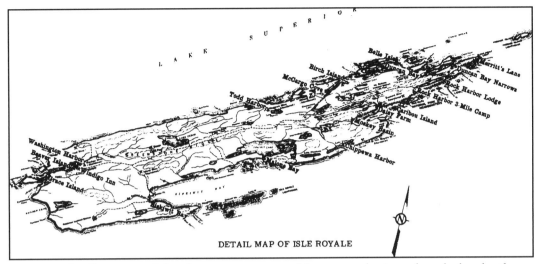

DETAIL MAP OF ISLE ROYALE

At Cemetery Island we saw some old graves, just sunken holes in the ground with crude, illegible markers. Who were these people? They were copper miners, I was told. They were Englishmen from a hundred years or so ago. Did they really work in the mines? Nobody knew, but Englishmen had worked several places on the Island. The more we explored the more evidence of digging we found.

"Who did all the digging?" I asked different adults who I thought would know some answers. I finally got a statement out of one leader, nothing detailed but more than I had ever learned before.

"Well, the last ones to mine here were the Americans," he said, "that was about 50 or more years ago. Before that it was the English, way back in the 1700 and 1800's. But most of the digging was done by Indians who dug for copper all over this island hundreds of years ago." I was more curious than ever. Imagine the history of people digging for copper here that went back hundreds of years.

Without even looking for it some of my friends had picked up nice pieces of copper mixed with rock. I was getting envious as I had been trying hard to find some, but I just couldn't seem to find a piece that was loose enough to take home. Eventually I was able to work a few small pieces free. Later I got some better pieces from friends until I had more than I really wanted. I still have most of this copper I obtained back in 1937, over 65 years later.

A Trip to McCargo Cove

When our ten days on Isle Royale were up, the boat couldn't return for us, so we actually stayed on the island for 18 days. With this extension of time we were able to take at least one more longer trip, so six of us decided to go to

Minong Mountain on the opposite side of the island, the northwest shore.

On that trip our leader was Bill Mudge, a premedical student at the time. Today Dr. Mudge is retired and lives in Marquette.

On a previous trip to nearby Mount Franklin we could see Minong Mountain on the distant horizon. Mrs. Carroll Paul, daughter of John M. Longyear of Marquette and head of the Marquette County Historical Society, had told me earlier that the Indian name for Isle Royale was "Minong." When a mountain with that special name was pointed out to me, I really wanted to go there. From what I had heard, that mountain must have some special significance. I was told to organize a group who would like to make the trip and Bill Mudge would take us. When we heard the boat would not arrive for at least four or five days, we got the go-ahead.

Until then we had not moved camp from the Siskiwit Mine on Rock Harbor near the east end of the island. The six of us, traveling in two canoes, made the first few miles on Rock Harbor as far as the CCC camp (Civilian Conservation Corps).[12] This location later became known as the Daisy Farm. (After being abandoned by the CCC boys, it grew a beautiful crop of daisies.) The CCC boys were there at the time and we left our canoes with them. We told them they could use them, but we would pick them up the next day.

Minong Mountain lies just up from the west end of McCargo Cove, a long body of water jutting inland from Lake Superior.

Following a swampy red-ribboned trail laid out earlier by the CCC boys, we sloshed our way northwest. We hiked about 17 miles to reach the cove at dusk.

It was on this trip that I became more and more inquisitive about the copper miners. It seemed to me that there was evidence of them everywhere on high ground. McCargo Cove and the sides of Minong Mountain had been carefully worked over, yet there was still copper to be found. In that area there were diggings everywhere. In some places there were square holes (vertical shafts) filled with water. Elsewhere there were addits, tunnels driven into the sides of hills, with depressions everywhere. There were remains of old machinery and railroad tracks (probably a tram-way), large clearings with dilapidated old buildings, and huge piles of tailings everywhere. Nothing has aroused my curiosity about copper more than the massive amount of surface disturbance that we saw that summer of 1937. What was so interesting at the time was so much obvious evidence of ancient and modern mining done in the same area.

---

[12] This was CCC Camp Siskiwit, No. 2699. The fires started on July 23, 1936. The men were sent from other CCC amps in Michigan and Wisconsin. The fire burned about 35,000 acres; the island's total acres is about 132,000. The camp was still manned again in the summer of 1937. No fires were allowed during the August dry season.

The modern miners left iron rails, now long overgrown with vegetation, and the tumbledown buildings and everywhere were more tailings, shafts and addits. Away from the modern workings, the ancient pits seemed spread out endlessly back through the woods in all directions. Possibly hundreds, even thousands, of these ancient pits had been reworked and then covered or destroyed by later mining.

Some 30 years later my memories of the scene were renewed and enhanced by an article from the American Antiquarian Journal-Vol. XXII, Jan-Nov, 1901, Chicago (found on page 119 of "Prehistoric Copper Mining in the Lake Superior Region" – Drier and DuTemple.

By J. H. Lathrop:

> *The most extensive series of continuous workings as yet discovered were those found on Isle Royale, on what is known as the Minong Belt. Here, for a distance of about one and three quarter miles in length and for an average width of nearly four hundred feet, successive pits indicated the mining out of the belt of solid rock to a depth of from twelve to thirty feet. Between the rows of pits are ridges of rock and soil, taken from successive pits, and indicating that they were left as dams to prevent the passage of water from one pit to another while the latter was being wrought. In another place a drain sixty feet long had been dug and covered with timbers, felled and laid across. In another the copper vein had been followed on an incline to a depth of more than thirty feet, and thirty inches in width, with large boulders rolled and wedged to keep the rock above from falling in on the miners, thus taking the place of timbering as in modern mines.*

These observations were made in 1867 and the pits were more extensively explored in 1871 and 1872, after which the Minong Mining Co. was formed in 1874. Most of what we saw in 1937 was left by modern American miners working in the 1880's.

Again quoting from Drier and DuTemple, page 171—A paper by George R. Fox—The Ancient Copper Workings on Isle Royale, circa 1911:

> *But even on the island alone the amount of copper mined must have been tremendous. Gillman says, page 385 of the Smithsonian report of 1873:*
>
> *"The amount of mining on three sections (3 square miles) of land at a point on the north shore of Isle Royale is estimated to exceed that in one of our oldest mines on the south shore of Lake Superior, a mine which*

has been constantly worked with a large force for over twenty years."

This is only on three sections, and there are several sections near Mc-Cargo Cove which were as thoroughly worked, to say nothing of the other pits in various parts of the island. Then, too, it must be remembered that the aborigines were working virgin ground; what must have been their finds when it has paid modern mining companies, employing high-priced labor, to work the same diggings.

At one time there were three hundred miners employed at McCargo Cove, and only on the north side at that; another three hundred worked at the Saginaw Mine on Rock Harbor.

According to the U.S. Statistical Report of Lake Commerce, the valuation of copper since 1887 to 1897 was constant at $200 per ton or ten cents per pound, so it is fair to assume that during the period when mining was being done on the island, the price was ten cents a pound. In order to make expenses, to say nothing of a profit, an average of at least thirty pounds of copper per man must have been found each day, or with a crew of three hundred, the production must have been fully four-and-a-half tons per day.

This inference is necessary in the absence of exact production figures. The mine at McCargo Cove was worked for a number of years, so to meet expenses and make a profit, several thousands of tons must have been produced from this one source alone.

Comparing modern mining with the ancient diggings shows that the work of the white man was only a small percentage of that of the prehistoric output. From this locality alone (the region around McCargo Cove), thousands of tons of copper must have been extracted by the earlier workers; for they had virgin ground teeming with copper nuggets through which to run their drifts, and they obviously worked this area very thoroughly.

It is interesting to note that the amount of copper passing through the locks at the Soo was 35,000 tons in 1887 and had increased to over 150,000 tons by 1910. From 1898 to present (1911), the amount shipped was constant; before 1898 growth was gradual. Total value of shipments from 1897 to date (1911) is more than $550,000, 000 during which time more than 2,500,000 tons were produced.

It is difficult to estimate the total amount mined by the first workers, but accepting the least given amount, or 35,000 tons, as the total found by them, there is a tremendous amount of copper yet to be accounted for. From the extent of the workings on Isle Royale, this estimate is extremely conservative; an estimate of one million tons (two billion pounds) would appear more nearly correct."

George R. Fox was archaeologist and Director of the Edward K. War-ren Foundation of Three Oaks, Michigan in 1911.[12a]

5720 pound piece of pure copper found at McCargo Cove raised on oak cribbing. Copper solutions kept the wood from deteriorating over the centuries. Notice how the piece must have been heated and hammered to break off ingots

This part of George Fox's paper is quoted here merely to show the importance of the McCargo Cove region.

There is another point that I will be coming back to, that few experts seem to realize. There would have been many large pieces of surface copper in the area and they were all missing by modern times. There was one 5,720 pound mass found near McCargo's Cove that was raised part way to the surface on cribbing in the same way the one in the Cliff mine and others were found. It would seem, since this had to have been a slow and laborious process, that others closer to the surface had been removed, this one having been left in the middle of the operation when the team working on it left, never to return.

We can imagine the tremendous amount of work involved, first to dig 10 or 15 feet down in the rock to discover this mass of copper, then excavate all around to break it free from the matrix and somehow build oak cribbing beneath it. The very task of cutting a tree with primitive tools must have been formidable enough, but raising a two-and-a-half ton object from the bottom of that hole in the ground seems positively awesome. This 5,000 pound chunk found on Isle Royale, raised upon cribbing, was one of the smaller ones. There were several much larger pieces found in the same position on the mainland in deeper holes. It would challenge a present day engineer to do this today with modern machinery.

[12a] In 2004 Dr. James Scherz located a long excavated trench (nearly a half mile long) on the Keweenaw Peninsula. From his early observation it appears it has been used as a drain and parts of it as a below ground level domicile.

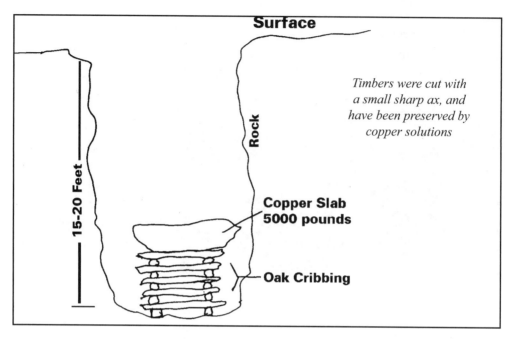

Surface

Rock

Timbers were cut with a small sharp ax, and have been preserved by copper solutions

15-20 Feet

Copper Slab 5000 pounds

Oak Cribbing

When climbing Minong Mountain in the dark that night (one flashlight among the six of us), we encountered pit after pit, shallow depressions in the rock some five and six feet in diameter. Some of these pits contained oblong rocks with chipped and broken ends. These seemed to be varieties of hard rock common to many sites around the shores of Lake Superior. The ones I saw varied in weight from perhaps five to ten pounds. Bill Mudge called them "Indian Mallos," or at least that's what I thought he called them. Later I found that some people called them "mauls" or, more descriptively, stone hammers.

I found one beauty in a pit on the side of Minong Mountain that just seemed to fit using two hands. It was all nicked up at the working end, but was still whole. Most specimens appeared to have broken under hard usage. I carried my find for miles on our return trip to Rock Harbor, but finally left it behind after I found a moose antler that seemed more rare and important at the time. I couldn't carry both prizes so I offered the stone hammer to the other boys who all refused it. So foolishly, I threw my probable artifact off a high cliff. On a trip ten years later, I recognized the cliff and spent a few fruitless hours looking for it.

When we reached the CCC camp at Rock Harbor, we found that some of our scouts had taken our two canoes. So, tired and hungry as we were, we had to walk the four miles back to our Rock Harbor site. I had discarded my stone hammer, but succeeded in bringing my moose antler (we always called it a moose horn) all the way home. I think the incentive for a moose antler was that the CCC boys were offering five dollars for one and I had the only one found on the whole trip. After 65 years I still have my moose antler and several more, but have regretted ever since tossing my stone hammer. Although I have since acquired many broken hammerstones, this particular one, at least in my mind's eye, was unique, very special and my first. It did not have the characteristic groove, but was still recognizable as a used, two-handled stone maul.

During the final few days on the island, I talked to nearly all of the different leaders and always asked about the ancient copper diggers. The obvious question was, "Who were they?" They all agreed, they were Indians. "And what did they do with the copper?" From that group I always got the same answer, "They made arrowheads with it."

The more I thought about that answer, the more I realized this could not be correct. All that copper and yet at that time, while I had seen many stone arrowheads, I had never seen a copper one or even heard of one. There were many collections of stone arrowheads around.

Returning from Isle Royale it was two more days of waiting at Copper Harbor. Four of us were taken in by a kind family who lived in and ran a gift shop in a ship's cabin. Three slept on the floor and I won the draw to sleep in a short ship's bunk. They fed us royally with pancakes and maple syrup.

As late as we were in getting home, as I remember, everyone took it all in stride, with no concern or worried parents calling as would certainly happen in today's organized world. But these were different times and everyone accepted different conditions.

Finding the Right People

Although Isle Royale had been proclaimed a National Park back in 1936, it took several years before anything was done as far as the government's taking it over. So while it was in the news from time to time, very few people knew much about it.

After my return from the island, I always tried to inform people about the place, but I found little interest. I was always ready to talk Isle Royale and copper with anyone. The one place I found a sympathetic ear was at the Marquette County Historical Society. Since I was very young I had known Mrs. Carroll Paul. She had been a friend of my mother and I had gone to school with her children and attended parties at their home. During my junior high school years, I had wandered into the upstairs rooms of the Peter White Public Library and found it to be the home of the Marquette County Historical Society and often found Mrs. Paul there. Around that period the Society had bought and renovated a building next door and had moved into it. I soon found out that Mrs. Paul was the president and executive director of the organization. It had been started by her father, John M. Longyear, just after World War I in 1918.

Mrs. Helen Longyear Paul, circa 1931

Mrs. Paul was a lady of many interests and I enjoyed talking with her. In some of my discussions with her about Isle Royale, the subject of native copper came up. She told me that Mr. Joe Gannon, owner of the Gannon Grocery Company in Marquette, was interested in Michigan copper and had been actively studying it for a long time.

She said, "If you want to know more about Michigan copper, Joe Gannon is the man to talk to."[13]

I didn't know Gannon, but I knew of him. He, too, was a person of many interests and was well known and

---

[13] Joseph Cuthbert Gannon was born in Dubuque, Iowa on March 19, 1876. His family moved to Fort Dodge in 1880. He attended school at Fort Dodge through two years of high school when he moved to Chicago in 1892.

In Chicago, Mr. Gannon went to work for the wholesale grocery company Sprague, Warner & Co. and joined the Illinois Naval Militia. He also became quite an athlete during this period (1892-98), taking part in many city track and cross-country meets.

In 1898, Gannon joined the Navy and took part in the Battle of Santiago in the Spanish-American War. In his later years, at the suggestion of Admiral Lahey, he wrote a book about his views of the battle to settle some historical conflicts that were going on in Washington between some historians and Naval officers. The book, "The U. S. S. Oregon and the Battle of Santiago," was published by Comet Press of New York in 1958. Gannon was the main signalman on the *Oregon* during the battle and was both sending and receiving messages giving him quite an overall perspective of what was going on.

In 1899, Joseph Gannon was transferred to northern Michigan as a salesman for Sprague, Warner, and again getting the overall picture of the business, organized the Gannon Grocery Company in 1909. He sold this company to Carpenter Cook Co. of Menominee, Michigan in 1950.

Besides being a leader in establishing the commission form of government in the City of Marquette in 1912, and a charter commissioner, Mr. Gannon was the main impetus and chairman of the Civil Defense committee during World War II, which was mainly responsible for bringing the K. I. Sawyer Air Force Base to Marquette County in 1956. Mr. Gannon's premise was that over the North Pole we were closer to Russia than anywhere in the continental United States and the mineral rich Upper Peninsula mines, Soo Locks and shipping routes that could cripple our nation were vulnerable.

From 1903 to 1918, Joe Gannon made five trips with the world famous naturalist and wildlife photographer, George Shiras III, into Canada.

Mr. Gannon was a world traveler with the ability and knowledge to see things quite differently than many compartment scholars and scientists. He would always look at things from several completely different perspectives to come to his conclusions. He died a man of considerable wealth in Marquette on February 16, 1965.

respected in Marquette. Both he and my father were in the grocery business and dad spoke of him often. Mrs. Paul added that Joe Gannon had been pondering the Michigan copper question for years, had traveled all over the world investigating this subject, and had been in touch with many authorities.

It turned out that my father and Joe Gannon were good friends. They were both in the local Masonic Lodge and years later my father worked for the Gannon Grocery Company in charge of their wholesale office in Marquette.

It was sometime in 1940 or early 1941 that I had my first talk with Mr. Gannon. In the fall of 1942, I enlisted in the Navy during

Joe Gannon

World War II, after which I attended Albion College from 1946 to 1948. In the summer of 1947 I returned to Isle Royale with two friends from college. We only stayed a week on that trip, but we brought a canoe along and did a more careful examination of some of the same places that had become fuzzy in my mind. It struck me as remarkable how things had changed in just ten years and yet we were trying to visualize back hundreds of years. It was another year or so before Gannon and I could get together to talk copper.

That first meeting gave me a whole new perspective, probably a much broader one ever held by most scientists today. Joe Gannon had indeed done a lot of thinking and a lot of traveling in his search for answers to his many questions concerning Michigan copper. Mrs. Paul and

Joe Gannon with President Theodore Rossevelt

Joe Gannon gave me my first good lessons in prehistoric copper mining. Those ideas kept me interested and thinking about that subject down through the years.

Isle Royale, to me, is a place of great mystery and intrigue.[13a] It holds the story of thousands of years of ancient history locked in its rock layers and caves and mines. Now that it is an organized National Wilderness Park, most people think it has been thoroughly studied and that there is little more to learn, so they have focused their interest on shipwrecks, lighthouses, hiking trails, photography, boating and fishing. But to those interested in copper, there is still much to explore, lessons to be learned and mysteries to be solved. While most tourists headed for the island today know what to expect and may not have the history of copper in mind, it can still be exciting to those who are looking for adventure with an open mind.

Before we get into the thoughts expressed to me by Joe Gannon, I must relate a story of discovery that was a complete mystery to me for many years, but in later years seems to be quite closely connected to the ancient mines of Isle Royale.

The Mystery Stone

In the summer of 1939 I had a job as head dishwasher (there were two of us) at the Bay Cliff Health Camp in Big Bay, Michigan.

In August, four people were lost in an area of thick slashings (cutover forest) on a high, flat sandstone cliff northwest of camp. They were three women counselors from the camp and their teacher, a geology professor from Northwestern University. The professor was only there for a few days. He was being shown some rock formations by the three girls. The party was to be back by 5:30 that evening for supper. When they didn't return, Miss Morse, the camp manager, became very concerned.

After the dishes were done and there still was no sign of the hikers, Miss Morse sent Paul Kotila, Jerry Grundstrom and me out to look for them. Shortly after we left, she called the State Police and the Conservation Department.

We went to the spot where the four had been instructed to leave their car. It was there as expected but no sign of people. It was getting dark and when

---

[13a] From "The Lake Superior County" by T. Morris Longstreth McClelland & Stewart (1924) pg 314: An enigma of archeology centers on Isle Royale, where certainly a prehistoric race once lived. Copper was mined here, and not by the Indians. A Mr. Ferguson of Pennsylvania stumbled on a prehistoric city's remains last fall and is coming back to complete his search. He found the ancient copper workings, the pits, still recognizable though over grown with century old timber. They employed the old way of mining by lighting fires on the rock and then pouring water on the hot stone.

we had only gone a short distance into the woods it started to rain. We decided to return to camp and reorganize as it looked as though the search would take longer and would be more difficult than we first had anticipated. Later, two State Policemen arrived and I was asked to accompany them.

About 3:00 in the morning we located the group huddled around a small fire, upset, but in good shape. Since it was still very dark and still raining, the state troopers decided we should all wait for daylight before starting out. I thought this was a good idea and slumped down by the fire. There were some very interesting stories, but by far the most interesting to me were those told by the geologist.

The more he spoke the more interested I became. I had never heard the story of the land in our area and I found myself more enthralled with every word. Then, at what seemed to be the peak of my interest, he mentioned a rock that he had heard about on the top of Huron Mountain.

Knowing that I was the only local person in the group, he asked me if I had seen it. He said the rock had been placed there in ancient times and that many people knew about it but few had seen it.

I told him I had lived here all my life, and my parents and grandparents before me, but I had never heard of such a rock. In fact, I had never been to the Huron Mountains.

The professor went on to describe the rock as being mounted on three smaller rocks. It was definitely not a natural formation. It had been placed there by man. It was supposed to be similar to one he had seen somewhere on the east coast. The story that he had been told there was that the eastern stone was thought to have been placed there by Norsemen. He said there was mounting evidence that Norsemen may have been in the Lake Superior region and that the stone may be a "Norse Altar" or some such thing. While I had no mental picture of the stone, what it looked like or its size, nevertheless, I was dumbfounded.[13b]

"The Norsemen here?"

"Oh, yes," he answered assuringly. "There was a Norse axe found in a river south of here, and there is evidence of them in Minnesota. Something about the three stones under the large one has to do with old Norse religion, and it seems like a logical place for them to put one of these altars if they were around Lake Superior."

The vague and unbelievable story of the rock may not have impressed the rest of the fire watchers that night and the conversation drifted on to other subjects. However, I don't think I heard the other tales. I was thinking about

---

[13b] It appears in retrospect that the professor had read "Here was Vinland" By John Kuran that was published that year. This is discussed again later.

the Norsemen. I didn't know much about them, had heard no mention of them in school, but had been told that some Vikings came from the southern coast of Sweden where my paternal ancestors had lived.

I thought about this idea of a "Norse Altar" here in Marquette County over the next few days and tried to talk to other people about it. No one had ever heard anything about such a stone, nor did anyone even seem slightly interested. I even asked the elderly truck driver from Huron Mountain Club who brought potatoes and Swiss chard to Bay Cliff from the club farm. Although he had worked there for many years, he had no idea what I was talking about when I mentioned the stone on Huron Mountain. As there seemed to be no one who knew about the stone, I soon forgot about it and turned my thoughts to more pertinent events of the day.

Two years later, in 1941, I was employed by Huron Mountain Club as an assistant to the store keeper. I worked as a clerk, brought supplies to the club kitchen, delivered ice to the cabins as well as laundry, freight such as trunks and luggage, and did small errands. Huron Mountain Club is a private summer resort that has preserved a block of land on the shores of Lake Superior for recreational use. The club is an old and respected organization. On their property, just a few miles from the clubhouse itself, is a small group of granite knobs known as the Huron Mountains. They are known geologically as some of the oldest mountains on earth. The most prominent of these granite knobs is Huron Mountain itself. It is situated north and west of the other mountains in the group and it can easily be seen from Lake Superior. All of these granite knobs are less than 2000 feet above sea level or 1400 feet above Lake Superior, which stands at approximately 602 feet. The position of Huron Mountain, to the north and west of the others, is such that anyone traveling east by water, within a mile or so of the shore of Lake Superior, sees only that mountain with its bare granite west end in full view. About three-and-a-half miles from shore further west of the mountains lay three groups of islands known as the Huron Islands. The mountain is most conspicuous from that direction.

To the south of the mountain is a rather large lake hidden in the hills named Mountain Lake. The northern extent of this lake goes right to the base of the mountain. That, too, is a rather bare steep rocky surface, but it was from this side that I first approached it.

It was a hot July afternoon when I found myself exploring Mountain Lake by rowboat on my day off. At the time I had no intention of climbing the mountain.

The north side was heavily wooded and I had learned there was a trail up through the woods on that side, but I had never been on that trail.

As I rowed around the lake, the steep rocky cliffs of Huron Mountain were always in full view and they beckoned me. An exhilarating swim in the cool waters gave me the ambition I needed to decide to try to climb that rocky slope.

Landing my boat near the east end of the mountain, I started to climb, picking my way from ledge to ledge, but always working toward the center of the south side of the mountain.

The mountain top had a round look to it, but from a distance I had noticed there were three gradual humps, with the center hump being only slightly higher than the other two. This high spot was where I was heading.

In those years I always carried a black metal box camera with me. It had been in the family for years. I thought

View of Huron Mountain from Lake Superior. What intrepid group of explorers could resist wanting to climb to it's top?

of it as an antique because it required a flat pack film rather than the roll film used in nearly all the other cameras I'd seen. The camera in one hand handicapped me somewhat in climbing. I paused often to observe the view which became more breathtaking as I climbed higher.

At length I was walking on fairly level rock, though still slanted to the south, scattered here and there were stunted, windblown pine, scrub oak and juniper bushes.

Suddenly, I walked right up to a strange rock table set on three stubby legs. The conversation of two years earlier about just such an object and in that very place never entered my mind. Either this was not the picture I had of the thing described to me at that time or I had forgotten about it.

This was a large rock, about 40 inches long and maybe two feet wide and two feet thick. It was balanced on the points of three small rocks that acted like three sturdy legs beneath it. It clearly had been set up like this purposely by someone.

I looked around. There was no evidence of anyone ever having been there. It was placed in the center of a flat area of a slightly rounded piece of bedrock, a part of the mountain. The view to the south was of Mountain Lake and beyond, ridge after ridge of hills stretching out to the distant horizon. Although I didn't know it at the time, the thin blue line just below the horizon was the Yellowdog Plains.

Many thoughts went through my mind. "Who put this here, and why is it here?" Then I had an impulse to get down to civilization as fast as possible to see if anyone knew anything about this

Mystery Stone as author first saw it in 1941.

strange rock formation. I started down to my boat at once, but not before I had taken a picture.

On my homeward trip, I began to think of the geology professor's Norse Altar.

"I'll bet that's the rock he was referring to. It has to be. Could that thing possibly be a Norse Altar? No, that can't be it, it's too crude and there is just nothing else around there. Someone at Huron Mountain will surely know something about it."

Back at the club I described the rock to several people and asked them what they knew about it. No one had the slightest idea what I was talking about. Finally I was directed to Miss Kate Brady, secretary to the club manager and in charge of the Post Office there for over thirty years, I had been told.

I described the rock to Miss Brady. She reached into a glass showcase in the office where they kept a few things for sale. Picking out a black and white glossy postcard, she handed it to me and inquired, "Is this what you're talking about?"

I was dumbfounded. "That's it," I said. "What is it?"

"Your guess is as good as mine," quipped Miss Brady. "It's been there forever; they call it the 'Mystery Stone.'"

"Is that the stone they claim the Norsemen put up there?"

"Well, I've never heard that—who told you that?"

"There was a fellow from Chicago at Bay Cliff a few years ago who told me there was supposed to be a Norse Altar on top of Huron Mountain."

"That's a new one," said Miss Brady. "Every few years someone has a new idea about it and I guess that's the latest." Then she laughed.

So that's the stone they were talking about, I thought to myself. Here I thought I'd discovered something new and they were selling postcards of it in the club office. The picture had been taken at least eight or ten years earlier. But I felt it was a real coincidence that I should run right into it the first time I was ever on the mountain.

Later I found out there were people who had known about that stone for many years, but couldn't find it. I wasn't sure if I could find it again myself.

I talked a lot about the stone that summer. Several people told me to ask Mrs. Paul at Ives Lake about it. She and her sister, Mrs. Abby Roberts, were the authorities on nearly anything in the area. They were born and raised there and their father was one of the founders of Huron Mountain Club. I knew Mrs. Paul well and made plans to see her that fall.

Mrs. Paul's' Theory

When I asked Helen Paul about the mystery stone, I learned a great deal. She told me she had known about it all her life, first seeing it when she was a child. She said her father, the famous (at least locally) John Munro Longyear, founder and first president of Huron Mountain Club, had run into it, as I did, on his first trip up the mountain in 1873 or 74. If a person is not following a trail, he would naturally gravitate toward the center and highest lobe of the mountain. It is just as obvious that the people who first marked out the trail did not know the stone was there and thus the trail goes right by it, only 40 or 50 feet away. In the 1880's and 90's, the south face of the mountain was much more barren than it was a century later. With very little vegetation, the strange perched rock was in plain view from three directions, while the trail passed by it to the north or sparsely wooded side; from the other three directions the full view stood out.

Mrs. Paul told me she never heard her father express any opinion on the rock as to who put it there or what its significance might be. He did realize it was unique.

I can vouch for the fact that the forest has closed in on it somewhat in the last 60 years. Pictures taken of the stone in the 1930's and 40's show it all by itself on a bare, bedrock area. Sometime in the 1970's a white pine started to grow on the east side of this bare spot. Despite such a severe growing surface, the tree is healthy and now of considerable size. One could never get a tree to grow in that sparse soil if he planted it. In the 1990's, to get a good picture of the whole monument, you would have to have someone hold the branches of the tree away. Now it seems the tree has grown beyond that stage and the stone is more visible. If the tree continues to grow, the stone will be under it, in the shade, and will appear quite different than it used to.

Mrs. Paul had her own thoughts about the stone and who might have put it there. There was never any question by anyone who saw it, that the stone was raised on its legs and placed there by men.

Helen Paul was a graduate of the Massachusetts Institute of Technology (MIT). She had spent a lot of time in and around Boston as well as up and down the east coast. She told me that she had seen several of these same distinctive stone monuments in that vicinity. They were similar, although much larger, and she felt quite sure they must have been put up by the same people for the same reasons.

In the east, she told me, they were thought to have been erected by the Indians for some religious purpose.

When I heard this, I said, "But Mrs. Paul, I've never heard of any stonework of any kind done by the Indians in this area."

She was quick to reply, "Yes, but these Indians are Algonquins and the Indians in the east, at least where the raised stones are, were Iroquois."

In 1651, a small band of Hurons, who were a sub-tribe of the Iroquois confederacy,[14] was chased into Lake Superior during the Iroquois Wars. This band of Hurons had lived on Huron Bay, just to the west of Huron Mountain. They had given their name to that bay, the big and little Huron Rivers, the Huron Islands nearby and the mountain itself. She believed the unique rock monument was an Indian Altar and that it was erected by the band of Huron Indians who lived nearby in the 1650's.

After several discussions with Mrs. Paul about the mystery stone, her explanation seemed quite logical and made sense to me.

There was one disconcerting event that took place about this time, however.

If these stone structures are found on the east coast with one on Huron Mountain, apparently they have been around for a long, long time. There must be some official explanation for them. There also must be some such structures elsewhere that have been called to the attention of the scientific community.

I made a stop at the Department of Natural Resources office in Marquette and asked if there was a geologist who might know about rock formations. I was directed to a gentleman and showed him a picture of the mystery stone.

Without hesitation he came out with the word: "erratic."

"What?" I questioned.

---

[14] Formerly inhabitants of New York State—Mohawks, Oneida, Onondaga, Cayuga and Seneca—and after 1712, Tuscarora.

*Drawing in Smithsonian Publications calling
the mounted stone a glacial erratic.*

"It's called an erratic, a glacial erratic," he said. "There are a lot of them around, they're left deposited by the glacier.

"Well, this one couldn't have been caused by a glacier, it's right on the top of a mountain and there are some like it on the east coast," I answered.

He went into another room and returned with a book. Leafing through it he found a picture and showed it to me. It certainly was the same type of formation as the mystery stone and the caption said it was a glacial erratic formed by the glacier. I was aghast and left the building bewildered.

When I told Mrs. Paul about it she wisely said, "There certainly are glacial erratics, all sorts, sizes and shapes of them, but these are different."

"But there was a picture of one nearly the same as the mystery stone in the book," I stammered.

Mrs. Paul smiled. "Both books and people, even experts, are wrong sometimes. We don't know everything."

I knew Helen Paul well enough to trust her judgment and so over the next few years I began calling it an Indian Altar. Since this required a long explanation, I often added, "or mystery stone." The thought of a Norse Altar had long ago left my mind and I never referred to that idea again.

Over the next decade or two the excitement of the mystery stone kind of died down. The subject seldom came up in conversations and people who climbed Huron Mountain seldom even went to see it. I don't believe I ever went up there without pointing it out to whomever I was with—mostly groups of children. Usually they were only mildly impressed.

For many years I was in charge of children's activities at the club and made many trips up the mountain. In all those years I never met anyone, young or old, who thought it was a natural formation. For the next 35 years (until 1982), the mystery stone was an "Indian Altar" to me.

A Second Trip to Isle Royale and Back to Joe Gannon

It was in the late 1940's when I next caught up with Joe Gannon again. Since we first talked, he had become even more interested in the subject of copper. In the meantime, I had been in the service, finished college, and by 1948 I had started a teaching career in the Village of Republic, a community in the western part of Marquette County. I lived there during the week, but was close enough to Marquette for me to go home and stay with my parents most weekends. In the fall and spring I spent time building a log cabin far out in the woods.

After my discharge from the service, I continued to work during July and August at the Huron Mountain Club, but during the month of June in 1947, I returned to Isle Royale with two college friends. We brought a canoe and camping gear so we could camp and explore at our leisure. Neither of my friends had been to the Island before so I was able to tell them what I knew of the various places I had visited earlier. We also toured islands, harbors and other locations that were new to me. We spent a few days at McCargo's Cove and took our time exploring other areas of the island. By then the Park Service was well established and there were rules to follow. Little displays of hammerstones imbedded in cement were at key points, maps were available and we were supposed to check-in at the Park Headquarters with a trip plan. We filled out a trip plan, but were unable to follow it.

A few years later I was able to meet with Mr. Gannon in Marquette while I was teaching in Republic. I had formed new, more intelligent questions and Mr. Gannon was willing to give me more of his time and we were able to speculate on the copper questions more intensively.

Joe Gannon was a deep thinker with boundless curiosity. He had traveled the world over and been a successful businessman. The one theme he focused on was that Michigan copper somehow must have gotten to Europe and elsewhere in ancient times. While I am unable to give all his reasons for this belief, word for word, the summary of at least some of the ideas that impressed me are as follows:

1.   Prehistoric people had far more knowledge and ability than they are given credit for today.

2. There was a great use of copper in Europe, Asia, Africa and India in ancient times, with very few and limited sources of that metal in those areas.
3. There was more pure, easily obtainable copper in the Lake Superior district than anywhere else.
4. There were several water routes from this copper to the oceans of the world.
5. Tremendous amounts of copper were removed in ancient times as is proven by the evidence in the Copper Country.
6. Such small amounts of copper artifacts have been found in the western hemisphere as compared with what must have been removed that there just could not have been the end of a copper trade here.
7. The Mediterranean definitely looks like the end of a large copper trade.
8. The period of mining was so long that there had to have been many groups of people involved over the years.
9. Some of the people who removed copper must have been highly organized; they must have had large boats and must have been seafaring people.

Joe and Mrs. Gannon in Egypt - Circa 1920's

10. They wore out more copper tools building the pyramids than they have over there.

11. There had to have been a long lapse of time between the end of the organized mining and the arrival of modern Europeans since all traditions of this large industry were lost.

Mr. Gannon proposed that the secret of the Michigan copper was one of the greatest mysteries of our planet and the answers are here in Upper Michigan. His claim was that little was being done about these mysteries; no one was interested enough to look for solid answers. He had read reports of several early studies, but found they posed the questions but gave only inadequate answers. He claimed he had contacted many appropriate institutions by phone, mail and in person trying to encourage some adventurous archaeologists to make more studies.

Among some noted places he mentioned were the Field Museum in Chicago, the American Museum of Natural History in New York, and the Smithsonian Institution in Washington. He also contacted several universities around the country, especially in the vicinity of the Great Lakes. He said they all had money to make archaeological investigations around the world, but that nothing was being done in the area where he felt the answer lay hidden. He was appalled by the lack of interest shown by everyone from all quarters. However, there was one sympathetic voice, a metallurgist from Calumet, Michigan, Dr. Roy W. Drier.

Dr. Roy Ward Drier

Roy Drier was a lifelong resident of Michigan's Copper Country. He was born on June 6, 1897 in Calumet to Adam and Winifred Drier. His great, great grandfather was one of the first metal workers and blacksmiths in the area.

After graduating from Calumet High School in 1915, he enrolled in the Michigan College of Mines (today's Michigan Technological University) where he received his Bachelor's Degree in 1926, his Master's Degree in 1928 and his Doctorate in 1934. In the meantime, he started a teaching career at his alma mater, Calumet High, and later, in 1930, became an

Courtesy of the Masonic Temple of Marquette

Dr. Roy Ward Drier

instructor at Michigan Tech. He was a member of the faculty research division for 30 years. He served in both World Wars. During World War I he was in the Army and in World War II he attained the rank of Lt. Commander in the Navy where he worked for the Bureau of Ordinance. His job was to increase production in existing ordinance facilities. Also during his career he did graduate studies at the University of Chicago and the University of Illinois. He was considered an expert in theoretical and applied x-ray field and it was he who established a program in this field at Michigan Tech.

Although Dr. Drier had many interests in closely related fields of science such as metallurgy, physics and electronics, his special fascination was in archaeology concerning the region's ancient copper mining.

During the 1930's, Dr. Drier made several sojourns to Isle Royale, later donating a large collection of mineral specimens and artifacts to museums. On these early trips to Isle Royale, Drier found pottery fragments that he put through a number of scientific tests such as x-ray diffraction, microscopic and metal lithography (making impressions from stones).

In collaboration with the Milwaukee Public Museum, he attempted to correlate his finds with pieces of its Indian collection. He found the pottery was fairly recent, probably brought by the copper-seeking Indians within the last 2,000 years. His tests showed great depth of correlation between many of the copper tools picked up near the pits. He reasoned that the prehistoric miners must have worked there at least 2,000 years prior to the less skilled Indian miners of more recent centuries. The more modern pottery matched modern Indian pottery, but there did not appear to be any pottery left by the much older miners. This lead to suspicions that these early miners were an entirely different people.

Drier also had compiled a collection of scientific reports and papers concerning earlier investigations by several groups or individuals who had studied the ancient mines. Since the evidence on Isle Royale was relatively undisturbed compared to that of the mainland, most of these reports concentrated on Isle Royale. Modern mining was far more intense on the Keweenaw Peninsula from 1845 on.

Even though Roy Drier, as a metallurgist, was not the archaeologist that Joe Gannon had been seeking, he was a man of great knowledge and sincere interest in the same subject. Also, he was close by and the two men both belonged to the same Masonic Lodge in Marquette. It was inevitable that they would find each other and would work together.

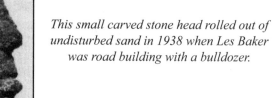

Photos courtesy of Mrs. Juanita Elinor Baker

Mrs. Juanita Baker 1987

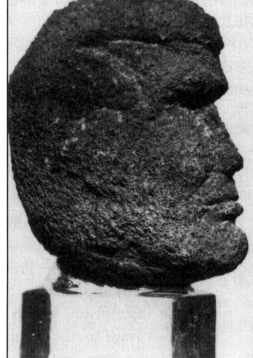

This small carved stone head rolled out of undisturbed sand in 1938 when Les Baker was road building with a bulldozer.

Chapter IV
Some Early Observations of Michigan Copper

Col. Charles Whittlesey

Courtesy of Marquette County Historical Society

Col. Charles Whittlesey

In the early 19th century, attempts were made to give order to the history of the American Continents. While some facts were known of South and Central America due to the Spanish in those areas, North America was a complete enigma. People were curious about the strange artifacts and ruins found in many places, artifacts that did not fit the prevailing picture of an undeveloped, wild continent with native tribes, some nomadic. Ruins were found bespeaking vast civilizations with no historical record.

By the 1830's and 1840's, some archaeological reports began appearing about the early inhabitants of the American Continent. The writings of Louis Henry Morgan, Henry Schoolcraft and Charles Whittlesey stood out for Joe Gannon because they all had connections with the Upper Peninsula of Michigan. Of these, Whittlesey in particular studied the ancient copper miners.

Charles Whittlesey had a nephew named Royal F. L. Whittlesey who came to Marquette from Cleveland, Ohio. He had a farm on Presque Isle (now a city park) in the late 1850's until 1872 or so. The Whittlesey farm was just south of Kawbawgam's[15] grave. Royal Whittlesey also ran a sawmill for a few years and in 1865 was the Postmaster in Marquette. Charles Whittlesey often stayed

---

[15] Kawbawgam—a local Chippewa Chief known to Marquette natives as the last chief of the Chippewas.

with his nephew when he was working around Lake Superior and sometimes used Marquette as a base for exploration.

Charles Whittlesey was born in Southington, Connecticut, on October 4, 1808. He spent his early years in Connecticut, Ohio and New York state. At the age of five, his family moved to Tallmadge, Ohio. When he was nineteen, he received an appointment to West Point (1827). After graduating, Whittlesey was assigned to duties at Fort Gratiot in Michigan and Fort Howard in Green Bay, Wisconsin, in 1831 and 1832. Upon discharge he opened a law office in Cleveland.

In 1837, Charles Whittlesey was employed by the State of Ohio as an assistant geologist to do mineral surveys. Ten years later, after the opening of the Upper Michigan copper and iron ranges, the U.S. Government hired him to do mineral surveys around Lake Superior and the upper Mississippi River. From 1849 to 1858 he surveyed Michigan's Copper Range, collecting vast amounts of data and making scientific evaluations of the ancient copper mines. He worked in and studied this region before the great mining era following the Civil War.

Whittlesey served as a Colonel in the Union Army from 1861 to 1863. He was a chief engineer and fought in the battle of Shiloh. Then in 1863 he went back to the Lake Superior region to complete his geological and archaeological report, which was immediately published by the Smithsonian Institution. This was the first comprehensive work done on ancient copper mining.

The summary of this report contained six points which did much to stimulate my interest in the ancient copper story as I went over them again and again with Mrs. Paul and Joe Gannon.

The six statements that summarized the Whittlesey report are as follows:
1. An ancient people of whom history gives no account extracted copper from the veins of Lake Superior.
2. They did it in a crude way—by means of fire, by the use of copper wedges or gads, and by stone mauls.
3. They penetrated the earth but a short distance, about thirty feet. Their deepest works were equal to those of the old copper and tin miners of Cornwall, wrought before the conquest of Britain by the Romans.
4. They sought chiefly for small masses or lumps, since they did not have tools for cutting large masses.
5. There is no evidence of cultivation of the soil nor of mounds, homes, roads or canals; however, the ancient miners did have darts, spears and daggers of copper.
6. They were numerous, industrious, and persevering, and the work must have been the equivalent of 10,000 men working for over 1,000 years.

We will discuss the progress and changes in thinking acquired by more advanced research and discoveries in each of these areas later on.

Joe Gannon held Charles Whittlesey[16] in high esteem. He was particularly interested in his first statement—"An ancient people of whom history gives no account, extracted copper from the veins of Lake Superior."

Gannon felt there had to be clues regarding the identity of these people. They would have left evidence. As there is no indication of large amounts of copper being used on this side of the Atlantic and every indication that there had been enormous use of copper overseas during the Bronze Age, he wanted to prove his thesis that overseas copper may have originated here. There was plenty of circumstantial evidence, but circumstantial evidence would never convince the scientists or the public.

Let's look into some of these objections and roadblocks that only hard, indisputable facts can overcome.

Off to a Bad Start

In the first "Contribution of Knowledge" published by the Smithsonian Institution in 1848, Ephraim George Squier and Edwin Hamilton Davis had the honor of seeing the results of their work on the "Ancient Monuments of the Mississippi Valley," and later, in 1851, "The Aboriginal Monuments of the State of New York."

Mr. Gannon did not consider these reports to be accurate because their observations were not well researched. Squier, who took credit for the writing, was also young and inexperienced.

Squier was born in Bethlehem, New York, in 1821. He taught school as a young man right off the farm and wrote for a local newspaper while studying engineering. In 1841, as a twenty-year old, he was employed by a newspaper known as the "New York State Mechanic." In 1843, he went to Chillicothe, Ohio, where he was on the staff of the "Scioto Gazette" and also became a

---

[16] In later years, Charles Whittlesey returned to Cleveland and from 1867-71 was with the Western Reserve Historical Society.

In 1849, while doing his geological surveys in northern Wisconsin, he discovered iron near Bayfield opposite the Apostle Islands in Wisconsin. He formed the Magnetic Iron Co. there.

Most of his early writings were concerned with copper and exploration, but after eighteen narrow escapes, he wrote mostly of a religious nature.

One of his near death experiences was a shipwreck on Lake Superior in October of 1845, the same storm in which Douglas Houghton drowned.

In 1882, Whittlesey wrote, "Considering how many of these storms I have passed through, it is a source of wonder and thankfulness that I am alive."

Charles Whittlesey died in Cleveland, Ohio in 1886 at age 78.

clerk in the Ohio State Legislature. In addition, George Squier began some spare time investigations into ancient mounds he had heard about in Ohio and neighboring states. There is no doubt that George Squier had great talent, and was obviously a remarkable and energetic young man, but the short time he spent in these investigations raised questionable assumptions that archaeologists would challenge for years.

During these years, Squier found a partner who shared his interest in archaeology and, fortunately, had some experience: a young physician named Edwin Hamilton Davis.

Davis was born in Ross County, Ohio, in 1811. About ten years before he met Squier, he had worked as a helper for Charles Whittlesey and developed a keen interest in archaeology. So at 32 he eagerly became a partner of George Squier, then only 22, and they were a good team. Davis supplied the funding while Squier did the writing, although both men were only part-time archaeologists.

During the early 1840's, when the Ontonagon Boulder was getting so much publicity, the National Museum in Washington, D.C., was being organized. The museum directors planned to publish outstanding scientific works in a series of publications to be known as the "Contributions to Knowledge."

Some Squier and Davis ideas contradicted those of experienced archaeologists and established some possibly erroneous theories. Because these ideas were sanctioned by the Smithsonian, they became dogma to many students of archaeology, anthropology and pre-history as such scholars often looked to that institution for guidance in the early days.

One special Squier and Davis concept that has held fast for 150 years deals with the strange rock formations, which I have already described and referred to as a "mystery stone" or Mrs. Paul's "Indian Altar" in the Huron Mountains. Their statement in "Contributions to Knowledge" has local inhabitants in the 1840's in New York State saying that such local stones looked like the ancient stone monuments commonly found in Europe, but when shown to authorities, it was explained that they were just glacier formations. Even though this explanation was proven wrong in the 1970s, today's academic authorities still stand by that original premise. In the 1990s, Chuck Bailey of Duluth, Minnesota showed me a documentary he had purchased which made the same claim.

The "Contribution to Knowledge" also went a long way to argue that Indians were the indigenous inhabitants and that no Europeans came to the Americas before Columbus. These ideas are still being taught in schools and institutions of higher learning across North America.

These so-called establishment "facts" have lead to the misinterpretation of artifacts and the suspicion of fraud or fakery concerning any artifact that even suggests its origin is overseas. For instance, if someone finds a Norse axe in Illinois, it must have been planted there recently as we "know" the Norse were never in Illinois. As such, most of these kinds of finds are ignored by the authorities.

The facile assumptions of some of these early archaeologists were carefully recorded and would be studied in the years that followed, often without adequate cross-checking. When a new interpretation or conflicting theory came along, it should have been the duty of the professionals to assess it thoroughly in the light of later discoveries and modern scientific methods. Instead they offered resistance and denial or the simple negation of the new circumstances.

Among early scholars working in archaeology were dedicated, conscientious, and competent men like Caleb Atwater, Albert Gallatin, Dr. S. G. Norton and James Foster. Both Whittlesey and the Squier and Davis team had conducted surveys in the vicinity of Marietta, Ohio, where there was so much evidence of ancient civilizations. By 1836, Whittlesey had completed a detailed drawing of an ancient town near the Muskingum River. The greater part of the neatly laid out village was unfortunately destroyed by later inhabitants of the area. The village was subsequently credited to the "mound-builders" who, because of their use of copper, were connected to the copper miners of Michigan.

A careful description and accurate plan of Marietta, Ohio was prepared by the renowned 19th Century antiquarian, Col. Charles Whittlesey. He completed this illustration of the ancient earthworks before the works were destroyed around 1836. The view is from the north. The Muskingum River is on the right, with the Ohio in the distance. In the upper left hand corner is Marietta's "Great Mound" which, alone of all the other Marietta structures, still survives. The Mound Builders. J. P. Maclean. 1879.

... or on the forehead of the body, were found three large circular bosses, or ornaments for a sword-belt or a buckler; they are composed of copper, overlaid with a thick plate of silver...

Courtesy Ancient America Magazine

And just who were these "mound-builders?" To this day we don't really know. Scientists have named three groups with distinct cultures who lived in what is now the central United States, beginning about 500 B.C.

All three of these cultures have left much evidence in the area which is now southern Illinois, Indiana and Ohio. The earliest was the Adena culture, which is believed to have developed around 500 B.C. and to have died out by 200 A.D. It was centered along the Ohio River in Indiana, Ohio, Kentucky and West Virginia. The Hopewell culture developed a little later, around 100 B.C., and died out about 350 A.D. While distributed over nearly the whole of the central United States, the main concentration of Hopewell sites are in the Mississippi and Ohio River Valleys and in Indiana and southern Illinois.

A culture known as the Mississippian arose about 800 A.D., and it is thought to have been in existence when the Spaniards arrived. It, too, covered a large area of the central U.S., but seems to have been concentrated along the Mississippi, as the name implies. The name "Hopewell" came from a farm in Ross County, Ohio, belonging to a Captain M. C. Hopewell, where the evidence of this culture was first identified. It is the same county where the Adena name originated. "Adena" was the name of an estate where many log tombs, skeletons and artifacts of the Adena culture were first located. Ed Davis was born in this county of numerous antiquities, which may explain his great interest in pre-history.

The unanswered questions concerning all three of these cultures are: Where did they come from? Who were they? Did one culture evolve from the other, or were different groups arriving? Finally, are they the direct ancestors of present-day American Indians?

The artifacts of the central area of the United States, so rich in antiquities, were almost completely destroyed, or at worst, overlooked by the rush of modern civilization. Luckily a number of competent early archaeologists had conducted studies there.

Atwater and Davis had identified about 30 furnaces at a place called Spring Hill in Ohio. They found evidence of the smelting of bog iron and the melting of copper, but later investigation negated these earlier observations.

Rewriting History

Squire and Davis apparently lost faith in their early observations about melting and casting of copper and smelting iron. They tried to establish that there was no overseas influence on American culture. They concluded that the copper in the mounds of Ohio had come from Lake Superior mines.

They decided that none of the copper was ever melted or cast, but was hammered into shape from thin sheets of what is known today as "leaf copper," found commonly in rock formations of the Keweenaw. Large objects were made by pounding many thin pieces together, a process known as "annealing." Thus the pieces were folded and pounded again and again to make larger tools.

While earlier writings of Squier and Davis were initially in favor of overseas contact, they were seriously challenged on the point. When considering their work as a whole, the theoretical seeds of the belief that the Americas had been

Hopewell Copper Repoussé and Cutout Items

Smithsonian Institution Annual Report 1916

isolated from global visitors for about 10,000 years were planted by these two men. But surpassing Squier and Davis, the man most responsible for putting to rest the idea of any advanced civilization distinct from the Indians was John Wesley Powell, and he was in a unique position do so.

Today Sheets of leaf copper are more valuable as art objects or wall decorations.

Sheet copper or leaf copper was quite common in rock formations of the Keweenaw. This is loaded on a flat bed ready to be shipped out. Circa 1910

John Wesley Powell

Powell was a geologist, born in Mount Morris, New York, in 1834. He attended Oberlin College in Ohio in 1857-58 and became interested in the natural sciences.

During the Civil War Powell enlisted as a private but rose to the rank of Major. He lost an arm in the battle of Shiloh and in 1865 became professor of geology at Illinois Wesleyan University. In 1867 he made his first journey of exploration to the Colorado Rockies. The adventures that put the Major in the public eye were two voyages of great danger and hardship: the first in 1869, through the Grand Canyon of the Colorado River. The scientific results of this first trip also brought him to the attention of other scientists.

Congress voted him the funds to continue his explorations, and in 1871-73 he made a second voyage down the Colorado, surveying an area of 100,000 square miles. In 1879, on the recommendation of Powell, Congress established the United States Geological Survey, of which he was the director from 1881until 1894.

During the years leading up to Powell's appointment as director and his elevated status among scientists, some still advocated overseas contacts and lost civilizations. But the politically powerful John W. Powell expressed strong opposition to the theory that there was ever a vanished civilization in America, stressing a new dominant theory that only Stone Age Indians had lived in prehistoric America. Everything suggesting otherwise was false, fake or misinterpreted and must be discarded or ignored. This attitude slowly worked its way into institutions of higher learning, museums and even the news media. Two or three generations of archaeologists were breast-fed with this "official" doctrine. Over the period of the 1890's to 1910, textbooks were rewritten to follow suit and the blinds were drawn on the distant past.

In issue #31 of the *Ancient American Magazine*, Barton and May give us a good idea of how, from that time on, the work of archaeologists and, therefore, history was directed and became so limited in scope:

> *In 1879, when Congress created the Smithsonian Institution's Bureau of Ethnology, Major John Wesley Powell, the Civil War hero, received additional power and prestige as the Bureau's first director. He was disposed to think that the Mound Builders were ancestors of the native Indians, and presented his theory as dogma in the Bureau's first annual report published in 1880. He wrote, "That vestiges of art discovered do not excel in any respect the arts of Indian tribes known to history. There is, therefore, no reason for us to search for extra limited origin through lost tribes for the arts discovered in the mounds of North America.*

So prestigious was the Smithsonian and its authoritative director that within a few years the scientific community unilaterally adopted Powell's conclusions while ignoring the vast amount of physical evidence previously accumulated. Scholars began to discredit and reinterpret the civilization of the Mound Builders in favor of Powell's theory. As one writer put it, "Evidence contrary to Powell's stated opinion was explained as fraudulent, as buried in the mounds intrusively, or simply reinterpreted to favor the new theory. From this time forward, anything that inferred to the original glorious Mound Builders theory was considered mythical. It was a very hostile academic environment for everyone who ventured to propose that there had ever been a highly civilized group of people in the New World."

Nevertheless, before this time there were literally *hundreds* of convincing written records of people coming to early North America. The latest of these ancient documents were, of course, the Norse Sagas, but in 1990 John L. Sorenson and Martin Raish published a two-volume set entitled "Pre-Columbian Contact with the America's Across the Oceans: An Annotated Bibliography." In this work they have listed over 2,000 books and articles of pre-Columbian contacts including the author, date, title and printer or publisher of each. They represent many foreign sources and authors.[17]

The first time I became acquainted with the inadequacy of the official version of our early history was in discussions of the Norse Sagas with an elderly

---

[17]Pre-Columbian Contact with Americas Across the Oceans: An Annotated Bibliography" by John L. Sorenson and Martin Raish, Research Press, Provo, Utah, 1990.

Fred Bang Johnson with model ship he was building, circa 1970's

Norwegian couple who were longtime friends of mine. They were Fred Bang Johnson and his wife, Helen.

Fred was born in 1903 and Helen in 1897, both in Norway. Fred went to sea as a young man and jumped ship at the port of Philadelphia in 1923. He had a sister then living in Chicago and went to live with her. Fred worked as a coal heaver, joined a Norwegian Lodge and was able to get jobs through some of the members. He also met his wife, Helen, another lodge member, and they were married in 1925.

He was soon working as a carpenter, then cabinet maker and finally boat builder, a profession he practiced the rest of his life. He worked in several shipyards in Chicago and in Wisconsin. In 1936, at the Thompson Shipyard, Fred met Louis Vincent from Upper Michigan, and in 1945 they came to Marquette to build boats. Here they built several fish tugs and two or three yachts, including the commercial boats for tourists to view the Pictured Rocks.

Fred was an interesting, cultured, self-educated fellow. He loved history and classical music, and played the violin in a Chicago orchestra for over 20 years.

I learned a tremendous amount of history from Fred and Helen, history that would be difficult to find in books, especially Norwegian history. In speaking of the Sagas, those interesting Norse family histories, he gave me a better background than those who write about them today. In fact, before he died, Fred gave me five, huge leather-bound volumes of the Sagas. However, they were in the Norwegian language and a few years later I returned them to him and have regretted it ever since. I hope they fell into good hands.

For example, the word "Viking," according to Fred, is an Icelandic word for "pirate." The Viking period lasted from around 750 or 800 A.D. until the battle of Hastings in October of 1066 A.D. Many of the people we speak of as Vikings were not Vikings but Norsemen or Northmen, later Normans. While Eric the Red was probably a Viking, his son Leif, born around 1000 A.D. in Iceland, was not a true conqueror-raider Viking, although he lived in the Viking period and was a brave seaman and explorer. He introduced Christianity to Greenland, and most certainly his followers were farmers and colonizers, not Vikings.

Sometime around 900 A.D., certain educated people in Norse families began writing family histories. It became quite fashionable and many families had their own written Saga. Some of the Saga writers were scholarly while others simply waxed eloquent as a novelist might do today. An untold number of sagas were lost over time and those that have survived would have been rewritten several times over the thousand years that have elapsed since they were first written. In the rewriting many were altered and because of this historians of the 17th and 18th centuries took them to be completely mythical. Fred thought that only 50 or 60 of the true, original sagas survive to this day.

The Leif Erickson story was one saga that seemed to fit and could be proven by other records and physical evidence, so it became accepted by historians toward the end of the 19th century. The Leif Erickson story was woven into the history texts of pioneer America. Pages were written about the Norse and the Irish monks in our older histories. Why didn't I hear anything about them, even in World History or American History, when I was growing up in the 1930's? Believe it or not, by the 1900s those stories had been eliminated, wiped from the records. So my American History started with Columbus. Our North American histories were rewritten just after the 19th century only to have it all rediscovered a half century later.

Two examples of these old histories are as follows. From the "Students American History," Genn & Company Publishers—A widely used history textbook, 1902:

> The Northmen: The Discovery of North America by the Northmen: Vinland the Good. The Scandinavians, or Northmen, were the most skillful and daring sailors of the middle ages. For them, "the Sea of Darkness" had no terrors. Before the mariner's compass had come in Europe, they made distant voyages in vessels often not so large as modern pleasure yachts. Their only guides on those perilous expeditions were the sun, the stars and the flight of birds.
>
> In the ninth century (875 A.D.), the Northmen planted a colony in Iceland. Their sagas or traditions inform us that late in the next century (981 A.D.), Eric the Red set sail from Iceland in search of a strange land which a Norse sailor, blown off of his course, had sighted in the far west. He found it, and giving it the tempting name of Greenland, lured a band of colonists to those desolate shores. In the year 1000 A.D., Leif Erickson, later known as "Leif the Lucky," a son of Eric the Red, set out from Greenland in quest of a land which a storm-driven mariner had seen

in the southwest. He discovered a beautiful country which abounded in wild grapes. From its products, Leif gave the land a name, and called it "Vinland." In 1347 the Norse records mention a ship going to this southern colony after a load of timber. That was the last that we hear of the settlement. The Norsemen ceased to make voyages to the west, the colonies they had planted died out, and all the records of them were forgotten.

This was about the extent of information in the textbooks at the beginning of the 20th century. Then a final declaration from the unenlightened scholars of that day was announced with great authority:

> *The descriptions of the country given in the records fail to throw any decisive light on this point and no Norse graves, inscriptions or ruins have been found on the mainland of America, although the ruins of buildings erected by the Northmen are still standing in Greenland. The conclusion of most eminent scholars respecting the settlements of Northmen is that the soil of the United States has not one vestige of their presence.*

And so the Norse presence in the mainland of America was dropped from our history books. We had already dropped the stories that came out of Iceland that predated the Norse. In fact, the Norse had stories of finding ruins of stone buildings when they arrived in Greenland.

The Irish were full of claims, notably vague, from the days before the printing press when stories of experiences never traveled far from the people who lived them,. Many were the adventurers who never returned to tell of their voyages and those that did often didn't know where they had been.

A summary of many long lost adventurers was reviewed in "The Irish-American History of the United States" (2 volumes) by Very Rev. John Conon O'Hanlon M.R.I.A. with introduction by Very Rev. Thomas J. Shanon, Catholic University, Washington D.C., published by Murphy & Son, 279 Church St., New York, 1907.

The following are some selections from some 25 large pages of fine print of early Irish contacts with America. "Early Irish Traditions Regarding Hy-Breasail or Great Western Ireland in Scandinavian Traditions":

> The Pagan Irish (before Christianity or during the time of the Megalithic Societies of Europe) had remote cherished traditions regarding some great magic Island, far away from them in the Atlantic Ocean. It was a land of enchantment for their imaginings, and in it lived an enchanted race of inhabitants. It bore a variety of names, and it was associated in their minds with vague mythological ideas.

The early Firbolgian and Fomorian colonists of Ireland—for the most part supposed to have been seafaring men—are thought to have placed their Elysium far out in the Atlantic Ocean. Sometimes they called it Oilean-na-m-Beo or Island of the Living, or Hy-na-Beatha, Island of Life. Again, it was designated Tir-na-Nog, the Land of Youth where Genii dwelt, enjoying lives of perpetual happiness. It had a delightful climate according to the ancient bards; while the heroes of Irish romance dwelt there in enchanted places. Sometimes it is styled Tir-na-m-Buodha or Land of Virtues: again it is poetically called the Land of Heroes or Land of Victories…This fairy land obtained, likewise, the name Hy-Breasail or the Island of Breasal…The 'Great Land' was the term applied to it in the Irish bardic poems and stories, many of these yet untranslated and unpublished; while still around the southern, western and northern coasts of Ireland, various fireside traditions are told by the peasants regarding Hy-Breasail, as also relating to the Firbolgs, Fomorians and Tuatha-de-Danaans—these fierce warriors of old, who have yet a fabled existence in the fairy or spirit land of the Immortals.

Hy-Breasail now dissolves, as a popular theme or vision; yet through its mists, a more distant region reproduces the spell of an Irishman's enchantment.[18]

Nor were such notions confined to Ireland alone, for similar superstitions had spread among other people of the Old World. For more than 400 years before the birth of Christ, the ancients held a belief regarding a lost island called Atlantis[19] or Atalantis, said to have been greater than all Libya (Africa) and Asia together, lying out in that ocean to which it probably gave name. It is alluded to in the Temoeur Dialogue of Plato. The descriptions given of its situation are vague and indefinite, and are thought to have been derived from ships and mariners that had ventured out into the great Western Ocean. The Carthaginians are reported to have established colonies in and visited frequently an island, far distant from the Pillars of Hercules.[20] Diodorus Siculus mentions a western island of great extent as also surpassing beauty and fertility, far away from Libya. The recollection of this fabled land seems to have been forgotten in a

---

[18] Hy-Breasail or Breasal—now recently in Brazil—deep in the jungle some of the world's largest megaliths have been found—discussed later in these writings.

[19] Atlantis still lives in the minds of many people. Several organizations are presently searching for it.

[20] A large ring of cut stones has been recently found when contractors were digging a hotel foundation in Miami, Florida—discussed later in these pages.

measure, during the Middle Ages, as few writers have reference to it under the original name. However, islands and curious legends connected with them were still reported to have been in the remote waters of the Atlantic. How far the original myths of Ireland had influenced maritime enterprise in Christian times is unknown, but it is possible the Greek and Latin accounts of discovery had been read in the schools, and that both sources of information were availed of to form vague conceptions of a land of promise or a Terrestrial Paradise, which still remained unexplored and which was destined as a future dwelling for the Saints…Frequent intercourse took place in very remote times between Ireland and Iceland.[21] So far as historic accounts throw light on such transactions, the Irish seem to have been the pioneers of maritime enterprise, antecedent to the Scandinavian development of ship-building and sea-roving. Long before the Northman colonization of Iceland in A.D. 847, the Irish, for sake of its productive fisheries, had reached its distant shores. With still nobler aspirations to guide them, Irish hermits had settled there when probably it was devoid of inhabitants; and the Christian religion was found to be established, when Gordar the Dane, and of Swedish origin, was the first Northman who discovered Iceland in 863, and when the Norwegian Ingolf began the colonization of that country in 874.

The people of Iceland and the Northern races of Europe have for many remote ages preserved national documents, in which there are very curious narratives of discoveries and of navigations relating to America, long antecedent to the times of Christopher Columbus. In those ancient chronicles, reference is often made to Ireland and Irishmen in various pages, and in relation to American maritime adventures. Those sagas have recorded various wonderful stories regarding an extensive Western Continent, and daring efforts of their hardy seamen to reach it. Even ancient Scandinavian records have applied the name 'Great Ireland' to a distant Western Continent which Columbus had not yet discovered.[22]

Not many generations had seen the light, after the first introduction of Christianity into Erin, when the adventurous and saintly men Barind or Barinthus and Mernoc, whether by accident or with a set purpose of discovery in view, reached the distant shores of the Land of Promise—the earliest Irish and Christian designation of America. They were enabled

---

[21] The Sagas tell of old building foundations on Iceland and Greenland.

[22] There are many recorded stories of isolated Irish colonies in the Northwest U.S. (See "The Pre-Columbian Discovery of America" by B. F. DeCosta—Joel Munsell's Sons, Publishers, Albany, NY, 1901.

to return once more to the island from which they had sailed, about the commencement of the sixth century. Wonderful were the rumors spread abroad, and the narratives of those navigators filled the minds of other with restless desires to witness scenes so graphically described and yet so vaguely portrayed. Among the many who sought information from the voyagers was one having manly courage and tenacity of will to second a lively imagination and an enterprising genius. Holy Brendan, in all the hagiological references called 'The Navigator,' formed a pious resolution to seek this distant land, there to spread the light of Christianity. He sailed from the coast of Kerry with a crew of sixty religious men, in quest of the unknown Western Continent.

It is probably this adventurous mariner who took his departure from the Land of Promise, from near the majestic headland and from out that bay, now bearing his name. both lie about seven miles northwards from Dingle. There is no mountain throughout that region of country supposed to approach in height St. Brendan's Hill in Kerry, nor which commands so extensive a view of Shannon, nor of its entrance to the ocean.

The narrative goes on to tell the story of St. Brendan's[23] voyage from his departure until his landing, "somewhere on the eastern shores of the present Transatlantic Republic." It then continues:

The holy man Brendan landed on the shores of a vast territory, the extent of which was unknown; and after a long term—seven years are said to have been spent in exploration—he and his hardy mariners returned to Ireland...Several Latin versions of St. Brendan's voyage are still in manuscript, and many of these are ancient. Never was popular romance more eagerly read in modern times than was this composition, not alone in Ireland but throughout Europe. It was recited in the Irish language; it was sung in the Norman-French; while it has been translated into various dialects, and published in prose and poetry.

The traditions of St. Brendan's voyage haunted the imagination of Irish navigators after his time; and a new-born zeal to spread Christianity in that new land excited the ardour of many inmates in monastic establishments.

The history goes on to record the futile attempts of religious groups that set out to reach the promised land. Among those who returned safely and told their story were St. Colman Ua Liathain in the sixth century who made several

---

[23] See St. Brendan's Voyage, Tim Saverin.

trips but was driven back, a disciple of St. Columba and his successor as Ablat of Iona, St. Baithen, also Maelduin, the son of a Munster chief, with a number of young men who spent three years and seven months on the Atlantic, among others.

There is good reason to believe, however, that several groups of Irish Christians had reached the trans-Atlantic shores at an early period. That they had settled there is on record, and it is even probable that they had propagated Christianity among the inhabitants—then briefly composed of the tawny or Red Men of the forest, whose origin, descent, and migrations have so often exercised, and still baffled, the researches of American Ethnologists and historians.

From Ireland, the accounts of the Promised Land and of other visionary islands in the great ocean spread throughout Europe. The Irish navigators had early and frequent intercourse with the Northmen of Iceland and of Scandinavia; and these daring seamen were anxious to hazard their lives around the coasts of Greenland to the points indicated. Attributing the honour of a first discovery to our (Irish) countrymen, and foreshadowing the Great Land as a colonial dependency, justly belonging to the County of their birth, the Northern Sagas called it Irland-it-Mickla, or Great Ireland.

The route towards it, commencing from the north of Europe, is described in this manner. The Sagas and Eddas relate, that to the south of habitable Greenland, enormous icebergs were to be found floating. Then wild tracts of uninhabitable wastes extended. Beyond these the country of the Scraelings lay. A region called Markland extended beyond their territory; while Vinland the Good stretched beyond the country just noticed. Icelandic records, and especially the Landnamabock indicated the Scraelings' land to be identified with the country of the Esquimaux; Markland with the present Labrador or Nova Scotia; Wineland or Vinland the Good with the New England states; and a tract called Haitranmanaland or Atlania, denominated also White Man's Land, is thought to have comprised the present southern United States. Formerly vessels are said to have gone from Ireland, while their crews landed in this particular region. Helluland is also a denomination found, but its situation is not so easily determined. However, it has been thought identical with Newfoundland, and that it is so called from its flat stones. Centuries before the Spaniards landed in Florida, and at a very early period, Irishmen had settled in that southern portion of North America, and had introduced a civilization, the traces of which remain. Even so far back as the eighth century, a people speaking the Irish language was found there; while, according to a probable conjecture, that country lying along the eastern coast, and stretching from Chesapeake Bay to the Carolinas and Florida, had been inhabited by Irishmen. Even the Shawnee Indians, who formerly lived in Florida, had a tradition that white men anciently occupied that region, and they were possessed of iron implements. In fact, the numerous antiquities discovered in various parts of the Eastern, Northern and Southern states prove that a race of civilized beings were residents there, and possibly anterior to the Indians. How they have disappeared as a race now comes to be unknown. It is probable they had been destroyed by the Red Men; or as some ethnologists have supposed, that intermarriages with native women took place, which merged the white race completely into the colored race.

That old Icelandic Scandinavian chronicles the Landnamabock relates that Ulf the Squinter, son of Hogni the White, occupied the whole of Reykianess—a south-west promatory of Iceland—which was situated between Thorskafiord and Hafrafell. He had a wife named Biorg, who was daughter to Eyvind the East-countryman. They had a son named Ari, and he was driven by a tempest to Haitranmanaland, which some called Ireland-it-Mickla or Great Ireland. This region was placed in the western ocean, near to Vinland the Good, and westwards from Ireland. Ari is said to have been baptized in this newly-discovered country. If so, it must have been by Irish missionaries, and among Irish colonists. He was held there in great respect, and elected as a chief, nor would the inhabitants permit him to take his departure from among them. Besides the forgoing, many Northmen settled in our Island and in Northern Europe, frequently sailed to those distant shores, a Northman merchant of Limerick called Rafu, and his kinsmen Ari Marson, Biron or Biorn, with a person named Gudlief, besides Madoc, a prince of Wales, with Antonio Zeno, a Venetian and others, are said to have landed there at various times, during the middle ages.

As we can readily see by these passages, there was much ocean travel of which we have little knowledge. The self-educated knew a great deal of the world, the heavens, mathematics and navigation; they had little time to write or record. The others were followers, they took orders, were hard workers and faithful but had no means to write or record. It was word of mouth or not at all. They were well aware of the travels of Europeans and Asiatics to these shores in the years before the voyages of Columbus.

But scholars of today have great trouble reading the signs; they have to see it in writing. If it isn't in writing, it didn't happen. They study the sagas

Helge Ingstad
Writer Adventurer
1900 - 2001

diligently without realizing they are getting only a small part of the story and only a few of those sagas have now become famous. And so it is this flawed and limited knowledge of most scholars that is being passed on to the younger generations and propagated by our news media.

We now have evidence of the Norse colonists in America but none of the evidence was accepted by the authorities until the discoveries of the Norwegian, Helge Ingstad,[23a] and his archaeologist wife at L'Anse aux Meadows in 1956.

There is one more interesting passage by the eminent Irish historian, the Very Rev. John O'Hanlon (1900):

...The aboriginal inhabitants of North America probably belong to various nations. It is generally thought that the great majority of the early colonists crossed over from Eastern Asia through the Behring[24] Straits at a very remote era. They are supposed to have arrived at different periods. Certain writers believe that the Phoenicians and Scythians sailed thither and settled there in times very distant from our own; but that those ancient mariners found themselves unable to return or communicate their adventures after they landed.

The earlier inhabitants of America are deemed to have been those most advanced in knowledge and skill. There can be no doubt that a civilized race had flourished—especially in the midland and southern parts of the North American continent—at a very remote time, as proved by the remarkable pyramids, dykes, causeways, idols, temples, hieroglyphics, paintings, and sculptures, and also other monuments found in the Yucatan Peninsula in Mexico and in Peru. Their agriculture and manufacturers were considerable, while their social and civil state was remarkably well-ordered.

[23a] Helge Ingstad, Norwegan writer and adventurer who followed a hunch and an ancient map to identify the place where Vikings landed in North America 500 years before Colunbus, died Thursday March 29th 2001 in a hospital in Oslo, He was 101.

[24] Behring=Bering—Vitas Jonassen Bering (1681-1741) was a Danish navigator employed by Russia to explore the northeast region of that country. He discovered the Bering Straits and Bering Sea in 1740.

Curious remains of antiquity abound in a variety of places throughout the United States, but those indications afford only objects for doubtful investigation. Mounds, monuments, earthworks, stone-cased graves, stone implements, flint spear and arrowheads and rock carvings are the chief antiquities hitherto discovered. They have been ascribed to various races and to different periods. In connection with primitive United States history, the Red Men seem to occupy the chief claim on our consideration. Since the white colonization many works have appeared, but these are almost solely descriptive of their habits and manners. The aborigines of America have an obscure history—if indeed it can at all be investigated, yet perhaps existing monuments and antiquities may help to throw some light on their origin and race.

Runic forts, tombs (one of these has been brought to light near the falls of the Potomac River and it is said to have had an inscription in the Runic character, purporting to be the burial place of Susie or Susa, a daughter to one of the Northmen) and inscriptions have been discovered, especially in eastern and middle states. These indications furnish evidence of a Scandinavian colonization. Axes, spears and arrowheads have been found in great numbers, especially in the middle, western and northern states. Numerous prehistoric monuments known as Indian mounds rise throughout the midland districts of North America. Frequently these are of considerable height and dimensions. Several have been explored, and they were found to contain human remains of gigantic proportions. But the great ethnological problem as to the race and period contemporane-ous with their erection, remains to be solved; nor does it seem likely that the nomadic habits of the Red Man could bear any relation to a state of society existing when those monuments were raised to such impos-ing heights.—The most extensive remains are to be found probably in southeastern Missouri and along the western bank of the Mississippi.

It has been supposed that the mound builders were a race of people whose remains indicate a state of advancement in the arts and manu-facturers, far superior to the savage tribes who succeeded them. Some archaeologists have adopted an opinion that the mound builders were not an extinct people, but were ancestors of existing tribes. Numerous wedges, chisels, hammers and other implements have been found in the ancient mining pits of Keweenaw Point, Lake Superior and at Isle Royale. Artistic forms of copper implements, both cast and hammered[25] cannot

---

[25] Professor Lewis has remarked that much greater number of prehistoric copper hammers were produced by hammering

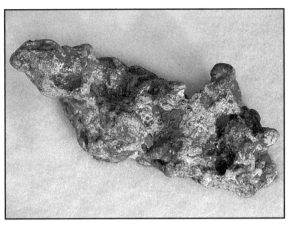

While heating the copper to spall the rock away with cold water, some hot fires would have softened it to a point of melting which would have been noticed.

fail to impress the observer, that a race of men existed in early times, and whose origin is enveloped in mystery, but whose skill rivals that of man in historic times, assisted by all the inventions of the iron age. Recent discoveries have shown that various forms of copper implements had been deposited in their burial places by mound-builders, with markings similar to those left by moulds in the process of casting. That these people were acquainted with the art of smelting copper,[26] besides that of hammering it, has been inferred on what seem to be reasonable grounds.[27]

The legend of St. Brendan had a reflex and shadowy light to throw on geographical science, down to a comparatively late period. In the Middle Ages, seven cities, with bishops and a great number of Christians, were thought to have been in the Land of St. Brendan, having fled thither in ships, at the time when Spain and Portugal had been conquered by the Moors.

Through the clouds of Irish recorded traditions, and through recent historic investigations, we may now trace the facts, but slightly obscured by the vivid cross-lights of old legend-mongers.

Soon after the invention of printing, Great Ireland was set down and also the Isle of St. Brendan. On the Map of the World, traced by Martin

---

[26] Colonel Whittlesey mentions that in all the pits examined by him, traces of fires were to be seen on the sides thereof, and fragments of charcoal and wood in the debris, indicating the use of fire in assisting the action of the wedges and in extracting the masses of copper. The melting point of copper 1098 degrees Celsius (correction $1083.0 \pm .1$ degree Celsius), which no doubt fused the small points of copper attached to the larger masses, and which the quick perception of those aboriginal people noticed, and thus it led them to utilize those particles in casting.—"Smithsonian Contributions to Knowledge for 1883."

[27] The fact, that in a collection made by Mr. Perkins, he saw copper implements of mound origin, and which bear well-defined traces of the mould, is stated by Professor Foster, "It is impossible," he adds, "to infer, after careful examination of the specimens, that the ridges have been left in the process of hammering or oxidation. The more I examine their arts and manufactures, the stronger becomes my conviction that they were something more than Barbaric people." *Prehistoric Races of the United States*

.

Behaim, A.D. 1492, and on most charts in the time of Columbus, it is noted. (See a reproduction of several ancient charts and an account of the pre-Columbian exploration in Justin Winsor's 'Narrative and Critical History of America," Vol, I, Chap ii) In an ocean space between the south of Ireland and the end of Guinea, it was represented. There can be little doubt, that from a very distant period, the inhabitants of Ireland had entertained widely spread ideas about the existence of a great and far-removed western continent. Some had even reached it and landed, still their adventures were unrecorded, and therefore during long ages a void continued in the history of those lost tribes.

All this coordinates reasonably with the many inscriptions (we will later read about) along with the huge numbers of ancient stone works found up and down our east coast and throughout the New England states. It also explains the tribe of white Indians (the Erie Indians) snuffed out of existence during the 19th century by other tribes in the area. This formerly unknown group is referred to again and again in the old histories.[27a]

A recent letter from Ireland addressed to me with the word "Erie" written across the top of the stamp was a gentle reminder that the name is so prominent south of Lake Erie around Erie, Pennsylvania, and along the Erie Canal. Truly these people were Irish and they left a tremendous amount of evidence of their having lived here for centuries. The same can be said for Scandinavians and many others before them.

Joe Gannon and some of his contemporaries had been trained in traditional schools of the 19th century. They learned Greek and Latin and read many of the classical histories referred to above, histories which by the 1920's, 30's and 40's had been taken out of the school curriculum.

Examples of Irish Stamps & Coins all with "Erie" on them.

Joe's idea was to start from square one and try to prove his own theory, one that

---

[27a] The Erie Tribe were close to or a part of the Iroqois Nation, but were all but annihilated by then. The surviving women and children were assimilated by the Oneidas, some of which are fair haired and light skinned today.

I thought was so logical. But he needed a lot of help.

By the end of the 19th century, when all these changes in our history were being made and the statements from authorities were decreed with such finality, there were discoveries to the contrary being made throughout the country. I will tell about three of these that are in the local (Great Lakes region) area. One was a carved stone found in Minnesota, another was a great controversy over thousands of artifacts (clay, slate and copper objects) found in Lower Michigan and the third was an inscribed clay tablet and three clay statues found near Newberry in Michigan's Upper Peninsula.

The Kensington Stone

The finding of the Kensington Stone in 1898 became so controversial that, at first, it did not get wide attention beyond the plains of western Minnesota. Here is what was known: a forty-four year old Swedish farmer, Olaf Ohman, while clearing land on his farm near Kensington in western Minnesota, found a large, flat stone bearing some kind of inscription. He was digging around the roots of an aspen tree when he discovered they were growing around this big stone—a stone almost a yard long, over a foot wide, and about six inches thick.

Ohman's ten-year-old son, Edward, noticed strange markings on one side of the stone and they called a neighbor, Nels Flaten, to come and look at it. At that time, even to experts, a large part of the inscription baffled all attempts at decipherment, but about ten years later a complete translation was published. Until then, the inscription was condemned as a "clumsy fraud" that had to have been perpetrated by the finder, Olaf Ohman.

Ohman   was   born   in Helsingland, Sweden, in 1859. He

Compliments of the Runestone Museum, Alexandria, Minnesota

Kensington Runestone

105

came to America in 1891 and worked as a laborer at whatever jobs were available to immigrant pioneers of that day at the going wage of one dollar a day. In 1891 Ohman was able to make a partial payment on a tract of land near Kensington in Douglas County, Minnesota, in the west central part of the state. His job of clearing land entailed cutting trees and removing the stumps.

Thus, in November of 1898, he felled an aspen tree with a ten-inch trunk, and found, tangled in its roots, this large, flat stone on which were chiseled hundreds of marks that were obviously an alphabet.

Within a short time, news of the strange find had spread to the surrounding countryside and many curious neighbors came to inspect the inscription. Even though the inscription was neat and orderly, no one could identify the language.

Ohman himself had only nine months of schooling in his life and though he could write, he needed help to compose a letter. He asked a local insurance man and real estate dealer, Mr. J. P. Hedberg, to help him write a letter to a weekly Swedish newspaper published in Minneapolis. The letter is as follows:

Kensington, Minn
Jan 1, 1899

Swan J. Turnblad
　Minneapolis

　　　I enclose you a copy of an inscription on a stone found about 2 miles from Kensington by a O. Ohman he found it under a tree while grubbing. he wanted I should go out and look at it and I told him to haul it in when he came (not thinking much of it) and he did so, and this is an exact copy of it the first part is of the flat side of the stone the other was on flat edge. I thought I would send it to you as you perhaps have means to find out what it is—it appears to be old Greek letters. please let me hear from you and oblige.

Yours truly
J. P. Hedberg

After a few months of inquiring around without success, Editor Turnblad

Hjalmar R. Holand
Historian, Author, Scandinavian Authority

printed the letter in his paper of February 28, 1899.

In the meantime, Mr. S. A. Sieverts, a bank manager at Kensington, sent a copy of the inscription to Professor O. J. Breda of the Department of Scandinavian Languages at the University of Minnesota. Breda knew very little about runes,[28] but was able to translate some of the inscription. He did recognize the word "Vinland," however. Since the runes on the stone did not correspond to the period of Leif Erickson (about the year 1000 A.D.), he determined the inscription could not be genuine. He sent his report to the University of Oslo and it was considered final.

Hjalmar R. Holand's translation of the Kensington Runestone (the words in parentheses are not on the stone):

("We are) 8 Goths (Swedes) and 22 Norwegians on (an) exploration journey from Vinland round about the west, We had camp by (a lake with) 2 Skerries (islands) one day's journey north from the stone. We were (out) and fished one day. After we came home (we) found ten of our men red with blood and dead. AVM (Ave Virgo Maria) save (us) from evil.

(We) have ten men by the sea to look after our ships 14 days journeys from this island. (In the) year (of our Lord) 1362."

In his book, "Explorations In America Before Columbus," Hjalmar R. Holand, who spent many years working with the Kensington Stone, wrote:

(In Oslo,) the story was used, publicly and privately, as a sample of "the irresponsible tricking that characterized the American people." This scoffing attitude was in part a result of jealous resentment because of the

---

[28] Rune=old Norse lettering.

great immigration to America in the closing decades of the 19th century. During the seven years from 1886 to 1892 about 300,000 of Norway's and Sweden's young men and women had been persuaded to leave for the United States. This was a tremendous drain of manpower from countries with small populations. The upper classes, therefore, had reason to feel unfriendly toward America, and the newspapers missed no opportunity to print stories about the depravity 'characteristic' of America with hope of checking immigration. The report came back from Oslo swiftly and sternly: 'the Kensington Stone inscription was a silly, meaningless forgery.'

Three groups of scholars investigated the stone: geologists, archaeologists and philologists (linguistic scholars).

The geologists agreed unanimously that the weathering on the stone must have taken at least fifty to a hundred years and most believed it to be of a much greater age. Since there were no Scandinavians in Minnesota even fifty years earlier and Douglas County had no settlers until 1867, it seemed there could be no possibility of a forgery.

The archaeologists decided there was nothing to be said either for or against the stone's authenticity from an archaeological point of view.

A larger number of philologists supported the authenticity of the stone; the

Olaf Ohman and the Kensington Stone - 1927

smaller, but persistent, group denounced it as a modern forgery. Based on their textbook knowledge of mainly formal legal documents, their idea of the spoken language at the time was quite different. In Norway local ethno-centrism has been successful in promoting regional dialectical differences and even today there is no single standard for writing the Norwegian language.[28a]

After several years had passed and the Kensington Stone had reached the Smithsonian Institution, the experts there declared it a fraud. Holand:

> This verdict left the people of Kensington and vicinity in great confu-
> sion. They did not question the verdict of the judges. If the great scholars
> in the home country said the inscription was a forgery, then, of course,
> it must be so. But a bothersome question persisted in their minds: How
> could a forgery be committed without a forger? The settlement was only
> thirty-one years old, and the disposition, aptitude, and education of every
> man was well known. There was no one who had the knowledge, skill
> and time to sit for days carving ancient inscriptions on rocks which could
> bring them no profit.

Over the years, while there have been many great researchers and scholars who champion the Kensington Stone as authentic, the run-of-the-mill professors and teachers who try to keep up with current thinking have condemned it as a fraud. The accused forger, Olaf Ohman, had to endure the burden of public ridicule the rest of his life. His children developed personality problems. A boy and a girl committed suicide and another girl changed her name and left home. A fourth sibling, who stayed on the farm, would not talk about the stone with anyone.

The story is told about a local pastor who went to visit the son on his deathbed. "Just tell me the truth about the stone," he asked. "I'm a man of the cloth and I'll believe whatever you say. I just want to hear you say it."

The son hesitated a long time and then a great tear rolled down his cheek and he looked at the preacher. In a firm voice, he declared, "The stone is real."

To this day there is constant wrangling as to whether the Kensington Stone is a fraud or authentic. In recent years it was still viewed as a forgery by the Smithsonian Institution, but a thorough scientific study is now underway led by a group of local scholars and their report should be available soon.[29]

[28a] Norwegian language variety is well documented.

[29] Recent investigation—is discussed later.

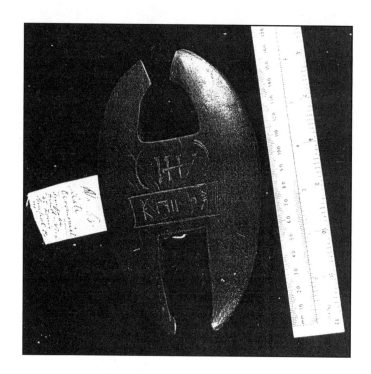

The slate shuttle, found in Crystal, 1874 which started public controversy.

The Michigan Tablets
(Soper Tablets)

This second enigma has a long history. I had heard about it for years but every time it was mentioned it was treated as a joke. In the 1950s I looked into it more closely. How could a story like this one be turned around so?

The best short history of the tablets was written by the late Kenneth Moore of New Jersey. It appeared in the *Ancient American* magazine, Issue #9. An excerpt follows below.

The first the public heard of the Soper tablets was in 1874. Near the small town of Crystal, Michigan, Gratiot County, in the central part of the Lower Peninsula, a farmer clearing land uncovered a large replica of a shuttle (used for weaving). It had been carefully carved out of a piece of black slate and then highly polished.

One surface displayed the incised drawing of a man's head wearing a helmet and the obverse side showed two lines of writing; a group of cuneiform[30] and a line of an unknown script. Over that 19th century summer more pieces were found in the surrounding countryside, including a

---

[30] Cuneiform=wedge-shaped characters of ancient inscriptions of Assyria, Babylonia, Persia, Carthoginian, etc.

copper dagger, a clay box, and some slate tablets, each item showing an unknown grouping of script, but each one bearing on it the grouping of script cuneiform, the same as that on the slate shuttle.

Note: This was not the first finding of such artifacts, it was only the first major public notice. From the 1840's onward, pieces with the same markings had been collected by a professor Edwin Worth and, although it was unknown to the farmers around Crystal, Professor Worth had exhibited some of these in Detroit. The collection begun by Professor Worth in 1848, exhibited for a time in New York, was finally destroyed in a fire at Springport, Indiana in 1916. Only a few copper pieces survived and these are illustrated by Henriette Mertz in her book, "The Mystic Symbol."

Local farmers, knowledgeable only about Indians, were surprised by these artifacts, which were unlike anything they had ever seen. No one could read any of the incised writing. Farmers began to display and compare their newly found artifacts and all agreed that there was writing on them, but no one could agree on what the writing purported to be. Between 1870 and 1920, farmers from seventeen counties had found artifacts, each piece having the same grouping of cuneiform. From these finds, some major collections developed, as did the earliest indications of controversy. The first professionals to view the artifacts could offer no explanation for them and, not able to recognize the writing as any script with which they were familiar, declared, in each and every case, that the artifacts were fraudulent.

In 1890, James Scotford made his first Michigan Tablet find; it elevated the controversy to an hysterical level which is only now beginning to subside. Scotford, a young hired hand on the Davis farm near Wyman, while digging post-holes, unearthed a clay jar covered with the unknown script. Scotford was uneducated and could make nothing out of the markings. Again, the curious came, this time to the Davis farm to see the tablets and speculate on their meaning.

Clay - Etzenhouser Collection. Found near St. Louis, Gratiot Co., Mich., Dec. 12, 1904.

Daniel Soper

This latest flurry of interest aroused the attention of archaeologists, even in Europe. By the end of 1890, Scotford had dug up more objects, such items as a sphinx, a vase and tablets; each one displayed the grouping of cuneiform along with other unknown scripts.

In nearby Stanton, people who were convinced that these relics were, in fact, remains of an unknown culture formed a society to study them. Photos were sent to museums and universities in the hope that someone could recognize the writing or identify the objects. Every answer was negative. A typical newspaper article was headed "Archaeological Forgeries at Wyman Michigan." At this same time, 1892, a man named Cornell of Battle Creek, Michigan, believing wholeheartedly that the artifacts were genuine, published a small monograph entitled "Prehistoric Relics of the Mound Builders." It describes the objects and illustrates some of them. After a description of the circumstances of the finds, he provides a detailed account of the mounds in which they were found, leaving us a very important eye-witness account. After summarizing some history of the Near East, he ends the pamphlet with a page of eye-witness testimonies signed by people who watched artifacts being dug from the ground.

The society of Stanton disbanded while the debate and condemnation continued sporadically in various newspapers and journals. Public notice gradually melted away until October 1907, when more artifacts again began to appear in Detroit. A man named Daniel Soper, who later went on to assemble one of the major collections of these artifacts, was responsible for this newest sensation. His own account, written some years later, is a most interesting narrative. He describes walking in the woods and seeing a mound where a woodchuck had dug a den. The sand thrown out by the woodchuck contained pieces of broken pottery which, when washed off, displayed the writing and markings. He got a shovel and dug into the mound where he found a clay lamp and a slate box which contained three copper spearheads.

On the same evening of the first find, Soper went to seek his friend, the Reverend James Savage, who, beyond being a pastor, was a knowledgeable amateur archaeologist and collector. Savage recognized that the artifacts resembled nothing in his present collection of ten thousand artifacts. Later, Savage was to build another major collection of mound artifacts.

In 1910, Bishop Rudolph Etzenhouser, a missionary of the Church of Latter Day Saints, enters our story. Etzenhouser proceeded to assemble his own collection and then published a formal brochure, "Engravings of Pre-Historic Specimens from Michigan. U.S.A." It featured forty-four pages of photos of artifacts and the tablets, including some from the collections of Soper and Savage. The engraved plates for this printing were made by Von Leyen and Hensler of Detroit. The brochure has an introduction which generally suggests that, although the language of the tablets has not been interpreted, it will be in the long run. "…yet an interesting chapter to the ancient history of this continent." A few copies of this booklet are still in circulation. [I have one which was generously given to me and I suggest that anyone who expects to do any research on these artifacts should get a copy, because it contains some reproductions which are not illustrated elsewhere.]

By now, many well-recognized experts were denouncing the artifacts as forgeries, some already accusing Scotford of counterfeiting them. This is interesting. In hindsight, their accusation is interesting, because what they were actually saying was that he forged artifacts which had, in fact, been found before he was born. Bishop Etzenhouser was on a lecture tour to acclaim the artifacts and well-known professors were lecturing just as vigorously to the contrary. At this time a committee was formed to settle the question by proceeding to Detroit to see a mound opened. Professor Frederick Starr of the University of Chicago and Roswell Field, an editor of the daily Chicago Examiner, were joined by a representative of the Mormon Church, Dr. James Talmage, Director of the Deseret Museum at Salt Lake City. Already there had been vague suggestions that the Michigan tablets could in some way throw doubt on those allegedly found by Joseph Smith; the Mormon Church now had a special interest in this study.

Along with the committee, a group of curious spectators watched as two mounds were opened. Professor Starr then wrote that even though he had himself removed one of the objects from the mound, they had been "introduced into the mound by sleight-of-hand even as everyone watched" (sic). His report was published without question. However, it was Talmage who became the loudest voice among all the denunciations, which have overshadowed the study even until most recently. Thank-fully, Talmage kept a diary of field notes and observations and, again thankfully, Dr. Fell, for reasons which remain obscure, published the significant section of Talmage's journal ESOP (1988).[31]

On first reading Talmage's notes, it becomes obvious that he went to Detroit with the explicit intention to discredit the artifacts (my personal evaluation). His story, published in the Deseret Museum Bulletin, in-cluding illustrations of some of the objects, is headed "The Michigan Relics—A Story of Forgery and Deception." He viewed the Soper and Savage collections and it is here that we find the first reference to the group of cuneiform characters appearing on the artifacts as the "Tribal Mark."[32] Concurrently, a Professor Kelsey had labeled this the "sign manual of the forger." The Talmage journal is readily available (ESOP), so to avoid lengthy repetition, I summarize the highlights.

The published story begins with a brief referral to the Soper and Savage collections and then poses a five-part theorem, which Talmage suggests must be completely true for the relics to be considered authentic:

1. That...the present State of Michigan was inhabited in the long ago...by people of the Caucasian race possessing a high degree of civilization.
2. That, living at the same time...same area, was another group of inferior culture, resembling the Indians of today.
3. That these two peoples, representing widely different cultures, were at enmity one with the other...
4. That the people of higher culture used a written language, both pictographic and characters, some of which had points of resem-blance to alphabets of Egyptian, Greek, Assyrian, Phoenician and Hebrew.
5. That the peoples of the higher class had knowledge of books of Jewish scripture, specifically Genesis, and later books of the Old Testament. [Note here a lack of reference to the New Testa-ment.]

---

[31] I spoke with Dr. Fell on this very subject. He told me one copper plate was a modern mixture of metals. I said there were no mixtures of metals that hadn't been experimented with in ancient times, and besides you don't condemn the whole collection on one piece. He did this with Burrows Cave also. Story later.
[32] Henriett Mertz named this group of letters "The Mystic Symbol."

From a perspective today, I suggest that in the light of progressive positive study, all of the five points which Talmage considered fanciful are being validated.

Talmage, curiously, brands everything a forgery. "He suggests that he open some mounds himself and everyone agreed that he should. He allowed Scotford to lead him and in November of 1909, he opened some mounds with Scotford's help. Talmage then describes an area near the Oldsmobile factory (in Lansing) and admits that some of the mounds appeared to be plainly artificial in origin. [His description of the first mound opened is important for us here now because it contains several facts which, at this later time, suggest a theory to me which I will detail later.) In the sand, 12 inches below the mound surface, a layer of charcoal was found. Both Scotford and Soper stated that the finding of this charcoal layer would prove the mound had artifacts. They continued digging and did find a copper axe. He describes the next mound, which the locals called the "Serpent Mound." Here he found the layer of charcoal and then a slate tablet inscribed on both surfaces. Scotford stated, "This is like what was found on one of the plates from Mormon Hill at Cumorah, New York." In this same mound they found a slate knife inscribed on one side.

Several days later, Talmage, with Scotford and Soper, went back to this mound and found another slate tablet. The next mound, with the charcoal layer, produced another slate tablet. Now, the next few mounds opened had no charcoal layer and produced no artifacts, all of the artifacts found displayed the "Tribal Mark." Talmage went to New York and then to Washington to show his six, newly fond artifacts to museum archaeologists, all of whom pronounced them as "fakes." He returned to Detroit and quietly went out to dig with the help of some hired men. The 22 mounds they excavated yielded nothing. Returning to Salt Lake, Talmage learned of Etzenhouser's book. He illustrates some of the plates from this work and adds his own very disparaging commentary. After stating his reasons for believing the artifacts as spurious, he directly accuses Scotford of forging them. In his (then) unpublished field-notes (June 6, 1911), Talmage records an interview with Scotford's stepdaughter, in which she states that Scotford "...had fraudulently manufactured many of the articles supposedly discovered in the ground."

We could certainly go on for many pages concerning "the great hoax," as the Michigan Tablets came to be known. On December 28 (1953), the *Detroit*

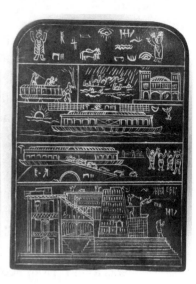

*Some examples of the Michigan Tablets
done on slate.*

116

News printed a story that demonstrates the attitude of the reporter. The article mentions the "Piltown Man" hoax as singularly lacking in imagination. Someone placed the mandible of an ape beside some fragments of human skull, thereby creating a missing link, until the hoax was exposed by carbon dating.

But this was trivial alongside the vast number of religious tablets and copper artifacts that were turned up in lower Michigan, some of which were so hardened that they rang like steel when struck, and were overlaid with a fine, green patina testifying to their long burial.

It all started about 1885 where the *Detroit News* story says, "James O. Scotford, one-time slight-of-hand performer turned sign painter, is displaying an almost clairvoyant ability to discover Indian artifacts in prehistoric mounds."

Scotford was selling Indian relics and soon became assisted by a Mr. Soper. No one was suspicious until 1890 when Soper was elected Secretary of State in Michigan, not a very important job in those days. He got into trouble accepting kickbacks and was promptly fired by Governor Edwin B. Winans in 1891.

Soper dropped out of sight until 1907, when he appeared in Detroit living near Scotford. At that time, Soper was offering rare Indian artifacts to collectors in Michigan, Wisconsin, Indiana, Illinois and Canada. He offered hundreds of objects—copper weapons, ornaments and all kinds of copper implements, as well as clay pipes and bowls which he claimed were unearthed by Scotford in Isabella County near Big Rapids, in places within three miles of Lansing and even in back of Palmer Park.

> From the *Detroit News*:
> On Nov. 14, 1907, a Detroit News reporter reveals that the firm has added a new line of goods. It is selling copper crowns—found on the brows of prehistoric kings—whose forms crumble into dust when exposed to air. It is peddling copies of "Noah's diary"…as well as the Tower of Babel tablet and the original Ten Commandments.

There should have been no question as to the authenticity of the relics because Scotford always had the presence of witnesses—usually the local editor, blacksmith, druggist, storekeeper and a neighboring farmer or two. All men of high repute, they signed statements that they had seen the articles taken from the earth.

"The scheme," writes the News reporter, "is so unique as to win absolute admiration for the perpetrators. If committed in a spirit of humor, it is the most colossal hoax of the century."

The reporter is not impressed with the fact that every piece of copper bears a curious cuneiform-like inscription. It is three vertical wedge-shaped marks on which a fourth is superimposed, horizontally, while a fifth slants off by itself.

The reporter interprets this as a crude "IHS," the cabalistic sign of the cross, and wonders what significance it could have in pre-Christian workmanship.

Indeed, these fakirs would have callow collectors believe that Michigan was the seat of the original inhabitants of the earth, that Noah's Ark floated somewhere around these parts and, finally coming to land, settled on one of Michigan's low-lying hills as the genuine Mount Ararat.

The reporter interviews Scotford, who takes umbrage at the reporter's questions while Scotford's 19-year-old son, Percy, "just laughs."

Scotford declares the finds genuine. He says some syndicate of sharpers once did offer him $500 to duplicate an article, "but I would not sell my honor for $10,000," he exclaimed.

The reporter calls on Father James Savage of the Most Holy Trinity Church, who bought 50 of the Indian and Biblical relics as well as one of the pre-Christian crowns.

Says Father Savage, "True, I may be duped. In buying them I felt this way: It is getting the most wonderful discoveries of the centuries, or it is getting fakes. I took the chance."

The director of the Detroit Museum of Art, to whom Soper offered a representative collection, declared them frauds.

When the University of Michigan refused an opportunity to buy "two caskets, a prehistoric beer mug, a bowl, three goblets and some copper coins" at $1,000, the items were offered at $100. The University again declined and Soper left them in Ann Arbor.

From Port Huron a collector said he had branded Soper a faker in1889. From Big Rapids came testimony that Soper had victimized Charles H. Throp, a real estate agent in 1895.

From Owosso came word that museums and private collectors were hurriedly going over their possessions and "many relics are disappearing by way of the trash heap."

From the Smithsonian Institution in Washington, W. H. Holmes, chief of the Bureau of American Ethnology, wrote, "I am exceedingly glad that you have succeeded in exposing this traffic and hope that some means may be found to break it up."

The story ought to end there, says the paper, but it doesn't. The relics were being sold in greater numbers and at a greater distance from Detroit.

Four years later, on July 27, 1911, a Professor J. O. Kinnaman of Benton Harbor, tells a News reporter that discoveries have been made "out North

Woodward," which will compel archaeologists to revise their theories of the origin and development of all civilization as it exists today. Professor Kinnaman:

> Tentatively speaking, we may say that historically and geologically, when the Detroit River and Lake St. Clair extended many miles inland from where they do now, a Caucasian race, with civilization developed to a point equal to any developed in the valleys of the Nile and Tigro-Euphrates, existed all over the present continent of America. Our knowledge of the Caucasian race will likely extend thousands of years back of the wildest dream of the most enthusiastic archaeologist.

On August 10, 1911, the News reports that Dr. James E. Talmage, Deseret Professor of Geology at the University of Utah, came to Detroit and examined Fr. Savage's collection. He pointed out that the battle axes bore file marks and the copper was commercially smelted and had none of the characteristics of native Michigan copper. He said the corrosion was affected with acid and was so thin that it could be wiped away. Talmage added that all the objects had been found within two feet of the surface—and it was mighty funny that none had been found except by Scotford or under his guidance.

Perhaps it was Granny Mary Robson who really gave the "Dawn Race of Caucasians" their quietus. She told the News on September 6 that one winter she had a room at 313-1/2 Michigan, next to the one occupied by Percy Scotford and his brother Charles, age 21.

She said, "Hammering went on day and night."

She went to the boys' room to borrow something and "they warned me out." Then they relented and told her that she was in Detroit's ancient relic factory.

Next day, Charles denied this and said that Percy had hypnotized Granny Robson using skills gained in a correspondence course.

"Never hypnotized me in their lives," said Granny firmly.

Later files of the News are silent on the subject.

This, then, was the great fraud: people digging up "Indian mounds" and finding any number of strange things that should have been completely unknown to Indians—copper crowns, pipes, small caskets, bowls and weapons, all with a strange mystic symbol imprinted on them, a symbol which seemed to be the Christian IHS.

The tablets were of clay, stone, slate and copper, and all were inscribed with some type of illegible lettering. All of the tablets depicted Christian Bible stories. They were taken from mounds in some 20 counties in the southern part of the state. About two of every ten opened mounds contained a tablet and other artifacts.

In the early years, the tablets were sent to archaeologists and scholars and received much acclaim; many were purchased by museums and universities.

Then people began to yell "Fraud!" The inscriptions were said to be a hodgepodge of Egyptian, Phoenician, Greek and cuneiform, probably gleaned from Webster's dictionary. People wondered how these men found so many of these things, and so often with star witnesses. Soper and Scotford were tried in the press and found guilty. People of repute, like Adolphe B. Covent, curator of the University of Cincinnati Museum, who at first had authenticated the finds, soon backed off and became silent in the light of the bad publicity. Testimony mounted against Soper and his friends, and the friends soon left him like rats from a sinking ship.

By the time the press declared Soper and his friends to be out-and-out frauds (that same press being backed by scholars and institutions), many things were quietly thrown out, packed away or kept as examples of what men will go through to dupe the public.

This was the period when textbooks were being rewritten to exclude the idea of people coming to the American continent, even by chance, prior to 1492.

To be sure, there were a few small voices too timid to be heard. They were so insignificant they would be trampled on and crushed if they tried to voice their opinion. But still some wondered about the multitude of strange and unexplainable artifacts and unreadable inscriptions in stone that kept turning up.[32a]

The Newberry Tablet
(McGruer's Gods)

The third enigmatic find that we will mention here was stumbled upon about the same time as the Kensington Stone.

An excerpt from a story written by Sprague Taylor for the *Newberry News* of April 7, 1966, gives us a good picture of what happened:

> It all happened in 1896, people said, when John McGruer sent two local lumberjacks, John Gordon and George Howe, out to cut wood for him on a forty he owned a mile west of Four Mile Corner, north of town.
>
> The story they returned with was that while putting up wood they saw a stray mink and chased it beneath the roots of an upturned hemlock. Peering underneath, they saw part of the exposed head of what seemed to be a crude sandstone statue. Quickly digging it out—and breaking it into several pieces in their haste—they poked nearby and unearthed two smaller ones, together with a slab or tablet of the same material.

[32a] Some of these inscriptions have recently been translated - See Chapter X

And so into Newberry they hurried, weighted down with certainly as strange a result of mink-chasing as ever turned up in a northwoods village.

News of the find spread quickly, and souvenir hunters descended on the woodlot site by the wagonload. Nothing more, so far as can be learned, was ever found.

For several weeks the images, set up on display in Newberry, caused widespread speculation. The largest was nearly four feet in height and, according to one observer, had been formed in a sitting posture. The next in size was standing, and the smallest, thought to be a child, was a little less than two feet long.

Weird as these supposed artifacts were, it was the tablet that caused most of the excitement. About 18 by 24 inches in size, it had one surface divided into 140 squares, each of which contained an undecipherable character.

Puzzled eyes focused hard on these tablet symbols. Clergymen dusted off volumes of ancient history that illustrated, some said, resemblances between the strange markings and Egyptian hieroglyphics—or letters of the Greek alphabet. A prominent lumberman, not to be outshown by men of the cloth, gave it as his opinion that McGruer's men had happened upon an ancient calendar. Either that, he declared, or a game board of a sort resembling checkers.

In all the furor that resulted, there is no indication that McGruer or the workmen, Gordon and Howe, or a local jeweler, L. N. Forbes, who was said to be 'interested in ownership' with McGruer, ever made any quotable comments on their good fortune. By their silence they seemed to be saying that they brought the things to light by happy accident: they were as mystified as anyone about their origin or significance, and they awaited whatever scientific judgment of the day might be forthcoming. (Here they differed markedly from the peddlers who operated in the Lower Peninsula, especially near Detroit, in the following decades, and who tested public gullibility with everything from copies of Noah's diary to prehistoric beer mugs.)

Clearly, no hint of connivance came into local print. Charles Brebner, editor of the *Newberry News* at the time, took a dim view of pranksters, whether they were announcing bloody attacks on woodsmen by timber wolves, or more innocently, reporting the capture of a seventeen-foot 'sea monster' in Miniscong Lake. He described the find as 'one of the wonders of the age,' sent photographs of the collection to the Smithsonian Institution in Washington, and published a reply stating inability to deliver any immediate opinion on authenticity, and asking more details.

Picture taken by Smithsonian Institute 1896
Photo courtesy of Chuck Bailey, Duluth, Minnesota

Note: Tablet was originally photographed upside down by the Smithsonian.

McGruer's Gods
Picture taken by Smithsonian Institute
Photo courtesy of Chuck Bailey, Duluth, Minnesota

Gradually the stir died down. John McGruer stored his unusual property in his barn on the bank of the Tahquamenon River. Occasionally, in the thirty years of forgetfulness that followed, local youngsters would interrupt their swimming hole fun to sneak in and take a furtive look at what had become to be known as "McGruer's Gods."

Then about 1929, some of the fragments that remained were pieced together and taken to St. Ignace for display in a small museum, Fort Algonquin, owned by Mr. (now Reverend) H. Vaughn Norton. There they remain today. (This written in 1966.)

The article continues:

Was, indeed, the whole thing nothing more than an engaging hoax? Obviously so, some present-day archaeologists have said, studying the figures and the tablet, or photographs of them.

Not necessarily so, said some older residents questioned at length in the late 1940's. They had seen the find in 1896; they remembered it well, and to them there remained a certain irrefutable logic in their unanimous assessment of the finders: 'They simply were not ingenious enough to think it up.'

Very possibly true, but also true, appears to be the fact that somebody once displayed a considerable knack of straight-faced tomfoolery—and got away with it.

If there is any last word, it remains a postscript elusively hidden.

This is the story of McGruer's Gods as it stood in 1966, written by Mr. Sprague Taylor of Newberry after many years of interviews with elderly residents who have wondered and questioned since they first saw the tablet and statues in the drugstore window fifty years earlier. No tricksters were ever named or even suspected, no one made any money from it and no one had ever come forth with an explanation of any kind.

The only word they had to go on was the pronouncement of a few distant

Mr. Sprague Taylor brought the "McGruer's Gods" story to light again in 1966. He died without finding answers

archaeologists that it was all a fraud. In the Smithsonian Institution the letters and pictures found their way into the "fraud file."

These three discoveries—the Kensington Stone, the Soper tablets, and the Newberry tablets—all in close proximity and all from 1900 or earlier, would have been viewed much differently had they been treated with an open mind or left as unresolved for further study. But like many other mysteries of that period, their declaration of fraud was final, with no further inquiry. Today, over one hundred years later, that is still the official verdict.

I don't believe these finds were considered or even known by Joe Gannon. Mrs. Paul never discussed any of them with me until 1956. But at this time in our story they were all considered frauds. As a scholar one would not question the authorities on these subjects. If one wanted to be accepted, one never discussed them—and the subjects never came up.

Small carved stone artifact found on Lake Superior shore 1990's,
It is about the size of a 50 cent piece

Chapter V

Building Toward an Expedition

Laying the Groundwork for an Expedition

As Joe Gannon was writing, calling and visiting museums, universities and historical societies across the country, trying to create interest in his idea that the "Greatest Mystery in America Was Where All the Copper Went," he generally received a polite, but cool, reception. The one exception was a metallurgist from Houghton, Michigan, Dr. Roy Drier. Dr. Drier had been interested in Michigan copper for years, especially the mysterious, ancient mining operations.

Dr. Drier did some publishing in connection with the history and archaeology of the Copper Country. Among his most famous books were "Boom Copper" (Boom Copper by Angus Murdock, 1943-1964) and "Copper Country Tales" (by Harley L. Sacks, edited by Drier).

During the 1930's, Dr. Drier made several expeditions to Isle Royale. He donated a large collection of mineral specimens and artifacts he discovered at that time to Michigan Tech. He also found pottery fragments that he put through a number of scientific tests such as x-ray diffraction and microscopic examination in an effort to classify and date them. In collaboration with the Milwaukee Public Museum, he attempted to correlate his finds with pieces in their Indian collection. After much study, his conclusions were that the pottery was fairly recent, probably within the last 2,000 years, from a people seeking copper more recent than when the pits were dug. His tests showed great correlation between many of the copper tools picked up near the pits, not from where the pottery was found, and he reasoned *that the prehistoric miners were a separate people from those who left the pottery. The miners would have worked there at least 2,000 years prior to the casual Indian miners who left the pottery.*

Dr. Drier's test results fascinated Joe Gannon. Here was a specialist right in his backyard who seemed to have the same interests and curiosity he did and was doing something about it. Both of these men had been investigating the copper question for a long time. Gannon was a layman and Drier a professional, but it wasn't until the mid-1930's that they finally got together. Mr. Gannon had the opportunity to study a lot of research on Michigan copper that Roy Drier had collected over the years.

After World War II, Joe Gannon and Roy Drier did a lot of conferring, with Gannon always pressing for information and pushing Drier to take positive steps to obtain answers. He thought there must be subtle clues to be found on

Isle Royale that were missed by earlier expeditions.

Joe Gannon wanted to find something that pointed to the Mediterranean as the end of a copper trade, but it had to be indisputable evidence.

In a discussion I had with Mr. Gannon during this period, he revealed an interesting idea concerning the Copper Eskimos who lived in the Northwest Territory of Canada. Their home was in the vicinity of the Copper River which flows north, just east of Great Bear Lake into Coronation Gulf. It is north of the Arctic Circle. Near its mouth is a settlement named Coppermine (formerly called Kugluktuk), but there is no copper mine there. It got its name from the lodes of pure copper that could be found on the surface of the land. These people were called the Copper Eskimos, as distinguished from the Mackenzie Eskimos to their west, and the Caribou Eskimos to their east.[33] They were known for making small items from the copper found in their area. The International Nickel Co. (INCO), with headquarters in Sudbury, Ontario, has spent millions of dollars searching for a "mother lode" or common source of copper in that area without success.

Mr. Gannon surmised that somehow copper from Lake Superior had reached Europe by way of the Arctic during the Bronze Age or before. The theory that he expressed to me was that at least some of the copper people were sea mammal hunters, an ancient people who lived in the Arctic region and were able to circle the North Pole as traders. While this opinion seems farfetched, I have found evidence since Mr. Gannon's death that gives his thesis some validity.

There is much evidence that the Polar Sea was without ice in the distant past. Also, Coronation Gulf, the home of the Copper Eskimos, is on one of the western routes of the famous Northwest Passage. At least 100 ships have now traversed routes of a Northwest Passage in the last century—the first were the Russians. Finally, there is some scientific support from the U.S. Navy. Dr. Louis Giddings, Jr. was on a Navy-sponsored expedition in the 1940's to gather climatic data in Northern Alaska and Canada. His findings support the theory that there was a prehistoric culture circling the top of the globe between 1,000 and 10,000 years ago. If so, these people could have been traders who took copper to the old world from the new.

While Mr. Gannon told me of these ideas in the early 1950's, to my knowledge he never put them in writing for publication. Perhaps he felt there wasn't enough supporting evidence. Today, knowing of the great water routes to the Beaufort Sea via the Mackenzie River, one could present a good argument

---

[33] All the Eskimos plus another group in the east known as the Central Eskimos are called Inuits today. The province there (in the east) is Nunevut, a new province formed in 2001, governed by the Inuits.

that at least some Michigan copper may have gone to the Arctic; but if any, it would have been only a relatively small amount. If the Chinese used this route of the later fur traders, it would not have been a convenient passage for carrying copper. I believe if Michigan copper went to China it went by way of the silk road via the Mediterranean, but the Chinese did know about Michigan copper, as we shall see.

By 1950, Drier and Gannon had been collaborating for a long time. They both felt there was still much to be learned from a thorough archaeological investigation in the copper region. There had not been enough knowledge collected to unlock the secrets of the ancient copper country mining and they were convinced the answers could be found on Isle Royale. Heavy mining in the U.P. had covered or destroyed most of the evidence they sought, but apart from some special areas that had been worked over in modern times, Isle Royale was relatively pristine. Several thorough investigations had been undertaken there by competent, qualified people over the past century, which yielded sizable collections or artifacts, mostly gads, points, awls and hammerstones. However, the burning questions of who these ancient miners were and when exactly did they mine, were still unanswered. The fact that there were no roads, no graves, and no evidence of ancient encampments along with so much evidence of mining needed some explanation. Some campsites had been identified for later miners, but as for inhabitation evidence of the earlier miners when the real work took place, there seemed to be nothing.

An expedition of wealthy Chicago and Milwaukee amateurs were earnestly looking for the answers to those questions. The principle participants were Eugene McDonald, Jr., President of Zenith Radio Corporation, Burt A. Massee, Vice President of Colgate-Palmolive-Peet Corporation and, to add archaeological respectability to the expedition, George A. West, who was president of the Board of Trustees of the Milwaukee Public Museum. This expedition, conducted during July of 1928, resulted in a huge collection of Isle Royale artifacts which can be found today at the Milwaukee Public Museum, and the Wisconsin State Historical Society in Madison.

During World War II there were tremendous advances in nuclear physics. While some of this information was being kept from the public because of the war and the frantic quest to produce an atomic bomb, certain bits of information were being reported and, being a metallurgist, Dr. Drier was watching these scientific advances carefully.

Much of this burst of knowledge, which came to light in the 1940's, was a direct result of the Manhattan Project at the University of Chicago. This secret project concerned the use of atomic energy for peacetime purposes. A

Photo by June Rydholm

Octave DuTemple circa 1990's in Lake Linden, Michigan

great number of young students of Roy Drier and others with Copper Country connections were involved with the work at the Argonne National Laboratories, also in Chicago. Among them were George Rapp, Jr., a pioneer in the fingerprinting of copper from the University of Minnesota (Ph.D. from Pennsylvania State University); Eiler Hendrickson, also fingerprinting and economic mineral deposit research from Carleton College, Northfield, Minnesota; Octave DuTemple of Lake Linden, Michigan, later director of the American Nuclear Society; Peter Gray, Nuclear Research for Phillips Petroleum; and Glenn T. Seaborg, the latter, both of Ishpeming, Michigan. During the war years, Seaborg had been chosen to lead the secret production of Uranium 235 and Plutonium with the hope of being able to produce enough of either to make an atomic bomb before the Axis Powers did. The committee, headed up by then President Franklin D. Roosevelt, consisted of a group of high-powered nuclear scientists such as Albert Einstein, Enrico Fermi and others. They chose Seaborg, then 29, because of his work at UCLA in the discovery or isolation of many of the transuranium (man-made) elements. Dr. Seaborg became the chairman of the Atomic Energy Commission (1961-1971). He rearranged the Periodic Table of the Elements and was awarded the Nobel Prize in chemistry in 1951 along with E. M. McMillan. He is the only person to have an element named for him while still living, Seaborgium. Dr. Seaborg died in 1999.

One of the atomic scientists doing research at the University of Chicago was Willard Libby, originally from Colorado. In his research in 1947, Libby

Courtesy of Glenn T. Seaborg

Glenn T. Seaborg, of Ishpeming, Michigan

developed the now famous Carbon 14 dating technique[34] for determining the age of organic material. He was granted a Nobel Prize for his work in 1960. This was the technology Drier and Gannon had been waiting for. While this method of determining the age of organic material has many problems of accuracy, it works reasonably well for objects up to 6,000 years old, plus or minus a hundred years or so. If the sample is not contaminated and has been handled properly, it should be adequate for determining the period of mining in the region. This is especially true if many samples are tested.

Even though there had been a dozen scientific investigations into the copper question between 1845 and 1945, Drier and Gannon felt that this scientific discovery was enough of an advance to launch another.

In September of 1952, a proposal to investigate prehistoric copper mining in the Upper Peninsula and Isle Royale was written, presumably for any interested party, but particularly Grover C. Dillman, then the president of Michigan Tech University. In this proposal, Roy Drier wrote:

> The problem can be simply stated and resolved into the following questions:
>
> 1. Who were these prehistoric miners and where did they come from?
> 2. When did the mining operation take place?
> 3. Why did the operations cease—seemingly so suddenly?
> 4. Where did the miners go?
> 5. How did they accomplish the magnificent distribution of the product (copper) of mining?
> 6. What was their means of transportation?

The proposal, written by Roy Drier with the encouragement of Joe Gannon, continues:

> From a survey of all available literature on the subject, it would seem

---

[34] Brief explanation of Carbon 14 dating: Cosmic rays constantly bombard the earth creating an isotope of carbon that is radioactive. The common form of carbon has 12 electrons in the atom and a stable outer shell, while the isotope, with 14 electrons is unstable and therefore radioactive. This unstable isotope begins to decay.

Carbon 14, the radioactive form, is in the atmosphere and like carbon 12, the regular carbon, it combines with oxygen to form CO_2 (carbon dioxide) which gets absorbed by plants and eaten by animals, thus becoming a part of all living things. When a plant or animal dies, it does not ingest anymore carbon of any kind.

In about 5,700 years, half of the radioactive carbon in a sample of organic material (plant or animal) decays and from the percentage left, its approximate age can be determined.

that the best approach to the whole problem would be item 2. Possible methods of solution of the problem of when the mining was done would be as follows:

a. Excavating some old mining operations to attempt to find charcoal, which would be associated with the mining. Determine by the radioactivity of the charcoal the approximate time the charcoal or wood was burned.
    (1) Perhaps in some museum, pieces of prehistoric cribbing are saved and can be tested.
b. Determine the age of the copper artifacts by measuring depth of oxidation of surface and estimating rate of corrosion.
c. Computing the time necessary for the old pits, on Isle Royale particularly, to fill in as they have.
d. Determine if condition of material thrown out of the mines indicates pre-glacial or post-glacial mining.
e. Other problems.

After the time of mining is determined or estimated, the question of who the miners were can more easily be investigated.

Roy Drier, looking at the situation broadly, did not believe any of the questions had been adequately answered, at least not to his satisfaction. He was most interested in knowing when most of the mining was done. Then, when he was reasonably sure of a timeframe, he could look at the historical record and see who was using large amounts of copper during that period. This should give a reasonable hypothesis of where the copper may have gone, a possible destination. Drier: "It would seem that the whole problem, other than such phases as age determination by radioactivity, would necessitate the searching for information in such places as various libraries and museums in the country (Library of Congress, Smithsonian Institution, Field Museum, Libraries of Universities of our Southwestern States) and also Mexico and Central America (to find out who was using a lot of copper at the time of the mining)."
Drier:

> It is to be expected that research on the subject will bring to light many more problems, probably of equal or greater interest and value than the ones listed.
> Once the questions of who and when are solved, the rest of the problem will, no doubt, set itself up in proper sequence and relative value.
> This problem is one which does not lend itself to a short period of

operation. Nor does it seem to be one which can be solved by many researchers working simultaneously. It would seem to be a problem to be solved mainly by the work of one, or a few, who has or have a personal interest in this particular search.

So wrote Roy Drier on September 27th of 1952, preparatory to organizing an expedition the following summer.

Gannon had done much prodding to get such an expedition organized, but there was always the question of funding. If he had been working with a bona fide archaeologist, one licensed to dig on state land, it would have been much easier to raise money. Dr. Drier was probably the most knowledgeable person there was on local copper and the most open-minded of the professionals, but he was not an archaeologist. He was a metallurgist. Even though the main purpose for the expedition was to collect samples for dating, there was a chance of encountering artifacts that needed archaeological interpretation, and this was considered out of his field. As we have seen, discoveries that were not seen or found "in situ"[35] by an archaeologist are always suspect. If some discovery is not accepted by the professional scientists, it is not accepted by the media and, therefore, the public.

Even without an archaeologist, Drier and Gannon hoped they would get permission from Michigan Tech to proceed with the expedition, with their blessing if not their cooperation. Both Drier and Gannon knew they had an ally in Dr. Grover C. Dillman, then president of the Michigan College of Mining and Technology. They knew he had a scientist's interest in ancient mining. He had studied it himself and had written about it.[36]

Gannon reasoned that the only justification Dr. Dillman could have for not allowing the expedition to be carried out with the sponsorship of the College would be money, so Gannon personally would finance it. Since there was no archaeologist on the staff at the time, it would follow that Roy Drier, with his knowledge and experience of the subject, would be a good choice to head up the project.

Dillman, as expected, was interested, but also as expected, he informed Drier that there just were no funds for such a project and it would take several years before such funding could be arranged. He did say, however, that if money could be found, Tech would cooperate in every way possible.

This was the spark that Gannon needed. He had never been this close

---

[35] In situ—in the place where it has been.
[36] Dee, James R. and Grover C. Dillman—First Account of Copper Country Published in France in Year 1936.

to his dream before. After much discussion between the three men in 1952 (Dillman, Drier and Gannon) it was agreed that Joe Gannon would supply the funding. He asked Dr. Drier to look into all aspects of the great expedition and let him know just how he should go about it.

On October 31, 1952, Joe Gannon received the following letter from Roy Drier:

Dear Joe:

I spoke with Dr. Dillman this morning and it was his idea (and mine too) that your check should be made out to the Michigan College of Mining and Technology, and it should be accompanied by a letter with any stipulations you wish to make concerning the use to which you want the money put. Perhaps the outline I sent you, or one of your own, could appropriately be attached. I think too, in this case, if your desire still is to have me head up the activity, it would be well to so state.

I am enclosing a copy of a letter from the U.S. Duty Tax Commissioner indicating tax exemption of such a contribution, and when Dr. Dillman acknowledges receipt, he will state that such contributions are considered allowable deductions in computing the income tax of the donor.

Please let me know your address when you get settled in Pasadena. I hope you have a pleasant trip and likewise a pleasant winter.

Sincerely,
Roy W. Drier

Less than a week later, in fact in the return mail, Mr. Gannon, following Drier's advice, wrote the following letter to President Dillman.

Mr. Grover C. Dillman, President
Michigan College of Mining and Technology
Houghton, Michigan

Dear Mr. Dillman:

For many years I have been interested in the prehistoric copper miners of the Keweenaw Peninsula and Isle Royale and it seems to me that no more worthy institution than the Michigan College of Mining and Technology could carry on an investigation to determine, if possible:

a.   Who these ancient miners were?
b.   Where did they come from?
c.   When did they operate?
d.   Why did they cease to operate?
e.   Where did they go?

In other words determine, if possible, through modern methods of investigation, the story of those ancient miners.

It occurs to me that Dr. Roy W. Drier, a member of your staff, is well qualified to head the investigation for the Michigan College of Mining and Technology and should be given the responsibility of heading this activity.

Trusting that this will meet with your approval and that the Michigan College of Mining and Technology be successful in solving this mystery, I enclosed my check for $1,000.00 to be used in the furtherance of this project.

Very truly yours,
J. C. Gannon

While $1,000.00 doesn't seem like a lot of money for such a project today, at that time (1952), teachers in Michigan's Upper Peninsula were being paid anywhere from $1,000 to $3,000 for a year's work. Mr. Gannon knew this was merely "seed money" to get things started. If things progressed as expected, he would give more as it was needed. Before he was through, he had donated over five times that amount and there were still some bills that came in a few months after the venture was completed. All such bills were turned over to Joe Gannon.

Through the winter and spring of 1953 many newspapers and a few periodicals carried stories of the proposed expedition which was to take place the following summer. While most papers only had one or two articles, the local papers carried updated stories regularly.

An article in the Houghton paper ran a headline stating: "Atoms to Help Find Age of Old Copper Diggers," and the sub-headline read: "Carbon-14 May Reveal When Ancients Dug Metal on Isle Royale in Lake Superior."

The article, a very thorough one, told of Roy Drier's accomplishments in the field of engine casting production, in rigging up an air-sea rescue device and as a layout engineer for Ford Motor Company's sprawling River Rouge Plant. However, in this new venture he would be picking up a cold trail, thousands of years old, of a long forgotten race. "He has studied the problem since 1933," it read, "but now with carbon dating, he may finally find the answers he's been searching for."

In his earlier work with the Milwaukee Public Museum, Drier determined that the age of the early copper diggers had to be at least twice as old as the Indian artifacts of one to two thousand years ago.

Roy F. Makens, a chemistry professor at Michigan Tech assisted Dr. Drier with this work. Makens had helped usher in the atomic age at Oak Ridge, Tennessee where the radioactive materials were first produced in commercial quantities.

When Drier and Makens first heard about Willard Libby's "time clock" being developed at the University of Chicago, they knew this was the ingenious device the world had been waiting for. All that was needed was someone with the interest and wherewithal to make the study possible. For Drier, Makens and Gannon, each step that was taken brought them closer to their goal.

While I never spoke with Drier or Makens, I did talk with Joe Gannon occasionally or would hear about his ideas and activities from Mrs. Caroll Paul at the Historical Society who was in contact with him regularly. It was easy to learn that Joe Gannon was hoping for some irrefutable clue as to the identity of at least some of these ancient people, other than local Indians. He was hoping for evidence of people coming from another hemisphere. If they had come from far off places for copper, certainly they would have left something distinct that would identify who they were or where they were from. He often mentioned the Copper Eskimos and his beliefs concerning them that they had definitely come from Siberia. Then there were the statements of Charles Whittlesey and others who suggested the engineering involved in raising five and ten ton boulders out of the earth indicates something more than a group going south in canoes with small pieces of copper to make metal points, axes and fish hooks. Something more was involved.

There were other things that made observers skeptical of the local Indian theory. There was the tremendous logistical problem of feeding miners and transporting them to and from their work areas as well as transporting large amounts of a heavy metal away. No one knew how much metal they were talking about, but all agreed it was an awesome amount.

Then there were the hammerstones, thousands, possibly millions of them, many of which were carefully grooved and again transported. It did not seem to be a haphazard operation.

Maybe the expedition could discover something out of the ordinary like the men who stumbled onto a leather bag back in 1863. They found it nine feet deep in one of the pits. It had been preserved for many centuries and was still pliable and tough as sheepskin. They found it lying on a mass of native copper, just as though "the ancients had gone out to lunch and never returned." Drier thought this bag might have been made of walrus skin. If so, this could indicate that some of the miners came from the north.

There had been other remarkable finds in the past, a crude ladder made from a tree trunk, a wooden shovel, three feet long, and the marks of a thin-bladed axe on the ends of timbers. These are the kinds of subtle clues that Joe Gannon would be looking for. If they were lucky, maybe something new and different would turn up. Anything significantly new that would add a piece to the puzzle would deem the effort a success.

There was much correspondence to and from the college. People and institutions were recommending people with various interest and areas of expertise that should be invited to join the expedition. Others were volunteering, some pleading, but all letters were answered politely.

By April 1, 1953, plans were still not complete. Joe Gannon, long back from California, was getting a little nervous but stayed in the background, not wanting to get in Dr. Drier's way.

What Gannon had in mind to be a tight-knit group of five or six scientists with a few kitchen helpers and some laborers, had now grown to well over a dozen people.

On April 20, Joe Gannon received the following handwritten letter from Dr. Drier:

Dear Joe,

Just a memo to tell you that in all probability, Dr. Griffin, the Director of Museums at the University of Michigan will probably be in the Island Expedition Party. He is the one the Smithsonian said knew the most about mid-west anthropology and archaeology.

Looks like we will go over to the Isle on June 12, and that the Park Service archaeologist, Dr. Beaubein will only stay a week, which very likely we will too. There's a camp at Belle Isle the Park Service said we could use and they will provide cots, blankets, dishes, and a stove. I will try to get the chef of the college cafeteria to act as chef.

A fish pickup boat oscillates between Minnesota and the island three times a week, so that transportation is available if necessary, and also, if necessary, we could telephone to the Park Office in Houghton and they would transmit the message, to have a local boat come over for us, if necessary.

We are making progress.

Cheerio, Roy

Just imagine the problems of the ancients, if there were thousands or even hundreds of them, to mine and transport food, hammerstones and copper, whoever they were.

When the group finally assembled on June 12th, Dr. Griffin had brought along his two sons.

That year I had been teaching in Vermontville, a small community in lower Michigan, but I was keeping track of the progress of the expedition in the newspapers. I might have been invited to go along if I had been in Marquette that winter, but this was probably wishful thinking as there was an effort to limit the numbers. Mrs. Paul told me I should ask Mr. Gannon, but I didn't feel it would be right on such short notice. If I had been asked I surely would have accepted, but I followed the stories in the papers intently.

I later learned that the news of the expedition was in papers across the country. The stories were all pretty much the same, but people were interested, local people especially so.

Joe Gannon was a prominent citizen in Marquette and many people knew how anxious he was to have the expedition be successful.

The story that appeared on the front page of the "Shillings Mining Review," a weekly periodical out of Duluth, Minnesota, had this to say in the June 27, 1953 issue. Headlines: "Scientists to Explore Michigan's Prehistoric Copper Mining Civilization."

An Expedition of prominent scientists left Houghton, Michigan on June 12 to study and explore the mystery of Michigan's prehistoric copper mining civilization on Isle Royale in Lake Superior. Archaeologists of the Smithsonian Institute call it an important journey, one of the major unsolved problems in North American archaeology.

Late last fall the Michigan College of Mining and Technology received a grant to conduct research into prehistoric copper mining in Michigan's Copper Country and Isle Royale from Joseph C. Gannon, Marquette business executive.

The investigation will center about seven questions:
(1) Who were Michigan's prehistoric copper miners?
(2) When did they mine?
(3) Where did they come from?
(4) Why did prehistoric mining cease so suddenly?
(5) Where did the miners go?
(6) How did they distribute the mined ore so extensively? And
(7) what were their means of transportation?

Prehistoric mining in Michigan has been the subject of research work for many years. Modern techniques, such as the determination of age by measuring radioactivity of materials found in old mine pits, and research entailing the supply of copper artifacts in museums of the United States, Mexico, Central America, Spain and England, as well as excavation of old mine pits in the Upper Peninsula and on Isle Royale may solve many related problems.

Reports of miners who opened commercial mining in the Copper Country during the 1840's tell of hundreds of prehistoric mine pits in this Upper Michigan area, some containing crude stone tools and cribbing. It is believed that ancient mine operations in Michigan may date back as far as the stone age, as indicated by the discovery of a copper knife in the remains of a mastodon in Missouri, and by the stone tools discovered in the mine pits. The early miners may have belonged to a race other than the American Indian and evidence indicates that they may have been destroyed or driven from their pits after developing a vast mining empire. Historians estimate that at least two million pounds of the "red metal" were extracted by ancient miners in Isle Royale alone.

Because of the purity of Michigan copper, making it usable without refining, it is believed that most, if not all, of the copper used by prehistoric North Americans originated in Keweenawland of Michigan's Upper Peninsula.

The expedition is headed by Dr. Roy W. Drier, professor of Metallurgical Engineering at Michigan Tech. Members of the expedition are Dr. James Griffin, director of Museums at the University of Michigan, Dr. Paul Beaubien, National Park Service Archaeologist, Drs. Walter White and Henry Cornwall, both of the U.S. Geological Survey and J. C. Gannon of Marquette, Michigan, sponsor of the expedition in cooperation with Michigan Tech.

Others in the group who journeyed to Isle Royale aboard the National Park Service Ship *Ranger II* were H. Staff, R. Lancott, C. Bryce, U. Usimaki, A. Archambeau, J. J. Lauren and W. Maki.

Roy Drier and Joe Gannon ready to depart for Isle Royal on the Royal Ranger II 1953

The Expedition on a dock at Isle Royale.

The expedition was carried out as planned. While Dr. Griffin added a great deal of prestige to the investigation, others in the group could not help noticing a slight animosity between Joe Gannon and Dr. Griffin. The main reasons, I was told later, were that he "outranked" Dr. Drier, so to speak and he was not invited but came at a later date. To Gannon it looked like someone was not trusting their team and they needed an archaeologist to look over their shoulder so nothing would be interpreted in error. Sometime after the trip Mr. Gannon remarked to me that at the last minute he brought his two sons along and they ate like horses. I knew the boys would have had a good time and I wish I'd been with them.

All of the professionals on the trip seemed satisfied that the whole adventure was a complete success. Many wrote letters to Joe Gannon, thanking him and congratulating him.

On July 22, 1953, a very friendly letter arrived from James. B. Griffin. One paragraph is a special report on the preliminary results of the Isle Royale trip.

Dr. Griffin:

> I think that you would be very much pleased to know that we have obtained a radio-carbon date for your specimen from the bottom of the pit. This one was down at the deepest level which men excavated and consisted of a piece of either white or black spruce which was a piece of wood and not charcoal. The date on the specimen is 3,000 years ago, so that is a date within the possibilities geologically as far as the lakes are concerned, and also a date that fits in pretty well with the use of copper, as we know it, by the Indians. I would not have been surprised at any date between 500 years and about 4,000, so this date hit very well in the middle range.
>
> The letter was signed "Jimmy."

This was good news, but Joe Gannon was looking for something more, something better that he did not feel comfortable discussing with Dr. Griffin because of his mindset. It seemed that Dr. Griffin's conclusion would always be that Indian people would be the miners.

The Expedition

Gannon had written to so many people, read so much history and traveled to so many places that he was hoping to find evidence of a people other than the Indians who came for copper. Everyone knew the Indians had been there, different ones at different times, but there were these traditional stories, lots of them, that had to have come from somewhere. He did not discuss these theories with any of the professionals for fear of ridicule; it had happened before. When he tried, it always ended in an argument and he was always the underdog.

An example was a letter he received on July 25, 1953, from Dr. Albert C. Spaulding, director of the Museum of Anthropology at the University of Michigan. It was a friendly letter of...

> ...sincere appreciation for the help that you gave during our stay in Marquette and encouragement. One of these days you are going to find something that will cast a lot of light on the copper tool problem (author: Spaulding knew what Gannon was looking for.) Then we can get together and have a fierce argument on just what it means, probably ending up with both of us wrong.

Just what were some of the ideas that Mr. Gannon discussed with me that he hesitated to communicate with the professionals? There were a lot of them that world travelers passed along to each other. Gannon associated with many scholarly types in the fields of geology, mining, engineering, anthropology and history. The geologists and mining engineers traveled to many remote parts of the world and were especially well versed in these often well-founded but little known ideas.

One such man, who was widely read, was a mining engineer named Harry C. Dudley. His wide interests and several communications from far-flung places, were an influence on Joe Gannon's curiosity. One letter received in October of 1953 was written while he was on a job in Mexico, from the Hotel Reforma. The letter read, in part:

> "My years of experience in mining in Mexico and South America have served to quicken my interest in the inhabitants of the Western Hemisphere in that long period prior to Columbus before our written history actually starts.
>
> There are so many legends, plausible, if not logical, as to the Norsemen, Eric the Red, Greenland and where many stone buildings are now emerging from the ice in the retreat of the glaciers, and also the Welsh Prince who is supposed to have been the founder of the Mandan-Sioux Tribe as described by Catlin,[37] the Indian painter, that we know Europeans, and Asiatics, maybe Semitic adventurers, must have roamed our country for thousands of years after the end of the glacial period. Catlin, some 130

---

[37] George Catlin—b. July 16, 1796 (Wilkes-Barre, PA) d. December 23, 1872; painter, engraver, writer. Traveled among the American Indians painted hundreds of Indian scenes, published travel books including *My Life Among the Indians* (1841).

Nobel and Roy in a mine Isle Royale 1953.

Roy Drier examining charcoal in mine. Charcoal from the bottom of the pit would presumably give the latest date the pit had been worked.

Belle Isle Resort, Isle Royale, Michigan

Joe Gannon on deck at Belle Isle Resort.

years ago (now over 180 years ago) described the Mandan-Sioux just before they were wiped out by small pox. A friendly, seemingly more cultivated people than the surrounding tribes, whose women had long, soft hair, blue eyes, and in many there were distinct European features. They observed a ceremony at Christmas, lived in square or rectangular houses, often with two stories and had stone fireplaces.

If the Atlantic Ocean presented no serious obstacle for a woman a few years ago to sail a 21-foot cat boat from England to the West Indies (aided by ocean currents), why would it be much of an obstacle to rough, tough sea-faring men of a thousand or many thousand years ago. Our growing interest in the bottom of the sea is producing new evidence of maritime excursions and trading in the early B.C. period.

Coming back from Rome by plane last spring my seatmate happened to be the President of Paramount International. When we were over the Azores I remarked that what we were over was an area which may

Dock of mine at McCargo Cove, Isle Royale

represent a sunken continent. He was much interested and said his friend Cecil DeMille had been talking lately about making a movie of Atlantis and had done some work on the subject.

He wrote DeMille of our discussion and some of the legends, even facts, which I had mentioned and sent me a copy of his interesting reply in which he mentioned that he had spend some $100,000 on this research of Atlantis, and still hoped to produce a movie. He did not know of Plato's notes on Atlantis which he made in Egypt after being kicked out of Athens by the Politicos, or of Plato's ambition to write an

Roy Drier at McCargo Cove

Epic on Atlantis to rival the Odyssey, which by the way is being filmed by Paramount in Italy.

DeMille did not know that very many of the words and roots of words of the Maya language today in Mexico are pure Greek. How come?

Very few, except some geologists realize that the great thickness of the sedimentary rocks along the Atlantic coast from north to south many thousands of feet thick, were formed by sediment brought from the northeast by ocean currents, produced by waves breaking against the rocks of a continent to the northeast. This represents the measure of time involved. There is so much more scientific evidence of a lost continent, or lost great islands, even if sufficient to definitely prove their existence. But it all adds up to the plausibility of legends of the more recent wonders of the last few thousand years.

Harry

These kinds of ideas filled Joe Gannon's mind for years. He heard bits and pieces of stories from scholarly people like this wherever he went and was always hoping to prove some of them. But whenever he tried to bring them up to the professionals, he was politely silenced. He had hoped his archaeological expedition to Isle Royale would produce some small questionable artifact with even a hint of a foreign look to it, but no such item was found.

Late that year the Wenner-Grenn Foundation supplemented the Gannon donation with a grant of $3,000 for some digging by Drier and Gannon in some old copper pits north of Sault Ste. Marie on the Canadian side of Lake Superior. Joe Gannon had received permission letters to explore several places.

And what did the expedition accomplish? It settled once and for all that the pits were indeed ancient. Subsequent testing gave a clear picture that most of the work was done between three and five thousand years ago and lasted until about 1100 A.D. Carbon dates from eastern Wisconsin and other places further south of copper cultures and copper artifacts fell well within those dates.

Secondly, it spurred interest in the ancient history of the region by scientific institutions and some other organized investigations followed within a year or two.

Third, this interest stimulated the need to make information available to an interested public. This information was forthcoming in the 1961 publication of a book containing a summary by each of its two authors, Roy Drier and a former student, Octave DuTemple. It is a collection of many of the more informative historical papers and reports that were written on ancient Lake Superior copper mining up to that time.

The book "Prehistoric Copper Mining in the Lake Superior Region," (1961) published privately by Roy W. Drier, in my opinion, did more to stimulate interest in Copper Country ancient history than any other publication. It was a stimulus that started several research programs and was the basis for magazine and newspaper articles that continue to be written to this day.

Courtesy of Ila Conklin

*This unusual looking stone was found in 1980
near a swamp in the eastern U.P.*

Chapter VI
The Work of Some Pioneer Amateur Archaeologists

Hjalmar R. Holand's Conclusions

No one studied the Kensington Runestone more thoroughly than Hjalmar Holand.[38] There was never any doubt in his mind that the Norsemen had been to America long before Columbus and possibly other adventurers. Few authorities agreed with him on that conclusion until sometime after his book was in print—after Helge Ingstad and his archaeologist wife, both from Norway, confirmed that there had been Norsemen who had spent at least a year or two at the northern tip of Newfoundland, at a place called L'Anse aux Meadows.

Holand had written a book back in 1940 that told the same story ("Norse Discoveries and Exploration in America, 982-1362, A.D." Dover Publications Inc., New York, 1940.) In this earlier book he pointed out the locations of the Eastern Settlement and Western Settlement in Greenland. He also showed possible locations of Vinland, Markland and Helluland as well as places where Norse artifacts and mooring stones were found west of the Great Lakes.

Mooring stones are usually large boulders near the waters edge where a typically triangular hole about four to seven inches deep has been drilled for the purpose of holding a ring bolt. There are hundreds of them in Norway and they are found on the east coast of the United States as far south as Cape Cod. The modern star drill creates a round hole while the flat chisel, used by the Norse, creates a distinctive triangular hole. One end of the ship would be anchored out and the other shore-end would be tied to the ring bolt which could be flipped out for a quick getaway. There now have been about 300 mooring stones identified

---

[38] Hjalmar Rued Holand—Internationally renowned authority on pre-Columbian explorations in America.

　　He was born in Norway on October 20, 1872 and came to America in 1883. Received his public education in Chicago and a Bachelor's Degree from the University of Wisconsin in Madison. After graduation he purchased land and started an apple orchard on the Door Peninsula. It is today Peninsula State Park.

　　Mr. Holand made the first accurate translation of the Kensington runestone and wrote a number of books about it. His first book was published in 1932. It was followed by *Westward from Vinland* in 1940 then two editions of *America 1355-1364* in 1946, *Exploration in America Before Columbus* in 1956 and *A Pre-Columbian Crusade to America* in 1962. He also wrote eight more books, all of an historical nature.

　　Holand was a long-time resident of Ephraim, Wisconsin and died there in August of 1963 at the age of 90.

Hjalmar Rued Holand as a young man when he started his research, which continued for over 50 years.

in the vicinity of the Kensington stone in Minnesota. There are no other mooring stones known in the central part of America. The Minnesota mooring stones are all near former shorelines. There is an unverified mooring stone reported on Keweenaw Bay in Lake Superior.[39]

During a trip to Norway in 1997, I discussed the L'Anse aux Meadows site with some Norwegian historians. They told me that traditionally Norse sailors always considered a new or unknown land as an island and would always attempt to circumnavigate it. These seafarers would follow a coastline for miles, checking both directions. The Norse were always curious world explorers and were known for following waterways in all directions.

L'Anse aux Meadows was obviously a temporary wintering site which may have been used several times. During this period of the known three-hundred years (982-1362) when the Norse were in Greenland, there would have been many unrecorded expeditions into the surrounding regions. The Norse were well-adapted to long hunting and exploring excursions. Their greatest need was timber and since Norway was over four times as far as southern Labrador, it became a frequent source of timber, free for the taking. Such timber was used for boats, roofs, floors, furniture and fuel. A few thousand Greenland colonists would have required many shiploads of it.

The "Norsetur" was a camp in the far north (Lat 72° N) of Greenland. The large landowners in the colonies to the south had vessels built to send to the Norsetur for seal hunting. Seal oil was the most common fuel for heat and light.

In 1823, Capt. W. A. Graah of the Danish Navy, while exploring the Arctic regions of Greenland, discovered a small runestone on top of a cairn, a heap or pillar of stones. Since it was found on the island of Kingiktorsauk, it is known as the "Kingiktorsauk Stone." While there were three cairns at this location, only one of them had a runestone inscription. This was translated to read "Erling Sigvatsson and Bjarne Thordavson and Endridi Oddsson raised these beacons

---

[39] The stone has been reported by several people but was rolled over during a storm in the 1990's and has not been located since.

the Saturday before 'gagndig' (April 25) and wrote…" and here follow six signs, which, to my knowledge, are still disputed. Professor Magnus Olsen gives the date of 1333, but Holand, after much study, believes the date to be 1291. In any case, three men must have wintered there in the region of the 73rd parallel which was not explored historically until 300 years later.

In the Greenland settlements, each family of settlers had their own boats and many had larger ocean-going vessels for carrying freight and cattle. Over these hundreds of years, expeditions explored the continent to the west and some of them left their mark.

There is the Heavener runestone in Oklahoma, the LaVerendrye Stone in the west Dakotas or Montana and the Kensington Stone in Minnesota as well as several others, all of which have either been ignored or declared a hoax by most modern scholars. This author believes that most, if not all, of these historical discoveries will some day be proven authentic as we learn more of our past history.

No one can say the LaVerendrye Stone was "planted" or can be a hoax. As shown below, it was found in 1738 and no European in recorded history had ever been in that western region before that date.

In an account received from Mr. de Verandrier (today known as LaVerendrye), commander of the expedition, and recorded by Mr. Holand in "Norse Discoveries and Explorations in America, 982-1362," he states in part:

> The governor-general of Canada, Chevalier de Beauharnois, gave Mr. de Varondier an order to go from Canada, with a number of people, on an expedition across North America to the South Sea, in order to examine how far these places are distant from each other, and to find out what advantage might accrue to Canada or Louisiana, from a communication with the ocean….as they came far into the country, beyond many nations,[40] they sometimes met large tracts of land, free from wood, but covered with a kind of very tall grass, for the space of some days' journey….When they came far to the west, where, to the best of their knowledge, no Frenchman or European had ever been, they found in one place in the woods, and again on a large plain, great pillars of stone leaning upon each other. These pillars consisted of but one stone each, and the Frenchmen could not but suppose that they had been erected by human hands. Sometimes they have found that such stones laid upon one another, and, as it were, formed into a wall….At last they met with a large stone, like a pillar, and in it a smaller stone was fixed, which was

---

[40] These would be Indian nations.

covered on both sides with unknown characters. This stone, which was about a foot of French measure in length, and between four or five inches broad, they broke loose, and carried to Canada with them, from whence it was sent to France, to the secretary of state, the Count of Maurepas. What became of it afterwards is unknown to them, but they think it is yet (1749) preserved in his collection. Several of the Jesuits, who have seen and handled this stone in Canada, unanimously affirm, that the letters on it are the same as those which in the books, containing accounts of Tartaria, are called Tartarian characters, and that on comparing both together, they found them perfectly alike. Not withstanding the questions which the French on the South Sea expedition asked the people there, concerning the time when the pillars were erected? What their traditions and sentiments concerning them were? Who had written the characters? What was meant by them? What kind of letters they were? In what language they were written and other circumstances, yet they could never get the least explanation, the Indians being as ignorant of all those things, as the French themselves. All they could say was, that those stones had been in those places since times immemorial. The places where the pillars stood were near nine hundred French miles westward of Montréal.

Pierre la Verendrye had spent fifty years among the natives of Canada. He certainly would have recognized Indian petroglyphs as would the Jesuits. A professor Kalm compared the writing with illustrations of Tartarian inscription and found the characters "perfectly alike." But Holand explains that the Tartars were not seafaring people and that they lived east of the Caspian Sea. Their presence in North America is almost an impossibility.[41] However, Tartarian and runic inscriptions have a remarkable superficial resemblance and most likely the LaVerendrye Stone was the work of the Norse.

If we look on a map, (see page 195) we can see that directly west of the Western Settlement of Greenland is the Hudson Strait. The Norse from that settlement would have explored the region and gone there on hunting and exploring expeditions over the centuries. When the climate went into the "Little Ice Age" (1240-1340?) and the weather became inhospitable to them, they would have packed up and headed into their Hudson Bay hunting ground with which they were familiar. Exploring up the Nelson River,[42] which was flowing from the southwest, would have brought them to Lake Winnipeg and from there they

---

[41] In light of the findings of Ethyl Stewart, it is very possible the inscription could have been made by people from Tartaria, having traveled the silk road to China and thence to America by the Chinese junks. Of course, it could have been Norse, as first thought. We will never know until the stone is located. Today many of these ancient scripts are decipherable.

[42] The Norse invariably were noted for exploring great rivers and waterways where possible.

easily could have immigrated into the Minnesota country via the Red River where the Kensington Stone and many Norse artifacts and mooring stones have been found. They also could have gotten to Lake Superior by the same route by heading southeast via the great fur trading route of later years through the "Lake of the Woods."

On a trip to Greenland in 2001, my wife and I went through a museum at a Danish and Inuit village[43] on the west coast of that huge island, the largest in the world, I am told. There were several sheds and buildings, all part of the museum complex where we freely wandered from one building to another. There was a young Danish anthropologist in charge and he was guiding a group of six or eight people, mostly women, from building to building, while lecturing in a strong but understandable Danish accent. I joined the group as did two or three other stragglers.

In one building there was a large map of Greenland on a wall and our guide was giving us an overall description of it, strangely not mentioning any of its interesting ancient history, in which I was especially interested.

During a pause for questions, a woman standing near me asked, "Where were the western Viking settlements?" She had obviously read some of the Viking history of the area.

The young man pointed to the early settlement locations, which were some distance south of us on the map. (See page 195)

"And what ever became of those people?" asked the same woman.

"Well," said our guide, "nobody knows, they just disappeared. There were a few stray sheep found wandering around, but no sign of the people."[44]

Then there was silence. Everyone in the group stood staring blankly at the map.

"They all went to Minnesota," I said, breaking the silence.

"What's that, what's that?" asked the group leader.

"Well, they all went west and south through Hudson's Bay and up the Nelson and Red Rivers to Minnesota," I said. "They have found hundreds of mooring stones besides Norse artifacts in the Dakotas, Wisconsin, Minnesota and Nebraska. Haven't you ever heard of the Kensington Stone?" I questioned.

Believe it or not, while there were about a dozen people there with the anthropologist, not one had heard or knew anything about the Kensington Stone. But I was just as surprised and pleased not to have gotten a negative lecture as I surely would have in the United States or Canada. The young anthropologist lit

---

[43] The village of Ilulissat, just north of Jakobshaun Glacier, which is considered the fastest moving glacier in the world, the source of the huge icebergs the Davis Straits are noted for.

[44] The inhabitants did not die out as there were orderly graves but no evidence of bodies that were not buried. They had obviously moved on.

up like a candle and in a very enthusiastic voice, he chirped, "I like that, I like that."

I said to myself, apparently this kind of thing is not as well known or as important to some people as I had thought, but it seems that an anthropologist certainly should have at least heard of the Kensington Stone.

Over the years I marveled at the work of Hjalmar Holand in his book, *Explorations in America Before Columbus.* Back in the days when I first read it, I couldn't wait to get Mrs. Paul's views on the subject. I remember being disappointed at her reaction. Her sister, Mrs. Abby Longyear Roberts, would not take sides on the subject. She was neutral or noncommital, but Mrs. Paul told me she had talked with Dr. Richard Sonderegger from the college history department. He was married to her niece. The doctor had gone to Minnesota to study the situation.

Dr. Sonderegger was a friend of mine and he convinced me the Kensington Stone had to be a fraud. He consulted with several historians in and around Alexandria, Minnesota, where the stone was housed. He said everyone, to a person, agreed it was a matter of pride to the many Scandinavians in the area that the "Vikings" were there five hundred years before Columbus.

Later, however, I realized there must have been people other than Scandinavians who believed the story: they named their professional football team the "Minnesota Vikings." When I was writing a local history ten or fifteen years later, I wrote that the "Vikings" could not possibly have been in Minnesota, but I tried to leave the question open. Ten years later, when finishing the book (*Superior Heartland—A Backwoods History; 1989),* I had changed my mind. Much new evidence had surfaced by then and I decided there were two strongly divided groups of people. My earlier friends and I had been only talking to one group.[44a] By the time I reached the end of that book (1600 pages), I had changed my mind completely.

The Joel Kela Stone
(now known as the Escanaba River Stone)

I visited the Marquette County Historical Society off and on for years. Often Mrs. Paul would have little jobs for me to do and eventually, sometime in the 1950's, I became a dues-paying member. In 1956 I was elected to the Board of Directors. I was a member of that Board for the next 33 years.

Mrs. Paul sent her son Phillip and I on a trip to investigate some alleged rock carvings on the Huron Islands and asked me to report on them at the annual

---

[44a] The group we were talking to were all of one mind, they were college professors.

Joel Kela, History Teacher from Gwinn Michigan. Circa 1957

meeting that following February (1957). The meeting was held at Northern Michigan College of Education—now Northern Michigan University.

Mrs. Paul had a report to give also and she asked another fellow from Gwinn, about 20 miles south, to report on a find he had made.

The man from Gwinn was Joel Kela, a history teacher in the high school there. I had only met Joel a few times, but knew his wife, formerly Helen Moody. I had worked with her years before at Bay Cliff. Mrs. Paul, Joel Kela and I sat together at the front table, facing the audience. On the table in front of Joel was a flat stone about eight inches long and almost triangular in shape. It definitely had some kind of strange writing on it. I couldn't take my eyes off it. Looking at it from the opposite end of the table I could see what looked like two lines of writing.

When it was Joel's turn to talk, he told the story of the stone. Some boys from the Gwinn School had been working on Highway M-35 near Gwinn during the summer. At noontime they had gone down to the nearby Escanaba River to eat their lunch. Having a little extra time, they decided to take a dip in the river to remove some of the road dust.

Just on impulse, one of the boys retrieved the stone from the river bottom in about four feet of water. They noticed what looked like some strange writing and threw it up on the bank. They brought up a few more flat stones but none with any markings.

That fall the boys told Joel about the marked stone at school. He said he would like to see the stone and within a few weeks time they brought it in.

At that time, Hjalmar Holand's book on the Vikings was out, and Viking fever was running high among a few historians who had read it. Joel was convinced that the writing on the stone was runic. He was very excited about it and had the boys take him to the spot on the river where the stone was found. Even though it was mid-October by then and some light snow was in the air, Joel stripped down and dove into the icy water looking for more stones. He collected many, but again, none had the peculiar markings of the one the boys brought in.

In his talk that night, Joel finished by slamming the table convincingly with his fist and shouting, "And I believe the gentlemen (referring to the Vikings) were here!"

When I had a chance to examine the stone carefully after the meeting, I said to Joel, "This isn't runic writing." He blew up at me.

"What do you know about it?" he growled.

"I don't claim to know a lot about it, but I sure know Norse runes when I see them," I answered. "They're like letters similar to ours and those aren't anything like runes."

He became very upset with me, but Mrs. Paul, kind soul that she was, calmed the waters. She had a professional picture taken of the stone and sent copies out to authorities on Norse culture across the country, seven or eight of them. Among them were

Dr. Alfred Kidder

Photo Courtesy of Marquette County Historical Society

Holand and Dr. Kidder,[44b] formerly of Marquette, then at the Smithsonian. All the letters came back saying that it was not Norse and not one of them had the slightest suggestion as to what it was, or even if it was writing at all.

I was convinced in my own mind that it had to be writing. If not, it was at least done by man, some man back in the darkness of time whose history was not yet known.

As I thought about Joel Kela's stone from the Escanaba river, I related it in a remote sort of way with a story I had heard from an elderly woodsman friend of mine, Curt Stone. Curt was never without something interesting to talk about, and on several occasions he alluded to a cave that Al Saari, a mutual friend from Champion, had described. It was over in the hills around Champion. Caves are rare or nonexistent in the local granite formations and anything similar to one should draw suspicion that it was manmade. This cave, according to those who saw it, had to have been manmade. It was said to have a huge flat stone over its opening to form a doorway.

When I sat down to get the information from Curt, I discovered that he had never seen it himself, but was interested in having me go with him to look for it. He had thought about it a lot. His idea was that it was constructed when the water was high and that the place where it was located may have been an island. Now, he told me, the cave, facing north, opened onto a spruce bog.

By the mid-1960's, I had a little collection of these unexplained oddities in mind. They all seemed related in some way to Charles Whittlesey's first statement, "An ancient people of whom history gives no account..." This was the only credible explanation: evidence of a race or tribe of people whose history

---

[44b] Professor Alfred V. Kidder of Marquette, Michigan honorary curator of Harvard's Peabody Museum - considered a pioneer in American Archeology and an authority of Southwestern U.S. died in 1963.

*Joel Kela's Stone
from the Escanaba river*

was lost in time. There were the ancient copper diggings, the mystery stone, the Soper tablets, the Newberry stone and Joel Kela's stone, all enigmas, or declared fake by the authorities. As far as I was concerned, none had a satisfactory explanation. If the Kensington Stone is authentic, then the Norse would have been here too, but that would have been a few thousand years too late for the ancient mining that took place 3,000 to 5,000 years ago.

Sometime in the 1960's, I heard Dr. George Cameron of the University of Michigan give a talk on some Persian stone tablets. He had deciphered them and found these small stone tablets were like checks: they were to remind the holder that he was owed money.

The tablets reminded me of the Joel Kela stone and I asked Dr. Cameron if he would take a look at it. By this time Joel had divorced and moved to Florida where he died. His ex-wife could not find the stone. She thought he had taken it with him because she said it was always in the trunk of his car.

I located a copy of the picture at the Historical Society and gave it to Dr. Cameron. It was a year later when I saw him again and I asked him if he had any idea about the markings on the stone.

He said, "Those lines are caused by the sun drying clay," and he had a name for such a process.

"But, Dr. Cameron," I insisted, "there are two distinct lines of writing and the rock was found in four feet of water."

"That may be so," answered the doctor, "but the sun caused it."

I was at a loss for words as that didn't make sense to me. Finally I stammered, rather quietly, "Couldn't we just say we don't know what it is?"

"You can say that if you want to because you don't know, but I know it was caused by the sun." He pronounced the technical term again. I was not convinced. The right person had not come along yet.

There is one more incident that I recall concerning the Joel Kela stone.

I was conducting a workshop on Upper Peninsula history at Northern Michigan University in 1976. It was the first course offered on this subject. The week-long program involved about 70 graduate students.

I was telling the group about the Joel Kela stone. I had just remarked as a closing comment, "Someday, maybe after I'm gone, somebody will come along who can read the writing on that stone—but we just have to wait."

With that, a young woman in the class raised her hand.

"I'm Joel Kela's daughter," she said. She looked much like her mother. I was very surprised. I didn't know that Joel and Helen had children.

"Do you remember seeing the stone?" I asked.

"Oh, yes," she said. "My dad carried it with him for years, but I don't know where it is now; it may be at camp." The stone never did turn up again, even though both Mrs. Kela and her daughter searched diligently for it.

Luckily, we had the excellent picture by a professional photographer that Mrs. Paul had taken for the Historical Society.

Courtesy of Bill Conners © 2005

Arlington Mallery

For many years, unknown to me (and apparently to Joe Gannon or Roy Drier), there was an amateur archaeologist diligently exploring the possibility that the old reports of Irish and Norse colonies in America were true. He reported many controversial findings in a book entitled *Lost America* in 1951.[45] The book was rewritten in 1979 by his associate, Mary Roberts Harrison.[46]

This picture of Arlington Mallery was taken by William Conner in May of 1963. He is standing in what was left of the bowl of the Overly Furnace, while trying to find charcoal for carbon dating. The Overly Furnace is in western Ross County, Ohio near the village of Austin. Conner has become a prime researcher as Mallery's successor to carry on the investigation of Ohio's Mysterious Furnaces

---

[45] E.P. Dutton, 2 Park Ave., New York, N.Y., 1006.
[46] Clark, Irwin & Co., Ltd. Toronto and Vancouver, Canada.

Arlington Mallery (1877-1968) was born in New York State. He followed a long line of bridge builders, but had many diverse skills and interests. As a young man and a trained engineer, he took over the family business, the Oswego Bridge Company, a pioneer in riveted steel construction. Mallery had a great interest in ancient history. He also owned a large motorized sailboat in which he did a lot of traveling.

Sometime in the 1920's Mallery was supervising the construction of a bridge near Shelbrooke, Quebec. This was the first steel arch bridge he had ever designed and he was very proud of it. During his early years with the company, Mallery had done all phases of bridge building. He had cut and laid stone for the foundations, forged and tempered stone drills, cold chisels, adzes, axes and other tools. He had experience in every job that involved building bridges.

On that summer day in Quebec, as he watched men working high in the air, he couldn't help but notice the ease and confidence they had as they walked the narrow beams and handled them with special skill and agility. He took special note of their physical appearance; they all seemed to be Scandinavian. When he inquired about them, he was surprised to learn that they all belonged to a bridgeman's union which only allowed Iroquois Indians to join. These men were all full-blooded Mohawk Indians.

According to his account of this experience in his 1951 book, *Lost America*, this revelation started him on the path as an amateur archaeologist, a path he followed faithfully until his death in 1968. He believed that many of the Indian tribes of the northeast were a mixture of Viking and Irish immigrants from prehistoric times.

Years later, when Mallery was working on a bridge in Ross County, Ohio,[47] he was told about the earlier finds there previously worked by Squire and Davis and Charles Whittlesey at Spring Hill on the Black Run. Here Mallery found what he described as pre-Columbian iron smelting furnaces. He has many detailed drawings and photographs of the various types of furnaces found in the area in his book, *Lost America*. He claims that some of these ancient furnaces are of the same type used during the Viking period in Norway and Ireland. The plague which devastated Europe in the 1350's and 60's, Mallery believed, decimated the populations of America as well. The remaining Celts and Norsemen melted into the indigenous populations which became the Iroquois Confederacy made up of the five tribes on the eastern seaboard.

Some of these same sites, especially those at Spruce Hill, had previously been assigned to the Adena and Hopewell cultures by professional archaeologists. Mallery either didn't know this or chose to ignore it. Needless to say, his ideas

---

[47] This is the same Ross County where Davis was born and where the first evidence of the Adena and Hopewell cultures were identified.

Photo by the author

Norse cairns at the edge of a plain high above
L'Anse Aux Meadows - seen in the distance.

did not meet with very wide approval among professionals. He identified evidence of Vikings and furnaces on Newfoundland as early as 1946 and several sites to the south along the Atlantic coast.

Mallery's discoveries were written up in the newspapers of that day but were never accepted by the vast majority of the scientific community.

However, about ten years later, when a site at the northern tip of Newfoundland was shown to a Norwegian, Helge Ingstad, and his archaeologist wife, Anne Stine Ingstad, by a local fisherman, they made an archaeological dig there. The place, known as L'Anse aux Meadows, was positively identified as a small, possibly temporary, Viking settlement, the only one accepted on mainland America to this day by American archaeologists. Mallery's sites have been ignored and all but forgotten.

In the course of his research, Arlington Mallery read of the Greek trip to Iceland in 300 B.C. He also studied the Norse Sagas, particularly the descriptions of Leif Erickson's trips to Newfoundland.

From page 172 in *Lost America:*

It will be recalled that Leif's camp was used both by his small expedition and succeeding ones, primarily as a makeshift base of operations, while the actual settlement was elsewhere in Newfoundland—with a consequent possibility therefore of confirmatory artifacts was revealed. And indeed, on at least seventeen locations in Newfoundland, archaeologists have actually found stone and iron tools and weapons indicative of prehistoric Scandinavian settlement.

Among the prehistoric Newfoundland site on Sop's Island, which I myself have excavated, are a number which were occupied in the eleventh and twelfth centuries. The age and dimensions of these sites and the stone implements found in them lead to the conclusion that they were occupied by Scandinavians, probably Danes—then confronted in Ireland with a compelling reason to be seeking new homes en masse. The wattle houses of the Danes would have disappeared without a trace as had the dwellings of the former inhabitants of these beaches.

When the Vikings turned their ships into the channel which was the northern entrance to Sop's Arm, early in the eleventh century, they saw on their right a rocky mountain coming steeply down to the sea. On the left was Sop's Island and a beautiful circular harbor, a rocky ridge separated the harbor from both White Bay and the channel and sheltered it from the northeastern gales prevalent in Newfoundland water. The entrance to the harbor was through a ninety yard gap in the ridge.

The Danish Vikings from Ireland who came to Sop's Arm found the Sop's Island harbor site more desirable for their purposes as seamen and fishermen than it had been for Karlsefni and his Greenland farmers. Needing natural meadows to provide wild hay and pasture, Karlsefni had gone to the southwest corner of the Arm, eight miles from the sea, where he found a salt water lake into which he could sail at high water. There he found a valley open to the north and northeast winds and at its southern end a natural meadow, where he built his settlement.

But the Danes stayed out on the easily defended island harbor sites, accessible only by water. There on the gravel beach, well above high tide, facing the land-locked circular harbor, they built their dwellings. Their boats could be drawn up on the broad sandy beach, then at level, for inspection and repair. While working on their boats, they must have dropped the iron boat spikes and nails which I dug up nine hundred years later.

Across Sop's Arm there is another sandy beach at about the same height above the seas as the Sop's Island beach. There my men dug up a Viking iron axe and a large iron chisel. The thin flat blade of the axe had been strengthened by cladding a sheet of carbonized iron on each side of the soft iron blade.

(Cladding is welding, at less than normal temperature, of thin sheets of steel or carbonized iron to a softer metal, a lost art for many centuries. This process has been revised for the manufacture of jet planes. Similar increased strength in wood has been made in plywood. *Author.*)

This method of manufacturing hard axe and sword blades (the famous Damascus blades, for example) was regularly used in ancient times, but became obsolete shortly after the new iron manufacturing process came into general use in the fifteenth century. Consequently, when iron tools, weapons and nails which have been intentionally carburized or fabricated by cladding are discovered in sites which are evidently pre-Columbian, it is most difficult to see how such iron artifacts can possibly be dated as post-Columbian. Carburized or cladded nails will not be found after on Viking sites. The Vikings used soft boat rivets and clinch nails in assembling their ships. In their later models, however, such as the Glokstad boat, they fastened the keel with hard nails.

Mallery describes these nails elsewhere in his book (*Lost America*). The book is profusely illustrated with drawings and photographs of artifacts he and his men found.

As one can see from the previous passage, Arlington Mallery has great knowledge of metals, maps and Vikings. He spent his own time and fortune on his hobby, but as far as I can tell he has been given little credit for his many important discoveries.

While he is seldom mentioned in any authoritative archaeological writings, there are some things he is noted for. Strange as it may seem, his work on Norse colonization is not one of them.

Support for Mallery

In 1963, a young science writer named William Conner of Columbus, Ohio, met Captain Mallery. Even at 86 years of age he was actively pursuing his hobby.

Conner seems to have taken up where Mallery left off in the study of melting and smelting of metals in ancient times.

Concerning this subject, Conner wrote in 1999 about his observations, some of which are quoted here with permission. He believes that there is much evidence of the melting of copper in ancient times and is completing a book on the subject at the time of this writing.

I too believe that copper would have been melted by some of the ancient people although most of the artifacts that I have seen have obviously been shaped by hammering and annealing.

I have two reasons for believing copper was melted and cast here. The first is logic. The ancients were building fires beneath rocks that contained native copper so that when water was thrown on it the rock would spall off or break up, releasing the metal. As they heated the copper it grew softer and with a very hot fire it would melt. They would have observed this. However, the later seekers of copper were looking for small pieces which could be hammered into shape without the elaborate heating process.

The more compelling reason for believing that copper was melted here is that I was with a friend, Matt Leff, the day he picked up a round, flat piece of copper that had definitely been melted. It has obvious bubbles in it and is covered

*Melted copper
found by Matt Leff in
Marquette County,
circa 1955*

Drawing By Katherine Savu

*The ancients were building fires beneath rocks that contained native copper so that when
water was thrown on it the rock would spall off or break up, releasing the metal. As they
heated the copper it grew softer and with a very hot fire it would melt.*

with the black oxide of copper,[48] which is formed when copper has been heated in the presence of copper carbonate.[49]

The piece was found at the bottom of a deep tire track in a two rut sand road a few hundred yards from Lake Superior in a very remote area. If one were to excavate in that vicinity I suspect other evidence would be found. The location would have been on an ancient beach, many of which were formed as Lake Superior receded.

Mallery used this same reasoning to determine that when cuprous oxide was present, the artifact would have been heated. Artifacts that were molded needed a harder material for a cutting edge. This was accomplished by hammering and thus it may be difficult to detect molded artifacts from hammered ones.

In a review of Mallery's report in *Lost America* in 1953 by Dr. Earle E. Caley, then a professor of chemistry at Ohio State University, while disagreeing with Mallery on many points, Caley said the "technical evidence he presents for the existence of the practice of melting and casting copper at an early date in North America is important and appears to be both sound and adequate." Apparently there are many artifacts in museums around the country that have not been examined closely in this respect. After Arlington Mallery died at 91 in 1968, William Conner, an avocational archaeologist and member of the Midwestern Epigraphic Society of Columbus, Ohio, wrote several articles about the furnaces for newspapers and magazines. Eventually he became a science writer for the Daily News in Springfield, Ohio, where he had a weekly column called "Science Scene." When studying the history of metallurgy, Conner learned that the first iron furnaces were indeed pit furnaces, similar to the copper smelters on the Sinai Peninsula that went back 2,500 to 3,000 years in Europe. He also found out they were used in Africa until about 100 years ago.

In 1973, at Joseph Mahan's first conference on pre-Columbian archaeology, William Conner met Clyde Keeler, also an amateur archaeologist who was investigating Mallery's furnaces. He was investigating a furnace called Haskins #2, a newly-discovered furnace in a mound just a few yards away from Mallery's Haskins #1 on Penny Royal Road along Deer Creek in Ross County. Conner visited the site, interviewed Keeler's partner B.E. Kelley and wrote a story about the excavation for the Springfield newspaper.

---

[48] There are two common oxides of copper in accordance to its valences. They are cuprous oxide (Cu_2O) and cupric oxide (CuO) Cuprous oxide is a red crystalline material, cupric oxide is a black powder.

[49] When copper is exposed to air it carburizes forming a blue-green protective layer of copper carbonate such as seen on the Statute of Liberty in New York Harbor. The 150 foot statue has a steel frame covered with more than 300 sheets of copper that are 3/32 of an inch thick. At the turn of this century repairs were made to the copper shell by annealing thin sheets of copper to weakened areas.

Conner knew that American archaeologists were not experts on pit furnaces and, frankly, denied that they existed, so he wrote to a British historian of metallurgy, Leslie Aitchison, author of *A History of Metals*. After much study of photographs of the Overly furnace which Conner sent him, Aitchison identified the remains as "almost certain" to be that of a pit furnace. This convinced Conner that Mallery's iron smelting theory was correct. He has been studying the furnaces ever since.[50]

Did Ohio's Prehistoric Indians Cast Copper?

The prehistoric fire pits in Ohio seem all to have been the work of the Hopewell Culture of Native Americans (200 B.C. to about 500 A.D.). These prehistoric fire pits lack complete evidence suggestive of iron smelting. However, slag and other materials associated with these sites show evidence of being exposed to high temperatures in the range associated with iron and copper metallurgy. (http://www.iwaynet.net/~wdc/copper.htm)

William Conner must have visited the property in Connecticut that belongs to the Gungywump Society. At the time (about 1997 or '98), David Barrons was the president of that organization and Dave showed us both the same site. It was up against a cliff with a small cave or crevice or fissure and a creek running by. Without an explanation, Dave asked me for a comment on the place. I looked around and pointed out pieces of rusted slag in the creek. He thereupon suggested that it could be an ancient smelting site. Certainly there have been any number of smelting sites discovered in Georgia, Virginia and Connecticut as well as Ohio; all of them need close archaeological examination.

---

[50] William Conner: In 1977, Mr. Conner joined AT&T's Bell Laboratories in New Jersey as a science writer. When AT&T broke up in 1982, he became the editor of a Washington Newsletter which reported on the satellite telecommunications and sensing industry. He moved back to Ohio in 1989 to be with aging parents and the following year was back in the field as an archaeologist investigator at a furnace site in Ross County. William Conner continues to pursue the question of iron smelting pit furnaces to this day. In 1990 he met a Ross County farmer, David Orr, who believed he found a new furnace site after plowing up some unusual burnt material. They have formed the Archaeo-Pyrogenics Society (APGS) to continue the scientific study of these furnaces. The APGS faded away in the mid-1990s when Orr became too busy with farming and his database on the Internet, which was one of the first on this subject. Since then Conner has been assisted by members of the Midwestern Epigraphic Society.

What Do The Archaeologists Have to Say About Mallery?
William Conner: http://www.iwaynet.net/~wdc/copper.htm

Mallery's excavating techniques weren't particularly subtle or scientific. In 1948 he enlisted local treasure hunters and relic collectors to help him dig. Like the mound diggers of old, he was looking for the goods and wasn't too particular about what got in the way between him and whatever it was that interested him. Mallery even used a bulldozer to rip into several features. Stratigraphy, pollen, charcoal, variation in soil color, and small artifacts that are so vital to archaeologists for interpreting sites were brushed aside to get at the iron furnaces Mallery was certain were to be found at the heart of every earthwork.

Mallery had little use for mainstream archaeology. His work completely ignored the preceding century of scientific exploration of the mounds and the culture that created them. The Adena and Hopewell are completely absent from his accounts. No mention is made of landmark excavations of the Hopewell Mound Group, Seip Mound, or Mound City, even though they are practically next door to his Viking homeland. He was either unaware or didn't care that these sites exist. He only referred to professional archaeologists to accuse them of ringing down an "Iron Curtain" over American prehistory and blindly destroying evidence of iron-smelting.

In his seasons on Spruce Hill, Mallery claimed to find multiple primitive iron-smelting furnaces of the type used in medieval Norway and Ireland. He also asserted that he found a runestone marking a Viking-style barrow and nine similar Norse graves nearby. Mallery further claimed to find a serpent mound on the hilltop, implying that the Great Serpent Mound of Adams County, Ohio might also be of Norse manufacture. Finally, Mallery identified the no longer extant stone enclosure in Black Run Valley as a Norse dam with several spillways.

Mallery's dig was followed with great interest by the press. Stories and photos appeared in the Chillicothe Gazette, the Columbus and Cincinnati press and papers through the Midwest.

The publicity brought forth information from other local residents and soon Mallery was poking into mounds all over Ross County. Amazingly, Mallery and his diggers found that they all held furnaces of one sort or another. One single mound even held nine furnaces. Ancient Ross County must have been the Pittsburgh of its day. Some of the mounds also held bothersome and hard-to-explain skeletons. No matter. Mallery would find a way to account for them.

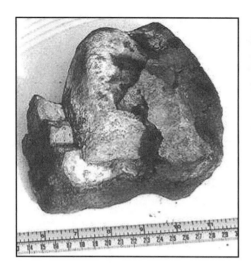

Photos courtesy of © Bill Conners

On June 30, 2003, William D. Conner, found what looks like a casting (two views above) inside its broken mold at the Garrett Site west of Chillicothe, Ohio. More information can be found at Conner's web site http://www.iwaynet.net/~wdc/garretmo.htm.

Copper that appears to have been melted in a crucible of some kind, was washed free from a sand dune on Lake Superior near Big Bay, Michigan found by Betty Waring.

Photos courtesy of Betty Waring

Photo by Jack Deo

Photo by Jack Deo

A dozen or so of these stones have been found near the mouth of the Iron River in Big Bay, Michigan. These two were found by Ed Rassmusen in early 1930's. The same area as the copper on previous page.

Photo J.-M. Labat © Casterman

Similar stone rings have been found in Africa and France. The French example pictured here are from Megalithic monuments in Morhihan France. Both African and French examples are thought to have been symbols of great wealth

This stone was found in Marquette County Michigan It is shown with a quarter for size.

A dozen or so of these worked stones have been found in the same vacinity as the melted copper shown on page 166 - near the mouth of the Iron River in Big Bay, Michigan.

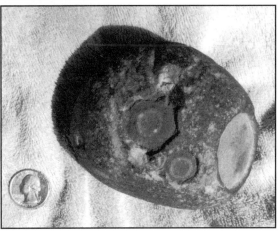

To the credit of Mallery, in July of 2004, in a letter addressed to this author, was a picture of a copper axe head in a mold. Across the top of the photo was a one-line message, "Fred. Bill Conners copper are still in the mold-smelting in America? Yes!" The envelope was postmarked from Eau Claire, Wisconsin.

As stated earlier, I had long believed there must have been the melting of copper in America as proved by many pieces of copper I have that appear to have been melted in ancient times.

Lost America

In 1951, Mallery published his theories in the book entitled *Lost America*. In this volume, Mallery claimed that the mounds, earthworks, hill forts, etc., of the ancient Ohio Valley were the handiwork of successive waves of Irish, Norse and Danish settlers driven westward by political religious and economic upheavals in Europe, Iceland, and Greenland in the years following 1000 A.D.

These settlements reached from the Maritime Provinces of Canada southward and westward as far as Virginia and the Ohio Valley. Some adventurers even made it as far west as Minnesota, he claimed.

The European settlers conquered the indigenous populations, multiplied, prospered and smelted lots of iron until they were struck down by the Black Plague sometime between 1350 and 1400.

This sudden mass death explains the presence of skeletons in iron furnaces. The many dead were buried wherever there was an empty hole.

After the plague, the few remaining Celts and Norsemen melted into the indigenous population giving rise to the mighty Iroquois nation and transforming everything from its genetic heritage to its language, customs and housing. Alas, however, the knowledge of iron smelting was lost in the plague and all or nearly all of the products of the Viking forges rusted away before the arrival of the Spanish, French and English in the 16th and 17th centuries.

The Evidence
ESTABLISHMENT review of Arlington Mallery's work

As evidence for this wild and revolutionary reworking of American prehistory, Mallery offers the following evidence.

- His own questionable excavations at Spruce Hill, other Ross

County sites, Oak Hill, Virginia and comparison of his finds to medieval iron furnaces in northern Europe.
- Metallurgical tests on iron items of unclear provenance.
- His reading of medieval Norse sagas as historic fact.
- The Kensington Runestone—An alleged Viking runestone found in Kensington, Minnesota in 1898. It supposedly recounted the fate of a 14th century Norse Expedition to the Gopher State. Generally regarded as a hoax perpetuated by Swedish-American boasters.
- The Newport Tower—A centuries old stone tower in Newport, Rhode Island long alleged to be Viking construction. Decisively proven to be a 17th century colonial structure by a 1948-49 dig.
- A list of alleged similarities between Norse and Iroquois culture, including curvilinear, zoomorphic designs, living in longhouses and using similar-sound words to describe the same object. Pretty unremarkable and the linguistic comparisons are filled with inaccuracies.

There is not much support here for overturning an interpretation of American prehistory based upon the work of many talented and highly educated scholars, rigorous debate and criticism, plus the fruit of hundreds of meticulously-documented excavations.

So as one can readily see, there are definitely two sides to the story and they are far apart. The sad thing about the situation is that there is no middle ground and no communication between the two sides.

Thus, here is an argument for the overturning of history as gathered by many talented people:

1872

From Pcanier Society of Michigan
"The Mound Builders of Michigan" by Henry Gillman of Detroit—
Read before the Detroit Scientific Association in 1874

Having seen the remark that the copper tools of the ancient miners have a rough and not polished exterior, inferences being drawn there from as to their rude construction, I wish to say that, having examined a large number of those tools, I believe this roughness to have been caused mostly by corrosion. In many cases this is quite palpable, the original surface being apparent in places and evidently confirming the fact that at least the external faces of the tool were originally approximately smooth, if not polished.

Excellent arguments have been advanced by Mr. Foster to prove that the mound builders understood the art of fusing copper, and at least some of their copper tools were made by being cast or molded. From the method pursued by this people in mining, in which the agency of fire bore so prominent a part, it would seem improbable, they could have long remained ignorant of the fusibility of metal; yet in most cases the evidence appears conclusive that the rudely-fashioned tool was simply wrought by being beaten into the desired form, often in the roughest manner. It is possible that the two classes of tools here referred to may mark two distinct eras in the history of the manufacture, and the molded tool designates an advance from the primitive method of hammering the metal into shape. Some of the beads taken from the "mounds" in Michigan display a wonderful degree of neatness in the manipulation of the metal, the junction of the bead being in many cases almost impeccable; yet the agency of fire was here evidently not employed.

1946-1950

Arlington Mallery: The widely accepted theory that the native North Americans used copper only as a malleable stone is wrong, because many of the heaviest pieces, such as axes and chisels, had never been touched by a hammer except at the cutting edge. Therefore, he concluded, these pieces could not have been hammered out of material from naturally occurring native copper deposits, but would have had to have been cast from molten copper.

1953

Statement by William Conner: David Orr and I met with Prof. Mabley in his office at O.S.U. in March of 1993. He was shown artifacts and photos of our Lynn Acres dig. The professor told us we had indeed found an iron furnace based upon the evidence he was shown.

It should be quite obvious that an attempt to overturn an interpretation of American prehistory built up from the life's work of many talented and highly educated scholars has been going on ever since the beginning of the period that the two theories were stated.

The Piri Re'is Map

There is another piece of startling information that Arlington Mallery is given credit for bringing to the attention of the public.

Mrs. Burt Sparhawk, a neighbor of mine who browses websites called and told me she had found something I'd be interested in, something called the Piri Re'is map.

I had heard of Piri Re'is Map before, but knew little about it except that it tied in with an old belief that the North Pole was once an unfrozen Polar Sea that drew several Arctic expeditions to explore it.[50a] Piri Re'is map was said to show the Antarctic continent free of ice. This condition has never existed since it was first explored in modern times. When I first heard of it I thought that this situation could be explained by the theory previously mentioned of a cosmic catastrophe in 9500 B.C. or about 11,500 years ago. That idea suggests that the earth's axis was nearly straight up and down with reference to the plane of its orbit around the sun. Therefore the two poles would have been free of ice. The result of the cosmic "phaeton" passing close to the earth tipped it to its present 23-1/2° from vertical, thus causing the severe winters at the poles with the permanent ice caps. This also goes along with the idea that ancient people traveled by boat to both poles prior to 9500 B.C. The legend of an open polar sea has persisted, but it has almost always been frozen within historic times. The one exception was in the year 2000, when my wife June and I traveled to 73°N Lat that summer. When we returned, the story on the front page of a Canadian paper in Ottawa said the polar ice had melted for the first time in 35 million years! So much for scientific stories in the news.

The story I want to quote, while extremely interesting, is too long and irrelevant to our subject to be included in total, but the last part is quoted here.

—In August of 1956, my grandfather (Colin Wilson speaking) was asked to take part in a radio discussion of a controversial new discovery: the so-called Piri Re'is map.

(A summary of the story follows)

That same year, a Turkish naval officer had presented a copy of a map whose original had been found in the Topkopi Palace in Istanbul in 1929. It was painted on parchment and dated 1513. It showed the Atlantic Ocean, with a small part of the coast of Africa on the right, and

---

[50a] In some recent years (since 1997) the Polar Sea Ice has melted considerably in summer bringing credibility to the ancient legends.

the whole coast of South America on the left, and at the bottom of the map, what looked like Antarctica.

The map was passed on to the Hydrographic Office's cartographic expert, W. I. Walters, who in turn had shown it to a friend named Captain Arlington H. Mallery, who studied the Viking Maps. It was after he had studied the map at home that Mallery made the astonishing statement that he believed it showed the coast of Antarctica as it had been before it was covered by thick ice. It appeared to show certain bays in Queen Maud Land as they had been before they were frozen over.

Now a few days before the broadcast, my grandfather had received a copy of the Piri Re'is map from the producer of the program. He compared it with the reports of the 1949 expedition, and was thrilled to discover that the bays corresponded exactly.

It was amazing enough that the 16th century map should even show Antarctica, which had not been discovered until 1820, but that it should show Antarctica as it had been in prehistoric times seemed preposterous. In the discussion, which took place at Georgetown University in Washington, D.C., indignant scholars had said as much and my grandfather then assured them that as far as he could see, the bays on the Piri Re'is map seemed to correspond to the bays discovered under the ice in 1949. I must be honest and admit that my grandfather did not press the point—he was an academic and had no wish to be thought of as a crank. But he certainly threw his authority on the side of the map and Captain Mallery. The discussion was lively, and was widely reported in the newspapers. My grandfather liked Mallery, who was a scholarly and friendly man. They had dinner together after the broadcast, and my grandfather told Mallery his story about Admiral Byrd and how this stimulated his interest in Antarctica. Mallery told my grandfather that maps like the Piri Re'is map were by no means uncommon. They were called portolans—which means "from port to port"—and they were used by mariners in the Middle Ages: the Library of Congress apparently had dozens of them.

A few months later, Mallery contacted my grandfather to tell him that he had been in touch with another academic who was interested in the Piri Re'is map—a professor of the history of science called Charles Hapgood, who taught at Keene State College, fifty miles or so from the University of New Hampshire in Durham. He gave my grandfather Hapgood's phone number and the two of them spoke on the telephone the same evening. They agreed to keep in touch and share their results.

It was some time later that Hapgood rang my grandfather in a state of great excitement. He had spent several days at the Library of Congress where he had been to study portolans. He expected to see a half dozen or so: instead, he found that the librarian had laid out a whole room full of them. (There were dozens, probably hundreds.). They appeared to show that these medieval mariners knew far more about geography of the world than is generally supposed. Moreover, said Hapgood, he had discovered a map that undoubtedly showed the whole of Antarctica, as if photographed from the air. The map had been drawn by a mapmaker called Oronteus Finaeus in 1531, and showed ranges of coastal mountains that are now deep under the ice. Hapgood was in the process of studying this map, but his preliminary findings indicated that the rivers on it followed natural drainage patterns, which meant that the coasts were then ice free. But inland, there were no rivers or mountains, suggesting that they were covered with ice.

We know that at the end of the last ice age—around 11,000 B.C.—Antarctica spent thousands of years free of ice. Then about 4000 B.C., the ice sheets began to return. That seemed to date the map—or the original map on which it was based—to around 4000 B.C.

Then why, asked my grandfather, were these amazing maps not better known—at least among scholars?

That, said Hapgood, was precisely the question he had.

The mainstream academic statement on the Piri Re'is Map:

A Turkish map from 1513 claimed by some to show the Atlantic coastline of the Americas in unusually accurate detail. Notable for its inclusion of the Antarctica coast. Said to have been assembled from ancient maps used by Columbus. Popular with the Von Daniken[51] Ancient Astronauts crowd and various theorists of Atlantis and other alleged prehistoric super-civilizations.

In 1966 Charles Hapgood published a book entitled *Maps of the Ancient Sea Kings*. The book was later reprinted (1996) by Adventures Unlimited of Kempton, Illinois. In a word of appreciation in the front of his book, Hapgood gives credit to Captain Arlington H. Mallery who first suggested that the Piri Re'is Map, brought to light in 1929, but drawn in 1513 and based on much older maps, showed a part of Antarctica. It was he who made the original suggestion that the first map must have been drawn before the present immense Antarctica

---

[51] Erick Von Daniken—Swiss author—postulated that in the remote past extraterrestrial space travelers visited the earth.

ice cap had covered the coasts of Queen Maud Land. Hapgood says Mallery's sensational suggestion was the inspiration for his research, stating categorically that Mallery was the impetus for his research and his book and it is "with deep appreciation that I dedicate this book to Captain Arlington H. Mallery."

These "Sea Kings" are the ancient Sea People that we have mentioned before, and are alluded to by historians, that must have been part of an advanced Ice Age civilization. The story relates to the first hard evidence that an advanced civilization preceded all the peoples now known to history. The charts of these Sea People were passed on by the Minoans (the Sea Kings of Ancient Crete), and the Phoenicians, who were for a thousand years and more the greatest sailors of the ancient world and were undoubtedly among the first to bring reports of the fabulous amounts of free, pure Lake Superior copper back to the Old World. They probably carried a few large pieces of copper just to compare with the relatively meager amounts of that metal being produced with great effort on Cyprus. I would assume that some early copper shipments were sold to the Cypriots for further processing to be sold as oxhides[52] to the city states of the Mediterranean. This gave Cyprus the reputation of having much greater copper deposits than it actually had, and the island became so highly prized as a source of copper that it passed successively to the Egyptians, Assyrians, Phoenicians, Greeks, Persians and finally the Romans. By that time practically the entire supply of copper came from Cyprus. And all the while this island was, in fact, mostly a brokerage house for copper coming from overseas, copper carried there by the last leg of a trade route involving the early Mediterraneans, the old Norse, later the Irish and the possibility of Vikings. Certainly the last leg of the route was carrying tin from Cornwall in the British Isles and from Turkey to the bronze processing works on Cyprus.

It was about 4000 to 3000 B.C. when Cyprus first began producing copper. The metal was first known as "aes cyprium" (ore of Cyprus) which was shortened to cyprium and later corrupted to "cuprum." This became the English word "copper" and the chemical symbol for the metal is Cu, the first two letters of Cuprum.

Hapgood is one of the few professionals (Professor of History of Science at Keene State College in Keene, New Hampshire) who openly gives credit to amateurs. He states that every scientist is an amateur to start with. Copernicus, Newton and Darwin were all amateurs when they made their principal discoveries. A footnote in "Maps of the Ancient Sea Kings" reads: "The late James H. Campbell, who worked in his youth with Thomas A. Edison, said that once,

---

[52] Oxhides—Copper ingots in the shape of oxhides for easy handling. They weighed about 65 pounds.

when a difficult problem was being discussed, Edison said it was too difficult for any specialist. It would be necessary, he said, to wait for some amateur to solve it."

Hapgood loved working with fresh, flexible minds. In his opening statement he discloses the advantage. "When our investigation started my students and I were amateurs together. My only advantage over them was that I had more experience in scientific investigations; their advantage over me was that they knew even less and therefore had no biases to overcome."

Although Arlington Mallery has been dead for nearly forty years, one by one his many revolutionary proclamations are being proven correct. Whether he will ever be given the proper credit for his many years of investigation remains to be seen.

I highly recommend Hapgood's "Maps of the Ancient Sea Kings" to any students of our lost history of the ancient world.

However, as mentioned, we must be careful when only one discipline has arrived at what they take as a foolproof conclusion; there is often another explanation. In this case, we quote Cyclone Covey:[52a]

> Amidst the 4-year continuing civil war in Alexandria, the longtime great mathematical genius at the Mouseion Hipparchos of Nicaea (Nicaca) in Bithynia (North Asia Minor, south of Nikomedia), in 131 BC, invented trigonometry, discovered the process of the equinoxes, and catalogued 1080 stars, among astounding achievements between 160 and 125 BC. Mapping of the Black Sea, Aegean, and Mediterranean could not have occurred (as on 13th-18th century that retained Alexandria as the base line) before Hipparchos' trigonometry notwithstanding, Mallery, Hapgood, and other grown men and women confused into believing these Alexandria-based portolani derived from the Ice Age, judging from Turkish Admiral Piri's 1513 Alexandria-based map of South America copied at the Hellesport from Amerigo Vespucci's 1501 data of pioneer eclipse-determined longitude, also his novice 1499 voyage, thus Piri's 2 equators and 2 Amazons. From Alexander and Burrow's Cave by Cyclone Covey © Covey 2004.

The above does not explain an ice-free Antarctica, however.

Viking Mettles

There was one strange story even more vague and enigmatic than that of the Kensington Stone, a story I heard from an old friend whom I met in L'Anse around 1962. He was Alf Jentoft, then president of the Lake Superior Archaeological

---

[52a] Cyclone Covey Noted Prehistorian Professor Emeritus Wake Forest University Salem, NC.

Society. This was a small but active group of interested amateurs trying to get someone to investigate some mounds at Sand Point near the town of Baraga on Keweenaw Bay.

Alf gave me a copy of a 70-page book called *Viking Mettles* written by Johan G. R. Baner, Norse and Indian scholar. It was printed in Ironwood, Michigan.

In 1930, Kendrick Kimball of the "Detroit Daily News" took a trip to see the author of the book. Some of Kimball's story from the December 28th issue of the "Detroit Daily News" is quoted here:

> Early in the eleventh century a band of Vikings, led by Vidor Viking, penetrated the Upper Peninsula and operated copper mines on Isle Royale."
>
> This surprising statement, conflicting with anything history tells, is made by Johan G. R. Baner, of Ironwood, writer, authority on Norse mythology, and antiquarian, who bases his belief on a runic inscription found in the Province of Helsingland, Sweden, and a story given him by an Indian.
>
> The inscription, which Baner has recently translated, tells of Vidor's voyage to the "big mouth" near Vinland, the Viking name for America, then a long and arduous passage up many rivers to an enormous lake, and a big island where copper was obtained.
>
> In his youth Baner took copious notes on the Helsingland rune (stone) which was found on a steep hillside near a lake. The Saga seemed fanciful, and was all but forgotten when some 40 years ago (1928) he came to America (1888).
>
> Baner lived for awhile in northern Minnesota. Then he went to Ashland, Wisconsin, where he edited a Swedish newspaper and found an Indian who talked broken Swedish and had the same name as one of Vidor's warriors mentioned in the rune. The Swedish words, the Indian said, were "magic" used by their ancestors many centuries before—men who were dressed in "ice," came from somewhere in a boat, and wore "eagles' wings" on their heads.
>
> Other evidence of a Viking visit to the Lake Superior region exists in runic inscription and an ancient weapon, obviously of Norse manufacture, discovered in Minnesota, Baner says. Both, he adds, have been authenticated by scientists.
>
> "Leif Erickson came to America in 1003, remaining a while at Martha's Vineyard or some other point along the Massachusetts coast," Baner declared. Previous Viking voyages had been made to the continent and a Norse colony on Iceland knew of the existence of the mouth of the St. Lawrence."

Johan G. Baner Circa 1930's

Vidor and 11 boon companions, among them Jarl Arnyat, set out for the St. Lawrence in Vidor's ship, which was named "Frekee," the fast-going.

It was undoubtedly smaller than the average Viking galley of the time, which was about 70 feet long. Fair weather was encountered and they made the mouth of the St. Lawrence without difficulty.

As they did not find the prophet immediately, the Vikings were forced to continue the search after they entered the St. Lawrence. They did not run into Niagara Falls, which would have been an impossible barrier, but apparently followed the Indian trade route, up the St. Lawrence to the Ottawa, up the Ottawa to the Mottawan and then into Lake Nipissing, and from this body via the French River to Georgian Bay in Lake Huron.

The early French explorers much later took this course, traveling in canoes 36-feet in length, propelled by eight paddlers. A number of portages were necessary. As the saga speaks of another ship, it must follow that Vidor and his men, unable to use their galley, constructed a smaller boat or dugout, or perhaps obtained a canoe to continue.

There is also another possibility. I believe one of the commonly used routes to Lake Superior and the north central United States was via Hudson's Bay when water levels were higher at the end of the big drain-off of that area. They could have easily traveled up the Nelson River to Lake Winnipeg and then to Lake of the Woods where they would follow the later canoe routes of the fur trade to Lake Superior from the north. Norsemen of the Viking period were renowned for exploring rivers and waterways wherever they traveled. The Norse from the western settlements of Greenland especially would have explored those waterways during their three hundred years of settlement there. While most of these people were farmers they were of the Viking spirit and owned both small boats for fishing and short excursions and larger ocean going boats with shallow drafts, capable of carrying cattle and cargo. Like the sea people of old, the Viking Norse could live aboard these during long excursions.

An even greater possibility for a water route to Lake Superior would be sailing down the east side of Hudson Bay into James Bay and on up the Albany River. One of the sources of that river is Lake Nipigon, from which they could have boated south to Lake Superior. One thing that makes this route a strong possibility is that Lake Nipigon lies close to the town of Beardmore where the Beardmore armor was found. This location can be used as evidence that Vikings did reach Lake Superior. Personally, I believe there is ample evidence that several Viking-period expeditions must have traveled in Lake Superior. When you examine the whole picture, one fact or situation gives credence to another.

The saga continues with an account of a voyage into a very big lake, heavy storms and the discovery of the island from which copper was obtained.[53] It also tells of friendly relationships with the inhabitants along the lake, a brief settlement, and the return trip with samples of the red metal. The ancient mines of Isle Royale point to this location as the source of supply.

Returning to Kimball's story; Baner:

> "One day in Ashland, about 1891, an office girl told me that an Indian was waiting to see me. I thought the matter a big joke—an Indian calling on the editor of a Swedish newspaper. An associate mentioned that there were several Indians in the vicinity with Swedish names. The name of this particular caller was Arnyat.

> "To my surprise, the Indian, who seemed to be a fairly intelligent chap, wished to take the paper. When I quizzed him he repeated some words I recognized to be corrupt forms of Swedish. He told me his people had always known them.[53a] Further questioning revealed that the words had been carefully preserved as "magic" and that they were given to his tribe many years before by white men from the east.

> "Believing I had blundered onto something of historical importance, I summoned the editor of a German newspaper and several friends for further questioning of the Indian.

> "His story left us absolutely breathless. He said he and several other Indians in the vicinity were descendants of the white men who came from the East. The men wore 'ice," which obviously was armor, and hats decorated with eagles' wings. This was a type of old Viking helmet.

---

[53] Discovering Isle Royale suggests the Beardmore route as they would have passed right by that island—with a southern route they would have missed it.

[53a] As we shall learn later, there are other possibilities of Swedish blood among Minnesota Indians.

They uttered strange words, which none of the Indians could understand, but were handed down from one generation to another as charms and instruments against evil. These were the corrupted Swedish words he had previously repeated.

"Where could the Indians have learned Swedish words except from the Vikings themselves? What other visitors to the northern section of America wore armor? As I pondered the story, I thought of the Vidor saga, obtained the notes from my trunk and found that the saga dovetailed exactly with what the Indian said."

"Baner's writings on the American Indian have been published extensively. He has gathered dozens of legends and folk tales from old men of the tribes. He writes Chippewa, Menominee, Choctaw and Arapahoe, and is an honored guest at ceremonials and pow-wows at the reservations in northern Wisconsin. The Menominees have christened him 'Inaqtik Atanaqken' or 'raven' legend bard; and the Cherokees call him 'Hatah Alepa' or 'harper of the red folk.'

"(Kimball): History records the first white visitor to northern Michigan as Etienne Brule, a French youth sent to Sault Ste. Marie by Samuel de Champlain previous to 1610. Brule was the guest of the Huron Indians and went to the Upper Peninsula to learn their language and customs. (This statement does not quite fit history, as we know it today—for a more correct version see "Superior Heartland—a Backwoods History" by C. F. Rydholm.)

"But 500 years before Brule set foot upon Michigan soil the Vikings were exploring Lake Superior," Baner concluded.

(Kendrick Kimball): In my mind there should be no doubt of their visit. One cannot dispute such evidence as the saga, and that given by a twentieth century Indian, who had no means of knowing he was supplying the concluding chapter to a story written centuries before in Sweden.

Kimball again in 1930:

The prehistoric copper mines on Isle Royale were begun 1,000 years ago or longer, believes Fred Dustin of Saginaw, archaeologist attached to the recent expedition of the University of Michigan to the Island. The object of the expedition was to learn, if possible, the identity of the original miners.

"I believe the Vikings instructed the Indians how to extract the copper from the ground," stated Baner. "It seems doubtful that the savages would recognize the value of copper without inspiration from other people. The fact that similar workings have been discovered nowhere else in the

United States seems very significant.

The Jesuit fathers of the seventeenth century found Ottawas and Chippewas of Michigan and Ontario holding the island in fear and awe. They presumed that the Indians had never ventured there to work the copper beds, but that mining had been done by a more intelligent people who disappeared without transmitting their knowledge and culture."

This was all written over three quarters of a century ago. It seems that there is little question that it could fit with what is known today except for some possible time variation.

As a footnote to Johan Baner's story, *Viking Mettles:* in the summer of 1997, my wife June and I went on a trip around Scandinavia. The purpose of the trip was to formally transfer eleven huge boxes of records of Mr. Longyear's coal mining venture in Spitzbergen (1905-1917)[54] to the Norwegen National Archives in Tromso, Norway. The records had been sent previously, but we were treated royally by the Government of Norway and took part in a great ceremony of the actual official transferring of the gift.

We had several other missions to accomplish during the trip, two of them on the eastern coast of Sweden. They concerned verifying the Baner story and identifying the carvers of the Kensington Stone.

I had sent a copy of Johan Baner's book to William R. (Andy) Anderson, who in 1962 founded the Leif Ericson Society and for 34 years was editor of a publication called "Vikingship." With his typical enthusiasm, Andy assigned these two tasks to us, sending out letters to friends for information, etc.

In one of the letters to a friend in Ann Arbor, he wrote that we would be visiting Sweden in June, "looking for evidence of the Baner fantasy and the carvers of the Kensington runestone of ill-fame but authentic. The inscriber was from Raby/Loharad, just west of Sodertalje."

He continues: "I got no help from Universities in Stockholm and Uppsala or newspapers there, so I wrote today to His Majesty Carl XVI Gustaf. (I start at the top when possible.) I told him enough to arouse his couriosity—I hope. Actually, few people have any interest in helping—obsolete books and discredited professors have little market."

We were to go to the village of Keelberg near the east cost of Sweden, where there is a vertical cliff with a base of gigantic stone blocks. On this cliff is an inscription carved in 1010 A.D. and evidently well known in 1876 when Johan Baner and a friend copied it in a notebook. They evidently found it without much difficulty, but had to climb a pine tree to see it. The message was said to

---

[54] There is a town there—Longyearbryn—named for him.

be 150 feet from the Rosta Skarning railroad bed. The inscription had survived for almost 900 years and must have survived 100 more, but no one seemed to remember it.

A second choice would be Baner's notes—so far not located. He died, leaving no children, but many friends, one of whom might have been aware of the importance of the notes.

Our other mission was to search the church records in the village of Raby/Loharad, which is located about eight miles northwest of Norrtalje. It was the home of Ulm Armlarl and a friend, who, according to Anderson, went with the expedition that traveled to Minnesota and carved the Kensington, Minnesota, runestone in 1362. The expedition probably left the area sometime around 1359 or 1360, and was of sufficient importance to be recorded in the church records. The return of these men may also have been recorded.

Before leaving for Scandinavia, we received a letter stating that the runic inscriptions were blasted away when they were building the railroad, but then Anderson pointed out that Baner read the inscription after the railroad was built.

It was on June 1st of 1997 that we headed for Lohorad, asking directions along the way. When we arrived there a young fellow who we asked for help hopped in his car and led us to a group of men who were restoring a very old house and adjoining farm buildings. They were members of the local historical society. After showing us around and telling many interesting stories, the president of the group, Perolof Johansson, a local school teacher, took us to their home and to the 11th century church (built in 1265). Unfortunately, all the records prior to 1600 had been sent to Stockholm and we were unable to locate them.

With directions to Keelberg, which was no longer in existence, we located a man who lived near its former location. We did not have time to walk the few necessary miles and then not know for sure if we were in the right place, so we made arrangements with the fellow for him to make the search later when he had time. We have never heard from him again and so failed to satisfy either of our missions. I feel it is as far as anyone has gone on these two very vague leads.

# # #

Alf Jentoft put me onto some other interesting things. For years I'd heard about cairns on Pequaming Point, right out on the north end. I went to see what was left of one some years ago, but was not impressed. Some tumbled down rock walls and some round circles of rocks were in disarray. However, Alf said the cairns had been destroyed some years before by loggers using bulldozers.

He located some pictures taken in 1906 of a few of the cairns. With these I was impressed. There were at least seven or eight of them, just up from the

The Hebbard family picnicking on Pequaming Point in 1906. Pictured L-R Maness Hebard (son of Wm) William Hebard and Manesses piano teacher. Notice 3 barrel cairns (of 6 or 7) in background.

Courtesy of Alf Jentoff

Courtesy of Alf Jentoff

Close-up of one of the cairns the gentleman in the picture is 6 ft. 4 in. tall

water. They were about five feet high and built in a ring form. The hollow in the center of each cairn was large enough for a man to stand inside. No one, up to that time, had ever come up with an explanation. In fact, their origin had faded into antiquity even in 1906, when the pictures were taken, although they tie in nicely with the story in *Viking Mettles.*

After reading the "Farfarers" by Farley Mowat (1998-Key Porter Books) where he told of a seafaring people called the "Albans" from the British Isles who sailed to Greenland and Baffin Island in fifty-foot, skin-covered vessels of the open Viking type in search of walrus (called Tuskers), we looked at the Pequaming Point stonework in a different light. Mowat describes these same types of hollow, barrel-type cairns far up in the Arctic. He calls them barrel beacons. The ones at Pequaming on Lake Superior in Keweenaw Bay are a shorter version of those in the Arctic. Lloyd Hornbostal of Rosco, Illinois, has reported similar cairns on the western shore of Lake Michigan and at Rock Lake (Lake

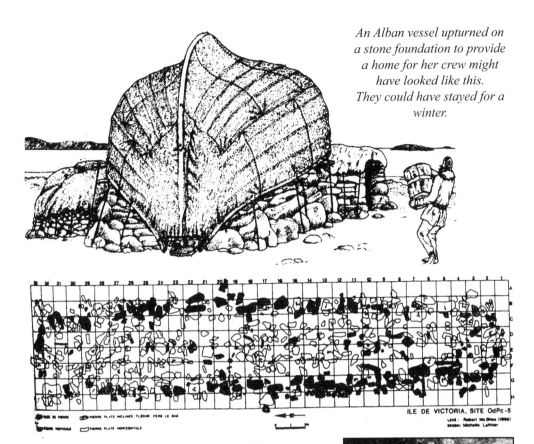

An Alban vessel upturned on a stone foundation to provide a home for her crew might have looked like this. They could have stayed for a winter.

A 50-foot vessel of 15-foot beam would have sufficed to form a roof over the foundation at Prince Patrick Sound, Victoria Island, shown here in plan above.

Drawings shown with permission of Rob Tuckerman, Warsaw, Ontario

Pictured here are members of an Ancient American study group stand on the rock foundation of an upturned ship about 85' by 15' in size.

Mills, Wisconsin). A very dramatic thing to me was a picture in Mowat's book illustrated by Rob Tuckerman of Warsaw, Ontario, of a long boat turned upside down, where seafarers lived for the winter. They would apparently excavate a living area under the boat and pile rocks to enclose it. Then when the boat was removed in the spring, the telltale jumble of rocks remained in the shape of the ship. At Pequaming, about twenty or thirty yards from the barrel beacons, which are along the shore, lies this same characteristic jumble of rocks, now in disarray, but plainly showing the shallow excavation and the shape of the ship about twelve to fifteen feet wide and 85 feet long. This could well be evidence of Albans, Norse or other early seafarers. But *Viking Mettles* is a written record of Norse in Lake Superior and according to Johan Baner, they were on Pequaming Point, Isle Royale and on the hills above Duluth.

Dr. Jim Scherz has made some exact surveys at this site and, as of this writing, will have a report available in the near future.

The Beardmore Relics

I have mentioned the Beardmore Relics and we should relate that story. All of my father's brothers and sisters were born in Marquette, but one of the brothers, my Uncle Ed, went to Canada to live. Uncle Ed had married Anna Touchette and lived the rest of his life in Port Arthur. For many years he worked for the Canadian National Railway. We lost track of his children except for one son who occasionally came for a short visit, and Ed himself who returned for a visit after the death of his wife.

It was sometime in the early 1950's that Uncle Ed came for a few days. In the course of a conversation I mentioned my interest in pre-Columbian visitors and Ed told me about a friend of his who had found some Norse armor in Canada on the north shore of Lake Superior.

I thought it strange that there was no publicity about it; it must have been a fake or a fraud of some kind. Ed assured me that this was no fake as he saw the armor himself and knew the fellow who found it. He said that all the scholars who had seen it declared it authentic. I was very curious about the story and decided to check it out. Before I could do any checking, I was reading about the "Beardmore Armor" in Hjalmar Holand's new book, *Explorations in America Before Columbus*.

Holand told about an axe found in 1880 near Cole Harbor, an indentation of Tor Bay just west of Cape Cansa in Nova Scotia. Nothing positive was ever known about that axe except Holand said it had "peculiar marks on the blade" and is a "duplicate of hundreds of similar axes in Norwegian museums from the 11th and 12th centuries."

The story of the other relics fit Uncle Ed's story perfectly. The fellow who had found it was Mr. James E. Dodd of Port Arthur, Ontario, a freight conductor on the Canadian National Railway. I didn't remember the man's name, but there was no doubt that this was Ed's friend. The book said that the items had been purchased by the Royal Ontario Museum in Toronto.

Within a few years, as I was researching a number of items, I wrote to the Royal Ontario Museum asking for the latest information on the Beardmore Armor. Within a few weeks I received a mimeographed copy of a small booklet telling the whole story. This, I am sure, is the last word on the subject and I will quote some of the important passages here:

(Booklet by A.D. Tushingham)

The Beardmore relics are either a practical joke—or a clue to one of the greatest adventures in Canadian history. Taken at face value, they tell a story 500 years older than Columbus, of a band of Viking rovers who sailed through Hudson Strait and Hudson Bay, on into northern Ontario and almost to the Lakehead.—

The Beardmore relics consist of three major objects, plus several small fragments. All are iron. The first object was obviously a sword. New, it would have been slightly more than a yard long from point to hilt end; over the centuries, however, the blade has corroded at the tip and been broken in the center. Two large portions are left, each about 15 inches long—one the hilt and upper blade, the other the lower blade—and three small fragments which may well have come from the missing central portion. Metallurgical analysis indicates that in its forging the blade was subjected to quenching and tempering. From the style and metal the sword appears to be Norse, 900 to 1,000 years old.

The second object is an axehead typical of those used in Norway during the 10th century or slightly later. Metallurgical analysis indicates that it was made of wrought iron without subsequent treatment. The absence of a hard steel cutting edge is strange, but as it was probably welded to the wrought iron body of the axehead it may have corroded or broken away completely, leaving no trace.—

The third item is a flat iron bar about 7-1/2 inches long, a little more than one inch at its greatest width and about 1/8 inch thick. The bar terminates at both ends in hooks which given an overall length of 9-1/4 inches.—The material is wrought iron, with no trace of hardening.

This piece is thought to be either a handle of a shield, which was made of wood and leather or a rangel (or rattle)—an object frequently found in Viking graves along with weapons.

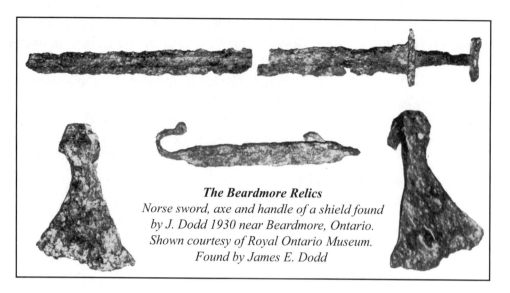

The Beardmore Relics
Norse sword, axe and handle of a shield found
by J. Dodd 1930 near Beardmore, Ontario.
Shown courtesy of Royal Ontario Museum.
Found by James E. Dodd

There is no reason to doubt the three objects—the sword, the axe, and the iron bar (whatever it may be)—are genuine. Their ages, however, apparently differ. Dr. Johannes Brondated, former director of the National Museum in Copenhagen, has suggested that the sword is an East Norwegian type made between the years 850 and 950, while the axe is later, from about 950 to 1025. In a letter to the Museum he added, "this combination: this sword together with this axe is unusual but not at all impossible. This Beardmore Viking had his own axe and his father's sword."

—The items were uncovered by a million-to-one chance in the rocky wilderness north of Lake Superior. Their name comes from the town of Beardmore, on the Canadian National Railway line east of Lake Nipigon. The actual point of discovery is said to be three miles southwest of the town, and about a quarter mile south of Blackwater River. If the story is true, we are faced with an astounding fact: that nearly 1,000 years ago a Norseman was in the region of the Upper Lakes.

—We know that the Norse were a wide-ranging group. Sailing fearlessly from the Norwegian fjords in their small but seaworthy open boats, they reached and colonized Iceland about 1,100 years ago. Some founded a settlement on the coast of Greenland around 985, and shortly afterwards Leif Erickson reached North America. Here, beginning about 1000, they tried to establish small settlements, particularly in the area they called Vinland. Some colonies may have lasted at least until early in the 12th century.

—Recent research appears to have settled the question of Vinland's location. The long-lost Vinland Map, published by Yale University Press in 1965, seems definitely to prove that the colony lay on the Atlantic coast, although in which part is not completely clear. Moreover, excavations carried out by Dr. Helge and Anne Stine Ingstad at L'Anse aux Meadows on the northern tip of Newfoundland have laid open the remains of a settlement which well may date from the 10th century.

—As for the Kensington Stone, it has been discredited by the careful investigation of Erik Wahlgren and must be regarded as a modern forgery—as it has always been considered by responsible scholars.

—The case rests ultimately on the credibility of James Edward Dodd of Port Arthur, a train man on the Canadian National Railway. Like many other people in that neighborhood, Dodd used to spend his spare time prospecting for gold. It was during one of these trips into the bush that he allegedly found the relics. When the Royal Ontario Museum bought his objects on December 3, 1936, Dodd made a statement to this effect:

"He had been sampling an exposed, nearly vertical quartz vein on a claim near Beardmore on May 24, 1931. Where the vein ran into the ground there stood a clump of birch consisting of one old tree that had died and a group of young trees sprung from the roots. To save cutting through that tangled mass, Dodd decided to use dynamite. Roots and all were blown over by the blast, and about 3-1/2 feet of overlay was dislodged, exposing rock. On the rock lay some rusty pieces of iron. Dodd was after rich metal—and threw them to one side. There they lay on the surface of the ground until 1933 when he carried them home to Port Arthur.

Eventually word of the find reached C. T. Currelly, director of the Royal Ontario Museum of Archaeology. He invited Dodd to bring the weapons to the Museum. As Dr. Currelly described the meeting some years later:

"It was obvious to me that the weapons were a set, that the axe and the sword were of the same date, which I judged to be about A.D. 1000. I asked Mr. Dodd if he had found anything else, as I knew that there should have been another piece. He said, yes, that lying over the bar of metal was something like a bowl that rusted into little fragments. He had just shoveled them out. This bit of evidence was as it should have been, and since no one unacquainted with Viking things would have known of this iron boss that covered the hand on a Viking shield, I felt, therefore, that there was no question that these things had been found as was described."

Nevertheless, Dr. Currelly asked Professor T. F. McIlwraith of the University of Toronto, an Indian archaeologist of much experience. To check the story, McIlwraith visited the site of the alleged discovery with Dodd in September of 1937. In his official report afterwards he supported Dodd's description of the physical features of the find, although dynamiting and trenching carried out in the intervening years had made it impossible check all the details. He concluded, "I believe the facts to be substantially as reported by him."

Dodd's story was supported by John Drew Jacob, who at the time of discovery was overseer in the Beardmore district for the Ontario Fish and Game Department. On December 9, 1936, he made a formal statement that he had visited the site soon after the weapons had been discovered and had seen there, imprinted in the rock, the rust stain left by the iron sword.

Six months later Jacob amplified his original statement. He explained that he had heard through an acquaintance of Dodd's find, had seen the objects in Port Arthur, had checked in reference books and identified them as Norse weapons, and had visited the site himself. In both these statements Jacob assumed the date of the discovery to be 1931, as Dodd had said. Soon afterwards, however, he checked his diary and found that he had visited the site and seen the rust impression between June 17 and June 21, 1930.

Dodd himself, apparently soon afterwards, independently revised his account to place the discovery in 1930 rather than 1931, and the earlier date is contained in a formal affidavit sworn by him on February 3, 1939. The same day, affidavits also were sworn by Walter Dodd, his foster-son ("I have read my father's affidavit, and can testify to its correctness."); by William Felthom, who said he had accompanied Dodd to the alleged discovery site about the end of May 1930 and seen the objects resting "on the banking of earth around the cabin"; and by Fletcher Gill, a railway man and Dodd's partner on the mining claims. Gill was not on hand at the time of the discovery but said he had a letter from Dodd in the summer of 1931 about finding an "old Indian cemetery."

Following this there are other affidavits of various citizens, some of which contradicted each other. A.D. Tushingham (author of the booklet):

These discrepancies would in themselves raise some doubts about the veracity of statements made by Dodd and some other witnesses. But in the absence of other evidence, the story, with some misgivings, could be accepted. There was no clear factual or testimonial evidence to disprove the essential features—that Dodd had found the Norse weapons while blasting on his mining claim and after some time had brought them to his home in Port Arthur were several people saw them. Besides:

- Why would Dodd have spoken of a "dome of rust" if he had not actually seen it?
- Why would Jacob, a reputable man well known to the Museum, have supported Dodd's claim so strongly before there was any newspaper publicity about it, if he had not actually seen the rust impression of the sword? It is difficult to believe in collusion between him and Dodd.

By such reasoning, Currelly came to believe that Dodd's story was, in fact, essentially true, and the Beardmore relics were proudly put on display in the Royal Ontario Museum.

There was little publicity for the weapons until January 27, 1938 when an article in the "Winnipeg Free Press" carried an interview with another CNR trainman, Eli Ragotte, who claimed to have discovered the rusty sword in 1928 in a pile of ashes in Dodd's basement. He gave a formal statement to that effect to the newspaper and that Dodd had made up the story of finding it on his claim. The statement contained some obvious errors.

Then there were letters degrading Dodd's honesty and insinuations that Dodd "salted" the claim. A lot of detective work followed attempting to straighten things out and at time things became heated.

During this period the weapons held a place of honor in the museum galleries and were mentioned repeatedly in many publications including textbooks as evidence that the Norse had indeed penetrated the Upper Lakes 1,000 years ago. Of course there were those who felt the museum was laying itself open to serious charges.

The Royal Ontario Museum decided to open the case in 1956 and asked the Toronto *Globe and Mail* to assign an experienced reporter to assess all the known data and look for new evidence. The first of five articles appeared on November 23, 1956, and the issue was also reported in *Maclean's* magazine in April 13, 1957.

By this time all the original players were dead except Walter Dodd, the stepson of James. He caused a sensation by making a statement that he was with his stepfather when he planted the weapons. His mother, James Dodd's widow, countered with an opinion that her foster son's second affidavit had been made—"not from any love for the truth or a guilty conscience—but simply out of spite. He disliked his adopted father, and had taken this method of revenge."

All this was 30 years later and there were statements on both sides—all of which were confusing and had inaccuracies. As far as I know, this is where the matter stands today. Tushingham:

> The weapons unquestionably are genuine Norse relics of about A.D. 1000. But did James Dodd really discover them, as he repeatedly said, under a tangled clump of birch roots on his isolated mining claim? Dr. Currelly retired in 1947, certain still that the story was true. In his autobiography, written before the later disclosures, he dismissed criticism with the comment that, "all the fuss in the newspapers came from the statements of a drunken brakeman and a cellar owner of more than doubtful honesty."

> Jacob's statement in particular about seeing the rust stains on the rock in 1930 demands special explanation. Nor are we any closer to understanding why Dodd would have carried out such a hoax. He made no direct moves to gain publicity or profit thereby, and it was only through the intervention of a Kingston school teacher, O. C. Elliott, that the Museum learned of the find at all.

> —At present the Beardmore relics lie in storage at the Royal Ontario Museum, in that particular limbo reserved for objects of uncertain history. From the evidence, circumstantial as much of it is, opinion leans toward the view that their "discovery" was a hoax. This does not deny the possibility that Norsemen did reach the central area of North America. Perhaps some day unequivocal evidence will be uncovered to support that theory. At present (early 1960's) there is none.

This is all that is known and the gist of Tushingham's report. However, at that time there were few followers of Hjalmar Holand, and Drier and others had not come up with anything conclusive that would prove otherwise. Therefore, the vast majority of the public who had any opinion at all and maybe 98% of the professionals were convinced that no one came to these shores before Columbus except the Vikings (Ingstad 1956) and that they were only temporarily camped at the northern tip of the Island of Newfoundland.

With the advent of our modern knowledge and the shedding of new light on the scoffed-at stories of the past, it all lends credence, one to another, that they have a basis of truth that can no longer be ignored.

Some of the New Light

While the establishment sticks to the standard, time-worn stories of our ancient history, there is new light shed on that dark and forgotten past every year or so. Though often ignored, it regularly appears, recorded for someone from the younger generations to discover and enlarge.

A case in point is the great breakthrough as told in a book by James A. Curran, who was the editor of *The Sault Daily Star* of Sault Ste. Marie, Canada. The book is called *Here Was Vinland.* It was published by *The Sault Daily Star* in 1939.

James A. Curran, editor of The Sault Daily Star of Sault Ste. Marie, Canada.
1865 - 1952

In my estimation, it is the most thorough explanation of the history of the Vikings in America that I have ever come across and leaves no doubt in my mind as to the location of the Norse "Vinland."

To really get to the bottom of any broad, unknown historical question, the very best anyone can do is to get the public involved. On the surface it may seem that the public is naïve and knows very little of these things. But collectively they have a vast amount of often misunderstood knowledge. If a way can be found to tap this storehouse of knowledge and collect it in one place so that it can be interpreted, it would be a far better source than all of the individual opinions of the scholars. This is really the basis for a democracy. Dr. Barry Fell[54a] collected wide input with his worldwide Epigraphic Society, as has Wayne May with his *Ancient American* Magazine. Also, many scholarly organizations are doing it across the country because they are concerned about the many flaws they see in the ancient history we are teaching in our institutions. They have chosen to take matters into their own hands.

James Curran did this with his newspaper. In a series of articles during 1937 and 1938, he asked people to come forward with their theories and their artifacts from the Great Lakes Region. Each individual find over the years had been quickly debunked by the authorities but it seemed to Curran that there were just too many of them. So each case as it came to him was thoroughly investigated. The conclusions that Curran arrived at are told in his book *Here*

[54a] Barry Fell Founder of the International Epigraphic Society is referred to in detail in this book from Chapter VII on.

Was Vinland.

From the wording of the few Sagas that describe the route to Vinland, Curran tells exactly where they traveled on their way to Vinland. While many have accepted Newfoundland, Nova Scotia and the east coast of America as Helluland, Markland and Vinland, Curran points out that one would have to travel directly south from Greenland, yet the Sagas say they traveled west.

West of Greenland leads one into the Hudson Strait, the route so many others have thought logical in more recent times. When I was in Greenland, I thought the Norse would have gone there often. It is shorter and in the direction which was always their destination. The Sagas, according to Curran, describe the Hudson Strait perfectly, the huge gorge, the birds, but mainly the treacherous currents, "whirlpools" and "abysses" caused by "violent tides" 38-½ feet high and the rock walls seldom less than 1,000 feet high. Through this chasm the water "ebbed and flowed violently." There is nothing to compare with this description down the east coast. The Sagas call this "Ginnungagap." It was through Ginnungagap that Vinland was reached.

Beyond the terrible gorge of Ginnungagap was another ocean, "the outer ocean," which we know as Hudson's Bay. Here again the Sagas describe it perfectly. The next area they passed was treeless with a huge area of flat rock which they called Hellaland (flatstone land). Then, farther on they came to an area covered with trees which they named Markland (woodland) and finally Vinland (wine land or, as is now claimed, "pasture land), the land of "self sown wheat," a great novelty for people who worked so hard to sow and harvest cattle fodder in Greenland. They had reached the great prairies, where the prairie grass grew for miles that fed the buffalo herds.

Curran proves his points a dozen ways, the description of the land, the language of the Eskimos and Indians, the regions of the polar bears, walrus and seals, the birds and the Norse relics with their wide distribution in the Great Lakes Region.

While there are two or three alternate routes to Lake Winnipeg, the usual suggestion is via the Nelson River. However, the Hayes River enters Hudson Bay only a few miles south of the four-miles-wide mouth of the Nelson, which has a long tidal bore. But the Hayes is a relatively narrow river with some lakes to pass through, a travel-way where practically every trading post was built and where the Hudson Bay Company had its forts. Thus Hayes seems a more logical Viking route to Lake Winnipeg, as this has always been a far shorter and easier river to navigate than the Nelson.

From Lake Winnipeg, the Red River would bring them to the continental divide where they could go on to the Mississippi. These waters were teeming with fish and the Norse were always fishermen. Another river, the Albany, took them

*Severe, austere thousand
foot cliffs from waters
edge so common in the
arctic.*

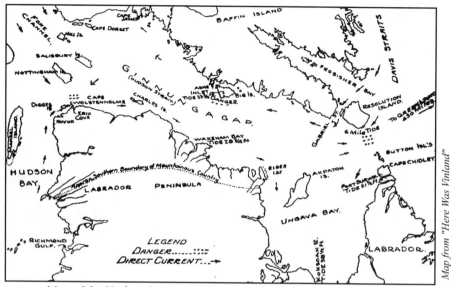

Map of the Hudson Strait - in Viking times known as "Ginnugagap"

to Lake Nipigon and from there they could enter Lake Superior. It was near this route that the Beardmore armor was found. In fact, there were far more Norse artifacts found in the Great Lakes Region than were ever found in the generally accepted Vinland of the east coast, although nearly everyone now accepts the premise that Vikings traveled there or even spent time around Newfoundland, at least temporarily. But now it seems to me that the overwhelming evidence leans toward Curran's deduction that Vinland was in the Great Lakes Region.

Among the artifacts he lists besides the collection of Beardmore relics, are the Norse axe from Batchawana Island (in Lake Superior) found in 1924; a spearhead from Gros Cap on Lake Superior (Canada) found in 1938; a socketed bronze axe found at Brantford, Ontario, found in 1907; an iron axe from Erdahl, Minnesota, found in 1893; a "Bearded" iron axe from Norway Lake, Minnesota, in 1908; the Brandon iron axe found by an early pioneer, a hatchet at Thief River Falls in 1919; a fire steel near Climax, Minnesota, found in 1971; and of course, the Kensington Runestone found in 1898. To this list we can add several more recent finds as well as the many mooring stones, the number of which grows yearly.

All the clues of Norse occupation that are discussed by Mr. Curran are too numerous to mention here. But getting back to our two main concerns: how does this connect with the copper and what happened to the Norse inhabitants? Both of these subjects will be discussed later in more detail. Briefly, Curran feels that the Norse had a lot to do with the many more skillfully made copper pieces that are found, especially the spear points that show great proficiency in design and experience in metal work. A good example of these are the spear

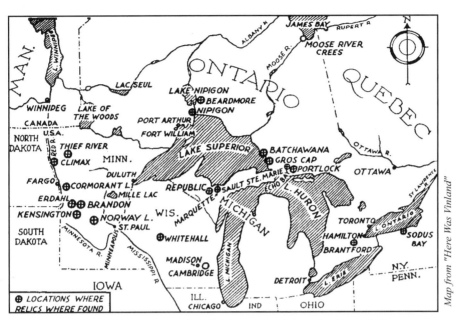

Where Norse relics have been found (cross in circle) in the Great Lakes area.

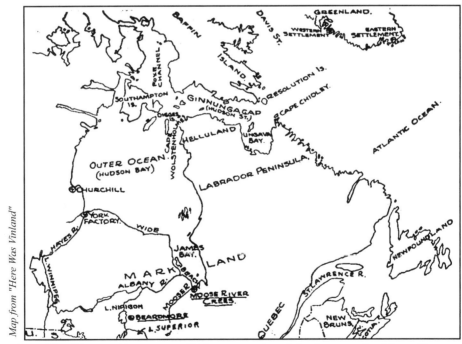

points found by Vernon Petersen of Marquette in a lake bottom in Alger County in Michigan. These were recently found at the beginning of this millennium. Curran states that no Indian tribe in America was known to have used spears, but it was a common weapon of the Norse during the Viking period.

As to the fate of the Vinland inhabitants, Curran claims there can be no

© 2001
Vernon
Peterson

doubt that the first Indians the Norse met in America were the Cree. The great bulk of the tribe formerly lived in the Lake Winnipeg area and on the adjoining prairie to the west. Since the Hudson Bay Company days (1670), the tribe has shifted a little towards Hudson Bay. At one time they lived on the banks of the Red River and were the leaders of the Algonquins against the Sioux. These are the Cree, especially those in the vicinity of the Moose River (known as the Moose Cree) who my friend Tom Wastaken (an Ojibway) says look just like white men. It seems that many Norse chose Cree wives. The Norse, who had moved out on the prairies eventually, after many generations of isolation, joined into a group we now know as the Mandan Indians, a tribe described by several early explorers as having fair skin, gray and blue eyes, many with fine blonde hair and living in completely different lifestyle than surrounding tribes, with palisade villages and homes of log construction.

The Mandans were decimated by small pox epidemics near the end of the nineteenth century. They certainly seem to fit the story of a lost population of Greenland Vikings.

It was a new idea at the time (1939) but his conclusion is being borne out more and

Two of these copper points were brought to me by a neighbor, Vernon Peterson, who works in a nearby State Police laboratory. Vernon found the copper points in a lake bottom a foot deep in sand.

My wife had been in Ireland that year and brought home a book with this similar picture but with no explanation. Obviously the same technique was used on the American pieces. I have seen the same strange tanged points in other collections, Irish pieces from Derrynananagh, Co. Galway - Celts Norse

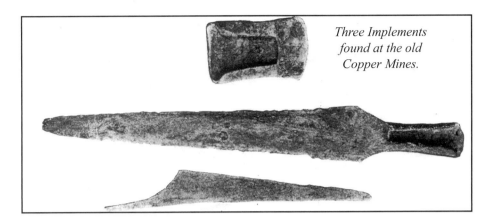

Three Implements found at the old Copper Mines.

The distinctive knife shape above and the two views below are commonly found in the Copper Country of Upper Michigan. Similar shapes have been found in Scandinavia.

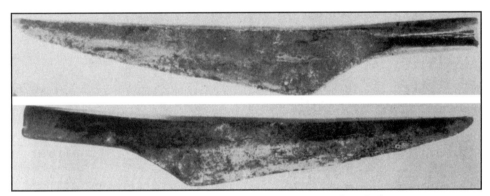

Echo Bay, Ontario, Copper Spear - Courtesy of Earl Alton

Red Rock, Ontario, on the north shore of Lake Superior - cast copper "spear" 8 1/4 in. long - Courtesy of John Stadler, Montreal

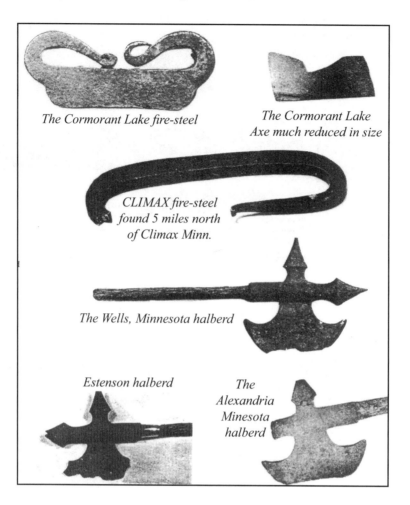

The Cormorant Lake fire-steel

*The Cormorant Lake
Axe much reduced in size*

*CLIMAX fire-steel
found 5 miles north
of Climax Minn.*

The Wells, Minnesota halberd

Estenson halberd

*The
Alexandria
Minesota
halberd*

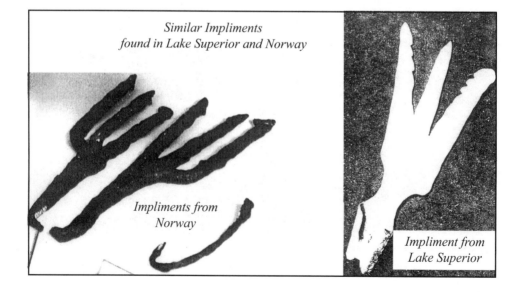

*Similar Impliments
found in Lake Superior and Norway*

*Impliments from
Norway*

*Impliment from
Lake Superior*

more in recent years. I believe that once you have read this book, you will be convinced that Vinland of the Viking period is in and around the Great Lakes, in the center of the North American continent.

How is it that such a thorough, remarkable book (*Here the Vinland*) has received so little publicity? It is my opinion that it was unfortunate timing. Germany marched into Poland that year (1939) to start World War II. This took the attention of the world for the next five years or more. To add to an already unfortunate situation, Curran had a stroke shortly after his book was published. He was confined to a wheel chair and became blind. There could be little or no follow-up. With only one inadequate printing and little publicity, Curran's great work went into obscurity.

Other 14th-century implements found in western Minnesota

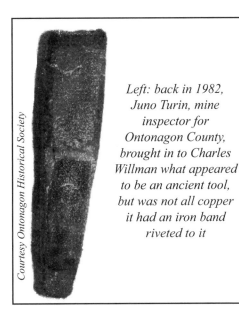

Courtesy Ontonagon Historical Society

Left: back in 1982, Juno Turin, mine inspector for Ontonagon County, brought in to Charles Willman what appeared to be an ancient tool, but was not all copper it had an iron band riveted to it

Norse Axe found in Copper Country circa 1950's

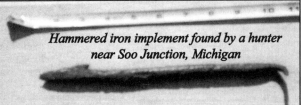

Hammered iron implement found by a hunter near Soo Junction, Michigan

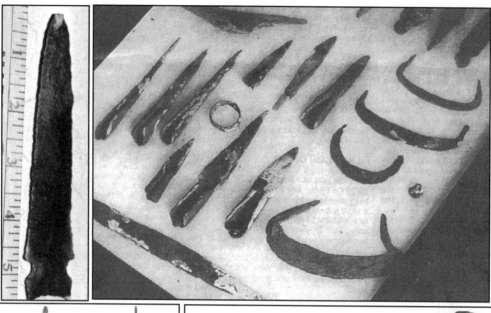

Bronze spear point from Sault St. Marie, Ont. suggested to be Viking by Wayne McKeachnic, but matches Sarsissa-heads from Macidonia & Greece in late Classical and Hellenistic Times - National Gallery of Art, Washington

Obsidion found in Marquette County by Bob Rydzewski of Trout Lake Michigan.

There have been so many styles of points found in the Lake Superior region. They represent many cultures.

Chapter VII
New Ideas Came to Life

Learning the Meaning of Joel Kela's Stone

Tread softly, white man, for the ground beneath your feet contains the relics and the bones of countless generations of people like yourself who had a civilization here ages before you came. They possessed an intellectual heritage as yet unknown to you, your ancestors destroyed this way of life before pausing to learn the wisdom built up through the ages. This is your loss; dare to disturb these poor fragments only if you seek to regain this lost knowledge.

> *Samuel William Brown, Jr.*
> *Zopathia Yuchi Tribe of Shawano*
> *(Composed at the request of Dr. Joseph B. Mahan)*

This message from Chief Brown Jr. should lead us to believe that we know very little of what went on in America before the time of Columbus. He is saying that there were many people here long before the Indian tribes as we know them.

I met and had several conversations with Chief Brown, a descendant of a long line of Yuchi chiefs. He was in Columbus, Georgia, on the occasion of the State of Georgia's returning to the Yuchi Tribe (now

Chief Brown with his daughters Dorthy and Jewel.

settled in Oklahoma) a piece of sacred ground taken from them in the 1830's when they were driven west of the Mississippi River by the U.S. Government. I also met Chief Brown's son and other members of his tribe at the same ceremony.

#

For several years, Jon and Bliss Clark invited my wife and me to their cabin on Lake Superior for a meal and lively discussions by the fire in their cozy living room.

As June and I entered the cabin one evening in the fall of 1982, Jon greeted me with his usual handful of some five or six books he wanted me to take home and read. The top book was called *Bronze Age America* and on the cover was a picture of a large stone mounted on three little stones. In the dim light where we were standing, it looked for all the world like a picture of the "mystery stone" atop Huron Mountain. For a moment I stared at the picture in wonder and disbelief.

Then I blurted out, "That's the stone on Huron Mountain!"

"What stone on Huron Mountain?" Jon asked.

By that time I was looking closer and had my wits about me. I could see that this stone was a little rounded and a slightly different shape than the one I knew.

"There is a stone almost like that on top of Huron Mountain," I said. "It looks like somebody knows something about those perched stones."

"No, this book's about copper," said Jon. "But that stone is called a 'dolmen.' They're believed to have been erected by the Celts or pre-Celtic, megalithic people of ancient Europe. I've never heard about that Huron Mountain stone."

Having that stone and copper mentioned in the same sentence made my heart skip a beat. I had wondered if there could be a connection. I had never heard the word "dolmen" in my life, but had known about the one on Huron Mountain for almost forty years. I was amazed.

That evening I told the Clarks about other strange phenomena that lacked proper explanations. One was a series of several small stone chambers reported to me each with a large stone above the entrance. Then there were some stone walls which could be natural or possibly manmade.

I thumbed through the book and found pictures of some of these stone chambers that had been described to me. Then I spotted drawings of some strange but familiar markings. The caption of one drawing said the picture was of "Ogam" writing. Immediately I thought of Joel Kela's stone from the Escanaba River.

I have had several stone chambers similar to this one described to me in the Upper Peninsula. One is in Alger County (Rock River), four in Marquette County (Escanaba River, Huron Mountain, Champion and the back of Sugar Loaf) and two in Ontanogan

County. I have been unable to locate any of them but have seen a dozen or so in the northeast United States. This picture by Malcom Pearson was taken near Bolton Massachusetts.

WINTER

SOLSTICE

SUNRISE,

21ST. DECEMBER

Calendar Site II, S.

Woodstock Vermont

© Warren Dexter

1986

Everett Davis, prospector, American Nepheline Mines, 1954.

"Some of this writing looks like the stuff on a stone found in the Escanaba River," I said.

"What stone?" Jon asked, whereupon I told the story of how Joel Kela acquired the stone and thought it runic, also how Mrs. Paul had sent copies of the stone's photograph to all the Nordic culture scholars she knew.

Jon asked me to send a copy of the photo to his winter home in Detroit as soon as possible. He also asked if I would take him to see the Huron Mountain dolmen the next day, which I did. He came with a tape measure and compass, and took measurements and alignments, something I had never thought of doing in the forty years I'd been going there. He also took pictures. Meanwhile the material in the book he lent me took on new reality.

It took me just a day or two to read Barry Fell's book, *Bronze Age America*. I became absolutely engrossed in it, studying each illustration over and over again. Here was a man who had never set foot in Michigan's Upper Peninsula, who knew little or nothing about the Copper Country, yet provided possible answers to a whole collection of mysteries I had been accumulating for years. The basis of his book was this:

At Peterborough, Ontario, in 1954, three geologists, Ernest Craig, Charles Phipps and Everitt Davis of Industrials of Canada, were examining mining claims a few miles north of Stoney Lake. While resting on an outcrop of bedrock they noticed some carving that eventually proved to be a remarkable collection of petroglyphs. Close examination by scholars concluded that the nearly one hundred prehistoric petroglyphs were ancient Indian graffiti of questionable meaning, possibly 3,500 years old (1500 to 1700 years before Christ!).

Dr. Barry Fell was an epigrapher, or translator of ancient inscriptions or extinct alphabets. He was, in 1976, the founder of the worldwide Epigraphic Society organized in almost thirty countries.

Fell claimed to have been able to lift off the more modern graffiti and read beneath the ancient Ogam[55] and Tifinagh inscriptions. The inscriptions tell of a

---

[55] Ogam and Tifinagh—two ancient forms of writing Ogam (or Ogham)—straight lines, Tifinag in dots.

© Warren Dexter

Barry Fell, OGAM Decipherer and Author of Bronze Age America.

BARRY FELL

Bronze Age America

The ancient inhabitants of N
with widely differing skull
pygmy (on the left, with pro
the right, and a common Ar
three skulls displayed by B
burials dating to the third ce

Below - rectangular form of internal plan of megalithic chamber, South Woodstock, Vermont. Photo with permission from Barry Fell - page 79 Bronze Age America

Nordic King named Woden-lithi who came from the head of the Oslo Fjord some seventeen hundred years before Christ to trade woven goods with the Algonquin Indians for ingots of copper. He left behind the inscription that records his visit, his religious beliefs, a standard of measures for cloth and cordage even an astronomical observatory for determining the Nordic calendar year. The glyphs make no claim to discovery or conquest, as the King's visit was merely one of many to prehistoric America.

I kept thinking to myself, this is just what Joe Gannon was looking for, facts far better than he had ever anticipated. He and Dr. Drier, with their scholarly attitude, had searched as many others had, looking for the slightest clue as to whom some of the ancient miners were. ***And here it was written out for them,*** not in the bottom of the ancient mines, not even near the mines, but at one of the trading places. It was all there, spelled out for them—if they could only have read it. Both Gannon and Drier were alive when the inscriptions were first located but at the time no one could decipher them. I'm sure they never heard about them as there was little or no publicity.

I looked up the definition of "Ogam" in an encyclopedia after failing to find it in several modern dictionaries. The only short reference described it as a straight line alphabet that came out of London about 200 A.D. There was a little more about it in a 1926 edition of the "Lincoln Library," for many years our family's trusted reference book:

> Ogham or Ogam (O'gam) Inscriptions. These are mostly Celtic names found on stones in Ireland, Scotland, Wales, the Shetlands, and England. A peculiar alphabet is used, consisting of straight vertical or slant lines arranged along a middle horizontal line. Different letters are represented by groups of lines, of varying number and direction. They are referred to in T. W. Rolleston's world-famous Irish lyric, "The Dead at Clonmacnoise."
>
> Tifinagh—a Libyan[55a] alphabet, apparently descended from the Old Libyan or Numidian characters (derived from the Punic cursive script) and still used by the Tuaregs." (Webster's International Dictionary, Second Edition)

These definitions are somewhat different from today's. Years later I asked Dr. Fell about the 200 A.D. date. He told me that could be true for the completed Ogam alphabet, but the first Ogam, called "Ogam consaine," was without vowels. The earliest known Ogam was found on Windmill Hill at Avebury, England. It was on an amulet similar to what is known as the Phaistos disc[56] and has been dated

---

[55a] In ancient times Libyan meant North Africa.

[56] Phaistos disc—a ceramic disc found on the island of Crete, explained later in these writings.

© Malcom Pearson

© WW Dexter

© WW Dexter

OGAM inscriptions

Left: SE Colorado - Hayes Canyon This photo was taken in 3 sections then spliced together for accuracy.

© WW Dexter

*Archaeological Photographer
Warren Dexter*

by British archaeologists at 2300 B.C. There are about 180 known ancient alphabets and only about 30 of them have been deciphered. There are also many different kinds and variations of Ogam.

Fell was not an archaeologist, an historian or an anthropologist. But his rare gift as a scholar made him all of these and more. He was a Professor Emeritus at Harvard University in the field of Marine Biology. He was also a geologist, but as far as I was concerned his greatest accomplishment was that he had opened up a whole new field of science: epigraphy, the deciphering of writings and inscriptions written in ancient or unused alphabets that, for the most part, have been lost to modern man. The ancients, in a crude sort of way, did what we might expect them to do. They told us they had explored areas and done things that we might never have thought them capable of if we had been left to our own speculation. They wanted to leave a record for future generations. Thus the Peterborough inscriptions revealed a whole era of history long suspected by people like Roy Drier, Joe Gannon, Octave DuTemple and others, because of the circumstantial evidence, but they always lacked irrefutable proof.

The whole idea of someone being able to read and date ancient marks and signs and obtain historic information first-hand about people who lived thousands of years ago was fascinating to me. Could it be that Joel Kela's stone contained a message in Ogam? If the Huron Mountain rock was a dolmen and the people who put up dolmens were Europeans, and it was also Europeans who wrote with the Ogam and Tifinagh alphabets, then it could be that this was an ancient message. Jon Clark and I both felt there could be a connection.

Up to that time, no one had ever had any luck in identifying Joel Kela's stone from the Escanaba River. There was that exchange with Dr. Cameron, but I could not believe his explanation that the sun baking clay could have caused those lines. To me they were too deliberate. I hadn't seen the picture of the stone since that time and had returned the copy to the Historical Society, so I knew it

ALPHABETS

Left: Mutwat's Tri- alphabet tablet Soweto Republic of South Africa Vowel less Ogam, Kufic Aribic and Egyptian Hieroglyphys.

Bottom left: Bi-Alphabet-Ogam (with vowels) correlated with English alphabet. National Museum, Dublin Ireland.

Bottom right: Tri-Ogam (vowel-less) alphabet type found in Burrow's Cave, Illinois

© WW Dexter

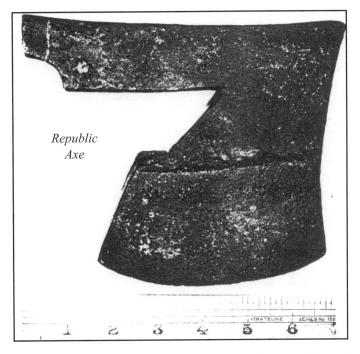

Republic Axe

was there and I could borrow it again. Many years had passed since the Cameron incident, but now I returned to the Historical Society to look again.

The staff at the society had completely changed, and no one knew what I was talking about. I had an idea that the stone itself might be there and made a thorough search through the unidentified rock drawer. It wasn't there, but I did find the famous "Republic Axe" mentioned by Hjalmar Holand in his book, an artifact found in the Michigamme River. Supposedly it had mysteriously disappeared, so I had to convince our new curator that this was indeed the "Republic Axe."

In the archaeology file, Kaye Hiebel, the curator, located the picture of Joel Kela's stone. A notation on the back of the picture said the markings were caused by salt crystals, signed by Dr. Albert Spaulding of the University of Michigan. That name I had heard many times from Mrs. Paul and had read some of his articles. Again I experienced that sinking feeling, but after studying the picture again very closely, I was convinced more than ever that the markings were manmade.

Both Dr. Cameron and Dr. Spaulding were from the University of Michigan. Both were great men in their field, and I do not mean to undermine in any way their contributions to science, but this was something they were unfamiliar with and their advanced training in archaeology had built no foundation for anything of this nature. My ideas from Gannon suggested that there was much more than we could only begin to understand. Only this attitude could lead to discovery. Who knows how much has been overlooked or discarded in the past by the experts?

I was looking at these markings from an entirely different point of view. The fact that some intelligent ancient people had dug copper here thousands of years ago has been accepted for years, but clues as to who these people were have

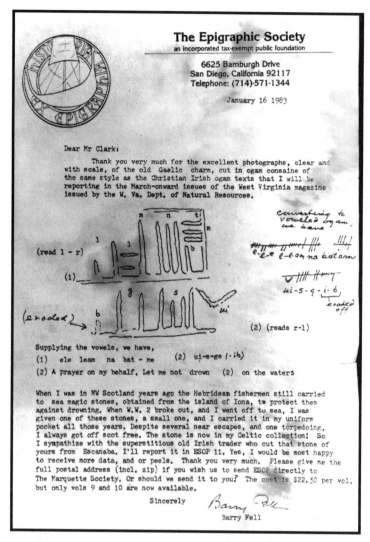

The Epigraphic Society
an incorporated tax-exempt public foundation

6625 Bamburgh Drive
San Diego, California 92117
Telephone: (714)-571-1344

January 16 1983

Dear Mr Clark:

Thank you very much for the excellent photographs, clear and with scale, of the old Gaelic charm, cut in ogam consaine of the same style as the Christian Irish ogam texts that I will be reporting in the March-onward issues of the West Virginia magazine issued by the W. Va. Dept. of Natural Resources.

Supplying the vowels, we have,

(1)   ele   leam   na   bat - me   (2) ui-a-ge (-ih)

(2) A prayer on my behalf, Let me not drown   (2) on the waters

When I was in NW Scotland years ago the Hebridean fishermen still carried to sea magic stones, obtained from the island of Iona, to protect them against drowning. When W.W. 2 broke out, and I went off to sea, I was given one of these stones, a small one, and I carried it in my uniform pocket all those years. Despite several near escapes, and one torpedoing, I always got off scot free. The stone is now in my Celtic collection! So I sympathize with the superstitious old Irish trader who cut that stone of yours from Escanaba. I'll report it in ESOP 11. Yes, I would be most happy to receive more data, and or peels. Thank you very much. Please give me the full postal address (incl. zip) if you wish us to send ESOP directly to The Marquette Society. Or should we send it to you? The cost is $22.50 per vol. but only vols 9 and 10 are now available.

Sincerely

Barry Fell

Barry Fell

been hard to discover. If they had left something linking them to Europeans, the very best anyone could hope to find was identifiable writing. Objects could be questioned, but writing was infallible.

When I was researching my family tree, I was surprised to find that very few on the Cornish side could read or write one hundred and fifty or more years ago. But the people who came here in ancient times would have had educated leaders among them, seafaring men of the world with knowledge of mathematics, geography, astronomy and navigation. They would have known many cultures and certainly many of them could read. They must also have included scribes, trained in the art of writing whatever language they spoke. Thus the dolmen, along with this writing (if it was writing) would certainly be two of my long sought clues as to who came here for copper, and from where. In other words, these may be clues to questions that had plagued me and others, since the time I was a Boy Scout on Isle Royale, where I first saw the copper pits and thought of the tremendous amount of work someone had done to get it.

So I sent the photograph of Joel Kela's stone to Jon Clark in Detroit. And almost in the return mail was a very enthusiastic reply.

"I think you've got something here," he wrote, and with some authority, having studied the Ogam illustrations in Barry Fell's book.

Jon phoned me in just a few weeks. His wife, Bliss, was on another phone and they were quite excited. Jon had received a letter from Dr. Fell, who not only said that the stone was written in the old form of Ogam, without vowels, known as Ogam Consaine, but he had actually sent a translation of it.

In Dr. Fell's letter to Jon Clark, dated January 16, 1983, he carefully drew a picture of the inscription from the rock, filling in the two or three spots on each end that were worn away. Then he gave each Ogam mark a letter meaning, and supplied the missing vowels. This gave him a message in old Gaelic, which he then translated into English.

The translated message, according to Dr. Fell, read "A prayer on my behalf, let me not drown on the waters." He explained that the stone was called a "prayer stone." Dr. Fell's letter:

> Thank you very much for the excellent photograph, clear and with scale, of the old Gaelic charm, cut in Ogam Consaine of the same style as the Christian Irish ogam texts that I will be reporting in the March onward issues of the West Virginia magazine issued by the West Virginia Department of Natural Resources.

Over half of the March 1983, magazine he mentions was devoted to these West Virginia Ogam inscriptions. The message had been found high up in the back of a shallow cave or overhang in Wyoming County, West Virginia. Fell continues:

> When I was in N.W. Scotland years ago the Hebridean fishermen still carried to sea magic stones, obtained from the island of Iona, to protect them against drowning. When World War II broke out, and I went off to sea, I was given one of these stones, a small one, and I carried it in my uniform pocket all those years. Despite several near escapes and one torpedoing, I always got off scot-free. The stone is now in my Celtic collection; so I sympathize with the superstitious old Irish Trader who cut the stone of yours from the Escanaba.

I was thrilled with the letter. We now had a few pieces of the puzzle and they seemed to fit. Joe Gannon had been dead for 19 years by then (1983) and Roy Drier for 11. I know they would have made much of this knowledge, and sent it to the proper scientists, but who would listen to me? I decided I would just have to look for more facts, building a case that someone would have to listen to.

Warren Dexter

My premise is that there were people from Europe who scoured the waterways of this continent for many centuries. Also that they could not have done so without learning about the free native copper and its source.

Despite my many years of interest in prehistory, I had never heard of a dolmen before I read Dr. Fell's book. For the next several years I tried to find out more about them. Occasionally I called Dr. Fell at his home in San Diego, California. We talked about the one I knew here in Michigan and I asked him how I could be sure that it was a dolmen. He mentioned that he would have someone come and take a look at it. He also wanted me to try to locate one in Minnesota that was pictured in his book. Eventually I was able to locate five dolmens around Lake Superior, two in Michigan, high on hilltops, one in Wisconsin, again high on a hilltop, one in Minnesota at the water's edge, and one in Canada at the top of a mountain. Prior to that I had only known of the one.

Late that summer of 1983 I had a call from a Mr. Warren Dexter. He was in Marquette and asked if he could visit with me about a dolmen. He eventually stayed with me and my wife for four days.

Warren Dexter was a soft-spoken, inquisitive gentleman from Rutland, Vermont. He told us he had come to Marquette at the suggestion of Dr. Fell. He himself was considered an expert on dolmens, having photographed well over a hundred of them in several parts of the world. But how had he become acquainted with Dr. Fell?

He said that in 1960, a woman named Betty Sincerbeaux invited Dr. Fell, at that time teaching at Harvard, to come to Vermont and investigate some strange rock structures that local people had been curious about for years. Archaeologists had said these rock structures were built by the early colonists, but the local inhabitants were not satisfied. There were large standing stones, walls and stone chambers, some with huge flat stones forming a roof. The archaeologists stated that these stone chambers were roothouses, but the locals could see that they were not built like conventional roothouses. They also knew the colonists had all they could do to build wooden cabins, some without even stone chimneys.

Dr. Fell had spent years studying ancient cultures and deciphering ancient inscriptions all over the world, especially in the British Isles, North Africa and New Zealand. He had been giving some different, controversial interpretations to many of the mysterious rock structures on the eastern seaboard, and many people wanted to hear what he had to say about those in Vermont.

Dr. Fell became so interested in what he was shown in the area that he ended up spending much time in Vermont over the next few years. Among some of the people he often worked with were the Vermont state Archaeologist Geovona Peebles, archaeologist James P. Whittall and Dr. Warren Cook, historian and archaeologist at the University of

Dr. Warren Cook

Vermont. During these years Dr. Fell had articles published by local papers and gave talks at the university and at various local group meetings. Warren Dexter attended one of Dr. Cook's lectures at the Rutland Public Library. Becoming interested, he started going along on many of the investigations and eventually became a close friend of both Dr. Cook and Barry Fell.

It was these east coast investigations that led Fell to many of the dolmens in that area.

In 1976, while still at Harvard, Barry Fell founded the Epigraphic Society and started to record his work and that of many of the Society's members in the Epigraphic Societies Occasional Papers (ESOP), published in soft cover book form. These came out at least once a year, and there have been years when there were two publications. This has continued for over 20 years and to this day.

It was also in 1976 that Fell's first controversial book, *America B.C.*, was published. Its subtitle, "Ancient Settlers in the New World" caused a great stir in established academia. Peter Tompkins, the author of *Secrets of the Great Pyramids*, wrote of it, "A stunning book…and authentic landmark destroys the premise of every previous text."

This book was followed by *Saga America* in 1979 and *Bronze Age America* in 1982.

Lessons from Warren Dexter

Warren Dexter arrived at our house in a big station wagon filled with boxes and crates of photographic equipment. Immediately he wanted to make plans to go and see things, he wanted to explore.

"We can always sit and talk," he said, "but you've got to get out and look for things. It isn't important that you don't find anything, but it is important that you keep looking."

His special project was to find the word "Baal"[57] written in Ogam. He told me it was such a simple sign, just three straight lines, two close together and the other a space away (11 1 or 1 11) that everyone of that culture could recognize. The pre-Christian Europeans wrote it on lintels, gorgets and other places as a Christian might draw a cross.

"Oh, you won't find anything like that around here," I remarked confidently.

"I already have," he said, showing me pictures of two little hand-held stones, "gorgets" he called them. He had found one in the historical museum in Ontonagon. The three lines he was looking for were there, but so insignificant and crude that you couldn't be sure if they were scratched there on purpose or

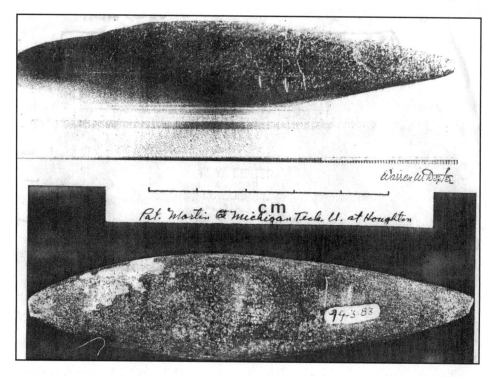

---

[57] Baal—A pre-Christian, Phoenician God—some wrote right to left and some left to right.

OGAM VOWEL LESS

Left: OGAM inscribed name of BAAL on LINTEL of Sesbrook Stone Chamber, South Woodstock, VT.

Above: OGAM, vowel less on sculptured Fallus, on top Fallus Hill, South Woodstock, VT.

Above: LARGALON STONE, (vowel less OGAM) "PRECINCTS of the Gods of the LAND BEYOND THE SUNSET".
© Warren W. Dexter 1986

Above: OGAM, Inscription, North of chamber Calendar Site II, South Woodstock, VT.

© WW Dexter

not, but he photographed the stone. A few days later he visited the Seaman Museum at Michigan Technological University and asked if they had any gorgets or prayer stones. They didn't know what he was requesting. I was unfamiliar with the term gorget also, but Warren explained that they were a stone or shell or piece of armor, notched or perforated, to be worn around the neck. The ones he was interested in were worn for religious purposes or held in the hand.

Looking around the museum he had found a gorget in a display case like the one he had photographed in Ontonagon and, sure enough, there were the three lines, the Baal sign. The people at the museum had almost covered it with paint when assigning a number to it. They could tell it was manmade by the shape and notched ring at each end, but had no name for it. Their records showed that it was found at Sault Ste. Marie.

We spent the better part of a day in the hills above Champion looking for Kurt Stone's and Al Saari's stone chamber with the big stone lintel over the entrance, but we didn't find it.

The next day we climbed Huron Mountain for a look at the dolmen, and Warren took pictures. Later we encountered scoffers who took the idea of a dolmen very lightly. When told by one chuckling fellow that, "We've always heard that the Indians put that up there," Warren grew very stern.

"That is a European dolmen, no matter who put it up there. It was put there for a very special purpose and had a very special meaning for whoever did it."

Warren showed us several hours worth of remarkable slides from all over the world, not only of dolmens in other lands but tombs, inscriptions and artifacts from Europe, Asia, Africa and South America. The demonstration left no doubt in my mind that there had been a great deal of intercontinental travel for thousands of years. He also showed us pictures of Ogam from five continents. The bickering we often hear about who came first, Leif Erickson or Columbus, seemed to me from then on like a children's squabble. It demonstrates the complete ignorance of the public about our ancient history.

Since that time (1983) my wife and I have traveled looking for dolmens. We have read and purchased many books on the subject, but only *Bronze Age America* said there were any dolmens in North America.

On the other hand, in a book called *The World of Megaliths*, by Jean-Pierre Mohen, the original edition of which was published in French, a map of the world shows where all the megaliths (big stones) are found. We have found megaliths where none are shown, but the only spot in the whole western hemisphere where Mohen shows megaliths is the country of Columbia on the northwest coast

Baal Ancient Canaaite God

Cimeron Springs, Colorado

Wyoming, U.S.

© WW Dexter

Ontario, Canada

218

of South America and on Easter Island in the Pacific Ocean west of Chile. Incidentally, there is also an appreciable amount of native copper in Columbia which was much mined in ancient times. But there was no mention of any dolmens in North America on Mohen's map or any other, to my knowledge, until Dr. Fell recognized them on the east coast. Even today many scholars do not believe real dolmens exist on the North American continent. To them they are all either glacial erratics or pranks.

Occasionally I would hear from people who seemed to have a very low opinion of Dr. Fell and I wondered how this could possibly be with his vast knowledge of ancient writing, his world-wide Epigraphic Society, his many writings and his knowledge of ancient mariners. But every once in awhile someone within earshot would belittle or attack Barry Fell. I had not known him very long, and had never met him, but I decided I had better take a second look at his credentials.

A friend of mine had an uncle who was an archaeologist at Harvard. I asked him to ask his uncle just what they thought of Barry Fell at Harvard; after all, he had a lifetime emeritus status since his teaching days there, and it was there in 1976 that he founded the Epigraphic Society that had now spread world-wide.

Within a short time I was sent copies of several pages from the archaeological journal called "Antiquity." They were copies of pages from three different issues—Vol. LIV, No. 211, July 1980; Vol. LIV, No. 212, November 1980; and Vol. LVII, No. 220, July 1983.

In the July issue of 1980, there was a review of Fell's second popular book on the subject, "Saga America." The reviewer, Marshall McKusick, went on for over a full page, but he stated his theme in just two sentences:

> (Fell's) current book has no redeeming features and in years past would have disappeared into merited oblivion without benefit of comment from *Antiquity*. Unfortunately today it provides much of the public with what they wish to read, and we may anticipate *Saga America* will achieve the international popularity of the previous book *(America B.C.)*.

In "Antiquity," No. 212 (November 1980), one paragraph from the editorial section on Fell's writing reads:

> It was not such a pleasure to visit the archaeological shelves of the main bookshops in Eastern America—the Co-op in Harvard, and Brentano's, Doubleday, Scribner's and the Strand in New York. We see in America, even more clearly than in England, the infiltration of lunatic rubbish into our serious, sensible, archaeological shelves. The good, sound, respectable books on archaeology in general, and American archaeologists in

general, and American archaeology in particular, sadly jostle with madness, folly and utter foolishness. We have often spoken about this in these columns and many have thought it was an editorial quirk. It is nothing of the kind: it is a statement of the danger that threatens archaeology, when it is becoming, very rightly, more popular and more properly understood than ever before. The danger is that the general public and the ordinary reader cannot be shown how to distinguish between carefully argued theories and established facts on one hand, and fantasy and folly on the other.

But it was the editorial of No. 220, July of 1983 of "Antiquity" that really came down the hardest on Barry Fell. It appeared about six months after Fell's third and most startling book, "Bronze Age America," came off the press. Established archaeologists of any repute then had to choose a side; many went with the establishment simply because it was the establishment, but there were others who went with Barry Fell. Most, however, sat back to watch without taking sides.

The editorial is quoted here in its entirety:

We had hoped that Professor Barry Fell had shot his bolt with 'America B.C.' and 'Saga America,' but alas, not so. Here comes 'Bronze Age America,' the third, and please God the last of these bizarre accounts of his invented past of America before Leif Erikson and Christopher Columbus: his trilogy of fairy tales for foolish fabulists. In 'America B.C.' (1976), he described roving Celtic mariners crossing the Atlantic from Iberia (Spain), establishing settlements in New England and Oklahoma, followed or accompanied by other colonists from Europe and North Africa speaking Basque, Phoenician and Libyan. Latin numerals, calendar systems, and ancient Greek astronomical knowledge were, he told us, brought to America then. This turradiddle of rubbish sold like hotcakes of apostasy, and in 1980 there appeared 'Saga America' in which we are told that pre-Columbia Europeans and North Africans crossed the Indian and Pacific Oceans as well as the Atlantic and settled in California and Nevada from the third century B.C., and that there is rich evidence of a Chinese presence, and an early Arabic presence, including (yes, believe it or not) the decorative signature of the Prophet Mohammed. The name America, according to the deluded Dr. Fell, has nothing to do with Amerigo Vespucci, but comes from a Libyan word meaning 'land across the ocean.'

So far, so bad—twice round the bend and well up to winning the lunatic stakes and the Von Danikan Cup. What fresh follies and fantasies were we to be subjected to, we wondered, as we opened the pages of 'Bronze Age America?' Had the Emeritus Professor of Biology at Harvard made it? Yes, he has. This beats all other runners from Elliot Smith to Mrs. Maltwood, John Mitchell, C.E. Joel, Alfred Watkins, Uncle Tom Cobbleigh and all. Here we are told that seventeen centuries B.C., a Nordic king called Wodin-lithi sailed across the Atlantic, reaching the neighborhood of Toronto, and established a trading colony at what is now Peterborough, leaving behind an inscription recording his visit, his religious beliefs, a standard of measure for cloth and cordage and an astronomical observatory for determining the Nordic calendar year. Flotillas of ancient Norse, Baltic and Celtic ships, he tells us, each summer set their prows to the northwest, to cross the Atlantic, to return late in the season with cargoes of raw materials furnished by the Algonquins with whom they traded.

When I am next in the Blue Bar of the Algonquin Hotel on West 44th Street in New York I will lift my glass in desperation and despair to learned professors from Elliot Smith to Barry Fell and Von Sertima who degrade scholarship and besmirch good, sound learning by their opinionated and ignorant oddities. Elliot Smith, himself, with Perry a prominent peddler of pernicious and private prehistories, once said 'The set attitude of mind of a scholar may become almost indistinguishable from a delusion: Fell is a sadly, badly, unhappily deluded man. Most readers of this journal will, fortunately, not share his delusions, or accept his flotillas of fantasies, but the commuters crowding round the bookstalls at Grand Central Station and Harvard Square will be tempted to buy the book. The title is good and a catch-collar, but it is outrageous that the publishers in England demand #10 for this fumbling farraginous charade.

This said, I am sure we could find more in the same vein written on Barry Fell. He has, with his new-found science of epigraphy, stepped on the toes of people in various fields. But how can we question a record written in stone from out of the past, if it says what Fell says it does? And if it doesn't say what he says it does, then what does it say? If there is Ogam on this side of the Atlantic, no matter what it says, those people were here! The messages and inscriptions that Barry Fell was reading have heretofore been attributed to plow scrapings on rocks, marks from sharpening arrowheads, salt crystals, and the sun. Some of it has been attributed to fraud and fakery and a few people have told me that Ogam doesn't exist.

I sent a letter to my friend from whom I received the pages of "Antiquity."

"Who are we to believe?" I asked. "I have to go with Dr. Fell, as I can find no other explanation for 40 or 50 dolmens on this side of the Atlantic, strategically placed and some of them 50, 60 and 70 tons. How do you explain away thousands of prehistoric copper mines in our area that by all estimates and scientific tests and measurements admittedly fall between 4000 B.C. and 1100 A.D., which overlaps perfectly the period known as the Bronze Age? Even if the writings don't say what Barry Fell attributes to them, how do you account for these alphabets being found on five continents?"

And as for these alphabets, at first we only had Dr. Fell to believe. He would certainly document and explain his methods of obtaining his translations, but now there is much supporting evidence coming to light and many other epigraphers are coming forward. When Fell's work was first made public, the National Geographic Society asked for an appraisal of Fell's decipherments from a British college professor. The professor stated that Fell's decipherments were not correct, but then the man was not an Ogam scholar. Since that time, many other students of Ogam in Europe and Africa are in full agreement with Dr. Fell's decipherments. Many have become members of his Epigraphic Society and contributors to its Occasional Publications, which (at that time) have been printed in one- and two-volume sets for the past 20 years (until after his death).

To give a contrasting opinion of Dr. Barry Fell, we can turn to a piece done by William R. McGlone and Phillip M. Leonard[58] in a writing called "The Epigraphic Controversy." It was reprinted in Vol. 15 (1986) ESOP ("The Epigraphic Society Occasional Papers").

> Professionally a distinguished marine biologist and geologist (having been the author of several books for the Geological Society of America), a fellow of the American Academy of Arts and Sciences (1964), a Fellow Emeritus (1980), the recipient of medals from the Royal Society of New Zealand, an Honorary Fellow of the Anthropological Society of Portugal, etc., and an Emeritus Professor of Harvard, Barry Fell has retired to full-time and very active involvement in epigraphy. He has been engaged in epigraphic research for over forty years, publishing more than one hundred and sixty papers in the field. His first, 'The Pictographic Art of the Ancient Maori of New Zealand' was published in "Man" in 1941. He is a man whose knowledge of ancient alphabets and languages is encyclopedic. Only those who have worked closely with

---

[58] McGlone and Leonard are authors of a book, *Celtic America*.

him can appreciate the rare genius he possesses in seeing the complex and often delicate relationships between symbol and language that lead to epigraphic denouement. His ability to bring together many aspects of a problem in order to gain insight leading to its solution is unequaled and, as Warren Cook (1978) said of him at the Castleton conference, 'You are a great generalist, who possesses the ability to see linkages between things that those of us who are specialists cannot see.' The manifestation of all this is a number of epigraphic breakthroughs that can be claimed for him. That list would include the following, all of special interest in the Americas:

1. Ogam Consaine—Not previously understood or readable by the Irish scholars, although it occurs in the Old World.
2. Ancient Basque—The ancient San Teima Stone of Portugal, believed to have the oldest form of Basque writing on it, was unreadable until Fell deciphered it, using (the) Cree Indian alphabet of North America, which was previously thought to have been devised in the 1840's by James Evans, a missionary in Canada. The implication of this epigraphic achievement, that the old Basque alphabet must have been brought to America in ancient times, has not been fully appreciated.
3. Ancient Libyan—Although this alphabet was known, it was Fell who first showed it could be read as an archaic dialect of Arabic language.
4. Tifinag—Norse—The realization that the famous Peterborough inscriptions in Ontario could be read using the old Norse tongue led Fell to also decipher ancient petroglyphs in Scandinavia.

Inca and Easter Island scripts as an earlier form of Micronesian script led Fell to the reading of the decorative phonic symbols on the robes of the Inca rulers.

It should be noted that some of these claims represent the ability to read for the first time Old World inscriptions by means of study of those in the New World. Fell has also published on Phaistos Disc, Minoan Linear A, and Etruscan, and although final results are not yet in, preliminary results are favorable. The scope of his work will surely surpass that of any other epigrapher in history.

A far more revealing and concise history of Barry Fell's life and work was printed in the Vol. 12, No. 4 (Winter 1999-2000) issue of "21st Century Science and Technology" magazine, P.O. Box 16285, Washington, D.C.) written by his son, Julian Fell, a zoologist with a specialty in systematics, evolution, and ecology.

This same issue contains stories of the two most famous epigraphers in the world, Jean Francois Champollion and Barry Fell.

The Champollion article, by Muriel Mirak Weissbach, was published exactly 200 years (1799-1999) after the discovery of the Rosetta Stone, an event which led to the successful deciphering of the ancient hieroglyphic script. The great scientific breakthrough came in 1822. Champollion's decipherment overturned the view held by the British that the Egyptian language existed only as a set of mystical symbols used by a cult of priests. Once these hieroglyphics could be read, it opened up a whole new field of Egyptology and the understanding of the history of the dynasties and Egypt's role in Biblical and Mediterranean areas. But now, because of the work of Barry Fell, the greatest of all epigraphers, we can get a whole new picture of the history of the world.

Although extremely difficult for the layman to understand, we can see how one of Fell's remarkable breakthroughs in the discovering the origin of the Polynesian language is illustrated in following chart.

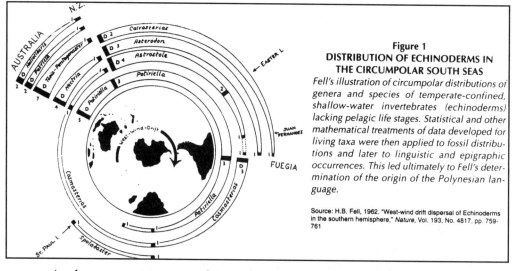

Figure 1
DISTRIBUTION OF ECHINODERMS IN THE CIRCUMPOLAR SOUTH SEAS
Fell's illustration of circumpolar distributions of genera and species of temperate-confined, shallow-water invertebrates (echinoderms) lacking pelagic life stages. Statistical and other mathematical treatments of data developed for living taxa were then applied to fossil distributions and later to linguistic and epigraphic occurrences. This led ultimately to Fell's determination of the origin of the Polynesian language.

Source: H.B. Fell, 1962. "West-wind drift dispersal of Echinoderms in the southern hemisphere," *Nature*, Vol. 193, No. 4817, pp. 759-761

And one more quote from that same article—"North American archaeologists utterly detest Barry for his works, but in the Arab world he is a hero."

Most copper region people seem to know, as it has been talked about on the shores of Lake Superior for decades, that there was much evidence of an intelligent prehistoric race who knew techniques of mining and engineering beyond that of the local Indians, and who came here and took away huge amounts of copper. In all those intervening years, no one could come up with a plausible answer as to who these people were until Barry Fell found some of the answers on the rocks at Peterborough, Newberry and from the Escanaba River. It was then that everything began to make sense. Strangely enough, none of the earlier major theories mentioned the obvious trade routes, but just as strange is that all of the theories may be partly correct, as the period of the ancient mining spread over at least five thousand years. By comparison, there has been only one hundred and fifty years of modern Keweenaw copper mining.

With our new insights on pre-history, it is now time to re-examine the great many fakes and forgeries that have popped up over so many years. Maybe the authorities are spending too much time trying to disprove their authenticity and not enough time trying to discover if they could be genuine. We may have been too willing to accept the snap judgments of a few "experts" and failed to investigate each case thoroughly. It seems that, with all the new, modern methods of detection, someone should take a second look at some of these old "frauds."

Meeting Dr. Fell and Learning About Some Early Inscriptions

Ever since I had been able to make connections between so many local enigmas that were so vague and misunderstood, I wanted to meet Dr. Barry Fell, the only man I had ever heard of who seemed to have a handle on these things. These were things I had wondered about for years and now they were coming into focus.

Jon Clark paved the way by introducing me to Dr. Fell by phone. I soon felt comfortable talking with him and he seemed very interested in what I had to say. I was surprised that he knew so little about Michigan's Copper Country and yet his book, *Bronze Age America,* was about that copper. He had never been there but had read about it on the rocks at Peterborough. It was over the phone that I told him about the amount of pure copper here. He was surprised that it could still be found quite easily. He did not seem to be aware of the full extent of the ancient mining or that it was still possible to find float copper near the surface. He asked if I could possibly send him some copper samples.

There were two dentists, both acquaintances of mine, who had done skin diving in the Keweenaw and picked up a lot of copper in Lake Superior. They offered me the pick of half a pail, hundreds of small pieces. This was smooth, washed copper. I sent several pieces that weighed less than a pound apiece to Fell. He also asked if I could get him a copy of the book by Roy Drier and Octave DuTemple. I had lost or lent out my first copy but had purchased a second that I refused to lend out. However, I called a friend of mine in Houghton, and he was able to get the last ten available copies from Mrs. Drier (Roy had died about ten years earlier). Dr. Fell was absolutely thrilled with the books and the pieces of copper I sent him. He called me about them and wrote several letters.

Photo by Kim Rydholm

Dr. Barry Fell and Author Fred Rydholm conferring in SanDiego, California.

I had so much I wanted to talk with Dr. Fell about that I wanted to meet him face to face. Very few people around here could grasp what I was talking about, and I did not feel confident in what I was saying. The only authority I could direct my listeners to was Barry Fell and I was getting pointed questions as to just who and what he was, and what kind of reputation he had.

I began to realize that there was just too much to explain in a short time, especially to people who had little or no background for what I was trying to tell them. I had done it many times, using slides, answering questions of reporters as best I could, but no articles ever appeared, except for one in the L'Anse Sentinel, which was fairly accurate. I was taped, both audio and video, and interviewed by newspapers, radio and television stations, but nothing was ever aired. My stories were just too bizarre and unconventional. At the same time, our newspapers were carrying articles about St. Brendan, the Ogam writings in West Virginia, and a front-page quip headed, "Were the Irish in America Before Columbus?" that came off the wire. I'm sure the editors didn't understand what they had printed, nor that there was a real story right here.

In the spring of 1984, I flew to California to visit our older son, Kim, and I took this as a golden opportunity to visit Dr. Fell in the same trip, as he was lecturing on a semi-retired basis at the University of San Diego.

Kim and I rented a car and drove down to see him, announcing our plans a few days ahead of time, and receiving a cordial invitation.

We were not the only visitors that day as at least three other parties from Berkeley, California, had also arrived, including Dr. George Carter, a well-known archaeologist formerly of Southern Methodist and now retired Professor Emeritus of the University of California at Berkeley.

There is just not time nor space to go into all the things we discussed but, in short, I was very impressed with the vast knowledge of Dr. Fell. He is not the only man in the world who has tackled so many of these ancient alphabets, but while several have mastered one or two, he is the only one who has translated works in 26.

During our visit he gave me copies of his two other books, *Saga America* and *America BC,*

Dr. George Carter and Dr. Barry Fell in SanDiego , California. Picture by Kim Rydholm.

and signed them both. My other son, Dan, had given me *Bronze Age America* for a Christmas present in 1982, and I had it along. Dr. Fell signed that one also. Before we left, he rolled out a 32-foot long, 30-inch wide latex mold that he had received from West Virginia, and told us its story. This was the latex that had been sprayed on the inscription in Wyoming County, written up in *Wonderful West Virginia* magazine that year.

Some years later, through a close friend, Tom Edgar, who lives in West Virginia, I was able to get the rest of the petroglyphs story. Also from some interested people I met in Washington, D.C., I was able to get remarkably clear pictures of the site.

The significant thing about this story is that these petroglyphs have been known for decades. The early explanation for these marks by scholars, historians and archaeologists alike, was that these strange lines in the rock, high up in a cave-like overhang, were made by Indians sharpening axes and arrowheads. This is still believed by some today.

But sometime in the late 1960's or 70's a man named David (Bugs) Stover who, like myself, was a local teacher who had become known as the local historian, was not satisfied with these "official" explanations. They seemed to him to be just too orderly. He wrote to the Raleigh Register-Herald, the local newspaper, arguing that the marks were just too complex not to say something. This is exactly what I thought when I first laid eyes on Joel Kela's Escanaba River stone.

It so happened that the "historian" for the paper read the article and called

Robert L. Pyle

Stover. Her daughter, Ida Jane Gallagher, worked with Barry Fell, then retired from teaching at Harvard and considered an expert on Celtic connections to the Americas. He had just written his book, *America BC,* on just those connections.

There were also archaeologists such as Robert L. Pyle of Morgantown, West Virginia, who, like Bugs Stover, believed the cliff markings to be some type of ancient writing. He, like Joel Kela, thought that they resembled Runic or Norse writing. He assessed the age at between 500 and 1000 A.D., or about one thousand years earlier than it had been assessed in an earlier government survey of the site. There had been talk of Norse explorers from Hjalmar Holand's and Arlington Mallery's books, but few had ever heard of Irish or Celtic writing.

As soon as possible, Gallagher contacted Dr. Fell in San Diego and he agreed to look at the inscription. Meanwhile, photographer Arnout J. F. Hyde, Jr., sent some clear photographs including some tracings that he and Gallagher had made. Fell's enthusiasm matched Gallagher's as soon as he saw the material and he immediately identified the script as Celtic Ogam, for it is one of the ancient scripts that he encountered regularly on American stone carvings.

The story Dr. Fell told me that day was that Ida Jane Gallagher had sent a drawing of the first part of the glyphs to him in San Diego. He roughly translated it, something to the effect that on Christmas Day, or during the winter solstice, the sun would shine through a notch and light up the message. Someone had called him to say that there was a notch in the mountain across the way but that the sun would never rise there.

Fell answered, "I don't know the situation there at all, but just go there on Christmas day and see what happens."

There were times when people were

Ida Jane Gallagher

© WW Dexter

228

*The Wyoming County
Petroglyphs
in West Virginia.*

*Pictures by
Mrs. J.H. Jones*

PREHISTORIC
PETROGLYPHS

Nearby are ancient rock
carvings of unknown age
or purpose. Some think
early Celtic explorers
carved them. Others be-
lieve Native Americans
more likely carved them
prior to 1000 AD.

WEST VIRGINIA DIVISION OF CULTURE & HISTORY

*Chalked in close-up of
one of the petroglyphs*

there during the winter solstice when it was cloudy and nothing happened but eventually Ida Gallagher and a group watched the sun rise, shining through a notch on the side of the cave, beaming creeping light across the whole message.

From the March 1983 edition of *Wonderful West Virginia* we follow Mrs. Gallagher's story as written by Arnout Hyde, Jr.:

> The sun figure on the petroglyph and the southeasterly orientation of the site made Gallagher wonder if the winter solstice sunrise might be observed from the rock shelter. The winter solstice occurs on the shortest day of the year, December 21-22. Ancient sun-worshipping people held important winter festivals on this day. As the days grew shorter, they feared that the disappearing sun would leave them to die. They appeased the sun god by making blood sacrifices, building huge bonfires and practicing other superstitious rites. As the days lengthened they celebrated the sun god's return.

Later, when Fell received the latex mould of the inscription, he was able to translate the Celtic Ogam into Old Irish or Gaelic. Next he translated the Old Irish into English.

According to Fell, the Wyoming County Petroglyph bears this astounding message:

> At the time of sunrise a ray grazes the notch on the left side on Christmas Day, a feast-day of the church, the first season of the (Christian) year. The season of the Blessed Advent of the Savior, Lord Christ (Salvatoris Domini Christi) Behold he is born of Mary, a woman.

This is not the only Ogam message found in West Virginia. There is another site in Boone County which Barry Fell says may be the longest stone-carved Ogam message in the world. It is called the Horse Creek inscription.

Full details of all the circumstances surrounding both of these sites, as well as each step of the translation by Dr. Fell, can be read in the March, 1983 issue of the *Wonderful West Virginia* magazine.

The Horse Creek inscription is also a Christian message. Dr. Fell's translation of the three-lined message is as follows:

> A happy season is Christmas, a time of joy and goodwill to all peoples.
> A virgin was with child: God ordained her to conceive and be fruitful. Ah, Behold, a miracle!

She gave birth to a son in a cave. The name of the cave was The Cave of Bethlehem. His foster father gave him the name Jesus, the Christ, Alpha and Omega. Festival season of prayer.

The inscription is overlaid with messages in other scripts, most likely done at later times, just as on the Peterborough inscriptions. Except here, one is in old Libyan script and says, "The right hand of God." There is also a short message in Algonquin which Dr. Fell says is a script taken from the Basques. Indeed, many Basque and Algonquin signs are very similar, some even identical.

Gaining Confidence

After my day with Dr. Fell and Dr. Carter, I became quite engrossed in our pre-history. I was amazed how little I knew about it and how much had been left out of our conventional education. I was invited to attend Epigraphic Society meetings in different cities across the country and became acquainted with the Epigraphic Occasional Papers. One or two volumes had been printed each year since the organization's inception in 1976. I purchased the current volumes and gradually acquired the back issues. Since then I have managed to build up a sizable library of books on ancient history, megalithic structures and pre-Columbian contacts with the Americas.

At Dr. Fell's urging, I joined the Epigraphic Society, and through that connection joined and became active in other organizations of similar aims. They opened a whole new, little known field of knowledge to me, as through them I was able to meet many people of specialized interests and expertise.

The first annual meeting I attended was in San Francisco, where I was able to add to group discussions with information about the Copper Country—a story which seemed new to many.

The first meeting where I gave a talk was in Albuquerque, New Mexico. At this meeting I spent a lot of time with Barry Fell and Henriette Mertz and met many people whose names I had become familiar. It was at this meeting that I was challenged by a group of young men who turned out to be archaeologists.

Three of their charges stuck out in my mind. First, they argued that there was not as much Copper Country copper as I claimed, nor was it as easy to find. They thought my story was exaggerated. Next, they insisted that dolmens in America were glacial erratics and not the same as those in Europe. Finally, they claimed that the Hopewells used tremendous amounts of copper.

"Where is it?" I questioned.

They answered, "They made tools, weapons, ornaments and breastplates with it."

"Breastplates!?" I exclaimed with alarm.

"Yes, breastplates," they answered with great authority.

"Well, if that is so, I stand corrected," I said timidly. "I've never read much about the Hopewells. Where can I see some of this copper?"

"If you want to see copper," explained one of the men, "just go to the Field Museum of Natural History in Chicago, you'll see copper!"

I had been to the Field Museum many times but had never seen any copper there. But apparently feeling a bit inadequate in my knowledge of the subject, I backed down and even retreated somewhat. Nevertheless I went directly to Chicago from that meeting, expecting to see a whole wing of the building devoted to Hopewell copper.

Hopwell Ohio

Following directions at the museum to a basement room where I had never been before, I walked up to a glass showcase containing what looked like 40 or 50 very small pieces of copper. I asked an attendant if I could see the Hopewell copper collection.

"This is it," he declared.

I stood with a blank stare. "I was told there were breastplates and many items of copper," I said.

"That's a breastplate right there," affirmed the man, pointing out a little bar of copper not much bigger than a fat cigar. To me it looked like one of Warren Dexter's gorgets.

To myself I muttered quietly, "I've got more copper on the hearth in my living room than they have here."

There was a bust of a man wearing a head ornament of antlers which seemed to be the largest piece of copper they had, but on close examination the antlers were made of wood covered with very thin leaf or sheet copper. I realized then that those young gentlemen at the meeting had no idea of the amounts of copper I had in mind. I was convinced they were wrong on all counts, and by then I had seen several instances in which the "experts" had been dead wrong. It also gave me great confidence that many such experts obviously had a lot to learn. Since then I have concentrated my interests on dolmens, the amounts of copper yet to be located in ancient societies and whether Copper Country copper could have gone overseas. Since then my wife and I have taken many trips with these mysteries in mind.

Meeting Russell Burrows and Jack Ward

Jack Ward

It was at a meeting of the ISAC organization (Institute for the Study of American Cultures) during the summer of 1988 being held in Columbus, Georgia, that I first met a fellow named Russell Burrows. I just happened to be sitting next to him during one of the sessions (see *The Mystery Cave of Many Faces* by Burrows and Rydholm 1992).

I had trouble concentrating on what speakers were saying as I was suffering from the heat, but I also was annoyed by the behavior of the audience toward one elderly presenter. The gentleman was Jack Ward from Vincennes, Indiana. He was telling a rather wild story of immigrants from the Mediterranean area who had settled along the Wabash River about 2,000 years ago. He was basing his account on artifacts brought to him by farmers around Vincennes, Indiana, an old and historic city on the Wabash River.

I discovered later that Jack was a retired stone, gravel and sand salesman. In the course of his work he learned much about the geology of his area.

Jack had been a fairly active and well-known community leader in his day and as such was chosen to put together a small museum as a part of the upcoming celebration of the 1976 United States Bicentennial. He had been chosen to head up a committee by the Old Northwest Corporation, which had acquired property with a small dwelling suitable for a museum. The company named an Indian mound there and their museum after their own patriot Indian, Francois Son of Tobacco, who was called "Sonoftobac." Over the next few years the displays grew rapidly, as many farmers from the area brought in their finds of arrowheads and other artifacts.

As Jack studied the stones at the museum, he noticed that some were so definitely not Indian that he began to separate the artifacts into two groups, Indian and non-Indian.

233

About this time Jack acquired Barry Fell's *America B.C.* and noticed that some of his museum stones bore inscriptions similar to those in Fell's book. He copied some of the inscriptions and sent them to Dr. Fell. These turned out to be Numidian (upper Egypt) and Libyan; the symbols were from ancient North Africa, Europe and the Mediterranean.

It was from these circumstances that Jack Ward pieced together two stories, both of which he put side by side in a book called *Ancient Archives Among the Cornstalks.* One was his story of discovery, the other a fiction based on his findings of what life may have been for ancient visitors to America. It was this story he told at the meeting, and it certainly was not met with much enthusiasm.

About the time his book came out, Jack discovered another collection of inscribed stones at an antique shop in Olney, Illinois, about 60 miles from Vincennes. The collection he saw there was far superior to the one in his Sonoftobac museum. He learned that the stones were being brought in by a "caver" (cave explorer) who was hoping to find someone who could tell him something about them. The caver was Russell Burrows from Olney, Illinois. The two were put in touch with each other.

Thus it developed that the speaker who followed Jack Ward at the ISAC meeting was the fellow who had been sitting next to me, Russell Burrows. He told his side of the story and, again, I was amazed and embarrassed by the reception he received. It was obvious that very few of those assembled believed what these men had to say. Later I learned that both men had attended the ISAC meeting the previous year with their story, and that this was part of the reason they were treated so shabbily. Those who had heard their story before were apparently appalled by the tenacity of these two to come and repeat such an unbelievable yarn.

But I was hearing it for the first time and without making any quick judgment, I wanted to hear more. Here were two men who with no apparent previous contact had arrived at the same conclusions about a prehistoric European Midwestern presence. The story was too good to have been made up independently. Who, with an outright lie, would come to such a meeting, several states away, twice!? The one aspect of the story that intrigued me was the fact that Jack Ward believed these people came to America in search of copper.

In his book and in his talks, he described how these Mediterranean people sent teams of workmen up to the alluvial gravel beds of the southern extremity of the glacier, a region teeming with copper nuggets. These were then rafted down the great Mississippi River systems to Poverty Point, now in Louisiana. Here, Jack said, was a spot where there was an inexplicable large half circle of pieces of copper. To him it was obvious that it was a storage place where copper was

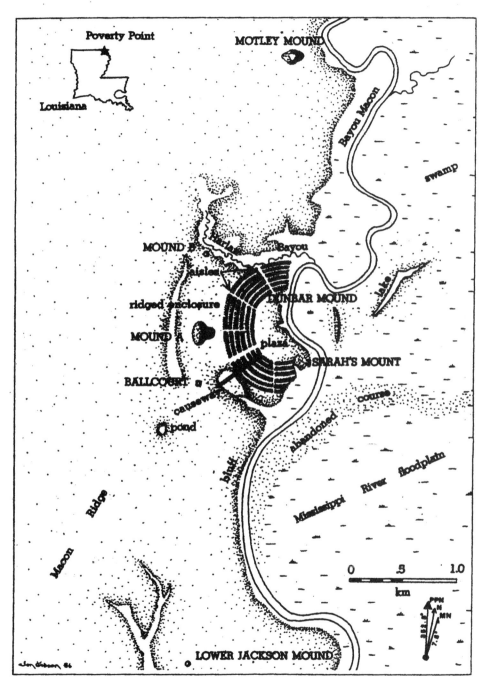

The Poverty Point Earthworks
Drawing by Jon Gibson

unloaded and the half circle was the remains of a large stockpile of bits of copper, half of which had been eroded away by the wash of the river over many centuries.

This all made sense to me, even though the whole idea was openly scoffed at by the majority of those present. After a private conversation with both Jack and Russell, I was invited to come to Vincennes to see for myself what had allegedly come from a cave Russell had discovered.

There were a few people among those at the meeting who had been to Vincennes and were open-minded about the story. One was my friend, Warren Dexter, who had photographed some of the Burrows Cave stones and another was a woman from New York

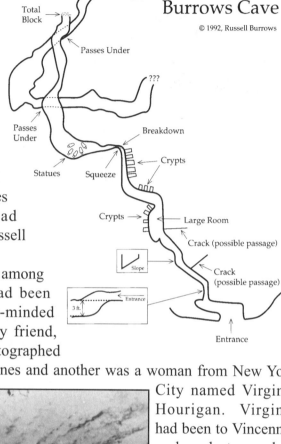

Burrows Cave

© 1992, Russell Burrows

City named Virginia Hourigan. Virginia had been to Vincennes and photographed several thousands of the cave stones. She generously sent the pictures out in a large package to anyone at the meeting who wished to study them for a few weeks. Then whoever got them was supposed to pack them up and send them on to the next person on the list. The photos were well done, very sharp

Russell Burrows in a bogus cave in Illinois.

Sketch of one of Russell's favorite pieces from Burrow's Cave site.

and of good color, all sorted into bundles of 20 or so.

Nearly everyone who took the time to go through the pictures was astounded by them. Most were openly skeptical and I couldn't blame them. Meanwhile, however, believers in their prehistoric authenticity thought it strange that in the four years since the cave was discovered there had been no publicity. Also, apparently only Burrows, its discoverer, knew exactly where it was. Thus many thought there was something very fishy about it all, that it had to be a clever hoax, a fake. When I showed the pictures to friends, they would ask me, "How much did these cost you?" "Who's making the money on this?" "Why are you being so gullible?"

The full cast of characters June 1987 - Left to right: Russell Burrows, Warren Cook, Jack Ward, Norman Cullen, Virginia Hourigan, and Warren Dexter, Vincennes, Indiana

I had no answers for any of their questions. I just wanted to find out more. I wanted to get to the bottom of it.

That fall I drove to Chicago where I met my friend, Jon Clark, the lawyer who had flown in from Detroit. Together we drove to Vincennes where we were met by Jack Ward and Russell Burrows, who invited us to view some of the artifacts that had been collected from Russell's cave.

I was absolutely astonished at what I saw. Jack Ward had two side by side rental homes on Fourth Street in Vincennes. One had been vacated in order to display the cave artifacts. You were only allowed to see them by appointment, yet there was no charge. There were at least three rooms full of items, plus more stuff in boxes or on the floor in a fourth room. I was told there were about 4,000 items in that house and another collection of about 1,000 that belonged to Mrs. Thelma McClain, an antique dealer in Olney.

Most of the artifacts were small enough to be held in one hand, but there were also a few large stones two and three feet across as well as some very tiny ones. I was much impressed by some very small, intricately carved cylinders of an obviously very hard, pinkish stone that Jack explained were roller seals, like a coded stamp that could be used for identification on sealing wax. There were several different sizes of these. A good number of the stones had faces and figures carved on them.

While many of the figures seemed to wear Indian headdresses, some wore armor and others resembled what I

© Warren Dexter

Some distinctly diverse pieces of rock art from Burrows Cave

thought of as Roman, Greek and Egyptian faces. There was just no question that if these carved stones were real—and I had no reason to doubt them with such an array—then the people who carved them would have come from the Mediterranean region. They would have come by boat, and they were familiar with the sea. Carvings included ships and whales, dolphins and camels. One large piece, delicately done in fine, faint lines, was a lion's head. It was a gray-blue stone that had a flat, broken bottom, perhaps six or seven inches across.

This upper stone has the Little Dipper above what looks like a reed boat and the Egypt hieroglyphic sign for water beneath. The boat is traveling west. All of these are from Burrows Cave.

I asked Russell about this particular stone and was told that one room in the cave contained several large, life-size statues, one of which had been broken, possibly by an earthquake, and that this was the top of the headpiece of that statue.

After a careful examination of nearly every piece on display I was thoroughly convinced that they had to be the product of many hands over a period of many years. There was no way a few people could have done all that work, all that artistry, or have that much knowledge or imagination in this day and age. If they were faked, they were faked many years ago and over a long period of time.

Not many had seen the collection as I had but, again, many of those who hadn't seen it, made up their minds almost immediately, that the whole cave story was one large hoax.

A lot of these people were followers of Dr. Fell and took heed of his advice. He had already published his first reaction to pictures he had seen of the cave artifacts, some of Virginia Hourigan's pictures, in ESOP 16 (1987). Dr. Fell's statement:

> Indications of another series of fraudulent inscribed tablets are coming from Illinois at this time. Of several hundred

Cuenca elephant tablet declared a fake by Dr. Fell.

Elephant Stela owned by Paul Chessman Crespi Collection Cuenca Ecuador.

photographs so far examined, some show objects that carry a jumble of letters of several ancient alphabets, making no readable words, and mixed together is a mélange that cannot be a real language or writing system. Most striking is an imitation of the Cuenca elephant tablet from the excavation at the airport of that Ecuadorian city. In 1976 an incorrect copy was accidentally used on the cover of ESOP, Vol, 3, Part 2. A corrected version was later published, both drawings by Fell. Ironically the Illinois forger chose the wrong illustration to copy, and thus the newly 'excavated' tablet is the 1976 version, with a misshapen 'ya' symbol, and copyrighted by the Society. Thus the ludicrous situation arises that the 'antique' from Illinois has infringed the registered copyright of a drawing first published in 1976.

I have long ago learned that one opinion, no matter whose, or one set of proofs is not enough. There are two sides to every story. The whole picture must be studied from many aspects to arrive at the proper conclusion. My opinion would be neutral until the whole story had an explanation that it was either true or false. Neither had been proven to me yet.

240

The Story Needs a Book

Between 1988, when I first met Jack Ward and Russell Burrows, and 1992, when a book was published, the three of us had several meetings, attended some symposiums and were in constant contact by letter and phone. Russell was getting a lot of bad publicity from all quarters and his reaction to it all was making things worse.

Every time I heard Russell speak you could almost tell he was getting tired of telling his story. But each time he told a little more, about the crypts he entered, the grand tomb with a stone sarcophagus and gold coffin, the statuary, the amphorae filled with scrolls, etc. Sometimes he didn't know where to start and would instruct the audience to ask questions which he would answer.

I told Russell that it was impossible to tell the story of his cave in just 20 minutes or a half-hour. There was too much to tell. I told him slides would help, but he needed to write a book.

Soon Russell was bringing in a stack of stapled papers. It was his book—mimeographed typing paper, 29 pages long.

After reading it, I could see that some things were over-explained while many important things were just mentioned or completely left out. The events were out of order and you could detect his frustration and paranoia throughout its contents.

I told him. "This book you've written just doesn't do it." Now I'm not a good writer by any standards, but I have written a few successful books with great effort and much time. I felt I knew and could tell Russell's story better than he could, as I had heard it many times, so I offered to write it for him. As fantastic as the story was, I had seen and handled over 4,000 stones from the cave. Whether the stories connected with it were true or not, there had to be a repository of some kind where these remarkable stones were coming from, and Russell had the only explanation.

Among the hundreds of doubters were some outstanding believers. Probably the greatest among them was the great Dr. Cyclone Covey. He never questioned that people had been traveling the seas for thousands of years, and he had such a background of prehistoric and especially pre-Columbian information that few would dare to openly challenge him; maybe to his back, yes, but never to his face.

Joe Mahan, founder of the ISAC organization, was also a strong believer, but with a different explanation. Then there were several who discovered answers for their questions on the stones from the cave.

One young, brilliant epigrapher named Paul Schaffranke was able to recognize writing in the Etruscan alphabet among the stones. He discovered

Paul Schaffranke, epigrapher, who claims some of the Etruscan writing in Burrows Cave translates into street Latin that was used in Rome at the time of Christ.

that it could be translated into street Latin of Roman times. His partner, Harry Hubbard, was convinced the body in the "royal" tomb was that of none other than Alexander the Great, whose tomb has never been found. A lone Jewish scholar from Syosset, New York, Zena Halpern, has found several connections between the cave and her research. She has gone into a lengthy study of the many Semitic influences found in ancient sites in America. Her book of great depth into this subject is being written simultaneously with this one.

The person who got into the cave stones probably more than anybody was Dr. James Scherz, then of the University of Wisconsin in Madison. His great interest in archaeo-astronomy, ancient structures, and his detailed study of effigy mounds resulted in a great interest in the cave. He became a close associate of Russell. Jim Scherz, Virginia Haurigan and I were among the first, and maybe longest lasting, of the Burrow's Cave Executive Committee, but there were many others over the years.

Since its discovery in 1982, Russell had shown no one the location of the actual cave. He brought several, including myself, to a bogus site, but he trusted no one, not even his closest associates to explore his find.

At some of the organization meetings we attended, some members were outright hostile. At the last ISAC meeting we attended together in Columbus, Georgia, a long-time, respected member of the Society, Paul Chapman, author

Russel Burrows, Virginia Haurigan and Fred Rydholm

of several books on Columbus, stood before the group and objected that Russell was an out-and-out liar, and that I, who had written the book, was never in the cave. I wanted to say, "You wrote two books about Columbus, but have never met him." But both of us held our tongues and took the criticism with stoical good grace. I know this was far more difficult for Russell than it was for me, as Russell was quick to take offense with any criticism.

We had had some public cave committee meetings here in Marquette, and I wrote a few articles in a monthly paper to keep my friends and the locals updated as to the developments as they happened. But with no source but me in the area, most people felt that I was riding on cloud nine, and as the stories became more unbelievable with no solid proof, many encouraged me to get over it, forget about it. But to me there were always the stones. Dr. Fell was especially upset with me. The first time he mentioned the cave on the phone his question was, "You aren't one of them, are you?" In several later phone conversations he told me to disassociate myself from the cave—"Just back off, they're a bunch of crooks."

My only answer was that I had to know where the stones were coming from; I wanted to see for myself. While many of the stories were unbelievable,[59] the many stones had no explanation and the only really distasteful thing about the situation was that Russell was selling the stones, in a sense, looting the

---

[59] See *Mystery Cave of Many Faces* by Burrows & Rydholm.

Mr. Beverley Moseley and Dr.. John White leaders in the Midwestern Epigraphic Society in Columbus, Ohio.

cave. His logic for these actions was that the laws protecting these things were not enacted in Illinois until 1992 and, further, the authorities, including the state archaeologist, denied the cave even existed, claiming the artifacts were fake.

It was easy to see Russell's side of the story. It was his discovery and he was putting his full-time effort into cave exploration. After being rebuked by the authorities on many occasions, he chose to ignore them. When he found that people would pay good money for his stones, of which there seemed to be an almost limitless supply, he began to sell them. Among the early, large collections that were purchased, besides those of Jack Ward and Mrs. McClain, was about 700 stones sold to Dr. Joe Mahan, president of the ISAC organization. Many were also sold to Mr. Beverley Moseley and Dr. John White, both officers in the Midwestern Epigraphic Society in Columbus, Ohio.

Russell did give me three small, inscribed stones early on, which I prize a great deal.

Wayne May and the Ancient America Magazine

By the time Russell and I were ready to publish our book, other scholars and researchers had come forth in defense of Russell's story. I wrote and published the book, but it was Russell's story, his discovery and his problem, and I could take no credit for it. I merely tried to tell his story, more often than not using his words from letters and phone calls.

We received great help and support from Mr. Buck Trawicky of Madison, Wisconsin, who edited the cave book. He did much research and fact checking on his own. Then there were Dr. Cyclone Covey, Dr. Warren Cook, Warren Dexter, Dr. Joe Mahan, and, of course, Virginia Haurigan and Dr. Scherz, all of whom wrote supporting papers included in the Mystery Cave book. There were also two other very competent scholars who contributed: Don Eckler of Houghton,

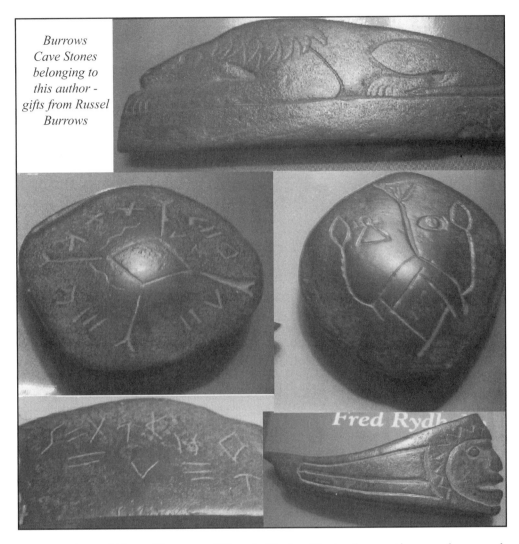

Burrows Cave Stones belonging to this author - gifts from Russel Burrows

Fred Rydl

New York, and Evan Hanson of Beryl, Utah. Their observations and research added greatly to the support of the cave. Most people who attended meetings designed to educate and enlighten the public concerning the cave just maintained a healthy, wait-and-see attitude, but as years passed many became impatient and lost faith. On the other hand, a few became more interested.

One such person who had attended some of these meetings was a young man from Colfax, Wisconsin, named Wayne May. It was sometime during this period that he showed up at our home in Marquette to discuss theories of ancient times. He brought with him a beautiful, solid, copper dagger, the likes of which I have never seen before nor since. I took pictures and had slides made of it. It appeared to be of modern design, but an all copper knife of any kind is unheard of today.

*Wayne May's
Copper Dagger*

Wayne spoke of other such anomalies he had come across and I told him I would be interested in seeing or hearing about any of them. I don't believe he mentioned his idea of starting the publication of a magazine at our first meeting, but later I heard him talk about such a venture. The only archaeology reports are by the professionals with which the public has little contact. The only articles a professional journal will accept are from the professionals, yet many of the great discoveries are made by amateurs.

Wayne's idea was a publication open to amateurs and professionals alike, a public forum where anyone could feel free to criticize anyone else's work or make comments. He hoped any attacks would not be personal, but generally directed at proving or disproving a point. To Wayne's knowledge there was no publication devoted strictly to the archaeology of the Americas at that time. Of course, there were the usual discouraging remarks claiming that he didn't have the necessary experience, that there wasn't enough interest or material out there to keep it going more than a year, that in general the project would surely fail. But apparently there was enough favorable sentiment that May was willing to give it a try; after all, he had been a journalist and certainly had a sufficient background in American archaeology from a long-time interest.

My personal feeling was that it was a great idea, a chance for the unfunded opinions and quiet work of a silent public to be heard. I have always felt that when there are open arguments on nearly any subject, the public will decide. It seems that one side of these ancient arguments has been covered up or at least denounced for years. Here would be a vehicle that could carry the opposing sentiments. I offered Wayne all the encouragement I could and told him I would help out whenever I was able. He asked me to prepare an article for the first publication, which was to be made available sometime in 1993, just a year or so after the book by Russell Burrows and I went on sale. Thus I have always hoped that our book may have been some of the impetus that created the

Ancient American Magazine, although there were several organizations that were publishing journals and papers that were reports from their members for some time then. The Amateur Societies that I was familiar with at that time, many of which I became a part of, are:

• American Institute for Archaeological Research - Mt. Vernon, New Hampshire

• Ancient Earthworks Society - Madison, Wisconsin

• Ancient American Artifact Preservation Foundation (AAAPF) -
  P.O. Box 216 - Skandia, MI 49885

• Early Sites Research Society - Long Hill, Rowley, Massachusetts

• Epigraphic Society - San Diego, California

• Midwestern Epigraphic Society - Columbus, Ohio

• New England Antiquities Research Association - Paxton, Massachusetts

• Institute for the Study of American Cultures - Columbus, Georgia

• Louisiana Mounds Society - Shreveport, Louisiana

• The THOR (The Hunters Ohio Rock) thor-thehuntersohiorock

• New World Discovery Institute, P.O. Box 491 Port Townsend, WA 98368

Today, while some of these no longer exist (2004), there are several other such organizations, both here and in Canada, which I have not listed.

My Essay on Dolmens

In the first copy of the *Ancient American* magazine, which was published in July of 1993, Wayne May, publisher and editor, asked me to write an article on dolmens. As far as I know, this was the first in-depth article ever published dealing with dolmens in North America. (There are literally hundreds of books about dolmens in Europe and elsewhere.)

The following essay on dolmens and other megalithic structures is a later revision of the one published originally. I am including it here as it shows the extent of old world travelers in America in ancient times. These people could not have missed the amount of free, pure copper being traded among the local inhabitants during this period and, therefore, would have laid the groundwork for a copper trade at that time. The essay could be revised again—we learn more regularly.

Courtesy of Joan Skelton

Dolman on top of Tip Top Mountain Ontario Canada

My Essay on Dolmens (Revised)

Although the word "dolmen" was not generally used in America prior to 1983, I discovered later it was a common term in Europe. However, the book *Bronze Age America* contained pictures of many dolmens of various sizes and shapes in America and Europe.

The word dolmen is defined in the dictionary (means table stone) as a "monument consisting of several megaliths arranged so as to form a chamber, usually regarded as a tomb. Cromlech and dolmen are practically synonymous terms, indicating any group of uprights supporting a flat capstone or table, this table being the original roof of the sepulchral chamber." I have found that while the word "cromlech" is sometimes used interchangeably with dolmen, it usually denotes something a little more elaborate such as a circle of standing stones or monoliths around a mound or dolmen.

Archaeologist Kevin Renfrew of the University of South Hampton, England, gives us an idea of how dolmens may have come about.

Dolmen on top of mountain in Wisconsin

He says that in the megalithic societies of Europe, they were impressed with the idea of what could be accomplished with a few simple tools and a lot of manpower. Mere humans, working together, could move huge stones.

As people lived in their own specified agricultural areas in enlarged family groups of possibly forty to sixty individuals, they had to have a special

Dolmen in Sweden on top of high rock hill.

Dolmen in Minnesota Sawbill Lake Courtesy of Chuck Bailey

"Table Stone" Dolmen one of several in Massachusetts. Photo bt James Whittall from Bronze Age America

N. West Coast of Ireland Karl, Lara, Rebecca Newman of Marquette

Photo courtesy of the Newman Family

For people who are especially interested in the megalithic remains in Europe and elsewhere there are literally hundreds of books out there. Some good ones are listed here:
Megalithic Mysteries – Michael Balfour
America's Ancient Stone Relics – Warren
    Dexter and Donna Marlin
In Search of Stones – M. Scott Peck M.D.
Ancient Irish Landscape – Iain Zaczek
Standing Stones – Kenneth McNally
A Land of Gods and Giants – Meck Sharp
Scotland BC - Anna Richie
The Megaliths of Brittany – Jacques Breard
The Dolmans and Passage Graves of
    Sweden – Unknown
The Countryside Companion – Wynford
    Vaughan-Thomas
Circles of Stone – Aubrey Burl
Classic of Stone – Max Milligan and
    Aubrey Burl

place to put their dead. Young men of the group, possibly with the help of men from neighboring groups, would erect a dolmen. The larger the capstone, the more impressive was the dolmen.

As time went on, dolmens were made in many shapes and sizes depending on what stones were available. The dolmen took on a deeply religious and spiritual meaning. Its location became a holy or magical place. Over the years the dolmen was elaborated upon. Sometimes the supporting stones were huge and varied in number. Sometimes the dolmen was underground and had a row of megaliths lining a passageway down to it. These passageways often have huge lintels across the upright megaliths to form a roof or doorway.

Some more elegant tombs had corbelled or built-up roofs and some were encircled by stone and earth forming a tumulus or sepulchral mound. In England, dolmens on hilltops were covered with stone piles to form cairns on the moors. The larger the cairn the greater the leader as each of his subjects were supposed to have carried a stone for his cairn.

I had a first cousin who was one of a long line of Cornish tin miners. He took us to see some of these conical rock piles he called tors out on the Cornish moors. He said he knew these people and the only reason they would ever carry a big rock to put on that pile was to make sure the one it was supposed to honor would never get out from under it.

The largest dolmen we found in southern England was called "Spinster Rock." It was being guarded by a lonely old Shetland pony. The big dolmen, maybe twelve feet high, was in the center of this comparatively small barnyard surrounded by a high hedgerow, on a quaint old farm.

The megalithic practices seemed to spread around the world taking on different forms of the basic idea, to raise a stone. In some places bodies were cremated and the ashes put in a covered urn which was placed under the dolmen. Some of these urns have the name Baal, the Phoenician or

Corbelled Chamber

pre-Christian god, inscribed on them. The dolmens are sometimes accompanied by standing stones also called menhirs or 'sarsen stones.[60] There are great circles of sarsen stones in many locations and there are places where they stand in groups, in lines or alone and they seem to have taken on various meanings.

The fact that dolmens are found in such great numbers in Europe suggests that the megalithic culture must have originated there, at least in much higher levels or advanced forms, but the very earliest megaliths are found in Nubia (southern Egypt) and may be as early as 6000 B.C. From there the skill and practice of moving big stones moved into Egypt where the building of the pyramids may have started around 5000 B.C.

Land of Many Megaliths

(One school of thought says they may have been built much earlier.)
The simplest dolmens, just a raised stone, seem to be in the north of Europe

---

[60] 'sarsen stone—heathen or pagan stone monument.

251

Black Sea portal tombs similar to those in western Ireland.

and the technique of raising stones seems to have spread rapidly through Scandinavia, the British Isles and France. They are also found in Spain, Portugal and North Africa and even Iraq. We found them in Finland where there aren't supposed to be any, and I am told there is only one known in Belgium.

On the west coast of Ireland, and especially the off-shore islands, there are some more elaborate megalithic tombs made of large slabs of stone. They call them dolmens, but they also have other names that are more descriptive like court tombs, box tombs and passage tombs. Some have a perfectly round hole or opening in one of the slabs.

Strangely there is another area where very similar tombs to the Irish ones are found. On the east coast of the Black Sea, in what is now Russia, there are about twenty-five hundred of these elaborate dolmens. They call them dolmens there, but they are certainly like the Irish portal tombs. They are almost identical, made of huge stone slabs with the round hole on one face of the tomb.

The most colossal megalithic collection seems to be around Carnac on the Queberon Peninsula in France. It is also in France where the Caves of Lascaux (Grotte des Lascaux) with their seventeen thousand year old paintings will send a chill up the spine of even the most naive of art connoisseurs. The cliffs along the Dordogne had people living on them for fifty-thousand years. There must have been a high degree of talent, culture, and civilization in that area. At Carnac are elaborate tumuli, huge dolmens and literally thousands of menhirs (standing stones). There are rows of standing stones that stretch for miles.

Stonehenge, built between 2000 and 3000 B.C. on the Salisbury Plains in England, has the most impressive and most famous megaliths, not only because of the great effort it must have taken to move 83 bluestone uprights that weigh tons apiece and 40 lintel stones a distance of over 200 kilometers (125 miles) but erecting them. Even more remarkable is the precision with which they were cut. They are the only known megaliths that are mortised, that is, when cutting the stone, protrusions were left on the top of the vertical stones that precisely fit into depressions cut into the horizontal lintels for an exact fit. The lintels were also tongue and grooved at each end so that they fit into each other. Then there is the precise alignment of the whole henge so that the first rays of the sun on the summer solstice shine down over the keystone and through the alignment making a perfect calendar.

An even more elaborate and older megalithic concentration of sarsen stones and stone circles, though not precision cut and fitted, can be found just a short distance north of Stonehenge at Avebury.

In a remarkable book, *The Stonehenge People* by Rodney Castleden (1987 Routledge & Kegan Paul Inc., 11 New Fetter Lane, London, he gives

us an account of how both Stonehenge and Avebury were constructed, apparently with the cooperation of the two groups of people.

Drawing of what Stonehenge would have looked like.

*Near Kirkwall,
the capital of the
Orkney Islands is
this chambered tomb
called Maeshowe built
around 2700 B.C.*

Orkney Islands

*Skera Brae
underground
domicile on the
Orkey Islands*

Orkney Islands
Ring of Brogar

Isle of
Lewis Heberdies

Orkey Islands

Many have reasoned that the huge stones were pulled on rollers but Castleden says they were levered onto large sledges using timber beams and skidded to their destination. He says, "a hundred people could pull a twenty-ton sarsen on a sledge all day without undue exertion."

At the town of Avebury there is a massive stone circle made with almost flattish sarsens that weigh up to 80 tons apiece. Inside the large circle are two smaller circles, these were made first. Around the whole structure is a moat or ditch 21 meters wide and 9 meters deep. It is 427 meters in diameter. This is a dry moat, that even today, with modern equipment, would be a considerable undertaking to build. Within a few miles of the town is a special religious spot with not much left to see except a few sarsen stones around which sheep are grazing. It is called Windmill Hill and it was at this location some years ago that there was found an amulet with the oldest known bit of Ogam writing on it. It has been dated by British archaeologists to the late Neolithic period of 2200 B.C.

Orkney Islands

Orkney Islands

Orkney Islands

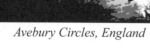

Avebury Circles, England

Then out in the Atlantic Ocean, north of Scotland, where some say are the most treacherous waters in the world, lie the Orkney Islands, with hundreds of megaliths and some very impressive stone circles, one called the Ring of Brogar. There is also a famous chambered tomb and mound known as Moes Howe that was used for thousands of years, having been reopened as late as the Viking period. It has many runic inscriptions date to that period.

These barren, windswept islands have been inhabited by daring seafaring people for at least 7,000 years, and they have left much evidence in the form of subterranean dwellings. Skara Brae is a complex of underground living quarters that has been restored. While part of it has been lost to the sea, what is left represents a home of possibly 30 to 60 people, in use some six or seven thousand years ago.

In 1958, high on the end of one of the islands at a place called Liddle in St. Margaret's hope, Ronald Simison found a corbelled roof tomb with four concentric stone walls around it. It was excavated in 1974-75 and proved to be about 5,150 years old. The skulls and thigh bones of 340 people were interred in the ten chambered tomb and their average age was 19. These people were an average of two inches taller than people of a later date. Because of the bones and claws of about ten eagles found in the tomb, it is called the Tomb of the Eagles. There are other stone tombs representing the clan of the dogs and the clan of the deer.

The stone circles of the Orkneys and those of Avebury and Stonehenge represent the very peak or climax of the early people's obsession with religion. But there are literally hundreds of stone circles in the British Isles. They seem to have developed in the late Neolithic period from about 3000 B.C. onward. They are of all sizes and the stones that make them up are of all sizes. Some were made of wood and many that were, were often later replaced with stone.

To quote Castleden again—"if there is one distinct and characteristic cipher of the Stonehenge people (megalithic society) one artifact that distinguishes their culture from all others, one single signature that identifies them, it is the stone circle."

These circles often defined a holy area, sometimes people lived within it or it was in a spot where they could easily get to it or had to pass through it. This was the idea of the causewayed circle[60a], the main road passed through the center of the circle. Most of the stone circles in the

---

[60a] Longbarrows and causeway circles were used in an increasing frequency in the period 3600 to 3200 BC (Stonehedge People page 26 Rodney Costedon.)

British Isles had this causeway and a well-traveled road passing through them. They were also a place for great religious ceremonies that must have evolved over thousands of years. The large circles may have taken hundreds of years to complete, and eventually became a temple.

But many of the dolmens and many standing stones present a complete mystery to scholars. The layout at Carnac in France is a good example. The stones cover miles of countryside and homes, and churches have been built among them. They can be found on the seashore, in the marshlands, and in the forests. In one area there are long lines of them of all sizes, running from three or four feet tall to fifteen and sixteen feet tall, and lines of them are miles long, sometimes five, six and seven abreast. Nearby are some elaborate tumuli and dolmens with fifty-ton capstones. Some of the largest capstones have been estimated at well over a hundred tons.

If old-world dolmens and menhirs present many mysteries, the North American dolmens are even more baffling. Many recognized authorities in the fields of geology, anthropology and archaeology say there are none on this side of the Atlantic and their arguments for this are numerous. They call the mounted boulders in North America "glacial erratics," that is, they are glacial boulders that were left by coincidence on smaller stones, or that material eroding away from stones in the earth by wind or water left them balanced on the points of several rocks.

They point out that what are called dolmens on this continent are not at all shaped like the stones in Europe and here they are usually on a rock surface rather than in a field. The premise of this school of thought is, how could there be dolmens on this side of the Atlantic when megalithic people were never here? (There is no way they could have gotten here.)

Until Barry Fell's books came out between 1976 and 1982 (*America B.C., Saga America* and *Bronze Age America*), all dolmen-like objects were shrugged off by scientists as being glacial erratics, or by some as being put up by the Indians, and few or no studies were ever made of them. They were merely curiosities, phenomena of nature.

Now, however, having seen many dolmens, menhirs and a host of other megalithic structures in other parts of the world, it is obvious to me that in most cases people used what stones were available. The structure was governed by the circumstances.

As dolmens seem to have different meanings in different places, I believe they may have taken on additional meaning in this country. What would people do to leave their mark in a far-off land? Today we would have our picture taken at a site, or a group could leave a plaque or raise

See Apendix Gamma Upsola Pictures

a flag. Some ancient seafarers definitely wanted to leave a "calling card" of some kind. The later Norse left some runestones. In the thinking of megalithic people, what could be more representative of their culture, more distinct to leave in a foreign land or more permanent than a dolmen? Later voyageurs planted a cross or raised a flag, but they are long gone. The dolmen had a deep religious and sentimental meaning to these much earlier travelers and it would be a dolmen that they would erect for future generations to witness. They would not have the time or the manpower to transport huge monoliths as they did in their home lands, but a dolmen in the right spot would be equally impressive and the dolmen was special.

Columnist Anthony Harrigan said it eloquently when he wrote:

> If Carnac does nothing else, it creates respect for our very ancient ancestors in Europe. They may have been unable to write down their thoughts, but their thinking processes were formidable. The boldness of their vision was tremendous. Their ability to cooperate and work together should inspire us.
>
> Contemporary men and women are arrogant. They think they know it all because they possess machines, including the new computing machines. They have much to assist them. Nevertheless, much of modern life consists of trivialities and an emphasis on superficial comfort and security. The builders of the alignments at Carnac had nothing but their hands and the rudest of tools made of sticks and stones, but they created a monument that has endured for 4,000 years and that may endure when the 20th century cities of the world are dust.

Yes, we continue to short-change these ancient people and keep asking questions that show our ignorance. How did they move those stones, how did they lift them, how could they cross oceans, how did they navigate? But they did all these things and more. It is very logical that megalithic people would certainly have erected a dolmen if they were in some far off land. Their courage, vision and persistence were awesome.

As for the argument that the American dolmens are all glacial boulders, it seems that it would follow that they would be rather unequally distributed over all the area where the glacier covered. This is certainly not the case, however. There is no doubt the glacier could produce a dolmen-like formation and a small percentage of American (and European) dolmens may have been formed that way, but their actual locations tell us quite a different story.

There are somewhere between 200 and 300 of these North American dolmens. With few exceptions, they all have similar locations. We find them mostly up and down the east coast or on offshore islands. We find them on the tops of high hills, often commanding a view, and along the waterways just up from the waters edge in a conspicuous spot. Everything indicates that their builders were seafaring people and that their penetration inland was by water.

Among the dolmens found inland, there are some in Colorado and Wyoming. I have seen pictures of some of these, but have not visited them. Nearly all of these are on the tops of high hills but here again, they seem to have taken on different meanings. In the March 1993 issue of the Louisiana Mounds newsletter, a beautiful "Turtle Dolmen" was pictured and mention was made of other animal-like dolmens in the area. Another dolmen that was pointed out to me by Chuck Bailey of Duluth, Minnesota, founder and president of the Upper Midwest Chapter of ISAC (Institute for the Study of American Cultures), is a typical North American dolmen. It is a large boulder raised up on three small (in this case, very small) boulders. The dolmen is situated right next to a canoe route, near its northern end. Just beyond this point is the divide where the waters

A portion of more than 3000 Menhirs that makeup what is known as the alignments of Carnac, France. Courtesy of Prehistoric de la France by Albert Ducoros and Fernand Nathan

Courtesy of Ancient America Magazine

Mrs. Janet Fisher, Nova Scotia

Peggy's Cove Nova Scotia

Algonquian Park, Canada

flow north. Anyone traveling on these waters would certainly see this huge unique marker. It is right out on a bold-faced rock island just above eye level; you're compelled to land there. All this is enough to make it seem as if someone in the past would have chosen this spot to erect a dolmen, but there is more. A group from Bailey's organization, led by Dr. James Scherz of the University in Madison, has discovered other marker stones in the area. It is possible the site may have further significance and an investigation of the whole area is continuing. Dr. Scherz has located, mapped and studied the alignments of hundreds of effigy mounds in Wisconsin.

There is another dolmen, much larger than the one in Minnesota, in Algonquin Park, Ontario, Canada. It is also placed conspicuously and strategically high on a rock ledge at the water's edge. This again suggests that it was put there for a purpose similar to the Minnesota dolmen. This brings us back to the original dolmen that I first laid eyes on in 1941. It is not on the water's edge, but high on the top of a rocky mountain.

If you were traveling east along the south shore of Lake Superior, east of

Courtesy of Chuck Baily, Minnesota

Sawbill Lake Minnesota

Photo by Chuck Bailey

*Author next
to Dolman in
Minnesota*

Huron Bay, this mountain alone rises above the land forms around it. While it belongs to a cluster of high hills, this one alone can be seen from the water when traveling east along the shore.[60b] It is so inviting to climb that many a fisherman has done just that in the past or been stymied by the distance, as it is not as short a walk as it looks.

And what would ancient travelers be doing on Lake Superior in the middle of our continent, one might ask.

Looking across the waters from that mountain, out as far as the eye can see, lies the Keweenaw Peninsula, containing the largest known copper deposits in the world. It is the only area on earth were any size pieces of pure copper could be, and still can be picked up or dug for, without having to free them from the rock matrix.

Even though there were once tons of it lying around in the free state (called float copper that has been freed by the glacier), someone was so anxious to get copper that when the free copper became difficult to find over a period of several thousand years, they laboriously dug some 5,000 mines and found copper in all of them. The bulk of the ancient digging was done between three and five thousand years ago although some digging preceded even that for a few thousand years and extended beyond that for a few thousand years. We are told that all of the ancient mining ceased about 1100 A.D.

Still today, in Michigan's Copper Country, people using metal detectors are turning up tons of copper and several huge five-to-ten ton pieces have been discovered in rivers or Lake Superior just in recent years. A

[60b] Picture is on page 72.

Photo by Professor William H. Manierre

Standing head stone on mountain top in Marquette County, Michigan.

remarkable fact is that even after six or seven thousand years of extracting copper, experts estimate that nearly 90% of the copper still remains in place, most of it under Lake Superior.

Yes, we would expect people from far off places who worked with stone and where dolmens had a very special meaning to have some erected in the vicinity of the greatest deposits of free pure copper on earth. When copper was in such demand during the Bronze Age, they would certainly have known about its main source.

If these people did mine copper and remain in the area for at least several months each summer, then there should be other evidence of them here, even after thousands of years, and there is. In fact, there seems to be quite a growing collection of things that can only be explained by the presence of European megalithic people.

Within a few miles of the Michigan dolmen, high on another granite hill, is a unique flat area about one hundred feet across. In the center of this area sits a large stone, maybe five feet high. It is not tall and narrow like the majority of European standing stones, nor is it implanted in the ground. But this stone has a strange natural face, making it look like a giant head.

This could all be natural, glacial and completely coincidental, except that the face of the stone looks right out over Lake Superior where the sun would rise out of the water on the equinox. The Colorado stones are similarly aligned. To add to its possible authenticity are clusters of stones just 5° off each of the four directions about 50 feet out from the stone. They could well have been cairns that toppled over in time.

Rocks with natural faces of people and animals that have been wrestled around so that they are upright have been reported in several other locations across the country, mainly on the east coast and in Colorado.

It seems that if we could find one dolmen on this side of the Atlantic

Photo by June Rydholm

Eric Mitchell and Author Fred Rydholm in Eric's home in Canada 2001.

Since this was written, two more stone faces have come to light under nearly identical circumstances— see later chapters.

that is absolutely above reproach, then everyone would just have to agree it was erected by man and not the work of the glacier, then it should follow that there are others.

The dolmen we are looking for, in fact many of them, turned up in the far north above the Arctic Circle, at the upper end of the Melville Peninsula.

In an article from the December 1953 issue of "The Beaver" magazine which is published quarterly by the Hudson's Bay Company, author E. H. Mitchell, a Scotsman, describes both menhirs and dolmens, but he had no idea what they were or why they are there. Ironically he raised the same questions and used the same terms that have been used to describe dolmens for years in this country. He calls them "mystery stones" and "altars," as we have here in the past. Mitchell states: "Nobody knows why they were thus raised nor how the primitive people who placed them in position were able to lift such enormous weights."

When Mitchell, who was a clerk at Igloolik and later a manager at Arctic Bay for the Hudson's Bay

Large "legged" dolmen, one of several on Melville Peninsula Northwest Territory, Canada.

Photo courtesy of Beaver Magazine

While visiting a museum in Tadoussac at the mouth of the Saguenay River, I showed a gentleman a picture of the stone head in Upper Michigan and told him about its alignments. He brought out a book showing a head there with identical alignments.

I wrote to the discoverer, Mr. Claude Le'gare of Quebec and got the whole story.

His stone was huge, four or five times as large as the one in Michigan, but with identical alignments. Facing east the top of the head aligned with the rising sun on the Spring Equinox looked toward the rising sun on the Summer Solstice and was aligned with the Fall Equinox.

The Canadian stone is on the top of Mt. Eternity overlooking Saguency Fjord.

This diagram and pictures show the Canadian rock, which is 9 ft tall, weighs an estimated 25 tons and is propped upright on slanted ground, supported by small rocks.

Le'gare says there are similar alignments in Europe photo at right shows the sunrise on the Spring Equinox.

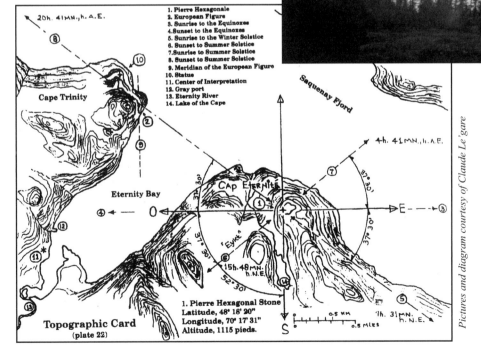

1. Pierre Hexagonale
2. European Figure
3. Sunrise to the Equinoxes
4. Sunset to the Equinoxes
5. Sunrise to the Winter Solstice
6. Sunset to Summer Solstice
7. Sunrise to Summer Solstice
8. Sunset to Summer Solstice
9. Meridian of the European Figure
10. Statue
11. Center of Interpretation
12. Gray port
13. Eternity River
14. Lake of the Cape

Cape Trinity

Eternity Bay

Saguenay Fjord

Cap Eternité

1. Pierre Hexagonal Stone
Latitude, 48° 18' 20"
Longitude, 70° 17 31"
Altitude, 1115 pieds.

Topographic Card
(plate 22)

Pictures and diagram courtesy of Claude Le'gare

Photo by Eric Mitchell

South Hampton Island

Map 9.   Somerset Island

There are 6 dolmens in the 20 mile stretch between Somerset Island and the Boothea Peninsula called the Belham Straights

Company, questioned the local Eskimos as to the origin of the stones, he says they call them "Estegaseemoute," which means "that which is raised from the ground." They had no knowledge of how they were raised, but they all knew who raised them. The Eskimos claim the stones were "raised by a race of comparatively large people. They call them the 'Toonikdoak' and refer to them as giants. They also claimed that once the "Illisimayoke" (the informed white men) saw the stones they would be greatly enlightened."

Indeed we are enlightened, as these stones are a whole new source of ancient history that has been unknown to us. These dolmens, in one unique way, prove beyond any doubt that they were erected by people for they not only stand on three or four supporting stones, but in some cases they are raised on legs made by a small pile of two or three stones. The reasons for this are purely speculative. Maybe it is so they would stand above the blowing snow or possibly just to make them more dramatic. I prefer the latter because in a region of so many rocks and no trees these legged dolmens really stand out. Also, we must remember that there have been great climatic changes in the arctic over the last three or four thousand years and these monuments could have been erected during an arctic warm spell.

Mitchell says the Toonikdoak lived in stone houses, many of which can still be seen today on the summits of small hills. The ancient Orkney Islanders, who were of Scandinavian descent, also lived in stone houses, as did early people in Scotland and Ireland, but these were either partially or totally underground.

I sent the article from the "Beaver" with pictures to Dr. Fell in California. He contacted Canadian Government officials in the area in 1992. They informed him that the stones in question were erected by the Inuits. These "official answers" are regularly given as they are probably confusing dolmens with "Inukshooks," a word that means "like a person." Eric Mitchell writes "from a distance they are just like that, forlorn figures silhouetted against the horizon, standing in a vast, treeless and timeless land, monuments to people and to a way of life that is now gone.

"Inukshooks are one of the salient features of the North, and they give to their place an air of serenity, at times mystery, as if all that had transpired in the past were embodied in their silent forms."[61]

These people, who built the Inukshooks, probably came fast on the

---

[61] Dr. W. E. Taylor, Chief Archaeologist for the National Museum of Canada says he knows of no Inukshooks west of Ellesmere Island and North of Viscount Melville Sound, and only three or four sites are known in that corner of the archipelago.

heels of the older megalithic north Europeans who had sailed the northern oceans sometime before 3000 B.C. They could have been the Firbolgs, Fomorians and the Tuotha-de-Danaans, also called the pre-Celtic and Old Norse. Even their ancestors left huge *cahirs* (memorials) of stone that still remain on the Aran Islands off the coast of Scotland. These monuments are said to demonstrate the power, strength and size of the people.

The Inuits say it was the "Tunrit" who built the cairns, fish weirs and Inukshooks, but occasionally Inukshooks are still erected today by modern Intuits.

According to Dr. Taylor, the Tunrits were Eskimos who lived in the region from 800 B.C. to 1300 A.D. But the Tunrits were preceded by the Dorset and pre-Dorset people (approximately 2500 B.C. to 800

B.C.). These dates put these people right into the megalithic period and I would suspect that they came from Europe. They would have put up dolmens and later Inukshooks.

The Inukshooks were "road signs"—they told where to fish, they sent migrating caribou in the proper direction so they could be killed, and they pointed to food caches, fording places and important stopovers in a vast, dimensionless land.

# # #

Inukshooks drawn by Liz Yelland

All this talk of people crossing the oceans in numbers long before Columbus does not agree with a great number of recognized authorities in the fields of history and archaeology. They firmly believe that the only early crossings to the North American continent were by foot via the well-known Bering Strait land bridge. This may have occurred, but even this time-worn theory is being seriously challenged today. There is more and more evidence that there were many early crossings in both oceans by water, in the west along the Aleutian Island chain and in the east via island hopping, Foroes, Iceland, and Greenland. This would have been even easier at an earlier time when the sea level was lower and the earth much warmer.

This is far from the original article I spoke of earlier; it has been updated considerably. Since it was written, I have learned much more about megaliths and the people who lived during that period. I have visited Norway, Sweden, Finland, France and the British Isles, and besides taking hundreds of pictures I have had many sent to me from all over the world. Nearly all of these places are where dolmens are supposed to be. However, I have tried to concentrate on places where they are not supposed to be, in an effort to locate where the people traveled. We found them in Finland where none had been identified. I did not find that so startling. But the many we located in the North American Arctic were a revelation. Here they seem to be in clusters.

Working with the Inuits, Eric Mitchell and a geologist friend of his, Henry Vuori, (chief geologist for INCO),[62] I was able to locate several areas where dolmens are found. Of Mr. Vuori, Eric Mitchell says he knows of no man who has covered the Arctic so thoroughly on foot than Hank Vuori. Vuori told me he had run into these raised stones often but had been told and always believed they were glacial. But the thing that amazed him was wherever he went there was always evidence of some ancient people having been there. Of course, recently a circumpolar culture has been accepted bearing out Joe Gannon's hypothesis of over 80 years ago.

There are three concentrations of dolmens on the north end of the Melville Peninsula, west of Hall Beach and south of Igloolik. There are several individual dolmens along the Bellot Strait, a narrow waterway about 20 miles long between the Boothia Peninsula and Somerset Island, some on South Hampton Island in the north part of Hudson Bay and, most revealing of all, is the trilathon, high on a point of land on the north coast of Baffin Island about 70 miles east of the village of Pond Inlet. This is extremely severe mountainous country and these had to have been a truly determined people, like the people who built Stonehenge, to erect a trilathon on the top of that cliff.

---

[62] INCO—International Nickel Co.

*Hank Vuori is shown in
photos from Fury Beach
on the east shore of
Somerset Island. Shown
are relics from HMS Fury
which was pushed around
by sea ice in 1829 while
Parry was looking for
a Northwest passage to
China.*

*Pictured are an anchor
and a 12ft ice saw that
was used to cut a channel
for the HMS Fury.*

Vouri with Inukshook in the Baker Lake area.

Modern Inukshooks

Photos by Liz Yellan

270

Beginning to Make Sense

Trilothon at Stonehedge

The finding of the Joel Kela Ogam prayer stone in the Escanaba River got my attention. What was it doing in this river, many miles from where Fell said it was made, in the islands off the coast of Scotland? Examining an Upper Peninsula map, one can see that the Escanaba came out of the central highlands of Marquette County. If people were looking for copper, which was further north, they could hardly reach it from the Escanaba. However, conceptualizing what the area might have been like some thousands of years ago when water was higher and land masses lower, I questioned if the Escanaba might have drained out of Lake Superior.

One day when my wife and I were taking a trip up to the Copper Country, I decided to look for the headwaters of the Escanaba River at Humboldt. Driving west on U.S. 41, the last time we crossed the Escanaba was just before we went through the cut of an extinct volcano east of the abandoned Humboldt mine (iron). The river came around the north end of that big rock hill from further west. There were broad, flat wetlands, and an old riverbed right through the town of Champion extending to Lake Michigamme. At the other end of Lake Michigamme there was again that big, broad riverbed, only this contained the Beaufort River coming from Beaufort Lake. We continued west on the highway to a cluster of three large lakes, Beaufort, as well as Ruth and Lake George; all a part of a huge drainage system coming from further west. As we traveled beyond this three lakes location, there were glimpses of an ancient, broad riverbed with a tiny stream in its center, sometimes crossing and recrossing the road. It disappeared to the north of the highway. Shortly afterward we crossed the Sturgeon River flowing south. It had obviously come from the vicinity where the east flowing

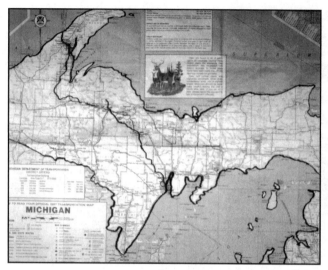

stream originated. Could that be the same Sturgeon River that flows into the Keweenaw waterway? A quick look at the map proved that it was. Yes, there was a water route from Torch Lake, the site of the greatest source of pure copper in the world, right to Lake Michigan, but the two rivers involved were running in opposite directions and the upper portion of each one was not navigable. Otherwise everything checked, they definitely came from a common area, one end was in the Copper Country and the other in Lake Michigan and an Ogam prayer stone was found along the route. To add to this coincidence, several stone axe-heads, just like some we saw in a museum in France and at the Marquette County Historical Society, were found on the Escanaba River.

At Chassell, a community just south of Houghton, the Sturgeon River broadens out into a giant slough of mud flats with a few branches of the river in it. It would have been a huge river at one time.

The very next day I called a geologist friend and asked him about drainage courses from Lake Superior to Lake Michigan.

Torch Lake to Lake Michigan

© - 2003 J.P. Farrell

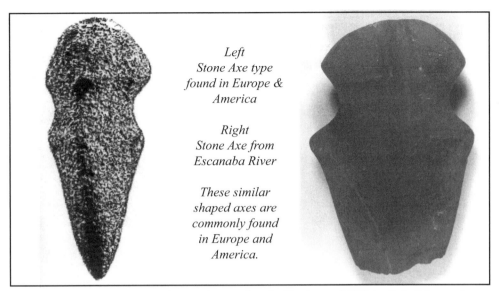

*Left
Stone Axe type
found in Europe &
America*

*Right
Stone Axe from
Escanaba River*

*These similar
shaped axes are
commonly found
in Europe and
America.*

He named a few, Eau Claire, Wisconsin, AuTrain and Whitefish Rivers (same situation—both flowing in opposite directions), the east end, etc., but he did not name the Sturgeon-Escanaba.

When I explained it to him he said he would have to check it out. The first thing he wanted to do was fly over the area next summer.

"Next summer!" I exclaimed, "How about tomorrow?"

I just happened to have a friend who had just flown a twin engine plane up from Texas. He was happy to oblige us.

The flight was amazing. You could see two great valleys connecting the two rivers parallel to each other. We flew low and fast and the geologist and I both got sick, but I was elated. I figured that with Lake Superior much higher three or four thousand years ago, and before the complete glacial rebound, the Sturgeon would have flowed south through that great funnel near Chassell (now a wide mud flat) and right down to Lake Michigan; the lakes along the way were part of the channel. With Lake Superior a hundred or two hundred feet higher than it is now, the row of storage pits that Henriette Mertz talks about in her book, *Mystic Symbol,* up on the hill above the Keweenaw waterway, could have been right on the shore. Loaded on rafts, copper could have been floated down the huge river all the way to Bay de Noc off Escanaba.

After we recovered I asked the geologist what he thought (I knew the pilot was convinced).

"Well," said the geologist, "we'll have to bring a team of students up some summer and make a series of borings and get some soil samples in the riverbeds." To my knowledge, no such borings were ever made and 20 years have passed. This all took place in the early 1980's.

But I was convinced. I spoke with several people about it and some were

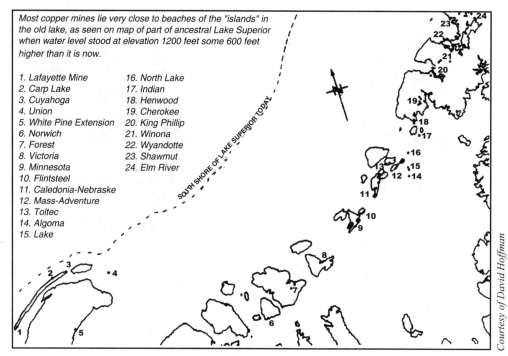

Most copper mines lie very close to beaches of the "islands" in the old lake, as seen on map of part of ancestral Lake Superior when water level stood at elevation 1200 feet some 600 feet higher than it is now.

1. Lafayette Mine
2. Carp Lake
3. Cuyahoga
4. Union
5. White Pine Extension
6. Norwich
7. Forest
8. Victoria
9. Minnesota
10. Flintsteel
11. Caledonia-Nebraske
12. Mass-Adventure
13. Toltec
14. Algoma
15. Lake
16. North Lake
17. Indian
18. Henwood
19. Cherokee
20. King Phillip
21. Winona
22. Wyandotte
23. Shawmut
24. Elm River

SOUTH SHORE OF LAKE SUPERIOR TODAY

Courtesy of David Hoffman

very sure that the Sturgeon could never have flowed south. However, when I was challenged on that idea while I was giving a talk on the subject, a geologist in the audience whom I had never met, spoke up and announced, "At one time all rivers flowed south out of Lake Superior." This was, of course, because the glacier was on the north.

# # #

That same summer (1985) June and I decided to explore the shoreline of Lake Michigan near the mouth of the Escanaba River. It seemed to me there should be evidence of a fairly large early population there. The ancient Copper Country mining venture, in my speculation, was no small time operation. It would have been well planned and highly orchestrated by well-organized, intelligent people. There would have been large gardens and artifacts that would have some connection with the Copper Country. If these ancients had left nothing distinctive at the mines, perhaps they had left something along their trail, like the prayer stone. Also you might expect to find remnants of housing, and although wood would not last and summer shelters would be temporary, there still should be clues as to who the early miners were.

We couldn't find anything, not even clearings (although they would have grown up) along the shore. There were some caves with petroglyphs but I was expecting something larger and more dramatic.

We drove south to Wisconsin and up the Door Peninsula where we heard stories of caves or tunnels that went through the peninsula, but these were on private land. We talked to a lot of people, but there didn't seem to be any evidence of a large prehistoric population.

Three years later, in 1988, we received a call from a Ms. Terri Bussi who was living on Beaver Island in Lake Michigan. She had heard that we had been poking around asking questions. She asked if we had heard of the Indian Medicine Circle on Beaver Island. We hadn't.

"I've only seen a few medicine circles out west," I told her. "Is this a big one?" The largest I'd seen was about 20 feet across with stones about the size of a five gallon pail.

"Yes," she said, "this is a big one."

"How big?" I asked. "Is it over 30 feet across?"

"Oh," she answered, "this is much bigger than that. It's 297 feet across."

"Two hundred and ninety feet!" I shouted. "I didn't know there were any that big. Who says it's a medicine circle?"

"The state archaeologist has put it on a list of places to be preserved. There is a developer who wants to build on the site and there is a road right through the center of it. The archaeologist called it a medicine circle."

We immediately made plans to go there as soon as possible.

I had never been to Beaver Island and didn't know what to expect. I had read and even written about its history of King Strang and his Mormon Colony,[63] but as far as I knew no one had ever written much about its prehistory, at least further back than Father Baraga in the mid-nineteenth century.

We reviewed some of the island's known history, learned about the fishermen who lived there, and found that many of the Irish families who took over the Mormon farms were still living there. Also much of the population was of Ottawa Indian ancestry. The Ottawa were the canoemen, the traders, a tribe of the Algonquin "Three Fires." This trio included the Otchipwe (puckered moccasins), Potowattami (keepers of the fire) and the Ottawa (the traders). The French called the Otchipwe Ojibway, and the English called them Chippewa (not to be confused with the Chippewaean of the northwest who are Athapaskan). But the Ottawa were the traders and the Ottawa River is the trading river named for them. As far as I can find out it was called the Ottawa River (the trading river) when Jacques Cartier arrived in the St. Lawrence in 1534. I always conjectured that the only thing they could have traded before that date was copper, as this

---

[63] King James Jesse Strang. From 1850 to 1856 Strang served as king of a dissident colony of Mormons on Beaver Island in Lake Michigan. His reign came to an end when he was murdered by the disenchanted followers in 1856.

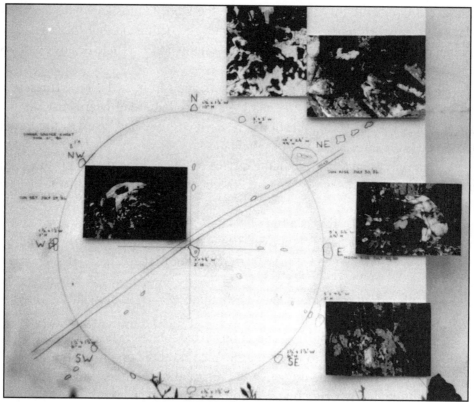

Photo courtesy of Terri Bussy Beaver Island

was long before the fur trade with Europeans.

A friend of mine had a daughter who married into one of the old time fishing families of Beaver Island and they made our housing arrangements on the island well in advance of our arrival. Terri Bussi, the woman who had discovered the circle, and some of her friends showed us around the whole area.

Our hosts took us on a sandy road to the site of the circle. It was the only road on that part of the island and there was no habitation nearby. The road headed right toward a large stone and then veered around it. The stone was actually right on the very edge and even partially in the road. It made you wonder why they hadn't made the road further away from the stone if they couldn't move it. You could see some large stones off to the right in an open field. It had been pointed out that this large stone was the center of the circle and when you walked out to the others, it was easy to see the large curve of the circumference. The other side was back in the woods. Part way between the center stone and the perimeter were seven stones in the pattern of the Big Dipper. It was obvious to me that this was a calendar circle, but later I realized it was much more than that, more like a causeway circle similar to many on the British Isles. A settlement may have been within it or at least nearby. No one could travel that road without going in and out of the circle.

"Do you know anything about this clearing?" I asked. They told me it was the site of an ancient Indian habitation. At the time it seemed a strange place for people to live, as it was not near water.

"Could there be any gardens nearby?"

"Gardens?" they exclaimed, wide-eyed and excited. "The whole place was a garden. There were raised gardens. You can see the lines in the earth down through the trees where the forest has taken over."

Indeed, the gardens stretched so far that the local airport had taken over large sections of it. Another island just to the north of Beaver is called "Garden Island" and there is a stone circle there also.

"Do you happen to have a museum on the island?" I asked.

"Not a real one, but there's a small collection of relics from the Mormon days at the old Town Hall in St. James," they told me.

Someone was kind enough to open the building for us so we could see what was there. We didn't really know anything that we were specifically looking for, but we were pleasantly surprised.

There was a large stone Irish Celt (stone axe) like many we had seen in Europe. Then I spotted a grooved hammerstone like many found in the Copper Country. There was no doubt,

Terry Bussey pointing out big dipper stones.

Photos by June Rydholm

Road going next to stone with hole in top possibly to put a post in.

from my superficial examination of the place, that this could be the base for at least one set of the ancient miners. It had the characteristics of the Neolithic people from the British Isles. Just a quick look connected these people to Europe

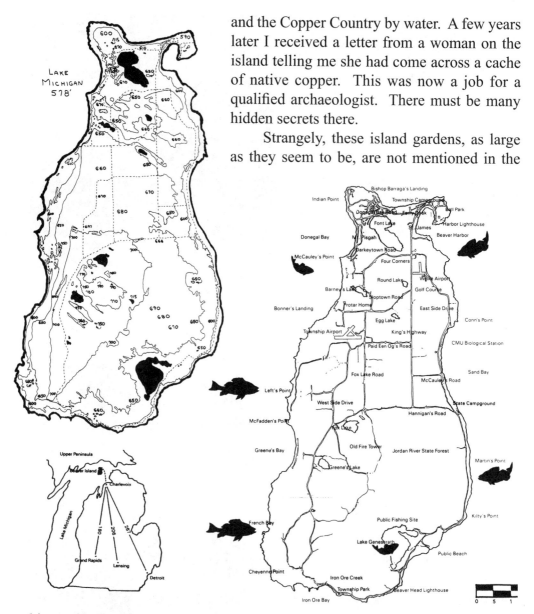

and the Copper Country by water. A few years later I received a letter from a woman on the island telling me she had come across a cache of native copper. This was now a job for a qualified archaeologist. There must be many hidden secrets there.

Strangely, these island gardens, as large as they seem to be, are not mentioned in the history books when they speak of the "Michigan Mystery Gardens." I believe these gardens are probably evidence of the same people but at a different period, maybe a few hundred years apart.

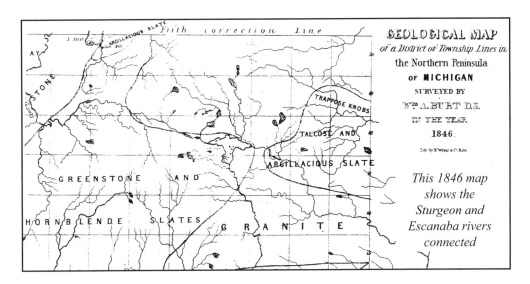

The Michigan Mystery Gardens

Scottish archaeologist Alexander Thom proposed—(the megalithic people) "as a peaceful and intellectual society that spent much of its time on geometry, astronomy and surveying as a background for monumental architecture."

There seems to be little information on the Beaver and Garden Island garden beds as to their exact shape or sizes except that they were extensive and there was at least one stone circle associated with each. There still may be enough left of them to make some fairly accurate observations as they can still be discerned. However, the famous Garden Beds of Michigan referred to in the history books are now all destroyed.[63a] Willis F. Dunbar writes of them in his *History of Michigan*:

> Far more mysterious of all North American antiquities consisted of low ridges of soil about eighteen inches high, arranged in almost perfect geometric patterns (rectangular and circular) and covering as much as 120 acres apiece. They were given their name because of their resemblance to a formal garden. Their function is a mystery. Were they simply artistic creations? Were they used for ceremonial purposes? Or were they used to kill buffalo by driving the herds across the ridges causing the beasts to stumble? No implements, pottery, arrowheads, or pipes have been found near these 'garden beds.' They had been abandoned long before

---

[63a] There seems to be no mention of stone circles in these Michigan Garden Beds, but like the Beaver Island ones they may not have been noticed or recognized

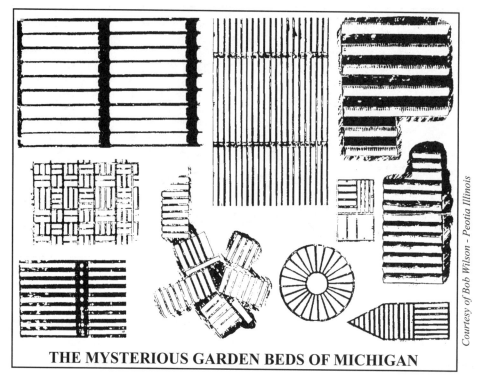

Courtesy of Bob Wilson - Peotia Illinois

THE MYSTERIOUS GARDEN BEDS OF MICHIGAN

the French came. Except for a few reported in Indiana and Wisconsin, they have been found only in Michigan. All of them have been destroyed by farmers. Bela Hubbard (1877):

> All opinions seem to agree that these relics denote some species of civilization and that they are different from those left by the field culture of any known tribes of Indians.

The following are excerpts from a paper read before the Michigan State Pioneer Society on February 7, 1877.

> An unusual importance attaches to these remains of a lost race, from the fact that they have been almost entirely overlooked by archaeologists, and that of those which were so numerous and prominent forty or even thirty years ago, nearly every trace has disappeared.

> The earliest mention of these relics is by Haven in his 'Archaeology of the United States.' It is the report of Verandier, who, with several French associates, explored this region before 1748. He found in the western wilderness 'large tracts free from wood, many of which are everywhere covered with furrows as if they had formerly been plowed and sown.'

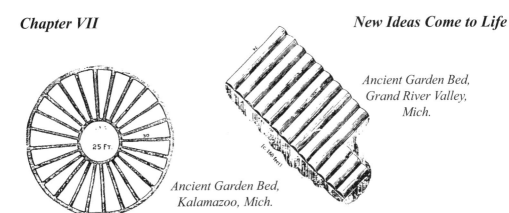

Ancient Garden Bed,
Grand River Valley,
Mich.

*Ancient Garden Bed,
Kalamazoo, Mich.*

Ancient Garden Bed, St. Joseph River Valley, Mich.

Editorial Comment:
This paper appears to be identical to that published later in the American Antiquarian, 1:1-9. 1878. *The beds were astonishing structures; nothing similar has come to our attention. Their purpose and their builders remain conjectural. Although their complexity argues against their being simple gardens. None remain to be examined; every trace had disappeared by the time Hubbard's paper was published.*

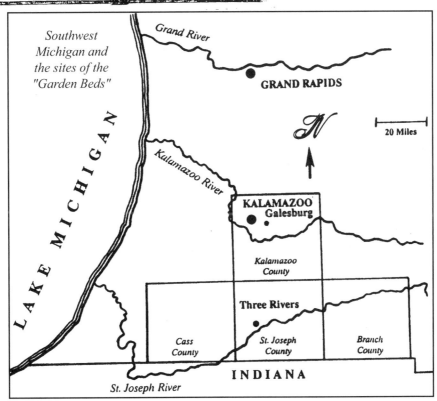

Southwest Michigan and the sites of the "Garden Beds"

Schoolcraft noted them in 1827. He records two kinds of beds and that the garden beds, and not the mounds, are the most prominent and, by far, the most striking and characteristic antiquarian monuments of this district of company.

John T. Blois (1839 Gazetteer of Michigan) gives detailed descriptions and diagrams of one kind of the beds.

Foster denotes less than a single page of his voluminous work to (the gardens) but says, "They certainly indicate a methodical cultivation which was not practiced by the red man."

Hubbard: "(The Gardens) were found in the valleys of the St. Joseph and Grand Rivers where they occupied the most fertile of the prairie land and burr-oak plains, principally in the counties of St. Joseph and Kalamazoo."

Hubbard: "The tough sod of the prairie had preserved very sharply all the outlines. According to the universal testimony, these beds were laid out and fashioned with a skill, order and symmetry which distinguish them from ordinary operations of agriculture, and were combined with some peculiar features that belong to no recognized system of horticultural art."

My own observations of these Mysterious Garden Beds are that they fit our presumptions of the megalithic culture so perfectly that I believe many others must have come to the same conclusion, but have remained silent because it may sound like such a ridiculous idea without the background I have presented.

Consider the following: By the perseverance and communal organization of these people, these gardens demonstrate the colossal organizational powers we attribute to the ancient Keweenaw mining culture, only here with these formal geometric gardens they could put into practice their love of surveying and (with the circles) astronomy. The gardens equate to the production of possibly a million hammerstones, the feeding and quartering of thousands of miners, the logistics of transportation to and from Isle Royale and the Keweenaw Peninsula, the creating of the storage pits filled with copper, plus lifting and transporting the copper that weighed tons from sometimes ten to twenty feet in the earth.

These people were obviously seafaring people and, having come by water,

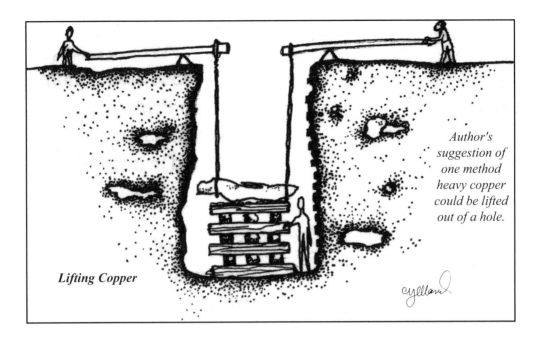

Author's suggestion of one method heavy copper could be lifted out of a hole.

Lifting Copper

lived and slept on their ships. This would account for the lack of domiciles in the mining areas or any signs of habitation. They most likely ate on their ships so any offal would have been destroyed.[63b] There are many places even today, around Isle Royale and the Keweenaw, where a large ship could be tied up close to shore, and this would have been even more true during times of higher lake levels.

Then there are the gardens, always accessible by water, on the rivers of Lower Michigan and the Lake Michigan islands, and it was at these places of good soil and growing climate that they were free to practice their religion and their obsession with surveying, astronomy and geometric design.

If we add all this to Joe Gannon's and Roy Drier's accumulation of circumstantial evidence concerning copper, we get a very clear picture of what went on in Michigan two, three and four thousand years ago. These gardens were necessary to provide food for the copper miners and there is no reason to believe there wasn't complete cooperation with the local inhabitants. Indications are that all encounters with these peaceful people were amiable. The indigenous people, especially from nearby Wisconsin and Minnesota, would have followed suit but in a much less aggressive way by working copper for their own needs.

[63b] Some broken pots have been found in Lake Superior near Isle Royal. They have been attributed to Indians, but they could have been thrown overboard from ancient ships. One such pot is said to be at Michigan Technological University

The entire collection from Newberry, Michigan 1898 - courtesy of the Smithsonian Institute

McGruer's Gods

Now that the Joel Kela stone led to such a clear picture of Neolithic people coming here for copper, I turned my attention to the three clay statues and a clay tablet that were found near Newberry, about a hundred miles east of Marquette, back in 1896. This "find" was virtually ignored by authorities until Sprague Taylor of Newberry resurrected interest in it in the 1950's. Even after more than a century, no one had ever come up with any answers about their possible significance.

I drove to Newberry to visit Mrs. Sprague Taylor. Sprague had died by then and I had to become reacquainted with the whole story.

First I wanted to know where the artifacts were now and who owned them. I was told they were in St. Ignace, Michigan. I drove there and discovered the bust of one of the statues in a glass case in the Fort De Brade Museum, which was in the same building that housed the St. Ignace radio station. The museum belonged to a Lansing dentist, Dr. Donald Benson. I called Dr. Benson to ask about the tablet. He told me it was in the back room of the museum in a deplorable condition, and gave me permission to look at it. It had indeed crumbled badly,

284

leaving only a few symbols recognizable. Dr. Benson said no one could tell him anything about it, and he personally felt it must be a hoax.

Mrs. Taylor was able to supply me with a copy of the symbols that were originally on the tablet taken from the 1896 papers. At that time all of the 140 spaces were readable except two.

It was when Mrs. Taylor sent this information to me that she told me some years earlier she had given the same information to a lady from Chicago named Henriette Mertz. This name had come up often in my research, and I was anxious to find out just who Henriette Mertz was.

With an address from Mrs. Taylor, I wrote to Henriette Mertz and found out that she had sent the information on to Barry Fell, exactly what I had planned to do with it. Fell had already reported it in Volume 9 of the Epigraphic Society Occasional Papers of 1981. The local experts of early Newberry had not been too far off in their assumptions. Fell had described the tablet as a puzzle-like religious chart that could be read across or down, and the script was Cypriot-Minoan, from Crete, Cyprus and some smaller Mediterranean Islands.

Again, it all fit so perfectly. Cyprus was where copper was first mined and named. It was where historians tell us copper was first discovered about seven or eight thousand B.C. The Cypriots knew as much about copper as anyone—they were the experts of their day. It is my opinion that Cyprus was a brokerage center for copper. Shipments of it came from Ireland and Cornwall and from overseas, the Lake Superior district. On Cyprus the copper was standardized into ingots and oxhides. [64]

> **Lincoln Library of Essential Information:** Crete—a large island in the Mediterranean. Extensive remains of palaces have established the fact that from about 2800 B.C. it was the seat of a highly developed civilization to which the name Minoan has been given after a lawgiver, King Minos. About 1500 B.C. the island established control over the sea as far as Sicily to the west and Canaan to the east. The people were possessed of a system of writing. The ancient Cretans showed much skill in engineering and architecture.
>
> **The Columbia Viking Desk Encyclopedia:** Extending 160 miles E-W, it is in the South limit of Aegean Sea.—There are iron and lignite deposits.—Crete's ancient Minoan civilization, named after King Minos, was one of the world's oldest; it reached its height in 1600 B.C., then

---

[64] Oxhides were shaped like a stretched animal hide, weighing about 65 pounds each for easy handling. At different periods the standard was different - some were 29 lbs etc. some Roman money was in the shape of oxides.

ended suddenly and mysteriously. Impressive remains have been found at Cnossus.

The Encyclopedia Americana: Crete, or Candia (called in the most ancient times IDAEA, from Mount Ida, afterwards Creta, whence the Turkish name Kirid, one of the most important islands belonging to Greece; situated in the Mediterranean, 81 miles from the southern extremity of the Morea, and 230 from the African coast; is 160 miles long, 7 to 35 miles broad and contains 3,326 square miles.—The air is mild; the summer is cooled by the north winds; the winter is distinguished only by showers of rain. Earthquakes, however, are not infrequent.—
Greek mythology made Crete the scene of many of the adventures of the gods and heroes. Here Saturn is said to have reigned and afterwards Minos.—

Archaeological exploration and excavation have revealed that a Neolithic period of evolution from abut 10,000 to 3315 B.C. was followed by the Minoan or Aegean period of civilization, which existed with the first dynasty of Egypt, from 3315 to 1450 B.C. and reached a culminating point in Crete.

—Minoan towns and palaces have been uncovered that exhibit architecture and engineering of a high order, unsurpassed for domestic conveniences in modern times.

—near Psychro and in the ruins on the neighboring islets of Pseira and Mochlos, the finds include archives of clay tablets in great quantities inscribed with the early forms of Minoan pictographs and linear script, polychrome decorated pottery, ivory and clay figures, mural paintings revealing the customs of the period, enormous decorated storehouses, jars, stone and bronze votive figures and objects of cult, sarcophagi, etc.

Of special note here are the "archives of <u>clay tablets</u> in great quantities inscribed with early forms of Minoan pictographs and linear script and <u>clay figures</u>.

While most of the early reports call the statues and tablet found at Newberry sandstone, they are definitely clay. Chuck Bailey made an analysis of the material and determined it was the same clay with fine wooden debris that is found near the Tahquamenon River close by.

#

When we were in Cornwall some years ago, we of course were given meals with all of the traditional Cornish favorites (pasties, saffron buns, clotted cream, etc.) and heard the legends connected with each.

The tale the locals told in connection with clotted cream interested me. They said that way back in the distant past a Phoenician cargo ship was wrecked on the Cornish coast near Land's End. This area at the southeastern-most tip of Cornwall between Land's End and St. Just was noted as a very dangerous spot and many sailing vessels were thrown against the rocks there. As the story went, the Phoenician sea captain wanted to do something for the inhabitants who had risked their lives to save his crew. He told them he would divulge the most valuable secret he knew, which was the recipe for clotted cream.

My question was, where was the Phoenician ship heading? They said it was a trading vessel headed for the north Atlantic. Their mission was probably getting walrus hides for rope, possibly fish for food or just maybe the ship would return with a load of copper. Henriette Mertz writes:

> This inscribed tablet found on the Upper Peninsula of Michigan represents only one of more than 5,000 inscribed artifacts recovered from Michigan mounds, roughly from 1870 to 1920—none of which survived. The enormity of this loss to history must be appreciated—5,000 inscribed artifacts sacrificed to the hypothesis that no ancient peoples, other than the historic Indian, were here. Blame for this tragic loss of priceless, irreplaceable material must be borne by the University of Michigan, whose responsibility it was to preserve these matters. The Newberry find represents only one artifact of the 5,000.[65]
>
> (And later:) No definitive study of this material has ever been published in spite of the fact that this extensive copper mining operation is known to have taken place and that artifacts recovered from mined out pits are comparable to those of Minoan Crete.

Fell:

> As reported by Dr. Henriette Mertz, a drawing was sent to me by Dr. Mertz, at my request, showing the form and arrangement of the symbols observed on the ceramic (clay) tablet when it was excavated. I informed Dr. Mertz that the syllabary, for such it is, a variant of the well-known Cypro-Minoan script, comprised an omens text similar to that of the Phaistos Disk (ESOP, Vol. 4). The language comprising the text appears to be a crolinized form of Minoan, having a vocabulary similar to that of Hittite, but lacking the formal declensions and conjugations of Hittite.

---

[65] Dr. Mertz is confusing the Newberry Tablet with the Soper Tablets - This author is sure there is no connection - The Newberry Tablet was in the Cypriot Manoan Alphabet and the Soper Tablet a much later period or Coptic Christian. From the 3rd to the 16th Century A.D. Coptic, a descendent of Ancient Egyptian language, was the tongue of ancient Egypt but gave way to Arabic, but the Soper Tablets may be connected to the Burrows Cave people.

The following is an exact copy of the figures on the Newberry tablet as found on page 133 of the Epigraphic Society Vol. 9, No. 218—June 1981—Occasional Publication. The decipherment and translation was done by Barry Fell.

National Decipherment Center

Newberry, Michigan   Henriette Mertz col.

The syllabary of this inscription, derived from Cypro-Minoan, is tabulated (Fell, 1980) on page 78, OPES vol 8, part 1. The numerals indicate the order, and the reading direction, in which each line is to be read. Thus the tablet is written in boustrophedon, alternate lines to be read in opposite directions. The tablet is also composed as an acrostic, to be read vertically as well as horizontally. The vertical reading logically precedes, thus line 1 is read downwards, line 2 upwards, and so on until line 10 is completed. Line 11 is then read horizontally, from left to right, line 12 from right to left, and so on to the end of line 24.

	1		3		5		7		9		
11	Pu	nu	si	wa	ko	se	lu	ya	ti	u	
	zi	ki	wa	lu	ta	li	ma	la	ta	wa	12
13	le	na	ko	li	li	pu	ri	se	ya	se	
	sa	le	na	ko	ze	no	po	li	nu	u	14
15	mu	so	no	ze	si	to	mi	li	lu	wa	
	sa	mi	sa	le	i	me	sa	zo	se	po	16
17	nu	pu	le	iya	le	mo	ki	li	mi	si	
	mo	ki	se	ze	we	(ma)	(sa)	la	ta	pa	18
19	lo	le	o	wa	me	lu	lo	lo	po	nu	
	no	ze	lo	sa	li	lu	ta	le	ke	re	20
21	pu	iya	zo	li	se	mu	sa	mi	o	so	
	zi	se	le	pa	ri	sa	sa	ki	na	ta	22
23	mu	sa	ki	li	lu	pu	na	sa	lo	sa	
	(sa)	na	sa	le	zo	pa	ze	se	si	ko	24
		2		4		6		8		10	

First stage in the decipherment of the Newberry Tablet. The phonetic values of the Cypro-Minoan signs have been substituted for the original elements. Three signs are inferred (for lacunae in the original text) and these are placed in parentheses.

On the next page the lines are taken in the numerical order inferred above, the reading direction of all the lines is rectified to flow from left to right, thereby yielding an intelligible sequence of Hittite-Minoan elements that are linked by hyphens to form recognizable words and language. See next page.

The vertical text, as now rendered in left-to-right horizontal lines
_____

1. Pu zi-le-sa mu-sa-nu ma lo no. Pu-zi mu-sa-
2. na. Sa se-ya-ze le-ki pu mi-so le-na-ki nu
3. si-wa ko-na no sa-le-se 'o-lo-zo le-ki sa-
4. le-li. Pa-li-sa-wa ze-ya-le-ze-ko li-lu wa-
5. ko-ta li-ze si-i-le we-me li-se-ri la zo-
6. pa mu-sa mu lu-lu ma no-me to-no pu li-se
7. lu-a-ri po mi-sa ki-sa lo te-sa sa-na-ze
8. se-sa ki-mi-le lo-la li-zo li-li se-la ya-
9. li ta iya. Nu lu-se mi ta-po ke o-na lo si-
10. ko sa-ta so-re nu pa-si po wa u-se wa-u

The horizontal text, as now rendered in left-to-right horizontal lines
_____

11. pu-nu-si wa ko-se lu ya-ti u-
12. wa-ta-la. Ma-li-ta lu wa-ki-zi
13. le-na-ko. Li-li pu-ri-se ya-se.
14. U-nu li-po-no-ze ko-na. Le-sa
15. nu-so-no ze-si to-mi li-lu-wa
16. po-se-zo. Sa-me-i le-sa mi-sa-
17. nu, pu-le Iya-le mo-ki li-mi-si
18. pa-ta-la-sa ma we ze-se ki-mo
19. lo-le o-wa me lu lo-lo po-nu
20. re-ke-le-ta lu. Li-sa lo-ze-no.
21. Pu-iya zo-li-se mu-sa mi-o-so
22. ta-na-ki-sa-sa-ri pa-le se-zi.
23. Mu-sa ki-li lu pu-na-sa lo-sa
24. ko-si se-ze pa zo-le sa-na-sa.

The Hittite-Minoan roots can all be found in Sturtevant's or Friedrich's
Hittite Dictionaries, as already described in detail in the various papers already published in OPES vol 4. On account of the exigencies of the
acrostic structure, many vowels are inconsistent; this may either be due
to the irregular spelling found in all American (and many North African)
inscriptions, or it may indicate that the syllabic signs were treated by
the composer as merely consonants. These vowel variations are self-evid-
ent, so a detailed vocabulary is not here given, for it can easily be as-
certained from the dictionaries cited, and from the papers in OPES vol 4.

The approximate translation of the foregoing text is as follows:

1. To obtain an omen from birds when a man is worried, the oracle
   is given
2. by birds. Put down grain, let it lie where it falls. Ensure now
3. that it lies secure, is not blown away, or destroyed as it lies
4. on the grass, Protect it and drive away from the prairie
5. any sheep that may come to crop the grass or feed on morsels.
6. A flock of birds, however, is a good omen. Allow them to peck at
   the grain
7. for good or bad fortune they deliver in this way. If they approach
   the grain
8. on the grass, and also eat it immediately on the prairie , it is
   a good omen,
9. for the gods speak by this sign. If they do not peck at it, however,
   by this same token the man knows
10. he is divined to be a victim, so let him be reconciled to his fate.
    To obtain an omen for his son and heir let him
11. ask an oracle for the boy. The man is to go to
12. the Seer. The man is to recite a prayer
13. and swear an oath. To the place of oracles on the prairie let him go
14. The man is to scatter grain. If peck
15. the birds the grain, the child will prosper,
16. and that is the omen. If the birds refuse to peck ,
17 a libation to the gods, imploring aid by the licquor
18. the priest is to pour on the grain on the grass
19. made from honey, pleading for the prosperity of the man and the child
20. in entreaty for the man. If they peck at it, he will be healed.
21. In this manner are given omens by the birds of oracular power
22. at the sacred precincts when a libation and grain are given
23. for the birds. A fee the man is to pay for the services of the oracle
24. in grain. He must deliver it to the oracle for the Sanusi (high priest)

These pages show excerpts from Epigraphic Society Occasional Publications
Vol. 9, No. 218, June 1981, Pages 132-136 By Dr. Barry Fell
Decipherment and Translation of the Newberry Tablet from Northern Michigan

The vocabulary of this American omen text from Michigan invites comparison with that of Cherokee language as well as with that of the linear tablets of Crete, and the Phaistos Disk.

The syllabary of the tablet has already (OPES, Vol. 8) been compared with other known Cypro-Minoan syllabaries, and requires no further discussion here.

The contained vocabulary is given in full later in this paper. A sample of the similarities of the vocabulary to other languages I have just named may be illustrated by these examples.

Meaning	Hittite	Minoan	Newberry	Cherokee
Grain	ziz, ve, se	zi	zese, segase	selu
Son	u was	(not known)	owa	aweje
Water	mu	mu	ma	ama
Pay, price	killam	(not known	kili	akwiyika

(Fell gives some more)

For a detailed discussion of the Crete Cyprus connection, see *Ancient Mines of Kitchi-Gummi* by Roger L. Jewell—Jewell Histories, Fairfield, PA, 2000.

Just too similar to be coincidences.
Left: Found in Derrynamanagh, Co.
Galeway, Ireland.
Right: Found on lake bottom in Alger Co.
Michigan, USA.
Other similar ones found nearby.

Chapter VIII
Early Ocean Crossings

Introduction

One of the great road blocks to getting people to believe that there could ever have been a copper trade is the crossing of the oceans in prehistoric times.

We must get over the idea that those oceans were barriers. They were highways and the literature just abounds with seafarers traveling long distances, some for religious reasons, some for exploration, some for escape, but many for trade. The trade routes were known only to the seafaring traders and kept as a highly guarded secret for several obvious reasons: first, this trade (walrus hides, furs, metals, etc.) was most valuable. Second, how do you explain where you've been without maps or printing to an ignorant population, many of whom thought the world was flat and that the oceans, were filled with monsters, or flowed off into an endless abyss at the edge?

But there were crossings, many of them. Let us examine just a few that are on record. Knowing of these will surely go a long way in visualizing a trade, and realizing the demand for copper—a copper trade. [64a]

In a recent letter (Jan. 23, 2004), Filip Coppens, an editor formerly from Belgium but now living in England, (He has a publishing business in both countries.) writes:

> One of the big mysteries of the past, I feel, is that in ancient times, metals were mined in the U.S. without knowing where they went, and in Europe, metals were used, without knowing where they came from. When we then know that in Europe, all these cultures are known as the 'Atlantic Arc,' because they traveled by boats from Norway to Morocco, you have to wonder whether rather than just North-South, communication also occurred East-West. And this goes back at least to 2000 B.C. (4,000 years).

[64a] Copper was the most sought after and valuable metal in the world at the time.

Ethel Stewart's Breakthrough

Ethel G. Stewart 1909 - 2001

It is sincerely hoped that by this time a picture of ancient seafarers to North America is becoming plausible to the reader. This may be difficult for people who were educated in the schools of the past century, which left no room for sea travel prior to Columbus.

However, let us take a look at some situations that clearly indicate travel by people in ancient times across oceans. It should be a forgone conclusion as every continent or great island that was "discovered" by Europeans was inhabited by people who had been there a long time, except for Antarctica—but even there the ancients may have seen and mapped its shores long before modern explorations.

The current thinking that has dominated the theory of the first Americans is that they all came from the west, across the Bering Strait 10 to 12 thousand years ago. It is evident that some did arrive that way, but the dates of their arrival are certainly in great confusion. There were many that came much earlier as we will see in the following pages. Had we taken the time to look up the pieces of historical written records as one Canadian woman did over a 40-year time period, we would see that the largest migration into America from the west, that of the Athapaskan people, was fairly recent and not by foot but by boat.

There is a book by Ethel G. Stewart, "The Dene and Na-Dene Indian Migration 1233 A.D." with a subtitle, "Escape from Genghis Kahn to America, 1233 A.D." (ISAC Press 1981). Dr. Joseph B. Mahan, the former president and founder of the ISAC organization (Institute for the Study of American Cultures), Columbus, Georgia, calls it one of the great historical breakthroughs of our time.

Dr. Mahan wrote in his preface for the book:

> It is seldom indeed that a book becomes available which presents a totally unprecedented interpretation of a mammoth segment of the world's history documented with such authority from so many substantiating areas

Dr. Joseph B. Mahan, Columbus, Georgia, the former president and founder of the ISAC organization. Dr. Mahan died in 1997

of study as does this pioneering treatise by Ethel Stewart. After almost forty years of persistent effort, this independent-minded Canadian scholar has produced a work that will, in time, be recognized as a very heavy "straw" which finally broke the camel's back of the historical fallacy of cultural isolation in pre-Columbian America. It may be ignored by those who spend their lives measuring and defining the results of this presumed isolation, but the revealing monument to vision and determination presented herein will not be forgotten.

The author has given a firmly-established history of the arrival in America of the Dene (the Athapaskan peoples whom eighteen and nineteenth century explorers found living dispersed from Alaska to Mexico) and the NaDene (the associated Haida and Tlinget tribes of the British Columbia Coastal islands). They came, she has discovered, in the best tradition of innumerable others, fleeing from intolerable conditions in their homeland to a refuge in America. In this case, flight was from conquest, oppression, and death at the hands of Genghis Khan and his Mongol hordes.

Ms. Stewart has found forbears of the Dene in the Kingdom of His-Hsia in Central Asia, among the Turkish tribes north of the Gobi Desert, and in the Uighur kingdom of Turfan. All of these were conquered and virtually annihilated by the Mongol invaders. Their history is recorded in numerous manuscripts and published sources the author used as she worked in some of the world's great libraries.

Details of the same history were preserved in the oral tradition of the Dene as it was recorded by nineteenth and twentieth century observers, including herself. By far the most comprehensive of these reports, however, were the work of Father Emil Petitot who resided in the Catholic Mission at Good Hope on the Lower McKenzie River from 1860 until 1875. He traveled widely with the Dene and recorded their traditional history and his observations of their customs, ceremonies, and religious rites. He prepared a dictionary of three of their dialects.

Father Petitot's work was completed before the native culture had been changed by European influences. It included the Dene contention that their ancestors reached this continent in ships via the Aleutians. Furthermore, I recorded their assertion that their ancestors fled to this continent to escape death at the hands of a terrible enemy, the leader of whom they called "The Crow Who Runs." Explaining the complex linguistic and other cultural details recorded for the American Dene and those from Central Asia, the author proves most adequately the historical accuracy of the five centuries-old oral account of the legendary migration.

Moreover, she has been able to identify specifically the origins of many of the individual tribes involved. For example, "fugitive groups from the Altoi and from Qara-Khodja in the Uighur kingdom of Turfan" are identified as ancestors of Kutchen tribes of the Dene; the Apache and several small Dene tribes of the Pacific coast are shown to be descendants of fugitives from the Southern Tarim, "largely from Khotan region." The name *Apache* means "warrior" in the Asian homeland as it does today among the American descendants. The Navajo are said to have come from Na-fo-po, the center of the Tibetan Administration from the seventh to the tenth centuries. By 1218 A.D. they had fled from the Mongols to temporary safety within the kingdom of His-Hsia. According to Ms. Stewart, the name Mescalera means "Mountain Valley of Meskar." She writes that "they were men of a regiment guarding the great Buddhist settlement of Maskar, which was situated in a mountain valley to the south of Khotan."

The Asian *Yueh-chih* (Yuchi) were among the ancestors of the peoples who fell victim to the ravages of Genghis Khan's Mongols. In *The Secret, America in World History Before Columbus,*[65] I presented evidence which indicates the Yuch-chih, who moved into northern India and established the Kushan Dynasty of Indian emperors (1st-2nd centuries A.D.) were descended from the same ancestral "Moon People," as were recorded for the people of the His-Hsia kingdom has further convinced me of this

---

[65] The Secret-American World History Before Columbus—published by the author Dr. Mahan 1983—also see North American Sun Kings—Keepers of the Flame, both books by Dr. Joseph B. Mahan, ISAC Press (1992), 1004 Broadway, Columbus, GA 31901.

relationship. Reading these sections of her book has given me the feeling of meeting old friends.

The same reaction will occur for other readers who will recognize elements of Buddhism, Nestorian Christianity, Manichaeism, and Islam in the Atkapaskan religious beliefs the author documents.. All of these influences were prominent in the twelfth century kingdom of His-Hsia which was home to persons of all these faiths because of a tolerance induced by the ethnic and cultural diversity of the people who had come there for centuries over the famed "Silk Road."[66]

This book opens a treasure chest of opportunities for investigating the untold number of research subjects it introduces.

> Joseph B. Mahan
> Columbus, Georgia
> March 30, 1991

Ethel Stewart's book gives the story of certainly one of the largest migrations into the Americas—that of the Athapaskan people. The migration was not across the Bering Strait 10 or 12 thousand years ago, but only 800 years ago. Beside the Navajo, Apache, Dene and NaDene, it includes the various tribes belonging to the Sioux Nation.

The fact is well known that the Winnebago (Ho-Chunk) were around Green Bay on the western shore of Lake Michigan when the French arrived there in the early seventeenth century. The Winnebago, A Siouxen tribe, were known to the French as the "people of the sea."

Correcting an Historical Error

For many years there was much mystery and confusion over the landing place of Jean Nicolet, a delegate of Samuel de Champlain who was sent to the western Great Lakes region in hopes of finding China along their western shore in 1634.

Champlain came to Canada in 1603 as a geographer on the third expedition

---

[66] The Silk Road was of great antiquity with the true beginning being, so far, lost in history. But Europe really became aware of its existence at the beginning of the second century B.C., when the Middle Kingdom succeeded in breaking through the ring of war-like nomads which barred its path to the west.

to attempt to start a colony there. He ascended the St. Lawrence as far as the Lachine Rapids, where Montreal now stands, following a written description made by Jacques Cartier almost 70 years earlier. From the Indians in that area he learned of the waterways to Lake Huron, Niagara Falls, the Detroit River and the copper of Lake Superior. He also learned of the shorter route of the A-da-wa (Ottawa), the traders, up the Ottawa River and the Mattawa to Lake Nipissing and down the French River to Lake Huron. He learned much more than Cartier had ever known—but this was knowledge accumulated over many years. The description of the copper region was very vague, but this and the hint of these great waterways and unbelievable inland seas beyond led to speculation that this might finally be the long-sought route to the western ocean.

In his early days, Champlain had begun a policy of sending promising young men back to the homelands of visiting Indians who arrived in ever-increasing numbers from the great inland seas to trade their furs at the French Colony in Quebec. Etienne Brule was the first of these "Coureurs de Bois," runners or messengers of the woods, and as a teenager he accompanied an Algonquian chief homeward in 1610. There were many of these young explorers sent into the Indian country to learn the language, water routes and geography of the land so as to pave the way for later trade and colonization.

For some time after Brule's first report, Governor Champlain had received other vague reports of a great inland sea far to the west that led him to believe that Asia was on its western shore. In 1634 he outfitted another famous coureur de bois, Jean Nicolet, with a beautiful Chinese-style silken robe and sent him off to meet the great Khan.[67]

According to an account by John Gillmary Shea, who used as his source the "Jesuit Relations," Nicolet went through the Straits of Mackinac into Lake Michigan and landed somewhere in Green Bay on the west side of the Door Peninsula, about 80 miles from the city of Green Bay, Wisconsin.

Today there is a bronze statue of Nicolet on the Peninsula, a gift to Wisconsin from all of her school children in 1939-1940.[68]

A sign at this Nicolet Memorial states:

Red Banks—Many of the explorers who followed Columbus were more interested in finding an easy route to Asia than they were in exploring and settling the continent. In 1634, Jean Nicolet, emissary of Gov. Samuel

---

[67] Genghis Khan was killed in 1229 A.D., but the rulers of the Mongols were all called "Khan."

[68] This was during the tenure of John Callahan, State Superintendent of Public Instruction.

Statue of Jean Nicolet on the Door Peninsula on Lake Michigan

de Champlain of New France, landed at Red Banks on the shore of Green Bay about a mile west of here. His mission was to arrange peace with the *People of the Sea* and to ally them with France. Nicolet half expected to meet Asians on his voyage and had with him an elaborate Oriental robe which he put on before landing. The Winnebago Indians who met him were more impressed with the "thunder" he carried in his pistols. Nicolet reported to his superiors that he was well entertained with "six score beavers" being served at one banquet, but it was the pelts and not the flesh of the beaver that were highly prized by those who followed him."

The plaque was created in 1957

In 1965 a lone researcher named Harry Dever from Cedarville, Michigan, made a

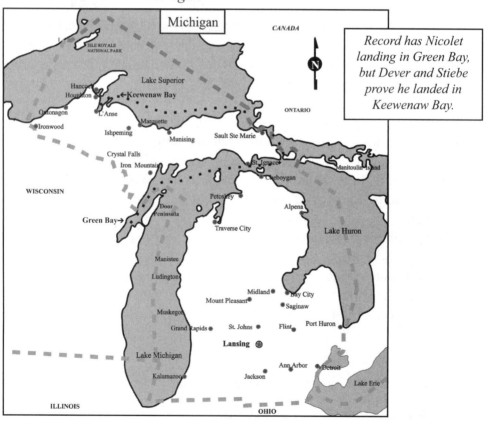

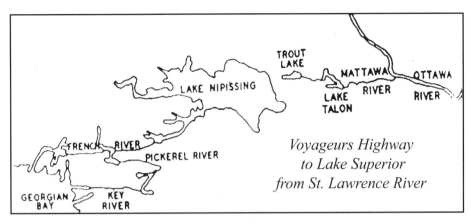

Voyageurs Highway to Lake Superior from St. Lawrence River

step by step analysis of Shea's story and although it was understandable, he discovered that Shea was way off base. True to form, all the historians and other scholars had followed his story to the letter down through the years and it became fact. Dever's argument appeared in the *Michigan History Magazine* (Vol. L, No. 4—Dec. 1966).

Without going into the many intricate details of Dever's reasoning, it comes down to the fact that Shea mistook the Ouinpegous, an Algonquian tribe, for the Winnebagos, who were then also called the Hochenogra or Otchagra, but are now known as the Hochunks, a Sioux tribe. Nicolet could understand some Algonquian but had never heard the Sioux language. Nevertheless he was able to make a treaty with them and they called him "Manitou Ininious," in an Algonquin dialect, which is slightly different from "Manitou Inine" as the Ojibway would have said it. But the Ounipigou clearly spoke an Algonquian dialect and would have been an Algonquin tribe as Nicolet had no trouble communicating with them, but he certainly could not conclude a major agreement with a Sioux tribe whose language he could not understand.[69]

Dever correctly follows Nicolet into Lake Superior by carefully reading the Relations and determines that the "west shore" where he landed was in Lake Superior, not Lake Michigan.[70] By following several studies and archaeological digs at and near Sand Point at the head of Keweenaw Bay near Baraga, Michigan, Ron Stiebe, in his book "Mystery People of the Cove" (Lake Superior Press, Marquette, Michigan, 1999) proved beyond reasonable doubt that this location

---

[69] Dever: The Ouinipigou reported in their neighborhood a tribe they described but did not name as "nadouesiu assinipour eriniouai," that is "foreign-speaking, stone-using men" or primitive foreigners. It has been universally accepted that this refers to tribes who later became known as the Sioux and Assiniboine. The Ouinipigou could not communicate with them as they spoke Sioux dialects. Some historians have suggested the Illinois, but that later denoted a group of tribes; it meant "the men."

[70] The "west shore" was the shore of the Keweenaw Peninsula in Keweenaw Bay.

is indeed the spot where Nicolet landed. Three hundred leagues west of Heronia on the south shore of Lake Superior would be about the right distance also. But the French did describe the Winnebago found later in the vicinity of Green Bay as people who had come from the coast of a distant sea, their ancestors having "come over the sea."

We can easily understand why we must prove ideas with evidence from at least two or preferably three or more completely different disciplines, or sets of circumstances, as any single method could have an invisible flaw not understood by an investigator. The following case could be a good example: Scientists endeavoring to trace the migration of a population by following the DNA could become very confused if they did not realize that people with the same origins, that is, west and north of the Mediterranean Sea, could have come to America from two opposite directions, and could have met in the Great Lakes region. In watching a television documentary of National Geographic origin on a scientist following global migrations by DNA, the immigration routes are correct but the dates and methods of migrations are way off according to Ethel Stewart's historical records. And then the scientists question, "How do some of the Great Lakes Tribes have European genes?"

The Possible Origin and Migration of the Tewa Indians of New Mexico

The following idea is implied by Ethel Stewart, but in my reading I ran across similarities in people from Asia and the southwest U.S. who might only be recognized by persons who are expecting to find such things.

Key hole foundation
Illustrated by Liz Yelland ©

There is an Indian tribe now living in New Mexico called the Tewas, who, like the Algonquians, have so many distinct traditions that by combining their oral history and their ingrained pattern of building, we can again compare them with a very old cultural group from Asia.

Briefly told, the Tewas believe that they originated in mother earth, living in partially underground houses of a distinct "keyhole" shape. The houses became

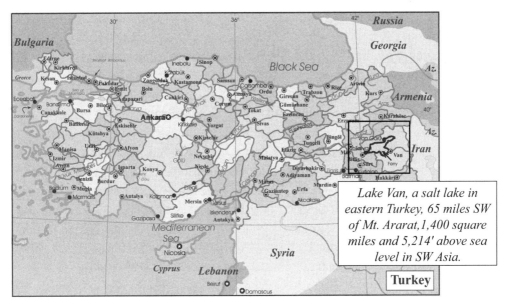

Lake Van, a salt lake in
eastern Turkey, 65 miles SW
of Mt. Ararat, 1,400 square
miles and 5,214' above sea
level in SW Asia.

Turkey

less and less underground and in more modern times were enlarged to multi-storied house blocks. The original homes had the door facing east so that the first rays of the morning sun shined in the entrance. These houses are known as kivas. While the traditional kiva was round, the newer ones are usually rectangular but still retain the old keyhole style with an opening channel toward the sunrise.

Since the new higher buildings tend to block out the sun, they have lost some of the tradition, but some of the Tawas have gone to the mountain tops and built the old traditional type kiva out of stones. The keyhole design reminded them of the original kivas that were partially underground and were used as a religious sanctuary. They continue to make journeys to these original style kivas as a place of renewal and to gain spiritual power.

The Tewa people also believe they came from the far north out of an unknown lake. They long ago had divided into two opposite groups, one known as the summer people and the other as the winter people. The two opposing groups tended to balance their life and this idea is carried out in many different aspects of the culture.

After emerging from the waters the Tewas started their migration south, traveling in the two opposing groups which would meet eventually. On their journey south they made twelve stops. They know where these places are but they do not have a time frame. In fact, they don't seem interested in knowing when this occurred, just that it was many years ago and is a part of their oral history. They don't know how long they have lived in their present homeland.[71]

---

[71] For details of this tradition, see The National Geographic Magazine, October 1991, Vol. 180, Nov 4, pgs. 6-14.

If, according to Ethel Stewart's book, many of the western Indian tribes came up the silk road from the area that is now Turkey, Iran, Iraq and Syria, or generally the region between the Black Sea and the Caspian Sea, known as "the Caucasus," then we can look there for the ancestors of the Tewas.

In ancient times there was a population there known as Helafians. Author James Mellaart has suggested they may have come from the north, possibly from the mountains around Lake Van,[72] where their ancestors were involved in the obsidian trade. They were also fine pottery makers and there were large cores of obsidian found alongside Halaf pottery of the highest quality at the settlement of Tilki Tepe, south of Lake Van. Obsidian here and at other Halafian sites may be the key to the origins of their culture, Mellaart believes.

In a book by Mary Settegast, "Plato Prehistorian," (Plato Pre-historian—10,000 to 5,000 BC—Myth, Religion, Archaeology, Lindisfarer Press, 1990), Ms. Settegast quotes Mellaart:

> The northern location of the Halaf sites also tends to suggest that in origin their occupants were hill people who had ventured into the plain in pursuit of agriculture and stock breeding like their Hussuna neighbors, but were loathe to sever their connections with their old homeland and native building traditions…Could it be that the early Halaf settlers had come originally from the mountains between the Assyrian steppe and Lake Van area, where for thousands of years, from Epipaliolithic times on, they had engaged in the obsidian trade? Once settled on the northern edge of the plain they might still have controlled the trade with their relatives to the north…

Mary Settegast:

> His reference to 'relatives to the north' and the 'native building tradition' are based in part on the similarity of Halafian round houses to the dwellings in the earliest agricultural settlements in the Kerr and Araxes valleys of Transcaucasia. Some of these northern structures also had rectangular or curvilienan annexes like the Helafian 'tholoi;'[73] <u>many were partly subterranean with a few steps down at the entrance</u>, recalling the ancient round house traditions of Natufian Ain Mallaha and the walled town of Jericho, stone foundation walls and outline of Halaf structure at Arpachiyah. The '<u>keyhole</u>' design of these buildings has been compared to the much later form of the 'tholoi' of the Aegean people.

---

[72] Lake Van—1,400 square miles—5,214 above sea level—SW Asia. See map on page 303.
[73] Tholoi—similar designed hut to Kiva.

And now I am comparing them both to the kivas of the Tewas in New Mexico.

There are possibly many comparisons we could make, but one that caught my eye and piqued my imagination first was the fact that in ancient times the Halaf people of Asia were somewhat nomadic traders of pottery and obsidian. And being traders they would have known about the Silk Road; in fact, they lived near this famous ancient trade route to China. Large caravans passed through their territory en route to and from China, loaded with trade goods. But, as we have learned, the Silk Road could also be used as an escape or an immigration route away from the tempestuous western Mediterranean of those times. For thousands of years these people had a deeply ingrained tradition of building keyhole-shaped domiciles, and they had lived in the mountains and on the plains. There is a great possibility that large groups of them, for reasons which would be fairly easy to determine, could have followed the Silk Road to China and boarded the great, five-tier trading junks which followed the Aleutian Island chain carrying on the sea otter trade.

The Tewas oral history starts with them coming out of the water far to the north. They then divided into two groups which traveled south and came together again. They can't really explain their traditional house, which was round, usually partly underground and of a keyhole design with the entrance facing east. Since modern living has made them alter this traditional design, many still go to the mountain top and build a house of stone with that same keyhole design, and go there for a renewal and a spiritual uplifting.

While this is just a thumbnail sketch of early Tewas home building, it could be greatly enlarged upon with the proper investigation and a discussion with Tewas elders. I know the feeling: for thousands of years the log cabin was the traditional home of northern Europeans. They're often cold, dark, drafty and difficult to keep clean—but even with the advantages of simpler methods of building and the many improvements of modern construction materials, there is always great satisfaction for descendants of these people to build a log cabin and spend time there for the spiritual uplift it brings. Strangely, you don't need a plan or a lesson to build such a refuge; to many it just comes naturally.

More Crossings from the West

A half century before Ethel Stewart wrote her authoritative book about the great Athapaskan migration via the Aleutian Islands in 1233 A.D., Dr. Henriette Mertz had told us of many Pacific Ocean crossings by the Chinese dating from 2250 B.C. to 400 A.D.

The noted philosopher, Confucius, proclaimed that "pale ink is better

Photo courtesy Warren Dexter

Dr. Henriette Mertz

than the most retentive memory." And so Dr. Mertz, like Ethel Stewart, went directly to ancient historical records for her source and wrote her findings in a book she named "Pale Ink."[74]

Any written record far exceeds archaeological digs in most instances. To learn about a culture and their travels requires the input of many disciplines. As John Tiffang, editor of the *Barnes Review,* points out, "Reconstructing ancient cultures by looking at potsherds and other artifacts is comparable to trying to deduce the plot of a stage play by examining the props."

For some years Dr. Mertz had been working with a Chinese guide and historian. From him she learned of two ancient documents that record specific locations on the American continent, long before the arrival of modern Europeans. These documents, which still exist in Chinese archives, are the oldest known works of geography. They are "Classics of Mountains and Sea" from 2250 B.C. and "Fu Sang" from 400 A.D.

Dr. Mertz explains that although the first listed dynasty recorded is that of Hsia 2197-1766 B.C., eight or ten preceding emperors, back to Fu-his, 2852 B.C., are known. (Different sections of China used different systems of chronology.) About 840 B.C. they appear to have been synchronized so that the dates after that all agree; earlier dates may vary as much as 100 years).

Yu was the Minister of Public Works under the Emperor Shun (2250 B.C.) for seventeen years. With the death of Shun there was a three-year period of mourning after which Yu ascended the throne. At the suggestion of Emperor Shun, Yu compiled the Shan Hai King—the "Classic of Mountains and Seas."

Yu sent explorers to all regions of the earth to survey the land. They used a method that is a variation of one that is still used today. They went to the top of the highest hills and mountains where they sighted to other high points which they then located on their map. In 1956, I observed a mapping crew doing the U.S. Coast and Geodetic Survey of the Huron Mountain region. They were doing the same thing. They built a tower within a tower (for stability) and triangulated

---

[74] "Pale Ink" by Henriette Mertz (1953 and 1972—The Swallow Press Inc., 1139 South Wabash, Chicago, IL 60605).

to other locations on high points.

The original books of the Yu survey numbered something like 136. They were kept in a cave where, over time, they deteriorated and had to be rewritten several times. Each time they were changed and condensed to thirty-some that exist today. To modern interpreters they seem almost whimsical, like myths (we had the same trouble with the Sagas and Greek myths), but Henriette Mertz had a brilliant deductive mind and through years of studying the various translations and comparing them with known places, she has been able to come up with some startling conclusions.

The Chinese told Dr. Mertz they were unable to locate any of these mountains mapped on the survey anywhere in Asia. But by carefully following the directions of the Classics, she compared them with the Rocky Mountain chain in America where they fit perfectly. From the Chinese map and descriptions, many specific and unique landmarks of our western region can be easily recognized.

I had no trouble believing this story as I heard local travelers from my hometown insinuate that the Chinese had been to America. I may have spoken earlier of Mrs. James Redi who, on her return from a trip to California in the 1920s, told of a man who found a small Buddha statue while digging a foundation for a fireplace.

A Discovery by Dr. James Acocks

Dr. James R. Acocks of Marquette

Then there was the story told by Dr. James R. Acocks of Marquette. He had been traveling in China and had visited the tomb of Qin Shi Huanghi, the Emperor from 221 to 210 B.C. He was the first Emperor to unite all China. The huge, mile square tomb, now world famous, was discovered in 1974. This is a tomb with thousands of terra cota soldiers, each with individual differences as they were in life. There are bronze chariots with full-size statues of horses in bronze. The points of the spears and standard bearers are bronze and Acocks was told that the bronze has minute amounts of gold in it. The scientists said they have examined all the sources of copper in Asia and could not find any that contained gold.

Many years ago Dr. Acocks heard me giving a talk on Lake Superior copper. He remembered me stating that Lake Superior copper was the only known gold containing copper mined in ancient times. For years, in modern times, both gold and silver were removed from the local copper as by-products. In fact, although the Craig and Daniels Mines, near the extinct town of Birch in Marquette County, were opened as copper mines, it was found that the ore assayed higher in gold than in copper. Today, older inhabitants still refer to the "Craig Gold Mine."

Courtesy of Dr. James R. Acocks

Above: Points of the spears and standard bearers of terra cota soldiers from tomb of Qin Shi Huanghi.
Below: Cavalryman and Pommelled Horse from tomb of Qin Shi Huanghi (Bronze)

Courtesy of Tom and Ling yu Edgar

Pale Ink

Henriette Mertz's "Pale Ink" is certainly a "must read" for anyone interested in the pre-history of the American continent. Most of us have heard of the mysterious bearded white god who visited the Americas sometime in the fifth century A.D. He was known to the Mayans as Kukalcan, Sume in Brazil and Bochica in Columbia. In Guatemala he was Gucamatz and in other places he was known by other names: Cipas, Wuepachocha, Viracocha and Contici. In parts of Mexico he was Quetzalcoatl, but all these names go back to the same general time period and they all have the same general description. Dr. Mertz was one of the first to spell out exactly who this person was, again by referring to an ancient document.

From "Pale Ink":

> During de Guignes', an eminent French sinologist,[75] study of the Classics, he came across a story retold by Ma Twan-lin, in his "Antiquarian Researchers" published in 1321, of a Buddhist priest, Hwui Shan by name, who, in the fifth century reported having been in a far country to the east of China. After translating the account, de Guignes believed that he recognized the country described as Fu-sang to be Mexico.

"Pale Ink" gives the complete English translation of the story. Hwui Shan was the Buddhist Priest who made his way begging alms as he traveled through what is now the southwestern United States and south into Mexico and Central and South America. As a traveler, explorer, missionary, teacher and recorder of events, Mertz describes him, without question, one of the 'greatest the world has ever known.' He was in China in 499 A.D. (according to the Classics) and told his story at court of having been to a far country 20,000 LI (about 7,000 miles) east of the Great Han country. He had established contact with people some 40,000 LI (13,000 miles) distant to the east. The people had writing, woven cloth and had some kind of paper. He goes on to describe a civilization with domestic cattle, their leaders and their culture. They had unwalled cities and were without weapons of any kind.

# # #

The fourth book of the "Classic of Mountains and Seas" is divided into four sections. Dr. Mertz has no trouble locating the mountains and landmarks

---

[75] Sinologist—one who studies the history, culture, language and literature of the Chinese.

described in the first part, along with the lakes and rivers. Her interpretation fits this country perfectly. It seems impossible that the story could have been written about any place but America. It describes pipe organ cactus and the birds that make their nests in them.

One very convincing quote from "Pale Ink":

> Nature's most magnificent display of her handiwork—the Great Luminous Canyon with the little stream flowing in a bottomless ravine—outspectacles every other natural extravaganza on this earth, with its brilliant yellows, vibrant oranges, deep subtle reds and its shadow pale lavenders turning into rich color—and nowhere else does it exist. To the ancient Chinese traveling east, this great fissure must be the place where the sun was born.
>
> Hundreds of Chinese apparently saw the canyon—it was a "must" on their travel adventure schedule. 'I saw the place where the sun was born'—Chinese poetry and literature fairly bulges with cantos of glowing reminiscence. They called it the 'Great Canyon" 4,000 years ago; we call it the Grand Canyon today. No one could stand on the rim of the canyon and be unmoved by it. The Indians could not; the Chinese could not; and we cannot.

To all appearances they traveled the ancient logical route of the Aleutian Islands, never over a day out of sight of land, the route of the Sea Otter trade that had gone on for thousands of years.

Among the many illustrations, both pictorial and descriptive as well as anecdotal, in the 1972 edition of "Pale Ink," there is one which caught my fancy because it mentions a locally famous name—a family I know well—John Munro Longyear.

#

John Munro Longyear III is the grandson of the (at least locally) famous J. M. Longyear of Marquette, Michigan, who developed the coal mines in Spitzbergen (1903-1917) and for whom the town of Longyearbyen is named. It is the most northern village in the world (population 1200).

John Longyear III was born on July 31, 1914 in Marquette and was graduated from Graveraet High School in that city with the class of 1931. He did his undergraduate work at Cornell and his Ph.D. at Harvard. Dr. Longyear did much of the early archaeological investigation at Copán and Chitzén Itzá on the Yucatan Peninsula in Mexico. He taught many years at Colgate and today

Photo courtesy of Joan Longyear, daughter daughter of J.M. Longyear III

Marion
Longyear
Sonderegger
and
John M.
Longyear III

(2004) lives with his daughter in Kennebunkport, Maine. His sister, Marian Longyear Sonderegger, is a life-long resident of Marquette.

# # #

From "Pale Ink":

In Edwin M. Shooks 'Research on the pre-Classic Horizons in Guatemala,' it reads; 'In speaking of pottery-making cultures throughout Mezo-America before 200 A.D., there has been found a three-legged incensoria (incense burner) and a special vessel set on three feet, dating from the archaic period. This form, he stated, continued through pre-Classic, Classic and post-Classic. It was the only pottery vessel with secondary supports found in pre-Classic sites. John M. Longyear III, writing on an 'Historical Interpretation of Copan Archaeology,' stated that 'Polychrome basal-flanged bowls and black tripod vases, so diagnostic of Early Classic refuse, suddenly disappear in Full Classic.' Both of these pre-Classic American tripod bowls have the same structure and design as the LI tripod identified by Dr. Creel. The colors found in slips and on most pottery found in Mexico and Central America, is close to that found in China—the shapes of the vessels are the same. Excellent photographs of tripod bowls and incensorias are shown in Dr. Morley's book on 'The Ancient Maya.' He dated the early beginnings of pottery making as being before 1000 B.C.—it arrived completed by that date.

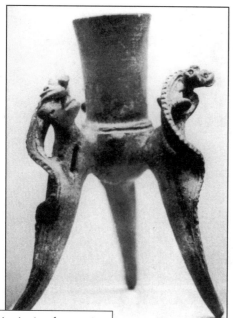

Chiriqui tripod ceramic vessel, Costa Rica (1000-1500 AD). Photo Camille, Museum of the American Indian Heze Foundation from Pale Ink.

Tripod ritual wine vessel, Shang dynasty (1800-1200 BC). Photo Camille Art Institute of Chicago from Pale Ink.

Above: Bas-relief at Chitzén Itzá (1000-1500 AD), a pre-Columbian horse. Photo: Emil Muench from Pale Ink.

Left: Seated figure-Late Classic Maya (c 900 AD-) Photo Camille-American Museum of Natural History from Pale Ink.

Right: Bodhisattva, China (600-900 AD). Photo Camille, of Art Institute from Pale Ink.

# # #

In the early days of my investigations, I corresponded with Dr. Henriette Mertz. Then in 1984 I had the good fortune to meet and spend time with her at a meeting of the Western Epigraphic Society in Albuquerque, New Mexico. She seemed fascinated with my story of Upper Michigan copper, and questioned me thoroughly on the subject. Little did I know that she was just testing me, for she knew the story of Michigan copper much better than I did.

"You'll be interested in a book I'm writing about Michigan," she told me. "It should be on sale in a year or two. There'll be some very enlightening facts in it for you." But she gave me no clue other than the hint that part of it dealt with Michigan copper.[76]

When I said goodbye to Henriette in Albuquerque that year, I had a sinking feeling that I would never see that book in print, for while her mind was keen, physically she seemed very feeble. I had to help her from the dining room to her hotel room. She confided to me that she was nearly 90 years old, had diabetes, and could not autograph my copy of her book, "Pale Ink," because of arthritis in her hands. I noticed, too, that her ankles were very swollen. The next day she made a special effort to sign the book and succeeded beautifully. I believe it was the last book she ever autographed. I was filled with admiration for her. Who, under these conditions, would leave the comfort and protection of a nice apartment in Chicago to fly alone to Albuquerque for a three-day meeting? She was indeed one of the great pioneers of pre-history of the world, but she is relatively unknown.

During the course of one of my discussions with Henriette Mertz, she told me that these Chinese books covered a survey of the whole American continent. Even though they had been greatly condensed in their several rewritings, she felt that the copper of the Lake Superior region was too important to have been left out. Her next project was to ask her Chinese contact if he could locate the book that spoke of the Great Lakes Region and see just what was said about the ancient Michigan mines.

Unfortunately she died the following year, even before completing "The Mystic Symbol."

Henriette Mertz, J.D., M.P.L., L.L.D., was a patent lawyer. She was admitted to practice before the United States Supreme Court, the United States Patent Office, the Canadian Patent Office, and the Supreme Court of Illinois.

---

[76] The book that Dr. Mertz was working on at that time was about thousands of clay, slate and copper tablets discovered in mounds in 27 counties of Lower Michigan between the 1860s and 1920s. The title of the book: "The Mystic Symbol" was published posthumously by a nephew. It is discussed elsewhere in this book.

She served as a Lieutenant Commander in the U.S. Navy during World War II as a special assistant to the Advisor on Patent Matters at the Office of Scientific Research and Development.

She possessed great knowledge, had an avid interest in ancient history and wrote a half-dozen or so scholarly books, all highly-acclaimed. Her best known works are, "The Wine Dark Sea," "Pale Ink" and "Atlantis, Dwelling Place of the Gods." "The Wine Dark Sea" was translated into Greek by the Greek government and published in Athens, and "Pale Ink" received an award from the Society of Midland Authors.

Henriette was born on June 22, 1896 in Chohio, Minnesota, but spent most of her life in Chicago. She was graduated from Marshall Law School there. She worked on the Manhattan Project and was advisor to Cordell Hull, Secretary of State during the Franklin Roosevelt administration (1933-1944). She was a contributor to the Greek Encyclopedia, a world traveler, photographer and artist. She died in Chicago on August 17, 1985, but her last book on Michigan, "The Mystic Symbol," was published posthumously by a nephew, Herbert Mertz.

Like many pioneers who went off on their own, Henriette Mertz, as well as Ethel Stewart, may have made a few errors in their far-flung historical deductions. But for the most part they will eventually be proven generally correct. Both Mertz and Stewart passed on knowing they were right and had done their part to set world views of history in the proper direction.

And Yet Again

Then, in January of 2003, as if no one had ever mentioned such a bold idea before, a Britisher named Gavin Menzies announced his own "new theory." In his book of that year entitled "1421," he offers many clues suggesting that the Chinese arrived here in 1421, examples that, in my opinion, are not as sound as those in Ethel Stewart's or Henriette Mertz's books.

One review (New York Times Magazine, January 2003), states that Menzies was given an advance of "more than $800,000" from Bantam in England. And Menzies, himself an amateur historian, was invited to speak at the Oxford Student Union after his book took London by storm in 2002. His book arrived in America along with a massive publicity campaign put on by his American publisher, William Morrow. His book signings have even taken him to China, where his stories received such a warm reception that there are now plans to build a modern replica of one of the famous huge junks that sailed the oceans a thousand years ago.

As with many claims of transoceanic travel in ancient times, while all offer possible proofs for their theories, all lack the dramatic, substantial proofs needed to sway academia and, therefore, the public. The evidence must be indisputable.

The situation that Menzies has hung his hat on is the historic fact that a fleet of huge Chinese junks was sent out in the 12th century to world ports. His research concludes that some of these ships visited ports in America, including one that navigated up the Sacramento River in California before grounding. His proof would be solidified if the remains of such a ship should ever turn up and be verified.

While Menzies' story is still being amplified by paid researchers and publicity people, as well as advertised in London, New York and twenty countries, in sharp contrast Henriette Mertz quietly published her own, "Pale Ink," in 1953 and then a second, revised edition, including pictures, in 1972.

Ethel Stewart's Dene Na-Dene book was deemed so radical that she could not find a publisher. All of the publishers she sent the manuscript to had it reviewed by college professors, who universally turned it down. When, however, she sent it to Dr. Joseph Mahan, president of the Institute for American Cultures, he was ecstatic, claiming it to be the greatest historical breakthrough of the century. Dr. Mahan persuaded me to handle the publishing and finance it under auspices of the ISAC Press, which I did. To my knowledge, Ethel never received a penny for her years of work. I am presently trying to accomplish a second printing. (The Dene and Na-Dene Indian Migration, 1233 A.D., Escape from Genghis Khan to America) (As of June 2005 it is once again in print.)

Still Another Discovery of Ancient Overseas Visitors

From the Boston Sunday *Globe* of November 10, 1985: Salem, Mass.—"The discovery in Mexico of a model of an ancient sailing ship with ten oarsmen with Asian features was offered yesterday as evidence that adventurers from Asia journeyed to the Americas before the birth of Christ."

Alexander von Wuthenau, a professor and specialist in pre-Columbian art at the University of the Americas in Mexico City, described his discovery at a conference reviewing evidence that ancient mariners visited the Americas centuries before the arrival of Christopher Columbus in 1492.

Von Wuthenau, who runs a foundation, "Humanitas Americana" in San Angel, Mexico, said, "The history books will all have to be rewritten because the evidence that the extremely important human activity of navigation evolved on our continent in ancient times is just too strong to ignore."

Von Wuthenau had been searching for evidence of such early contact between the Americas and other cultures for about 40 years, his curiosity sparked by discoveries of many other investigators which prompted him to wonder how people with such non-Indian faces came to be on this continent.

One figurine found in the Guerrero area made him wonder: "What is a Japanese wrestler doing in the mountains of Guerrero?" It was then that he determined the Guerrero area would be the place to find the evidence he was looking for. Over the years, more and more figures with Asiatic faces—as depicted in stone and in terra cotta by ancient artists—came to his attention, including two completely Asiatic "baby faces" found in the Olmec region of Guerrero.

Of course all this reminded me of how curious I was in the 1930's when Mrs. Emma Redi, who had just returned from California, told us about the man who, while digging a hole for the foundation of a fireplace for a mountain lodge, found a small statue of a Buddha. This discovery, I'm sure, was never reported to the proper authorities for fear of ridicule.

Von Wuthenau's article in the Boston Globe goes on to say that one of his greatest surprises was that this very Asiatic group of early immigrants to America, found at the most unlikely site of Xochipala, was also on the edge of the Olmec region. But the artifact that seemed to impress the professor most, the one that solidified the whole picture as to who these mysterious Asiatics were and how they got here, was the foot-long terra cotta boat model containing ten human figurines with what he described as distinctly Japanese faces. The artifacts were discovered in a burial site along with a number of other figures which had features of other cultures as well as Asian.

We have only mentioned a small number of these discoveries which indicate early people arriving in the Americas by water. Even if only one such case is true, our whole concept of pre-Columbian history is wrong. Even though these discoveries by responsible people are often reported at symposiums and published in various scientific journals, I have yet to see a break in the old traditions in a modern textbook. Old, ingrained ideas die hard.

Chapter IX
Ocean Crossings from the East

Evidence in the Arctic

Picture By Jason Mikki

Melville Peninsula Dolmen.

When speaking of ocean travelers arriving on the east coast of America, it is only fair to mention that according to Gavin Menzies,[77] the Zheng He treasure fleet first traveled to Kenya; they then sailed south, rounding the Horn of Africa and went to the Americas. His research has ships traveling up the Mississippi and along the American east coast during the 1420's. It seems quite possible that some of the Menzies story may be true. It will be years before the proper artifacts can be examined and dated.

This all takes time, but the momentum he has gained from the media (periodicals and TV talk shows) should hasten the research. In the meantime, Admiral Zheng He is a Johnny come lately, according to other research.

The finding of many dolmens in the high Arctic proved beyond a doubt that megalithic

Picture By Jason Mikki

---

[77] *1421 A.D.*, by Gavin Menzies, 2003.

Picture By Jason Mikki

Jason Mikki and friend 2003

Europeans covered all possible water routes in the Arctic. [76a]

Up until the 1980's, dolmens on this side of the Atlantic were seen as glacial erratics. They were just taken for granted and went unstudied.

In a publication by Victor W. Sim for the Department of Mines and Technical Surveys of Ontario, Canada, entitled "Maximum Post-Glacial Marine Submergence in the Northern Melville Peninsula," and based on observations made during the summers of 1957 and 1958, geologists seemed to have encountered many dolmens along these water routes, but tried to explain their existence as caused by land submersion and a glacial rebound. They speak of an uplift from at least 450 feet to possibly 650 feet before reaching equilibrium. Geologists also expect that much rise in the Hudson Bay region. One clue to the rising land or submersion was the finding of marine shells above present water levels. The highest they were found was 477 feet. Much of the report concerns the study of boulders, which are plentiful in some places and missing in others. It was quite obvious what had been submerged and what had not, and one section of the report specifically addresses "Perched Boulders" or in my way of thinking, dolmens. It says they may have been deposited by the "dumping

Picture By Eric Mitchell 1953

Melville Peninsula Dolmen.

[76a] The Era of Dolmen aproximatly 4500 BC to 1000 BC.

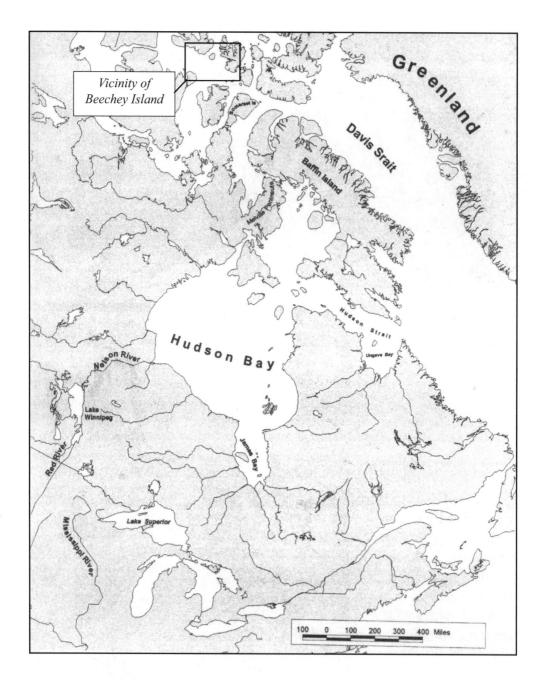

of englacial debris during deglaciation." It also states that such boulders could not survive wave action and ice push along the edge of a post-glacial sea, so their altitude must indicate that they were above a marine limit. The report suggests caution in interpretation, however, since "other perched boulders are occasionally seen at altitudes between sea level and the marine limit."

One man (H. R. Thompson, 1954) suggests "that rocks may be perched as the result of rock falls or by rolling down snow banks to lodge on the boulders at the base of the slope." Sim does not agree, however, believing they can almost invariably be recognized for what they are (glacial erratics). But he is quick to add that "others are less easy to explain, as several large perched boulders no more than 30 feet above sea level were observed on a low saddle between two pre-Cambrian knobs near the south entrance to Bunn Inlet in Garry Bay." Sim suggested that they were rafted into the area on ice floes and dropped into position when the ice grounded and later melted on the saddle. The report also supports the idea that the perched rocks would have been close to the water's edge, but would have survived the forces of the ice when the water further receded. To me, however, the fact that most of these dolmens are along present or earlier water routes indicates that these are practically all man made. The geologist Hank Vuori, after many years of working in the Arctic, was amazed to find that everywhere he went there was evidence that someone had been there in the distant past. Of course the solid evidence, as mentioned before, that megalithic Europeans had been there are the dolmens photographed by Eric Mitchell in 1953, those that had the multi-stoned legs, three stones in each leg. No glacier could make these. Besides the ones along the water routes, there are some lined up high on the rim of a valley that has the remains of underground domiciles such as those found on the Orkney Islands and Scotland, in a valley below. Then there are some along the sea coast and on the tops of mountains. The clincher as to who some of the people were is the trilothon on a peak along the north coast of Baffin Island, about 70 miles east of Pond Inlet, as reported by village elder, Nutarak Cornelius of Pond Inlet, Nunavut.

The Dorset people might have come from the east as their evidence is mostly east. But the early Eskimos say that the dolmen builders were giants and that they were not very bright. Anyone who did not know how to live in the cold and who died out would seem to be rather dumb to the Eskimos. The British[78] who tried to escape from the Arctic in their army uniforms fell into that category, so we must keep an open mind about the idea of real giants. We will discuss them later in these writings.

---

[78] Sir John Franklin led two expeditions into the Arctic in search of an open Polar Sea (1819-22 and 1825-27).

Set out in 1818 and again in 1825 to find a Northwest Passage. The entire expedition of 129 men were lost.

More than 40 rescue parties later sought traces of the expedition gaining immense geographical knowledge. Evidence of the expedition's tragic fate finally discovered in the 1850s. The author visited some grave sites of the Franklin Expedition on Beechy Island in July-August 2000—73 degrees N. Lat, Lancaster Sound. (See map on previous page)

Tracing the Algonquins

My good friend, Jim Dakota, 1937.

When we consider ocean crossings from the east in ancient times, we again clash with established history which emphatically states that all of the early crossings were from the west via the Bering Straits. Remember that we have already pointed out many other possibilities: the Irish, the Norse plus numerous Mediterraneans and Africans.

This is how I learned of the migration of the Algonquin Indians:

It was in 1941 that I first met "Indian Jim" Dakota as he was affectionately called by all who knew him. I knew nothing of the history of the Indian Tribes in our area at that time, but was always curious about them. During the summers of 1941 and 1942, I had much contact with Jim, living with him in the Huron Mountains in a tent on several occasions, sometimes up to a week. He had been born in 1873 and so, in my mind, was a very old man at almost age 70. Jim was full of stories, some that could not be believed, but many turned out to be true.

One thing I was confused about was the different local Indian tribes. Jim straightened this out for me. He said he was a Menominee and Chippewa, but his tribe in L'Anse where he lived was called Ojibway.

According to the writings of Bishop Baraga, a Jesuit who compiled an Algonquin dictionary, these people were all Algonquin (or Algonquian); they were a part of the Algonquin Nation, which consisted of many tribes loosely joined by a common language root. While they spoke different dialects, there were enough similarities that they could easily understand one another.

The Ojibways and the Chippewas were formerly called the "Otchipways," but the French pronounced their name "Ojibway" while the English pronounced it "Chippewa." Some groups retained the name Ojibway and others Chippewa, but they are all a part of the largest local group of Algonquins, known as the "Three Fires," who settled the western Great Lakes Region. The other two tribes belonging to the Three Fires are the Ottawas, who were the traders (they were the canoemen) and the Potowatamies, which meant "keepers of the fire," (they were farmers).

Jim was a Menominee, which means "wild rice gatherers," a sub-tribe of the Otchipwa," (Chippewa) Later I learned there are over a hundred tribes in the Algonquin Nation and even more with the same language roots.

**An Incomplete List of Algonquian Tribes
Odishquagumees-Algonquins Proper-Last Water People**

Abenaki
Agawams
Allumettes
Appomatic
Arapaho
Armouchequois
Aroonagnticook
Attikomeques - Whitefish
  Nation
Beatkuk
Blackfeet
Blood
Cambus - Norridgewocks
Caniba
Cheyenne
Chickakoming
Chippewa
Chowan
Connecticuts
Connoy
Cowesit
Cree—Kenistenoag
Delawares—Waubunukeeg
Eries
Fox—Odugameeg
Gaspesians
Hammonassets
Illinois
Iroquets
Kaskaskias
Kikapoos
Kaskakans
Kristineaux
Lenape (Delaware)
  Loup A/Loup B
Malecite
Mangunks
Massachusett
Massacoes
Massapequa
Mattabesec

Menominee
Menunkatucks
Miamies—Omaumeeg
Micmac – Souriquois
Missisaigas
Mohican
Mohegan
Montagnais
Montauk
Motinecoc
Munsi
Muscouien
M u s k e g o e s —
   Omushkegoag
Nanicoke
Nansemond
Narrangansett
Nashau
Naskapt
Nassauakuetouns
Nateck
Nauset
Nebicenini
Nehantics
Nepmucks
Nez Perce
Niantic
Nipmucks
Nipnaic
Noke—Noquet
Ojibway
Ottawa—Outonaes
Ouinpegous
Outchetaguin
Pamlica
Pammisnkey
Passamoquaddy
Pegano—Black Feet
Pennacock
Penobscot
Penticket

Peorias
Pepipenisoi
Pequaket
Pequots
Piegan
Pocamtuck
Podunks
Potowatami
Quinnipiacs
Sacnnet
Sauk—Saukies—Osaugeeg
Schoghticoke
Secotan
Senagos
Setauket
Shawnees—Shawunoag
Shinnorock
Sicoogs
Siwano
Sokoki
Tunxis
Tunris
Unami
Unalachtigo
Uncas
Unquachog
Wampana
Wampanaag
Wangunks
Wappinger
Weitspekan (Cal)
Wepawang
Weskarima
Wishoskan (Cal)
  California—long lost brothers of the Algonquin nation. Compiled from several sources.

Tom Wastaken

I often asked Jim Dakota where his people had come from. At first I got vague answers about his immediate family, but later, when he understood what I was looking for, he admitted that he didn't really know, except he was always told that they came from the east. At least one time he said "they came from the land of the rising sun." This statement stuck with me. Of course, it just meant "from the east," but the phrase had a kind of poetic ring to it as if it could have meant some far off land.

The reason this statement seemed important was because after World War II I began to hear theories that all Indians entered North America by crossing the Bering Straits, which, of course, was contrary to Jim's traditional story. At the time I put it aside and went along with the scientists.

Many years passed. In the early 1960's, I traveled north into the Canadian bush country where I met a lone Ojibway Indian named Tom Wastaken. He was the hunter for his tribe, which turned out to be all his close relatives. He would deliver meat and fish over vast distances by canoe or toboggan pulled by dog team.

After several trips meeting Tom, a tragedy occurred when his tent burned and he lost everything; the wind had changed and his only possessions were destroyed, his rifle and a sleeping bag an aunt had made for him from the hides of 200 rabbits.[79] We (my wife and two sons) brought Tom home to Marquette where he lived with us for about eight weeks. What seemed like a tragedy to us, Tom thought very funny and had a good laugh over it.

Tom had never been away from the Canadian Wilderness before, let alone to the U.S. It was a great experience for all of us and we learned a great deal from Tom. He spoke the Ojibway language fluently and read and wrote the language in the syllabulary characters used by the Cree. He was surprised by the abundance of Indian words used throughout the Upper Peninsula and enjoyed telling us the meaning of them (Ameek—beaver, Ishpeming—high place, Munising—bay with an island in it, Negaunee—the one who goes ahead, etc.).

---

[79] The inside layer had the fur inside, and the outer layer had the fur outside.

This Indian Cemetery near L'Anse, MI was established in the early 1840's after a change in custom from platform graves to pine "spirit houses".

Courtesy of Clyde Elmblad

Chief Herbert Welsh

We decided to take Tom on a trip west of Marquette to meet some Ojibway-speaking people. On our way through the little village of Three Lakes we passed a big teepee. Standing in front of it in a white, beaded buckskin suit and wearing a Sioux war bonnet was Chief Herbert Welsh,[79a] whose home was in L'Anse, a small village on Keweenaw Bay, about 25 miles farther west. Tom was very curious and we stopped to talk with him.

Tom tried to speak with Chief Welsh in his native tongue but the chief had to explain that he was not Ojibway, but Sioux. Grandson of the famous Sitting Bull, Chief Welsh had moved to Upper Michigan and married an Ojibway woman. Mrs. Welsh spoke Ojibway fluently and the chief wanted Tom to meet her, so we invited Chief and Mrs. Welsh to come to our home the following Sunday for a meal and a chat. Tom was looking forward to the meeting with great anticipation.

When the Welshes arrived at our home, by coincidence *Life Magazine* had recently arrived with a picture story of the migration across the Bering Straits.

After the meal, while we were still seated at the table, I announced that I

[79a] Tatanka Iyotare Hoksila - Sitting Bull Boy Grandson of "Chief" Sitting Bull - Sioux Tribe, Member of the "Standing Rock" Sioux Tribe of South Dakota.

Chief Herbert Welsh

would read them the story of where their people came from and I proceeded to read the article from the magazine. As I remember, there were large, two-page pictures of the migrating people and just a comparatively small amount of reading material. As I read, I would occasionally glance up at the three Native Americans. They were smiling at each other and occasionally they would wink or laugh politely. I stopped reading.

"What's the matter?" I asked. "Don't you believe this?"

Chief Welsh looked straight at me and with a very serious tone said, "Do you see my eyes?"

Yes, I could see his eyes very plainly. There was that conspicuous epicanthic fold so characteristic among oriental people.

"I came from that direction (West), but they don't have that fold; they came from the other direction."

"Well," I said, "this story is supposed to be the result of scientific investigation. Archaeologists have concluded that the American Indians all came across the Bering Straits about ten or fifteen thousand years ago."

"Yeah," said Chief Welsh, "But they didn't ask us."

Tom agreed. "I always heard that we came from the east, from the land of the rising sun."

"That's right," chimed in Mrs. Welsh.

"Isn't that strange?" I said, "I've heard that before from an old friend, Jim Dakota, but he never elaborated on it. He used the same phrase Tom used—'from the land of the rising sun.'"

"You don't go along with this story then?" I questioned. "The authorities apparently have settled on a theory that all the early inhabitants of North and South America come from the Bering Straits and spread across the continent. What are your ideas about that?"

Chief Welsh spoke again. "It's pretty clear to me that many people came here in ancient times from different directions. The scientists can believe what they like, but all the tribes of Indians are so different. The white man lumps us all together as one people, but we have different physical characteristics, completely different customs and traditions, many different languages, and even colors of skin. People came to this land in wave after wave at different times."

I put the magazine away and we talked about this idea which was new to

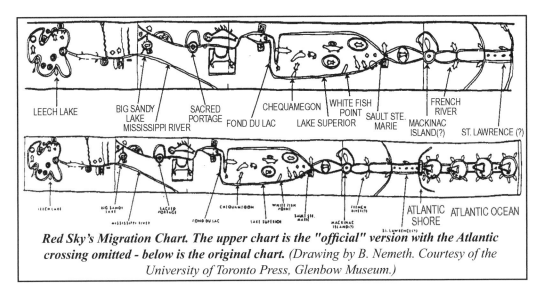

LEECH LAKE   BIG SANDY LAKE   SACRED PORTAGE   CHEQUAMEGON   WHITE FISH POINT   FRENCH RIVER
MISSISSIPPI RIVER   FOND DU LAC   LAKE SUPERIOR   SAULT STE. MARIE   MACKINAC ISLAND(?)   ST. LAWRENCE (?)

ATLANTIC SHORE   ATLANTIC OCEAN

Red Sky's Migration Chart. The upper chart is the "official" version with the Atlantic crossing omitted - below is the original chart. (Drawing by B. Nemeth. Courtesy of the University of Toronto Press, Glenbow Museum.)

me. Tom told how you could always tell that someone was from a different tribe and always recognize people from his own tribe. He knew immediately when he was in Cree country by the people, but they all recognized that there had also been a certain melding of characteristics and customs over the centuries. He said the Cree all look like white people except that they all have dark eyes and black hair.

Mrs. Welsh told of how the Algonquin people were spread out to the east along the waterways of the Great Lakes system, and down the east coast of the U.S. You could follow the language and customs of the people.

I thought about the ideas of this meeting over the ensuing years. Chief Welsh's statements were so logical, he spoke with such confidence and though I had never heard this before, I thought it was worth further investigation. If the Algonquin people came from the west and wandered across Canada there should be evidence of them in Alaska. The people there were Athabaskan stock. Yet if you follow the tribes strung out to the east, they are all Algonquins.

Then the first real clue presented itself. Over the years I spotted in books and museums a picture of Red Sky's migration route. I assume he was a respected Algonquin elder. The last place I had seen the drawing of this event was an enlargement high on a wall at an Indian Museum in St. Ignace, Michigan. Whenever I saw that chart, it always started at the St. Lawrence River. However, there was no indication that the Algonquins had wandered across Canada ten thousand years ago to assemble at the St. Lawrence.

I talked about this to a close friend, Wilson Turner, who had been a Navy pilot for years. He and his family summered at a cottage a few doors away from where my parents lived near Marquette.

Turner was an avid reader of history. He read nearly everything I suggested to him as well his own books, plus what he could find in the local bookstores and libraries. Sometime after our discussion of the local Indians coming from the east, Turner brought me a book on a period of Canadian history that included Red Sky's migration chart. At first glance I recognized the distinctive drawing I knew well, but then I noticed that it started in the east with Red Sky's people *crossing the Atlantic Ocean.* How could the scholars see fit to cut off the transatlantic migration?

Now it all made sense. There are no signs of the Algonquins in the region of the Bering Straits. A people with such a rich and distinctive culture certainly would have left signs of that culture wherever they came from. If they came to these shores from somewhere else, then the place to start looking would have to be at the mouth of the St. Lawrence.

Following the Trail to Europe

If the Algonquins, or "water people,"[80] came from Europe they would have followed the route used by all of the early travelers who arrived at Newfoundland. So they undoubtedly came by way of Iceland and Greenland. All indications are that some came at a very early date, possibly when the glacier was receding from the northern hemisphere. So much water was bound up in the miles thick glacier that sea levels would have been much lower than present and many more islands would have shown themselves along this route, with Iceland much larger than it is now. A lot of that island on the Greenland side has disappeared in historic times, and it was warm during the period of melting ice.

If the Algonquins did cross the ocean to the mouth of the St. Lawrence they would have spent much time planning such a journey at their northern landfall

---

[80] From William Whipple Warren, born at LaPointe, May 27, 1825; died June 1st, 1853, 28 years old. ("History of the Ojibway People"—Minnesota Historical Society Press, St. Paul, 1984.) Page 46: "They also claim that of the six beings who emerged from the great water (at the mouth of the St. Lawrence) and originated the totems, their progenitor was the first who appeared, and was the leader of the others." Author: I interpret this to mean there were six migrations. Page 30: The principal and most numerous of these several primitive stocks, have been euphoniously named by Henry R. Schoolcraft, with the generic term of "Algic," derived from the word Algonquin, a name given by the early French discoverers to a tribe of this family living on the St. Lawrence River. Most numerous Ojibways (Otchipways) puckered moccasins; next most numerous O-dah-waug (Ottawas), trading people; then Po-do-waud-um-eeg (Potawatomies), those who keep the fire; Waub-un-uh-eeg (Delawares), Eastern earth dwellers; Shaw-un-oog (Shawnees), Southerners; O-saug-eeg (Saukies), those who live at the entry; O-dish-quag-um-eeg (Algonquins proper), last water people.

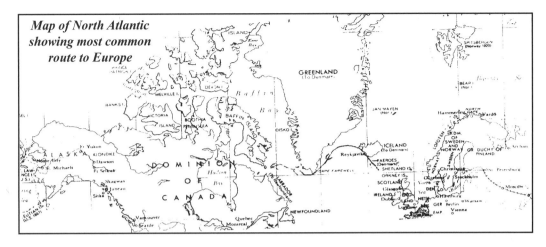

Map of North Atlantic
showing most common
route to Europe

*Hundreds of Dolmens in one flat area-Island of Oland,
Baltic Sea.*

in Europe. Judging from the number of Algonquin tribes strung out along the Great Lakes waterways and down the east coast of the United States there were probably a lot of people involved. There may have been many crossings. Certainly if these people spent much time in any one place some of their distinct culture would remain there.

It so happens that my wife has many relatives in Finland. They were known as Swede-Finns, Swedish speaking people who lived in Finland. Finland used to be a part of Sweden and has only been an independent country since World War I.

We decided to make a trip to Scandinavia and look for any signs of our local Indian culture there. We thought whatever we found would be hard to recognize after so many centuries, but if you know what you are looking for, you may recognize it. One piece of evidence would not be enough as that could pass as coincidence; there had to be at least three or four distinct similarities.

We spent a month in Scandinavia, and eventually made a second trip there a few years later collecting information along the way. First we were looking at the megaliths. We were told by authorities that those in America were not the

Tom Wastaken's Grandson
2004 - Canada

Saami family with cradle board (Tikkinagan)
Circa 1920's

Author exiting a Saami lavu

Cooking in the lavu

same as those in Europe. This was not true. We found many dolmens exactly like many of those in America. There was a whole field of them on the island of Oland off the coast of Kalmar, Sweden, in the Baltic Sea. There were probably more than a hundred in one field there, but we also found many single ones in many other locations.

On our second trip we concentrated on the people formerly known as the Lapplanders or Lapps. Today they want to be called Sami (or Saami) though the term Lapp is still used. The land where most of them now live is spread across northern Norway, Sweden, Finland and Russia. It is called Finnmark. This is where the many similarities with our Algonquins began to jump out at us.

Spending time with a Sami family, the first similarity we noticed was the teepee. There they are called a lavu (pronounced Lá-voo). While Ojibway people traditionally used a round-top wigwam, they also used a teepee.

Then we saw an Indian cradle-board, called a tikkinagan by our Ojibway friend Tom Wastaken. He claimed the family always kept the youngest child in the tikkinagon to keep it out of trouble. It could be hung in a tree, laid against a rock or stood in the bow of a canoe. The Saamis even had the familiar bentwood support over the baby's face for hanging a bug netting, to keep out wind and rain, and to protect the face should the board fall forward.

These people showed much reverence toward their own stones, the dolmens or menhirs. We soon discovered they formerly even had the typical Algonquin tom-tom, although we only saw them in museums. We were told that although Christian missionaries took their tom-toms from them, they soon adopted the single-skinned Inuit-type drum, as they loved to dance and sing. If you have ever heard an Algonquin drum group sing, you probably marveled at the very high throaty chant they start with. Even this is found in the Sami but it too was condemned by Christianity. The Saami call it "Yoiking," and it is coming back strong in their culture.

All these similar cultural customs were enough to convince me that there had been a close association at one time between the two groups. But there was more, much more.

Our local Indians call themselves the "Anishenaabeg," which means the "first people." The Saami have a word that also means "the first people," which they call themselves. Much of the folklore of both groups consists of slightly different versions of some of the same stories. We found there is much spirituality in both cultures. The Saami believe that Nature is a gift while the Anishinaabeg believe Nature is a relative and that they are a part of it. Both people try to live with Nature and leave it undamaged.

The word "Ochipway" means "puckered moccasin." The Sami also puckered their footwear to bring the toe up to a point. The purpose of this

Below: Saami Puckered Moccasin
Right: Ojibway Puckered Moccasin

was to keep a ski or snowshoe on. When I asked an Ojibway woman why she puckered her moccasins, she told me she didn't know why, she thought it was tradition. How else would you do it?

At a Sami museum we saw a little scene of what they did with the older women when they could not travel anymore. There was a small birch bark lavu (teepee) with an old woman sitting by a fire inside. There was a small pile of cut wood nearby. It was explained to us that when old women could not keep up, they were left with food, shelter and firewood, to fend for themselves. I've read of the exact same custom with our local Indians. In one local account, a daughter crept back during the night to kill her mother, an honorable thing to do so that she would avoid a lingering death. The old and helpless Sami males just take care of themselves. I also recall that when I was a school boy, friends playing along the Lake Superior ice found an old Indian man, whom we all knew, seated on a berg and wrapped in a blanket, but frozen stiff. He had gone there alone and waited to die. Both groups believed in sharing, both live in extended family villages, and both do beautiful beadwork. The similarities go on and on.

We met a very popular Sami vocalist who did yoiking. She explained that this had been banned along with the tom-toms. I told her how our Indian songs all seemed to start with the same high falsetto tones as hers. We stayed with her family and were given recordings of some of her own songs. We later wrote back and forth to members of her band and some of them even came to visit us in our home in Marquette.

I kept thinking, with all these almost identical peculiar features and customs, why hasn't some anthropologist noticed this before. The only answer to me was that those educated in such specialized fields were handicapped by a learned mental block—the unquestioned belief that no one crossed the oceans

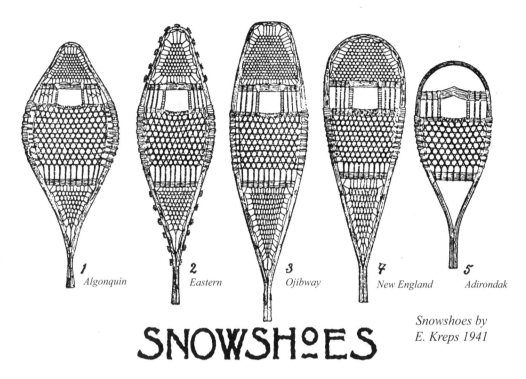

1 *Algonquin*   2 *Eastern*   3 *Ojibway*   4 *New England*   5 *Adirondak*

SNOWSH͜OES

*Snowshoes by
E. Kreps 1941*

in early times, or before Columbus. You would be ridiculed if you so much as mentioned such a thing.

But the real shock came when we were visiting a six-thousand-year-old archaeological dig in northern Norway. When I entered a rather small building that served as the archaeologists' office, there in the corner stood a Michigan-type snowshoe. Our home area has the honor of housing the U.S. Ski Hall of Fame. It is in Ishpeming, twelve miles from my home. In this part of the country everyone knows that skis were invented in Scandinavia and snowshoes were an invention of the Michigan (Algonquin) Indians. It just went without saying—there were no snowshoes in Norway.

And so I said to the man at the desk, "What is that doing here?!"

The man stood up and in all authority stated, "That is called a 'snowshoe.'"

"I know what it is," I said

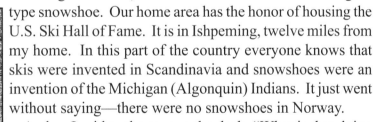

*Carvings of Michigan style snow
shoe are found in several locations in
Norway and Sweden, said to be 6,000
years old.*

333

One Pair of my Triple Bridge Snow Shoes Outlast Two Pairs Any Other

Typical Indian Made Snowshoe called "Michigan Style"

FOR LUMBERMEN AND CRUISERS

Oil tan shoe straps with wide toe slip, 50c pair.   Straight Toe sent only when ordered.   Make any size shoe to order

No. 0. Bent Toe, size 13 to 15 inches wide by 50 inches long, per pair, $6.50
No. 1. Bent Toe, size 13 to 15 inches wide by 47 inches long, per pair, 6.00
No. 2. Bent Toe, size 13 to 14 inches wide by 43 inches long, per pair, 5.00
No. 3. Bent Toe, size 13 inches wide by 43 inches long, per pair,   5.00
LIGHT FRAME AND LIGHT FILL

Goods shipped the same day order is received.   All Snow Shoes strictly finished in oil.

in alarm, "but what's it doing here?"

The fellow took it to a nearby rock cliff where it fit, precisely, into tracks carved in the stone, maybe six or eight of them going up the rock. All the while he was explaining that they had to go to Canada to find the technique to make the snowshoe. Later we were shown ancient rock carvings that showed Michigan-style snowshoes. They claimed the carvings were 6,000 years old.

There were still more exciting discoveries at a Saami Museum near the southern end of the Finnish-Swedish border. There was a festival of some kind going on and for a small village there seemed to be a very large crowd of young people. We were told they were Samis. Up to this time the Sami we met all seemed to look like people from the Ural Mountains, where we were told they had come from long before the Finns, Swedes or Norwegians. But then we noticed many that looked just like Swedes. I am half Swede and live among the Swedes and for the most part I recognize them, like the Indians recognize people of their own tribe. But here in that crowd of young people were many dark-skinned, black-eyed, black-haired Sami[80A]. To me they looked exactly like most of the Indians I knew from my home area. I spoke to some of them, and although they didn't know what I was saying, I really felt I knew them. In the nearby museum we found grooved hammerstones, just like the ones in Michigan, and arrowheads of several distinct shapes that are the same as those in my fireplace hearth, all found in Michigan.

I could go on in this vein, but there is one more thing that seemed so out

---

[80A] The Sami are often referred to collectively as "The Lapps" in much the same way that American Indians are lumped together as the "Indians" actually there are more than ten Sami cultural areas, each with its own style of dress and language.

[81] Torque—a collar or neck chain, usually twisted, especially one such as worn by ancient barbaric nations, as the Gauls, Germans and Britons.

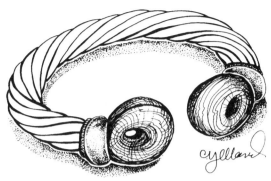

Wooden Torque from Saami Museum

of place to me. In books on ancient Celtic artifacts or Mediterranean metalwork, you often see a piece of jewelry called a torque.[81] It was strange to see this item in a Sami museum, but what was even more strange to me was that these were made of *wood*. Could some of the Saami people have come from much further south, from central or southern Europe or the Mediterranean area? Certainly they bore those physical characteristics, the darker skin, the black hair and the dark eyes. This was another question to ponder as among them there was a distinct mixture of races.

Years later I ran across a possible answer. In a book entitled "Ships and Seafaring in Ancient Times" (University of Texas Press, 1994—ISBN-0292-71163-X) by Lionel Casson, is a picture, on page 89, in a section called "The Age of Supergalleys," of a large, two-level galley underway. It is the magnified portion of a huge mosaic found in the Palazz Barberini at Palestrina, Italy. I wrote to the Mayor of Palestrina, my last resort after several other attempts fell through,

Top Part of 2200 year old mosaic found in Palestrina, Italy.
Small section outlined here is enlarged on page 338 showing tile detail.

2,000 year old mosaic in Palestrina, Italy, 1 st century BC

and received an illustrated booklet and a nice letter in return. The large mosaic covers the floor of an ancient building that dates from the first century B.C., but the mosaic depicts a scene from a few centuries earlier. It shows the Nile River in one of its annual flood stages, when boats of all sizes could move about areas that were usually under cultivation.

The part of the mosaic that caught my eye was not the galley but the bow of what looked like a "birch bark" canoe just above it. In the canoe sat a fisherman

Sami museum has the same style of arrowheads and hammerstones as found in Michigan.

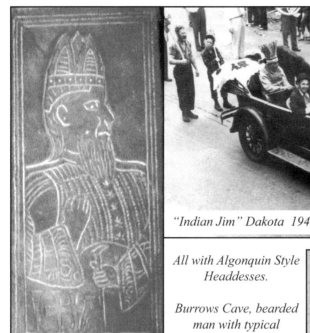

"Indian Jim" Dakota 1949 Parade

All with Algonquin Style Headdesses.

Burrows Cave, bearded man with typical Algonquin headdress.

with his pole and wearing what struck me immediately as an Algonquin feathered headdress.

Back in 1949, the city of Marquette was celebrating their centennial. I had a 1922 Oldsmobile (which I was driving at the time). I had asked my friend "Indian Jim" Dakota to ride in the parade with me in my old car. It so happened that Carter Harrison, a former mayor of Chicago who owned a cabin on Lake Superior and summered there, had a genuine Algonquin head-dress. It had been presented to him when he was adopted into

Kawbawgam - Last chief of Chippewas, Marquette, circa 1880's.

an Algonquin tribe in Minnesota in the 1890's. It was a distinctive head-dress with the feathers straight up all the way around. It was the first one of those I had ever seen, but Jim explained to me that it was authentic and he wore it with great pride.

The second Algonquin headdress I found in a picture of our local chief, Kawbawgam. He was known as the last chief of the Chippewas in Marquette County. The picture was taken of him in the 1880's. This Algonquin-type of headdress is rather rare now as it seems many of the tribes have adopted the

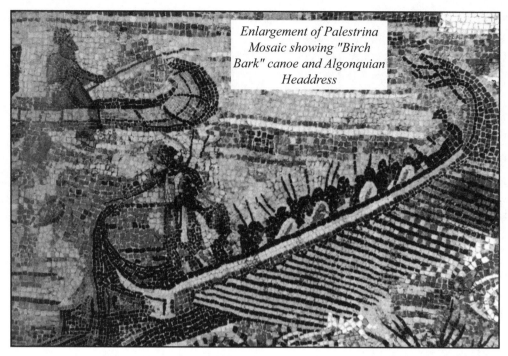

Enlargement of Palestrina Mosaic showing "Birch Bark" canoe and Algonquian Headdress

beautiful "war bonnet" style of the Sioux or plains Indians. But the remarkable thing in the Palestrina mosaic is that the fisherman in the canoe is wearing an Algonquin-style headdress, the third one I have ever seen.

Every boat in the mosaic typically has a high bow and stern. It seems that all of them were modeled somewhat traditionally after the reed boats of the ancient Nile as they were built that way out of necessity. All old canoes had the high bow and stern and it is only in the last 150 years that this tradition has changed. It was the Algonquins who changed it first.[81b] From what I can find out about the canoes on the Nile, the first ones were made out of papyrus. They were called then and still are called "canoes."

A possible scenario is that during the period of the Old Testament, many populations were utterly destroyed, some taken into bondage, but many driven from their land as the boat people of today. They escaped and became nomadic, looking for a new homeland. These same populations could have been split up, some traveling east

Chuck Bailey, long-time amateur researcher of Duluth and Paula Baker Sten, student of language origins.

[81b] See illustration on page 433.

up the silk road and eventually, after years of roaming and fighting, running from Genghis Khan by traveling on huge Chinese junks that were traveling to Kodiak Islands in quest of sea otter pelts.

Some Conclusions From Another Source

It seemed very confusing to me to have followed the Algonquin people to southern Europe. I had never heard any inkling of that before. I figured some day someone would back up this theory or completely disprove it.

Sometime during the 1980s, I received a call from a young researcher who lived in western Upper Michigan, the part known as the "Copper Country." Her name was Paula Sten and she was working on the origins of languages. We were to meet at a gathering of the Ancient Earthworks Society in Madison, Wisconsin. Paula and her young son were late for the meeting but we connected later on a field trip that followed the meeting.

It was hard to grasp exactly what her intent was at first, but over the years we communicated a few times and met on several occasions. She was in touch with Dr. Cyclone Covey who was following her work as well as Dr. John White of Columbus, Ohio.

Paula became very ill with lyme disease and her symptoms progressed over the years until at times she was bed-ridden with the effects of the disease.

In the winter of 2004, Paula called and asked if I could go to her home with my truck and pick up her books—boxes and boxes of them. She wanted me to see that they got to Dr. White; she felt only he would be interested in them.

In April I made the trip to pick up the books and we had a long conversation about her work. She did most of the talking. She was explaining from a 25-page, carefully illustrated booklet entitled *In Search of Old Europe* that she had published and copyrighted.

Now I had long known of a connection between Algonkin and Basque language and writing. Years ago I had heard that a priest in Canada[82] had taught the Indians (Cree) the Basque syllabary. But Dr. Barry Fell says, "In reality, as inscriptions from pre-Roman and Spain and also the Peterborough site in Canada show, the script is of very ancient origin and is due to Basques."[83]

An interesting book, *The Roots of Civilization* by Alexander Marshack (McGraw-Hill Book Company, NY, 1972), shows how sticks and bones were marked for counting days, full moon to full moon, summer and winter, etc.

---

[82] It has long been supposed that the script was the invention of a missionary, James Evans, in 1841.

[83] In 1979, Basque inscriptions in Spain and Portugal were deciphered by Fell using Algonquin syllabary. These were confirmed by Basque scholar Imanuel Agiré.

Meaning	Basque		Algonquian		
sun	guzki	ᒡᣔᐸ	gisis	ᐸᣔᣔ	Ojibwa
			gischuch	ᐸᣔᒍ‾	Delaware
star	šita	ᣔᑕ	skwita	ˆˋᐊ·ᑕ	Natick
mist	alphorra	ᐊᶜᗄᒧ	awan	ᐊᐊᐊᣄ	Ojibwa
dew or fine rain	babada	ᐸᐸᑕ	papad-	ᐸᐸᑕ	Natick
cloudy weather	gohin	ᒡ"ᐊᣄ	guhn	ᒡᣄ	Natick
wind	aize	ᐊᐊᣔ	aiowastin	ᐊᐊᐊ·ˆᑎᣄ	Cree
	aitše	ᐊᐊᒣ	outšou	ᐅᣔᑕ	Abenaki
	ulauza	ᐅᔆᐅᓴ	lutin	ᔆᑎᣄ	Old Algonquian
	etc.		etc.		
water	uds*	ᐅ‾	utan (-quench)	ᐅᑕᣄ	Natick
to wash	kusi	ᒡᣔ	kusit (-flow)	ᒡᣔᣔ	Natick
to wash	babi	ᐸᐱ	papen- (-drip)	ᐸᐯᣄ	Natick
drink	ziba	ᣔᐸ	sipe (-water)	ᣔᐯ	universal
river	šipa	ᣔᐸ	sipu (river, etc.)	ᣔᗴ	universal
flood lake river waters	ibai ibaiak	ᐃᐸᐃ ᐃᐸᒣᣄ	(n)ipe ipog	ᐃᐯ ᐃᗴᣄ	universal universal
ocean ("confluence of waters")	ur-keta	ᐅᣄᕱᑕ	kehta	ᕱᑕ	universal
land	uts	ᐅ‾	uto	ᐅᔆ	Natick
			wuto	ᐅ·ᔆ	Natick

*(dim. ustinta)

This comparative table, taken from my 1979 paper on the decipherment of ancient Basque, shows also that the language of the Algonquian Indians contains words of Basque origin. The last two columns compare the related pairs of words as written in the Cree-Basque syllabary.

Chart from Bronze Age America comparing Basque and Algonquian.

Paula took me through step by step, how female animals denoted summer, male denoted winter, and how certain marks were for words, Algonquin words. I was still under the impression that the early Basques brought their writing and language to America but Paula said the Algonquins developed it in Europe! I was shocked.

"Do you mean the Algonquins originated in Europe?" I asked. "I had traced them there myself," I said. "I followed them back to France, Spain, Italy, even north Africa, Egypt."

Paula said that she believed the Algonquins were the indigenous people of southern Europe, the first Cro-Magnon people to appear there some 37,000 years ago.

There is no way I could even summarize the many intricacies of Paula Sten's analysis. She brings in comparisons with Iroquoian, Finnish, Sami/Laplander, Norse, and Creole. I was especially interested in a mention of two entry points to America, one within the St. Lawrence watershed and another at the Carolina Susquehanna River. Both of these lead to the interior and I was aware that these two Algonquin-speaking peoples have two traditional histories. It is the northern group who say they came from the east while the southern, east coast group claims to be the indigenous people of the area. These could be the people of Virginia, the Savannah of South Carolina, and Pennsylvania's Meadowcraft Rockshelter.

Paula Sten says she is through working on her baffling project, but I am thankful for her many hours of work seeking answers to migrations through language.

There is one bit of information that illustrates how delicate the handling of information among professionals must be.

Alexander Marshack[83a] tells the story in detail of getting his work published so it would be accepted by other scientists. In the course of his efforts he spoke to Professor Hallam L. Movius, Jr., of the Peabody Museum of Archaeology and Ethnology, Harvard.

In the course of his talk with Professor Movius, Marshack speaks of the steps he must go through to get his discoveries accepted. These steps seem to be in direct opposition to what would be my attitude. The advice he was given was: "Proceed both with haste and caution—leave France at once, talk to no one, and show no one the manuscript. Publish as soon as possible to establish a priority—check European materials first-hand to see if his ideas held in the field. They agreed that one could not trust the scientific renderings of archaeological material."

As a teacher of science, I have always believed you should tell those interested what you know or have found out. Openly accept the criticism of others but keep an open mind until some definite proof is arrived at.

[83a] In his book "The Roots of Civilization" (Mcgovern-Hill 1972)
[84] Proverb by Frank Crane: "You may be deceived if you trust too much, but you will live in torment if you don't trust enough."

I may be showing too much trust in human nature, but I have always felt the way to learn is to be open and honest. Yes, you may get carried away by some strange ideas but eventually they will fall into place, usually the right place—but it may take time.[84] I believe this method would advance science more rapidly than to teach students that this or that is fake or this or that idea is wrong based on tradition, religion, or biased opinion. Secrecy or cover-up never sets right in an open society. It all comes down to attitude. The advice Morshack was given speaks of distrust, professional jealousy and a certain amount of arrogance.

A short paper by Marshack was approved and he did receive some grants to proceed with his work. One of these was from the Wenner-Gren Foundation, which, incidentally, had given supplemental funding to Dr. Roy Drier and Joe Gannon almost thirty years earlier.

And also, incidentally, Dr. Barry Fell had also suggested that the Algonquin people had migrated from southern Europe, an idea I had completely missed or had forgotten earlier. It was implied through the similarities with Basque writing. [84a]

Professor Discovers Another Clue

As I have often stated, one of the best proofs that an idea is on track is if several people arrive at the same conclusion independently.

The following is a case of a father gathering material so he could better teach his two young daughters some nearly lost history.

I came across Professor Mark McMenamin's article in the December 26th (1996) issue of the *Chicago Tribune*. Not so strangely, I haven't seen or heard a word about it since, as it is another case of an idea that clashes with our established archaeological history. The piece of history that we are looking for here is proof or evidence that many people were traveling to and from the Americas in ancient times.

McMenamin, a professor of geology and paleontology at Mt. Holyoke College in South Hadley, Massachusetts, made his discovery while carefully

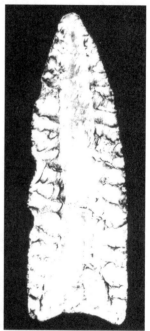

Clovis points are fluted a thin groove down the middle of each face. Dennis Sanford of the Smithsonian believes they originated in the Salurian culture of Spain

---

[84a] Recently a report of the same theory has come to light from archeologists Dennis Sanford and Bruce Bradley of the Smithsonian, who again may have followed the Clovis point to Europe. See chart page 340.

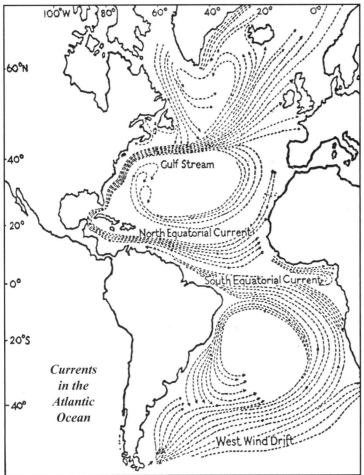

Currents in the Atlantic Ocean

studying Phoenician coins. He had read that some Carthaginian coins from the fourth century B.C. had been found on the Azores Islands, 800 miles west of Portugal. This raised McMenamin's suspicions that Phoenician sailors may have reached the Americas if they had ventured that far west.

He kept looking for clues and eventually found some in the

Folsom, New Mexico points are also fluted but more carefully made. They are thought to be a later form of Clovis points.

1778 diary of a Swede by the name of Johannes Podolyn. Podolyn claimed he had been given some Carthaginian coins by a Padre in Spain who had gotten them from Spanish sailors 30 years earlier. The sailors told the priest they had gotten the coins on Corvo, the westernmost island of the Azores, from a pot in the corner of an old foundation recently exposed by a storm. The sailors also found a statue of a horse, but had destroyed it. McMenamin was unable to locate Podolyn's coins, but in a book on Carthaginian gold coins from the University of Massachusetts Library, he spotted strange markings on the reverse side of coins called "staters."[85]

Coin experts had long been baffled by these

---

[85] Staters—local coin of gold or silver issued by ancient city-states.

seemingly sloppy marks when the rest of the coin was sharp and clear.

But when McMenamin enlarged the images on a computer, he realized they were maps similar to those of the Greek geographer Ptolemy.

Professor McMenamin was able to locate all of the 14 specimens of this type of coin and all had similar maps. Though slightly different from one another, they clearly showed the Mediterranean at the center of each, with Sardinia, an island, shown as a dot, the north coast of Africa across the bottom, Europe arched above, and the Phoenician homeland to the east and far India beyond that.

Tribune staff writer, Charles Leroux, writes, "But there's more. As McMenamin notes in an article in the November 1996 issue of *The Numismatist Magazine,* of compelling interest is the landmass portrayed to the west of the Iberian Peninsula (Spain)."

Compelling indeed. For depicted as far larger than any of the islands of the Mediterranean, the landmass, McMenamin wrote, presents "the intriguing possibility" of representing the coast of South America.

Of course initial scholarly reaction was harsh and critical; it seems that it always is as those who believe they know the whole picture react automatically. However, as the more scholarly make their own observations and are able to study the maps on the coins, the criticisms soften and someday I am sure the new discovery will be accepted.

McMenamin adds in support of his discovery that there are, "Traces of roads in Florida that seem to be Phoenician, as well as artifacts—up and down the coast from Massachusetts to Brazil." He also noted on maps of ocean currents that there are only two recirculating currents that would make very long return journeys possible. One links the waters off Spain with Brazil, the other links East Africa with India. (See map on previous page)

Some ancient writers spoke of a Carthaginian discovery beyond the Mediterranean, where they could go to escape their enemies. But, writes Leroux, the Punic Wars with the Romans, beginning in 264 B.C. and lasting over a century, demolished Carthage—and they were lost to history from then on. But the legends of another world across the sea persisted as we have read earlier in the 1900 volumes of the "Irish—American History." (See Chapter IV)

Today the average student knows very little of the Phoenicians. They are losing their place in history. About 30 years ago I was giving a talk and slide show to a group of lighthouse historians. At one point I heard a very audible comment from someone in the audience, "If he's going to start talking about Phoenicians, I'm getting out of here."
Later I was interrupted by another fellow who stood up and gave me quite a lecture, saying that I was undermining the historians and archaeologists of the world and belittling the Native Americans—I was a racist. Later I learned that

both of these men were teachers. I would hope that the average person should know that the Phoenicians were the greatest sailors of the ancient world. They are now thought to be remnants of the Sea People who were the original traders. They eventually settled in Lebanon, marrying into the Semitic race and using the famous cedars of Lebanon to become great ship builders and carry on the traditions of the sea. Their two most famous cities were Sidon and Tyre, but they also built the city of Carthage in North Africa. The Phoenicians built ships for several countries and they showed up wherever there was a trade route by sea, beyond the Gibraltar Strait (the "Pillars of Hercules") or by caravan to India and China. For a thousand years they controlled the commerce of the world (1500 B.C.-500 B.C.) and they most certainly would have at some period been involved in the copper trade from America.

Another Professor Discovers Evidence of Romans in Texas

In the *Dallas Morning News* of June 13, 1993, we find an article by Victoria Loe, staff writer, telling about a discovery by Valentine Belfiglio, a professor of history at Texas Women's University. Belfiglio became interested in "the Book of Mormon" that had been given to him by two young proselytizing Mormons. In it he found passages describing the voyage of the followers of Jared.[86] According to the book, the Jaredites traveled on barges for 344 days across "that great sea that divideth the lands" and came ashore "upon the shores of the promised land."

Belfiglio decided to investigate this further to see if he could find any corroborating evidence to prove such a statement. With the 500th anniversary of Columbus's voyages coming up he thought it would be an appropriate time to make such a search.

The professor discovered several things which could prove the likelihood of such a voyage, but in each case he was shot down by the experts in various fields; nevertheless, historians and archaeologists agreed that the Romans had vessels capable of making such a voyage.

The first of Belfiglio's discoveries was the report of a mysterious shipwreck in Galveston Bay. From his reading of Plutarch:[87] and Pliny the Elder[88] he learned that the Romans knew the earth was round and that they had been to the Canary Islands far out in the Atlantic. From these islands, currents sweep southwesterly

---

[86] Jared—A Hebrew leader and teacher from the Old Testament.

[87] Plutarch (50 A.D.-125 A.D.)—Greek moralist and biographer. He accumulated vast stores of historical and mythological lore, wrote "Parallel Lives," one of our best records of antiquity.

[88] Pliny the Elder (23 A.D.-79 A.D.)—Roman naturalist and encyclopedist—died trying to save lives during the eruption of Vesuvius.

around the tip of Florida and into the Gulf of Mexico.

In the Galveston library, Belfiglio found an article from 1886 describing the discovery of the wreck of an ancient ship of unusual design. The paper reported, "Her stern is put together in such a manner as to contradict any reasonable supposition that she was a vessel fashioned even as early as the sixteenth century. It is composed of the most massive solid oak, fully six or seven inches in thickness, and pieces laid crosswise over each other secured with huge iron spikes. The ship had width of about fifteen feet. Dr. Belfiglio decided that this construction was similar in every respect to a Roman cargo ship.

But then an expert, Barta Arnold of the Texas Historical Commission, the state's nautical archaeologist, said that Roman vessels didn't use iron spikes. He said they were held together by an intricate mortise and tenon construction in which a tongue carved in each plank fit into a groove in the adjoining plank.

Another nautical archaeologist, Dr. Fred Hocker from Texas A&M University, agreed with Arnold that this was not a familiar Roman construction. However, both archaeologists agreed that Roman ships would have been capable of making it to the Gulf Coast either purposefully or by accident. Dr. Hocker said Roman ships were fully capable of sailing across the Atlantic or being blown off course and ending up there.

Dr. Belfiglio also read a 1915 account of timbers found buried 15 feet below the bottom of Galveston Bay. Dr. Hocker claimed this could happen in just 100 years, not 1500. But then Belfiglio had two examples of positive Roman artifacts. This time it was an account of two Roman coins found in Texas. One was discovered in a sand dune on St. Joseph's Island, the other was recovered from the bottom of an Indian mound near Round Rock; this would appear to date the coins arrival in America sometime around 800 A.D. He speculated the coin could have reached central Texas on a Roman canal boat plying the Colorado River.[89]

There is objection to this also from Jeremiah Epstein, a scholar who first investigated the Round Rock coin and decided it probably was not original to the mound but was dropped on the surface of the mound much later and carried to the bottom by rodents or tree roots. (Can you imagine?) Dr. Epstein, an emeritus professor of anthropology at the University of Texas in Austin, is one of several scholars who have pointed out that it is well known that Roman coins have been found all over Western Europe. Some of them, they say, could have made their way to America mixed in with beach pebbles used as ballast on European ships.

But Dr. Belfiglio had even more connections in his repertoire. He noted

---

[89] This is the Texas Colorado, not the Colorado River that empties into the Gulf of California.

Lookout at Poverty Pointe

that by comparing various words in Latin (the Roman language) with the dialect of the Korakawas, a now extinct Gulf Coast tribe, he found many similarities, too many to be coincidental. Some examples: Karabikawa caha (house), Latin casa (hut); mal (die), mala (death); notawa (swim), nature (swim); tal (this) and tale (that). He also noted that the Karakawas, like the Romans, enjoyed wrestling, archery and ball games.

This society would have occurred nearly 2,000 years ago, but when my wife and I visited a museum on the grounds of Poverty Pointe[89A] in Louisiana, we marveled at a large table covered several inches deep with stone arrowheads. When I remarked to the curator there (a young woman) that I had never seen so many arrowheads in one place, I was told, "these are not 'arrowheads,' we just call them points." She explained that "the bow and arrow was not introduced to America until 400 years ago." We did not argue with her but called her attention to two other glaring errors. The museum wall had a timeline showing the advance of civilization around the world. The beginning of the Egyptian Dynasties was almost 1,000 years too late.[90] On a huge map of America, with lines from Poverty Pointe to the source of certain trade materials, there was a line going to the center of lower Michigan as the source of copper. I pointed out that this spot was just south of Mount Pleasant, while the source of copper was 400 miles northwest in Michigan's Upper Peninsula.

Her remark was, "Well, these exhibits were made by professionals who work for the federal government and we can't change them."

There are always people eager to tell Dr. Belfiglio that his ideas are "absurd" and "ridiculous," but then there is more to the story than even Dr. Belfiglio may realize.

Apparently, completely unknown to researcher Belfiglio (at least he did

---

[89a] See Poverty Point Map on page 235.
[90] I believe it read 2400 B.C.—it should have read 3100 B.C., with a build-up of civilization of possibly 500 to 800 years.

not mention it), there have been reports for years that Romans had landed on the Gulf Coast in southern Mexico. The first time I heard of such a thing was at a meeting around 1989 or 1990. A gentleman was telling me about some historical research he was doing when he discovered that there were two Roman Legions[91] which had been abandoned on the Iberian Peninsula (Spain) after the fall of Rome in 455 A.D. He suspected they had gone by ship to the New World.

None of this seems to budge academia or those in charge of the large museums, big publishing establishments or the people in the great halls of science.

(And More)
Comalcalco, Mexico

There was a man I spoke with at two or three different meetings I attended in my quest to learn more about pre-Columbian history. His name was Neil Steede and he impressed me as one of the harder working field researchers I have met. He was always dressed as though he had just come from an archaeological dig and was on his way back to one as soon as possible.

Neil's talk was very convincing and I sat down with him after a meeting to get a few facts straight. He had worked for some years at a site called Comalcalco, an ancient city in the state of Tobasco in the extreme southern part of Mexico. It is on a broad coastal plain about sixty miles northwest of Villahemosa. It is not on the coast but lies on the banks of what was the Rio Seco, a part of a river system which drains the Chiapas highlands and flows north into the Gulf of Mexico.

The unique thing about Comalcalco is that it was a city made largely of fired bricks. This is rather unusual for a Mayan City but what makes things more interesting is that many of these bricks were inscribed with strange signs and even some pictures.

Steede told me that many aspects of the buildings were very similar to Mediterranean architecture, the brick work, the art styles in stucco, and even the way tombs were built. In the building that was determined to be a palace, the walls and floors were tiled.

The best argument for Roman influence, in my opinion, is the similarity of the marks on the Comalcalco bricks. It would be strange to find two cultures on opposite sides of the ocean and of the same period to even mark their bricks,

---

[91] Roman Legion—3,000 to 6,000 infantry men with cavalry self-supporting unit.

but in this case many of the marks are identical. Neil Steede brought these marks to the attention of Dr. Barry Fell.

In an article written by Steede for the *Ancient American Magazine* (Vol. 2, Number 7, Sept/Oct 1994), he writes:

> Two wonderful photographers made up the team which came from the United States to document the bricks. Stele Bryant and Ted Freddle went with me to the site for the study. Having hired six people, the 4,612 bricks were moved from their storage area to an improvised photographic studio some 40 feet away. An average brick weighs ten pounds, which meant that over twenty tons of bricks were moved in the following ten days. The photography was done in high contrast black and white 35mm film. This, with the lighting, helped to draw out the many fine inscriptions found on the bricks.
>
> An extremely varied group of inscriptions were revealed. All of the inscriptions had been inscribed on bricks while they were wet. Upon firing the bricks, the inscriptions were fixed into the surface. They consisted of drawings of animals, plants, houses, temples, humans, artifacts, ships, calendars, sacred symbols, religious rites and letters.
>
> Later the bricks were used in the construction of the temple at Comalcalco. The inscriptions were never intended to be seen, and were covered with mortar, which was most fortunate for us since it left a great deal of information in pristine condition. Millennia later we would find the inscribed bricks among the fallen walls of the site. We were additionally grateful to the builders of the site, who did not wet the brick before applying the mortar. This allowed the mortar not to bond with the brick and pulled away readily.
>
> Before his death, Dr. Fell had recognized and translated several hundred of the bricks in question. Several of these were published in ESOP (The Epigraphic Society Occasional Papers). In fact, he was still translating them at the time of his death. His working table was strewn with brick photographs and notes. The middle of the pile was topped by two pictures of your author (Neil Steede). Fell was trying to decide which to use in the new edition of *America B.C.* He planned a whole chapter on Comalcalco.

In an earlier conversation with Neil Steede, I remember asking, "With such startling news as Romans in America, why didn't you write this up or publish it in scientific journals?" His answer was to the effect that surely he had seen

European comparisons with Comalocalco Bricks. Country-ESOP, Vol. 19 © Barry Fell, 1991.

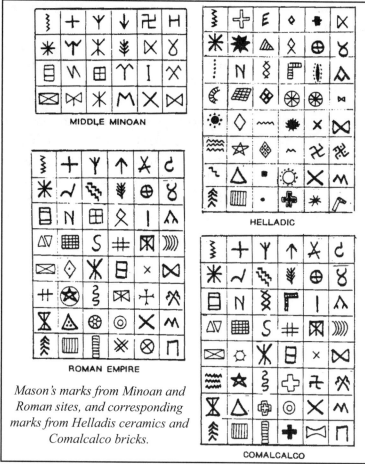

Mason's marks from Minoan and Roman sites, and corresponding marks from Helladis ceramics and Comalcalco bricks.

The spread of the Christian religion through Roman Empire and beyond brought new suites of symbols to the brick masons' resources. Here we see in sign number 53 the widespread Christian symbol known as the

Cross Calvary, (a Latin cross mounted on 3 steps). Sign 54 is the so-called Greek Cross, and sign 56 is one of the forms of the Chi-Rho symbol.   Barry Fell © 1991

350

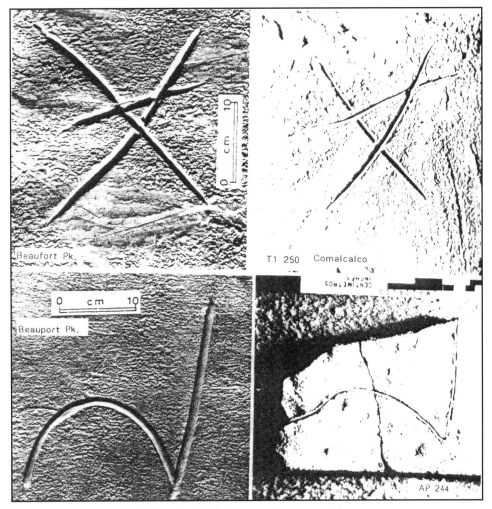

Comalcalco bricks are shown on right.

what to him was a strong Roman influence, but only about 6% of Comalcalco had been archaeologically excavated. He wanted to see what later archaeologists found.

In a later issue of the *Ancient American Magazine* (Vol. 3, Number 24) there appeared an article by David Escott, a British archaeology investigator and writer for England's *Quest Magazine*. He was a little more cautious than Steede and had a few minor criticisms about what the brick inscriptions meant. However, David Escott did acknowledge the Roman marks on the bricks and reported Fell's opinions and translations. He even went so far as to show a picture of a ceramic head with a Roman-style beard and mustache that was on display in the Museum at Comalcalco.

In speaking of the bearded stucco head he writes:

It is hard to understand, especially in view of the controversy surrounding Comalcalco, why this specimen has not received the same publicity as the carved, bearded head which was professionally excavated in 1933 from a truncated pyramid at Calixtlahuaca, 45 miles west of the present Mexico City. Experts confirmed that the Calixtlahuaca head reflected a style belonging to the Hellenistic/Roman culture and dated it to 200A.D. This date has also been confirmed by thermo luminescence.

The Botanists Get Into the Act

In the early 1990's, I spotted an article in a New York paper telling of the finding of cocaine and nicotine in the tissue of Egyptian mummies. The discovery was made at the "Institut fur Anthropologie und Humangenetik der Universtat" in Munich, Germany. Sometime later I watched a television documentary on the same subject. I have lost or misplaced my garbled notes long since, but then an article by A.J. Julius, a biologist from Austin, Texas, appeared in the *Ancient American* magazine (Vol. 2, Number 8, page 13) describing this discovery. The researcher was an elderly, respected female scientist who made the discovery. While the article did not name the researcher, it said the following appeared in the scientific journal, *Naturwissenschafen* in 1992:

> Cocaine and nicotine are members of a chemical class of compounds known as alkaloids. Plants containing alkaloids have been culturally and economically important for thousands of years. Nicotine is found in a number of plants around the world; the same cannot be said of cocaine. Cocoa plant (erythroxylum) was unknown in the Old World until after the Spanish expeditions to South America during the 15th and 16th centuries; since then it has been cultivated in other parts of the world.

The mummy materials tested were dated from 1070 B.C. to 395 A.D. Every mummy tested contained cocaine and nicotine, and we can assume that this study is still going on today because of its controversial nature. However, the fact is clear that if these drugs are not of a local origin, the only possibility is that their findings are good forensic evidence for pre-Columbian contact. A.J. Julius:

> Nearly a year after the report appeared—the journal published several controversial letters they received from the scientific community. Some felt the editorial staff had been sloppy in reviewing the manuscript, and that the project was either a bizarre hoax or an experiment gone wrong. The researchers were attacked because they failed to include proper

controls, and the possibility of instrumental error was not sufficiently ruled out.

There were other suggestions such as that the mummies might have absorbed tobacco smoke while being studied in the museum.

Dr. Franz Parsche, one of the mummy researchers, responded: —"Our analysis provides clear evidence for the presence of alkaloids in the ancient human remains."

Again we must remind ourselves that there is always the chance of some unknown explanation for an extraordinary and bizarre result of a scientific finding.

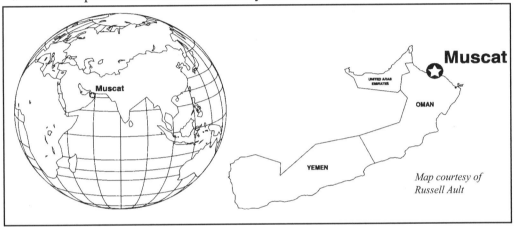

Map courtesy of Russell Ault

But if two or more findings prove the same conclusion in unrelated settings, then we can say we are on firm ground.

An unrelated but similar situation was brought to light some years ago. It was sometime in the 90's that I received a phone call from a Mr. John Fitzhugh Millar. He did not tell me how or where he found my name and address, but he fascinated me with another story of a botanical nature that had aroused his curiosity. The gist of his story was that a certain grape from the Arabian Peninsula, on the northwest coast of the country of Oman, on the shores of the Gulf of Oman (entrance to the Persian Gulf) had found its way in ancient times to the southeast coast of the United States. I jotted down his name and address. Some years later, as I was organizing materials for this book and wanting to get my facts straight, I wrote and asked Mr. Millar for some details. On February 4th of 2002 I received the following letter:

Dear Fred Rydholm:

Thank you for your letter of 29 January inquiring about grapes possibly brought to America by Phoenicians or other early Mediterranean voyagers.

I am an historian specializing in 18th century, so I have to confess that I have absolutely no expertise in botany or history of the early pre-Christian Mediterranean history, as every book or magazine article I pick up on the subject seems to disagree with every other one. I graduated from Harvard in 1966, so I took a course about 1965 from Professor Sterling Dow on that period of history; he told us that the Phoenicians were essentially the same people as the Mycenaeans and Minoans, hence the path of the Phoenician alphabet. Then I talked to some other great authority on the subject last year and he said that we had gone way past that primitive view, and it was no longer regarded as so. Then another authority said that that view had been reinstated, and another said (probably the most truthful) that we really have very little idea who the Phoenicians were and who was related to them.

Anyway, here's how the grapes came to my attention. I run a small bed & breakfast. My wife is a good gardener and has various plants in the garden that we incorporate into our meals. One is the SCUPPERNONG, a Muscatine grapevine (the name is an Algonkian word) that produces grapes with tough, leathery skins and lots of seeds inside. The grapes are green when young and they turn bronze when ripe in September. If you don't mind the skins and the seeds, they have a good, if different, taste, and they make good jams and jellies, also a sweet, syrupy wine. The vine grows from Virginia to Florida and west to Texas, but not north of that zone, and it is known to have been growing in that range when the Spanish conquistadors arrived. Muscatine grapes, though, are native to the Middle East (the word Muscatine comes from the Arab state of Muscat), so I began to ask out loud, how did these grapes arrive here far enough ahead of the Spanish to have naturalized over such a wide area. We know they cannot be propagated by birds (that's one of the good aspects of the vine: birds, squirrels and other animals leave them alone, and they are immune to all the diseases that regularly attack other grapes).

One day, about five years ago, I was telling all that to a guest from Indiana at breakfast, and I said, "I wonder if it could have been the Phoenicians who brought the grapes. They sailed completely around Africa, they sailed to India, and they sailed to England, so they probably have sailed here too."

"Oh, we know all about that," he replied. "The Phoenicians sailed up the Mississippi on a regular basis sometime before 1000 B.C. all the way to the Great Lakes. They lived in the Bronze Age, so they needed lots of copper, and the price of copper in the Mediterranean had gone through the roof, so they came over here looking for it."

When I asked for references, he referred me first to an amateurishly-written book, but which seemed to hold genuine evidence in it, Jack Ward's *Ancient Archives Among the Cornstalks,* and then to the journal *Ancient American.* That's all I know, other than what I have read in those places, which is very fascinating but occasionally confusing. I would be delighted if you could put it all into one clarifying framework. I would also like to see Ward's information made more available to those interested in the subject. Please feel free to write or phone me if you have any further questions. I am here most of the time, as I have to run the B&B and write historical books, although I am often at a part-time job in the evenings. Good luck with your book.

Very sincerely, John Fitzhugh Millar

Ms. Zena Halpern, authority on Hebrews in America.

Of course, John Millar's letter hit a nerve with me. I had many long talks with Jack Ward. In fact I was at his home the night he died. I have a better opinion of Jack than many others who share interests in discovering antiquity. I had a dozen of Jack's books which I used to lend out. They have all disappeared except one hard-cover which he signed; I do not lend that one. We will read more of Jack Ward in these pages.

The latest I have heard from a botanist's point of view was in a phone conversation in the recent past from Ms. Zena Halpern of Syosset, New York. She had been in contact with Carl L. Johannssen, Ph.D. Dept. of Geography, University of Oregon who had read in a publication by Dr. Steffy that the Kyrenia shipwreck, a Greek vessel[91a] discovered off the coast of Cypress had agave fibers used in its caulking. Agave is a cactus plant found in Mexico. Dr. Johannssen is a world expert on the Pre-Columbian diffusion of plants across oceans such as maize which was carried to China and India before the 15th century AD.

Years ago I heard a talk given by Dr. George I. Carter of Southern Methodist University. He was a pioneer in the subject of archaeological botany. He spoke of a long list of plants that were native to one continent, but had somehow been carried across oceans—most of them transplants which could only have been accomplished by human transportation.[91b]

[91a] The ship sank about 300BC off the north coast of Cyprus. It had a well preserved wooden hull which was excavated and a replica of the ship was built by Dr. Steffy, the world's expert on ancient wooden ships

[91b] In reading accounts of early ocean voyages, it seems that many carried a cargo of plants and animals to other parts of the globe. A good example is Captain Cooks 3rd Voyage See *American Traveler* - James Zug - Basic Books - 387 Park Ave, NY - 2005

Then there are stories of the intricate and advanced manipulation of breeding plants to eliminate their seeds, a common practice today, yet it happened in the banana sometime in the distant past.

No, Not Egyptian!

We have spoken about my book, "The Mystery Cave of Many Faces." Except for a very few, the vast majority who knew about it ridiculed the very idea of the possibility of anyone bringing all that stuff from the Mediterranean. For my part, I could see no other explanation. To me it could not possibly be a fraud, but I didn't have any answers.

From "The Mystery Cave of Many Faces" by Burrows & Rydholm (Superior Heartland 1992):

In the fall of 1990, my son Dan, who was in a Ph.D. program at Union Theological Seminary in New York, called with a message for me. Dan had become very interested in the cave, naturally, and had by this time

stepped beyond the bounds of skepticism and was truly trying to help out. Almost monthly he was sending me packets of background material that he had run across.

Dan had met a man from the Peabody Museum in Massachusetts and had spoken to him about the cave.

Not wanting to get into too deep a conversation with his limited knowledge of the cave, he obtained a telephone number and asked me to contact the gentleman.

I made the call. The fellow was obviously interested and made an effort to be helpful.

He asked, "What kind of a cave is it and where is it?"

I told him it was in Illinois

Burrows Cave, Southern Illinois
Egyptian looking piece.

Mrs. Gloria Farley

and held any number of inscribed rocks and numerous other artifacts, but it was mostly buried and filled with silt.

"From what I've seen of the stuff it seems to represent many Old World cultures but there is definitely a strong Egyptian influence there," I said.

"Well," said the museum man, "it wouldn't be Egyptian, they never went anyplace, but there are any number of other groups it could be." And he listed several.

"I didn't mean to say it is Egyptian," I said, "but there seems to be Egyptian infl—"

"Not Egyptian," he said emphatically.

This idea seemed to prevail throughout academia: "The Egyptians never went anywhere."

Apparently this is the view of the establishment and of the history we've been taught in school.

But let's look into this subject (Egyptian travels) from the perspective of more recent independent researchers.

One pioneer in this field is Mrs. Gloria Farley of Heavener, Oklahoma. Gloria has been studying and researching signs, glyphs and artifacts of ancient travelers and explorers for nearly half a century. In 1994 she published a 475-page book on her life's work (see *In Plain Sight, Old World Records in Ancient America* by Gloria Farley, 1994).

One distinct icon of the Mediterranean region, including the Iberian Peninsula, is the tanith or tanit (pronounced Tanith). It is a figure which represents the principal goddess of Carthage, which is now Tunis on the North African Coast. There are many variations of the Tanit, but it is always considered female, the spouse of the

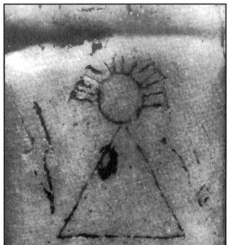

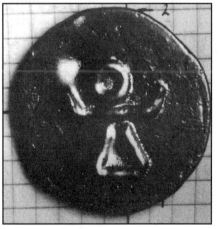

Burrows Cave Tanits

357

Phoenician God, Baal. We find the Baal sign, Ogam, and the Tanit in America. While many tanits have been found, if people knew what to look for, I'm sure many more would turn up. Gloria Farley discovered the first known Tanit in America. She didn't know what it was at the time (1975 in Colorado), but it was immediately recognized by Dr. Fell.

Ms. Farley had made a tracing of it along with many other glyphs which she kept. Dr. George Carter sent it to Fell, who acknowledged it gratefully in a letter to Mrs. Farley; a portion of that letter is quoted here (from *In Plain Sight,* page 163):

> Again congratulations and heartfelt thanks at the privilege of being able to see your extraordinary finds…The large goddess figure from Colorado is the sun goddess Tanit (pronounced Tanith), spouse of Baal, and peculiar to Carthage and Cadiz. As usual, the head is a sun disk, both arms are raised and she holds aloft the Phoenician word for sun-disk. As usual she is draped in a doll-like, crudely represented dress. This is the first known representation of a Mediterranean divinity in America, labeled with the name. Congratulations on an epoch-making discovery.[92]

Gloria Farley adds (in her book): "Fell modified his first translation of the inscription at Tanit's knee after he was able to study in Tripoli and Leptis Maga, Libya. Adding to what he learned there with evidence found in Tunisia and Morocco, he concluded that Roman, Carthaginian, Greek and Berber [92b]-Arab influences all were contemporaneously present in ancient Libya." (In ancient times, Libya meant all of Africa.)

Later Gloria Farley discovered another Tanit in Vermont which was interpreted by Fell.

While Tanits are commonly found in Spain, Sardinia, Carthage, Bosnia, Lebanon and Egypt, they have also been found, in the last 30 years, in Tennessee, Ohio and Oklahoma. Two sheet copper images of Tanit were found in a Hopewell Mound in Ohio, and in Spiro Mound in LaFlore County, Oklahoma, there was one carved on a conch shell similar to one from Sardinia in the Mediterranean.

The Tanit design has been found in the artwork of southwestern Indians in Mexico, New Mexico and Nevada, and in Owens Valley, California, there is a Tanit just one inch away from a drawing of an Egyptian-type boat, eleven inches long.

Sometime in the early 1990's a close friend of mine, who I have known since she was a baby, was working as a volunteer at an archaeological dig in

---

[92] Dr. Fell had already written two books that told of Mediterraneans being in America.
[92b] Berbers - most important people on northwest Africa - Mohammeden religion - Semetic related language

Peru. She told me that a high percentage of the artifacts they came across were Egyptian.

There is another researcher I have read about who believes King Solomon's copper mines were in South America. Something else to explore.

More on Egyptians in America

It seems that if the Chinese, Irish, Basques, Phoenicians, Hebrews, Old Norse, among others, had been sailing the oceans of the world for thousands of years, then certainly the Egyptians should have come to America. They were a highly sophisticated civilization and early users of copper and bronze, so they would have left more evidence of their presence than an occasional petroglyph, although they seem widespread. Could there have been a settlement of some kind that has been lost to modern historians like the rest of history?

Searching the literature from records written in the 16th and 17th century, we find it pretty well devoted to exploration. But when Europeans began settling in the American hinterlands, they found many inexplicable things. There were heathen idols, unknown scripts, mystery caves and many artifacts. But with the settlers' limited background in early history, all of these things naturally had to be attributed to the Indians; after all, no one else, to their knowledge, had ever been to these shores. But later, in the 19th century, a few curious people began to analyze and wonder. They had done a lot of world traveling and reading, and were better equipped with background information than the first settlers

The late Dr. Joe Mahan, founder and former president of the Institute for the Study of American Culture (ISAC) of Columbus, Georgia, has been a student of pre-history for many years. At the 1991 ISAC conference, Dr. Mahan read a paper, "Historic and Ethnological Context of Burrow's Cave." Part of that paper piqued my curiosity as I had never heard of this reference before. The reference I am referring to is a story of mummies found in a cave in Kentucky. His statement was as follows:

> Since the earliest settlement of the Ohio River Valley, there have been found numberless bits of evidence attesting to millennia—old contacts with European and ancient Mediterraneans. A cache of three hundred or more Egyptian-style mummies was found in caverns beneath what is now Lexington, Kentucky in 1775 by the first settlers there. The intruders, finding nothing of value to themselves, burned the entire lot of mummies, their wrappings and accoutrements. This has, until now, been the greatest loss that is known to have occurred to American archaeology.

A little book of 5 sheets of copper and a lead plate were sent to me from Bountiful Utah, said to be found in a cave (tomb) there. They have been returned to the sender but many magnified pictures of them were taken by Dr. Donald Snitgen of NMU.

Since the time of that conference, I have heard vague references to this tragic incident and was searching diligently for the source of this story when it was sent to me in August of 1999 by a friend and author of the book, *Ancient Mines of Kitchi-Gummi,* Roger Jewell, of Biglerville, Pennsylvania. His book is about one phase of the ancient trans-Atlantic copper trade.

The reference I was searching for came from the *Excitor*, Vol. 1, page 358, for 1827. But the article was quoted in 1838, in a book by Josiah Priest ("American Antiquities and Discoveries in the West"). The lengthy subtitle: "Being an Exhibition of the Evidence—that an ancient population of partially civilized nations, differing entirely from those of the present Indians, peopled America many centuries before its discovery by Columbus, and inquiries into their origins." In this book, Priest examines some of the perplexing stories of the early settlers. One of these enigmas, he determined, could only have been Egyptian.

The article, in its entirety:

A Catacomb of Mummies found in Kentucky

Lexington, in Kentucky, stands on the site of an ancient town, which was of great extent and magnificence, as is amply evinced by the wide range of its circumvallatory works, and the quantity of ground it once occupied.

There was connected to the antiquities of this place, a catacomb, formed in the bowels of the limestone rock, about fifteen feet below the surface of the earth, adjacent to the town of Lexington. This grand object, so novel and extraordinary in this country, was discovered in 1775, by some of the first settlers, whose curiosity was excited by something remarkable in the character of the stones which covered the entrance to the cavern within. They removed these stones, and came to others of singular appearance for stones in a natural state; the removal of which laid open the mouth of a cave, deep, gloomy, and terrific, as they supposed.

With augmented numbers, and provided with light, they descended and entered, with obstruction, a spacious apartment; the sides and extreme ends were formed into niches and compartments, and occupied by figures representing men. When alarm subsided, and the sentiment of dismay and surprise permitted further research and inquiry, the figures were found to be mummies, preserved by the art of embalming, to as great a state of perfection as was known among the ancient Egyptians, eighteen hundred years before the Christian era; which was about the time that the Israelites were in bondage in Egypt, when this art was in its perfection.

Unfortunately for antiquity, science, and everything else held sacred by the illumined and learned, this inestimable discovery was made at a period when a bloody and inveterate war was carried on between the Indians and the whites: and the power of the natives was displayed in so savage a manner, that the whites were filled with revenge. Animated by this vindictive spirit, the discoverers of the catacomb delighted to wreak their vengeance even on the mummies, supposing them to be of the same Indian race with whom they were then at war.

They dragged them out in the open air, tore the bandages open, kicked the bodies into dust, and made a general bonfire of the most ancient remains antiquity could boast. The descent to this cavern is gradual, the width four feet, the height seven, and the whole length of the catacomb was found to be eighteen rods and a half (almost 100 yards) by six and a half (36 yards); and calculating from the niches and shelving on the sides,

The Egyptians had a long history of trading and ocean travel, dating back to 3000 B.C. Here, an ocean-going Egyptian ship around 1500 B.C., as drawn from a reliel in the temple of El Bachri.

it was sufficiently capacious to have contained at least 200 subjects.

I could never, says Mr. Ash, from whose travels we have taken this account, learn the exact quantity it contained; the answers to the inquiries which were made respecting it were, "Oh, they burnt up and destroyed hundreds!" Nor could he arrive at any knowledge of the fashion, manner, and apparel of the mummies, or receive any other information than that they "were well lapped up," appeared sound, and consumed in the fire with a rapid flame. But not being content with the uncertain information of persons, who, it seems had no adequate knowledge of the value of this discovery, he caused the cavern to be gleaned for such fragments as yet remained in the niches, on its shelving sides and from the floor. The quantity of remains thus gathered up, amounted to forty or fifty baskets, the dust of which was so light and pungent as to affect the eyes even to tears, and the nose to sneezing, to a troublesome degree.

He then proceeded on a minute investigation, and separated from the general mass several pieces of human limbs, fragments of bodies, solid, sound, an apparently capable of eternal duration. In a cold state they had no smell whatever, but when submitted to the action of fire, gave out an agreeable effluvia, but was like nothing in its fragrance to which he could compare it.

On this subject Mr. Ash has the following reflections: "How these bodies were embalmed, how long preserved, by what nations, and from what people descended, no opinion can be formed, nor any calculation made, but what must result from speculative fancy and wild conjecture. For my part, I am lost in the deepest ignorance. My reading affords me no knowledge, my travels no light. I have neither read nor known of any of the North American Indians who formed catacombs for their dead, or who were acquainted with the art of preserving by embalming.

The Egyptians, according to Herodotus, who flourished 45 years before Christ, had three methods of embalming; but Diodorus, who lived before Christ, in the time of Julius Caesar, observes, that the ancient Egyptians had a fourth method of far greater superiority. That method is not described by Diodorus; it had become extinct in his time; and yet I cannot think it presumptuous to conceive that the American mummies were preserved after that very manner, or at least with a mode of equal virtue and effect.

The Kentuckians asserted, that the features of the face and form of the whole body were so well preserved, that they must have been the exact representation of the once living subjects.

This cavern, indeed, is similar to those found in Egypt, where the once polished and powerful inhabitants bestowed their dead, wrapped up in linens, spices, and aromatics of that country. It is probable that the cave where these were found was partly natural and partly artificial. Having found it suitable to their purpose, they opened a convenient descent, cleared out the stones and rocks, and fitted it with niches for the reception of those they had embalmed.

This custom, it would seem, is purely Egyptian, and was practiced in the earliest age of their national existence, which was about two thousand years before Christ. Catacombs are numerous all over Egypt, vast excavations under ground, with niches in their sides for their embalmed dead, exactly such as the one we have described.

Shall we be esteemed presumptuous, if we hazard the opinion that the people who made this cavern and filled it with the thousands of their embalmed dead were, indeed, from Egypt? If they were not, whither shall we turn for a solution of this mystery? To what country shall we travel? Where are the archives of past ages, that shall shed its light here?

If the Egyptians were indeed reckoned as the first nations; for so they are spoken of, even in the Scriptures: if from them was derived the art of navigation, the knowledge of astronomy, in a great degree with many other arts, of use to human society; such as architecture, with the science of government, etc.; why not allow the authors of the antiquated works about Lexington (together with the immense catacomb as evidence), to have been, indeed, an Egyptian colony; seeing the art of embalming, which is peculiarly characteristic of that people, was found in their state of perfection not exceeded by the mother country itself.

A trait of national practices so strong and palpable, as is this peculiar art, should lead the mind, without hesitation, to a belief, that wherever the thing is practiced, we have found in its authors either a colony direct from Egypt, or the descendants of some nation of the countries of Africa acquainted with the art.

But if this is so, the question here arises, how came they in America, seeing the nearest point of even South America approaches no nearer to the nearest point of Africa, than about seventeen hundred miles? Those points are, first, on the American side, Cape de Verd.

But such is the mechanism of the globe, and the operation of the waters, that from the west coast of Africa there is a constant current of the sea setting toward South America, so that if a vessel were lost, or if an eastern storm had driven it far into the ocean or South Atlantic, it would naturally arrive at last on the American coast. This is supposed to have been the predicament of the fleet of Alexander the Great, some hundred years before the Christian era, as we have before related. The cause of this current is doubtless the flow of the waters of the Mediterranean into the Atlantic; the Mediterranean being fed by a vast number of the rivers of Europe.

The inquiry to be pursued, is, whether the Egyptians were ever a maritime people or rather, anciently so, sufficient for our purpose?

By consulting ancient history, we find it mentioned that the Egyptians, as early as fourteen hundred and eighty-five years before Christ, had shipping, and that one Danus, with his fifty daughters, sailed into Greece and anchored at Rhodes; which is three thousand, three hundred and twenty years back from the present (1835) (3500 from today). Eight hundred and eighty-one years after the landing of this vessel at Rhodes, we find the Egyptians, under the direction of Necko, their king fitting out some Phoenicians with a vessel, or fleet, with orders to sail from the Red Sea, quite around the continent of Africa, and return to the Mediterranean which they effected.

It is easy to pursue the very track they sailed, in order to circumnavigate Africa; sailing from some port on the Red Sea, they pass down to the strait of Babelmandel, into the Indian Ocean; thence south, around the Cape of Good Hope, into the South Atlantic; thence north along the African coast on the west side, which would carry them along opposite, or east of South America.

Pursuing this course; they would pass into the Mediterranean—at the

Strait of Gibraltar, and so on to Egypt, mooring at Alexandria, on the south end of the Mediterranean, a voyage of more than sixteen thousand miles; two thirds of the distance around the earth. Many ages after their first settlement in Egypt, they were the leading nation in maritime skill and other arts.

It is true, that a knowledge of the compass and magnet, as aids to navigation, in Africa or Europe, was unknown in those early ages; but to counterbalance this defect, they were, from necessity, much more skillful in a knowledge of the heavenly bodies, as guides to their courses, than men are at the present day. But in China, it is believed that a knowledge of the magnet, and its application to the great purposes of navigation, was understood before the time of Abraham, more than two thousand years before Christ, of which we shall give a more particular account in another part of this work.

But if we cannot allow the Egyptians to have visited South America, and all the islands between, on voyages of discovery, which by no means can be supposed chimerical, we are ready to admit that they may have been driven there, by an eastern storm, and, as favoring such a circumstance, the current which sets from the African coast toward South American, should not be forgotten.

If it be allowed that this mode of reasoning is at all conclusive, the same will apply in favor of their having first hit on the coast of the West Indies, as this group of islands as they now exist, is much more favorable to a visit from that particular port of Africa called Egypt, than in South America.

Egypt and the West Indies are exactly in the same latitude, that is, the northern parts of those islands, both being between twenty and thirty degrees north.

Sailing from Egypt, out of the Mediterranean, passing through the straits of Gibraltar, would throw a vessel, in case of an eastern storm, aided by the current, as high north as opposite the Bahama islands. A blow of but a few days in that direction, would be quite sufficient to have driven an Egyptian vessel, or boat, or whatever they may have sailed in, entirely on the coast of the West Indies. The trade winds sweep westward across the Atlantic, through a space of fifty or sixty degrees of longitude, carrying everything within their current directly to the American coast.

If such may have been the case, they were indeed, in a manner, on the very continent itself, especially if the opinion of President Jefferson and others be allowed, that the Gulf of Mexico, which is situated exactly behind those islands, west, has been scooped out by the current which makes from equator toward the north.

Kentucky itself, where we think we have found the remains of an Egyptian colony, or nation, as in the case of the works and catacomb at Lexington, is in latitude by five degrees north of Egypt, so that wheather they may have visited America on a voyage of exploration, or have been driven on the coast against their will, in either case it would be perfectly natural that they should have established themselves in that region.

Traits of Egyptian manners were found among many of the nations of South America, mingled with those who appeared to be of other origin; of which we shall speak again in the course of this work.

But at Lexington, the traits are too notorious to allow them to be other than pure Egyptian, in full possession of the strongest complexion of their national character, that of embalming, which was connected with their religion.

The Mississippi, which disembogues itself into the Mexican gulf, is in the same north latitude with Egypt, and may have, by its likeness to the Egyptian Nile, invited those adventures to pursue its course, till a place suited to their views or necessities may have presented.

Other tokens of the presence of Egyptian population are not wanting in North America; as in the vale of Mexico, a few years since, "several curious specimens of sculpture have been discovered, and sent to Charlestown, South Carolina, by the American Minister at Mexico, Mr. Poinsett; which articles are now in the Museum of the Literary and Philosophical Society, at Charleston. The collection consists of several images and a large figure of a snake, which was doubtless a favorite object of adoration. These images are well worthy of attention, as they bear the evident marks of antiquity; and though the sculpture is rude, it is impossible for anyone who has examined the remains of ancient times, not to be struck with the strong resemblance they bear to the workmanship of the ancient Egyptians."

General Statement by Dr. Covey

In 1994, the famous pre-historian, Dr. Cyclone Covey, writing the preface for our book, "The Mystery Cave of Many Faces" (by Russell Burrows and myself, 1991), gives us a most remarkable historical background, completely unknown to mainline historians and teachers and therefore the public. I have known Dr. Covey for about 20 years and believe him to be one of the greatest living authorities on ancient history in this country, if not the world. He is now emeritus Professor of History at Wake Forest University in Winston-Salem, North

Dr. Cyclone Covey

Carolina. He is so far above the few colleagues in his field that there is just no comparison. His knowledge in this field is encyclopedic and authoritative.

An excerpt from Dr. Covey's preface is most enlightening:

Conventional theory of inconsequential transoceanic contact with America before Columbus, Leif Erickson, Brendan, circumpolar Red Paint People, Shan hai jing explorers, Huui Shan, Madoc of Wales, or Mandinga Emperor Abu Bakr II (whichever discussant's 5th grade teacher happened to know enough to recognize), retreats in ever more frantic epicycles which may work to the good in the long run: the fellow who finally proved continental drift had set out to disprove it. We should welcome skeptics willing to test instead of burn Copernicans at the stake.

Nicole Guidon did not expect hearth charcoal she excavated from Pedra Furada, Piauf (Brazil) to carbon date 48,500 years ago. Neanderthals rafting by Gulf Stream to Brazil! Unthinkable as tectonic plates.

We may wonder at the vast Egyptian Akkadians substrate in the Americas. Egyptians surely preceded displaced Mycenaeans (also Minoans and Akkadians before them), as well as Phoenicians and Carthaginians, voyaged into the Atlantic with their respective imperial expansions and metal-searchings, then again in flight with their calamitous reverses…The Maya calendar base date, 13 August 3114 B.C. Gregorian, comes as close as have managed to pinpoint the founding of the 1st dynasty and may commemorate this era-change…

Corresponding with Jim Bailey

In one of my conversations with Dr. Fell, I told him of Joe Gannon's theory of a copper trade between Lake Superior and the Mediterranean. I told him how Joe and Roy Drier were looking for clues from people from overseas as there seemed to be such strong circumstantial evidence. Other than the fellow from Ireland who detected such a definite parallel in mining methods, the local scholars seemed to have their minds made up: "There was never any trade with Europe." But now, after Drier and Gannon were dead, Fell had come out with his book[93] spelling out such a trade. I told him that for years I thought I was the only living person in the world who suspected this trade until I read his book, *Bronze Age America.*

Fell's book gave me a whole new insight into ancient history. He told me that many of the great scholars of ancient history from all over the world were interested in such a trade and many were well acquainted with Roy Drier's work.

I asked him if he knew anyone from overseas who spoke English and who I might write to, just to get an idea of their thinking. Fell gave me the name and address of a Professor J. R. A. Bailey who lived in the Republic of South Africa. Mr. Bailey and I corresponded maybe two or three times a year for a few years in the 1980's. He said that several African and European scholars were convinced that some of the early Mediterranean copper had come from America. I was astonished to hear this; here I thought I was almost alone with this idea.

In September of 1986, I received a letter from Professor Bailey that summarized his thoughts very clearly. He wrote that while he has no direct evidence of usage of North American copper in the Old World at an early date, there is much indirect evidence. It sounded like Mr. Gannon talking.

Bailey goes on to state his reasons:

1. According to papers issued by duTemple and partners, the extraction of pure copper from Isle Royale began 5300 B.C.—adjusted by Dendrochronology, this makes 6000 B.C. the start of the Copper Age.
2. Until 4000 B.C., the only copper that could be used was native copper; the temperatures for smelting oxides and sulphides weren't reached until 4000 B.C.
3. The only place in the world where native copper existed in economic quantities was around Lake Superior with a little bit admittedly at Cora Cora in Bolivia.
4. The earliest monumental architecture in the world is on the Atlantic shores of Western Europe, in Brittany, going back to 4800 B.C. (almost 7,000 years ago).
5. The climate in the North Atlantic reached an optimum in 6000 B.C. as shown by pollen analysis in Britain so the North Atlantic was then fairly Mediterranean in point of wind and temperature.

---

[93] "Bronze Age America"

6. The only people using copper in that early date were living around the Black Sea from the Balkans to Turkey and Jordan.
7. According to Diodorus, the start of God-kingship took place in North West Europe among peoples who were a mixture of Pelasgian[94] from the East Mediterranean and the local natives.
8. This system of government was taken right around the world and I have always supposed that it was financed by the copper trade.
9. For example, the oldest and most sacred city of Sumer was called Eridu, which was the Sumerian name for copper.

#

Professor Bailey says he could take this theory much further for the Bronze Age, but communicating by mail makes complicated ideas difficult to get across.

Jim Bailey had been studying the history of ancient Europe for many years. In 1973 he released a book entitled *God-Kings and the Titans*. It was then that he realized the importance of copper and first suspected a trade with America concerning that metal.

Then in 1994 he released another book, *Sailing to Paradise: The discovery of America, 7000 B.C.*: It concerned the copper trade. A year later, he revised this book and republished it in 1995 as *Sailing to Paradise: The discovery of America in 5000 B.C.* Jim Bailey died in 2001.

It is easy to see that the possibility of an ancient copper trade was being considered by scholars on both sides of the Atlantic. Professor Bailey has many followers on both sides of the ocean and around the world.

The question here in America was: "Where did all the copper go?"
The question overseas was: "Where did all the copper come from?

---

[94] Pelasgian: One of an early people or group of peoples mentioned by classical writers as the primitive dwellers in Greece and the eastern islands of the Mediterranean, Minoan, Mycenaean—or a member of the branch of the Mediterranean race which Sergi holds to have formed the pre-Hellenic population of this region.

Axe may be 500,000 years old

Greek artifact significant find for dating habitation.

BOSTON (Reuter) – Archeologists said Wednesday they have unearthed an artifact that provides verifiable evidence that humans inhabited Greece as long as 500,000 years ago - and credited pure luck and slow goats to the find.

The artifact, an axe, was discovered by Boston University Archeologist in what was once a lake bed near the Greek region of Nikopolis, about 300 kilometers west of Athens.

The axe resembles an oversized arrowhead. It was found imbedded in an eroded gully that allowed scientists to date it from the lower Paleolithic period of the early Ice Age - about 200,000 to 500,000 years ago.

In December 2002, it was announced that a skeleton that had been in Mexico City's National Museum of Anthropology since 1959 had been identified as more than 13,000 years old—the oldest skeleton yet found in the Americas. Dubbed the "Penon Woman III," the skeleton's skull—typically dolichocraniac, or "long-faced"—was what attracted the attention of scientists, as the Amerindian population has Mongolian shape skulls. Scientists speculated that the skull was of Ainu extraction, just as the Kennewick Man remains.

Detroit Free Press, April 4, 1989

Historic remains

Broken stone tools, charcoal and bison bones discovered on Oklahoma may be evidence of the earliest known humans in North America.

Analysis has yielded dates going back 26,000 to 40,000 years, said Don Wycoff, of the Oklahoma Archeological Survey. If further research confirms preliminary findings, the discovery would push evidence of human activity on this continent at least twice as far back in prehistory as thought.

Chapter X
A Look at Some of the Faults in the System

Some Situations I Have Stumbled Into

The bodies of research we've discussed so far are those I have read about or with which I am familiar. I hear of others constantly and think that, despite the barrage of TV documentaries and magazine articles upholding the official view of ancient history, much of the public knows that what is being taught in our institutions is grossly outdated. Hundreds of observations have gone unnoticed or unreported, with still more to be recognized.

We have already pointed out two separate powers that have distorted early academic thinking. One was religious beliefs. The other consists of dogmatic attitudes by the most powerful leaders in archaeology, history and other disciplines devoted to discovery of our ancient history. Today the established dogma guardians argue: "How can a century of scientists be wrong?"

In my years of independent research, I have run into many situations which illustrate how closed-minded this branch of the scientific society can be. Some of these you may have already detected, but there are specific situations that I would like to share.

My first experiences with this closed-mindedness were trivial alongside some of the later ones. Imagine for example my frustration when I enthusiastically described my first dolmen, only to have it ridiculed emphatically as nothing more than a glacial erratic. There was no question, no further doubt, the "experts" had been taught and they knew all about it.

Then within a very few years, when I was excited about what appeared to be strange writing on the stone from the Escanaba River (the Joel Kela Stone), the experts said, first, that these marks were caused by the sun baking clay and, second, that they were caused by crystallizing salt. No further questions, no alternatives, nothing curious about it.

Moreover, who could believe that Indians mined all that copper in those thousands of mines, including masses weighing several tons apiece, still propped up on cribbing? Who could believe the Indian theory when all that has ever been found for the use of that copper has been axe or arrowheads, with just a very few larger artifacts? Who could believe those scoffing academics when it has been known for years that huge amounts of copper were used overseas in statues,[94a]

[94a] Websters International Dictionary - Colossus of Rhodes - A Statue of Appollo, about 120ft high made by Chares about 280 B.C. One of the seven wonders of the Ancient World.
"He doth bestride the narrow world like a colossus" – *William Shakespear*

armor, chariots, warship rams and many other large objects—all this when ancient sources of European copper were quite limited, while in our "Copper Country" copper fairly burst from the earth?

A New Look at the Kensington Stone

Barry J. Hansen, Author of the 2 volume "Kensington Runestone—A Defense of Olaf Ohman Accused Forger"

Photo Courtesy of Barry Hansen

My next challenge was the story of Minnesota's Kensington Stone. The authorities claimed that Olaf Ohman, a simple, honest, dirt farmer, cut those intricate runes, the only ones he ever cut in his life, just to fool somebody. One look at that stone and I could never believe those runes were cut by anyone but a master rune cutter with much experience.

In 2002, Barry J. Hansen of Maple, Wisconsin, published a two volume study of the Kensington Stone (*Kensington Runestone—A Defense of Olaf Ohman the Accused Forger*, Morris Publishing, 3212 East Highway 30, Kearney, Nebraska, 68847).

Working with Dr. Richard Nielsen over a period of many years, these two men put the stone and the runes, as well as the circumstances, through every type of analysis they could think of. They worked with many inhabitants of the Kensington area. They learned that there had been very few scientific tests ever made in the years following the discovery

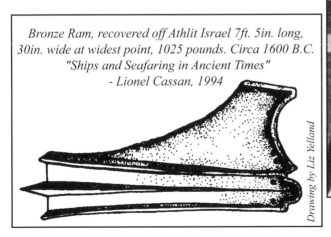

Bronze Ram, recovered off Athlit Israel 7ft. 5in. long, 30in. wide at widest point, 1025 pounds. Circa 1600 B.C. "Ships and Seafaring in Ancient Times" - Lionel Cassan, 1994

Drawing by Liz Yelland

Dr. Richard Nielsen

Courtesy Ancient American Magazine

Olaf Ohman and his family

Olof and Karin, *who were married 11/27/1886, lived in Holmes City where Olof worked in the flour mill and did carpenter work as it was available.*

Olof, Jr. *(6/1887-2/1938) was born in Holmes City and lived at home until homesteading in Alberta, Canada, where he lived until he died.*

Shortly after Olof Jr. was born, the family began purchasing and clearing the land that would eventually become their farm.

Arthur *(2/7/1891-2/18/1984) spent his life on the farm, except for the last few years in a nursing home in Alexandria. He is buried at Solem Lutheran Church Cemetery*

Oscar C. *(3/14/1897-1/7/1918) died of meningitis and is also buried at Solem.*

John G. *(4/11/1899-2/10/1960) remained on the farm and is buried in the Solem Lutheran Church Cemetery.*

David Edwin *(8/12/1902-7/17/1929) developed a spinal tumor, was wheel- chair bound, committed suicide and is buried at Solem.*

Edward Carl *(11/20/1888-12/9/1950) went to North Dakota in the early 1910's and was a veteran of WWI. He spent most of his life in Appam and is buried in Williston.*

Betsy Amanda *(12/9/1892-4/19/1951) married Joel Carlson on 8/9/1924, lived in Minneapolis, committed suicide while visiting her family at the farm. She is buried in Lakewood Cemetery, Minneapolis.*

Ida C. *(12/1895-?) married Abraham Kolberg. Their son, Lalard, was put on a train when he was 3 years old and sent to live with Olof and Karin. She was a teacher in Detroit, MI for many years.*

William *(10/1905-10/1973) died in Pinewood, MN. He married and had a family.*

Dr. Gunnar Thompson, a great American Pre-Historian, author of many books of pre-history.

of the stone, and that most of the conclusions were the opinions of "experts."

To me, a very impressive part of the two volumes (over 90 pages out of 750) was devoted to a thorough study of every "expert" who offered an opinion on the stone. The few who meekly offered believing reports were quickly overwhelmed by the sheer numbers of those crying fraud. As Hanson points out, there were no "experts" as no investigator was historically attuned to the variations of runes from Norse history, nor had anyone ever previously seen a runestone in the heartland of America. Most of the opinions were given at a time (1901-1912) when the "authorities" had just gone through a long campaign to rule out any rumor that the Norse had ever been to America. The 400th anniversary of the landing of Columbus, as far as academia was concerned, had proven once and for all that no one had come to America before him. This was pointed out by one of the great, but so far relatively unsung pre-historians, Dr. Gunnar Thompson, in his book, "American Discovery: The Real Story" (Seattle, Argonauts O.MT.I, 1992):

> Most historians and anthropologists are loyal to a doctrine of cultural isolation that was originally promulgated by a medieval religious fraternity. During the 1800's, the Columbian Order promoted the ethnocentric belief that Columbus was chosen by God to bring the first Christian civilization to America.

Thompson:

> Although modern scholars abandoned the religious premise of American discovery, they adhered to the belief that no significant voyagers preceded Columbus to the New World. This belief is often referred to as the 'Monroe Doctrine of Cultural Isolation.' Because of this doctrine, establishment scholars automatically dismiss evidence of pre-Columbian cultural diffusion as heresy. The resulting academic myopia is a clear indictment of scholars who claim that their beliefs are based on scientific principles. Indeed, "the practice of science demands an open-minded examination of <u>all</u> the evidence, no matter how unorthodox it might seem."

An almost humorous example of unscientific thinking is that of a former science teacher friend of mine who went to his doctor with a nagging skin condition he had had for years.

The doctor suggested that it could possibly be caused by an allergic reaction to the soap he was using.

"Oh," said the teacher, "it couldn't be that, I've used the same soap nearly all my life."

Dr. Jim Scherz, Professor Emeritus of the Department of Civil and Environmental Engineering, University of Wisconsin in Madison, tells a story of a prominent archaeologist in Wisconsin who was making an archaeological dig into a Wisconsin effigy mound. Jim previously had surveyed over 200 effigy mounds in an area around Madison.

When the archaeologist came to what were obviously bones of a horse, she stopped the dig.[94b]

When Dr. Scherz asked to read her report, she stated that she didn't make one. Asked why she hadn't, the reply was, "Well, it was a horse," implying that obviously some farmer had buried a horse there in modern times.

If the dig had been properly done, the bones would have been carbon-dated. If their age had been determined to be six or seven hundred years, or even older, it certainly would have been a great archaeological discovery. There are those who believe the Norse may have brought horses into that area a thousand years earlier. In fact, there have been petroglyphs of a horseshoe found at the Jeffers site in Minnesota, according to Chuck Bailey of Duluth. Here is a case of a

---

[94b] The story in Dr. Scherz own words - quoted from *Rock Art Pieces from Burrows cave in Southern Illinois Volume 1* by Scherz & Burrows.

One summer, I learned from a farmer, who lives near Aztalan, Wisconsin, that archaeologists dug up a small horse from an Indian mound on his farm. He said it was a Shetland pony. Recognizing that this is the type of horses that the "Vikings" would have had in the days they were known to have had New World settlements at the mouth of the St. Lawrence River in Newfoundland, I was very excited and wanted to know more about the pony from the mound. I thought that these bones might provide supplementary data to the Indian legends of "Red Haired Giants" that the Winnebagos preserved in their verbal traditions, and about the legend of the great boat with white wings and shiny scales on its side, preserved by the Prairie Island Sioux north of La Crosse, Wisconsin.

I called up the prominent archaeologist who dug the site and requested a report on the horse bones that were dug up from the mound. Also I asked, "What was the age of the bones?" "Oh," was the reply, "We never had the bones analyzed." "Why not?" I asked. "Well, the Indians did not have horses." was the reply. "How did the horse get into the mound?" I asked. "Well, a farmer must have buried a pet Shetland pony in the mound." I protested that farmers do not normally bury horses, but send them to rendering plants or haul them out into the woods. But I was told that some unknown farmer must have not only buried a horse, but did so in an ancient Indian mound, and that the state of Wisconsin did not have money to analyze bones of a farmer's horse.

Courtesy of Milwaukee Public Museum. from "Here Was Vinland"

Courtesy of Wm Grasley. from "Here Was Vinland"

Above: Norse axes found in Minnesota at Erhahl, Right: 5 1/2lbs. edge 8 1/4 in. At Norway Lake, Left: 5 lbs. edge 16 in.

Left: Portlock, Ontario, cast copper "spud," Weight 3 lbs 11 oz. Length 8 1/4 in.

Below: Norse Axe found in the Keeweenaw Peninsula.

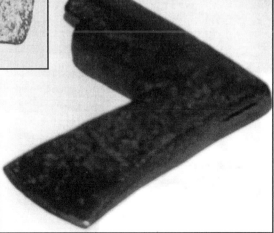

possible real discovery disregarded because of an archaeologist's preconceived belief. But shouldn't the fact that the bones were actually in an effigy mound have raised the curiosity of any researcher as to their age? We could have learned much from that dig alone, but we will never know.

Some might say if my first look at the actual Kensington Stone was all I needed to convince me that it was cut by an experienced rune master, then it was just my opinion. This is certainly true, it was just that—and not even an expert opinion. But I have probably seen as many runestones as those seen collectively by the whole roster of experts who passed judgment on the Kensington runestone in the early 20th century. And I don't consider myself an expert to any degree.

Barry Hansen has listed the qualifications and analyzed the testimony of every one of the "experts" who have condemned the Kensington Stone, and universally found their expertise in this very specialized field sorely lacking. However, with all of Dr. Richard Nielsen's years of experience and research, I would be comfortable in classifying him as an "expert" on that particular stone, as I would Barry Hansen himself. After years of study, these two men, as well as Chuck Bailey, Judi Rudebusch, Oscar and Ilene Anderson, Katie and Paul Weiblen, and a host of others who have spent a great deal of time and effort proving the authenticity of the Kensington Stone, certainly deserve as much respect as a century of condemnation by "authorities" who have done little more than echo the hollow opinions of the "authorities" of the last century.

There have been many related discoveries in a four state area (Minnesota, Iowa, North and South Dakota) that tie in closely to the Kensington Runestone. There have been fire steels, Norse axes, a harpoon, halberds and what many have said are grave sites and evidence of longhouses. Also, in the last decade or so more and more mooring stones have been located.

One of the arguments used that artifacts were being "planted" by overzealous Scandinavians was that so many of these things have been found. How could a band of ten or twenty Vikings lose things over such a wide area? But we are now realizing that hundreds of Norse farmers once moved into the area, presumably from the western settlements of Greenland. There were also many boats involved that could travel in a large flooded area, the remains of Lake Agassiz.[95]

With the introduction of GPS satellite locating computers, Judi Rudebusch, a Minnesota farm wife, has taken great interest in mooring stones, as have Carol Swayze-Hansen and others. They have located many such hole-cut boulders over

---

[95] As previously stated, this pre-historic lake was named for Jean Louis Rodolphe Agassiz (1807-1873) of Switzerland, who discovered in 1840 that glaciers and ice had once covered large parts of northern Europe and America. The Agassiz Museum of Comparative History

Triangular mooring hole 7/8" in 2 ton granite boulder, found on Eldon Hubbard Farm near West Mud Lake in Chactauqua County N.Y, known to have existed well over a century ago.

a large area, over 350 so far.

Up to now most people thought that these could not be mooring stones as they seem to be haphazardly scattered, even up on hills. They were thought to have been Indian horse tethers, or maybe holes drilled by farmers splitting rock for building use. These explanations don't seem to stand up for various reasons. Others have dismissed them, saying that some of these types of stones have been found up and down the east coast, but then many believe the Vikings had been there also. After all, we are just now learning what great explorers the Norse were.

Traveling from the Scandinavian Peninsula and Denmark, they established a dukedom in Normandy (France), occupied much of the British Isles, populated Iceland and Greenland, and founded the Kingdom of Russia, settling in such far-flung places as Kiev and Novgorod. We now know for certain that they were traveling in America hundreds of years before the arrival of Columbus.

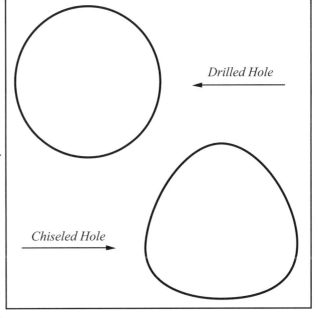

From *Here Was Vinland,* Curran, page 168: "According to the Anglo-Saxon Chronicle, three Viking ships raided the South Coast of England near Dorchester, in 787 and carried off spoils. This was the first of many raids. In 793 and 794, they raided the North-Umbrian coast. The following year 100 Viking ships appeared off the south coast of Wales. Probably it was this same

This lichen-covered granite boulder in Clay County Minnesota has an eight-inch-deep triangular hole about the size of a quarter.

Judi Rudebusch has mapped 57 holey rocks in Roberts County.

Right: Judi Rudebusch and Brenda Seewafen, Corona, S. Dakota. Judi's grandfather homesteaded this farm, Brenda lives on it now. Stone is believed to be a carved horn with possibly some religous meaning - others have been found like it.

Left: Richard Alfstrom 94 yrs old and Judi Rudenbusch at Wheaton Minn. on exact spot of burial site where Wheaton Ruestone was found. Marion Dahm was involved in 1985 and by then it was lost by the Minnesota Historical Society. This photo was taken in Sept. 2000, by Marion Dahm.

Marion Dahm with broken Mooring Stone

party that raided Leinster in Ireland. St. Columbia's shrine was ravaged in 802 and again in 806. From 812 to 814, Vikings were reported far inland in Munster, Ulster and Connaught. In 826 the Viking Torgils founded Dublin. Limerick was another city founded by the raiders."

This was similar to what happened in France where the Vikings showed up with 30,000 fighting men to capture Rossen and besiege Paris. In 877 a permanent colony was established on the Loire, acknowledging the Norse Kings of Dublin as their ruler.

# # #

"When the Swedish Vikings invaded Russia in the 9th century, the inhabitants spoke of Roders as Rots, Routsi, etc. Swedish settlers in Russia were therefore called 'Russ' by Arabs and Slavs, and so the word Russia came into being."[96]

As the raids on Britain continued, the Norse occupied the Orkneys, Shetlands, Hebrides and much of Scotland, and some claim there is evidence of them along the river systems of both North and South America.

Until recently, what we have known about the Vikings was written by their defeated enemies, Arab, English and French historians, along with Irish monks. They gave us the classic Viking picture of wild, brutish marauders, thieves and murderers. We have heard such stories about enemies in our own wars. But the Vikings had another side as lovers of art, fine metal works, and elegant furniture. They were even among the first to have a laundry day, called lordag, and seem to have been the inventors of hot irons and ironing boards. They named the days of the week after their Gods, some of which are used in our everyday English. But they are best known for their shipbuilding and seafaring: As explorers they were second to none.

By plotting the exact location of the many mooring stones on a contour map, Judi Rudebusch and her friends have discovered that they are all between 1,100 and 1,200 feet above sea level. Thus these stones would have been at the edge or along the shore of islands or waterways when they were used.[96a]

Rudebusch and Swayze-Hansen have hunted tirelessly for more stones over a vast area. The key to what they have been looking for is a stone with a triangular hole four to seven inches deep. This peculiar shaped hole is the result of using a flat chisel in contrast to the round holes made by a star bit used to drill rock in modern times. And as they are commonly found on the coasts of northern Europe, there seems to be no other logical explanation for them but Viking

---

[96] *Vikings—North Atlantic Saga,* Fitzhugh & Ward, 2000.
[96a] *A new explanation for "out of the way" mooring stone holes being considered by Judi Rudebusch is, she has learned from Iceland, that they were also used as property markers.*

period mooring stones. The Kensington runestone was found at an elevation of about 1,300 feet according to Judi Rudebusch. These new finds explain a lot of things and add a lot to our overall picture of Norse life in the heartland of our continent.

Barry Hansen, in his book, has even taken on the Smithsonian in their attempts to squash the age-old Viking legend. He takes a number of quotes from a three-page letter (1999) from Ives Goddard of the Smithsonian to the Kensington Runestone Museum in Alexandria, Minnesota (October 10, 1999) that was answered by a 32-page letter from Dr. Richard Nielsen (January 3, 2000) pointing out the many questionable assumptions and their dependence on the opinions of earlier experts.

Hansen points out that "Goddard alludes to 'the experts' eight times in three pages and yet when the Smithsonian was asked directly to name just one 'expert' who could identify any feature of the Kensington Runestone that could not have been done in the fourteenth century, they could not do so."

Reaction to Smithsonian Exhibit

In the year 2000, the Smithsonian Institution assembled a major exhibit entitled "Vikings: The North American Saga." It traveled from Washington, D.C. to New York, Ottawa, Los Angeles, Houston and Chicago. In connection with this exhibit, the Smithsonian had two authors, William W. Fitzhugh and Elisabeth I. Ward, assemble a beautifully and profusely illustrated book by the same name as the exhibit. Both had been supported by the kings and queens of all the Scandinavian countries, the Nordic Council of Ministers and Valvo, along with such great industries as the Phillips Petroleum Company of Norway and organizations such as the National Geographic Society, the White House Council on the Millennium and others.

Both the book and the exhibit (true to form) disclaimed each and every shred of Viking or Old Norse evidence in America. Among the more controversial articles of interest were the Heavener Runes in Oklahoma, the Spirit Pond Runestone from Maine,[96b] the Vinland Map, the Newport Tower and, of course, the Kensington Runestone. Their conclusions, without reservation, decreed all to be modern fabrications and frauds.[96c]

The reaction from independent researchers and pre-Columbian study organizations from across the country was to point out the many errors in the publication and sharply challenged their point of view.

[96b] *See Spirit Pond Runestone - A Study in Linguistics by Paul Chapman, Part II, Volume 22 ESOP. Distribution address Mail Station, Suite 680, 2482 Jett Ferry Rd. Dunwoody, GA 30338*
[96c] *See Appendix*

In the journal of the New England Antiquities Research Association (NEARA) for the summer of 2000 (Volume 34, Number 1), the president of that organization, Donald Y. Gilmore, wrote an introductory letter stating the indignation of some of its members at the Smithsonian's long-standing ridicule of so many artifacts. Many NEARA members were quick to pick up the gauntlet. Gilmore states:

> Not only do they (the members) disagree with the categorically negative conclusions of Fitzhugh and Ward, but they also point to a plethora of errors and an abundance of bias in the Smithsonian's account——
> ——in this case we would have hoped for at least a glimmer of objectivity from supposedly qualified scholars, perhaps some recognition that those whose research they attack are also reputable scholars and that their views should be weighed carefully—even if there is disagreement on interpretation—pending further scientific evaluation. We expect higher academic standards at a distinguished institution such as the Smithsonian.

Further on in the letter he cites Bill Conner's work on Arlington Mallory and researcher Michel Zalar, saying he found "no less than 37 factual errors in the chapter on the Kensington Stone." He then rebuts each of these errors with the actual facts.

Retired chemical engineer and archaeological researcher Jim Guthrie challenges the Smithsonian's position on the Vinland Map.[96b] He thinks the "jury is still out on this one," while Sue Carlson, longtime scholar of Old Norse and runic inscriptions, is outraged "by the errors and distortions in the catalogue" (the book *Vikings—The North Atlantic Saga*).

Gilmore ends his letter with the statement which should be the objective of all honest and serious researchers, "Our goal, like that of other objective research organizations, is diligently seeking the truth, letting the chips fall where they may. This is the meaning of science."

The NEARA Journal goes on for some 40 pages of critical comment on the Smithsonian exhibit and the accompanying publication.

Anyone wishing to read a thorough critique of the Kensington Runestone should certainly review Barry Hansen's two volume work on the subject. He and his collaborators scrutinized the stone from every possible angle. They have conducted all the scientific and linguistic tests that the public would have expected the Smithsonian to have done before organizing an exhibit such as the one they assembled in 2000. But for the unsuspecting public, the Smithsonian's

---

[96b] *This author takes no stand on the Vinland Map - there are "Scientific tests" and experts that prove both sides.*

seems to be the final word. Then, as usual, the "experts" sentiments are picked up by such popular magazines as *Time* and *U.S. News and World Report,* thus further solidifying their one-sided arguments.

Time Article Criticized

A *Time* article (May 8, 2000), though informative and well written by Michael D. Lemonich and Andrea Dorfman, specifically and categorically states that the Newport Tower in Rhode Island, the Kensington Stone and Yale's Vinland Maps are all bogus.

Among others was the response of the great prehistorian Dr. Cyclone Covey. A reprint of his letter to the editor of *Time, Inc.* is as follows:

Dr. & Mrs. Cyclone Covey with Ethel Stewart (left)
June 15, 1991

The Newport Tower

Courtesy of Urungo Mutu

Dear Editor Sutter,

It's a terrible shame that *Time* blew its opportunity to tell the more newsworthy truth about Vikings (May 8, 2000).

The reason the Kensington Stone and Viking Map are "widely believed…a modern forgery" is that widely circulated articles like this week's *Time* suppress the current state of scholarship. And an early governor of Rhode Island built the Newport Tower? Name him. (Rhode Island became a state in 1790.)

Newport Tower. Verazzano inspected this "Norman villa" in 1524. Mercator depicted the tower flanking a Romanesque church on his 1569 Mappemode. Christopher Jones used it in navigating the Mayflower in 1620. Sir Edwin Plowden cited the "Round stone tower" in a charter application to Charles I. Quaker colonists built plain meeting houses when they did not use each others houses, never 14th century churches, but did use the immemorially standing tower for a windmill in 1675 or 1676.

English units of measure do not divide any of the tower dimensions, which prove (it was) built on the 12.35 "Rhineland foot." The Danish archaeologist C.C. Rofu detected it in 1838, a Scandinavian church dating no later than 1200 (actually than 1400). Magnus Bjorndal and Prof. Peer Lovfald discovered the runic inscription in 1946 fourteen feet upon the west side: HNKSR, "of the stool," that is, the bishop's chair – Latin Cathedra, thus cathedral church [O.G. Landsverk 1967; Earl Syverson 1973; Barry Fell 1980]. It took Dr. Clyde Keeler's Crowngraphic camera to catch another inscription in 1974, one foot to the right and 1.5 feet higher; abbreviation of *In hoc signa crux* [Keeler 1985]. Verazzano's very word Norumbega = Narragansett abbreviates Norse gang = settlement [Paul Chapman 1994]. Roger Williams[97] in the 1630's tried in vain to find an explanation of its origin.

A clam digger discovered the partially submerged Narragansett Stone in Narragansett Bay in 1985 that warned disembarkers, in runes, to be aware of wild animals. Fell abstracted a Norse vocabulary creolized in Algonquin (1976). These are little overlooked details.

Kensington Stone—Olaf Ohman in Nov 1898 with great difficulty despite a winch pulled out an aspen whose roots clasped the Kensington Stone. Neighbors and family witnessed and townsmen marveled. "Experts" promptly persecuted the hapless farmer, who was glad to sell his farm in 1907 to Hjalmar Holand. In the next 50 years, Holand disproved most of the charges of fakery. Numerous genuine experts continued to find

---

[97] Founder of Rhode Island, born in London in 1604, immigrated to America in 1631.

medieval Scandinavian and Greenland runestones and manuscripts for every usage the scoffers had called in question, including the bugaboo word opdagelsford (discovery voyage) and Arabic numerals in the runes, etc., etc. Verification culmination in the systematic explications by three of the world's leading runologists, Robert Hall 1950/1982, Albert G. Hahn 1987 and Richard Nielsen 1986-89. (Did your authors not think to consult them?)

One way to take evidence is at face value. If scoffers had not expended all their energy fantasizing how the Kensington Stone could have been faked, they might have tested the stone's message itself. It memorialized, 10 men found dead by 10 who returned from fishing to their camp beside two skerries[98] a day's journey from the stone site. Another 10 men had been left "by the sea" to guard the ships (possibly Lake Winnipeg). The expedition had been on a discovery-voyage from Vinland. This account in 14th century runes consonant with stone's self-date of 1362 grows more plausible on considering navigable watercourses from Hudson Bay to Minnesota, a hope of finding refugee colonists, 26 Viking mooring-stones in the Stone's vicinity, runic epitaphs in the nearby cemetery, foundations of Viking longhouses, ship sections and iron implements (Margaret Leuthemer 1983; Orville Friedrich 1993; et al]. The 10 who reached this "metropolis" had a secure place for indicting their memorial the winter of 1362, done probably by a Goth of the party because of the Swedish rise instead of Norse raise. No one in the 16th, 17th, 18th, 19th or first 75 years of the 20th century knew enough to fake 14th century runes (including "spiked" and dotted with colon word divisions and other idiosyncrasies lately authenticated).

L'anse aux Meadows. The National Geographic of November 1964 disclosed the Ingstad's already over 3 centuries behind Norse discovery of Newfoundland—little detail).

Iroquois. Your article missed Iroquois canoes modeled on Norse boat shape, longhouses modeled on Norse longhouses, intertribal organization, physical stature and language replete with Norse cognates.[99] Mallory could not distinguish between "full blood" Mohawk laborers and Norwegian Swedish. Not only Iroquois but Wampanoags, Mohegans and Narragansett's in once Viking New England were described as unusually tall, sachems (chiefs) perhaps 7 ft—Massasoit Uncas, Canonicus, Miantonomy. Hybrid vigor?

If your authors were ignorant of these long-known empirical data, they

---

[98] by a lake with two skerries (islands).
[99] Cognate—word root.

were unprofessional. If knowing but suppressed, they were unprofessional. Whatever your biases, the scholars who ferreted and analyzed the evidence have been at least as intelligent, industrious, conscientious, devoted, and learned as those who sit at the scoffer's seat, and have worked many decades longer at the Viking problem than promising young reporters.

Cyclone Covey
Prof. Emeritus History
Wake Forest University

Dr. Covey has so much knowledge of these ancient subjects that he jams a tremendous amount of information into a relatively short letter. Books have been written about each artifact he writes about, but in his sharp, quick style it is almost too much for the average reader to absorb. I suggest you read the letter again so as to get a clearer picture of the many documented historical facts that the Smithsonian authors had either ignored or of which they were entirely ignorant. One would think Smithsonian scientists would consult working historians like Dr. Covey during their research and deliberations. But they seem to prefer old books and old paradigms.

Gloria Farley

Another Article Criticized

It was in the July 12, 2000 issue of *U.S. News and World Report* that author Bruce B. Auster attacked the authenticity of the Heavener runestone along with the Newport Tower and the Kensington Stone.

Just before the turn of the century, my wife and I spent a few days in Heavener with Gloria Farley, the longtime pre-historian researcher and author of *In Plain Sight* (1994).

Ms. Farley, besides feeding us and spending two evenings going over her huge collection of stones, artifacts and antiquities, took us on several interesting field trips in the area. By far the most interesting was the one to the Heavener Runestone. Its site had been made into a state park with a visitor's center and attendants on duty. There was a long wooden stairway that descended into a valley where the huge, flat stone stood upright. It was protected by a locked wooden building with a large glass window just a

*Gloria Farley, author, and attendant at
Heavener Runestone Center, Heavener
Oklahoma, July 2000.*

Gloria Farley explaining the Runestone

*Newport Tower
Rhode Island*

*Heavener Runestone
Heavener Oklahoma*

few feet from the stone so that visitors could see the carved runes close up. The park had been established some thirty or more years earlier.

The huge slab of stone is about twelve feet high, ten feet wide and a little over a foot thick. It looks as though it may have been stood up by man. The runes are about seven or eight inches high. There are eight of them, well made, about a half-inch into the rock. Gloria had been taken there with a friend in 1928. The man who took them to see the rock (the other girl's father) had first seen it in 1913.

Although there have been several interpretations of the runes, there is certainly no doubt that they are runes.

A few days after our visit with Gloria, when June and I were visiting Spiro Mounds, we were told by a man working there that those runes (on the Heavener Runestone) were carved back in the 1920's by a group of Boy Scouts who had camped there. My first thought was that he certainly never had a scout troop! Scouts would be no more capable of carving those runes than Olaf Ohman was of carving the Kensington Runestone.

When we told Gloria Farley about this state employee saying the scouts had carved the runes, she said that rumor had come up some years earlier. She had located most of those scouts who were still living and they had each signed affidavits that none of them had carved the runes, also that the runes were old when they camped there. The most they admitted to was that a few of the boys had tried to carve their initials in the rock and indeed we did see where people had scratched such things in several places.

Gloria's comments to the editor of *U.S. News and World Report* (July 12, 2000) included the following paragraph:

> There are five runestones in Oklahoma, four of which are near Heavener. How does he account for the fifth in Shawnee, Oklahoma, 175 miles away? He says, 'the rock carvings were made by a local resident fond of things Scandinavian.' The local resident, Lester Shipley, during a runestone exhibit in Oklahoma City in August-October 1971, attended by 140,000 people, claimed on television that at age 11 he and a friend made the runestone. But records show that he was born in 1925, and the Smithsonian had a record of the Heavener stone in 1923. The friend denied ever having done this.

It seems there is always someone eager and ready to offer an explanation to prove their point one way or another, and there is always someone on one side or the other ready to pass along bogus information, regardless of how ridiculous. We should move beyond this. Gloria also sites a book by Robert Hall Jr. in her letter (when speaking of the Kensington stone), "It is a 1994 publication entitled

'The Kensington Runestone—Authentic and Important.'"

My Experience with the Davenport Stone

There have been several blatant cover-ups that I would like to relate. To the perpetrators they may seem innocent and logical, but whenever people try to hide something from the public it raises hackles, and suspicions are aroused. There is a sense that something dishonest is going on.

We had such an experience while trying to view an interesting stone found near Davenport, Iowa, in 1874 by a Rev. Gass. It was somewhat similar to the experience we had in Peterborough, Ontario, while viewing the rock inscriptions that were the subject of Barry Fell's book, *Bronze Age America*. In that case we had asked the attendant why Dr. Fell's book wasn't listed along with the dozen or so they suggested (none of which were written specifically about those particular glyphs). We were told at that time that a woman from Ireland claimed Dr. Fell's interpretation was wrong!

A recent photograph of the Died Festival tablet, here shown photographically enhanced by Malcolm Pearson, presents certain discrepancies from the original published engraving. In particular some letters appear to have been abraded from the area of the mirror, on the left. The suggested decipherment, is based on the engraving; it is possible that the inferred reading "Mirror of the Egyptians" and "Metal reflecting" may have to be discarded, but they are left as a plausible interpretation of the now-lost signs.

Some years later, a highly respected archaeologist, Dr. David Kelly from the University of Calgary in Alberta, Canada, generally agreed with Dr. Fell, but whether or not this was enough to place *Bronze Age America* on the reference list or not, I am unable to say.

Anyway, we traveled to Waukon, Iowa, a small town in the extreme northwest corner of the state, to visit a 94-year-old step-aunt of my wife. From Waukon to Davenport was about 400 miles, and we decided to go there to see the famous Davenport Stone, on display at the Putman Museum. I had heard and read about it from time to time and thought that this would probably be my only chance to see it.

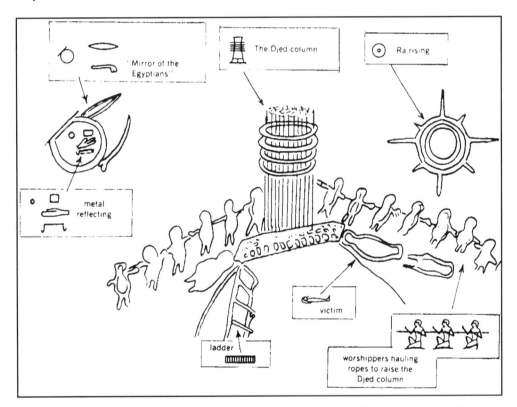

The Died Festival of Osiris as celebrated in Iowa around 700 B.C. Explanation of the scene depicted on the Davenport stele, the hieroglyphs incorporated into the picture being here translated, and also rendered in the formal Palace style. The Died column, made of bundles of reeds encircled at the top by rings, represents the backbone of Osiris, in whose honor the Died column was erected each year on the day of the spring equinox, This information, originally obtained by Adolf Erman from a tomb inscription of the XVIII Dynasty in Thebes, Egypt, is here completely confirmed by the inscription and illustration on the Davenport stele of Iowa. The mirror of reflecting metal, shown to the left of the picture, relates to the Egyptian text of the stele, which instructs the reader to attach a mirror to a column in such a way that the rays of the rising sun, on the morning of the spring equinox, will be reflected onto a signal stone called the "Watcher." (ESOP Vol 20-1991 Page 244)

It was my understanding the stone had been discovered somewhere along the banks of the Mississippi River. I had read that Barry Fell had interpreted it as a kind of Rosetta stone, with possibly the same message in three ancient alphabets, making it a most important artifact. The alphabets were all difficult to decipher, as one was said to be a rare form of hieroglyphics while the others are (according to Fell and Charles Moyer) Punic and Libyan. Fell: (ESOP Vol. 20, 1991, pg. 244). Fell:

> Charles Moyer inquires as to whether similarly corrupt hieroglyphic inscriptions are known: they are, I have seen many desert rock-cut examples in the collections of the Egypt Exploration Society. The excavations of Dr. Beno Rothenberg brought to light some very corrupt Egyptian texts in the Timna Valley south of the Dead Sea, where Egyptian miners were active around the twelfth century B.C.

Fell also mentions a text from Almuneca, Spain, where XXII Dynasty objects have been found in local tombs. Spanish archaeologists believe that Phoenician (or Punic) traders may be responsible for them. Dr. Fell thought they could have been left by Libyan or Iberian traders, since Punic and Libyan texts occur on the Davenport Stone, but he admitted there are problems. My main impression was that the Davenport glyphs were seriously being studied by the great epigraphers of both Europe and America, and I wanted to take a first hand look at the original.

We left Waukon rather late for the 400 mile drive and were wondering if the museum would close at 4:30 or 5:00. We were rushing to make the 4:30 deadline, just in case.

We arrived at the museum at about 4:25 and asked the attendant how much time we had. She calmed our fears when she said they were open until 5:00 and we had a full half hour. I told her we had specifically come to see the Davenport Stone that we assumed was still on deposit there.

"You do have the Davenport Stone here, don't you?" I asked.

"Yes," she answered. "It is in the basement, but I'm afraid you won't be able to see it."

"Why can't we see it?" I said with alarm. "We've come a long way just to look at it."

"Well, it's a fake and it's locked up in the basement," said the lady with a finality.

I had trouble believing what I had just heard, but I could see she was serious. When I finally loosed my tongue, I asked, "Who says it's a fake?"

"Our Board voted unanimously that the stone is a fraud and we took it out of the display case," she said.

I was dumbfounded. "I don't care if it is a fake or not. I would just like to see it. This is a museum, isn't it? If your Board thinks it's a fake, put a sign on it—Our Board Thinks This Is A Fake—but let the public see it. Who do you think would fake such a thing?"

"We think some of our museum staff planted the stone where Reverend Gass was digging, just as a prank," said the attendant in all seriousness.

"This seems very strange to me. You're giving your staff an awful lot of credit. I understand there are inscriptions in two or three unknown alphabets that have only recently been identified. I would really just like to take a look at it, or do you have a picture of it I could have? I have a camera, would you be able to take a picture of it for me?"

But no amount of persuasion would move her. I did not blame the woman as she was following the rules of the institution. She was just doing her job, as they say. I found out, or so I was told, that the basis for the Board's decision came from the Iowa State Archaeologist, Dr. Marshall McKusick. This was the same person who had written the very unflattering critiques of Dr. Fell in the archaeological journal "Antiquity" (no. 212, November 1980) and (No. 220, July 1983). (See pages 219 - 221)

So we had driven 800 miles for nothing—we were not allowed to view the famous Davenport Stone—and I kept thinking, what are they afraid of, why are they hiding it? I detected a flaw in the character of the scientist involved. My idea has always been, just put all the pieces where everyone can look at them. Then and only then will the truth of the matter be decided. [99a]

A Similar Story in Lower Michigan

An almost identical story can be told concerning the Michigan Tablets or what are sometimes referred to as the Soper-Savage tablets, which were mentioned earlier in Chapter IV of this book. It happened to be the subject of the book Henriette Mertz had told me she was writing when I met her in Albuquerque, New Mexico. She died before her book was in print but it was later published by her nephew.

I had been given pictures of some of those tablets by my friend Jon Clark, and had ruled them out as obvious forgeries when I first saw them. The reason I had ridiculed the tablets when I first received a small sampling of the pictures was because of their child-like portrayals of holy scenes and Bible stories. I made no attempt to analyze the way they were made, the materials they were made of, what was written on them, or who could have made them. I didn't even know what their history was, but blindly went along with what I had read about them years before. The words "Noah's Diaries" were on my mind, and

---

[99a] This author understands that the Davenport stone was put on display again, I'd like to think I may have had something to do with that.

A Sampling of the Soper Collection

with them was my ingrained disgust for the perpetrators of such a fraud.

However, some years earlier, Judge Claude Stone of Peoria, Illinois, who was well aware of Henriette Mertz's expertise in the field of ancient history, asked her if she would re-examine the surviving specimens according to the rules and procedures of law—to give them a fair trial, so to speak, which they had never had. No one had ever put them to modern tests, some of which were developed only recently. In fact, many archaeologists and other experts refused even to look at them.

Henriette took them through each step and to each expert in many of the various fields of science. She estimated that somewhere between 3,000 and 10,000 of these artifacts had been recovered under almost identical circumstances in mounds from some 27 or more counties of lower Michigan, as well as a few northern counties in Ohio, Indiana and Illinois, possibly even many more whose whereabouts were unknown. The tablets were of copper, slate and clay. She believed the copper came from Michigan's Copper Country and the slate from Arvon Township's slate beds in Baraga County.

Several of the examining authorities said that no two of the known tablets were done by the same person. The tablets were turned up between the Civil War period and through World War I (1860s to 1920) in Michigan, and one or two artifacts would turn up in about every ten mounds. The artifacts were made in different ways, using a variety of techniques. No forger or team of forgers could have carried out such an elaborate plan.

They did have a mixture of Mediterranean languages and alphabets on them, such as Phoenician, Egyptian and Greek, but Ms. Mertz points out that these were a mixture of peoples who would have had a mixture of languages and alphabets. We don't have to look far for a parallel, as our own English is a mixture of words and phrases from many origins. We commonly use words from Latin, Greek, German, French, Indian, Swedish, Finnish, Spanish and other sources, as these early settlers must have when they came together to live so many years ago.

I will not try to defend the authenticity of the Michigan tablets here, but merely ask those who are interested to read Henriette's book, *Mystic Symbol,* named for the one sign that is so prominent on every tablet and artifact. It is the symbol:

which was the cuneiform character for HIS or YHW (Yahw-eh), the Christian sign for Jesus. I should add that in two separate phone calls to Dr. Fell, he stated emphatically that the tablets were proven fake years ago, and that one of the copper plates was determined to be made of a modern alloy of copper and other metals. This may be true, but I don't believe there is any alloy of copper that wasn't tried in ancient times. And, as we have seen, the final conclusion should never be based on any one test, opinion, or conclusion. I believe the final analysis should be on the evidence of many disciplines, and on how an artifact or group of artifacts could fit into the whole historic picture. Only then can some sense be made of the transcriptions of the messages on the tablets themselves. While this is a monumental task, headway is being made in several seemingly unrelated branches of learning at the present time.

Dr. Mertz's conclusions to Judge Stone, after lengthy tests and deliberations, were that there was no sign of fraud. She believed the artifacts and inscriptions to be the work of possibly up to 20,000 refugees "fleeing from Decian or Diocletian (Roman Emperors of the 3rd and 4th centuries A.D.) persecutions sometimes after 321 A.D. and sailing out from the harbors of Rome, Naples, Alexandria, Carthage and other Eastern Mediterranean ports and, to the known world of that day, assumed lost in the turbulent waters of the North Atlantic."

Two points are brought out in Henriette's book of which, up to that time, I had been unaware. One was the mention of a huge storage pit full of small pieces of copper discovered by Edwin J. Hulbert in 1858 and opened by him in 1865, in the Torch Lake region on the Keweenaw Peninsula. The Calumet and Hecla Mining Company sank a shaft through the storage area that was rich with handpicked copper nuggets. Henriette felt that this was storage for copper coming from Isle Royale, but it seems more likely to me that copper was brought to this pit over land from various locations on the peninsula, to be shipped out from there. In my later studies I learned that there were several such storage pits along the Keweenaw waterway and others on the eastern end of Lake Superior in the vicinity of the ancient mines on the Canadian shore there.

The other reference of great interest concerned the mysterious copper-bearing (in the form of oxhides), red-skinned Keftui who were often referred to in ancient literature as coming from the "outer isles." All references of them ceased about 800 B.C., and there are no later records (*Mystic Symbol,* page 50-57). Warren Dexter as well mentions them as possibly being Indians from North America. He sent me pictures of them which were painted in the tomb of Rekkamara at Thebes on the Nile River.

Mr. Dexter states in the accompanying letter to me, "If the Phoenicians took Indians from our eastern seaboard, that may be where the Micmac Indians come up with their Libyan-Egyptian hieroglyphics." These hieroglyphics he

Oxhides of Copper

Courtesy of © Warren Dexter

Keftui - Tomb of Rekkamara at Thebes on the Nile River, 2nd and 5th figures are shown carring oxhides of copper

speaks of are described in the Epigraphic Society's Occasional Papers.

We must remember that Dr. Mertz's conclusions were made in the 1970s and 80s after exhaustive analyses from many people, while the prevailing academic conclusions were arrived at before anyone had flown in an airplane, heard a radio or seen a television picture. It seems most appropriate that the authorities should take a second look now.

But here is the state of affairs at the beginning of the twenty-first century:

At an Ancient American Conference held in Utah in 1997, publisher Wayne May made arrangements for a group in attendance to view one of the largest known collections of the Michigan relics. The story heard was that the University of Michigan[99b] had housed it years earlier, but when "experts" decided it was all a fraud, they wanted to get rid of it. Not wanting to see the collection destroyed, the Church of the Latter Day Saints offered to take it. So hundreds of pieces of all descriptions were packed in barrels and sent to Utah by the University. When they arrived, many of the more fragile clay items were broken.

The museum staff at the Mormon Church, even though they were told in no uncertain terms that the collection was all fake, took the time to repair what they could and very carefully placed the items in storage, handling them with cotton gloves. They were never put on display but were stored for the next 40 or 50 years.

That Sunday morning after the conference a small group of people were allowed to view the collection and photograph much of it. However, only the museum staff was allowed to handle any of the pieces, and then, with the utmost care and again wearing cotton gloves, they took some pieces out for photographing. There was never any mention of either fraud or authenticity but definitely an air of reverence as many of those items had been brought to light well over 100 years earlier, and nothing was ever proven either way. As far as I can find out, no tests or scientific analyses were ever conducted except by the

---

[99b] Later I was told they were from Notre Dame University

The Soper/Savage collection artifacts were donated to the church by Milton R. Hunter, who acquired the pieces from Notre Dame University (Father Savage's collection) and Elliot Soper, son of Daniel Soper in the 1960's.

Speakers at 1998's Ancient American Conference. Left to right, Professor James Scherz, Ronald Garf {President, Triple A Productions) Fred ("Mr. Copper") Rydholm, Cecil Abbott (President, Indian Ministries), Dr. John White, Dr. Gunnar Thompson, Frank Joseph (Editor-in-Chief, Ancient American), Marion Dahm (Founder, Viking Research Group), Wayne May (Publisher, Ancient American).

Thirteen Month Calendar

These Clay Tablets require a special set of styles, seems too complicated for a forgery.

Soper Collection

direction of Henriette Mertz.

Over the course of the next year, Wayne May made some formal overtures to have the collection (then estimated at 1500 pieces) be returned to Michigan. A group was being formed in the Copper Country in hopes of finding a home for many small (and a few large) collections of copper artifacts from local residents. The people in Utah said they would, at their expense, pack and ship their collection to this group.

When no funding could be located for this private organization, a request was made to house the Michigan items from Utah in one of several museums that were being set up by the National Park there.

At first this was acceptable, but when local archaeologists were told of these arrangements, they said these items were known fakes and should not be a part of any display of national importance.

Then in the summer of 2002, with the collection packed and the Mormons ready to ship, they were sent to state archaeologist John Halsey.

I called John Halsey and he assured me that the collection was on its way and would be put on display at the Michigan Historical Museum in Lansing.

Then in the October 27, 2003 issue of the <u>Marquette Mining Journal</u>, the following article appeared. Headline:

Church Donates Fake Artifacts to Museum.

Grand Rapids, Mich (AP) Some of the now-debunked Michigan relics—once considered by some influential Mormons as evidence of the church's connection to a Near Eastern culture in ancient America—have a new home.

For decades, the Mormon Church kept a large collection of artifacts in its Salt Lake City museum, but never formally claimed them to be genuine.

This past summer, after scholars examined the relics and declared them fake, the Church of Jesus Christ of Latter Day Saints donated the 797 objects to the Michigan Historical Museum, which will display them next month.

The relics were once hailed as the greatest archaeological discoveries since Pompeii. But there are many clues they are really fakes, Michigan State Archaeologist John Halsey told the Grand Rapids Press.

Among the relics are engraved slate tablets. One scene depicts the crucifixion of Christ.

One disturbing fact is that this group of collections, said to be one of the largest known, was supposed to number about 3,000 pieces. At Salt Lake City it was estimated at about 1500. The article in the paper now gives the figure as 797 artifacts, so what happened to the missing pieces? While I have heard of several other Michigan relic collections, I have never heard a figure given as to how many pieces they involve.

In the Volume 9, Number 55 issue of the *Ancient American Magazine,* researcher and author David A. Deal writes a five-page commentary in answer to the John Halsey article, expressing the opposite view. The following are some excerpts from that article:

> Mr. John R. Halsey, a highly-placed archaeologist for Michigan and the curator of a newly-returned, but much maligned and grossly misunderstood, major Michigan Artifact corpus, "The Soper Savage Collection," a large body of ancient American artifacts, which is now ensconced at a proper state institution called the "Michigan Historical Center," has written a document that conforms perfectly and quite nicely to the long-standing dogma of John Wesley Powell. Powell was the formidable and dictatorial director of the Smithsonian Institute Bureau of Ethnology, who in the century before last set down a dictum which has ruled the academic roost in American anthropology, that is, for more than a hundred years. No American antiquarian, archaeologist or anthropologist worth his academic salt, ever wavers from Major Powell's hard-core line. In Mr. John Halsey's case, the pattern is predictably familiar. He toes the mark quite nicely.
>
> As positive proof of this writer's (Deal) conclusion that Mr. Halsey's opinions are simply those of other higher ups, we see that he has provided for us a large portion of the standard set of the well known and much disparaged, valid ancient American artifacts, among them the Kensington Rune Stone.
>
> —He has given nothing more than his opinion. Please remember he is a state archaeologist, trained in America for American tastes and not of, or for, the "old world," where these languages were studied by academics. American archaeologists were trained not to expect such things here in America. In fact, American archaeologists refrain from using words such as "necropolis," for new world cemeteries, primarily because they are trained to separate the two worlds, old and new. A word such as "necropolis" carries with it a hint of ancient Greece or Egypt. And that would never do for American archaeology. Simply not permitted! No diffusion is allowed. Of course, Mr. Halsey does not know that the Maya Indians came from the eastern Mediterranean. They were some of the first diffusionists. They were Hivites. (The NEXUS, Deal, David, ISAC Press, 1993).

…Time and the general advancement in knowledge have refuted Hulbert H. Bancroft's (and others) wild, outrageous and ignorant claim(s). But its effects are still rolling along in the narrow-minded ivy-covered halls of that ever so pompous American academy.

However, Mr. Halsey will continue to promulgate the lie by 'explaining yet again to an innocent public why they are not what they seem.' It seems the effete and supercilious fox has been put in charge of the hen house, as is usually the case on this continent.

These kinds of unconforming artifacts have been turning up for several centuries here in the Americas, and the party line we hear from the academics is clear, 'They are all fakes…frauds…and humbugs!'

Why is this? For what possible reason, does – what appears to be, the entire academic community, respond in such a foolish way? Is it their higher indoctrination? They never questioned their professors while being instructed at university. The nominal professor who is spouting the party line drivel that he learned from his professors that he learned from his professors before him, was never amenable to such questions. These students later matriculate to go onwards and regurgitate the same hierophantic flummery they consumed in university…ad nauseum.

Here is the underlying dogma and compelling reason. The two words "evolutionary theory." Major Powell's idea was: '…that all early immigrants to North and South America came by way of the hypothetical Bering Sea "Land Bridge."' This hypothesis continues: 'that the American Indians are all descendants of Orientals." Any subsequent archaeological evidence found in the Americas that would tend to contradict Powell's hypothesis, 'must be' interpreted in the poor light of Powell's dictum and properly condemned (debunked, destroyed, hidden or disappeared), and we all know what peer pressure is like. Powell's hypothesis has become carved in flinty stones, and many generations of archaeologists have been trained to conform to its dogma. It got them through school, didn't it? Why change horses once the professional fees start to come into hand? And Mr. John R. Halsey is a professional archaeologist. Professionals do it for money, amateurs do it for love, it follows then, and is well to keep in mind, that the Ark of Noah was built by an amateur, and the Titanic was built by professionals.

—(Mr. Halsey) has classified all non-doctrinally approved evidence. It has to be "fraudulent" in his mind, and he really believes it. But he is not being scientific in any sense of the word. He is pontificating and condemning all of these classics of diffusionist, (disestablishmentarian) evidence, by any and all means at his disposal. Must we let the establish-

404

ment think for us and thereby conform to their "higher" but effete and useless erudite knowledge?

John Halsey's argument would, most likely, be that he relies on peers who have published on these items. Peers that went through the same, or similar training as he did, and then specialized Peers; we should note, they bear the same prejudices he bears. Peers that carry the Powell doctrine in their hearts and minds. Peers that must protect the 'innocent public' from the truth.

—We can, and should all agree, that Mr. Halsey[99c] is entitled to his opinion or belief.—He is a state archaeologist, after all. A politician once said, 'Everyone is entitled to his own opinion, but not his own facts.'" Analyses briefly told—complete article pages 22-29, *Ancient American Magazine,* Vol. 9, #55.

'—There is a consistent graphic, illustrative theme running throughout these Michigan artifacts—on the overwhelming majority of these tablets there is a might Elohym being called YHW 𐤉𐤄𐤅 —written in a totally discrete 4th century AD ciphered alphabet, and deciphered by this writer (David Deal) some years ago, a cuneiform-styled paleo Hebrew alphabet never seen before or since. (See *Ancient American Magazine,* Issue 11, pp. 10-19).

This highest of Elohym beings is usually not shown in full facial likeness. On nearly all the tablets he has called 𐤉𐤄𐤅 YHW, (Yahw-eh) and is nearly always shown above two subordinate Elohym (deity) beings, who are in constant competition—no, actually in warfare, even to the point of death on some tablets. One is a younger (son of the right hand—also called 𐤉𐤄𐤅, and the other is the finally defeated and burned-on-a-pyre, evil son of the left hand, the elder of the two subordinate "gods." Both are Messiahs. Both intent on winning power of mankind. One for good and one for evil. This is not a recognizable, Trinitarian Christian doctrine.

The individual symbology of these subordinate Deities is detailed in the aforementioned *Ancient American Magazine* articles (i.e., 'son of the right hand' and 'son of the left hand').

In common parlance, we might say the high Elohym   (Yahw) YHW is a great mighty one, who created the universe, and whose son (the good one) created all life on earth, whose brother is trying to defeat him; this is graphically portrayed on several tablets, and clearly not a modern Christian concept.

[99c] While David Deals comments appear to be especially harsh toward State Archeologist Halsey – his comments are directed to the vast majority of archeologists the world over. We must admit, however that there are a growing number of them who have broken with tradition.

David Deal

No, not your nominal Christian fare, in fact, no Christian religious sect in the 1860s (or even now) could have produced this doctrinal statement, either in written or graphic form, that is, if we are, logically, to base the idea of artifact creation on the overall doctrines and dogma of their creators. This specific religious doctrine is anathema to Christians and Jews alike. It is surely not a "Trinity" doctrine.——Additionally, there is the life and deeds of the Messiah Yahwshua (commonly called 'Jesus') and some very readable Egyptian hieroglyphs in contrast to what Mr. Halsey claims 'ersatz Egyptian hieroglyphs' indicating gross 'fraud by Mr. Scotford'—"

David Deal goes on to further explain the ancient Christian beliefs that are accurately portrayed on the tablets and giving references where this information can be found. He also explains that the traditional Jewish version of Satan is "the devil—Samael, evil son of the left hand," and he compared the Michigan tablets to Gnostic Coptic Christianity.

On the basis of this simple, easily understood, consistent graphic doctrinal content, found widely spread throughout the tablets of Michigan artifacts, compared to the then unknown Coptic (Egyptian Church) religious doctrine, which is very foreign to nominal Christianity it may be concluded: that these artifacts are real, ancient American documents, created by escaping refugees from the Mediterranean. They were nothing more than Coptic, Egyptian, Gnostic Christians who had been persecuted by Emperor Constantine's Post Nicean Council, anti-Arianism programs. These specific anti-Arian edicts were codified in 325 AD at the Council of Nicea, with Constantine having the only vote. Also, it can be concluded a truism, that absolutely no Trinitarian-based American Christian religious person, assumed to be a forger, could have created this precise, ancient and long-lost Coptic Christian doctrine out of thin air, particularly based on a work yet to be published anywhere in the world or remotely known, at the time of the first Michigan Artifacts finds were made by post hole diggers and sewer workers, certainly not by Mssrs. Scotford and Soper and Savage as Mr. Halsey claims in his fabulous document dismissing these ancient artifacts as 'fakes—.

The article goes on, but David Deal ends it with a challenge for the archaeologists to offer a contradictory pamphlet (to his opinions) so that the public will know there are definitely two sides to the story and may be free to make up their own minds. Deal even offers to pay for the opposing pamphlet. He finishes his challenge with the statement: "Just let Mr. Wayne May of the *Ancient American Magazine* know, and if I need to pay for the work myself, in the name of the 'innocent public,' I will do so. This will allow them to do their own thinking instead of having you doing it all for them."

To my mind David Deal is the world authority of the explanation of the Michigan Tablets. I first met him at the "Los Lunas Stone" mountain in New Mexico in the early 1980s. He was pointing out the Zodiac on a stone. At that time Dr. Barry Fell was there telling me that David Deal did not know what he was talking about, but again it was a case where Dr. Fell would not listen. There are several cases that I could mention where Dr. Fell would have nothing to do with them; the Michigan Tablets were among them and Burrows Cave another.

When I first tried to study the Michigan Tablets in the late 1980s, one thing that caught my eye on several of them was what looked like a thirteen-month calendar. I had read something about such a thing somewhere and while I knew nothing about such a calendar, I knew that somewhere back in time one did exist. This was something I felt was too authentic to have been made up by a forger. I just didn't know how to go about looking up information about a 13-month calendar.

Finally, many years later, I found the explanation in the book *He Walked the Americas* by L. Taylor Hansen, Amherst Press, Amherst, Wisconsin (1963).

In this book a calendar of this type is called a "Venus Calendar."

It is common knowledge that the ancients studied the stars thoroughly and the average person in those days knew the heavens far better than the average person today and this ancient calendar was used in the old world and by the Indian Tribes of both North and South America. Its use is explained as follows:

Venus, being the second planet from the Sun and Earth the third, swings around its internal orbit making thirteen revolutions to eight[99d] revolutions of the Earth. Thus among all the Indian tribes, the Earth number is eight, and the number of the Morning and Evening Star (depending on time of year viewed) is thirteen. Eight thirteens then would bring the planets into their original position. This would be a full cycle, or one hundred and four years. A half cycle would be fifty-two years. upon this most American Indian reckoning is based. However, it is often checked by other reckoning. The Mayans have four inter-revolving

---

[99d] This author has run across the number 8 in Indian lore several times in the past but never understood it. (8 stones in a medicine wheel, 8 feathers in a headdress etc.)

Thirteenth Month Calendar

calendars—one like ours, the Sun-year and its ¼ day which is comparatively simple—the Moon, etcetera. I would not suggest that anyone study the Mayan Calendar system unless he has a major in mathematics and a minor in astronomy. It makes for pretty stiff studying when the mathematics is to be translated on a twenty basis instead of the ten we use, and then each number is a different god in various positions. The Mayans wrote a date usually four times. They were well acquainted with the weight and measurement of the earth and the swing of the sun from Capricorn to Cancer and back, moving through space, carrying our family of planets along. They believed the Sun is circumnavigating a Central Fire located in the Heavens near the Pleiades which they called Mya (this is the way their name is pronounced.). On many of their great stone stele, which the Spanish were unable to destroy, we are able to read the dates, but the events thus far are still a mystery. The dates are of themselves fascinating, a few going back to fantastic antiquity. Perhaps some day we shall learn what happened on these dates.

The Gungywamp Incident

There are many stories that fall into the category of "holding for further study," "it seems to have disappeared" or "it was sent to so and so to be tested."

I will relate just one of these as an illustration. It was told to me by David P. Barron, then president of the Gungywamp Society in Connecticut.

I had an invitation to view the Gungywamp site. There is a lot of old stonework there and I was given a two or three-hour tour by Dave himself.

The Society had purchased much of the acreage encompassing the site and was in process of buying more.

There was a lot of interesting and various types of stonework in the area that looked as though it could have spanned two or maybe three periods. One place in the side of a cliff near a small creek looked as though it could have been a primitive iron forge; there were some rusty pieces of iron in the creek.

Without going into the many interesting aspects of the Gungywamp area, I will focus on one stone chamber that appeared to have a corbelled roof[99c], common in ancient European construction.

The story Dave told me was that some teenagers had had a party in and around the chamber and had destroyed some of the stonework at the entrance.

Gungywamp personnel had a cleanup day when they picked up bottles, repaired the damaged entrance and did some raking in the area. In the process of raking, one of the members uncovered a tunnel about four feet long and five or six inches in diameter that led to the inside of the stone chamber. It was determined that this was an alignment where on a certain date the sun shown down through

Photo Courtesy of Ancient American Magazine

David P. Barron at mouth of Tilley Street Tunnel.

[99e] See Corbelled roof page 251

the tube into the chamber. This, of course, was a new and exciting discovery and was much discussed by the group.

A few days later, when an elderly gentleman came to see the new find for himself, he wanted to know exactly where in the chamber the stream of sunlight was directed. Being somewhat handicapped, he could not get inside, but was able to peer in. He was told that the light just hit the top of a flat rock that stood near the wall of the chamber. But the man stuck the end of his cane behind the rock, tipping it just enough to reveal another larger tunnel beyond. The new tunnel led into a completely buried beehive chamber, not unlike two or three others I was shown in other northeastern seaboard states. And the big surprise was what appeared to be a bronze pot in the second chamber, obviously very old.

When Mr. Barron told me this, I immediately perked up. "Where is the pot now?" I asked.

"Well, we brought it over to the University of Connecticut," he said.

This had all the makings of one of those sad stories that I had heard so often before, but I was eager to hear the rest.

Mr. Barron went on, "We went to check on it the next spring and they said, 'What pot?'"

The very worst I have heard of this kind of loss of potentially important artifacts was told to me by a young archaeology student from Arizona.

Way back in the 1870s, twenty-eight mule train loads of artifacts were sent to the Smithsonian Institution. About a century later, this friend of mine was assigned a summer project to work with these objects. He went to Washington, D.C., showed his credentials and told them about his project. He was told it would take a few days to locate the collection. He checked in day after day, to no avail. Finally, after some three weeks, he was notified the collection had been found. He went there, was given a key and taken to a storage area where he was shown a large drawer with the name of the cave on it. Opening the drawer he found one clay pot.

I have not mentioned the names here, but some years later I wanted to check on this story. I called the friend, who was no longer in archaeology, but he insisted that I call his professor, then retired but living in the area. I did this and the story was verified.

So many of such stories come to mind that I don't think it worth my while to relate them; it's like kicking a dead horse.

Consider the following from:

Arizona Gazette, Phoenix, AZ, Monday evening, April 5, 1909:

Explorations in Grand Canyon
Mysteries of Immense Rich Cavern Being Brought to Light
Jordan is Enthused
Remarkable Finds Indicate Ancient People Migrated from Orient

The latest news of the progress of the explorations of what is now regarded by scientists as not only the oldest archaeological discovery in the United States, but one of the most valuable in the world, which was mentioned some time ago in the Gazette, was brought to the city yesterday by G. E. Kinkaid, the explorer who found the great underground citadel of the Grand Canyon during a trip from Green River, Wyoming, down the Colorado, in a wooden boat, to Yuma, several months ago. According to the story related yesterday to the Gazette by Mr. Kinkaid, the archaeologists of the Smithsonian Institute, which is financing the explorations, have made discoveries which almost conclusively prove that the race which inhabited this mysterious cavern, hewn in solid rock by human hands, was of oriental origin, possibly from Egypt, tracing back to Ramses. If their theories are borne out by the translation of the tablets engraved with hieroglyphics, the mystery of the prehistoric peoples of North America, their ancient arts, who they were and whence they came will be solved. Egypt and the Nile and Arizona and the Colorado will be linked by an historical chain running back to ages which staggers the wildest fancy of the fictionist.

A Thorough Investigation

Under the direction of Prof. S. A. Jordan, the Smithsonian Institute is now presenting the most thorough explorations which will be continued until the last link in the chain is forged. Nearly a mile underground, about 1480 feet below the surface the main passage has been delved into, to find another mammoth chamber from which radiates scores of passageways, like the spokes of a wheel. Several hundred rooms have been discovered reached by passageways running from the main passage, one of them having been explored for 854 feet and another for 634 feet. The recent finds include articles which have never been known as native to this country, and doubtless they had their origin in the Orient. War weapons, copper instruments, sharp-edged and hard as steel, indicate a high state of civilization reached by these strange people. So interested have the scientists become that preparations are being made to equip the camp for extensive studies, and the force will be increased to thirty or forty persons. Before going further into the cavern, better facilities for lighting will have to be installed, for the darkness is dense and impenetrable for the average flashlight. In order to avoid being lost, wires are being strung from the entrance to all passageways leading to large chambers. How far this cavern extends no one can guess, but it is now the belief of many that what has already been explored is merely the "barracks" to use an American term for the soldiers, and that far into the underworld will be found the main communal dwellings of the families, and possibly other shrines. The perfect ventilation of the cavern, the steady draught that blows through, indicates that it has another outlet to the surface.

Mr. Kinkaid's Report

Mr. Kinkaid was the first white child born in Idaho and has been an explorer and hunter all his life, thirty years having been in the service of the Smithsonian Institute. Even briefly recounted, his history sounds fabulous, almost grotesque.

"First, I would impress that the cavern is nearly inaccessible. The entrance is 1486 feet down the sheer canyon wall. It is located on government land and no visitor will be allowed there under penalty of trespass. The scientists wish to work unmolested without fear of the archaeological discoveries by the curious or relic hunters. A trip there would be fruitless, and the visitor would be sent on his way. The story of how I found the cavern has been related but in a paragraph: I was journeying down the Colorado River in a boat, alone, and looking for mineral. Some forty-two miles up the river from the El Tovar Crystal Canyon I saw on the east wall, stains in the sediment formation abut 2,000 feet above the river bed. There was no trail to this point, but I finally reached it with great difficulty. Above a shelf which hid it from view from the river was the mouth of the cave. There were steps leading from this entrance some thirty yards to what was, at the time the cavern was inhabited, the level of the river. When I saw the chisel marks on the wall inside the entrance, I became interested, secured my gun and went in. During that trip I went back several hundred feet along the main passage 'til I came to the crypt in which I discovered the mummies. One of these I stood up and photographed by flashlight. I gathered a number of relics, which I carried down the Colorado to Yuma from whence I shipped them to Washington with details of the discovery. Following this, the explorations were undertaken.

The Passages

The main passageway is about 12 feet wide, narrowing to 9 feet toward the farther end. About 57 feet from the entrance, the first side passages branch off to the right and left, along which are a number of rooms about the size of ordinary living rooms of today, though some are 30 or 40 feet square. These are entered by oval-shaped doors and are ventilated by round air spaces through the walls into the passages. The walls are about 3 feet 6 inches in thickness. The passages are chiseled or hewn as straight as could be laid out by an engineer. The ceilings of many of the rooms converge to a center. The side passages near the entrance run at a sharp angle from the main hall, but toward the rear they gradually reach a right angle in direction.

The Shrine

Over a hundred feet from the entrance is the cross hall several hundred feet long, in which was found the idol, or image of the people's god, sitting cross-legged with a lotus flower or lily in each hand. The cast of the face is Oriental, and the carving shows a skillful hand and the entire are remarkably well preserved, as is everything in this cavern. The idol most resembles Buddha, though the scientists are not certain as to what religious worship it represents. Taking into consideration everything found thus far, it is possible that this worship most resembles the ancient people of Tibet. Surrounding this idol are smaller images, some very beautiful in form, others crooked necked and distorted shapes, symbolical, probably, of good and evil. There are two large cacti with protruding arms, one on each side of the dais,[100] on which the god squats. All this is carved out of hard rock resembling marble. In the opposite corner of the cross hall were found tools of all descriptions, made of copper. These people undoubtedly knew the lost art of hardening this metal, which has been sought by chemists for centuries without results. On a bench running around the workroom was some charcoal and other material probably used in the process. There is also slag and stuff similar to matte,[101] showing that these ancients smelted ores, but so far no trace of where or how this was done has been discovered, nor the origin of the ore. Among the other finds are vases or urns and cups of copper and gold, made very artistic in design. The pottery work includes enameled ware and glazed vessels. Another passageway lead to storage granaries such as are found in the Oriental temples. They contain seeds of various kinds. One very large storehouse has not yet been entered, as it is twelve feet high and can be reached only from above. Two copper hooks extend on the edge, which indicates that some sort of ladder was attached. These granaries are rounded, and the material of which they are constructed, I think, is very hard cement. A gray metal is also found in this cavern, which puzzles the scientists, for its identity

---

[100] Dais—raised platform.
[101] Matte—a mass with a dull finish.

has not been established. It resembles platinum. Strewn promiscuously over the floor everywhere are what people call 'cat's eyes' or 'tiger eyes,' a yellow stone of no great value. Each one is engraved with the head of the Malay[102] type.

The Crypt

The tomb or crypt in which the mummies were found is one of the largest of the chambers, the walls slanting back at an angle of about 35 degrees. On these are tiers of mummies, each one occupying a separate hewn shelf. At the head of each is a small bench, on which is found copper cups and pieces of broken swords. Some of the mummies are covered with clay, and all are wrapped in a bark fabric. The urns or cups on the lower tiers are crude, while as the higher shelves are reached the turns are finer in design, showing a later stage of civilization. It is worthy of note that all the mummies examined so far have proved to be male, no children or females being buried here. This leads to the belief that this exterior section was the warriors' barracks.

Among the discoveries no bones of animals have been found, no skins, no clothing nor bedding. Many of the rooms are bare but for water vessels. One room, about 40 by 70 feet, was probably the main dining hall, for cooking utensils are found here. What these people lived on is a problem, though it is presumed that they came south in the winter and farmed in the valleys, going back north in the summer. Upwards of 50,000 people could have lived in the cavern comfortably. One theory is that the present Indian tribes found in Arizona are descendants of the serfs or slaves of the people who inhabited the cave. Undoubtedly a good many thousands of years before the Christian era a people lived here which reached a high stage of civilization. The chronology of human history is full of gaps. Prof. Jordan is much enthused over the discovery and believes that the find will prove of incalculable value in archaeological work

"One thing I have not spoken of may be of interest. There is one chamber the passageway in which is not ventilated, and when we approached it a deadly, snaky smell struck us. Our lights would not penetrate the gloom, and until stronger ones are available we will not know what the chamber contains. Some say snakes, but others boo-hoo this idea and think it may contain a deadly gas or chemical used by the ancients. No sounds are heard, but it smells snaky just the same. The whole underground institution gives one of shaky nerves the creeps. The gloom is like a weight on ones shoulders,

---

[102] Malay type—a brown skin people from the Malayan Peninsula.

and our flashlights and candles only make the darkness blacker. Imagination can revel in conjectures and ungodly daydreams back through the ages that have elapsed 'til the mind reels dizzily in space."

An Indian Legend

In connection with this story, it is notable that among the Hopis the tradition is told that their ancestors once lived in an underground world in the Grand Canyon 'til dissension arose between the good and the bad, the people of one heart and the people of two hearts. Machetto, who was their chief, counseled them to leave the underworld, but there was no way out. The chief then caused a tree to grow up and pierce the roof of the underworld, and then the people of one heart climbed out. They tarried by Paisisval (Red River), which is the Colorado, and grew grain and corn. They sent out a message to the Temple of the Sun, asking the blessing of peace, good will and rain for the people of the one heart. The messenger never returned, but today at the Hopi village at sundown can be seen the old men of the tribe out on the housetops gazing toward the sun, looking for the messenger. When he returns, their lands and ancient dwelling place will be restored to them. That is the tradition. Among the engravings of animals in the cave is seen the image of a heart over the spot where it is located. The legend was learned by V. E. Rollins, the artist, during a year spent with the Hopi Indians. There are two theories of the origin of the Egyptians. One is they came from Asia; another that the racial cradle was the upper Nile region. Heeren, an Egyptologist, believed in the Indian origin of the Egyptians. The discoveries in the Grand Canyon may throw further light on human evolution and prehistoric ages.

#

We must remember, this article was written about a century ago, and to my mind we know no more about this cave now than they knew then .

Was this cave, along with several others blocked out from public knowledge, covered up in order to keep the paradigm of the scholars in charge, sterile?

If we read the story carefully we can see that the author didn't know how many feet there are in a mile nor did he or they have a clear idea of what may be Egyptian or Chinese. But after reading Henriette Mertz's *Pale Ink,* it seems more logical that the seated god was Buddha and the people of the cave were Chinese. If so, there was no question as to what they were eating: it was rice!

In 1950 I was on an expedition down the Colorado River and we saw where people had lived up on the canyon walls. There were granaries at the various places of inhabitation and small stepping holes, like crude ladders where people could climb up in the steeper places. We were told that these were made thousands of years ago by the Moki Indians, a tribe long since extinct.

The above article is just one of many told about elaborate caves in the Canyon Country.

Some of the worst of these tales were told to me by a man who has been studying the North in the region of the Great Plains (Minnesota, North and South Dakota, and Iowa) for half a century. His name is Marion Dahm from Chokio, Minnesota, the same town where Henriette Mertz was born.

Marion was a farmer who, in his early 40s, came down with leukemia. He gave up farming, started looking after his health and got a job at the Kensington Runestone Museum in nearby Alexandria.

Without knowing much about either side of the runestone controversy, but completely confused by the strong stance of the two opposing sides, Dahm decided to do a thorough analysis of the whole picture.

Checking out every lead, both old and new, Dahm soon arrived at the same conclusions as most other independent researchers, that there was evidence of Norse occupation. Over the next 30 or 40 years, he built his own airplane and got deeply into infrared photography, topography and the geography of the region. He interviewed hundreds of people who had found evidence of any kind, artifacts, mooring stones, stories of Olaf Ohman, relatives, neighbors, etc., yet he got no cooperation from the academic community, who stood solidly entrenched in opinions set down a century earlier.

Marion is now 86 years old and still researching. He tells many stories of the stubbornness and arrogance of archaeologists to whom he has tried to explain some of his observations. I don't want to go into the details here, though I've heard many, but would prefer they come from Marion himself. In my opinion, some of these tales could backlash and cause the establishment to further dig in its heels. I feel that, in time, as more knowledge is learned, a true picture of the Kensington Stone's validity will surely emerge. Marion certainly has done his part to get many competent people interested in his project.

The Marion Dahm Story

I did write to Marion Dahm asking about the particulars of one story. In answer, I received a huge packet of information that he thought I would find useful. My job is to abbreviate it to a page or so, if that is possible. Dahm's letter of January 21, 2004 states: "You have my 'total permission' to use any of it,—'the material shows what we the amateurs face from the powerful few.'"

It turned out that there were several stories of discouragement—but none of them dampened the enthusiasm of Marion Dahm.

As Marion told this one story, he had been taking infrared photos from the air in 1971. The photos from Runestone Park, where the famous Kensington

Stone was found, showed large rectangular areas which he said showed places where the earth had been disturbed by construction of Viking period longhouses. The shapes on the photographs indicate the existence of five separate buildings scattered throughout the park area. Dahm showed the photos to a university archaeologist, who looked the ground over to match up the ground with the photos.

As the story was told to me, Marion explained that the area near the end of a large possible lodge would have had a fire pit and presumably a lot of activity—a logical place to look for artifacts.

Marion Dahm

That July the archaeologist and others returned with a backhoe and dug two trenches, neither where Dahm had suggested.

In the packet that Dahm enclosed was a 20-page report of the dig. The title, *Report on the Archaeological Survey and Test Excavations Carried Out at the Runestone Hill, Stevens County, Minnesota, during the fall of 1975 and summer of 1976,* was submitted January 21, 1977 by the Department of Anthropology, University of Minnesota. Then in longhand it states, "A Review by Marion Dahm R-1 #60, Chokio, Minn 56221, July 20, 1994."[103]

Without going into great detail, I will quote just a few of the more relevant statements. I have intentionally omitted the name of the archaeologist who authored the report for reasons which will be apparent:

> Report:—Stage I involved a traditional test excavation, undertaken during two weekends, Oct. 11-12 and 25-26, 1975, the writer, assisted by Dr. Guy Gibbon, Dept. of Anthropology, University of Minn. and Ms. Kim Hohnesohlager, Carleton College, tested two areas identified by Marion Dahm as two "house foundations." The locations of the test excavations, as well as the results, are described in Appendix B. None of the tested areas yielded evidence of either any cultural material or

---

[103] Dahm's comments are written in longhand throughout the report and they have been watered down somewhat by the author

any soil disturbance that could be attributed to human settlement in the past.

Dahm (in longhand):   I have very definite reference points on the infrareds. It's so simple to pinpoint—She came out with results in the wrong area.—We had a $15,400 grant from State of Minn—also a match from U.M.M., they used it all up for nothing.—Mr. Olson, who ran the payloader, was from Cyrus, Minn. He said, "What a (— —expletive deleted) project" they had done.—M.D.

Report:—It was therefore arranged that a local and highly skilled backhoe operator would come to our help.

Dahm (in longhand):   Had never done a job like this before in his life.—She went swimming and beer drinking for hours while Olson backhoed the hell out of Runestone Hill.

Report: It seems beyond doubt that we have identified and test excavated at least two of the areas claimed by Mr. Dahm to be Norse house foundations.—

Dahm (in longhand):   There is no doubt in my mind that you dug in the wrong area.—

Report:—We did not recover any cultural material, any buried humus horizon, any charcoal or any soil changes of any kind that one would associate with such house foundations. The surface disturbances that show up on the aerial photographs must therefore be assumed to have a different origin and to be the result of natural, non-human factors. What these factors might be has been suggested in Appendix C.

Dahm: She did not dig and would not dig where I told her to. I know where to dig, in light of my infrared pictures, on west and south house where Runestone was made in winter of 1361 and 1362. She used her electrical sensor devices to pinpoint an area west of house.

She could not keep her positive and negative readings in relationship to positive and negative poles. (They) meant nothing to her…

While the backhoe operator tore the whole area to hell, she went to Red Rock Lake and swam with Dr. Kramer. Then she came back and sat by the car and drank a 12-pack of beer with him. Then she threw the empty cans in the trenches and told him to cover it all back up.—but Mr. Hoffman of Indian Mound site in Alexandria told her to get the hell down in the trench and bring the cans back out so some scientist won't come along a hundred years from now and detect metal here, and it will be your damn beer cans. She went down and took them out.

——There were a number of us there, myself, Cliff Roiland, Karl Skogland, Joana Dahm (Vern Hoffman) and others.

The archaeologist kept all her notes up in an area of flagpoles. When lightning struck up there, she got so scared she ran off and forgot her notes. Later on she couldn't find them, so like a good fellow, I got them and gave them to her. M.D. (Marion Dahm)

The report goes on for the next fifteen pages of graphs and scale drawings of the trenches, etc. Two of the pages have objections to the material written by Marion Dahm and on the last page Dahm writes a P.S. stating: "In 2001 I took infrared pictures of the area and it plainly shows her dig on the south side of the north house."

At the end of the report Dahm wrote a very unflattering report concerning the archaeologist and attached a very hazy infrared photo showing all the locations spoken of here.

Obviously there is no love lost between holders of the two opposing views and, again, only one view gets the headlines.

The Lake Region Echo, Aug 4, 1976, headlines "After Weekend Excavation—No Evidence of Vikings Found" and another note there from Dahm to me—"Write Dr. Hahn, from Space Center! He gives you the right answer."

I knew Dr. Hahn from several ISAC meetings in the past, but he died a few years ago. Just before his death he had plans to move to Duluth, presumably to be closer to the situation.

The above incident, just one of many, was, of course, a great defeat for the cause of the Kensington Stone supporters. But it did not discourage Marion Dahm or the growing number of believers. This type of apparent closing the book on a subject has gone on for years. But it is like keeping clean, you just keep at it or you soon get dirty again.

This all happened decades ago, but recently we've had the book by Barry Hanson and the work of Richard Nielson.

In one of their recent efforts they sought out the expertise of a Mr. Scott Wolter who owns and runs an independent laboratory. His credentials included the testing of concrete from the Pentagon after the 9-11 disaster.

When contacted he frankly told them that he would not take sides in the matter and that he had no feeling either way. He said they should be prepared to be disappointed in his findings. They agreed and hired Wolter to run his tests on that basis. On tests measuring the rate of decay and loss of certain minerals

Scott Wolter and Richard Nielson, authors of new book "The Kensington Rune Stone - Compelling New Evidence".

as compared with known hundred-year-old tombstones, his conclusions were that the stonework had to be at least 200 years old. After the first year, Scott Walter became so enthused with his findings that he volunteered to continue the work at no charge.

Then, because of the enthusiasm generated by the work of Hanson, Nielson, Rudebush, Wolter and Cal Courneys, the Kensington Runestone, in 2003, was sent to a Swedish museum for a first-hand look (The Historiska Mustet—Stockholm). There, because of the runestone's hidden message, plus the mooring holes on both sides of the Atlantic, as well as the words, terms and letters in Kensington verified in Sweden from the same period, Swedish scientists have decided that, rather than a complete fraud, the stone merits cautious reconsideration—a view, to my knowledge, still resisted by the Smithsonian. But now (as I write in February 2004), a group of those working on the stone have been invited back to Sweden.

I might add that when I was in Sweden and Norway (two trips in 1990s), my efforts to talk with historians were all cut short—in their mind, the Kensington Stone was proven fake many years ago.

Opinions on the Viking Helmet

In recent years the great institutions have tried to debunk the "myth" that Viking helmets ever had horns or wings (one recent reference, Vikings—North

Atlantic Saga—published by the Smithsonian Institution Press associated with the National Museum of Natural History, pages 365-373).[103a]

[103a] No problem finding horned headgear in ancient times see page 422.

It is hard to understand why some authors devoted so much time and energy to arguing that Viking helmets never had horns. There are a few reasons to believe that some Viking helmets may have been adorned by horns or wings, but how would anyone ever prove that they never had them?

Quoting from the reference above, "Archaeologists regard this helmet (a horned helmet) with perplexing amusement, because no material dating to the Viking Age includes a horned helmet or even a nonhorned helmet. The single Viking grave in which a helmet was found is in Germandbu, Norway."

First, as stated before, the vast majority of Viking period settlers in America were farmers, not warriors. However, for several hundred years artists' pictures of Viking warriors often depicted one or two among them with horns or wings. Of these two icons, horns would be the easier to get and far more simple to attach. The Viking war or raiding parties were led by individual chiefs or kings and they would have had no prescribed set uniform; it seems many may have made up their own, like today's motorcycle gangs, and some ideas are contagious. If the halberd, sword, spear and shield were essential, why not the helmet, with its ancient European traditions?

Then there is one legendary account (Johan Baner's *Viking Mettles*) that specifically describes the men wearing "ice" and wings on their helmets.

I believe it is quite probable that some Vikings wore such classic military adornment. It is not an area for a scientist to get into, and it will be as difficult for the public to change that image as it will be to deny Columbus as America's discoverer.

But there is still one more important aspect of where academia, and especially the archaeological community, has painted itself into a corner. This is the shoddy way they have treated members of their own profession who have come to conclusions that do not fit their paradigms.

My first knowledge of this internal squabbling or what some people call professional jealousy, came from an article in *Antiquity,* the journal of and for professional archaeologists, a copy of which was sent to me from Harvard. Included was a diatribe against Barry Fell by Marshall McKusick, part of which appeared earlier in this book. Since that time I have read other articles and books that treat Dr. Fell as some kind of a newcomer to the field.

Here is a person who studied ancient languages in the four corners of the world for over fifty years, who has established the global-wide Epigraphic Society, who was one of the first persons on earth to learn how to decipher messages in unknown scripts without another known script to go by; one who has salvaged the secrets of some twenty-six different unknown alphabets and has been acclaimed as the greatest epigrapher who has ever lived—and yet some write about him as though he had made up those alphabets himself.

Bath
England

Hopwell
Ohio

Four humanlike figures hold
hands on a sacred scroll;
horns traditionally were signs
of supernatural abilities.

*It is not hard to find people or headgear adorned with horns or antlers in sculptor or among
petroglyphs from almost any period - but not the Vikings (according to the Smithsonian). Most
significant is a Cree Ice Sculpture in China pictured here lower left.*

Severe Internal Squabbling

Here is the story of some other frustrating situations with which I have had remote contact. One concerns a woman I met at a conference in Provost, Utah. She told her story at the conference and later I had lunch with her and one or two others who took part. She was Virginia Steen-McIntyre, formerly with a U.S. Geological Survey team.

I was somewhat familiar with the Hueyatloca site, having first heard of it in a letter from Dr. George Carter some time in the early 1980s. He referred to it as being a 250,000 year old site, mentioning it along with a 200,000 year old date for the Colico site in the Mojave Desert. He said there was also a 100,000 year desert varnish date for the surface of that site (Oberlander, Geography, UC, Berkeley). That same letter stated that it seemed likely that Man originated in East Africa, but "all we can say with great certainty is that it was somewhere in the warm belt that stretches from Southeast Asia across India into Africa." He says, "It now appears that Man moved into Europe a bit earlier than 800,000 B.P. He was living in northern Greece by 1,000,000 B.P.[104] (before present)."

Since so few agree with each other, especially on dates, I don't suppose many will agree with Dr. Carter on his statements, but at least he is headed in the right direction.

And so I was at least aware of the Hueyatloca site being estimated at 250,000 years old, but knew little about it.

It was in the 1960s that some stone tools as advanced as those found with Cro-Magnon man in Europe were found by Juan Armenta Camacho and Cynthia Irwin-Williams at Hueyatloca, about 75 miles southeast of Mexico City.

A controversy arose when the team of geologists working for the U.S. Geological Survey dated them at about 250,000 years old. The team of geologists, besides Virginia Steen-McIntyre, consisted of Harold Malde, also of the U.S. Geological Survey and Roald Fryxell of Washington State University. They were working under a grant from the National Science Foundation.

This whole episode was written up in a very straight-forward manner in a remarkable 900-page book written by Michaela A. Cremo and Richard L. Thompson, entitled *Forbidden Archaeology: The Hidden History of the Human Race* (Bhaktivedanta Book Publishing, Inc., Los Angeles, Sydney, Stockholm, Bombay—1993, revised 1996-1998).

According to Cremo and Thompson, the geologists said four different dating methods were used independent of each other. They were (1) Uranium

---

[104] In recent years several scientists have told me they believe "man" goes back much further than one million years.

series dating, (2) fission track dating, (3) tephra hydration dating, and (4) study of mineral weathering. (The average layman has probably not even heard of these highly technical dating methods, but in a book sent to me by Dr. Bruce Marsh,[105] Professor of Earth and Planetary Science at Johns Hopkins University, it gives five general areas of dating material. Within the subdivisions of each of these general areas are almost 40 different dating methods. At Hueyatloca, carbon 14 dating was not applicable because the artifacts were all inorganic.

The report goes on to tell who did the dating of the material, where it was done, every step of the methods used and the theory behind these methods and, of course, the results. The calculations yielded dates of about 245,000 years before present. This date was determined, after comparisons, to be the minimum age of the site, the lower levels of which could be substantially older.

"Cynthia Irwin-Williams, who originally discovered the tools, suggested that the real age of the samples should be around 25,000 years. But careful study of the data supplied by Szabo, who performed the uranium series tests, appears to rule out the hypothesis that migration caused falsely old dates."

Every conceivable method and idea was thoroughly discussed and reexamined.

> "We have examined in some detail the cases of Hueyatloca and El Horno in order to show that the dates for these stone tools from these sites were solidly based on serious scientific analyses, more rigorous than in many accepted dating studies. However, due to the anomalous character of the 250,000 year figure, this dating has proven to be extremely controversial. The daters declared themselves to be 'painfully aware' of the dilemma they had caused and 'perplexed' about how to resolve it. Roald Fryxell said: 'We have no reason to suppose that over decades, our understanding of human prehistory is so inaccurate that we suddenly discover that our past understanding is all wrong…On the other hand, the more geological information we've accumulated, the more difficult it is to explain how multiple methods of dating, which are independent of each other, might be in error by the same magnitude'" (Denver Post, November 13, 1973).

This date of 250,000 years, arrived at with such scientific care, was a great shock to established archaeologists. The truly scientific attitude should be to just record it along with other data and wait. I have waited 50 years for answers to some of my questions that have been answered to my satisfaction and I have many

---

[105] Dr. Marsh is originally from Negaunee, Michigan.

other questions pending. But those who have arrived at their answers through opinion or other unscientific ways tend to throw out any data that doesn't "fit."

Then the true scientist, who wants the correct data recorded and accepted, is ostracized, banished from the fraternity.

This was the story of Virginia Steen-McIntyre who tried desperately to report her undoctored findings and "stick to her guns." From *Forbidden Archaeology:*

> Among the social processes that discourage acceptance and reporting of anomalous evidence are ridicule and gossip, including attacks on character and accusations of incompetence. Furthermore, discoveries have almost no impact in the world of science unless they are published in standard journals. The editorial process, especially the practice of anonymous peer review, often presents an insurmountable obstacle. Some submissions are met with a wall of silence. Others are shunted around for months, from editor to editor. Sometimes manuscripts are mysteriously lost in the shuffle. And while positive reports of anomalous evidence are subjected to protracted review and/or rejection, negative critiques are sometimes rushed into print. Occasionally a maverick report eventually does appear in a journal, but only after it has gone through such extensive modifications that the original message has become totally obscured—by editorial deletions and, in some cases, rewriting of data. (Cremo and Thompson, page 362)

Steen-McIntyre could not get her paper printed. She was relegated to an office in the basement; they would not return her paper. It languished in Los Almos for almost five years. During all this time she wrote letters, called often, but the party she called was always in conference or out of the office—she could get no response, but in the meantime there was a lot of false information being bantered around.

> The competence of Steen-McIntyre's associates was also called into question. She informed Porter: 'There's the old saw that Fryx wasn't in his right mind when he did the work. Those folks forget that I saw the stratigraphy too, and once you get into a cross-trench, it was relatively simple, thanks to a magnesium-stained bed that traced on the excavation wall like a pencil mark!'

> In March of 1981, Steen-McIntyre wrote to Estelle Leopold, the associate editor of the Quarternary Review: "The problem as I see it is much bigger than Hueyatloca. It concerns the manipulation of scientific thought

through the suppression of 'Enigmatic Data,' data that challenges the prevailing mode of thinking. Hueyatloca certainly does that! Not being an anthropologist, I didn't realize the full significance of our dates back in 1973, nor how deeply woven into our thought the current theory of human evolution had become. Our work at Hueyatloca has been rejected by most archaeologists because it contradicts that theory, period. Their reasoning is circular. Homosapiens sapiens evolved ca 30,000-50,000 years ago in Eurasia. Therefore any homosapiens sapiens tools 250,000 years old found in Mexico are impossible because homosapiens sapiens evolved ca 30,0000—...etc. Such thinking makes self-satisfied archae-ologists but lousy science."

Eventually, Quartarnary Research (1981) did publish an article by Virginia Steen-McIntyre, Roald Fryxell, and Harold E. Malde with the 250,000 year date for Hueyatloca. It was severely challenged by Cynthia Irwin-Williams but her objections were answered point by point by the original research team. But Irwin-Williams did not relent. She and the American archaeological community in general continue to reject the 250,000 year date that has been so valiantly defended by Virginia Steen-McIntyre and her team.

In a letter to Steen-McIntyre, Dr. George Carter called the "dominant clique" of New World archaeologists "priests of the High Doctrine" and complained that they bragged among themselves about having blocked him from publishing in the major journals. He compared his treatment to a modern Inquisition. Steen-McIntyre answered, "I had thought to circumvent these 'true believers' by publishing in an obscure symposium volume, but no such luck." But years later, Virginia Steen-McIntyre did publish an article in the *Ancient American* magazine.

The above information is written up in detail in *Forbidden Archaeology*. Quotes are from that work.

Another situation I was somewhat familiar with was closer to home. It is a site known as Shequiandah, located on Manitoulin Island near the north shore of Lake Huron. My wife and I visited this site, expecting to see a museum nearby that told about it. Instead, we were told the site had been sold, and there were several buildings where the archaeological dig had taken place.

At this location archaeologist Thomas E. Lee, digging through several layers of glacial till and a layer of boulders, found a "broken bifacial implement and several stone flakes " apparently struck by human beings (T.E. Lee, p. 49). It looked to him as if these tools could be older than the standard views of peopling of the New World.

There were four geologists who were most concerned, Dr. John Stanford of Wayne State University (Detroit), Dr. Bruce Liberty and Dr. Jean Terasmae, both formerly of the Geological Survey of Canada and Dr. Ernst Antevs of Arizona. All but Dr. Antevs thought the site could extend back to interglacial times, but opinions as to how far back ranged from 30,000 to 100,000 years. The date made public at the time was "a minimum of 30,000," which agreed with some opinions as to the earliest peopling of the New World. However, in another paper Lee (1981) said that some of the geologists had suggested the stone implements may be as old as 150,000 years.

Even though all agreed that the site was very old, and Stanford supported Lee's base of geological evidence, the idea of that age was openly ridiculed and there were efforts to discredit Lee.

Most scientists then didn't believe the New World had been inhabited for more than 12,000 years. But after careful study of the interglacial periods, they determined the implements could possibly be as old as 125,000 years.

Cremo and Thompson's account goes on for 8 to 10 pages, giving proof of a more than 30,000 year date for the implements, even though 70,000 years was thought to be more accurate by those closest to the study.

Lee's own account recalled, "Several prominent geologists who examined the numerous excavations in progress during the four years at Sheguiandah privately expressed the belief that the lower levels of the Shequiandah site are interglacial. Such was the climate in professional circles—one of jealousy, hostility, skepticism, antagonism, obstructionism, and persecution—that, on the advice of the famed authority, Dr. Ernest Antevs of Arizona, a lesser date of '30,000 years minimum' was advanced in print by some of the geologists to avoid ridicule and to gain partial acceptance from the more serious scholars." Cremo and Thompson:

> But even that minimum was too much for the protagonists of the 'fluted-point-first American myth.' The sites discoverer [Lee] was hounded from his civil service position into prolonged unemployment, publication outlets were cut off and the evidence was misrepresented by several prominent authors among the Brahmins.[106] The tons of artifacts vanished into storage bins at the National Museum of Canada, while its director [Dr. Jacques Rousseau], who had published a monograph on the site, was himself fired and driven into exile for refusing to fire the discoverer. Official positions of prestige and power were exercised in an effort to gain control over just six Sheguiandah specimens that had not

---

[106] Brahmin—highly cultured person, exclusive intellectual.

disappeared, and the site has been turned into a tourist resort. All this without the profession, in four long years, bothering to take a look while there was still time to look. Sheguiandah would have forced embarrassing admissions that the Brahmins did not know everything. It would have forced the re-writing of almost every book in the business. It had to be killed. It was killed.

Of course, this is just a small taste of Cremo and Thompson's remarkable and revealing book, which goes on for nearly 900 pages and describes hundreds of examples of case after case where authorities in the field have refused to examine alternative views for fear they could be proven wrong.

It should be obvious to the reader that archaeology, anthropology, geology, history, etc., are not exact sciences. These often have to be dealt with in general terms—but if enough data is gathered to show a trend, instead of condemning the research or attacking the researcher, the trend could be examined openly by more people. It is often the broad picture we are looking for, not an exact date.

Such a startling revelation of extreme human antiquity as found in *Forbidden Archaeology* did not go unnoticed by the scientific establishment. Hundreds of letters poured in, both complimentary and disparaging. In the true spirit of honesty, in 1998, Michael Cremo published most of the letters and reactions in another book entitled *Forbidden Archaeology—Impact* and subtitled *How a Controversial New Book Shocked the Scientific Community and Became an Underground Classic.*

We cannot do much of a review of that book here, but going down the list of respondents, I picked out two whom I knew.

For forty years our family has known the family of Mutu Gethoi of Kenya. His father spent a week with us in our home, and we have watched his children grow for years. They all come to visit occasionally and have often stayed with us. In Kenya, the Gethoi family is close friends of the Leakey's, whom we talked about regularly but had never met. However, when Richard Leakey, son of the famous Lewis Leakey, came to Marquette to speak at the University, I was eager to visit with him. After our initial introduction and discussions about our mutual friends, I asked him about just a few of my ideas, only to be met with some most unwelcome comments. There certainly was no open discussion or flow of ideas. And so I was not surprised to hear his reaction to *Forbidden Archaeology*. His letter was summed up in one sentence on the dust cover of *Impact*.

Richard Leakey: "Your book is pure humbug and does not deserve to be taken seriously by anyone but a fool." Richard Leakey, Anthropologist and Author.

I then turned to the letter of Dr. Joseph Mahan, archaeologist, anthropologist and historian, and founder of the Institute for the study of American Culture (now deceased). He was a kind and understanding elderly southern gentleman who listened to all comers. We had corresponded for years, and just before his death he asked me if I would be an officer in his organization. I felt I lived too far from the headquarters (Columbus, Georgia) and until I met Joe Mahan felt I was out of the loop so to speak. At the time of his death, Joe was writing a book called *The Presumption of Fraud*, an attitude he encountered regularly among his co-horts. I have never seen that book in print.

I quote here two unrelated sentences from his letter. This and the Leakey quote dramatically illustrate the polarization of the archaeological community. Joe Mahan (*Impact*, page 352):

"You have documented and most effectively called attention to the stubborn stonewalling by students of ancient man in the manner I have tried to do to American archaeologists and anthropologists for the past thirty years. Congratulations!" —and— "This will provide the Establishment a challenging opportunity to use their 'presumption of fraud' defense. It should create interest elsewhere as well."

We should all realize that there are often two sides to the seemingly most fundamental questions. No matter how deeply we are imbedded in one view, a true scientist must listen to the opposing view and be able to openly weigh both sides and change, if necessary. If one has honestly made a discovery himself, those views are well engrained; if his position has been learned from others it can be challenged by honest researchers on the same subject.

More Rough Treatment

There are readers that will believe there is exaggeration here. I used to think something along these lines myself. Things can't be this bad or people in high positions just can't be that unreasonable. But over the years, I have changed my mind, after hearing the stories of archaeologists who "learned too much." I have had calls from people whom I never knew from other states telling me to "stick to my guns," "don't give up," etc. I try to explain that I just tell what I have learned, I try to examine both views when there are opposing sides.

I have talked to young archaeologists who have expressed the view that "we believe what you are saying, but we are working for someone with different views."

I would like to tell some of these stories but in this atmosphere it would be best not to.

However, there is one man with whom I have been corresponding for a few years. I have never met or even spoken with John Henderson of Manassas, Virginia, but by letter I asked if he would tell his story for this book. A first-hand account from a relative stranger would be valuable.

His answer came by letter on March 3, 2004:

> I always wanted to be an archaeologist. I studied and did field work on my own and with organized parties whenever I could, and finally was part of several major expeditions to sites in Yucatan, Chiapas and Guatemala. I was told I did good work and had a solid future in the field.
>
> Then I made some discoveries that pushed the age of man in these areas back thousands of years but also showed distinct evidence of advanced technology and contact with other cultures across both oceans. First my work was ignored, then ridiculed, then my honesty, intelligence and character were viciously attacked, and I went from 'fair-haired boy' to 'bumbling amateur.' I was sent home and no one would hire me.
>
> In the 1960s I read a book *He Walked the Americas* by L. Taylor Hansen in which she showed that white bearded robed culture heroes like Quetzalcoatl had visited many, many tribes in North and South America. One of these was called Puants who were said to have built cities in the Midwest near the Great Lakes, and that their capitol was situated at a point where all waters flowed away in the four directions of the compass. I decided to research that point to see if it could possibly be true. I found the spot, actually indicated by a roadside plaque, east of Watersmeet and on the shore of the strangely named lake, Lac Vieux Desert (lake of the ancient desert) just inside the Michigan-Wisconsin border. I discovered there was a buried city there which could have been one of the great archaeological discoveries of North American history, and I, as still a licensed archaeologist, requested a permit to excavate. I was refused. To this day nothing has been done at that site to my knowledge. To orthodox science, if it rocks the boat, it's best not to know…

It just so happened, a year or so earlier, I was invited along with some other interested people, to go to Eagle River, Wisconsin, by Mr. David Hoffman. He has a family cottage in the area where we stayed for a few days. One of the people in the group was Dr. Jim Scherz, who has been mentioned several times in these writings. Jim has a nose for archaeological sites.

One of our trips was to an island in Lac Vieux Desert. The Michigan and Wisconsin boarder runs through that island. Jim wanted to look at some mounds there. We couldn't break him away and I understand he spent much time there in the following weeks.

Incidentally at least four other sites (of buried cities) have been mentioned to me by other interested people (all amateurs) that have never been examined by professionals. North America should be an archeologists paradise of Pre-Columbian civilizations.

New Ancient city found by David Deal in lower Michigan - See article in Ancient American Magazine #63, June 2005, page 36.

*This group of interested people on the island in Lac Vieux Desert 2004.
l-r: David Hoffman, Susan English, Mr. & Mrs. Rob Robinson, Dr. Jim Scherz and Laurie Zie. This is private property and the group had the owners permission.*

Some enlightening conclusions.

Many people crossed the oceans in pre-historic times.

There were methods of navigation unknown to us today.

The ancients had writing systems that have been lost to time – some not yet recognized.

Ancient civilizations were far more innovative and sophisticated than they have been given credit for.

One of the very early routes to Lake Superior copper must have been through Hudson Bay and Lake Michigan and exiting via the Mississippi River (Marian Dahm and others point out the only against current travel were the rivers to Lake Nipegon. Dahm says besides copper the ancients got lead in Iowa. It was a three-year round trip journey).

Could These Be Misinterpretations?

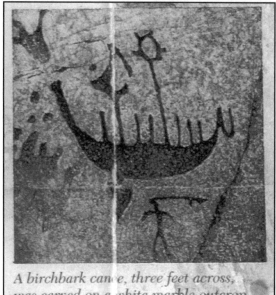

A birchbark canoe, three feet across, was carved on a white marble outcropping before the arrival of Europeans. The sacred site of 900 petroglyphs is

On a large inset map printed by the National Geographic Magazine is a picture of a boat from the Peterborough inscriptions.

Beneath the picture it states: "A birch bark canoe, three feet across, was carved on a white marble outcropping before the arrival of Europeans, the sacred site of 900 Petroglyphs - "

In my mind I don't see how anyone could interpret this as a "birch bark canoe."

Some of the Petroglyphs at Peterborough

These could be birch bark canoes---

---but the glyphs to me look much closer to ancient boat drawings from Europe, such as those illustrated here:

Sketch from ancient drawings and stone work in England and Scandinavia.

Several variations of this bird are often shown with Hopewell artifacts made of sheet copper. One was said to be found beneath the "Death Mask Mound" near Chillicothe, Ohio.

It has often been referred to as a peregrine falcon. I cannot

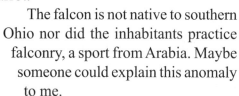

see what there is about it that would make someone think it is supposed to be a peregrine falcon, one of the fastest flying birds on earth. They are streamlined, small tearing beak, eyes looking straight ahead. This bird has eyes on either side of its head and beak that, to me, looks like a parrot.

The falcon is not native to southern Ohio nor did the inhabitants practice falconry, a sport from Arabia. Maybe someone could explain this anomaly to me.

In the Journal of Columbus (1492) he tells of the natives owning parrots.

I keep running into these strange discrepancies that seem to have no explanations and they go unchallenged.[106a]

Peregrine Falcons

[106a] In recent publication (2005) Ohio Archaelolgy by Bradey T. Lepper, he questions the Peregrine falcon as "possible".

Chapter XI

An Entertaining Story—But All Too True—And Now Lost History

The following is quoted in part from a story entitled *A Dramatic Discovery,* a collection of articles found in Merion Newspaper Ltd, New South Wales, published in 1973 by Castle Books.

True Life Stories of Freaks, Fate and Fortune

On March 1st, 1924, Emile Fradin, a peasant living in a French village of Glozel, was working in his grandfather's field when he noticed a large circular hole in the earth. With a torch, he dropped into the hole and found himself in a small cavern. At one end stood what appeared to be a tomb made of baked clay bricks. Looking inside he could see clay pots, stones bearing unusual carvings, stone rings, flint fishhooks, clay masks and several inscribed clay tablets.

Intrigued by the tablets, Fradin took two of the larger ones to a local archaeologist the next day. During the next month, he became famous.

Leading authorities on ancient history declared that Fradin had stumbled onto the greatest archaeological discovery of the century. They thought the letters on the tablets constituted the world's first alphabet and could be as much as 5,000 years old. Their existence proved that Stone Age man had achieved a degree of civilization thousands of years before the eastern world and this meant that man's conception of prehistory must be radically revised.

Then came the bombshell that was to destroy or damage some of the greatest scientific reputations of the time.

An independent scientific committee visited the site of the cavern and after some explorations and some tests declared that the entire Glozel affair as a hoax.

An amused public learned that the so-called "relics" had been manufactured only a short time before Fradin found them in the field.
Immediately Fradin took two more tablets to the Glozel archaeologists, word of the discovery spread and several scientists traveled to the village to examine the relics.

Among them was the celebrated French ceramics authority, Franchet, who said the tomb-like object was an ancient glassmaker's furnace.

Franchet announced that it was probably made during the early Stone Age period in the territory which later became Gaul.

Shortly after Franchet had completed his analysis of the furnace, a local antique collector named Perot appeared on the scene and said some of the pieces in his collection bore inscriptions the same as those on the Glozel tablets.

Then in 1925, a Vichy doctor and amateur antiquarian named Morlet arrived in the village and examined the recently discovered relics.
Morlet declared that the objects unearthed represented the greatest archaeological find of modern times and the inscriptions proved that the art of writing had been developed during the Stone Age.

After making these profound utterances, Morlet leased the field, gave Fradin funds to start a Glozel Museum in his house, and poured funds into further diggings.

As months passed, more of the strange objects came to light. These included tablets bearing numerals, pictures of animals and complex designs suggesting that the Stone Age had advanced artists.

As more discoveries were made, overseas archaeologists poured into Glozel and at Morlet's invitation made their own diggings.

Soon they were unearthing more tablets including several which bore mysterious crossed and half-moons.

The famous authority on prehistory, Dr. Marcell Budin, said that in his opinion the Glozel discoveries dated from the Bronze Age rather than from the Stone Age.

Another authority, Seymour de Ricci, disagreed violently. He said that apart from one stone fragment all the discoveries were fakes. But he was ignored.

As time passed the discoveries grew more dramatic, culminating in the finding of two vases carved to resemble death heads.

According to several experts, the death head vases were the world's first representations of dead loved ones while the fact that no mouths were present represented the eternal silence of death.

Now it was decided that in aeons past, Stone Age man held primitive religious rites in the Glozel area.

Portuguese scientists found a resemblance between the Glozel inscriptions and those on similar vases unearthed in western Portugal.

Said Professor Michael Rostovstoff of the Yale Classical Society: "The discovery solves the main problem of prehistory proving the cultural independence of the West and the priority of literature as compared with the East."

Camille Jullian, the world's leading authority on Galle-Roman life and customs, dismissed the theory out of hand. he declared that the relics were of far more recent origin. He said they were Roman and that the inscriptions were nothing more than a variant of the Roman script. The only reason why it had been difficult to decipher them, he added, was that they appeared to have "no rational significance." But this could be explained by the fact that the people writing them had developed a strange argot[107] of their own.

The controversy raged throughout 1927. Then excitement reached its peak when M. Dussaud of the Louvre Museum published a statement denouncing the Glozel discoveries as a practical joke. Dussaud sent a letter to Dr. Salmon Reinach that the bricks in the furnace were comparatively soft. Over centuries, they would not have kept their shape let alone their inscriptions. Furthermore, Dussaud continued, the so-called prehistoric glass-making furnace was of 16th century origin while the markings on the bricks indicated they had been made with a sharp steel instrument in recent months.

Denouncing Morlet and Fradin, Dussaud said they had perpetrated the hoax between them and "were incredibly stupid in their choice of letters from the original alphabet."

One inscription when deciphered read "Glozel" while another read "Christ be with us."

Dr. Reinach angrily denied the charges contained in the letter. Then either he or someone else made the mistake of telling Fradin about the accusations the letter contained.

Immediately Fradin and his father took out a libel suit against Dussaud and the magazine which published the scientist's original charge of fakery. Apparently the suit was withdrawn, for it never came to court.

Meanwhile the Glozel affair showed now sign of fading. The illustrated London News published two pages crowded with photographs of the site. They also published a full-page article b the Australian, Sir Grafton Elliot Smith, an authority on antiquities and a distinguished anthropologist. Smith suggested in the article that the objects were of genuine historical importance. Further publicity in widely respected American journals led to debates on the subject at various international science congresses.

In an attempt to settle the controversy, the French Minister of Public Instruction ordered two museum authorities to super-intend all future excavations and catalogue the relics as they were found.

---

[107] Argot—special vocabulary.

Then in November of 1927 the International Institute of Anthropology appointed a commission to examine and test the site and make a conclusive report on the subject.

The institute's committee members ordered a director of the Paris Laboratory of Legal Identification, Edmond Boyle, to subject every item in the Fradin museum to a close examination.

In his laboratory Boyle broke down each of the clay tablets and explored their contents.

He found that the tablets were full of swarming microorganisms which proved that they could not have been properly baked when made. If not properly baked they could not have survived long in the ground. Yet they were supposed to have been buried for about 5,000 years.

Boyle then took a tiny piece of grass from a fragment of earthenware, put it under a microscope and found that all its cells were intact.

In the clay, Boyle discovered threads that had been colored with aniline dyes, a 20th century product. Also some of the "ancient" bones discovered on the site were found to be full of marrow.

When Boyle's findings were published, l'affaire Glozel became the greatest sensation to have swept France since the Dreyfus case.

Extraordinary scenes took place in several scientific academies as the pro and anti-Glozel factions actually came to blows or ripped up seats and attacked each other with them.

After a bitter fight in one institution, the anti-Glozelians were driven from the hall. They returned with an angry mob, smashed the hall's windows and climbed over the sill to engage in further combat with their enemies.

Felix Regnault, President of the French Society of Prehistory, made headlines by suing Fradin for having charged him four francs to see his museum.

Regnault claimed that in the light of Boyle's discoveries the four francs had been illegally obtained.

After that police broke into Fradin's home, took all the relics not already appropriated and carried them off in packing cases.

Violent scenes took place in court as Fradin and Regnault screamed abuse at each other. Finally the case was settled out of court.

Then tragedy struck. Boyle, whose report on Glozel had virtually smashed the pro-Glozelian's case, was shot dead in the street. Police arrested scores of Glozelian's but the killer was never discovered.

On February 24th of 1928, Glozel again hit the headlines when Dr.

Morlet found seven corkscrews buried at a depth of 20 feet.

Morlet claimed that the corkscrews belonged to the seven members of the International Institute of Anthropology Committee. He said they had deliberately been buried by the committee in the hope that when he and Fradin found them they would claim they were relics of the Iron Age.

This would conclusively prove their dishonesty and they would then be forced to admit they had seeded the earth with other "antiquities." Once more the world laughed as the scientists continued to squabble over the matter of the corkscrews.

The Glozel affair ended with a report to the Government by various French Scientific organizations. But even this report was inconclusive. It simply said nothing had been proved.

Fradin and Morlet slipped back into obscurity while the pro-Glozelian scientists went to work to forget the whole business as quickly as possible.

Now A Similar Cave Found In America

When an archaeological discovery is made of which nobody can be sure of the age or circumstances, no one can assess it before many studies are completed. But people want answers, right now! So the very bold make up their minds immediately. If they say it is a fake, then there is no further investigating; it's final. If one chooses to wait and consider, he can easily be talked down or outmaneuvered by the bold ones who are sure of themselves—even if they are dead wrong. They just have to keep stressing the fraud. This can be the outcome in history, politics, theory and the kind of discovery we are talking about, Burrows Cave.

It seems that if a colossal discovery is made and handled in the right way by the right people, it has to be accepted. Because of so many unusual circumstances Burrows Cave was not handled correctly and so most of the people and practically all of the professionals believe the Burrows Cave story is a trumped up hoax.[107a] There are, of course, those who do believe and I happen to be one who wants to keep the question open. So far it has not been handled right and no one but Russell Burrows has been inside the cave to know if he is actually telling the truth. The reason I am more of a believer is because I am one of a few who has actually seen and handled seven-thousand carved stones that supposedly have been taken from the cave. I don't believe there is anyone alive today who would

---

[107a] See "The Mystery Cave of Many Faces" - Burrows & Rydholm.

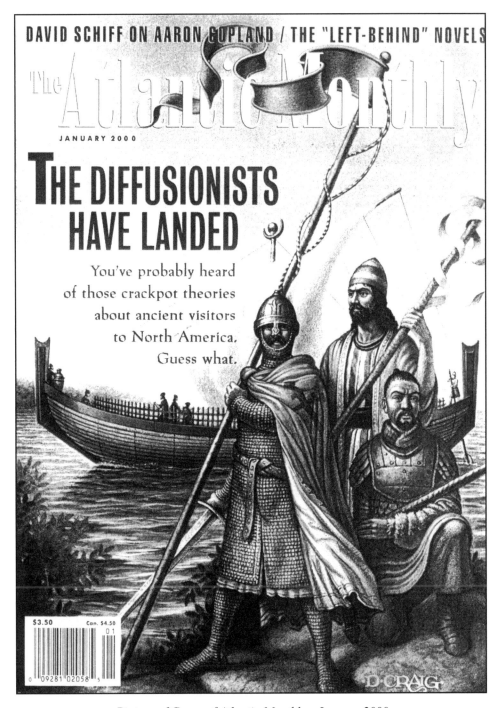

Picture of Cover of Atlantic Monthly - January 2000

Russell Burrows, Jack Ward and Norman Cullen

know enough to present such huge amounts of evidence, let alone do all the work of carving them. They have to be authentic.

There is a small group of knowledgeable people who feel the same as I do, but there has been much written expressing the opposite view.

Luckily there is one man who has been willing and able to do something about this exasperating situation. He had the courage to start a magazine (*Ancient American*) in which he has, in almost every issue, mentioned or featured stories about Burrows Cave. The person, of course, is Wayne May. Burrows Cave is either the greatest archaeological discovery in history or the greatest hoax ever perpetrated on the public. I don't believe Russell Burrows, Jack Ward and Norman Cullen are capable of perpetrating such an out-and-out public fraud.

Among the great steadfast news media and scientific institutions of higher learning, few will even mention the cave.[107b] However, there are some who are beginning to accept the idea of diffusionism and one or two who have actually championed Burrows Cave itself; none, however, to the extent that the *Ancient American* magazine has.

I have followed the ups and downs of the situation step by aggravating step, through the years since I first heard about it in 1984. I had great faith that someday Russell Burrows would take me to the cave. He did take me to a bogus cave along with a few others. Then, in the course of time, I followed Harry Hubbard and company but I could see he was making enemies. But Wayne May was a straight shooter, honest, friendly to all parties. He listened to everyone

---

[107b] A few specific magazines – Ancient American (most issues) Barnes Review (four or five issues and two conferences) and The Atlantic Monthly (January 2000). Articles have also appeared in several newspapers over the last decades.

and then made up his own mind.

Wayne, on his own, convinced a lot of people to have faith in the cave. If anything was going to happen, he would have to make it happen. I took up with Wayne and in the early days of his investigation I made two trips to Olney, Illinois.

I was there to meet the land owners and to watch the people he hired run some ground-penetrating radar equipment.

Year after year I watched him struggle to get in a cave he had decided was the right one. Russell fought him every step of the way (but from a distance). He told me several times that Wayne's cave is 41-2/10 miles from the real location. Harry Hubbard was putting his money at still another location.

While planning this book, I had always hoped that one of the final chapters could be about the opening of Burrows Cave. As the ending of the story came into sight, I decided to keep chapter eleven for that story. It would be the natural climax that was needed to settle all the questions.

Wayne has promised me that when he gained entrance he would call me. When and if that call came I would jump in my truck and head south just as soon as I was able. But as we all know, the best laid plans of mice and men can go wrong. Luckily I have had enough life experience to know there should always be a Plan "B."

My Plan B may turn out to be the best after all. In case everything in this story is ready to go and the cave is still not open, I would ask Wayne if he would write the story of his efforts. This, at least, gives the reader an accurate description of what has happened and where things stand now. Wayne said, in his usual upbeat attitude, he would be honored to do so.

As of this date, however, there has been one giant step taken by Frank Joseph, editor of the *Ancient American* magazine, that must be briefly told.

Over the years, scholars have been working with the tantalizing carvings and scripts on the Burrows Cave stones to see if they can detect just who these people were and how they fit our known history. How did this elaborate collection of strange and valuable artifacts come to be hidden in a cave in southern Illinois for possibly two millennia or more?

Several highly qualified historians (Dr. Warren Cook, Dr. Cyclone Covey, Dr. Joseph Mahan as well as some younger scholars) have been able to fit this episode into a blank spot in known, recorded history.

Wayne May's magazine has done more to advance the cause of pre-history than any periodical or institution in existence. His magazine has also been the focal point of all of the great research that is being done on the cave artifacts and a clear picture has finally begun to emerge.

Frank Joseph, as editor-in-chief of the magazine, has been privy to all the information on Burrows Cave.

To many with little background for such a story, it will be startling and difficult to believe, but the book he has written puts it all together: *The Lost Treasure of King Juba* (Bear & Company, Rochester, Vermont: 2003). The book gives the background of the people who are the cave's history.

Joseph's book follows in detail, commonly-accepted historical facts about ancient history over seas—history that can be found in any encyclopedia that he believes is linked to Burrows Cave.

His theory dates to thousands of years ago when Cleopatra Selene, daughter of Cleopatra the Great of Egypt, was the ruler of Mauritania (where Morocco and Libya are today in North Africa) with her husband, King Juba II. At that time, Mauritania was a province of Rome.

Caligula, the Roman emperor, was envious of King Juba's treasure and lured Juba's son Ptolemy to Rome under false pretenses and had him executed. This caused a revolt that eventually led to war. Caligula was after Juba's treasure and especially the famous library of Ptolemy.[107c] The library contained information about the American continent that had been passed down from their Phoenician ancestors for thousands of years.

With the help of the Senegalese people, Alexander Helios, the last of Cleopatra's children and twin brother of Cleopatra Selene, led a great fleet and sailed to America. Traveling up the Mississippi River to the Ohio and then the Wabash rivers, they landed in what is now Illinois on the banks of the Embarras (pronounced Aham-bar-ahs), a tributary of the Wabash, where they cut out their underground tombs in a natural limestone cave. The thousands of artifacts from the cave have now borne out this remarkable piece of history. While all of this could go the way of the Kensington Stone, Joel Kela's Stone or the Soper Tablets if left to the interpretation of the establishment, it all may hinge on the ability of someone besides Russell Burrows to finally gain entrance to the cave. Of course, there will still have to be the subsequent study of the artifacts, but once someone is in there it won't take long to know if the cave and its contents are authentic.

Now we can turn to Wayne's story of what has recently happened and where things stand now.

It appeared in Volume 9, Number 59 (October, 2004) in the *Ancient American* Magazine. The entire report is printed here with the permission of

---

[107c] This is the last Ptolemy, there were several. The first historic Ptolemy was a general in the army of Alexander the Great.

Mr. Wayne May and the *Ancient American* Magazine.

Tomb of the Embarras River, or Burrows Cave?

Twenty-four years ago, a subterranean collection of stones illustrated with human portraits and inscribed in several written languages from the ancient Old World was accidentally found in southern Illinois.[107d] Since their source was deliberately concealed in early 1989, attempts to relocate it are finally beginning to succeed, as described by <u>Ancient American</u> publisher, Wayne May. His report brings out readers and project investors up to date concerning the latest progress in accessing the Embarras River find. The painstaking work of discovery goes on there, as investigators are about to pin-point the underground location's lost entrance. Mr. May's article features exclusive photographs of artifacts removed from the so-called "Burrows Cave." They were purchased by <u>Ancient American</u> and <u>American Diffusion, Inc.</u> at the John A. Ward estate auction in Vincennes, Indiana. A special note of thanks to Tom Elkin of Vincennes, Indiana, for alerting <u>Ancient American</u> to the recent auction of John A. Ward's personal collection. Tom Elkin is Mr. Ward's grandson.

Editor

Ancient American and *Discovery Resources* have been funding a research and exploration project known as *Tombs of the Embarras River* for six summers. More recently, they formed an Illinois Corporation: *American Diffusion, Inc.* (A.D.I.). Investors have been acquired and exploration continues.

In *Ancient American's* previous issue, readers learned about the Vincennes, Indiana auction of the Jack Ward estate. *A.D.I.* and *Ancient American* purchased 90% of the artifacts which were displayed at the Sonoftobac Museum in Vincennes during the mid-1980s. Also obtained were Mr. Ward's personal files.

John Ward was a partner of Russell Burrows in their organization, *Archaeological Recovery Exchange,* "a parole agreed partnership of three members, Russell Burrows, of Olney, Illinois, Norman Cullen and John A. Ward, of Vincennes, Indiana which at some future date evolve(d) into a regularly constituted business for profit partnership" (*Papers of John*

[107d] The complete story of the discovery of the cave, with some variation, is told in *"The Mystery Cave of Many Faces"* by Russell Burrows and Fred Rydholm.

A. Ward). Ward explained the origins and purpose of forming such a partnership:

"Early in 1986, the above partners agreed to form a nucleus of an organization called ARE (Archaeological Recovery Exchange) for the express purpose of exploring certain areas for artifact material which may be marketable.

"In order to expedite this objective, it was determined by the three partners that to proceed with the exploration they needed some form of economic transportation to provide Burrows with transportation to and from the archaeological sites and conveyance of supplies and recovered artifacts. So, a used Datsun pickup was purchased and licensed in Illinois, and domiciled (sic) at Burrows' residence in Olney, Ill. The three partners each share in paying for the truck, which was financed at the American National Bank, Vincennes, Indiana. The obligation of truck payments to conclude in February 1987.

"After the truck was purchased, it was necessary to make certain repairs, and two of the partners shared the responsibility to pay for the repairs, understanding that the ultimate sharing of the cost would be bourn by the three partners.

"There are two archeological sites, at hand, to be worked. One being;

• **cave found by Burrows some 75 miles west of Vincennes.**
The other is:

• **site along the Ambraw River in Richland County, Ill.**
Each of these sites had the permission of the landowners to Russell Burrows by a parole agreement.

"Russell Burrows was to pursue obtaining a legal document, lease or deed to the cave property which is now in a Trust, or some form of a conveyance to the partnership for its development. A temporary lease was given to Burrows for interim working the cave site.

"In addition to the operation and maintenance of the truck, the partners also contributed to the expenses encountered by Burrows in the recovery of artifacts from the cave.

"Burrows had a contact in West Virginia who disclosed that similar findings had occurred there. Samples of the cave's artifacts were sent to Egypt, to the Department of Antiquities, who purported to have become very interested in that these things were a part of their lost history. A team came to West Virginia and requested that Mr. Burrows meet with them. The matter was brought before the three partners, and it was agreed to pay Burrows expenses to go and meet with this Egyptian team. Other

Russell E. Burrows (left) with Ancient American publisher, Wayne May, 24 March 1999, at what Mr. Burrows claimed was the entrance to his "Mystery Cave of Many Faces," in Richland County, Illinois. Following this declaration, Mr. May and fellow American Diffusion, Inc. researcher, Ralph Wolak, secured a signed agreement with the landowner on which the site is located for archaeological exploration and excavation. That same week, however, Mr. Burrows reversed his claim: The Richland County location was not his, his site is really forty miles away, but it is "a" site nonetheless. Thereafter, Ancient American and A.D.I. investigators examined the area in question with a broad array of ground penetration radar and supplementary electronic scanning technology. Results of these thorough sub-surface sweeps yielded sufficient evidence to show that an artificial complex of some kind was indeed present at the site. Since it is distinct from all previous claims, the location is not referred to as "Burrows Cave," but known as the "Tombs of the Embarras" (pronounced, "Ahmbrah"), after the nearby river. The area has been posted by the landowner, and security is in place. Exploration for the entrance is under way, as it has been for the last six summers. A certified archaeologist, geologist and anthropologist have been engaged to examine the site when its entrance is finally exposed.

than verbal confirmation as to what some of the artifacts were, the only result was that they were desirous to have the cave's location, so that they might confiscate it and return the artifacts to Egypt, or that we would pay them a fee of $135,000.00 for them to come and look at the artifacts that we had already recovered, which would not preclude them from trying to confiscate them.

"Circumstances necessitated that some authoritative person be allowed to visit the cave to confirm its existence and that it contained similar artifacts. To pursue this permission, the partnership sent Mr. Burrows to meet the land-owner, who, at this particular time, was at one of his industries in the vicinity of Detroit, Michigan. From this meeting, the land-owner took it upon himself to seek authoritative opinions, one being an anthropologist at Ann Arbor, MI. Subsequent contacts with the

Items from the cave.

land-owner, we are informed verbally, that the anthropologist visited the cave with the land-owner, and he would make a report to the land-owner. The anthropologist, through the land-owner, instructed Burrows to take a sample group to a friend of his who operated an analysis laboratory at Norman, Oklahoma, who would examine the specimens, and report back to the anthropologist in behalf of the land-owner. A third evaluation of similar research was also to be done by a researcher in Alexandria, Louisiana. The latter has not been done.

"The anxiety on the part of the partnership to establish full control of the cave and its contents resulted in Mr. Burrows having to meet the landowner and his attorney on several occasions in the St. Louis area. The time and place usually determined at the will of the land owner. At the times of these meetings, the partnership agreed to pay the traveling expenses for Mr. Burrows to attend." (*Papers of John A. Ward* now owned by *Ancient American*}.

In the foregoing excerpt from his personal papers, John Ward writes of not one, but *two* underground locations in Illinois: one in Marion County and another in Richland County on the "Ambraw" River (Embarras River). In his book, *The Mystery Cave of Many faces,* Russell Burrows states that he made his discovery in Marion County. Taking him at his word, independent investigator, Harry Hubbard (Melbourne, FL), spent several hundred thousand dollars in a fruitless search for the site. Six years ago, Mr. Burrows pointed out a location in Richland County by saying, *"this is the cave."* John Ward's papers indicate that the site may indeed have been found in Richland County.

'Also found among Ward's papers were two maps of the cave site matching the map published in *The Mystery Cave of Many Faces.* They differ in that the Ward map reveals more precise size/distance measurements. More importantly, it shows what appears to be the famous "hole" into which Mr. Burrows claims to have fallen. The maps, dated 1984 and 1987, and are reproduced on the next page. They do indeed seem to indicate Burrows Cave. Of course, final verification will not be possible until the tunnel system is actually entered. But our investigations have

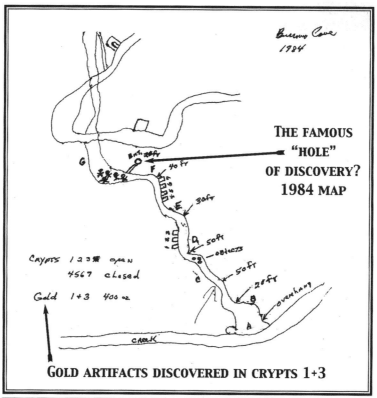

THE FAMOUS "HOLE" OF DISCOVERY? 1984 MAP

GOLD ARTIFACTS DISCOVERED IN CRYPTS 1+3

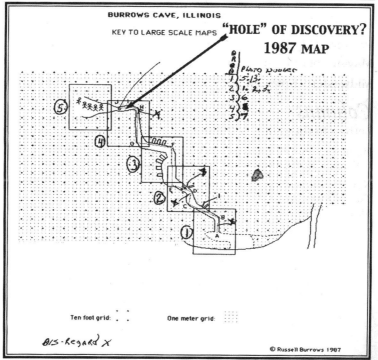

449

shown that Burrows' entry was not made at the creek near the overhang, as described in his book.

In 1989-90, he published and distributed a pamphlet before his co-authored book with Fred Rydholm. Entitled *The Discovery of Burrows Cave,* it describes how Russell crawled through the subterranean entrance before finding five large statues, followed by a dozen portals:

"...I again find myself nose to nose and eyeball to eyeball with another figure. This one however, is black and very well executed. Here I am, looking at this fellow and trying to decide whether or not to make a new entrance when I see four more of these handsome fellows in a half-circle. After getting my heart rate back down to about twice normal, I am at last conscious of the fact that I have found something that should not be there. I can see that these statues are not Amerindian; rather, they have a totally different look about them, maybe Egyptian...these fellows are in excess of eight feet tall.

"I now begin to look closely along the walls of the cave, and in so doing, I locate yet another portal which is also sealed with cut and fitted blocks of stone. I have found twelve of these to date. Being rather nosy, I have to find out what is behind these portals, and so I begin to work toward removing one of the blocks. After doing this and shining a light into the area behind the seals, I find myself looking at a full skeleton. As the blocks of stone are large, I have no trouble getting through the opening."
The Discovery of Burrows Cave, pages 10-12.

In his *The Mystery Cave of Many Faces,* however, he claims (pages 36 through 49) to have entered under the overhang, discovered all twelve portals, and then found the statues, everything being in reverse from the booklet story of two years earlier. While his word-portrait of the pit with a stone face and fitted blocks of stone might be accurate, they could not have occurred under the overhang near the creek bed, as described.

Burrows' discovery of the "hole" is presented in the private papers of John Ward:

"It was on such an occasion while walking along a bluff wall in a very remote area, that he fell into a hole up to his chest.

"Stunned by the fall, (his) first thought was to get out of the hole. While still in the hole, he noticed that he was standing on several stones which appeared to be hand-fitted together. After cleaning out the debris of the forest that was in the hole, he could see that the stones hade been deliberately arranged.

"This intrigued him, and the next day he brought a relative to help him, and after a full day's work they found that (a) particular stone, if removed, would unlock the others. When they had all of the stones removed from the pit, they could see that they covered an entrance to a cave.

"Crawling in with a flashlight into a room filled with silt which had washed into the cave, left only about three feet of crawl space. Not far into the cave, they found several artifacts of rough black spear-points and odd shaped stones with faces carved on them."

Here is a very different version of the actual discovery. Which one is correct? In view of the evidence, Mr. Ward's version appears to be the more reliable account. Burrows deliberately disseminated misinformation via false maps, as placed with Dr. Joseph Mahan (Columbus, Georgia), and Thelma and Sherman McClain (Olney, Illinois). These were supplemented by photos and data at the Marion County site, as published in *The Mystery Cave of Many Faces,* to screen all his moves at the Embarras site.

It seems certain that Burrows first entry into the cave was made at the "hole" of discovery, and that he worked down that passage toward the original door made by the ancient builders. The 1987 map shows by a dotted line his direction of movement down the tunnel toward the creek bed and overhang, but an exit or entry was never made at this opening.

Here we were instructed by Burrows to dig in 1999. At the time, he knew that this part of the tunnel was closed long ago by its builders. We did excavate to a depth of forty-four feet, but stopped after we could not find any disturbed rock or dirt. The builders had cut the rock face overhang causing it to drop on top of the entrance, sealing it under several tons of solid rock.

The gold artifacts shown on page 447 are replicas from the Ward collection. He was careful enough to reproduce the metal artifacts for future study and recorded the actual pieces which have since become lost. It is generally believed that the original gold artifacts were melted down and sold for their bullion value.

The following page reproduces a March, 1989 letter from the A.R.E. to Frank McClosky, asking the Illinois congressman for help in selling gold to the United States government.

American Diffusion Inc. will remain at the Embarras site until its investigators gain entrance to the underground site. We do have a signed

FRANK McCLOSKEY
8TH DISTRICT, INDIANA

100TH CONGRESS

ARMED SERVICES COMMITTEE
SUBCOMMITTEES:
RESEARCH AND DEVELOPMENT
INVESTIGATIONS

POST OFFICE AND CIVIL SERVICE
COMMITTEE
SUBCOMMITTEES:
CHAIRMAN, POSTAL PERSONNEL
AND MODERNIZATION
HUMAN RESOURCES

WASHINGTON OFFICE
127 CANNON BUILDING,
WASHINGTON, DC 20515
202-225-4636

DISTRICT OFFICES
501 S. MADISON
BLOOMINGTON IN 47401
812-334-1111

FEDERAL BUILDING, ROOM 12
101 N.W. SEVENTH STREET
EVANSVILLE, IN 47708
812-465-6484

10 N.E 4TH STREET
WASHINGTON, IN 47501
812-254-6646

Congress of the United States
House of Representatives
Washington, DC 20515
March 31, 1989

Mr. John A. Ward
Archaeological Recovery Exchange
819 N. Fourth Street
Vincennes, IN 47591

Dear Mr. Ward:

   Thank you for contacting my office concerning your questions about gold.

   My office has been in contact with the U.S. Department of the Treasury concerning your questions. In regards to your questions, Mr. Michael Iacangelo, contracting officer, Fort Knox, KY is only a storage place for gold. The U.S. Mint in Washington, D.C. buys gold directly. Correspondence is used to form a relationship between the two parties involved. A great deal of information is needed to actually sell the gold, according to Mr. Iacangelo.

   For further information about the possible sale, please contact : Mr. Michael Iacangelo, Contracting Officer, U.S. Mint, 633 Third St., N.W., Washington, D.C. 20220.

   Again, thank you for contacting my office. If I can be of further assistance, please do not hesitate to contact me.

         Sincerely,

         Frank McCloskey
         Member of Congress

FM:rgc

agreement with the landowner. He is fully aware of our intentions, and is kept abreast of all exploratory work carried out at his property.

A university-trained, state-certified archaeologist is on call, ready to travel to the Olney area, as soon as our excavations have opened the tunnel system. This part of our search is considered exploratory and not in violation of an archaeological laws in the State of Illinois. If, in the course of our investigations, any human remains are uncovered, the A.D.I. will comply with all state regulations under the professional guidance of our appointed archaeologist.

As publisher of *Ancient American*, I would like to thank the many readers who have phoned in to offer their voluntary assistance with all kinds to help in this venture. We are not in a position, as yet, to

Hypothetical burial scene inside Burrows Cave, based on the finder's testimony and artifacts removed from the site. Original painting by the late Charles Platt (Columbus, Ohio), republished from Ancient American, The Face of Asia in Prehistoric America, Volume 1, Issue number 4, page 40.

take advantage of their generosity, which would require a great deal of physical labor, but sincerely appreciate their voluntary spirit.

Trusting in the accuracy of Burrows' 1984 map, we hope to discover the "hole" into which he fell, and make our own entrance, as he did with the assistance of his relative. If the entrance is plugged or collapsed, it may still give us the proper angle to drill a new tunnel at the opening. If the entrance continues to elude us, we have the landowner's permission to lay open a trench by surface excavation, which, unfortunately, could destroy a portion of the tunnel system with its artifacts. This is our last resort if entry cannot be obtained by any other way. It is our intention to thoroughly begin a new search in the area indicated by the 1984 map from John Ward's papers which hopefully will open a new chapter and possibly final of discovery at the Tomb of the Embarras River.

As you can see, there is still a lot of confusion and a lot of unanswered questions concerning Burrows Cave. And we can't blame anyone in their right mind for taking the whole story with a grain of salt, or at least not swallowing it hook, line and sinker. And now to add to this dilemma, I have to give a whole new twist-Russell's story of what has transpired recently.

In a recent talk with Russell (January 2005), he told me that two years ago he turned the cave over to an anthropologist from Michigan-the same one who entered the cave previously with the landowner. The man, says Russell, is employed by a university (not identified and no name). The anthropologist has been working in the cave continuously for over a year and had sent Russell a lot of artifacts, which he returned.

Russell also stated "just as soon as this weather gets a little better, he will take me to the cave." This has been a longstanding promise and I just don't know what to think-but as usual, we just have to wait and see. I have lived with the story of the cave for over twenty years now and it is not easy to forget.

The following are some additional pictures of cave artifacts.

For more pictures of the Cave Stones see "Rock Art Pieces of Burrows Cave" by Jim Scherz and Russel Burrows and "Mystery Cave of Many Faces" by Burrows and Rydholm

Burrows Cave Artifacts

Cartouche similarities recognized by Virginia Hourigan. Left - A cartouche of Merneptah on a sword from Ugarit. Note the similarities between it and the artifact from Burrows' Cave on the right.

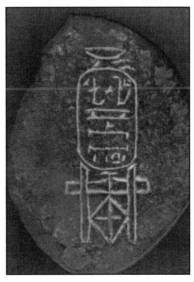

455

The following chapter is what this author believes to be a far more accurate and complete picture of events in earlier World History than is being taught today. Of course there will be many revisions and additions in years to come, but this should change the minds of many and present a much clearer picture of ancient history.

Chapter XII
A Thumbnail Sketch of Early History

and a Copper Trade
A General Assumption

If humans originated in East Africa some time over a million years ago, it seems unlikely that it took them 750,000 years to reach America. Dr. George Carter says man was living in Greece by 1,000,000 years ago.[108]

However, if the earliest date that we can find evidence of man in the Western Hemisphere is 250,000 years,[109] then we can rest with that for now. In my opinion, since scientists have only had the wherewithal to date these early sites for the last fifty years with the greatest advances only in the last 30 years, it seems that as time goes on earlier sites may turn up or at least a much clearer picture will develop. As we have seen, these early dates have not been officially accepted, but as more are discovered, they will be. There are other early sites that have not been discussed in these writings, such as the 200,000-year-old date for the Calico site in the Mojave Desert, the Folsom points found in Sandia Cave, New Mexico dated at 250,000 years and the great enigma of the handmade mortar and pestle and other tools and implements made by human hands that have been found imbedded in ancient rock formations at Table Mountain, Tuolumne County, California. I'm sure there are others I haven't heard about. It seems that several civilizations may have risen and fallen before us.[110]

In the million years that man has been in existence, the earth has gone through so many surface changes, so much plastic bulging, some violent and some that took hundreds of thousands of years, that we just don't know how many islands have disappeared, how many land bridges have come and gone or where they all were. Over time we may be very surprised at what we may discover. There are new ones coming under suspicion all the time. Much of the ocean floor, or at least most of the continental shelves, were above sea level at one time and likewise much of our present land surface was under water.

Then there are the constant movements and migrations of humanity, both

---

[108] Personal letter to the author April 4, 1983 from Dr. George Carter.

[109] Hueyataca Site in Mexico (Male, Steen-McIntyre and Fryxell).

[110] Many other early sites are mentioned in Cremo & Thompson's *Forbidden Archaeology* and John Henderson says, "I firmly believe man is much older than 1,000,000 years. There have been many races here that have evolved, disappeared, and others were put down here to evolve as well. (Expressed in a recent letter to the author.)

Dr. Jim Scherz, Dr. Gunnar Thompson and Wayne May at conference in Utah

by land and water.

Probably the most remarkable book I have read pertaining to these early movements of human migration is *American Discovery* by Dr. Gunnar Thompson (Argonauts Misty Isles Press, Seattle, Washington, 1992). The book (about 400 pages) is profusely illustrated with many of the ancient types of watercraft and drawings of hundreds of artifacts found in various parts of the world that prove where people have come from or traded with.

I recall in a World History class in high school being told that ships plied the ocean waters for 10,000 years. This was a bold and unbelievable statement then (1930s). Later I read it was 40,000 years, then 70,000. But quoting an early paragraph from the prologue of Dr. Thompson's *American Discovery*:

> From the beginning of human migration and exploration, watercraft provided our ancestors with the means of crossing rivers and seas. The earliest evidence of maritime travel comes from Southeast Asia where natives called 'Australoids' crossed the sea between Southeast Asia and New Guinea about 100,000 years ago. At that time, the combined territories of Australia and New Guinea were separated from the mainland by more than 90 miles of open seas.[111] Using primitive Stone Age tools, the Australoids constructed rafts which they sailed or paddled toward distant islands off the New Guinea coast. As far as we know, the Australoids were the first ocean sailors.

Over the centuries different populations used bamboo rafts, reed boats, skin boats, and dugout canoes with woven reed sails, later hide, bark fiber sails, and finally plank ships. Thompson believes that Asians were the first people to reach America on foot from Siberia over the land bridge to Alaska, but beyond that the

---

[111] Davies 1986, pg. 31—Lists many references where people have rowed distances up to 9,000 miles between 1969 and 1991, plus numerous single person yacht crossings. Today, even families sail around the world in small boats for adventure.

vast majority of the migrations were by water. Yes, there were many people in the Americas before and during the many natural disasters, the earthquakes and the floods.

After the Flood

Almost yearly new discoveries are being made that answer questions that have plagued us for years. Many books written in the 1960s and 1970s are no longer relevant. Some of these questions were: What happened to Neanderthal man? Why did he go extinct? Did he mix with Cro-Magnon man?

In 1856, the first remains of Neanderthal man were found in the Neander River in Germany. About 28,000 to 20,000 years ago, both Neanderthal and Cro-Magnon man were living together in Europe. They were found together in caves on Mt. Carmel dated 30,000 B.C. ...this is documented in several sources.

In 1998, a child skeleton with human and Neanderthal genes was found near Logar Velho, Portugal. Anthropologist Erik Trinhaus of Washington University said the 24,500 year old bones prove conclusively that this is clear evidence of mixture. This had been suspected by a few scientists earlier, but this is the first proof. The Neanderthal disappeared from the earth about 20,000 years ago.

Then there was the great Biblical flood or possibly several floods. This flood has been referred to time and again in the histories of ancient people.

We know very little of the people who lived before the flood, but we do get quick glimpses of them in the writings of Plato who tells us of the civilization of Atlantis that was supposed to have existed about 12,000 years ago. These stories were also reported on 4,000-year-old Egyptian scrolls. The story of Atlantis has been debunked by many modern scholars, but as we have seen, so has nearly every other story of discovery that has come up over time, but there seems to be too many plausible facts, findings and global connections to just ignore these stories completely. (See *Atlantis—The Antediluvian World* by Ignatius Donnelly, Dover Publications, Inc., New York, 1976—originally published by Harper and Brothers, New York, 1882 or write to William Donato, President of the Atlantis organization—Buena Park, California.) [111a]

But there are indications everywhere that there was flooding of colossal proportions in which people, in some cases whole populations, must have been wiped out as a result of this natural catastrophe. There was also violent volcanic action, tidal waves of monstrous proportions and darkness.

It was during or because of this flooding that many people took to the seas. Many were looking for new lands that had not been destroyed and others who had survived by taking refuge on higher ground, and who eventually set out,

---

[111a] William Michael Donato - 6599 Via Grandso Circle, Buana Park, California 90620

as soon as ships could be built, to find new places to live. It was these roving sailors who realized for the first time the vastness of the earth, the variations of the climate and the sources of many different foods, furs, forests, metals, ivory and other useful materials. These were the mysterious people who have come to be known as the first "Sea People."[112] They traveled the oceans wherever the wind and currents took them. Their ships were their homes. Some settled on the first habitable land they found, while others went on to explore the earth. It was these people who inhabited the far-off islands of the great oceans and it was their descendants who spread to other islands and continents. As they adapted to new climates, new foods and new environments, their physical characteristics changed over the years, as did their language, which although different, still clung to its ancient roots. This became one scientific way to trace their origin; another was their method of writing. Each of these societies also developed some form of religion, some belief in a higher power.[113]

While some societies did not change rapidly, there were a few early civilizations that began to emerge, such as that of the Indus Valley in India, the valley of the Tigris and Euphrates in Persia, then known as Mesopotamia (modern Iraq), the Valley of the Nile in Egypt, Coral on the Sope River on the coast of Peru, and others, such as the Island of Sri Lanka.

All of these early advanced civilizations had some things in common. They were all in fertile valleys or on rivers where there could be irrigation. Their rapid advancements were due to the ability to grow food and other useful crops, and have access to the sea for trade and travel. This type of activity required communication and navigation skills. They developed first an appreciation for and then a demand for art, science, labor-saving utilities and technical skills. They all built megalithic structures, pyramids and temples.[114]

The ancient Paleolithic[115] people of the Great Lakes region, that have already been described at Sheguiandak on Manitoulin Island, Canada (in northern Lake Huron) according to Thomas E. Lee, former anthropologist at the National Museum of Canada, may go back 20,000 or 30,000 years or more. Several geologists and Lee himself have stood by an even earlier date,

---

[112] Sea People—There are other explanations as to who the Sea People are; this is mine. These are not to be confused with the people of the sea who contended with Egypt during the Bronze Age as evidenced on Egyptian based beliefs.

[113] A recent *Time* magazine (Oct. 25, 2004) featured an article that scientists have discovered that some people carry a gene for religion—they call it the "God gene."

[114] See *Voyage of the Pyramid Builders* by Robert M. Schoch, Ph.D.—2003, Penguin Putnam Inc., New York. Note to author from Dr. John White: Fred, did you know there are four pyramids in France?

[115] Paleolithic—earliest period of the Stone Age.

Photos courtesy of Jim Paquette

Left: Photo was taken by Jim's wife Karen Paquette in July of 2002 while they were visiting an ancient Marquette County archaeological site.

The morning of March 22, 1987 at the newly discovered Gorto Site on Deer Lake, Ishpeming. John and Jim Paquette at the exact spot where the day before, on March 21, we together discovered the incredible cache of 10,000-year-old Paleo Indian projectile points. For more information see the book "The Find of a Thousand Lifetimes: The Story of the Gorto Site Discovery"

Photo by Bob Paquette

up to 70,000 years. But in the Lake Superior region, it took the keen eye of an amateur archaeologist, Jim Paquette of Negaunee, Michigan, to find similar stone artifacts on the south shore of Lake Superior. Although the official date for the beginning of copper digging in the Copper Country is about 6000 B.C., Paquette's discoveries could push that date back another two or three thousand years. Paquette just locates the stone and copper artifacts, but he leaves the aging of them up to the professionals, thus they have settled on a date of about 8000 B.C. or 10,000 years ago. Jim Paquette has discovered any number of copper tools that go back to this period.

And further west, but still nearby in Minnesota, we have the "Brown Valley Man."

In 1933, William H. Jensen, an amateur archaeologist, uncovered a broken skeleton of a man in a gravel pit. It had been on a plateau, formerly an island in the ancient river Warren, an outlet of Glacial Lake Agassiz. In 1987, carbon

Note: Jim Paquette is actually one of a team - in his book "The Find of A thousand Lifetimes" he gives full credit to his partner John Gorto and three professional archeologists. Dr. Marla Buckmaster, John Anderton, and John Franzen.

dating revealed the skeleton is 9,000 years old, one of the earliest found in the New World. He is known as "Brown Valley Man."

According to Dr. Barry Fell, there were trans-Atlantic crossings as early as 7,000 years ago. These crossings were made by the Maritime Archaic Red-Paint Cultures of western Scandinavia and northwestern Europe. The archaeological remains of these people, carbon-dated in Norway to 5500 B.C., are very similar to those of the Maritime Archaic Red-Paint People of Labrador and New England, carbon-dated back to 5000 B.C. Fell says on both sides of the North Atlantic these people operated sea-going wooden vessels and used similar fishing devices for hunting swordfish and marine mammals.

The Ice Man

One might imagine what went through my mind when I read in 1991 of the discovery of a body, found in the Swiss Alps (Tyrolean Alps or in the Similaun Glacier), that had been frozen for 5,500 years. This was the first report, later they decided it was 5,300 years. Also the first report said he was carrying a bronze axe. I thought to myself, they had moved the Bronze Age in Europe back 500 years. Later reports said it was a copper axe, and this axe is almost identical to

Copper Arrowhead, knife and axe collections like these are common among residents in the Copper Country.

several copper axes of about the same age that were found near the mouth of the Carp River here in Marquette. Knowing of the several possibilities of how the axe could have gotten to Europe from here through trade, I waited anxiously for years to find out if they ever discovered whether or not it could have been Michigan copper. I never heard.

But it seemed strange to me that certain things surprised the scientists. People had survived in the northern climes for thousands of years by that time, yet the scientists thought it quite remarkable that he carried a long strong bow and that the arrows were so well made with the feathers at a slight angle to give them a spiral movement in flight. There have been several types of copper arrowheads found in the Copper Country that are much older, all of which would have been useless if the arrow didn't spin. Without this spin, an arrow has no accuracy. The scientists marveled at his stone knife and flint scrapers, his needle-like awl, all of which were in common usage for thousands of years previous. The first reports said he had stuffed hay in his shoes to keep his feet warm. When we were in Finnmark (Lapland) there was always a beautifully large, neatly twisted rope of hay hanging in the bedrooms. For thousands of years it has been standard practice to stuff this hay in your boots in the winter; some still do it today. We could go on, but this man was equipped the same as those counterparts living in America at the same period, right down to the backpack, deerskin tunic, birch bark canisters, quiver, leather pouch and grass-spun cordage. Later some more copper axe heads were found near where the Ice Man was found. If we had a melting glacier here, the same type of man could have been found here. In fact, there have been much older bodies found in America, but they were not preserved. The Ice Man is the oldest preserved human body ever found, and this is because it was frozen.

Spirit Cave Man

Discover Magazine, February 1999, front cover, "Europeans Invade America 20,000 B.C.," author Karen Wright. "Not long ago we thought the first humans in the New World were mammoth hunters from Siberia who crossed the Bering Strait at the end of the Ice Age. Now we are learning none of that may be true—not the who, not the where, not the how, and certainly not the when."

Doug Owsley: (Physical anthropologist at the National Museum of Natural History in Washington, D.C.) "When you think of this time period, you imagine those people running around chasing big game." But for Spirit Cave Man—no—not the skins, not the spears and not the Siberian looks. "He wore a carefully constructed blanket woven from thin, twisted strips of rabbit pelt and cords of hemp." He had been eating fish, not game; apparently he gleaned his meals from netting fish in the marshes that once filled the desert basins rather than going on grueling hunts on the plains."

In fact, in recent analyses of some ten early American skulls, anthropologists have found just two individuals who could pass as kin of either contemporary northern Asians or Native Americans.

Monte Verde

There is a site in south central Chile known as Monte Verde. It was excavated by Tom Dillehoy of the University of Kentucky at Lexington.

Hundreds of stone tools and artifacts of bone, wood and ivory, as well as caches of leaves, seeds, nuts and fruits were found. There was also evidence of crayfish, birds, an extinct camel and a mastodon. There were hearths and huts and a child's footprint.

The problem with the discovery was, what was evidence of man 12,500 years ago doing in Chile, 10,000 miles south of the Bering Strait? Many scientists had considered the Clovis point people as the first to enter America about ten or twelve thousand years ago.

Theodore Schorr, a molecular anthropologist at Emory University in Atlanta, Georgia, says these people may be 20,000 to 40,000 years from their Old World relatives.

Then a second excavation at Monte Verde on a promontory overlooking what used to be a lagoon about 200 feet from the 12,500 year old village was a site dated at a very cautious 30,000 years.

But these aren't the only sites that are older than Clovis. There is the Meadowcraft Rock shelter in Pennsylvania said to be 17,000 years old (James Adovasia of Mercyhurst College in Erie, Pennsylvania), the Penago Cave, 30,000 years old (Richard MacNeish, Andover, Mass) and in the mid-1980s a French-Brazilian archaeologist, Niede Guidon discovered a cave painting at Pedra Furadu, Brazil that was 17,000 years old and tools that were 32,000 years old.

Author Karen Wright states: "Like Spirit Cave Man, the early Americans suggested by these sites are forcing experts to revise their model of the spear-chucking Clovis-type of textbook lore. The possibility of maritime immigration is also turning the model for New World settlement upside down." Anyone who could paddle a boat could go anywhere.

Clovis points were thought to be a New World invention from the southwestern United States, but some unusual points turned up 50 miles south of Richmond, Virginia that were dated at 5,000 years old., precursors of Clovis. They looked like Old World spear points from Spain. They look like the points crafted by people called Solureans from western Europe 24,000 to 165,000 years ago. There are other similarities between the Solurean and Clovis cultures. One scientist stated, "Never once thought of them crossing the ocean, but that would explain Madam X in the gene pool."

It was also in Chile that archaeologists unearthed a city over 4,600 years old. They call it Coral. It had six pyramids around a massive central plaza and a huge dominating stepped pyramid. It grew as a trade center for people living many miles away. Work continues at this site and we will be reading much more about it in years to come.

In the *Columbus Dispatch* of October 12, 2004, the section on science featured a full-page story entitled *Bone of Contention.*

It told of a discovery by a teacher of anthropology and paleontology, Federico Solórzano, 83, who has taught at the University of Guadalajara for generations.

In his collection of bones he has made over many years, mostly from the shores of Mexico's largest lake (Chapala lakebed) when drought exposed a large ring around it from 1947 to 1956, there were some human bones. One, especially, was a mineral-darkened piece of a brow-ridge bone and a bit of a jawbone that didn't match any modern skull. But they did match perfectly when placed beside a model of the Old World's Tautavel man—a member of the species, Homo erectus, who some believe is an ancestor of modern man. There has never been any trace of homo erectus ever before found in the Americas and he is believed to have died about 100,000 to 200,000 years ago. So much for the arrival of humans in the western hemisphere in the last 20 or 30 thousand years.

There have also been the skulls of 12 long-extinct horses found in the area, all of which have been smashed between the eyes. The scientists believe they must have been killed by humans. It is estimated that the horses lived 10,000 to 20,000 years ago. Another find in the area was a cache of swamp deer teeth, several of which were grooved, apparently for use in a necklace. Carbon dating showed these to be roughly 20,000 years old.

Obviously these finds will draw several studies to this area and it will be some time before any solid scientific conclusions will be forthcoming, but again it goes against our accepted theories of human history in the Americas.

This same article mentions a possible hand scraper (splotched with blood) more than 34,000 years ago at Monte Verde, Chile, some possible stone tools in Brazil that are 40,000 to 50,000 years old, and a report of human remains found near Puebla in central Mexico dating 28,000 years ago.

There is also the claim of 250,000 year old human tools found near the Valsequillo reservoir in Mexico which the article says were laughed at in the 1970s, but researchers are working there again today. These early dates are becoming more common and some scientists are beginning to take them seriously.

Stone Circle discovered many years ago on the Sillustani Peninsula near Umaygo Peru, reminds us of Stonehedge.

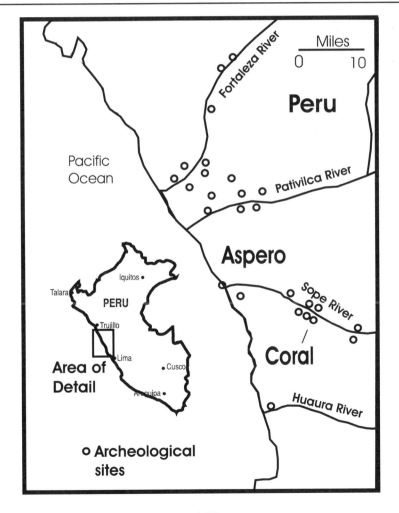

It is becoming obvious that archaeology is still in it's primitive stages in the Americas, We have much to learn.

Other Ancient Bodies in America

There were the remains of a human, a woman, found buried in Colorado, estimated to be 9,000 years old. Also in Colorado, 10,000 feet high in a mountain cave, amateur cave explorers found the skeleton of a man who died 8,000 years ago (San Jose Mercury News, National, Sunday, October 3, 1993). Anthropologists estimated his age at about 35 to 40 years and his height at about 5 feet, 5 inches tall. He had to have been well equipped to live there. Two interesting quotes from the article by John Noble Wilford: (Patty Jo Watson, an anthropologist at Washington University in St. Louis) "Watson said it took special clothing and skills to hunt at such altitudes. Once again we are realizing that ancient people were a lot smarter and stronger than many people previously thought." And: "The cave skeleton is thought to be twice as old as most Egyptian mummies and almost twice as old as the frozen corpse known as the 'Ice Man' found in 1991 at an altitude of 10,500 feet in the Tyrolean Alps at the Austrian-Italian border." The article also said: "Some researchers suggest, however, that the Ice Man is a hoax." These had to be real scientists.

Kennewick Man

In July of 1996 in the eroding bank of the Columbia River, near the town of Kennewick in southeastern Washington, some human bones were reported. There was a skull and a hip bone that were most important but several other bones of the same man were also found in the river.

Dr. Jim Chatters examined the bones and had decided they belonged to a European, probably an early settler of one or two hundred years ago. The features of the skull were definitely that of a European. However, with the cleaning and close examination of the hip, Dr. Chatters discovered a stone spear point of a very primitive kind imbedded in it. There was also evidence of many broken bones and presumably much suffering. It was estimated that the man would have been about 5 feet, 9 inches tall and in his 40s.

The prehistoric spear point raised some perplexing questions to the scientists so against the wishes of the local Indians, who claimed all ancient bones from that area belonged to their ancestors and insisted they should be reburied.

Because the skeleton raised such burning questions, the bones were sent to California specialized technologists such as Kate McMillian and David Glen Smith, who performed further tests. The carbon-dating proved that the bones were 9,000 years old, a date that was unbelievable to all the scientists. They are still talking about Indians as if they are one people and can't seem to bring themselves to believe that people of all types have been migrating around this world for many thousands of years. But they sit up and take notice when a scotch plaid is found on a red-headed mummy in a grave on the Gobi Desert or they hang their hat on a single dyed thread of European wool found among the Inuits in the Arctic, but ignore the many Norse artifacts found in Minnesota.

Minoan Crete

As the more advanced early civilizations of the eastern Mediterranean began to emerge, there was on one of the Greek islands a seafaring society, that because of their long experience in the sea trade took on a leadership role there. This island state had been developing for a thousand years on the island now known as Crete. Excavations there, some of the oldest in the world, have uncovered extensive remains of elaborate palaces. Archaeologists have established that about 5,000 years ago a highly developed civilization was building on that island, which became known as the Minoans. The name came from the legendary King Minos.[116] By 2900 B.C. (4900 years ago), the Minoans were the first to dominate the trade routes of the world. They developed their own written language now known as Linear A and Linear B.

Probably because of their trade with India, the Minoans were the first to introduce bronze to the Mediterranean world and, of course, were seeking sources of copper.[116a] The alloy, bronze (90% copper, 10% tin), a much harder and stronger metal than copper, soon became in great demand.

The copper mines of Cyprus were the earliest in that region but there were others, such as Ireland, Sinai Peninsula, Turkey, Danube Valley, etc. These

---

[116] In Greek legend, Minos was a king of Crete who kept a monster called the Minotaur—half human, half bull—in a labyrinth in his palace. The Minotaur was the offspring of the King's wife, Pasiphae, as a result of her mating with a white bull sent to her by the god Poseidon, a form of revenge on her family. King Minos spent the last years of his reign living at the center of his labyrinth with Pasiphae and her strange love-child.

Archaeologist Arthur Evans, digging into an ancient mound at Kephala (Knossos) discovered the remains of a palace far older than those of the Mycenaens (civilization which preceded the Greeks, 1900 BC-1100 BC).

Beautiful frescoes, a throne and massive granary containing enormous storage jars indicates that the palace had belonged to a wealthy ruler of a highly developed civilization. Evans named this civilization Minoan after King Minos.

[116a] In a private letter from Dr. Fell to this author he had a note in the margin stating that bronze was apparently produced in india 1000 years before it reached Europe.

were mostly low grade ores, and the Minoans must have found it to their great advantage to follow their ancient explorations to the one place on this earth where copper was pure, plentiful and in the free state.

There are several irrefutable proofs that the Minoans came to Lake Superior. Probably the most convincing are the clay statues and clay tablet found north of Newberry in Michigan's Upper Peninsula. The Minoan traders of 2800 B.C. most likely went into Lake Superior by way of the Mississippi River as the ancient maps of even 2,000 years ago show it draining from the west end of Lake Superior and also from the south end of Lake Michigan, or they might have came through Lake Nipegon via Hudson Bay.

Since the Cypriot-Minoan script and telltale clay statues were found north of Newberry, just east of another important drainage system between Lakes Superior and Michigan at Au Train, it is likely that at least during some period they may have taken the route through Lake Michigan and into Lake Superior, or more likely exited that way.

Dr. Fell identified and translated the Newberry Tablet. He says it is a variant of the well-known Cypro-Minoan script. comprised an omen's text similar to that of the Phaistos Disk.[117] The language comprising the text is a form of Minoan, having a vocabulary similar to that of Hittite. The vocabulary of this American omen's text from Michigan invites comparison with that of the Cherokee language and the Linear A tablets of Crete, and the Phaistos Disk. It compares with other known Cypro-Minoan syllabaries.

From that very part of the world comes the early beginnings of art and

---

[117] The disk was discovered by Italian archaeologist Luigi Pernier while digging in the magnificent Minoan city-palace called Phaistos. Besides many archaeological treasures, thousands of clay tablets are inscribed with unreadable scripts of the Minoans, which they labeled Linear A and Linear B. The disk was special because it had been ceramically fired, the only one among thousands of tablets that had been accidentally baked in fires that ravaged the temple. Finally in 1953 an amateur British philologist, Michael Ventris, was able to translate Linear B characters.

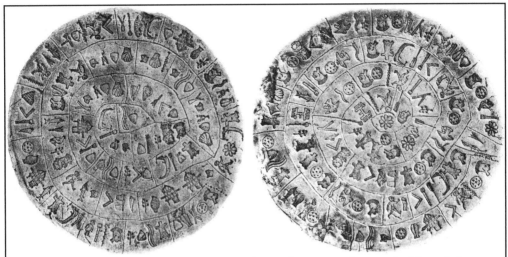

This disk was slightly more than six inches in diameter and covered with symbols on both faces. Altogether 45 different symbols are used to make 241 separate impressions. These symbols are clustered in groups of two or more into 61 compartments, 30 on one face of the disk and 31 on the other. The compartments are along a spiral that coils into the center of the disk.

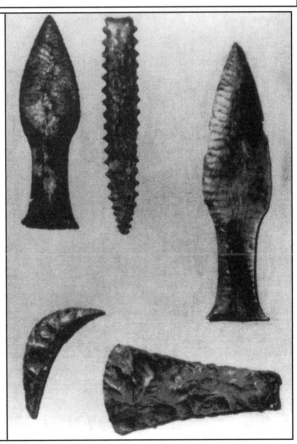

Stone Points - stone saw, axe and sickle.
North German flint implements from circa 2000 B.C. Skillfully worked Neolithic tools. Probably produced at a manufacturing center as trade items.

From "Conquest by Man" Harper 1954 - page 8.

sculpture, democracy, music, astronomy, mathematics, architecture and even the kilt. We have already discussed the many clay statues and tablets excavated on Crete.

The Minoans established the copper brokerage on Cyprus. They founded the cities of Chytri, Lapethus, Golgi and Athienon all on that island. But there were other stepping stones in the Mediterranean on the route to Spain where they obtained silver and copper. But they had also gone to the Azores and the Canarys in the Atlantic and to some far off secret, unbelievable source of copper and to the British Isles for tin. Another lesser source of tin was the Iberian Peninsula.

There are three possibilities for a Minoan water route to Lake Superior and they must have known all three. They could have come from Hudson's Bay, the St. Lawrence River or the Mississippi.

The shortest would have been Hudson's Bay, Lake Nipigon and directly to Isle Royale. [118a] The Mississippi via the west end of Superior would be the best route to the Keweenaw. In either case, they would have found the huge chunks of copper on the surface, undisturbed by the local inhabitants who were only interested in smaller pieces. At either location they would have been safely docked at the water's edge in the mouths of rivers, McCargo Cove or the Keweenaw waterway. They would have lived on their ship and needed no camp site. By 3000 B.C., they had bronze saws and all the world's major civilizations had plank-built boats capable of sailing to America (Thompson *American Discovery*). By building fires around the large pieces of copper, it could be softened enough to cut with a bronze saw,[118] and pieces of a few hundred pounds could easily be loaded aboard their vessels to be taken to the metal works on Cyprus to be cast into oxhides for sale or trade items in the Mediterranean ports. A small fleet of ships could handle a tremendous load of copper. The Minoans were fishermen and Superior was teeming with fish; there was no food shortage.

The Evidence: The Newberry Tablet and statues now have a positive identification. The script is Cypriot-Minoan, a form of Linear A and has been translated.

There is a bronze axe from Thunder Bay that very well could go back to that era.

In the May-June 1972 issue of the Michigan Natural Resources Magazine is a story about a sandstone face that was found by Julie Stockmeyer, a junior

---

[118] There are photos of Michigan relic copper saws on the web and ancient bronze saws in Cairo museums that are thousands of years old. Bronze saws are mentioned in Thompson's *American Discovery* and even stone saws from over 4,000 years ago.

As more and more new discoveries are made, the antiquity of civilization constantly recedes further back in time. Saw picture see earlier page.

[118a] See the last paragraph on page 431 "Some Enlightening Conclusions"

Brantford, Ontario, socketed bronze axe possibly 3000 years old. 3 3/4 in. long; 2 4/5 in. wide. shown courtesy of the Museum of American Indian, N.Y.

Sandstone face found by Julie Stockmeyer

high school student. She picked it up near an excavation along the Saginaw-Tuscola County line in the town of Reese, Michigan, about ten miles south of Saginaw Bay on Lake Huron. The face has two similarities—the statue of McGruer's Gods from Newberry and some found near Burrows Cave in Illinois. Dr. Moreau Maxwell, anthropologist from Michigan State University, said there is nothing characteristic about it to link it to any time period but microscopic examination revealed no indication it was carved with modern tools.

In a March 4th letter to this author (2004) from Marian Dahm, he states he has four sites he can relate to the Minoan period; Glenwood, Minnesota, Hancock, Minnesota, the Howard Sitter Site, south of Johnson, Minnesota, and Corona, South Dakota. He says these sites "are all much earlier than the Viking sites as the mooring stones are a lot lower altitude, by as much as 100 feet. This puts us into an area of history 5,000 years old!"

Finding any evidence from 5,000 years ago is difficult, and then recognizing it as such is even more difficult.

The Demise of the Minoans and Rise of Phoenicians

Excavations of the Palace of Knossos and surrounding area showed that it had been inhabited since Neolithic times (6000 BC and earlier). Since the earliest times the Palace had been destroyed by earthquakes at least three times. After each it was rebuilt more elaborately than before.

Through all these centuries (5000 BC to 1450 BC), Knossos was a great city, at its peak of prosperity, having a population of no less than 100,000 people. Its trade with Egypt, Greece, Mesopotamia, Spain and other ports on the Mediterranean flourished along with its monopoly on the sea trade.

But then around 1450 BC, with the eruption of the Santorini volcano on the island of Thera, only 60 miles from Minoa (Crete), the island was covered with volcanic ash and thousands of inhabitants were killed. Knossos was eventually restored, although nearly a century later; the other city states on Crete did not recover. The Minoans were no longer the sovereign of the seas.

For many years, the Minoan sea trade had been challenged by the Phoenicians who then inhabited a strip of land about 100 miles long and 10 miles wide on the eastern coast of the Mediterranean. First, as fishermen they were developing a commercial fleet which, with the destruction of Crete, soon took over the Mediterranean all the way to the Strait of Gibraltar and beyond into the Atlantic.

By 3000 BC, the city of Babylon, about 500 miles east of Phoenicia, was the marketplace to which precious metals, grain, wool, and other materials were brought from all directions. By 1600 BC well developed trade routes existed, over which Arabs conducted caravans transporting silks, spices, wine, gold and other commodities from the Red Sea district, from Phoenicia, and even from Asia, to Egypt, where they were exchanged chiefly for grain and linen. Soon the

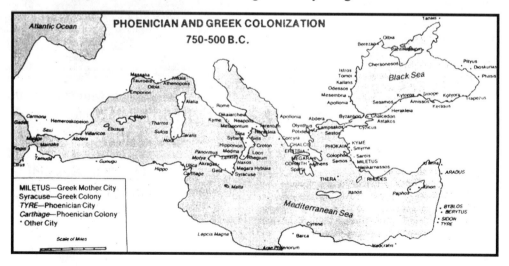

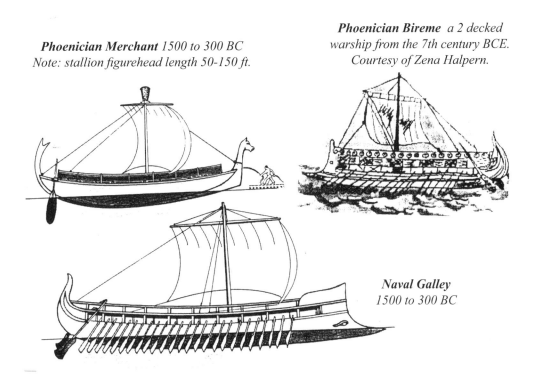

Phoenician Merchant *1500 to 300 BC*
Note: stallion figurehead length 50-150 ft.

Phoenician Bireme *a 2 decked warship from the 7th century BCE. Courtesy of Zena Halpern.*

Naval Galley
1500 to 300 BC

23 inches

Left: Strange flat copper tempered blade found by Rudy Arkelin in 1980 on a rock pile near Caledonea sometime called the Neboska Mine in Upper Michigan. These same types have been found in Kensington.

Right: Copper Vase about 4 1/2 inches high found near Port Arthur Ontario, Canada. Container could also be Greek.

Phoenicians were taking over these land trade routes and, along with their sea trade and became the world leaders in commerce. They, too, had developed a written language, were skilled navigators with ancient traditions of sea travel and within a short time they established base stations and stopover sites on islands down the African coast and on the shore of the western Mediterranean Sea. Some of these became great cities. Sidon and Tyre came into existence and a colony on the North Coast of Africa, Carthage, was to become a thriving city-state which later became a rival of Rome. With its colonies at vantage points and its spider net-like land trade routes, the Phoenicians, for perhaps the next 1,000 years, controlled the commerce of the world.[119]

The Phoenician vessels ventured into regions where no one else dared to go, and always with an eye to monopoly, they carefully guarded the secrets of their trade routes and their sources of trade goods as well as their knowledge of winds, ocean currents and far off navigable rivers. We are finding more and more rare scripts of where they have been in the British Isles and North and South America.

---

[119] From Henry H. Ritez—*The Mound Builders and Their Work in Michigan 1879*—"Those maritime rovers, who spread their sails in the face of the Greek philosophers (who despised commerce), planted colonies on the shores of the Mediterranean, and explored that 'extensive ocean, so much talked about by people of their day' and to have visited that 'great Saturnian continent,' which in some way had been brought to their notice and in the existence of which they fully believed. The Phoenicians were bold navigators, and may have sailed up and down our great rivers when the kings of Egypt were building the pyramids."

476

They even kept the design of their ships a secret. Stories are handed down how Phoenician merchants would land on a beach at night and unload their merchandise, then move the ships out of sight. They would trade during the day and move the ships in again under darkness, pick up their trade goods and be gone.

Recently, with new evidence, some believe the Phoenicians had bases on the American continent. There is mounting evidence that they were able to navigate the Mississippi into the Great Lakes as the Minoans had done a thousand years earlier. They have left telltale evidence in many areas of the American continent that has only recently been recognized and interpreted. Their distinctive, Phoenician alphabet and their Phoenician goddess, Tanit, have been identified worldwide with Carthage and Egypt where the Phoenicians had established trading bases.

It seems that nearly all of the early traders and explorers got into the Mississippi River system at one time or another.

Gene Ballinger, former editor of the *Courier* of Hatch, New Mexico, writes of this evidence. He has been a long-time follower of area archaeological finds. Editor Ballinger writes in the 1990s:

In the last several weeks we have brought to you several authenticated petroglyphs and sites found in our region of New Mexico that clearly indicate that not only were the Celtic people here in our land for a long period of time, some of them clearly came from Carthage via Iberia (Spain).

Dating and translation of the petroglyphs, including several central Ogam alphabet scripts, were completed by Dr. Arnold Murray and his staff over the last ten weeks.

The incised petroglyphs, including Ogam alphabet script at the sites reported over the last three weeks in the *Courier*, were dated between 300 and 100 B.C.

Confirmation of incised figures of pagan Phoenician goddess Tanit and a Celtic water goddess as well as Ogam script advising water locations, game and fish locations, trail

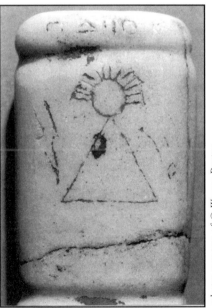

photos courtesy of © Warren Dexter

Tanit from Burows Cave

markers and refuge, all in the same central area along with mineral markers (incised cups and rings) are all indicative of a Celtic presence with the Tanit goddess identified worldwide with Carthage long before it fell to the Romans.

In the past 15 years, Celtic Ogam script in several ancient languages has been found, identified and often translated throughout Canada, the United States, Mexico, Central and South America.

Many of those petroglyphs had been noted and recorded as much as 150 years ago, but until very recent times had not been recognized for what they were, much less translated.

Languages using the Ogam alphabet include, but are not limited to, ancient Hebrew, Iberian, Gaelic, North African, Egyptian, Libyan and Greek, all languages associated with the Celtic people.[120]

The earliest confirmed time period thus far for those early visitors and explorers in our southwest is about 2500 B.C. and the latest about 1100 A.D., with a later Viking presence as far west as Oklahoma about 1100 A.D.

Although numerous artifacts have been discovered, including edged weapons, funerary items, armor, crossbows, long bows, clothing, etc., many so-called experts still refuse to admit that those early people were here, and not by accident.

But it does not matter what they may or may not think. The facts are clear and become clearer each day.

And there are still many problems, mainly because in the United States (not elsewhere), there has been a major reluctance by some professionals in various fields of archaeology, anthropology and associated disciplines, to admit the presence of those ancient visitors because it causes them to have to rethink their work, teachings and re-write centuries of history. Too bad.

The article goes on in the same vein and is accompanied by a picture, also by Mr. Ballinger, of petroglyphs on a rock cliff. The caption states that the ""Glyphs are identical to those found in caverns in the Grand Canyon and in Illinois. But these are in southwestern New Mexico and date to 300 and 100 B.C. They are directly associated with the now-emerging truth of ancient ones in our land." (Author's copy of the picture is too poor for reprint.)

The Egyptians came to America too, possibly on Phoenician ships, but

---

[120] Ogam is an alphabet and can be used to write any language. Its most modern use is by African tribal shamans who still use it as a secret code. (Warren Dexter)

478

it is certain that they picked up the copper trade soon after the destruction of Crete. They became involved with the metal experts of their day on the island of Cyprus and built-up the cities of Chytri, Lopethus, Golzi, and Athienon there. It appears that Cyprus continued to be a great brokerage for the receiving, casting and distribution of copper. The copper was standardized into oxhides and ingots for distribution. Almost certainly the Phoenicians took the last of the large pieces of float copper that were available on the surface from Michigan and by that time beginning to trade with the local American inhabitants who would come to the Copper Country when the snow left and collect the smaller pieces for the storage pits to be taken abroad when the next fleet arrived. Among the trade goods from the east were highly polished stone tools.

Zena Halpern on the beach at Kibbuto Ma'agan Mikkael in the Eastern Mediteranian where an ancient ship sank in 12 ft of water, 210 ft off the beach. Zena is a researcher of ancient seafarers of the eastern Mediterranean.

Yes, the Israelites Also Came

Probably the best evidence of Jews (also known as Israelites) in America will be forthcoming in a book by Zena Halpern of Syosset, New York. She has collected a great deal of intriguing information on the subject.

From Ms. Halpern's research - she writes of Seagoing Israelites

Archaeological evidence from underwater excavations along the Mediterranean coast of Israel has revealed significant maritime activity in the 10th century BC, the time of the Solomonic kingdom. Ancient shipwrecks, submerged harbors and cargoes attest to the maritime policy of Israel in the early Iron Age. We now have solid evidence of the construction of ships and their seaworthiness from the actual excavation of an amazingly preserved 2.400 year old ship found off the coast ofIsrael.

Discovered 10 km south of the harbor of Tel Dor, a 3000 year old major maritime center, this ancient harbor has revealed shipwrecks dating from Canaanite to Byzantine times, evidence of wide spread sea trade. The harbor of Tel Dor and her famed lagoon where eighteen shipwrecks lie waiting to be explored is still revealing secrets of the seafaring activity of the Israelites in the 10th century BC. Phoenicians and Israelites launched voyages to distant lands in search of metals such as copper, tin, iron, gold, silver and precious gems. We cannot underestimate this driving force which motivated these ancient states to form a generally unrecognized seafaring partnership. They spread west across the Mediterranean, establishing colonies along the rim, reached Iberia by the 11th to 10th centuries BC and went on to Britain and the tin mines of Cornwall. The lure of wealth from metals pushed them into the North Atlantic and into the coasts and rivers of America. Ancient inscriptions on rocks across America are testimony to their presence; records from a period of intense exploration of areas which held minerals. It was the quest for economic and military power that led to these voyages.

During the Solomonic period, fleets sailed from the ancient harbor of Ezion-Geber, to India, Africa and South America. Underwater archaeology has revealed the remains of the ancient harbor of Ezion-Geber, entrance to the Red Sea and the Indian Ocean.

The recent dramatic discovery in 2005 of a complete Israelite alphabet indicates literacy at time of the Solomonic kingdom and gives substantial credence to evidence that it was a sophisticated state, well able to engage in an extensive policy of seafaring. We can thus project a new recognition of the potential for transoceanic voyaging in the tenth century BC given the use of a concise alphabet which enabled seafarers to keep records efficiently.

The ancient harbors that were in use along the Mediterranean coast and at Ezion-Geber offer solid evidence of the seafaring skills of these ancient Israelite mariners from the eastern Mediterranean coast and the Red Sea. Their awareness of the importance of seapower effectively connected two oceans; the Atlantic, the Indian Ocean and ultimately the Pacific Ocean.

There are three findings which are constantly referred to which seem to imply there were Jews in America. Of course they are all controversial but their defenders as authentic are growing as more information is gathered.

In the 1860s, five stones were found in mounds in Newark (Ohio) and other locations in Licking County with Hebrew letters carved in them. Bradley Lepper, an archaeologist for the Ohio Historical Society, claims the stones were faked to support the theory that the mounds were built by the lost tribes of Israel.

A friend of a summer neighbor introduced me to the work of retired biology professor at Denison University, Robert Alrutz, who has written a booklet titled "The Newark Holy Stones—The History of an Archaeological Tragedy." Alrutz

The Bat Creek Stone (left) and The Newark Decalogue Stone

photos courtesy of © Warren Dexter

is an amateur archaeologist, as a hobby. He says he cannot believe the one found at Jacksontown is a fake. There is no supporting evidence to say it is a hoax.

The stone is about seven inches long and three inches wide and was inside a stone box carved especially for it.

The stone was recovered from a great stone stack 45 feet high and 500 feet in circumference and contains the Ten Commandments written (according to David Deal) in a more modern form of Hebrew (400 BCE).

A second inscribed stone was unearthed by Smithsonian archaeologists in 1885 near Bat Creek, Tennessee. It was on display at that institution for many years and thought to be written in Cherokee. However, Dr. Cyrus Gordon of Brandeis University claimed the stone had been displayed upside down. When reversed he said it was paleo-Hebrew script. His translation, "A Comet For the Jews," dated ca. 200 AD.

Then there is a third rock, which I have visited three times. The first time, both Dr. Fell and David Deal were present. This was, I believe, in October of 1984. David Deal has done much study of the area there and written about this Las Lunas Stone in New Mexico. It will also be treated thoroughly in the forthcoming work of Zena Halpern.

Two excellent David Deal sources for the story of the Los Lunas Stone are *Discovery of Ancient America,* Kheren La Yah Press/Irvine, California, 1984 by David Deal, and also an article in the *Ancient American* magazine by Deal.

Above: Author at Los Lunas stone, New Mexico.
Photo by June Rydholm
Inscriptions shown here enlarged.

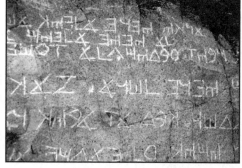

The Los Lunas Stone is located at a very obvious spot about half way to the top of what is called "Hidden Mountain" or "Mystery Mountain." At this point there is a large fallen rock, which has a flat surface and seems to be balanced just above eye level. There is a long inscription covering the whole face of this rock. It is without any doubt written in ancient Hebrew.

Dr. Robert Pfeiffer of Harvard University Semitic Language Department was the first to recognize "Inscription Rock" to be the Ten Commandments. The translation was made in the late 1940s.

To be sure there are the many usual denouncements and cries of fraud, but Deal says, "The letters of the inscription, cut deeply and accurately in very hard, flinty igneous rock, are by no means a mystery. They are clearly and unequivocally a form of paleo-Hebrew. A comparison of alphabets easily proves this point."

On the top of this mountain is what appears to be some type of well laid out

482

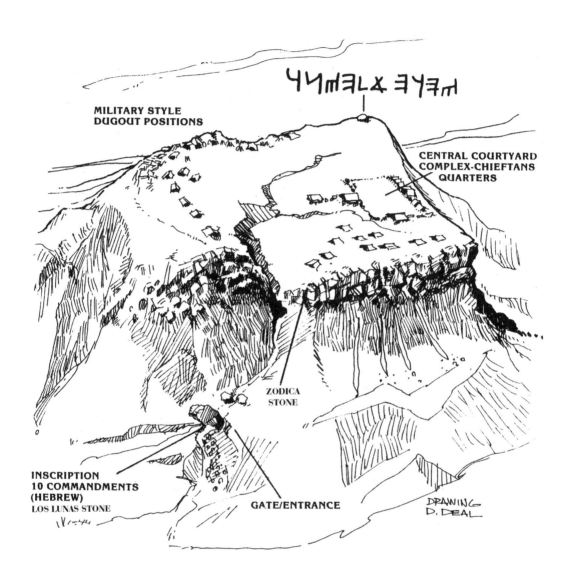

Overview looking S/SW expeditionary encampment

From; "Discovery of Ancient America"
by David Allen Deal, 1984

Jewish hilltop forts similar to Hidden Mountain in Africa and New Mexico.

fortification which Deal claims are "surprisingly similar to finds in the Middle East" and unlike formations of other Indian sites. There are many rock carvings and inscriptions in the "camp" area on the top of this mountain. There seems to have been a lot of time spent here by a large group of people and the inscriptions seem to point to one group of people. These inscriptions have been accepted as authentic by Fell and other competent epigraphers.

The water route to this location would most likely have been the Rio Puerco, a tributary of the Rio Grande, flowing into the Gulf of Mexico. This waterway brings you to less than a quarter of a mile of the site, a natural highway to the sea. This area is rich in semi precious stones; garnet, agate, and turquoise. Mt Taylor is known as "Torquoise Mt." There was ancient mining up there!

Competition

By 2500 BC the old Norse had begun to penetrate the Arctic. They traveled all of the then swollen water routes and left the telltale marks of their religion throughout the far north. The islands and waterways of that area are fairly littered with huge dolmens and as their travels took them further south they became interested in the fabulous, free copper.

It was also about 2500 BC that a Beaker Culture appeared in Scotland. The name came from a most distinctive type of drinking vessel decorated with parallel zones of designs produced by the impressions of twisted whipcord in clay.

Cord pattern pottery shards from illustrations and from Lake Superior.

In the early 1950s, Richard Saari of Marquette, a young boy at the time, discovered what seemed to be an ancient Indian camping site in some sand dunes along the Lake Superior shore a few miles east of Marquette. In the area he uncovered hundreds of various sized gray pottery shards and two beautiful copper arrow or spear points. They did not compare with the cruder ones so common in the Copper Country. At the time that I first examined the collection, the first thing I noticed was the cord imprints on the shards, but I was far more interested in the copper points. Many years later, when pondering those cord imprints, I contacted Richard's mother to look at the collection again. The copper points were gone and there seemed to be fewer shards and they were smaller than I remembered them. I made imprints of several of the shards in molding clay before returning them. It was at that time that I realized that they just had to be connected in some way to the Beaker people; this was the mark of their culture.

These pictures are admittedly poor but very revealing. The pottery shard found by Steve Kyllonen of Calumet has the exact round patterns as the one illustrated on page 150 in Dr. Barry Fells "America B.C. That one came from an area in New Hampshire believed to have been occupied by Iberian Celts during the Bronze Age.

In the book *Lake Superior* by Grace Lee Nute (Indianapolis: Bobbs-Merrill Co., 1944), she speaks of the early Irish fur trader, John Johnson, finding pottery shards in the mouth of a small creek west of Marquette (Compeau's Creek) which flows into Lake Superior.

Johnston 1792): "In the bed of the river, I found a part of the earthen pots used by the Indians before they had the use of copper and tin kettles. It is the only specimen of the kind that I ever saw. There was no indication as to whether there were imprints on them.

This is all we know about this early find of pottery, but pottery shards have turned up in the Copper Country in very recent times.

Almost identical pottery shards have been found in New Jersey in areas suspected of having been inhabited by Bronze Age Iberian Celts. They are the same as found near Lake Superior in the Keweenaw Peninsula and near Marquette.

The Beaker communities were responsible for the spread of copper metallurgy in Europe in the third millennium BC. There seems to be at least two separate but contemporary groups. The earliest group which had the cord pattern over the whole vessel came from Central Europe and spread to Holland and Great Britain. The other group probably originated in Iberia where they developed a bell-shaped vessel. This group was known as the Bell-Beaker or Maritime-Beaker culture. In England the Beaker people are associated with Avebury and other ritual monuments. (Source: EDANIN-BRAVENET web services)

From 3000 to 1000 BC, the Megalithic Societies of Britain, Iberia (Spain) and western Europe were erecting dolmens, stone chambers, menhirs and other stone monuments. These were the Irish and Iberian Celts. But the megalithic culture seemed to spread to all the coastal land of Europe. It was especially strong in the British Isles, Denmark and France.

The Celts were writing religious messages in several types of Ogam, and since both megaliths and Ogam are found in many areas of the American continent, we can be assured that they were here often and in numbers.

Several things that fit the Celtic culture that are connected to the copper fields are Ogam, found on the Joel Kela stone from the Escanaba River (and some lesser stones, gorgets from the St. Marie River and Ontonagon), the mystery gardens of Lower Michigan and on Beaver Island and also the causeway Calendar Circles on Beaver Island and Garden Island in Lake Michigan.

The Celts seemed to have been well established along the east coast, as witnessed by the many dolmens, menhirs, etc., and the elaborate stonework at Mystery Hill in New Hampshire (About 1500 BC—Fell). The dolmens in the

Arctic could also be Celtic or Old Norse, but the two known Trilithons there (70 miles east of Pond Inlet on Baffin Island and on Akpatok Island (in Ungava Bay) seem to be the work of people from the British Isles. There are trilithons there (Stonehenge is a ring of Trilithons), but I know of no other place where they are found except Burma. However, the ones in Burma are distinctly different.
Both the Celts and Norse were skilled metal workers and worked in bronze. Both Runic and Ogam alphabets are found in many places throughout North America.

Unexplored Evidence in West Virginia

West Virginia seems to have been the home of Celtic people for centuries, both before the Christian era and after, for at least several hundred years. The evidence of ancient Europeans in this area is no fly-by-night operation. When we consider the country of the Untied States of America is less than 250 years old, we must compare that with the five or six thousand years we have been discussing that people have been traveling to America.

In various places in Wyoming, Boone and Raleigh counties of West Virginia, there are the remains of many prehistoric, enormous stone dams. In the Clear Fork of the Gayandotte River in Wyoming County, according to a local resident who died in 1904, the ruins of 16 huge stone dams were discovered; the largest was said to extend three-fourths of a mile across the valley and to be 100 feet high.

Author F. Elizabeth Collier, writing for the *Wonderful West Virginia* magazine, discusses an article she found in the Archives Search Room Library at the Science and Culture Center in Charleston. It had neither date nor name but from the business ads and prices listed she determined it was a Lexington, Kentucky paper from around the 1890s maybe to 1910. (With our present knowledge it seems like it had to be before 1900—Author.) The article was written by I.E. Christian. Investigating information on Mr. Christian, Collier discovered he was born in Logan County on September 5, 1855. During his lifetime, he was engaged in farming, lumbering and was eventually a clerk in the store of L.B. Cook & Co., before starting his own grocery store, which, over the years, enlarged and did well.

In speaking of the ancient stone dams found in the three counties, the article states:

They are attracting no small amount of attention from archaeologists. During the last two months over 50 men, under the management of Prof. J.P. Jones, have been making excavations in Wyoming County for the purpose of more thoroughly investigating these obscure works of what was certainly one of the most ancient races of the human family. In McDowell County also I am told that J.D. Cyphers is having a number of excavations made for the same purpose.

The work already done in this county has furnished facts which prove beyond the possibility of a doubt that the antiquity of these ruins is vastly greater than that of any other work of man now known.

The great antiquity of the mound-builders of North America is well known; the remains left by them antidating by several thousand years anything yet found in the eastern world (remember, this was written in the 1890s), but even back in the prehistoric age of the Mound Builders, these dams were then, as now, only crumbling ruins left behind by a still more ancient people who had lived and passed away so long before them that even the mystic thread of tradition could not reach back to them. This fact was clearly proved by excavations made about two weeks ago on Geo. W. Cook's land, one mile below Oceana, where it was found that one of the largest mounds to be found anywhere in this part of the county had been built right over the foundation of one of these old dams which, even in remote age, was entirely covered up with alluvial deposits which had been ages in accumulating.

So far as I have been able to learn, there are, in this county, seventeen of these ruins, all of them except one being on the waters of the Clear Fork of the Guyan River. In Raleigh County there are three; two of them on Marsh Fork of Coal River, and one on the waters of Piney Creek. In Boone County there is only one, and in McDowell County, perhaps seven or eight, mostly on the waters of the Dry Fork of Tug River. This completes the entire list of these ruins, as no others have ever been found so far in any other part of the world.

These dams, in their original condition, extended entirely across the valleys of the streams, from one hill to the other, and according to very conservative estimates made by Col. J.R. Irwin, were in many cases over one hundred feet in height and two hundred feet in width at their base. They are now in most cases covered up almost to their tops by alluvial accumulations, and the streams have worn passages down through them in places almost to their very foundations, which is not be wondered at when we consider their great age.

These dams are composed of very odd-looking, wedge-shaped stones, the largest of which would weigh less than one hundred pounds. The stones in any one dam are all the same size, but are of different sizes in different dams, the stones of some dams being almost twice as large as they are in others. The reason for this no one has ever been able to conjecture.

On account of the peculiar shape of these stones they of course do not fit together like they would have done if they had been square: the crevices between them have all been nicely filled with a composition which seems to have been made of coarse sand and small fragments of crushed stone. By carefully beating this composition into the open crevices, it apparently answered the purpose of these ancient architects as well as the best cement would have done. Just why these wedge-shaped stones should have been used instead of square ones in building these dams is a question which no one has ever yet been able to answer.

"Dr. W. G. Cooks who has given the matter considerable attention is of the opinion that it shows that they were built in an age, so remotely ancient, that the cube or square was yet unknown and inconceivable figure in the crude minds of the architects; the shape of these stones representing the nearest approach to it which they had ever yet been able to conceive."

# # #

Comment by Archaeologist John Henderson:

The "scientist" in the article who says the architect was ignorant of square blocks or cubes of stone for building because he built with wedge shaped stones is dead wrong, as wrong as the archaeologists who claim the Mayans built wide roads and causeways for nothing because they never invented the wheel.

This child toy of burnt clay, unearthed in New Mexico about a half century ago, seems to prove that the Mayans were well acquainted with the wheel. They may not have used it extensively for some reasons, but they certainly knew about it.

Builders who can erect a dam ¾ mile long, 100 feet high and 200 feet wide at the base made of identical wedge-shaped stones bound by a type of cement they invented, like the Mayans, DID SO BY CHOICE—NOT OUT OF IGNORANCE. But just think of the incredible difficulty of such erections, finding millions and millions of identical sized and shaped stones for each dam and assembling them, and look how many dams there were! These structures had to be very ancient, especially if they were crumbling when the mound builders showed up. They were a lot older than 2000 BC and absolutely not in the AD range. I am sure the Celts were there and probably used the pre-built structures, but did not create them. That construction is not their style. The only place I have ever found a series of dams across streams like that is in the Negev Desert south of Palestine. Some long-gone people created arable land that way and raised crops, some remnants of the dams remain, yet there are no traces of the West Virginia dams 100 years later. They must still be there, buried.

And Back to the Article by Collier

The largest one of these dams is situated just below Sun Hill on J.E. Toler's land. It extends completely across the valley of the Clear Fork, a distance of three-fourths of a mile, and was originally over one hundred feet high. All of the level land between Oceana and Sun Hill was no doubt originally formed by alluvial deposits which accumulated in the bottom of the great lake or pool which the dam once formed in the Clear Fork valley. The stream has now worn a narrow passage through this dam down almost at its foundation, and Mr. Toler has constructed a modern dam on the foundation of this ancient one and is using it to furnish water power for a fine flour mill at that place. Another one of these dams is also being utilized in the same manner by Capt. C.S. Canterberry, near Cramey P.O. in this county.

"What object these primitive people could have had in view of building these enormous dams is beyond the power of the present generation to even conjecture, unless it was simply an insane and unholy determination on their part to everlastingly and eternally dam this part of the country for all time to come, before leaving it to their successors."

Isaac E. Christian
Oceana, W. Va.

Artist's interpretation of an excavation near Oceana where a huge, deteriorated dam was said to have been discovered under a mound.

Imaginary scene of a huge dam being constructed in ancient times.

For supporting evidence - see Ancient American Issue Number 62
West Virginia's 5th Century Statue - By Nancy Clark.

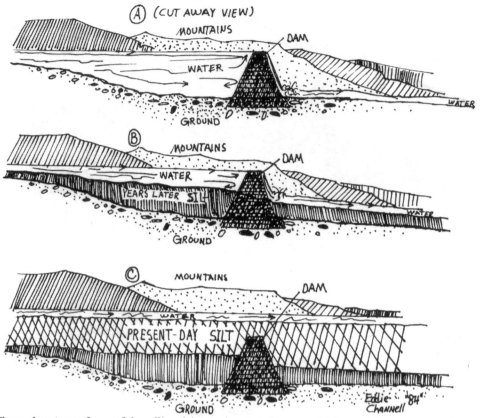

Three *drawings* of *one* of the *alleged* dams *showing* changes *which would* have *occurred* through the ages: *(A) Soon after* the dam *was built, sometime between 2000* BC and AD *800 approximately. (B)* Many *centuries late, after silt would have covered* about *half* of the *structure. (C)* The present *time. when* the dam *would* be *entirely covered* by *sediment.* Eddie Channell

A more logical and modern thought, in view of what we know about the ancients nowadays, would be that the dams were built for water power and irrigation.

F. Elizabeth Collier accompanied the 1890s newspaper piece with eight pages of analyses, which included photographs and three drawings by artist Eddie Chamell. Permission was granted by the West Virginia magazine to reprint these and the article itself in this work.

For brevity I have chosen just three sections of the article by Ms. Collier here. Collier:

> "A personal visit to the Oceana area proved equally unproductive. Two old stone mill walls in the Clearfork Valley on two separate tracts of land, one presently and the other formerly owned by the Toler family, still stand. It is possible that these walls were built over the ancient dams, but there is no way to determine if that is the case without digging. I did

Massive stone work fitted perfectly without mortar, by unknown ancient builders in South America.

note that the Clearfork Valley is an alluvial flood plain area, as Christian mentioned, which means that at one time was under water. Two tall mountains near a present day golf course at the head of the valley suggest a natural location for the construction of a dam to form a lake in what is now the valley.

Christian's article says that the ancient dams were old at the time that the mound builders inhabited West Virginia. Works of the mound builders have been carbon-dated to a few centuries before Christ, 800-500 BC in some areas. Other mounds were built during a later time period, until approximately AD 1000. According to information given in the article, then, the dams could have been constructed anytime between 2000 BC (or earlier) and AD 800.

It is not impossible that such mammoth stone structures could have been built during the ancient era. Egypt's famed pyramids were erected about 2680 BC (now some say earlier). Huge stone structures were built in the Americas beginning some time between 1500 BC and AD 317 by people of the Maya Culture, one of the greatest and advanced of the pre-Columbian civilizations.

Every few months reports come in of new discoveries and new progress being made about old questions.

In the September 29th (2002) issue of the *Sunday Gazette-Mail* of Charleston, West Virginia (Section B, Valley and State), there is a story by Rick Steelhammer about a skeleton found by archaeologists Robert Pyle, the man who did much of the work on the Ogam message in Wyominig County first brought to his attention by Bugs Stover. [121a]

Long ago I had surmised that there was so much evidence of ancient Irish in West Virginia that sooner or later someone would come along to prove it. This is where the great dams were, the Ogam messages, the ancient tales and

---

[121a] Refer to page 227

Irish legends, etc.; all we could ask for are some bones from Ireland. Robert Pyle believes he has found these in a cave, which he first visited in 1981. Not only did he find Ogam markings on a bone needle, but he also found human remains, human teeth. Working with Brigham Young University, where DNA tests were made and carbon dating arrived at a date of about 710 A.D.

Of course the professorial archaeologists say these findings are doubtful and Pyle himself probably would not have come to these conclusions if he had been a trained archaeologist with a degree in that field. However, he says he is a federally certified archaeologist who performed archaeological surveys for the state division of archaeology in the 1970s and 80s. He studied archaeology at Northwestern university and geology at West Virginia University.

At least the professionals are willing to make their own investigation of the 1300-year-old evidence. Pyle hopes that when all is said and done, he will be given some credit for his discovery.

We must also look at a new theory as to the time of building and use of the Egyptian pyramids.

Over recent years it has been discovered that the base of the Sphinx has been warn away by water, which certainly has not occurred in the last few thousand years. As usual, the present group of Egyptologists and archaeologists are reluctant to accept this analysis. The new thinking is that the Great Pyramid, for example, was built 10450-10350 BC and some Gaza structures even older—such as the base of the second pyramid, the valley and sphinx temples, the so-called funerary temple in front of the second pyramid, the causeway past the sphinx, and, of curse, Osiron. This redating of sphinx was the work of two scientists, John A West and Robert Schoch, but now an Englishman now living in Danville, Illinois, master craftsman and engineer, has added a whole new dimension to the original pyramids in general.

In a book named *The Giza Power Plant—Technologies of Ancient Egypt* (Bear & Company—1998), author Christopher Dunne gives us a completely different perception of the Giza pyramids. He says they are not, and never were, tombs for the ancient pharaohs. This thought-provoking book claims that the pyramids were built as power plants using and magnifying the earth's sound vibrations. "The author shows how the pyramids' numerous chambers and passageways were positioned with deliberate precision to maximize its acoustical qualities. This may be the same technology discovered by Nikola Tesla[122] and the solution to our own clean energy needs."[122a]

---

[122] Nikola Tesla (1856-1943) Electrical Engineer - one of the most brilliant men in history - developed principles and devices that made alternating current, contributed much knowledge of electronics.

[122a] Quoted from the book's back cover.

Ancient Pyramids in China

Dunn says that this is the source of the energy that was used to cut miles of underground waterways beneath the Gaza plateau as well as the cutting and moving of huge granite beams and sarcophagi. This would, of course, explain why there has never been a body found in any of the 50 or so remaining pyramids of Egypt. Before you dismiss these ideas, out of hand, I would suggest you read *The Gaza Power Plant* by Christopher Dunn.

For some very significant reason, the idea of pyramids has been taken around the world in ancient times. We find them in places now where we would never have expected them to be, such as the remote parts of China, islands of the Pacific, both North Central and South America, Japan and Polynesia.[123] I have had this note on my desk for years from Dr. John White.

4/23/96
Dear Fred:

>   Did you know that France has at least <u>four</u> ancient pyramids? I found this claim on page 44-45 of *Mystery of the Ancients* by Eric & Craig Umland, 1974. They quote Robert Charroux, author of *Forgotten Worlds.*

>   John White

Dr. John White is a long-time leader and principal researcher and writer of the Midwestern Epigraphic Society based in Columbus, Ohio.

---

[123] See *Lost Cities and Ancient Mysteries of South America* by David Hatcher Childress, Adventures Unlimited Press, Stelle, IL (1986) and *Voyage of the Pyramid Builders—The True Origins of the Pyramids from Lost Egypt to Ancient America,* Robert M. Shoch, Ph.D., Torcher/Putnam, 2003.

Back to Collier's article:

In an effort to pinpoint the spot mentioned by Christian where a mound had been built over an ancient dam, I again consulted the *Reference Book of Wyoming County.* On page 3 I found this: "Two small mounds are known in the county, one by the mouth of Toneyfork in the bottom in front of Bill Walker's place and the other on the Tom Davis form on Trace Fork of Little Cub. Neither has ever been excavated...On the Walnut Gap Trail, six miles across the Wyoming-Boone line, near Echert post office, and on the farm of the late Rev. A.H. Perry, there is another mound. Some years before his death, Rev. Perry reported that he had commenced excavation of this mound, but found it had been lined with long broken slabs of stone, some of which were 12 to 14 feet long, which he could not handle, so he gave up the work."

Could the slabs of stone under the mound on Reverend Perry's farm have been the top of the dam, which Isaac Christian said was being excavated by Professor Jones? The location of the site does not conform, however, with the location of the large mound on land then owned by George W. Cook, one mile below Oceana, described in the old newspaper article. It is conceivable, however, that Perry's mound could have been built over another ancient dam.

# # #

And finally, Elizabeth Collier asks: Who was J.D. Cyphers, said by Christian to have been 'having quite a number of excavations made,' to investigate the ancient stone structures in McDowell County? Did Cyphers write any notations or reports on his findings?

Who was Professor J.F. Jones, and what were the results of his excavations in Wyoming County? Surely, if Jones had over 50 men digging, he must have been doing a serious study and almost certainly recorded his findings. Where, then, is his written report of the excavations?

Did any local citizens or others living at that time who took an interest in the excavations record any information other than the newspaper article which Isaac Christian wrote? If so, can these writings be located?

# # #

Did Isaac Christian record any additional data about the dams and excavations? Do his descendants have any information?"

Photo by Tom Edgar

Stover at the site of the Ogam petroglyphs near the town of Oceana in West Virginia.

Looking at the preceding story from our modern perspective, it is easy to imagine what might have happened to any such reports or information at that specific period (1900). It certainly would have been "covered up" along with the many other disturbing facts and finds that were being discovered at that time.

But now we can add the information that has been recently brought to light by David "Bugs" Stover.

In April of 2004, a friend of mine, Tom Edgar of Wolf Creek, West Virginia, took the time to videotape Robert Nolley interviewing Bugs Stover at the site of the Ogam petroglyphs near the town of Oceana in West Virginia. This is the Christian story deciphered by Dr. Fell that explains very well who these people were. It does not tell us how long they had been in this area but with the well-established massive dams and the Horse Creek petroglyph nearby in Boone County, West Virginia, reportedly the longest Ogam inscription anywhere in the world, tells us that these Celtic colonists were here for a long, long time and they were here in great numbers and had contact with the "old country." Since Ogam inscriptions have been found in many places in America, we can see that they explored the river systems thoroughly and were undoubtedly a part of the Edena, Hopewellean and Mississippian cultures, which were eventually absorbed into many of the Algonquin tribes along with other European, Mediterranean and Asian peoples. America has always been the great international melting pot.

There is an area where Bruce Watson of Berlin Center, Ohio, who runs an underwater salvage company, claims to have found much evidence of Celtic

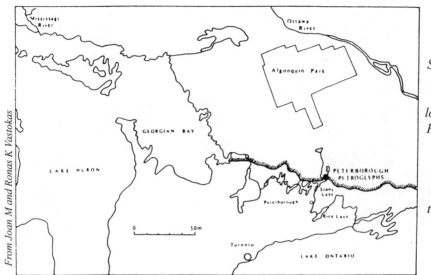

From Joan M and Ronas K Vastokas

South-central Ontario, showing location of the Peterborough Petroglyph site on southern boundary of the Canadian Shield.

activity in that area. Geologically, a few thousand years ago, the ocean had an inlet right to where Lake Ontario is now. This was a very logical area for the Irish to settle that was far more convenient than Beaver Island and was probably settled at a later date. There were water routes from Lake Ontario to Lake Huron and then to the Lake Superior mines. It was on one of these water routes, north of Peterborough, Ontario, that Wodin-Lithi left his records on the rock giving details of his trading mission in 1700 BC.

Since the Norse and Irish Celts were making this ocean crossing quite often, this became a part of a trade route from America to Ireland. The copper was then traded to the Phoenicians who took it south to the Mediterranean. There were trade routes by land from England to the Mediterranean but copper was too heavy and difficult to handle until it was converted to ingots or oxhides on Cyprus. It therefore makes sense that it was carried by water directly from the northern leg of the trade route to Cyprus.[123a]

Carthage, which had become the seat of Phoenician trade and power, had changed a great deal over the centuries of its existence. It had become the rival of Rome. In about 69 BC, Roman legions besieged Carthage, but even before this time it was no longer bringing copper down from the north to the southern end of the trade route. They were trading for it with the Northmen.

About 1000 BC iron began to replace the use of bronze. It was strong, very plentiful and the technique of smelting had reached the point where many cultures were beginning to use it, although it had been known since before the days of the pyramids.

[123a] See *The Incredible Bronze Age Journey,* a well-researched fiction by James P. Grimes (Infinity Publishing Co., Haverford, PA, 2002).

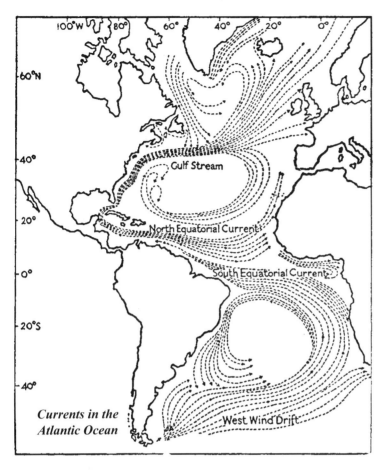

During the final millennia of digging for copper in the Copper Country, local Indians made many forages north to dig and select small pieces. They were traded far and wide.

While tales of Greater Ireland[124] still lingered with some of the Irish, the lands of the Western World were long forgotten by most of Europe. The copper trading had long ago ended, but except for the Leif Ericson stories in a few of the Sagas there was no reliable record of any of the lands to the west, only vague legends.

When the Viking expeditions began to arrive in Lake Superior, they had to rediscover and were still fascinated by pure copper and collected small amounts. The local Norse living in the Lake Superior region lost interest in it because they were already using iron, but mining continued by the local Indians and Norse, many of them more or less reverted to Indian ways; after all, they were thoroughly adapted to the Great Lakes environment.

The Irish of the eastern Great Lakes became known to the later Europeans as the "Erie"[124a] (Irish) Indians. They were living primarily where north eastern Ohio and western Pennsylvania and New York are today. They were all but annihilated by the surrounding Iroquois tribes.

---

[124] As the Americas were called by the ancient seafaring Irish. See the *Lost Treasure of King Juba* by Frank Joseeph
[124a] Erie, the name of old Ireland.

Yet To Be Determined

Among the immigrants to America that must be considered are the people who established Burrow's Cave near Olney, Illinois, or what is now being called the Tomb of the Embarras River. Frank Josephs (and others) have already proclaimed them to be followers of King Juba II, king of Mauritania but, of course, it may be too early as of this writing (2004) to know if this prediction is actual fact.

The finding of the "mystic symbol" on some of the artifacts in the cave definitely connects them in some way with the group, which David Deal has identified as Coptic Christians out of Egypt. They appear to have arrived about the same time period. David Deal has recently discovered an ancient habitation site in lower Michigan in an area where a lot of Michigan relics were found.

Again, too early for speculation, but these people could have set the stage for the great religious development which appeared at Cahokia a few centuries later. There are many other possibilities that must be considered.

Various Farfarers

It seems that many writers insist on finding a discoverer of America. Their minds are obsessed with "Who was first?" It is hoped, after reading this book, we have dropped that idea. America was "discovered" over and over again and there have been many migrations. The real "firsts" are lost in the depths of time. We should be reminded of the sagestic words of Chief Welsh, "They came in wave after wave after wave."

After the "red paint people" and others in the north from Europe there were the old Norse and the old Irish, pre-Celtic or the megalithic people of Europe—those people that the Irish legends referred to as "Firbolgian" and "Formorian," who were known to be seafaring men, probably another remnant of the Sea People who often traveled to their "Elysium" far out in the Atlantic Ocean. There must have been many places as they had many names that were handed down from generation to generation. Some spoke of Oilean-na-m Beo (Island of the Living) or Hy-na Beatha (Island of Life). These places were sung about by the ancient bards, or told about by the raconteurs. But there is one place held above the others that was soothfast, the "Great Land," Hy-Breasail. This was the land of Firbolgs, Formorians and Tuatha-de-Danaans, the fierce warriors of old.

Whenever I read of this Hy-Bresail, I thought of Brazil. It's a huge land far off in the Atlantic Ocean. My archaeologist friends hadn't heard of it but my historian friends had called it "Hi-Brazil."

In the 1950s, there were unsubstantiated reports of menhirs and stone circles in the north of Brazil. Then at the turn of the twenty-first century, two independent researchers, Antonia J. Cardosa and Arthur Franco of Rio Grand do Sul, Brazil's most southern state, discovered some of the biggest dolmens in the world. This is possibly the site of the largest megaliths on earth.[124b] From ceramic fragments found in the region estimates are that the site could be two to ten thousand years old. Local farmers claim that aligned menhirs and ancient sites have been destroyed by development in the recent past.

And so it seems obvious that there was truth in the tales and legends of the sea rovers of the Irish and the old Norse. They have left their marks in many far flung places from the waterways of the far north to the islands of the Pacific. We know they traveled to the Mediterranean area during the Viking Period, but there had to have been some connection during this earlier time as the two places where a distinctive type of dolmen are found, often called a portal tomb, are on the islands off the west coast of Ireland and on the east coast of the Black Sea! There are reportedly 2500 of them there.

As we have read there is a close association between the old Scandinavians and the British Islanders. It looks very much like both groups were putting up megalithic monuments during the same time frame. It was one of these seafaring populations, or both, that took over the Atlantic leg of the copper trade. It could have been the megalithic societies from Ireland and Scandinavia that followed the same water routes to southern Russia as the Vikings did later. This is a new concept that must be explored.

But in the western hemisphere, at first the Norse were traveling the Hudson Bay route and later, with the help of the local Algonquins, they were meeting at a place between Lakes Erie and Huron, in the vicinity of the present Peterborough, Ontario. It was most likely the Norse who took the large pieces of copper that were left by the Minoans and Phoenicians, neither of whom were coming to America at this late date (1700 B.C., Fell).[124c] Those Mediterraneans were re-using their copper and bronze and there were other sources of copper being discovered that did not require the long ocean voyages. The new sources were, however, all lower grade ores that required processing.

It was the Norse who learned to get smaller pieces from the large chunks of copper by heating and hammering off smaller ingots of five to ten pounds.

[124b] See Appendix E

[124c] They did not cut them, but hammered off five to ten pound pieces from the larger piece freed by earlier civilizations.

See Appendix pictures of big Dolmens.

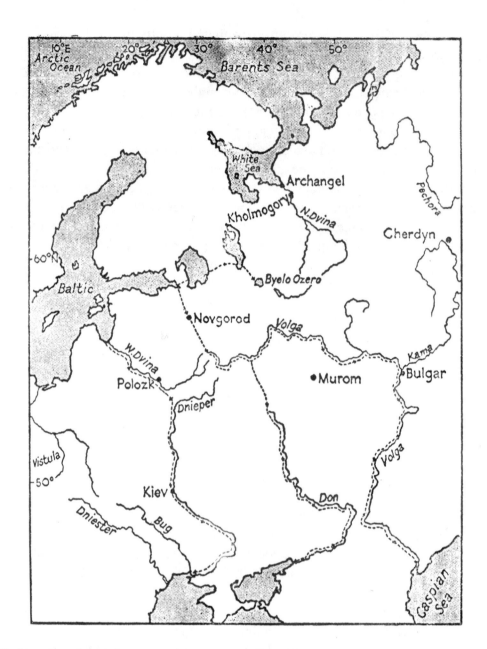

Prehistoric and proto-historic trade routes in Russia. In addition to the Vistula-Dniester route to Olbia and the Baltic road along the W. Dvina and the Dnieper, the N. Dvina-Volga and the Percha-Kama-Volga routes were much used. Amber from the Samland coast (N. Prussia) and furs from western Siberia, Which were carried as Far as India, were the principal commodities transported along these roads. The precise position of Gelonos is unknown; it probably stood on the site of the later Bulghar. Holmgard was, of course founded during the Middle Ages. This colony, which was greatly influenced by Norway, was probably established on the site of a prehistoric village of hunters and fishers.

Portal tombs, although still called dolmens on the east coast of the Black Sea

There is an estimated 2500 of them up and down that coast.

This 5000 lb piece of copper was found on cribbing in one of the ancient mines near McCargo Cove on Isle Royal. The author speculates, it was freed and raised by Minoans or Phoenicians and left. Later found by Norse, it was heated and hammered to take many 5 to 10 lb ingots from it.

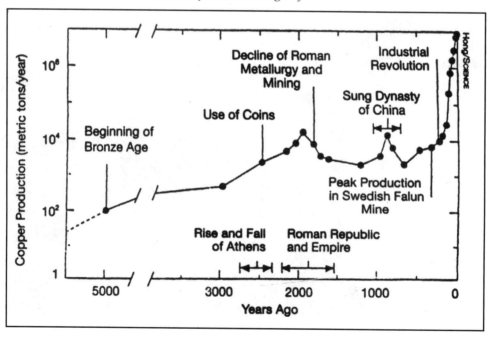

In volume 149 of *Science News* (April 13, 1996), it told of a study by Sungmin Honey of Domaine University in France measuring the copper concentrations in glacial ice layers from different parts of the earth. They found the layers from Greenland correlate nicely with those of other parts of the world for a period of the last 7,000 years. Each year the ice caps build up a layer of ice that can be read like tree rings.

The Norse and Celtics or Celts produced fine bronze work on their own, but metalwork seems to have reached a peak in the Roman Empire around the time of Christ. This, by volume at least, was far surpassed during the industrial revolution of the past one hundred and fifty years. (See chart on previous page.)

Discovering Lost Cities

Sometime in the 1990s, I received a letter from a friend which has since been misplaced. In it was a page from Forum (Omni Magazine) telling the story of a lost city in Brazil by Rene Chabbert of Phoenixville, Pennsylvania.

There is a long discourse on his efforts starting in 1956 to locate some of these lost cities in Brazil that he had heard about. His first target was an ancient city named "Z" which he believed was inhabited by white Indians, thought to be descendants of Atlantis. His second target was a city he named "1753." This city was said to have been discovered by Portuguese adventurers seeking the lost Muribeca silver mines, a fabled site of great wealth. The mines were said to have been discovered a century earlier by natives but were since lost and forgotten. The Portuguese expedition vanished without a trace in 1754 after sending the Portuguese viceroy of Bakia a notice of the discovery.[125] The letter describes buildings, temples and inscriptions found on them.

Studying aeronautical charts over a period of several years, by 1981 Chabbert had located 13 probable locations for ancient cities on a map. He was much puzzled by some inscriptions on the last page of the letter. He knew three of them were ancient Greek but the fourth was a complete enigma until Dr. Barry Fell determined that both alphabets contained in the glyphs "were used by mariners roughly 2,000 years ago. The lost city then wasn't built by Atlantean survivors but by Mediterranean seafarers."

With computer-enhanced satellite images of the Amazon rainforest—images supplied by General Electric—Chabbert found the city of 1753. It was just as it had been described by the Portuguese. The river, which started near the city's main square, was clearly visible, a key feature mentioned in the letter of 1753.

---

[125] That letter exists today as document 512 in the archives of the National Library in Rio de Janeiro.

The images had been examined by Richard M. Foose, Hitchcock Professor of Geology at Amherst College, and a recognized authority on satellite photo interpretations. He confirmed the images appear man-made and not odd geological formations.

Rene Chabbert:

> *Portuguese navigator Pedro Cabral is credited with discovering Brazil in 1500. I feel that Cabral, like Columbus before him, rediscovered a country known and explored during classical times and whose location was lost for centuries following the Dark Ages. Last year, Aurelio de Abresi, a Brazilian archaeologist from Sao Paulo, found the lost city of Ingrejil, north of Bahia. Other sites will no doubt be found and although I may not be the last person to do so, I believe I was the first one to find a lost city by using modern satellite technology.*

By 1000 BC and onward, while it was not written (though some remote maps did exist), there was no question among the seafarers as to whether or not there was a far off land across the sea. It was probably very vague to most, but there was no doubt that it was there. They had many names for it, however, only a relatively small number of sea captains and navigators knew exactly where they were headed when they left eastern ports. The copper trade had dwindled down to the Norse/Irish/Celtic by whom the copper was then relayed to the Mediterranean but in much smaller quantities than in the previous millennium (2500 BC to 1500 BC).

Copper from Michigan, by this time in less demand than earlier, that came to the Mediterranean ports was finding its way to China in small quantities by way of the silk road. Egypt, Mesopotamia and the Indus Valley in India were reaching their peak of development, and bronze art of all sizes was being produced. In these places it was common practice to reuse old copper artwork to make bronze, as we use scrap iron today.

About 2000 BC Sumerian power was waning and came to an end in Mesopotamia under the assault of Semitic invaders. Sumerian refugees began to colonize South America from the Mediterranean. They introduced animal husbandry and plant cultivation to the Andean population (Fell).

Some copper was making its way south through Lake Michigan via the Escanaba River to Beaver Island and also into the copper culture of Wisconsin via the Ontonagon River and the Wisconsin River to be traded, in some cases, further south.[126] The Hopewells, one of the mound building societies, were using relatively small amounts of copper in a number of art forms. Some of it was

---

[126] See *The Lost Pyramids of Rock Lake* by Frank Joseph.

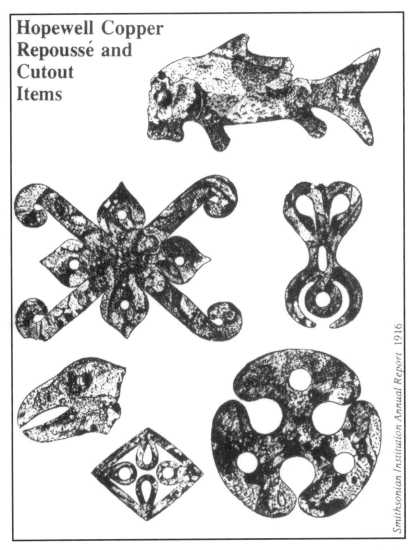

Hopewell Copper Repoussé and Cutout Items

Smithsonian Institution Annual Report 1916

Hopewell copper was often made from very thin sheets. Other than some tools, nothing weighed more than a few pounds or so.

making its way down the Mississippi to a great trade center at Poverty Point.

In regards to the stone circle on Beaver Island with the road going through the center of it and the huge prehistoric garden beds nearby, I had it all explained to me in a book entitled *The Stonehenge People*. There are two books by that name, one by Rodney Castleden subtitled *An Exploration of Life in Neolithic Britain 4700-2000 BC,* and the other by Aubrey Burl subtitled *Life and Death at the World's Greatest Stone Circle*. They are both very informative and I highly recommend them.

Burl is teaching at the National University of Ireland in Galway. In 2002 I wrote to him explaining how there is a huge calendar circle on Beaver Island in Lake Michigan that has the road going right through the center of it, typical of several hundred such circles on the British Isles. I mentioned the ancient gardens, the copper, the Irish Celt at the museum and the many copper mines in the Copper Country. I'm not sure I told him about the Ogam prayer stone but I did say we saw the same shaped stone axes and other things in European museums that have been found here in America. I truly thought he would be interested in my comparisons or at least ask some pertinent questions.

I knew how some of our local archaeologists thought about this or any thought of foreigners coming here for copper, that is why I had written to Ireland.

The answers I received could well have been written by one of our own; they seem to think alike. The answer:

I'm afraid I am not convinced by your parallels—in stone or in metal. It is now widely recognized in archaeology that tools and indeed other cultural developments may appear in very similar ways in many different places. The challenge is to explain why different societies did this in very different circumstances and not to seek explanations in terms of which migrations.

Good wishes.
Aubrey Burl

I did not answer this letter. But I would like to give a few examples that I have noticed how people have come up with different ways to do the same thing when in isolated circumstances.

1. Gus Anderson mining iron in Greenland.
2. English drivers driving on the left.
3. In England I noticed their five panel doors were mounted upside down.

They told me ours were upside down, they had them first.

4. In Africa they all peel a banana from the top, we peel them from the stem, and hang them upside down when in a bunch.

5. Even though we use the same eating utensils (knife, fork and spoon), Europeans use them quite differently than we do.

6. Simple games and puzzles are entirely different on other continents.

7. Have you ever seen anyone in the Americas carrying things on their head? If you have, they probably came from Africa.

8. People who are comfortable sitting on their heels for long periods are probably from Central Asia.

When we see things done in identical ways on different continents, we should be suspicious and look for other similarities.

More Irish and Vikings in America

There was a period of time from the decline of the Roman Empire until the 15th century that has often been referred to as the Dark Ages. During this time most forms of education ceased to exist, very few records were kept, famine, plagues and disease were rampant, there was little or no sanitation and superstition reigned.

History for that period was scarce or written often in a fanciful style that made it unbelievable and much of it from the previous era was lost.

The trade centers of the Mediterranean had moved to a rivalry between Genoa and Venice and the trade was with Egypt, India and China in the far east.

The Venetian naval superiority and wealth was due to her great galleys built by a state run Arsenal. The Arsenal could build and outfit 80 galleys at a time. With lateen sails and 150 oarsmen, they were capable of great speed and maneuverability in war or entering harbors. Their merchant galleys were divided into seven great convoys that sailed throughout the Mediterranean, and Venetian sailors accumulated much knowledge of seamanship from their travels.

In northern Europe, men of power and wealth formed their own armies and became first chieftains and later kings of their own territories. They built great castles and their subjects were serfs who tilled the land and paid taxes in the form of grain or produce to the Lord of the castle or the king. In exchange, they received the protection of the King's army.

In the year 312 AD, Constantine[126a] marched to Rome where he was

---

[126a] *Constantine the Great (274 AD – 337 AD) born in Naissus, now Nish Yugoslavia – At the death of his father in Britain in 306 AD he was proclaimed Emperor by the troops. Challenged by relatives he defeated both their armies. He was said to have seen a cross in the sky with the Greek words "By this Conquer." Under this sign, known as the Labrum, which he adopted as his standard, he marched to Rome where the Senate acknowledged him as Emperor in 312 AD.*

Irish Monk stone bee hive huts, 600 plus steps up to the top of Skellig Michael on the remote Skellig Islands

acknowledged as emperor by the Roman Senate and in 313 AD he issued the edict of Milan, which granted toleration to Christians. Constantine was baptized in 337 AD as a Christian but three years earlier, he had proclaimed Christianity as the state religion. Thus, it spread throughout Europe and the Mediterranean.

There was one group of people who kept history alive during these centuries. These were the Irish monks, religious devotees of Christianity who belonged to various religious orders. While some lived in monasteries, some often chose to live a solitary and cloistered life devoted to asceticism, prayer and self-denial. These zealous religious men spent their lives copying by hand everything of importance they could find to preserve. Many of these Monks did not want to associate with people for fear of being tempted into unholy ways or falling into the depths of damnation. Some just left society. They built small stone beehive huts to live out their lives in. Many were known to go in groups of two or three and some alone, in skin boats into the western ocean, to see where God would take them. One well-known group was led by St. Brendan the Navigator, who was said to have returned after spending seven years in some far off land in the western ocean. Their tiny stone huts have been found on inaccessible mountain heights on inaccessible islands. Some of these beehive huts have been found on Greenland and the east coast of the American continent. This activity was common in the fifth and sixth centuries and the stone remains of the Irish of this period were found by the first Viking parties that arrived a century or so later.

It was the monasteries of these devout and humble people that became the objects of the first Viking raids in England in 789 AD. This then is the beginning of the Viking period that lasted for the next three or four hundred years. European history of this period is filled with stories of the marauding Northmen who showed

Viking Ships Bent on Plunder.

up everywhere in their long, sleek, shallow boats, bent on plunder.

The only written record of them being on the North American continent is in a small number of the Icelandic Sagas. But the archaeological evidence is growing rapidly. Many artifacts found over the last 200 years are just now being understood and the Viking period picture in America is beginning to take shape. It is every bit as bold as it is in Europe.

As an active local historian, I keep finding well-documented history that has been completely left out of our history books. But I have also found that we have learned those history lessons that we were taught so well, that we are reluctant to change our minds with the gaining of new evidence and knowledge.

It is well documented that the Norse reached Iceland in 863 AD. The Sagas tell us that Eric the Red was exiled to Iceland for murder in 950 AD. Then he was banished from Iceland for three years in 982, also for murder.

Eric the Red used his three summers of banishment to make a thorough inspection of Greenland. When he realized the southwest end of Greenland was habitable and had chosen the deep "Eric's Fjord," now called Tunugdliorfik, for himself, he returned to Iceland.

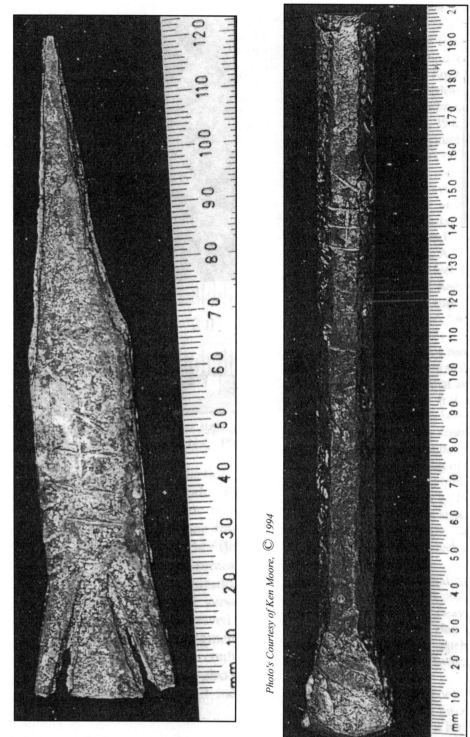

Photo's Courtesy of Ken Moore, © *1994*

Left: A copper spear-point found by Daniel Soper.
Right: One of the octagonal copper chisels which were proven, after many tests, to have been cast and forged with a high degree of technology.

Greenland with Eystribyggd and Vestribjggd. Vestribyggd, the Western Settlement, lay some way north of the Eastern Settlement. The distance between the two was about 200 miles, or, in the words of an old chronicle, 'six days' rowing with six men in a six-oar boat'. Since the seaway ran past dangerous glaciers, whose sharp-cornered calf-ice often blocked the channel completely, contact between the two colonies cannot have been particularly close.

The very next summer (986 AD), twenty-five ships,[127] with families and supplies, equipment, livestock and household goods, set out to colonize Greenland. There must have been nearly 700 people in all. Their settlements were invariably on the fjords and there were two,[128] the western settlement Vestribygd and Eystribyggd, the eastern settlement. They were about 200 miles apart.

The climate of the region must have been more temperate and the flora richer then. Ruins of the farm of Eric the Red showing clearly four cowsheds with a total of 40 stalls were found, and the farm of the Bishop's estate nearby was even larger, with cowsheds to accommodate about 100 animals.

Lack of timber hindered their development. They had to depend on imports from Europe and America. In later centuries, when they no longer traded with Europe, the Northmen depended entirely on the east coast of North America or Markland (wooded land), which could have been Newfoundland, Nova Scotia or

---

[127] Not all of the ships reached Greenland. Some may have been lost, others could have reached places on the east coast of America, accounting for the early reports of "white Indians" in several places.

[128] The settlements described in detail in Heimskringle or Lives of the Norse Kings, written in Iceland turn of the 12th century.

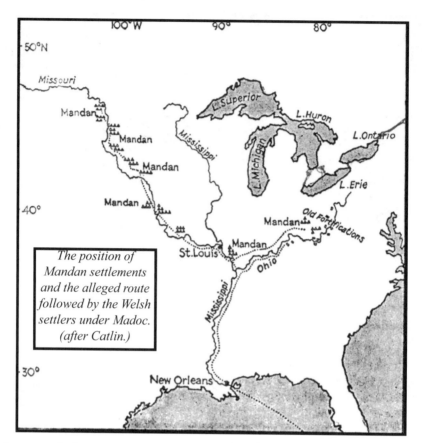

The position of
Mandan settlements
and the alleged route
followed by the Welsh
settlers under Madoc.
(after Catlin.)

as we have read, the west coast of James Bay. Traveling west from the western settlement would have brought them to the Hudson Strait.

The predominant theory today is that sometime around 1250 there was a dramatic climatic change known as the "Little Ice Age." The already struggling western settlement ceased to exist. It was sometime before 1350 that the inhabitants of the western settlement moved on. To the rest of the world, perhaps as many as a thousand men, women and children, just disappeared. A Norwegian priest from the eastern settlement traveling there in 1350 found only a few wild cattle and sheep wandering around. There were some orderly graves but no mass of dead people which there would have been if there was starvation or plague. So the only alternative seems to be that they migrated to a more hospitable location.

Pages of arguments have been written as to what happened to the people of the western settlements. The one I prefer is one that has not even been considered by any but a small group of scholars. The earliest of these seems to be the author of the book *Here Was Vinland,* by James W. Kuran in 1939. Without even hearing of that book, Marion Dahm, Judi Budibusch, Barry Hanson and others had all in the last decades arrived at the same conclusion: *That Vinland was in the vicinity of Lake Superior, Minnesota, North and South Dakota, Iowa, and even Upper Michigan and Wisconsin.*

The scholars of the great institutions have apparently given up on ever finding the answers to that question years ago, as they have pointed out continuously in their publications.

The only idea I might add to these many competent researchers is the idea that in the last few hundred years of the Viking occupation of America is that it looks very much like Helluland and Markland become less and less important and that Vinland became the Norse word for America. It is probable that the last few hundred years (1100 to 1300) or so, that as many Norse found their way down the east coast as those taking the northern route to James Bay and the Great Lakes.

The Viking Period Norse followed the coast south to the Mississippi and in 1116 may have built the church (Newport Tower) at Newport, RI. The Irish also must have landed on the east coast in numbers. [128a]

Massachusetts seems to qualify very well to be Vinland and I have an idea the name may have fit both places in Viking times.

But it seems clear that Helluland, Markland and Vinland were the isolated western settlement clearly on the south end of Hudson's Bay. Its route there is described too clearly in the Sagas. They encountered Eskimos, polar bears, huge cliffs with thousands of birds, etc, etc.,—all of which are in Hudson Strait and which are not found going south to Nova Scotia and Cape Cod. But both areas have good descriptions in different Sagas.

Around the year 1000 at the request of the King of Norway, Eric the Red's son, Leif, introduced Christianity to Greenland. Eric did not embrace Christianity himself (nor did he adhere strictly to his pagan religion).

But in 1350 when King Magnus Erikson of Norway learned of the disappearance of the population of the western settlements, he ordered Paull (Powell) Knutsson, a respected member of his royal bodyguard, to pick what men he needed from his bodyguard and using the King's Knorr (his personal ship) travel to Greenland to locate and give aid to the lost Christians.

We do not know the rest of the story, but since this order was given in 1354, it seems logical that the trip was taken within a few years.

As to the fate of the Western Settlement, there are vague reports of Eskimo raids but also there was a sudden drought. This catastrophe must have devastated their livestock industry and their only choice would be to go look for a better place to settle. They certainly knew of the channel to the outer sea (Hudson Strait to Hudson's Bay) and must have made many excursions there to Markland for

---

[128a] Alf Monge - Chief Cryptographer for the US Army during WWII has translated a date found on the tower as 1116 AD. Also see Appendix B.

lumber, and to the outer sea for hunting and fishing purposes during the centuries they lived there. Likewise, some of the sailors on the Knutson expedition must have known about such a route to the west.

With the finding of the Kensington Stone in Minnesota, the Norse words used by the Indians and Norse appearing Indians among the Moose River Cree, and the many Norse artifacts in the Great Lakes region, there is no doubt that there had to be a sizable Norse population that spent many years and spread out over a large area.[129]

The explanation for one group of Norse is the tribe of blonde, blue-eyed Indians (the Mandans) as described by the artist Catlin, explorer LaVerendry, Lewis and Clark, and others. This involves another story of pre-Columbian visitors that came from Wales on the west coast of the British Isles, just north of Cornwall. The report can be found in a 1622 publication by Francis Bacon (*History of the Reign of King Henrie the Seventh*). The story came from a 12th century Welsh historian, Gwynede ap Grono, who says that Prince Madoc, son of Owain, Prince Gwynede sailed with a fleet of ten ships from Abergwili, Carmarthen in the year 1170. He was said to have landed in the New World, built a fortified settlement and returned to Wales, leaving 120 men there. On a second voyage in 1190, he found most of the original 120 men missing.[129a]

Over the next few centuries, Welsh-speaking Indians were reported in Florida, West Virginia and several locations along the Mississippi and Missouri Rivers. Probably the most famous reports came from the Lewis and Clark Expedition of 1804-05 and George Catlin, who, in 1832 spent much time among the Mandan Indians on the Missouri and painted many authentic pictures of them. These men and others were always very intrigued to meet the Mandans and some closely related tribes. They all remarked that there could be no doubt that they were descended from European stock; a high percentage of them had blue or green eyes fine blonde hair and light skin. Their facial features were also decidedly European. Everything about these people hinted of European ancestry. The Mandans themselves said they were descended from people who arrived in a big canoe and although their only vessels were round skin boats for crossing the river, they had a large wooden replica of what looked like a half of a great canoe standing as a religious shrine in the center of their village. Unlike other tribes, their dwellings were of log construction and their social customs were unique.

---

[129] See *Here Was Vinland* by J.W. Curran (1939).

[129a] John Henderson, who has studied the Mandans situation thoroughly says "there is no doubt in his mind that the Madoc's second expedition was in 1171 or 1172, he went right back as soon as he could as there was nothing to keep him in Wales at that time. The second sailing was almost certainly from Lundy Island off the English Coast, as there is evidence of his presence and activity there.

It seems to me there is good evidence that they could be descendants of the nearby Norse farmers who had mixed with the native tribes and converted to an Indian way of life. Also, there seems to be a legitimate argument that they could be remnants of Madoc's Welsh colonists that disappeared from their downstream homes some years earlier, as there are reports of the use of Welsh words in their language.

No one seems to have thought of the possibility that the two groups found each other on the same river system and recognizing their common European heritage, joined together in a common society. This could account for the number of Welsh words that were recognized by several early explorers. The Mandans also were said to have some oral traditions that vaguely resembled Old Testament Bible stories.[130]

There are many enigmatic structures in the Arctic that give us quite a different and clearer picture of what has taken place possibly in those same centuries that we have just lightly reviewed (1200 to 1400 AD).

We have mentioned the dolmens of the Old Norse and pre-Celtic megalithic societies of which there must have involved many voyages. Then there were the Thules and the Dorset people who had come and gone by that time. The Dorset preceded the Vikings by 1,000 years. Even earlier were the pre Dorsets (2500 to 800 BC) [130a]

Other Europeans involved were the Basque fishermen who came to the fabulous cod runs in and around Iceland and Greenland. They could have been as late as the 15th century, although they left their unique syllabulary writing system to the Algonquin tribes, most especially the Cree and Otchipway. Those Algonquin tribes themselves, as we have seen, had been migrating to America via the same northern route of the others, although it seems as though they may have come in many waves that started much earlier.

The intellectuals of the period prior to Columbus' voyage at the end of the 15th century were so concentrated on the travels of Marco Polo and Nicolo Conti with their fantastic description of India and the Orient (the Spice Islands, China and the fantastically wealthy Cipangu (Japan), that they knew nothing of the continent in the other direction. They didn't even have any idea of central Africa before David Livingstone and others began their explorations of the dark continent. Except for the romantic and almost forgotten legends like Hy Brasail, etc., the Americas just didn't exist.

But even with these populations here mentioned, some who stayed and some who returned homeward, there were others. The ancients left megaliths,

---

[130] The Mandans were unfortunatly wiped out by small pox in the 19th century.
[130a] A recent report from William Smith of the Thor Group in Ohio, says a fireplace at the Ales Stenan site in Sweden had been carbon dated to 3300-3600 BC.

the Eskimos built Inukshuk, the Vikings left cairns, but there is still another characteristic stone monument found in the far north. They seem to be the work of another seafaring group from the British Isles. These people were walrus hunters. The walrus hide was cut into strips to make hawsers and sail ropes. This product was a trade item that went all the way to the Mediterranean and was in great demand. Along with these sail ropes was a demand for ivory in the form of walrus tusks. Over the centuries the walrus herds or tuskers were driven out of their former habitat that was as far south as Newfoundland into the far north of Davies Strait and Lancaster Sound.

With the tales of St. Brendan and his search for "The Promised Land of the Saints" to the west, a "St. Brendan's Isle" appeared on maps of the western sea. It had many locations but for sure, the British sailors sought it out and came on to the unknown lands. British England was the jumping off place for fishermen and walrus hunters in the far north. It was the place where John Cabot, who was born in Genoa (the family name was Cabatos) about 1450, migrated. The British fishermen and walrus hunters were already making these trips into these same waters where Cabot went on his voyage of discovery in 1497. In his book *The Farfarers,* Canadian author Farley Mowat calls them the Albans, British Isles seafarers who were at sea for tuskers. Their mark is a large hollow cairn known as "barrel beacons," of which there are many examples in the Arctic and a few places in the Great Lakes, Lake Superior, Lake Huron, and Lake Michigan. (See page 182)

It is well known that there had to have been some maps of these waters. While we don't even know the methods these early sea captains had for navigating, latitude was no problem. But even some of the early maps had longitude marked on them and navigating by the needle, dead reckoning, the birds migrations, the winds, and ocean currents were all known. [130b]

We have all heard the story of the *Vinland Map* declared to be a fraud by some experts, but declared to be authentic by others. Fraud or not, there were maps like it in existence, but the question is, is this one of them? (See portolans Page 172)

We certainly have not covered all of the little known ocean travelers who preceded Columbus, but it is hoped that enough of them were mentioned to whet the appetite and arouse the curiosity of history-loving readers. The books are out there waiting to be read.

With the mention of John Cabot's voyage in 1497, just five years after the first voyage of Columbus, we have lightly reviewed the gamut of what must have gone on during those endless lost centuries before the invention of the printing press. We have a fairly clear picture of the happenings on our globe for

---

[130b] See Appendix D Methods of Navigation.

the last four or five hundred years, but we should never be complacent about our knowledge of history—we will <u>never</u> know it all; there will always be more to learn about than our limited minds can imagine. Like time and space, there is no end and no beginning. All nature is cyclical.

We Know So Little About So Much

To add to these confusing stories of all these immigrants to the Americas in the distant past, we could add many others that we hardly dare mention. Pygmy skulls have been found in the central United States and the skeletons of giants. There were indeed both little and big people.

Giants have existed in fables, nursery rhymes, the Bible and folklore for generations, but most people think of them as pure myth.

When the Inuits of the north speak of giants erecting dolmens they could mean they were just big people relative to themselves. What we would call giants today would have to be as tall as the tallest basketball players of seven feet or more.

Archaeologists have turned up skeletal remains (and miniature remains) of most species that are on the earth today. Living organisms weren't always the size that we know them. There were giant beaver, bears, porcupine, rhinoceros, orangutan, giant sloths, giant alligators, giant buffalo, etc. Certainly many of the extinct animals such as mammoths, mastodons, bats, tigers, etc., were huge. Of course, many millions of years ago some of the dinosaurs weighed many tons.

The largest known primate ever to have inhabited the earth was gigantopithecus, a huge (now extinct) ape that is said to have weighed as much as 600 pounds. It was reported in the 1974 issue of *Scientific American Magazine* by authors Elwyn L. Simons and Peter C. Ettel. Discoveries of this huge ape were made in cave deposits in two districts of Koangsi province in southwest China and in the Sivalik Hills north of New Delhi, India. He is believed to have lived perhaps five to nine million years ago. One scientist who has studied it, Franz Weidenreich, has published a paper suggesting that modern man may have evolved from earlier and larger descendants by a process of diminution.

In a book called *Lost World of Giants* (Prestige Copying and Printing, Adelaide, Australia, 2002) by Jonathan Gray, an international lecturer, there are literally hundreds of references to giants, real giants, some over 20 feet tall. He lists reports of bones of 448 giants found in 30 different locations in the United States, 23 more in South and Central America and many others from around the world.

Strangely, there are no reports from Michigan in that book and yet there is plenty of evidence of them being in our area in the past. I have had a report of a giant grave on an island in Lake Erie, which was common knowledge to the locals. Dave Hoffman of Eagle River mentioned the grave of a giant in northern Wisconsin and there must have been a whole population of them at one time living around Detroit.

In a talk on the Mound Builders in Michigan read before the Pioneer Society of Michigan in Detroit on February 5, 1829, Henry H. Riley of Constantine tells about the mounds in that Lower Michigan area:

> The mound builder was an early pioneer. The banks and streams upon which he built declare this to be true. Their channels have been cut deeper since he laid out his grounds by their sides and erected his cities thereon. Terraces have been evidently formed below his work since he passed away; for it may still be seen where the same stream has destroyed a portion of his enclosures higher up where they now stand.
>
> Skulls are found at the bottom, showing that the mounds were raised over them and that the body was not afterward buried in them, although subsequent burial remains of Indians are found near the top, and almost always there is the evidence of an altar having been erected upon which the body was laid and consumed by fire, the rites and ceremonies over some great chieftain perhaps, who is now forever forgotten.
>
> It is through these skulls, more than any other way that physiologists have been able to determine that the mound builders, whoever they were, were not Indians; the shape and outlines of the head being different and indicating an entirely different race of people. We frequently hear of the discovery of the skeletons of a gigantic race, and we therefore are more puzzled to know to what race the mound builders belonged, for although we are called a new country, comparatively speaking, we may be the

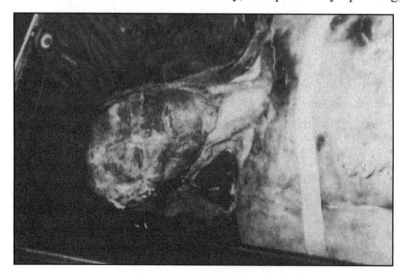

Mummified Giant Compliments of Wayne May of Ancient American Magazine.

520

oldest.

A few years ago an article appeared in the Toronto Telegraph stating that the township of Cayuga in the Grand River, on the farm of Daniel Fredenburg, five or six feet below the surface, were found two hundred skeletons nearly perfect, a string of beads around the neck of each, stone piles in the jaws of several of them, and many stone axes and skimmers scattered around in the dirt. The skeletons were gigantic, some of them measuring nine feet, and few of them less than seven. Some of the thigh-bones were six inches longer than any now known. The farm had been cultivated a century and was originally covered with a growth of pine. There was evidence from the crushed bones that a battle had been fought and these were some of the slain. Decayed houses had been found near this spot before, and there were indications that the region had at some time been inhabited. Were these the remains of Indians or some other race?

These references to giants all seem to have been eliminated from modern histories like so much other information. But some years ago Wayne May lent me a picture of one of these giants that he obtained in Colorado. It is a subject that needs some good solid research.

What Can Be Done to Educate the Public in our Pre-history?

One thing that has always bothered this author is the complete stubbornness of most of the professionals to even discuss openly the alternatives to their beliefs. No funds are allotted to the alternate theories, no museums will display the evidence and, in the case of Upper Michigan copper, many of the facts have been dismissed and downplayed or in some cases even eliminated.

Here is My Plan

My proposal is to have a private museum in Michigan's Copper Country to tell the other side of the copper story.

The museum should be built around this fact: There is nowhere else in the world known to have such indescribable quantities of pure copper, free from any matrix, lying in loose soil; pieces of copper that can be picked up and carried away.

The largest exhisting piece of float copper that is known anywhere on earth is located right where it was found.

It was discovered a few years ago by two men from Calumet, Rudy Kastelic and Jim Meneguzzo. Both are lifelong residents of the area and are employed by the Houghton County Road Commission. Rudy works in Calumet as a mechanic

Rudy Kastelic of Calumet, Michigan, one of the finders of this big copper slab.

James Meneguzzo with the historic treasure.

and Jim works in Ripley as a machinist. Ripley is located just east of Hancock along the Portage Canal. They have been close friends for some time.

In the early 1990s, the two men decided to go into a purchase agreement to buy a 40-acre piece of wooded land, log it to make some extra money and then sell it. This is a fairly common practice for people in timber country, who are so inclined.

In 1992, they purchased 40 acres just south of Calumet in a remote area. They claim they did cut a few trees, but in the fall of 1996, they decided to go over the land with a metal detector. They made their first strike in late September and, of course, they knew what they had but decided to wait until the next summer to do any digging.

In the meantime, the men had time to check the title of the land and see that all the legal work was in order, right of access and mineral rights.

It was on the 8th of July in 1997 that Kostelic and Meneguzzo went to their land with two large pieces of equipment, an excavator and a front-end loader. The weather was bad, raining with thunder and lightning. This proved to be a worry, as raw metal in the ground has been known to attract lightning.

The copper was laying at an angle just under the surface of the ground, the upper edge a few feet down and the lower end maybe six or seven feet below the surface.

After digging down to the copper and clearing off the overburden, they raised it out of its ancient resting place and up onto some timbers, where it rests today.

There have been some huge pieces of copper found in mines that were several hundred tons, but these were part of a vein. Large pieces of float have not moved far from their vein because of their weight. But this particular piece is a perfect example of float copper, it has the typical flat shape and smooth surface and was found in sand and silt of glacial till, nowhere near its source. It had been moved along by glacial action and deposited in the sand where it was found.

If there were larger pieces of float found in the past, they have long since been cut up and sent to the furnace. This piece, which is not yet famous and does not have a name, is surely the largest known piece of float copper in existence and should be preserved to be believed.

The huge specimen has an irregular flat leaf shape that varies from 4 to 18 inches in thickness. Its surface area is roughly 14 feet by 14 feet with its greatest diameter at one spot 15 feet and the least diameter is eight feet, ten inches.

With this largest piece of float copper in existence as its centerpiece and drawing card, my proposal is to raise about $500,000. This amount would purchase the forty acres of land, the piece of copper, and provide a suitable building for the only museum in the world that tells the story of the copper trade. It would be perfectly located in the heart of the Copper Country in a National Park that, as of this writing, has only a scant idea of the true importance of this area to the ancient world.

The *Ancient American* magazine is set up as a nonprofit repository for donations to the cause. Tax exempt contributions payable to *The Ancient American Copper Museum* can be sent there or to this author at:

Pre-Columbian Museum Fund
221 Lakewood Lane, Marquette, MI 49855

(or) Pre-Columbian Museum Fund
C/O Ancient American Magazine
P.O. Box 370 Colfax, WI 54730

(or) Ancient American Artifact Prservation Foundation (AAAPF)
P.O. Box 216 Skandia, MI 49885

This is a ten year project until 2017. The seeds for such an undertaking were planted over one hundred and fifty years ago by people like Whittlesey, but they lay dormant for many years.

They were watered by Joe Gannon and Roy Drier, to whom this book is dedicated, in the 1920s and 30s, but again the results were feeble. However, because of their efforts and the book (Prehistoric Copper Mining the Lake Superior Region by Drier and DuTemple), the interest and impetus has spread worldwide to a scattered group of people who set out to answer some of the old, gnawing questions that hounded the early investigators.

The seeds really began to grow with the work of Dr. Barry Fell in the 1970s and 80s and they blossomed at the turn of the century, primarily due to the work of pre-Columbian organizations that have sprung up across the country.

The full extent of the knowledge will not be fully accepted by the public until the professionals become fully immersed in the study and the story finally finds its way into the textbooks. Eventually it will be accepted. An ancient Copper Museum, built around the largest known piece of float copper in existence featured in the prehistoric Keweenaw National Park will help a great deal with this quest.

As we have already stated, history, like time and space has no end or begining.

Our limited minds keep trying to put a limit on all three, Most of us cannot fathom eternity!

Appendix A
Subject to change as knowledge is gained.

Many years ago, perhaps in the 1960s or 70s, maybe even the 50s, a man called me from somewhere in the Copper Country. I am very vague on the recollection but the story that is in my mind now is that the fellow with a Finnish name (not uncommon in our part of the country) said he had a coin that he found on Isle Royale when he was there in the CCC's (Civilian Conservation Corps) about 1939. They were digging a foundation for a building when he found it. I asked him to describe the coin to me. He answered that it was as big as a silver dollar and that he would send it to me.

When the coin arrived, I could tell the gentleman nothing. It looked to be copper or an alloy of copper and I remember it had what seemed to be a Buddha on a truncated pyramid. On the reverse was a heart and a wishbone. I had no answers so I returned the coin.

Some time in the 1990s, I was in Madison, Wisconsin with Jim Scherz and was absolutely amazed to have Dr. Scherz show me the exact same coin!

"Had I ever seen that coin?" he asked. "Yes," I said, "I had seen that coin many years ago. It belonged to someone from the Copper Country. He told me he found it on Isle Royale."

Jim had gotten the coin from Dr. Peter Carmody, a local physician from L'Anse. Dr. Scherz had been surveying the barrel beacons on the Carmody land and knew the Carmodys well.

Scherz was trying to run down the origin of the coin. I told him that years ago I drew a blank. I could find nothing about it.

Jim had discussed the coin with several people. Two of the opinions he had heard were, first, that it came in a Cracker Jack box years earlier and the other was that the Masons "Masonic Order" had given them out for some reason.

While I was in Madison, at that time, Dr. Scherz introduced me to a man from India who ran a restaurant, and a student from Nepal. Later I was told that this student could identify the writing on the coin. This was the first bit of positive information he, or anyone, had found.

Sometime later, on the cover of the *Ancient American* magazine (Volume 8, Number 50), there appeared a beautiful enlargement of that very coin.

The article in that publication, written by Editor Frank Joseph, told the whole story in detail. The locating of the coin differed slightly from my memory,

but I certainly would not argue the point.

According to the story, it was in 1983 that Scherz received a picture of the medallion from Dr. Carmody. The owner from whom I had obtained it had died by that time.

Scherz published a drawing of the coin (token) in several newspapers and eventually in the October 2000 issue of *Ancient America*. A Mr. Paul Tolonen of Tularosa, New Mexico saw the picture and recognized the medallion immediately. He telephoned publisher Wayne May. Tolonen told May that his uncle had found the piece on Isle Royale in 1929 while digging a foundation. This is a ten year discrepancy from the year I remember, but the CCC reference rings in my mind because they were there in 1939, but not 1929.

Regardless, Paul Tolonen now owns the medallion and sent it to Wayne May and Wayne photographed it and gave it to Dr. Scherz. It was a great surprise to me when it surfaced again and I saw it in Madison.

After much study and research, Professor Scherz concluded that the token appeared to describe an honored leader who was a Buddhist from Borobudor.

However, in Ancient American Issue # 65, Frank Joseph offers an updated correction to these first conclusions. He states that the original identification has since been incorrect.

The Temple building depicted on the medallion is the Mahabodhi Temple at Bodk Gaya, in northeastern India. In the article he states:

> This proper identification is important because it makes sense of the Buddha figure prominently portrayed on the token: the Mahabodhi Temple marks the place where the founder of Buddhism, Siddhartha Gautama,

achieved enlightenment. Maha Bodi refers to the bodhi or pipal tree under which he reached illumination, and the most important place for pilgrimage for Buddhists around the world: hence the crowd of robed figures and the prominence given to trees depicted on the token.

The temple was completed during the 7th Century A.D. but has been subsequently embellished and renovated. While the structure depicted on the Tolonen Medallion is un-mistakably the Mahabodhi Temple, it differs markedly from the building as it appears today. Missing is the stupa, a bell-like shrine added to it's summit sometime in the early 16th Century .D. The Isle Royal object must have been manufactured before the stupa was in place and therefore brought to Michigan in pre-Columbian times.

It is now estimated that the Medallion was manufactured between 750 A.D. when the Mahabodhi Temple was completed and 1300.

For Frank Joseph's complete article, see *Ancient American Magazine*, Volume 10, Number 65.

Note: As with most of the objects and theories mentioned in these writings, these represent on-going studies and there may be changes as new information is learned and new discoveries made.

One Example of a newer find is this rock used as a mold to make a sundial from the impression in the rock. It has a rounded bottom and 26.4 degree angle. The sun dial made from the rock could be on display to show how measurement was taken. This rock was found by Gloria Smith at the Willian Smith Farm in Ohio, in the 1970's .

527

Appendix B

Alf Monge, a native of Norway, was the chief cryptographer for the U.S. Army during World War II. Early in the war, he succeeded in breaking Japanese enciphered codes. After his retirement from the army, he became interested in various Norse runic inscriptions that contained cryptograms. He became the first person in recent times to solve these often complex and long forgotten types of, secret messages in medieval runic inscriptions.

Without going into detail on this complicated topic, we will list some of these more famous inscriptions arranged according to the year they were carved, as follows:

1.	The Vango Inscription (Sweden)	A.D.	1008
2.	Byfield No.1 (Massachusetts)		1009
3.	Heavener No.1 (Oklahoma)		1012
4.	Heavener No.2 (Oklahoma)		1016
5.	Heavener No.3 (Oklahoma)		1022
6.	Maeshowe No. 18 (Orkney Islands)		1100
7.	Maeshowe No.8 Orkney Islands)		1102
8.	The Norumfont Inscription (Sweden)		1103
9.	Maeshowe No. 11 (Orkney Islands)		1109
10.	Maeshowe No. 12 (Orkney Islands)		1112
11.	Newport Tower (Rhode Island)		1116
12.	The Burserud Inscription (Sweden)		1193
13.	The Hoppenstad Church (Norway)		1225
14.	The Kingigtorssuag Inscription (Greenland)		1244
15.	The Urnes Church Inscription (Norway)		1297
16.	Maeshowe No. 16 (Orkney Islands)		1306
17.	Maeshowe No. 21 (Orkney Islands)		1308
18.	Maeshowe No. 15 Orkney Islands)		1312
19.	Kensington Inscription (Minnesota)		1362

For 70 years, runologists have been saying that these runic carvings contained so many mistakes that they could not be authentic, but Monge discovered that what appeared to be mistakes were really clues that there is a hidden coded message. Only a few scholars, mainly Hjalmar R. Holand and O.G. Landeverk, defended the Kensington Runestone as authentic, but hundreds of others, many who had never seen it, did so much damage with their presumptions of fraud that it will be years before it can be fully reconciled.

Monge flatly states, "There is nothing more left to solve in the Kensington enigma everything is now accounted for."

Appendix C

When I was first becoming interested in ancient history (1930's) I was led to understand that the reason there could have been very little ocean travel was because there were no known methods of navigating. I was told that the Chinese had discovered the magnetic qualities of lodestone about 4500 years ago which lead to the invention of the compass.

Now, however, according to the Encyclopedia Britannica, the Chinese, the Arabs, the Greeks, the Etruscans, the Finns, and the Italians have all been claimed as the originators of the compass. There was a lot more sailing around the oceans in ancient times than we were led to believe.

It also states "There is little doubt that many writers on history of the subject have lost sight of the fact that the ancients could and did make many voyages out of the sight of land using a steady wind to give them their direction and an occasional sight of the sun or stars to inform them of any change." The first use of the compass was not to show the direction of travel but to tell the direction of the wind.

Now, of course, we know that there were many different means and methods of navigation used, many of which we don't really understand today. An example is a recent television documentary of a Polynesian navigator hitting an obscure island dead-on after a trip of a few thousand miles with no apparent navigational aids.

Beside the use of winds, currents, sun, stars, (as well as other heavenly bodies) the flight of birds, sunstones, moonstones (see Norse America by W.R. Anderson (1996) Valhalla Press), portolans , etc. We are just now discovering some of the other means of navigation that were used in ancient times.

One of these is described in a book by Ralph E Robinson of Port St. Richey Florida. In it he explains the use of a "Norse Beating Dial", which he says was probably similar to the astrolabe, which the ancient Greeks had used before 150 B.C. The Greek astrolabe was a carved wooden disk with a rotating straight edge. It allowed them to find their latitude at sea by determining the azimuth, the position of a star in its regular arc across the sky.

A Viking navigational instrument.

William Smith, researcher from Ohio, will be explaining a Celtic navigational device at a conference to be held in Big Bay, Michigan (Oct. 2005). In a communication he explains that he will be showing photos of 17 sun-god symbols with their specific information. One photo will show a world map and when the sun-god symbols are plotted on it (using Smith's theory of early navigation) it can be shown that they will have one point on the earth that will be common to all.

Still another possibility for a navigational device are depicted in some photos sent to me by Barry Hanson (Kensington Runestone researcher) of Maple, Wisconsin. It is a strange globe-like stone found in the area at the west end of Lake Superior.

To my knowledge, no one has the slightest idea of what it could be but the fact that it is girded by these peculiar, equally spaced notches, gave me the idea of a zodiac-like navigational device. If there are 17 of them it could have something to do with Smith's theory. If there are 12 it could be the zodiac, which I understand, goes back to the Minoan times.

I'm sure some readers will have other ideas.

This stone was found by Lake Superior. Its origin is unknown, but could it have been used for navigation?

Appendix D

A Skeleton Chronology

1,000,000 years ago	Humans begin to move out of Africa into Greece and Asia
250,000 years ago	Earliest located habitation sites of humans in America (Valsequetla Reservoir in Mexico)
100,000 BC	First known ocean travel (Astroloids)
30,000-12,000 BC	Possible earliest inhabitants of U.P.
29,000 BC	Evidence of possible huge stone structures appearing (some say the Sphinx was built)
28,000-20,000 BC	Neanderthal and Cro-Magnon Man living together in Europe
20,000 BC	Neanderthal Man becomes extinct in Europe—Spirit Cave Man found in America
14,000-12,000 BC	Early sporadic habitation of Western Hemisphere
9500 BC	Catastrophic worldwide flood—land bridge crossings— possible sinking of Atlantis
9500-8000 BC	Era of the first Sea People. Discovery of native copper around the world. First workings of Lake Superior copper fields.
8000-7000 BC	Rise of early post-deluvian civilizations
7000-6000 BC	First known Atlantic crossings. Old Norse, pre-Celtic, Maritime Archaic Red-Paint cultures, seagoing wooden vessels.

531

5000-4500 BC	Megalithic societies in Europe, Africa, Asia, South American. Dolmens appear. Minoans dominate world trade.
4500-4000 BC	Beginning of Lake Superior copper trade to overseas ports, rise of Copper Age.
4000-3500 BC	Beginning of bronze making in India. Rise of Egyptian Dynasties.
3000-1000 BC	Bronze Age in Europe. Megalithic builders active in Europe and America.
2500 BC	Old Norse and Northwestern Europeans penetrate the Arctic. Stone structures in America.
2250 BC	Emperor Shun, Classic of Mountains and Seas, Survey of the World.
2000 BC	Possible early Algonquin migrations from Europe to America.
1700 BC	Woden Lithi trading at Peterborough with Algonquins.
1500 BC	Iberian, Celtic and Egyptian contacts with American Indian nations.
1450 BC	Eruption of Santorini Volcano near Crete. Minoan cities destroyed by tidal waves and ash. Abrupt end of Minoan trade dominance.
1300 BC	Rise of Phoenician sea power. They take over the copper trade.
800-500 BC	Mound builders become active in America.
750 BC	Rome founded.
600-450 BC	Rise of Roman power.
400-300 BC	Golden Age of Greece

390 BC	Celts invade city of Rome.
350 BC	Celts settle in Ireland.
284 BC	Building of Colossus of Rhodes—sixth wonder of the ancient world—bronze statue (120 feet high)
280 BC	Building of the Lighthouse at Alexandria (550 feet high). Seventh wonder of the ancient world.
250 BC	Celtiberian and Ogam inscriptions on bone and stone artifacts buried with skeletons of both American Indians and European types in Tennessee (early Woodland Indians)
221 BC -206 BC	Qin Empire Qinshihuang - First Emperor in Chinese History
70-14 BC	Golden Age of Rome
47 BC	Cleopatra VII becomes Cleopatra the Great, Queen of Egypt.
46 BC	Juba II taken to Rome—brought up as a soldier and a scholar.
36 BC	Antony and Cleopatra become lovers.
35 BC	Twins Cleopatra Selene and Alexander Helios are born to Antony and Cleopatra. Born on the winter solstice.
31 BC	Antony defeated at the Battle of Actus. Octavia becomes Emperor Caesar Augustus.
30 BC	Cleopatra the Great commits suicide.
25 BC	Cleopatra Selene married Juba II.
6 AD	Cleopatra Selene dies.

40 AD	Roman legions invade Mauritania.
Circa 46 AD	Mauritanians flee to America, arrive in present Illinois.
300-500 AD	Many Christians, Jews, and others sail to America to escape turmoil in Europe.
312 AD	Constantine marches into Rome.
313 AD	Edict of Milan granting tolerance to Christians.
400 AD	Coptic Christians arrive in present Michigan.
409 AD	Roman garrisons abandon British Isles. Romans arrive in America.
410 AD	Goths plunder city of Rome.
400-800 AD	Cloistered Irish Monks record ancient documents.
Circa 300 AD	St. Brenden's Voyage to America.
780 AD	Beginning of Viking Age. Viking raids on England begin.
863 AD	Vikings reach Iceland. Irish had already been there.
986 AD	25 Viking ships head for Greenland to colonize. Irish had already been there.
1100-1300 AD	Norse exploration and colonization in America.
1109 AD	Newport tower constructed.
Circa 1170 AD	Welsh Prince Madoc in America.
1271-1275	Travels of Marco Polo.

1350-1450 and beyond	European Basque fishermen fish off Nova Scotia. Albans after walrus in the Arctic. Explore the Great Lakes.
1492	First voyage of Columbus.
1497	First voyage of John Cabot.
1513	Balboa, first European on record to sight the Pacific.
1534-1542	Cartier in the St. Lawrence River.
1588	Defeat of the Spanish Armada by England.
1650-1700	Jesuits in America, report native copper. Many French migrate to America.
1700-1820	Thousands of Africans brought to America.
1763-1776	English first mining copper in Lake Superior. Many English and Scotch migrate to America.
1840-1850	Beginning of Lake Superior copper boom.
1845	Potato famine in Ireland. Many Irish migrate to America.
1850-1900	Tin mines of Cornwall close. Many Cornish migrate to America.
1870-1913	Golden Age of Lake Superior copper mining. Many Scandinavians, Italians and other Europeans migrate to America. Also Chinese.
1903-1905	Amunsen located the North Magnetic Pole and Northwest Passage.
1997	End of Copper Country copper mining, but there are new possibilities on the horizon.

Appendix E

The Discovery

The discovery of this archaeological site had been made by independent researchers Antonio J. Cardoso and Arthur Franco, from Porto Alegre, capital of the southern Brazilian state, Rio Grande do Sul. At the present time, we are studying other structures in the local, jointly to archaeologists who work in order to raise evidences of the human presence in the sites. One of the sites showed us dozens of fragments, from shaped stones to guarani (a primitive local tribe) ceramics, whose age could vary from 2 to 10 thousand years, according to previous similar artifacts found in the state.

Illustration by Judy Johnson

536

Bibliography for Reference
and Further Reading

Allan, D.S. & Delair, J.B. *Cataclysm! Compelling Evidence of a Cosmic Catastrophe in 9500 B.C.*, Bear & Company, Santa Fe, NM, 1995.

Ancient American Magazine.

Antiquity, Vol. 16, Number 292, June 2002.

Anderson, W. R. *Norse America: Tenth Century Onward*, Leif Ericson Society, Evanston, IL, 1996.

Arms, Myron. *Riddle of the Ice: A Scientific Adventure into the Arctic*, Anchor Books, Doubleday, New York, 1998.

Beaivi, Ahcazan. *Nils-Aslak Valkeapaa*, Goalmmar deattus, Girji lea prentejuvvon Vaasa Oy prentehusas Vasas jagi, 1991.

The Book of the Dead, Citadel Press.

Burl, Aubrey. *The Stonehenge People: Life and death at the world's greatest stone circle*, J.M. Dent & Sons Ltd, London, Melbourne, 1987.

Burrows & Rydholm. *Mystery Cave of Many Faces,* Superior Heartland, 1991

Capri, Donald L. *The Crystal Veil. Avant-Garde Archaeology,* Stonehenge Viewpoint, Santa Barbara, California, 1995.

Casson, Lionel. *Ships and Seafaring in Ancient Times*, University of Texas Press, Austin, TX, 1994.

Chapman, Paul H. *Columbus, the Man*, Isac Press, 1992.

Childress, David Hatcher. *Lost Cities & Ancient Mysteries of South America*, Adventures Unlimited Press, Stelle, IL, 1986.

Cohen, Daniel, McGraw- Hill. *Ancient Monuments and How They Are Built*, 1971.

Coxe, William. *The Russian Discoveries Between Asia and America*, Readex Microprint Corporation, Library of Congress, 1966.

Cremo, Michael A. *Forbidden Archeology's IMPACT*, Bhaktivedanta Book Publishing, Inc., Los Angeles, CA, 1998.

Cremo, Michael A. and Thompson, Richard L. *Forbidden Archeology: The Hidden History of the Human Race*, Bhaktivedanta Book Publishing, Inc., Los Angeles, CA, 1993.

Cuthbertson, Brian. *John Cabot and the Voyage of the Matthew*, Formac Publishing Company Limited, Halifax, Nova Scotia and Seven Hills book Distributors, Cincinnati, Ohio, 1997.

Danziger, Edmund Jefferson, Jr. *The Chippewas of Lake Superior*, University of Oklahoma Press, Norman and London, 1979.

Deal, David Allen. Discovery of Ancient America

De Costa, B.F. *The Pre-Columbian Discovery of America by the Northmen with Translations from the Icelandic Sagas*, Third Edition Revised, Joel Munsell's Sons, Albany, NY, 1901.

De Poncins, Gontran. *Kabloona: Among the Inuit*, Graywolf Press, St. Paul, MN, 1996.

Dexter, Warren W. and Donna Martin. *America's Ancient Stone Relics: Vermont's Link to Bronze Age Mariners*, Academy Books, Rutland, Vermont, 1995.

Diamond, Jared. *Guns, Germs, and Steel: The Fates of Human Societies*, W.W. Norton & Company, New York/London, 1997.

Donnelly, Ignatius. *Atlantis: The Antediluvian World* (with a New Introduction by E.F> Bleiler), Dover Publications, Inc., New York, 1976.

Donnelly, Ignatius. *Atlantis: The Antediluvian World*, Gramercy Publishing Company, New York, A Modern Revised Edition, 1949.

Drier, Roy W. and DuTemple, Octave J. *Prehistoric Copper Mining in the Lake Superior Region*, Published Privately, 1961.

Ducvas, Albert. *Prehistory de la France*.

Epigraphic Society, Occasional Papers.

Erdoes, Richard and Ortiz, Alfonso. *American Indian Myths and Legends*, Pantheon Books, New York, 1984.

Farley, Gloria. *In Plain Sight: Old World Records in Ancient America*, Isac Press, Columbus, GA, 1994.

Fell, Barry. *America BC,* Pocket Books, NY, 1976.

Fell, Barry. *Bronze Age America*, Little, Brown and Company, Boston/Toronto, 1982.

Fell, Barry. *Saga America*, Times Books, a division of Quadrangle, New York, NY, 1980.

Fitzhugh, William W. & Elisabeth Ward. *Vikings – The North Atlantic Saga*, Smithsonian Institution Press, 2000.

Friedrich, Johannes. *Extinct Languages*, Dorset Press, New York, 1957.

Gallagher, Ida Jane and Warren Dexter. *Contact with Ancient America*, 858 Sovereign Terrance, Mt. Pleasant, SC 29464.

Gant, Tom. *Discover Dartmoor*, Baron Jay Publishers, Plymouth, Canada, 1978.

Glob, P.V. *The Bog People: Iron-Age Man Preserved*, Barnes & Noble Books, New York, 1965.

Golding, Morton J. *The Mystery of the Vikings in America*, J.B. Lippincott Company, Philadelphia and New York, 1973.

Griffin, James. *Anthropological Papers Museum of Anthropology University of Michigan,* No. 17, Lake Superior, Copper and the Indians, U of M Press, 1961.

Hapgood, Charles H. *Maps of the Ancient Sea Kings*, Adventures Unlimited Press, Kempton, IL, 1996.

Harbison, Peter. *Guide to National and Historic Monuments of Ireland*, Gill and Macmillan, Dublin, Ireland, 1970, 1975 and 1992.

Harrington, Richard. *The Face of the Arctic: a camerman's story in words and pictures of five journeys into the far north*, Abelard-schuman, New York and Thomas Nelson & Sons, Canada, 1952.

Hawkes, Jacquetta. *A guide to the Prehistoric and Roman Monuments in England & Wales*, A New Edition, Chatto & Windus, London, 1976.

Hawkins, Gerald S. *Beyond Stonehenge*, Harper & Row, Publishers, New York, 1973.

Hawkins, Gerald S. *Stonehenge Decoded*, Doubleday, Garden City, NY, 1965.

Higgins, Reynold. *Minoan & Mycenaean Art,* Thames and Hudson LTD, 1967-1981.

Houston, James. *Confessions of an Igloo Dweller: Memories of the Old Arctic*, Houghton Mifflin Company, 215 Park Avenue South, New York, NY 1003, 1995.

Howard, Philip K. *The Death of Common Sense: How Law is Suffocating America*, Random House, New York, 1994.

Imbrogno, Philip and Horrigan, Marianne. *Celtic Mysteries in New England*, Llewellyn Publications, St. Paul, MN, 2000.

James, Peter and Thorpe, Nick. *Ancient Inventions*, Ballantine Books, New York, 1994.

James, T.G.H. and W.V. Davies. *Egyptian Sculpture,* British Museum Press, 1983.

Jane, Cecil (Translator). *The Journal of Christopher Columbus*, Bonanza Books, 1989.

Jennings, Jesse D., McGraw - Hill. *Prehistory of North America*, 1968

Jewell, Roger. *Ancient Mines of Kitchi-Gummi: A Case Study*, Jewell Histories, Fairfield, PA, First Edition, 2000.

Jimenez, Ramon L. *Caesar Against the Celts*, Sarpedon, New York, 1996.

Johanson, Bruce H. *Victoria: The Gem of Forest Hill* (The story behind the Victoria Mine of Ontonagon County, Michigan), The Society for the Restoration of Old Victoria, Inc., Rockland, MI, 1993.

Joseph, Frank. *Atlantis in Wisconsin: New Revelations About Lost Sunken City*, Galde Press, Inc., St. Paul, MN, 1995.

Joseph, Frank. *The Lost Treasure of King Juba*, Bear & Company, Rochester, Vermont, 2003.

Leakey, Richard and Lewin, Roger. *Origins Reconsidered: In Search of What Makes Us Human,* Doubleday, New York, NY, October 1992.

Mahan, Joseph B. *North American Sun Keyings. Kleopatra of the Flame*, ISAC Press, Columbus, GA, 1992.

Mahan, Joseph B. *The Secret: America in World History Before Columbus*, The Author, Columbus, Georgia, 1983.

Martin, Susan R. *Wonderful Power: The Story of Ancient Copper Working in the Lake Superior Basin*, Wayne State University, Detroit, 1999.

McGlone, William R., Phillip M. Leonard. *Ancient Celtic America*, Panorama West Books, Irena, California, 1986.

McNally, Kenneth. *Standing Stones and other monuments of early Ireland*, Appletree Press, Belfast, 1988.

Mehl, Bernard. *Viking Head*, Apollo Books, Inc., Winona, MN, 1984.

Mertz, Henriette. *Pale Ink*, The Swallow Press, Chicago, IL, Second Edition, 1972.

Mertz, Henriette. *The Mystic Symbols: Mark of the Michigan Mound Builders*, Global Books, Gaithersburg, MD (published posthumously), 1986.

Midwestern Epigraphic Journals.

Milligan, Max and Burl, Aubrey. *Circles of Stone: The Prehistoric Rings of Britain and Ireland*, The Harvill Press, London, 1999.

Morahan, Leo. Archaeology, Landscape and People, Croagh Patrick, Co. Mayo, 2001.

Morrison, David and Germain, Georges-Hebert. *Inuit: Glimpses of an Arctic Past*, Canadian Museum of Civilization, 100 Laurier Street, Hull, Quebec, Canada J8X 4H2, 1995.

Myers, Philip Van Ness, *Ancient History*, The Atheneum Press, Ginn & Company, Boston, MA, 1904.

NEARA Journals.

Nielsen & Wolter. *The Kensington Rune Stone, Compelling New Evidence,* 2006

Norman, James. *Ancestral Voices: Decoding Ancient Languages*, Barnes and Noble Books, New York, 1975.

Northwest Passage: An Overview for travelers with Marine Expeditions, Marine Expeditions, Inc., 890 Yonge St, Toronto, Ontario, Canada.

Paquette, Jim. *The Find of a Thousand Years,* 2005

Peck, M. Scott, M.D. *In Search of Stones: A Pilgrimage of Faith, Reason, and Discovery*, Hyperion, New York, 1995.

Pringle, Heather. *In Search of Ancient North America*, John Wiley & Sons, Inc., New York, 1996.

Reading the Past Runes, British Museum Press, 1987. Page, RI.

Robinson, Tim. *Stones of Aran: Labyrinth*, Penguin Books, London, England, 1995.

Robinson, Tim. *Stones of Aran: Pilgrimage*, Penguin Books, The Lilliput Press, London, England, 1990.

Rollen, Duane W. *World of Juba II and Kleopatra Selene*, David Brawn Beak Co., Routledge, 2003.

Rothenberg, Beno. *Were These King Solomon's Mines?* Stein and Day, New York, 1972.

Sawyer, Peter (Ed.). *The Oxford Illustrated History of the Vikings*, Oxford University Press, Oxford/New York, 1997.

Scheny, James P. *Fred Kingmans Roman – Style Coins from Wisconsin Risen (1907s)*, University of Wisconsin, Madison, 1994.

Scheny, James. *Wisconsin's Effigy Mounds*, Ancient Earthworks Society Inc, Madison, Wisconsin 53701, 1991.

Scherz, James P. and Burrows, Russell E. *Rock Art Pieces from Burrows' Cave in Southern Illinois*, Volume I of a two-volume set, 1992.

Schoch, Robert M. with McNally, Robert Aquinas. Voyages of the Pyramid Builders, Jeremy P. Tarcher/Putnam, a member of Penguin Putnam Inc., New York, 2003.

Settegast, Mary. *Plato Prehistorian: 10,000 to 5,000 B.C. Myth, Religion, Archaeology*, Lindisfarne Press, Hudson, NY 1986.

Sharp, Mick. *A Land of Gods and Giants*, Fraser Stewart Book Wholesale Ltd., Abingdon, Oxon, 1989.

Shavhey, John. *Celtic Mysteries*, The Ancient Religion, CS Graphics, Singapore, 1971.

Sodders, Betty. *Michigan Prehistory Mysteries II*, Avery Color Studios, Au Train, MI, 1991.

Sodders, Betty. *Michigan Prehistory Mysteries*, Avery Color Studios, Au Train, MI, 1990.

Spedicato, Emilio. Apollo Objects, *Atlantis and the Deluge: A Catastrophical Scenario for the End of the Last Glaciation*, Instituto Universitario Di Bergamo, Bergamo, Italy, 1990.

Stevene, Horace J. *The Copper Handbook. A Manual of the Copper Industry of the World,* Vol. IX, Houghton, Michigan, 1909.

St. John, John. *A True Description of the Lake Superior Country*, William
	H. Graham, Tribune Buildings, NY, 1846, Reprinted by Black Letter
	Press, Grand Rapids, MI, 1976.

Stewart, Ethel G. *The Dene and Na-Dene Indian Migration 1233 A.D.: Escape from Genghis Khan to America*, Winter Cabin Books, Superior
	Heartland Books, Marquette, MI, 1991.

Stiebe, Ronald. *Mystery People of the Cove: A History of the Lake Superior
	Ouinipegou*, Lake Superior Press, Marquette, MI, 1999.

Storm, Hyemeyohsts. *Seven Arrows*, Ballantine books, New York, 1972.

Thompson, Gunnar. *The Friar's Map of Ancient America, 1360 AD*, Laura
	Lee Productions & Argonauts of the Misty Isles, Seattle, WA, 1996.

Thurner, Arthur W. *Calumet Copper and People: History of a Michigan Mining Community, 1864-1970*, Privately published, 1974.

Tilley, Christopher. *The Dolmens and Passage Graves of Sweden: An Introduction and Guide*, Institute of Archeology, University College, London, 1999.

Trento, Salvatore M. *Field Guide to Mysterious Places of Eastern North
	America*, An Owl Book, Henry Holt and Company, New York, 1997.

True Life Stories of Freaks, Fate & Fortune, Castle Books, New York, 1973.

Waddell, John. *The Prehistoric Archaeology of Ireland*, Wordwell Ltd., Bray,
	Co. Wicklow, 1998 and 2000.

Walker, CBF. *Reading the Past Cuneiform*, British Museum Press, 1987.

Ward, John A. *Ancient Archives Among the Cornstalks*, MRD Associates,
	Vincennes, Indiana, 1984.

What Life Was Like on the Banks of the Nile, Egypt, 3050-30 BC, Editor of
	Time-Life Books, Alexandria, VA. (from a series).

Zaczek, Iain. *Ancient Irish Landscapes*, Gill & Macmillan Ltd., Dublin, Ireland, 1998.

Zug, James. *American Traveler; The Life and Adventures of John Ledyard;
	the Man Who Dreamed of Walking the World*, Basic Books/Perseus
	Books Group, New York, 2005.

Index

A

B

C

396, 397, 476, 477, 480
diffusionists, 3, 403
Dillman, Grover C., 130, 132, 133
Diodorus, 96, 363, 369
Dodd, Mr. James E., 185-190
Donato, William, 459
Dordogne, 253
Dorset, 268, 321, 516
Dr. Griffin, 136, 137, 140
Drier, Roy Ward Dr., 63, 80, 81, 126, 128-136, 138-140, 142, 144-146,
157, 190, 207, 209, 213, 225, 283, 342, 367, 368, 523
Dudley, Harry C., 141
Dunbar, Willis F., 279
Dunn, Christopher, 493
DuTemple, Octave, 129, 145, 209, 225

E

Edena, 496
Edgar, Tom, 227, 496
Egyptians, 174, 357, 359, 361, 363-367, 390, 415, 477
Eldred, Julius, 27, 28, 32, 33
Embarras River, 445, 448, 453, 499
Enormous dams, 489
Epigraphic Society, 163, 164, 191, 205, 215, 219, 222, 231, 244, 247,
285, 288, 291, 313, 349, 397, 421, 494
Eric the Red, 93, 94, 141, 510, 512, 514
Erie, 104, 464, 498, 502, 518
Erikson, King Magnus, 514
Escott, David, 351
ESOP, 114, 215, 222, 239, 240, 349, 350, 382, 391, 392

F

Farley, Gloria, 357, 358, 387-389
Fell, Dr. Barry, 191, 205, 222, 225-227, 291, 339, 342, 348, 407, 462,
468, 484, 504, 523
Field Museum, 80, 131, 232
Firbolgs, 96, 268, 499
Fitzhugh, William W., 382
Folsom points, 343, 457
Fomorians, 96, 268

Heavener Runestone, 150, 387-389
Heberdies, 255
Hecla Mining, 45, 52, 396
Helluland, 99, 148, 192, 514
Henderson, John, 430, 457, 488, 515
Hendrickson, Dr. Eiler, 9
Henry, Alexander, 21, 22, 24, 27
Herodotus, 363
Hoffman, David, 274, 430, 431
Holand, Hjalmar R., 107, 148, 211
Hopewell Culture 350 A.D., 89, 185, 164
Hopewell, 232, 422
Hopewellean, 496
Hopi Indians, 415
Houghton, Douglas, Dr., 27, 36, 37, 86
Hourigan, Virginia, 236, 237, 239, 455
Huanghi, Qin Shi, 307, 308
Hubbard, Bella, 27, 280 ,282
Hubbard, Harry, 242, 442, 443, 448
Hueyatloca, 423-426
Hulbert, Edwin, 45
Hyde, Arnout J. F., 228, 230

I

Iberian Peninsula, 344, 348, 357, 471
Igloolik, 264, 269
Illisimayoke, 267
Ingstad, Helge, 101, 148, 159
Inukshooks, 267, 268, 270
Irwin-Williams, Cynthia, 423, 424, 426
ISAC, 233, 234, 241, 242, 244, 260, 295-297, 315, 359, 403, 419
Isle Royale, 2, 10, 11, 16, 20, 22, 23, 53, 58, 59, 60-65, 67-70, 78, 81,
102, 126-128, 130, 131, 133, 134, 137-140, 142-145, 176, 178, 179,
184, 212, 282, 283, 368, 396, 471
isolationist view, 3
Italian Hall Disaster, 49

J

Jackson, Dr. Charles T., 39
Jakobshaun Glacier, 152

Jensen, William H., 461

Jentoft, Alf, 175, 181

Jesuit Relations, 20, 299

Jewell, Roger, 360

John Hays, 41,

Johnson, Fred Bang, 93

Jordan, S. A., 411, 414

Joseph, Frank, 398, 443, 499, 505

K

Karlsefni, 160

Kawbawgam, 84, 337

Keeler, Clyde, 163, 385

Keftui, 396, 397

Kela, Joel (Stone), 153-157, 202, 205, 209, 211, 212, 227, 228, 271, 284, 372, 444, 485

Kelly, David, 391

Kennewick Man, 467

Kensington Stone, 105, 107-120, 123, 149, 150, 152, 153, 156, 175, 180, 187, 373, 375, 377-379, 381, 383-389, 405, 417, 419-421, 423, 425, 427, 429, 431, 433, 444, 515

Keweenaw Waterway, 272, 273, 396, 471

Keweenaw, 2, 11, 12, 16, 17, 19-23, 25, 27, 29, 31, 33, 35, 37, 39, 40, 41, 43, 45-49, 51, 53, 65, 81, 90, 102, 133, 138, 149, 176, 182, 225, 262, 272, 273, 282, 283, 301, 325, 396, 471, 485, 523

Khan, Genghis, 296, 297, 299, 315, 338

Kidder, Dr, Alfred, 155

Kimball, Kendrick, 176, 179

King Juba, 444, 498, 499

King Solomon, 359, 478

Kinkaid, G. E., 411, 412

Kinnaman, J.O., 118

Knapp, Samual O., 43, 44

Knutson, 515

Kushan Dynasty, 297

L

L'Anse Aux Meadows, 101, 148, 149, 159, 187, 386

Lake Agassiz, 15, 16, 378, 461

Lake Van, 303, 304

M

Melted Copper, 162, 167

Melville Peninsula, 264, 269, 318, 319

Meneguzzo, Jim, 521, 522

Menhirs, 251, 253, 258, 260, 264, 331, 485, 502

Menorah, 362

Menzies, Gavin, 314, 318

Mertz, Henriette, 111, 231, 273, 285, 287, 305-307, 309, 313-315, 393, 395, 402, 415, 416

Mesopotamia, 460, 473, 505

Michigan Mystery Gardens, 278, 279

Mikki, Jason, 318, 319

Millar, John Fitzhugh, 353, 355

Minoan Crete, 287, 468

Minoans, 174, 354, 367, 468, 469, 471, 473, 476, 502

Minong Mountain, 61, 62, 66

Mississippian, 89, 496

Mitchell, Eric, 264, 266, 267, 269, 319, 321

Monette, Clarence J., 53

Monge, Alf, 514

Monroe Doctrine of Cultural Isolation, 375

Monte Verde, 464, 465

Mooring Stone, 148, 149, 152, 194, 378-382, 386, 416, 472

Morgan, Louis Henry, 84

Moseley, Beverley, 244

Mound builder, 88, 89, 92, 102, 103, 112, 169, 170, 475, 486, 487, 489, 492, 519

Mowat, Farley, 182, 517

Murray, Arnold, 476

muscatine grapes, 354

Mystery Stone, 70, 74

Mystic Symbol, 111, 114, 119, 273, 313, 314, 395, 396, 499

N

Na-Dene, 295, 296, 298, 315

Narragansett Stone, 385

Navajo, 297, 298

Newberry Tablet, 120, 124, 287-289, 291, 469, 471

Newport Tower, 169, 382, 384, 385, 387, 388, 514

Nicolet, Jean, 298-302

Nielsen, Richard, 373, 378, 382, 386

Noah's Diaries, 393
Northmen, 93-95, 99, 100, 102, 497, 509, 512
Nunavut, 321

O

Ogam Consaine, 207, 213, 223
Ogam, 205-210, 212, 213, 216-218, 222-223, 226, 228, 230, 255, 271, 272, 358, 476, 477, 485, 492, 496, 507
Ohman, Olaf, 105, 108, 109, 373, 374, 385, 389, 416
Old Norse, 71, 107, 174, 223, 268, 359, 382, 383, 483, 485, 499, 502, 516
Olmec, 316
Ontonagon Boulder, 17, 18, 22, 24, 25, 27, 28, 30, 33-35, 38, 87
Orkney Islands, 254-257, 321
Owsley, Doug, 463
Oxhides, 174, 285, 396, 471, 478, 497

P

Palace of Knossos, 473
Pale Ink, 305, 306, 309-315, 415
Palestrina, 335-338
Paquette, Jim, 461
Parsche, Franz, 353
Paul, Carroll Mrs., 62, 67
Pearson, Malcom, 204, 208
Peggy's Cove, 261
Pequaming Point, 181, 182, 184
Peregrine Falcons, 434
Petitot, Emil, 296, 297
Pfeiffer, Robert, 480
Phaistos Disk, 287, 292, 469
Phoenicians, 101, 174, 344, 345, 353, 354, 359, 364, 367, 396, 473, 475, 476, 478, 497, 502, 503
Polar Sea, 7, 127, 171, 321
Poverty Point, 234, 235, 347, 507
Powel, John Wesley, 90-92, 403
Priest, Josiah, 360
Ptolemy, 344, 444
Puebla, 465
Pyle, Robert L., 228, 492, 493

Pyramid(s), 80, 101, 215, 251, 353, 460, 465, 475, 492-494, 497, 505

Q

R

S

T

V